Does Foreign Aid Really Work?

Does Foreign Aid Really Work?

Roger C. Riddell

OXFORD
UNIVERSITY PRESS

OXFORD

UNIVERSITY PRESS

Great Clarendon Street, Oxford OX2 6DP

Oxford University Press is a department of the University of Oxford.
It furthers the University's objective of excellence in research, scholarship,
and education by publishing worldwide in

Oxford New York

Auckland Cape Town Dar es Salaam Hong Kong Karachi
Kuala Lumpur Madrid Melbourne Mexico City Nairobi
New Delhi Shanghai Taipei Toronto

With offices in

Argentina Austria Brazil Chile Czech Republic France Greece
Guatemala Hungary Italy Japan Poland Portugal Singapore
South Korea Switzerland Thailand Turkey Ukraine Vietnam

Oxford is a registered trade mark of Oxford University Press
in the UK and in certain other countries

Published in the United States
by Oxford University Press Inc., New York

First published 2007

First published in paperback 2008

British Library Cataloguing in Publication Data

Data available

Library of Congress Cataloging in Publication Data

Data available

Typeset by SPI Publisher Services, Pondicherry, India
Printed in Great Britain
on acid-free paper by
Ashford Colour Press, Gosport, Hampshire

ISBN 978–0–19–929565–4 (Hbk.)   978–0–19–954446–2 (Pbk.)

10 9 8 7 6

For Eliza, Becky and Zoe

■ CONTENTS

■ LIST OF FIGURES

■ LIST OF TABLES

■ LIST OF BOXES

■ PREFACE

The origins of this book

Twenty years ago, I wrote a lengthy book entitled *Foreign Aid Reconsidered*. It was written in part as a riposte to the popular and influential view at the time that the answer to development lay in expanding and deepening free markets. According to the strongest free-market adherents, aid actively impeded rather than contributed to development.

On a number of occasions since then, I have been asked to write an updated edition of this earlier book, surveying and reviewing new evidence and the new ways that aid has been provided to see what light this sheds on the continuing debates about the merits of providing aid. Though I was keen to 'reconsider aid' again, until recently other commitments prevented me from doing this. From mid-2004 onwards, however, I have had the opportunity to examine anew the overall contribution and impact of foreign aid. This book is the result of nearly two years' intensive work.

Rather than simply updating the earlier book, however, it quickly became apparent that what was needed was a new and quite different book on aid because of the changes that have taken place and are continuing to take place in the complex worlds of aid. Three are of particular importance.

First, *Foreign Aid Reconsidered* focused overwhelmingly on official development aid—assistance provided by governments and international agencies. Emergency and humanitarian aid, and aid provided by non-governmental organizations (NGOs) and civil society organizations were hardly mentioned. Even today, most published studies which seek to answer the question 'Does aid work?' still focus their attention exclusively on official development aid. This is no longer adequate. Over the past 20 years, aid provided for emergencies has expanded more than fivefold, and there has been a huge expansion in aid provided by NGOs. Indeed, today (in current price terms), emergency and NGO aid account for more than the total value of all official aid provided in the mid-1980s ($29bn). Surprisingly, however, no book has been published to date which has attempted to examine the impact of all aid: development aid provided by official agencies, development aid provided by NGOs and emergency aid provided by both. This book is a first attempt to do so. It is based, in part, on my own involvement in these 'new' areas: over the past 15 years, I have undertaken a succession of major studies, often in collaboration with others, involving numerous field visits, which have examined the impact of the development activities of NGOs, and from 1999 to 2004, I was responsible for overseeing the emergency and development work of Christian Aid, with an annual budget of over $50mn, trying to ensure that the funds deployed achieved their objectives.

The second reason why I felt that a new and different sort of book on aid was needed is due to the changes taking place in the wider world of international relations which are altering the traditional discourse about the role and purpose of aid. Historically, the discourse on aid has been dominated by the donors, and located within the context of each individually deciding how best to help those in extreme need. Today, however, aid-giving is increasingly being discussed and provided within a human rights framework, where the needs, capabilities and rights of the recipients are taken as the starting point for determining how much is given and the ways in which it is given. It is also being discussed in international fora, in which individual nations are increasingly beginning to acknowledge that they have joint responsibility for helping to address violations of basic human rights, including those linked to extreme poverty. These evolving changes challenge some of the longest-held assumptions about aid, such as the view that it is up to each donor to decide, largely on its own, how much aid to give, in what forms and for how long. Responding to the changing environment, this book discusses new thinking about and approaches to aid, and outlines ways in which they might further influence and shape future aid relationships.

The third reason why I thought that a different sort of book on aid was needed is based more directly on my own experiences and encounters in working in the worlds of aid and development for more than 40 years. Let me explain. In the mid-1970s, I was fortunate to participate in one of the first post-graduate multi-disciplinary courses on development, which was established at the Institute of Development Studies at Sussex in England. It was run by the late Dudley Seers, whose commitment to and questioning of development was to shape and influence my own work in this field. As the decades passed, a number of Dudley's views became conventional wisdom: his early recognition that development is an extremely complex process, which is difficult to define, and difficult for outsiders to help in promoting without an in-depth understanding of the attributes and constraints of each poor country.

Encouragingly, the growing acknowledgement of the complexities of development has led to increased specialization within the development profession. But this has also led to the compartmentalization of different subgroups within the field of development, often leading to isolation from, ignorance about, and sometimes even indifference to other dimensions of development. Regrettably, these weaknesses are also present in the aid world. The longer I have worked in the field of aid and development, the more concerned, and at times alarmed, I have become about the limited knowledge and appreciation of so many full-time aid professionals (including some in quite senior positions in offical aid agencies and in some NGOs) of the complexities of development and the gaps in our knowledge of the role that aid can play in assisting the process of sustainable development. Sustainable development is unlikely to be achieved by slavishly following the 'how-to' guidelines of off-the-shelf manuals.

Most aid professionals are good at their own particular jobs. But the world of numerous aid and development workers is narrow and self-contained, with many unaware of, and, more worryingly, a number seemingly unconcerned about, the wider world of aid, the different roles and potential of different aid agencies, and the lessons to be learnt from past aid interventions. For example, in recent years, officials in donor agencies have supposedly 'discovered' the importance of good governance as a critical factor contributing to aid effectiveness, with many seemingly unaware of the importance placed on this issue fifty years ago. Likewise, donors are beginning to channel their aid to infrastructure projects, with many officials not realizing that this was one of the most important forms of aid provided in the 1950s, and little evidence of a wish to learn the lessons of past aid interventions. It is for this reason that the early chapters of this book provide a history (albeit a short one) of aid-giving, and draw attention to the very different ways that individual donors have understood why they give aid, and how they believe poverty might best be addressed. These differences remain important to this day.

Unless the lessons of history are learnt and absorbed, we will be responsible for sustaining a development profession where aid does not make enough difference to the lives of those it is meant to help. This book is written, in part, to help those engaged in different parts of the complex worlds of aid to understand better how they 'fit in' to the whole. It is also wrtten for a more general readership, providing, I hope, a readable discussion and update of the issues most central to debates about the importance of aid, and the evidence of its impact.

A counter-blast to the sound-bite

There are many ways that development can take place in poor countries: through raising savings and investment levels, through the judicious expansion of trade, and by forgiving unpayable debt. This is not a book about trade or debt relief, important though they often are. This is a book about aid and the contribution it can make to saving lives and in helping to accelerate the process of development and the reduction of poverty. Emergency aid is often necessary to help save lives; development aid often contributes to development but it is not usually the crucial ingredient. This doesn't mean it is unimportant. It can and sometimes does play a vital role. The fact that trade or debt relief also can sometimes play a vital role in development does not mean that a study of aid and its impact is redundant.

When I set out to write this book I assumed that it would be as simple as it was twenty years ago to trawl through, read and absorb the 'literature on aid' in order to synthesize and update what we know about the impact of aid. Though a major part of the book presents this data and information, I would not be honest if I did not acknowledge the mammoth task I had set myself. In the intervening period since I worked on *Foreign Aid Reconsidered*, the number of books, articles and detailed studies on different aspects of aid have expanded exponentially. Today, the 'aid literature' consists of vast array of different sub-literatures, each expanding almost on a daily basis. In the course of eighteen months of almost full-time reading, research and writing, I read drozens of books and scores of evaluation reports. I have printed out and read almost 20,000 pages from articles, studies and books on aid and development—not half the number that I left unprinted and saved on my computer. Surveying the literature to try to assess the 'overall' impact of all aid remains important. But it is going to be increasingly difficult to do this in the future: in the ten years to 2010, official aid levels are set to more than double in size, creating a further massive wave of studies examining how effective such aid has been.

We live today in the age of the sound-bite, where the public increasingly wants to know, in one simple sentence, the answer to complex questions. Does foreign aid really work? One of the key messages of this book is that this question cannot adequately be answered with a simple 'yes' or 'no'. I hope that the pages of this book both help to explain why this question cannot be answered simply, and provide a considered answer to this complex question. In many ways, the book is a counter-blast to the simple sound-bite.

Acknowledgements

This book is the culmination of many decades of work and reflection on aid and aid issues. From the early days, I owe a particular debt to the late Dudley Seers, to Sir Richard Jolly and to many colleagues at the Institute of Development Studies who taught me to think rigorously about development and to question conventional wisdoms. I am also grateful to Tony Killick, a former director of the Overseas Development Institute, who encouraged me to undertake research on aid, and who, to this day, remains one of the most renowned scholars on international aid.

More immediately, I would not have been able to complete this book without the help of very many people. Some have provided advice on the structure and balance of the book; some have steered me to studies I would otherwise have missed; some have provided me with aid data and information and answered questions I have had about official aid statistics; and some have helped search out and photocopy articles I was not able to access myself. Others have been generous in the giving of their time to comment on draft chapters of the book as they have emerged. Among those who have provided assistance and support I would like, in particular, to thank the following: Peter Cox, Alex Duncan, Peter Harris, Stephen Jones, Hans Lundgren, Peter McCaffery, Ida McDonnell, Simon Maxwell, Kelly Scott, Simon Scott, Paul Spray, Olav Stokke and Wendy Tyndale. I would also like to thank my editor, Sarah Caro, for her continual interest and support while the book was being written, and for her helpful, constructive and detailed comments and suggestions for improving its structure and content; and also her colleagues at Oxford University Press who have helped to steer the book to publication. I am also grateful to T. W. Bartel for his invaluable assistance in copy-editing the manuscript. It has been a major undertaking. However, the errors, gaps and mistakes remain my own.

Last, but by no means least, I would like to thank and acknowledge the help and support I have had from my family as this book has taken shape and eventually been completed. I am grateful to my daughter, Becky, for substantial assistance in creating the book's tables, graphs and figures, and to Eliza for trying to move my mid-twentieth-century English style into the twenty-first century. However, my greatest asset and standby has been my wife Abby, without whom this book would never have been either started or completed. She cast her critical eye over successive drafts of all the chapters, and provided constant help and assistance, not least in helping me regain my composure after my computer crashed two-thirds of the way through the writing and when, for two dreadful weeks, I thought I had lost everything on both my hard drive and backup discs.

RCR

■ PREFACE FOR THE PAPERBACK EDITION

Since the first edition of this book was published, in the spring of 2007, its key themes—whether aid "works" and how its impact could be enhanced—have continued to be keenly debated.

The attention of most major donors and recipients has been focused on the Paris Declaration (pages 46, 381-2), with the months leading up to the follow-up conference in Accra, Ghana, in September 2008, witnessing a plethora of studies analysing the extent to which donor pledges to work more closely with each other and with aid-recipient governments have been fulfilled. In turn, the analysis of harmonisation, alignment, co-ordination and developments results—the current "buzz-words" of contemporary aid discourse—has raised awareness of the critical relationship between aid impact and the way aid-giving is organised. More concretely, if the impact of aid is to be enhanced, it is increasingly recognised that donors need to focus far more than they have done in the past on a number of key systemic factors which today continue to have a profound, adverse effect on aid's effectiveness. These include the unpredictability of aid flows and their volatility; the multiplicity of donors and the ever-expanding numbers of discrete projects and programmes; the failure sufficiently to integrate emergency aid-giving with development aid-giving; and the continued distortions of and disruptions to development aid impact caused by the influence of commercial and short-term political interests on aid decisions. It is against this backdrop that the continued appeals for more aid—seen as vital to the chances of achieving the Millennium Development Goals by 2015—need to be placed. More aid without addressing aid's systemic problems is likely to continue to mean more aid unnecessarily wasted.

This, in turn, adds to the urgency of both politicians and the public needing to re-visit the way that the aid system is currently organized, and to consider afresh how to create and replace the old and tired aid system with one based on contemporary international relations and attuned to the needs of the 21st century -the subject of Part IV of this book: *Towards A Different Future for Aid*. The ending of the Bush Presidency provides a pivotal opportunity to re-invigorate this debate, and there are already encouraging signs that the United States might be poised for a radically new approach to aid-giving centred more on helping to achieve the development goals of poor countries.

I hope that the launching of the paperback edition will widen access to the issues raised in this book, giving more people, including especially students and the members of the general public, the opportunity to understand the current aid system better, its strengths and weaknesses, and why it needs to change.

RCR
April 2008

■ LIST OF ABBREVIATIONS

AA	Auswärtige Amt (Federal Foreign Office, Germany)
AAI	ActionAid International
ACP	African, Caribbean and Pacific
ACT	Action by Churches Together International
ADB	Asian Development Bank
ADRA	Adventist Development and Relief Agency
AfDB	African Development Bank
AFESO	Arab Fund for Economic and Social Development
AIDS	acquired immunodeficiency syndrome
AKRSP	Aga Khan Rural Support Program
ALA	Asian and Latin American regions
ALNAP	Active Learning Network for Accountability and Performance in Humanitarian Action
APP	Africa Progress Panel
AusAID	Australian Agency for International Development
BMZ	Bundesministerium für wirtschaftliche Zusamenarbeit und Entwicklung (Federal Ministry for Economic Cooperation and Development, Germany)
bn	billion
BRAC	Bangladesh Rural Advancement Committee
BWI	Bretton Woods Institution
CAE	country assessment evaluation
CAFOD	Catholic Agency for Overseas Development
CAP	Consolidated Appeals Process
CARE	Cooperative for Assistance and Relief Everywhere
CAS	country assistance strategy
CBO	Congressional Budget Office
CDB	Caribbean Development Bank
CDF	Comprehensive Development Framework
CERF	Central Emergency Response Fund
CFA	Commission for Africa
CGD	Center for Global Development
CHD	Centre for Humanitarian Dialogue

CIDA	Canadian International Development Agency
CPIA	Country Policy and Institutional Assessment
CREDIT	Centre for Research in Economic Development and International Trade
CSAE	Centre for the Study of African Economies
CSO	civil society organization
DAC	Development Assistance Committee
DAG	Development Assistance Group
Danida	Danish International Development Agency
DEC	Disasters Emergency Committee
DFID	Department for International Development
DG	Directorate-General (European Commission)
DG DEV	Directorate-General for Development (European Commission)
DG RELEX	Directorate-General for External Relations (European Commission)
DI	Development Initiatives
DSK	Dushtha Shasthya Kendra (Bangladesh)
EAA	Ecumenical Advocacy Alliance
EC	European Commission
ECA	Economic Commission for Africa
ECDPM	European Centre for Development Policy Management
ECHO	European Community Humanitarian Aid Department
ECOSOC	Economic and Social Council (of the UN)
EDF	European Development Fund
EFA	Education For All
EPTA	Expanded Programme of Technical Assistance
ERC	emergency relief coordinator
ESF	Economic Support Fund
EU	European Union
FAO	Food and Agriculture Organization
FCO	Foreign and Commonwealth Office (UK)
FONDAD	Forum on Debt and Development
FY	financial year
G8	Group of Eight Industrialised Countries (Canada, France, Germany, Italy, Japan, Russia, the UK and the US)
GAVI	Global Alliance for Vaccination and Immunization
GBS	general budget support
GDP	gross domestic product
GEF	Global Environmental Facility

GFATM	Global Fund to Fight AIDS, TB and Malaria
GHD	Good Humanitarian Donorship
GMR	Global Monitoring Report
GNI	gross national income
GNP	gross national product
GRD	global resources dividend
GRO	grassroots organization
GTZ	Deutsche Gesellschaft für Technische Zusamenarbeid (Agency for Technical Cooperation, Germany)
HDI	Human Development Index
HDR	Human Development Report
HIID	Harvard Institute for International Development
HIPC	highly indebted poor countries
HIV	human immunodeficiency virus
HPG	humanitarian policy group
HPN	humanitarian practice network
IAF	Inter-American Foundation
IAO	International Aid Office
IASC	Inter-Agency Standing Committee
IBP	international budget project
IBRD	International Bank for Reconstruction and Development
ICC	International Criminal Court
ICCO	Interchurch Organisation for Development Co-operation
ICESCR	International Covenant on Economic, Social and Cultural Rights
ICHRP	International Council on Human Rights Policy
ICISS	International Commission on Intervention and State Sovereignty
ICRC	International Committee of the Red Cross
IDA	International Development Association
IDAF	International Development Aid Fund
IDB	Inter-American Development Bank
IDEA	International Development Ethics Association
IDG	International Development Goal
IDP	internally displaced person
IDR	Institute for Development Research
IDRC	International Development Research Centre
IDS	Institute of Development Studies
IFAD	International Fund for Agricultural Development

IFC	International Finance Corporation
IFF	International Finance Facility
IFFIm	International Finance Facility for Immunization
IFI	international financial institution
IFRC	International Federation of Red Cross and Red Crescent Societies
IHL	International Humanitarian Law
IIEP	International Institute for Educational Planning
ILEAP	International Lawyers and Economists Against Poverty
ILO	International Labour Office
IMF	International Monetary Fund
INEE	Inter-Agency Network for Education in Emergencies
INGO	International non-governmental organization
IRC	International Rescue Committee
ITDG	Intermediate Technology Development Group
KfW	Kreditanstalt für Wiederaufbau (Bank for Reconstruction and Development, Germany)
LDC	less developed country
LIC	low-income country
LICUS	low income countries under stress
LLDC	least developed country
LOLF	Loi Organique Relative aux Lois de Finances (Institutional Act on Financial Legislation, France)
LSE	London School of Economics
MAE	Ministère des Affaires Étrangères (Ministry of Foreign Affairs, France)
MBO	membership-based organization
MBRLC	Mindanao Baptist Rural Life Centre
MCA	Millennium Challenge Account
MCC	Millennium Challenge Corporation
MDG	Millennium Development Goal
MIGA	Multilateral Investment Guarantee Agency
MLF	Multilateral Fund for the Implementation of the Montreal Protocol
mn	million
MPF	Montreal Protocol Fund
MSF	Médecins Sans Frontières
NAIA	National Aid Implementation Agency
NAO	National Audit Office
NCA	Norwegian Church Aid

NGDO	non-governmental development organization
NGO	non-governmental organization
NORAD	Norwegian Agency for International Development Cooperation
OA	official aid
OCHA	Office for the Coordination of Humanitarian Affairs
oda	Overseas Development Administration (UK)
ODA	official development assistance, official development aid
ODC	Overseas Development Council
ODI	Overseas Development Institute
OECD	Organisation for Economic Cooperation and Development
OED	Operations Evaluation Department
OFDA	Office of US Foreign Disaster Assistance
OHA	official humanitarian assistance
OPEC	Organisation for Petroleum Exporting Countries
OPM	Oxford Policy Management
PBA	programme-based approaches
PEPFAR	President's Emergency Plan for AIDS Relief
PRDE	poverty reduction in difficult environments
PRGF	Poverty Reduction and Growth Facility
PRS	poverty reduction strategy
PRSP	poverty reduction strategy paper
PVO	private voluntary organization
RLEK	Rural Litigation and Entitlement Kendra
SCF	Save the Children Fund
SDC	Swiss Agency for Development and Cooperation
Sida	Swedish International Cooperation Development Agency
SMART	Standardized Monitoring and Assessment of Relief and Transitions
SSA	Sub-Saharan Africa
SWAp	sector-wide approach
TA	technical assistance
TC	technical cooperation
TEC	Tsunami Evaluation Coalition
TI	Transparency International
ULRTF	Urban Land Reform Task Force
UN	United Nations
UNAIDS	(Joint) UN Programme on HIV/AIDS
UNCTAD	United Nations Conference on Trade and Development

UNDG	United Nations Development Group
UNDP	United Nations Development Programme
UNESCO	United Nations Economic Social and Cultural Organization
UNFPA	United Nations Fund for Population Activities
UN-HABITAT	United Nations Settlements Programme
UNHCR	(Office of the) United Nations High Commissioner for Refugees
UNHSP	United Nations Human Settlements Programme
UNICEF	United Nations Children's Fund
UNIDO	United Nations Industrial Development Organization
UNRISD	United Nations Research Institute for Social Development
UNRR	United Nations Relief and Rehabilitation Administration
UNRWA	United Nations Relief and Works Agency for Palestine Refugees in the Near East
UNTA	United Nations (regular programme of) Technical Assistance
UNU	United Nations University
USAID	United States Agency for International Development
WC	Washington Consensus
WCC	World Council of Churches
WDM	World Development Movement
WFP	World Food Programme
WHO	World Health Organization
WIDER	World Institute for Development Economics Research
WTO	World Trade Organization
ZSP	Zone de Solidarité Prioritaire (France)

1 'A good thing'?

Those who can should help those who are in extreme need. What could be simpler? This is the principle that underpins and drives support for foreign aid. In turn, the belief that aid is 'a good thing' is sustained by the assumption that the resources or skills that aid provides do indeed make a difference to those being assisted. Yet, as this book explains, foreign aid is anything but simple.

With little public awareness of foreign aid before the early 1950s, it has expanded from small beginnings to become a large and complex enterprise that reaches all corners of the globe. Every country is either an aid donor or aid recipient, and a still small though growing number both give and receive aid. Development cooperation, as aid is also called, is now established as a key component of contemporary international relations. People have strong views about aid. For both individual donors in rich countries and for their governments, foreign aid has always been viewed as a moral issue. Yet the benefits and virtues of aid have always been contested and challenged.

Helping and providing assistance have been viewed by many cultures with scepticism and suspicion. Altruism has not always had a good press, and it is widely believed that handouts often come with strings attached. Such suspicion goes back at least to the time when the ancient Greeks won a famous military victory against the Trojans, who unwisely accepted the gift of a large horse which concealed Greek soldiers who infiltrated the city at night. The phrase 'Beware of Greeks even when they bear gifts' has become a synonym for suspicion. In German, the phrase *ein Danaergeschenk* means 'a fatal gift', one that brings misfortune or causes problems. Less poetically, the British have a saying, 'There is no such thing as a free lunch'. Some of the recipients of this new form of gift-giving—foreign aid—have a nuanced way of discerning between different forms of gifts and gift-givers. For instance, the Shona of Zimbabwe have a variety of different words to distinguish various kinds of gift (*chipo*). They differentiate between a 'free gift' (*handwa*), a 'generous gift' (*gomborero*) and a 'gift given to predispose the receiver in the giver's favour' (*tsinzo*).

In today's world of aid-giving, few voices have questioned the provision of *emergency* aid to help save lives when crises strike, especially natural disasters. However, almost since the modern idea was raised of providing aid continuously in substantial quantities, its critics have doubted the extent to which, in practice, *development* aid brings the poverty reduction expected. Aid's harshest critics have continued to question whether it could ever produce the desired effects, with some asserting that the very process of giving aid sets up perverse incentives which undermine or, at the extreme, completely eclipse the intended beneficial outcomes. Government aid has also long been criticized because of the way that decisions about who to give it to, and for how long, have been influenced by the political, strategic and commercial interests of the donors, rather than being driven and shaped by the urgent needs of the recipients.

Against the backdrop of decades of theoretical debates about what aid potentially *might* achieve, attention has increasingly been focused on what aid *has* achieved in practice. Today, examining the results of aid projects and programmes, and sifting through the evidence to try to understand the relationship between the aid provided and the wider performance of aid-recipient economies, are seen as fundamentally important in deciding whether—as its supporters argue—aid really works, or whether—as its detractors contend—it really doesn't.

The aid revival

Over the past fifty years, support for aid has waxed and waned. But what has particularly characterized the post-war foreign aid enterprise has been its durability: aid has managed, repeatedly, to reinvent and renew itself after repeated bouts of uncertainty, doubt and pessimism. Some fifteen years ago, as the Cold War drew to an end, aid levels experienced their sharpest and most prolonged period of contraction in four decades. This led some to question whether foreign aid would survive in our new, emerging and globalizing world. Some thought it would wither, and eventually disappear, as another relic of the Cold War. However, towards the end of the 1990s, aid levels bottomed out and then slowly began to rise again. Today, foreign aid is in the midst of another phase of revival.

The first years of our new century have witnessed a steady expansion of aid and growing attention of political leaders to the problems of global poverty. This has resulted in aid being given a new prominence, with repeated pledges being made at successive world summits to provide more aid. For instance, against the backdrop of the Global Call to Action against Poverty and campaigns to 'Make Poverty History', in June 2005 the leaders of the main industrialized countries (the G8) met in Scotland, where most pledged to increase aid levels more rapidly than ever before, as a major contribution to achieving the objectives of the Millennium Development Goals (MDGs), to which they had earlier committed themselves: most notably to halve acute poverty by the year 2015. In the year 2005, the total quantity of aid provided by the rich countries of the world topped the $100bn mark for the first time ever, nearly doubling the amount of official aid given in the year 2001 ($52bn).

A record of over $7.5bn was raised by the general public in 2004/5 in response to worldwide appeals to help those affected by the Indian Ocean tsunami. This serves as an indicator of global concerns with the rising number of natural disasters and the generosity of the responses to them. If aid levels expand in line with the recent pledges made, then, following a small dip in official aid levels in 2006 and 2007, the aggregate amount of aid is set to continue its expansive path for at least the next five years, and probably longer. On this basis, it is estimated that in the six years to 2010, the total amounts of aid provided will have doubled again from their 2004 levels, rising in real terms (allowing for inflation) by over 60 per cent. It would seem that the first decade of the century is on track to record the fastest expansion in official aid since records began (OECD 2006a: 16).

The revival in aid-giving, and growing public interest, has also led to old questions resurfacing, and the posing of some new ones about the good that aid will do in practice. How can we be sure that the aid provided today will reduce poverty, given the record of previous decades? In donor countries especially, it is asked if poor-country recipients have the capacity and ability to absorb more aid, and the will and commitment to use it wisely. Won't more aid simply encourage corruption, the extra aid merely lining the pockets of their elites, and failing to reach down to, and make life better for those who really need it? In contrast, in aid-recipient countries it is asked why we should believe the donors when they state that they are serious about helping to make a real difference to poverty and human suffering, when one, two, three and four decades ago they made similar pledges to help, and used similar words to say they cared, and most didn't deliver.

If history is our guide, enthusiasm for aid will not last. Old doubts and questions will mingle with new ones to cloud again the whole aid enterprise, its long-term expansive path, and possibly the public's view that it can make a lasting difference to the lives of poor people in poor countries. Indeed, as early as 2006, doubts were already being raised about whether all major donors would honour the pledges made only one year earlier to increase aid levels. Careful analysis of the massive jump in aid—from $80bn in 2004 to over $100bn in 2005—showed that the additional aid provided was absorbed almost entirely in debt relief, emergency aid and other special-purpose grants, leaving next to no additional aid for recipient countries to further their development goals (World Bank 2006c: 81).

However, the current revival could be different in one key respect from earlier decades. Development and development aid used to be relatively minor concerns of governments, managed and overseen by small departments or agencies of government. Today, in contrast, development, poverty and aid issues have become a central focus of attention of world leaders and a top agenda item at successive meetings of donor governments, and at UN summits. This is not only (as in the past) because extreme poverty and human suffering are still viewed as moral problems, but, in a world of growing global inter-dependence, poverty and underdevelopment are seen as contributing signifi-cantly to terrorism, conflict and global instability. Against this new backdrop, it will not be so easy to reduce aid levels significantly, unless the actual and potential effectiveness of aid are substantially called into question.

The more aid governments provide to poor countries, and the deeper citi-zens dig into their pockets to fund the activities of voluntary agencies working to help relieve suffering and contribute to poverty reduction in poor countries, the more important questions about what aid achieves have become. Future levels of aid and the future of public support for aid have been seen as fundamentally linked to two inter-related and crucial questions: whether aid works, and what measures and steps should be taken to improve its effectiveness. These are the questions which this book sets out to answer.

A different book on aid

The recent revival of aid has been accompanied by an increased interest among both donors and the research community in the impact of aid. Donors have upgraded the importance they attach to assessments of aid. They have under-taken or commissioned far more evaluation studies than in the past, and more funds have been available for research on the impact of aid. This has resulted in a massive outpouring of literature on the performance of different aid projects and programmes, as well as an increase in the number and range of studies which focus on the wider impact of aid, at the sectoral, country and cross-country level. Compared with fifteen years ago, the aid industry is awash—some would say saturated—with books, studies and reports, providing more and more data and information on aid, much of which aims, directly or indirectly, to shed light on the central question of whether aid works. An increasing number of these are accessible on donor and development research centre websites.

Herein, perhaps perversely, lies the first reason for writing a new book on foreign aid. Most recent studies on aid have tended to examine a narrow part of the aid sector and have been written for specialized audiences. None has attempted to trawl through the evaluation literature, bringing this together to draw conclusions about the overall impact of aid, and of different types of aid. Some wide-ranging books and studies have been produced, such as the *Africa Commission Report* (Commission for Africa 2005) and *Investing in Development: A Practical Plan to Achieve the Millennium Development Goals* (UN Millennium Project 2005). But these have focused more on explaining how to use more aid more effectively, and less on analysing, in depth, the impact that aid has had. Ironically, too, the outpouring of new evaluation reports has not led to any new consensus about the overall impact of aid: aid's supporters and critics, and different groups of researchers, still claim, as trenchantly as they ever did, that the evidence supports their respective views that aid works, or that it doesn't.

Stepping back from the immediacy of contemporary debates that dominate current discourse on aid, *Does Foreign Aid Really Work?* takes an in-depth and dispassionate look at the whole aid enterprise, placing this within a wider historical and political context. It focuses particularly on the impact of aid, providing a review and overview of the best evidence available to show what aid has achieved, isolating those factors which limit and constrain aid's greater impact, and summarizing what we have learned—and now know—about when and why aid is most likely to work and why that is so. It also discusses how many of the key factors impeding and constraining its greater impact might be addressed, both those which are part of contemporary mainstream discourse, as well as those which currently are not. The book helps to explain why controversies about aid continue, and why the impact of aid continues to be disputed.

ASSESSING AID IN ITS NEW CONTEXT

Over the past two decades, a number of key books and articles have been produced which have reviewed the evidence of the impact of aid in order to inform debate about the role of aid in development.[1] Is the present book merely an update of these earlier analyses, inserting new evidence from recent aid projects, programmes and studies, and providing a new synthesis to add to our knowledge? At one level, the answer is 'yes', as a major part of the book does indeed review recent evidence of aid's impact to provide an updated contribution to ongoing debates about aid effectiveness. But in a number of important ways the answer is also 'no'.

Many of the most influential studies assessing aid's overall impact, and the relationship between aid and development, were undertaken not merely before the recent revival of aid, but in a setting notably different in a number of key ways from the present era of aid-giving. The last major overall assessment of aid, *Does Aid Work?* by Robert Cassen and Associates, was first published twenty years ago, and researched well before the end of the Cold War. Many of the more recent major studies on aid and development, published some ten years later, were written not only when aid was in a period of decline, but prior to two factors which have had a significant influence in shaping contemporary approaches to aid: the adoption of the Millennium Development Goals and the combating of global terrorism. But behind these headline issues, other changes have occurred which have influenced, or are beginning to influence, not only the way that the role and purpose of aid is understood, but also how one should go about judging and assessing its impact. The following five areas of change are particularly important, and all are discussed in different parts of the book.[2]

From needs to human rights

Traditionally, aid was provided within the framework of meeting 'needs'. Today, increasingly, development is viewed and approached through the prism of human rights. A rights-based perspective attaches great importance to the role of aid's recipients, the beneficiaries, not merely in participating in the implementation of aid projects and programmes, but in engaging actively in decisions and choices about how aid should be used, and the forms in which it is provided. Consequently, assessments of aid informed by a human rights perspective need to include recipients' views on aid's performance and impact. The importance of recipient perspectives is confirmed by the emerging consensus that the impact of aid is crucially determined by the commitment and capacity of recipients to use aid well.

Changing notions of international obligations

Changes have taken place and are continuing to take place in the realm of international relations which are altering the ways in which states understand their obligations and responsibilities. Perhaps this is best illustrated by new international agreements which acknowledge the obligations of the international community to intervene to protect citizens from extreme human rights abuses when these take place within the borders of their own countries, and when other approaches have failed. Major shifts in understanding the nature of international obligations in our contemporary world raise fundamental questions about the role of the international community in protecting people in poor countries from extreme human rights abuses caused or perpetuated by acute suffering and extreme poverty—not least the nature of the obligation for rich countries, individually and together, to provide aid to protect these people. These changes broaden the focus within which the impact of aid is assessed well beyond what aid achieves. They raise fundamental questions about whether aid is being provided in sufficient amounts to those who need it, and challenge current practice, in which official aid funds are provided almost entirely on the basis of voluntary contributions made by individual governments.

A step change in collaboration

For many years, donors have recognized that the impact of aid is not only determined by the efforts and activities of individual donor agencies, but is critically related to relationships and interactions among different donors and between donors and recipients. What is different today is that both bilateral donors and the main United Nations aid agencies are in the process of implementing concrete measures to coordinate and harmonize their activities, and to align them more closely to the development plans and strategies of aid-recipient countries. For a number of major donors, this has already led to very different ways of providing aid and running aid programmes. Consequently, assessments of aid and future prospects for enhancing its impact need to include assessments of the impact of these new forms of interaction and cooperation.

Changing relationships between aid and politics

The end of the Cold War and the prominence given to the MDGs led some to believe that the political influences on aid and the impact of aid would decline. In practice, however, the political dimensions of aid remain central to understanding both the giving of aid and its impact at the recipient end. It is the nature of some of the relationships between aid and politics which have changed. Following the end of the Cold War there has been a sharp increase in conflicts within a growing number of states, which aid funds (often mixed with military assistance) have tried to address, opening up new and different roles for aid, and new dimensions for aid assessment. In more recent years political factors have lain behind the massive increases in official aid to countries such as Pakistan, Iraq and Afghanistan. But perhaps most important has been the growing recognition that the impact and effectiveness of aid is crucially dependent upon the political structures and processes of the country to which it is given, and that weak clientelistic states, in particular, provide a particularly difficult environment for aid to be effective. Consequently, assessments of the impact of aid, and the prospects for its greater effectiveness, require an analysis of the different political dimensions of aid.

Reducing poverty: balancing the short-term and the long-term

The link between aid's revival, expanding aid levels and the adoption of the MDGs has sharpened the focus on the role of aid in achieving short-run and tangible inroads into poverty in the poorest countries. Indeed, this has led to increasing support for the view that the *only* way that aid effectiveness should be judged is in relation to its ability to make an immediate and concrete difference to poverty levels in aid-recipient countries. Yet, the more aid is used to help address immediate poverty problems, for example by helping to expand and provide free basic health and education services, the less is available to be channelled into projects and programmes which aim to address more systemic structural problems and which contribute to accelerating the wealth-creating potential of recipient country economies. Indeed, the more aid that is channelled into welfarist-type projects and programmes—welcome and desirable though they often are—the longer aid will be needed, and the more dependent poor countries will be on continual aid flows from rich countries. These dilemmas have direct implications for how aid's impact is assessed. To judge the impact of aid merely by focusing on short-term improvements in poverty levels provides a partial, and thus incomplete, picture of aid effectiveness.

DOES *ALL* FOREIGN AID WORK?

Foreign aid is not only a large and complex enterprise, but it consists of three different and major 'aid worlds': the world of official development aid, the world of development aid provided by non-governmental organizations (NGOs) and civil society organizations (CSOs), and the world of humanitarian and emergency aid, provided by official donors, UN agencies, those that are part of the Red Cross movement, and NGOs.

Historically, the literature on aid and its impact has focused overwhelmingly on only one of these worlds: the world of official development aid. For the majority of studies, the question 'Does aid work?' has meant—and for many still means—'Does official development aid work?' Indeed, so obscure has the world of NGO aid been that the term 'official development assistance' (ODA) is still widely used interchangeably with the word 'aid', even though ODA is defined solely as aid (grants and concessional loans) provided by the official sector: governments and inter-governmental agencies.[3] Likewise, mainstream discussions and debates about the role and impact of development aid have taken place largely without reference to, and often ignorant of, the growing literature on and increasingly lively debates about the impact of humanitarian aid. Additionally, though a growing number of books on NGOs and development have been produced in recent years, studies which attempt to review the evidence on the impact of the range of NGO development activities—aid projects and programmes among poor communities, NGO advocacy and campaigning activities, and the overall impact of NGOs on development and poverty reduction—are still a rarity. This was more understandable in the past when the development activities of NGOs were relatively few in number, and their influence and impact far weaker than they are today.

There are two related reasons why any contemporary assessment and stock-taking of the role and impact of aid needs to encompass all three 'aid worlds'. First, all three aid 'worlds' are becoming increasingly interlinked. Each year, NGOs receive over $10bn in official aid from governments to fund and support both humanitarian and development activities. Additionally, there is no longer as sharp a dividing line between development and emergency work as there used to be. A growing proportion of funds raised for emergencies is used to fund projects similar, and in some cases identical to, projects funded with development aid money.

Secondly, the overall amount of aid spent on emergency and humanitarian projects and programmes and the funds spent by NGOs for both development and emergency work have grown rapidly and now make up a significant part of the overall aid effort. Humanitarian activities have quadrupled in scale in the past fifteen years. By 2004 (and prior to the Indian Ocean tsunami), total humanitarian aid amounted to over $15bn, equivalent to over 20 per cent of total ODA for that year. Likewise in 2004, NGOs utilized around $23bn in aid funds for their different development and emergency activities, equivalent to over 30 per cent of total ODA.[4] Many of the largest NGOs receive funding from both governments and private contributions. The amount of money that NGOs raise through private donations to finance their own development and humanitarian aid activities is both large and growing: in 2003 it topped $10bn for the first time, rising to almost $15bn when in-kind contributions are added, and it has continued to expand since then. More than two dozen of the largest NGOs, such as ActionAid and Caritas, have annual budgets in excess of $100mn; some, such as Save the Children, Oxfam and the Red Cross, double or triple that amount; and the giants, the Cooperative for Assistance and Relief Everywhere (CARE) and Catholic Relief Services, have annual budgets in excess of half a billion dollars. Each works, directly or indirectly, in more than twenty countries across the developing world. To grasp the importance of the size and scale of contemporary NGO activity, it is sobering to note that the biggest international NGOs today have budgets and oversee aid portfolios larger and more complex than those managed in the late 1960s and early 1970s by more than half the leading bilateral governmental aid donors, including Sweden, Norway, Denmark, Switzerland, Austria, Finland, Italy and New Zealand.

This book is unique in taking up the challenge of providing an analysis of foreign aid which encompasses all the main worlds of aid. It looks in turn at official aid, development aid provided by NGOs, and emergency aid, examining the impact of aid provided at both the macro-level and micro-level.

Outline of the book

The book is divided into 22 chapters, split into four parts. As far as possible, the text has tried to use 'non-technical' language in order to make the discussion of the key themes accessible to the more general reader. However, for those who are interested in some of the more rigorous analyses and discussions, the main chapters contain numerous endnotes and citations of the main texts, which, together with the extensive References section at the end of the book, should enable development specialists and practitioners, as well as students, to delve more deeply into each of the issues discussed, aided by the numerous links given to the key websites of the main donors, NGOs and development research institutes, where major new impact studies, appearing almost on a daily basis, can be found.

PART I: THE COMPLEX WORLDS OF FOREIGN AID

Part I provides the book's scene-setting chapters. Chapters 2 and 3 present an overview of the evolution and development of aid, from its early origins to the present day. Though aid has always been provided to contribute to the development process, the ways in which it might do this have been subject to constant change. These two chapters describe how, in successive decades, aid has been provided to achieve different objectives—to fill different 'gaps' in order to contribute to poverty alleviation, and more recently, to human development, in very different ways. To this day, development remains a complex process, still not sufficiently understood. As researchers have identified yet more factors that have constrained and held back the development process, so, too, have donors discovered yet more roles that aid can play, and different forms in which it can be provided to help address those constraints. If history is our guide, this process will continue in the years ahead.

Chapter 4 and 5 look at the policies and approaches to aid-giving of the main donors which together have created the current complex web of aid-givers. It discusses, in turn, the main bilateral donors (Chapter 4) and then the main multilateral agencies, including the international financial institutions, such as the World Bank, as well as the different United Nations agencies which provide aid (Chapter 5). As the discussion in Chapter 4 shows, the world of bilateral aid consists of a very mixed bag of different agencies whose thinking about aid differs, sometimes sharply—why they provide it, and what they hope it will achieve. Those readers living in countries which for many years have given high priority to solidarity and poverty reduction as the main thrust of their aid efforts may be surprised at the extent to which this outlook and these priorities are still not universally shared. As discussed in Chapter 5, the world of multilateral aid is even more complex, and is characterized by considerable overlap of roles and responsibilities between and across agencies. Part I ends (in Chapter 5) with a discussion and assessment of initiatives being taken to begin to move away from forms of aid-giving based on the independent decisions of individual donors. Efforts are under way to try to introduce a more rational, coherent, consistent and efficient way of providing aid, based on greater coordination and collaboration among donors, and greater alignment with recipient countries' priorities and development plans. Though advances have been made, much still remains to be done.

PART II: WHY IS AID GIVEN?

Part II shifts the focus from what aid has achieved to the different reasons why donors provide aid, and why individuals support the development and humanitarian work of NGOs. As Chapter 6 makes clear, the profound influence that strategic, political and commercial interests exercise on the allocation of aid provided by almost all bilateral donors continues to have a major (largely adverse) effect on its potential to make a greater developmental impact. Chapter 7 looks at the strength of public support for aid and the relationship between such support and the levels of aid governments provide. It finds high levels of public support for aid, but also high levels of public ignorance about aid across most donor countries. Perhaps surprisingly, a significant proportion of people appear to be supportive of aid, even though they believe it often fails to achieve its poverty-reducing objectives.

Both individuals and governments support aid on ethical grounds. Chapters 8 and 9 examine the moral case for aid: what people and governments mean when they say there is a moral case for providing aid, and what theories lie behind these assertions. Chapter 8 looks first at why the rich should give aid to the distant needy, and then discusses the different theories of ethics, justice, capabilities and human rights that have been deployed to argue the moral case for providing aid. Against this backdrop, Chapter 9 starts by looking more closely at the moral arguments governments use in providing aid. It then discusses changes taking place in the field of international relations and international law which suggest that governments are facing a number of new and different moral challenges in aid-giving, though most have not begun seriously to consider their implications. As a result, a gap is beginning to grow between donors' assertions that they provide aid, in part, for moral reasons and how in practice they provide it. On the basis of recent trends, some quite different approaches to the ethics of aid-giving are discussed which challenge contemporary approaches, based as they are on the individual and voluntary decisions of each donor government. Chapter 9 ends with a discussion of individual motives for giving aid, and draws attention to some new ethical questions and dilemmas facing NGOs, especially the larger ones which many have hardly begun to address.

PART III: DOES AID REALLY WORK? REVIEWING AND ASSESSING THE EVIDENCE

Part III is by far the longest. Based on an enormous number and range of assessments, evaluations and reviews of aid, it takes stock of, and discusses what the evidence tells us about, what aid has achieved. Assessing aid is not easy. Part III starts (Chapter 10) with a crucial discussion of the key, and often complex, methodological issues involved in trying to assess its impact. This is followed by nine chapters which look, in turn, at the impact of different forms of development aid provided by governments (Chapters 11 to 15) and by NGOs (Chapters 16 and 17), ending (Chapters 18 and 19) with a discussion and examination of the evidence of the impact of emergency aid. The different chapters also seek to shed light on why and how foreign aid has been successful, and why and how, too often, it has failed to live up to the hopes and expectations of successive generations. There is still to this day a surprising lack of rigorous and reliable evidence upon which to draw firm conclusions about the impact of aid: rising quantities of such material have not been matched by a rise in the quality of material available.

Chapter 11 focuses on the impact of project aid provided by official aid agencies, Chapter 12 looks at programme aid and donor efforts to build the capacity and strengthen the institutions of aid-recipient countries, and Chapter 13 discusses the impact of official aid at the individual country level and across countries over time. Chapter 14 moves on to the important discussion of the influence and impact of the policy advice which donors have encouraged, and often demanded that recipients pursue, as a condition for receiving aid. Chapter 15, 'Does official development aid really work?', summarizes what we know (and what we don't know) to give an overall assessment of the impact of development aid provided by governments and multilateral institutions.

Chapter 16 discusses and provides an assessment of the impact of NGO development projects and programmes on poor people and poor communities. However, these activities constitute only part of NGO development activities funded by aid money. Chapter 17 summarizes the findings of studies which have looked at the impact of NGO advocacy, lobbying and campaigning efforts, which growing amounts of aid money have been used to undertake and promote. It ends with a discussion of the growing popularity of using aid funds to help to 'strengthen civil society', and assesses the contributions this use of aid funds is making to development and poverty reduction.

Chapter 18 discusses the growth in the number of natural, man-made and complex emergencies we are facing today. In spite of huge amounts of money provided by both governments and by individuals, there remains a large gap between the funds and resources needed and those which are currently provided. Against this backdrop, Chapter 19 examines the evidence of the impact of humanitarian aid, in relation not only to saving lives but to helping to restore livelihoods and to protecting those whose basic human rights have been violated. Included here is evidence of the impact of the billions of dollars of aid provided to help the victims of the 2004 Asian tsunami.

PART IV: TOWARDS A DIFFERENT FUTURE FOR AID

Part IV draws together the threads of the earlier chapters, and incorporates insights from the growing literature on the relationship between aid and governance, to take stock and discuss the future of aid. Chapter 20, 'Why aid isn't working', summarizes the key factors which are influential in impeding aid's impact and effectiveness. It looks particularly at the issue of governance and the relationship between 'bad' governance and ineffectual aid. On the basis of this assessment, Chapters 21 and 22 look forward. Chapter 21 assesses the prospects for aid on the assumption that donors and recipients remain committed to the reforms which they have collectively agreed to pursue, and that they will continue to learn from the new wave of studies aimed at shedding light on the key constraints to aid effectiveness, especially in what are termed 'fragile states', which they have begun to identify. The main conclusion is broadly positive: if donor cooperation continues, and the lessons that have been learned are acted upon, then aid will increasingly have a more positive impact.

However, as explained in Chapter 22, there remain a number of fundamental problems with aid which remain untouched by current reforms. Confronting and successfully addressing these hold out the prospect of even greater gains being made. Drawing largely on the work of others, Chapter 22 lays out a series of proposals and recommendations for fundamentally recasting and reshaping a number of key aspects of contemporary aid relationships, challenging both official donors and NGOs to bring these ideas more centrally into the mainstream of contemporary discourse about the future of aid. The chapter ends by providing a number of specific recommendations to enhance aid effectiveness. Among these are proposals to address some of the systemic problems impeding the greater effectiveness of humanitarian aid, and proposals to extend and deepen the accountability of NGOs, especially those involved in large projects in the poorest countries.

Part I
The Complex Worlds of Foreign Aid

2 The origins and early decades of aid-giving

Defining aid

FROM FOREIGN AID TO DEVELOPMENT AID

What precisely is foreign aid?[1] At its broadest, it consists of all resources—physical goods, skills and technical know-how, financial grants (gifts), or loans (at concessional rates)—transferred by donors to recipients. Yet this definition leaves many crucial questions unanswered. It makes no mention of who the respective donors and recipients are, why the transfer of resources is taking place, what its impact is, or the extent to which the giving and receiving are voluntary acts or based on some degree of conditionality, or coercion. Donors do not have to be rich or recipients poor; the short or long-term impact could be positive, negative or neutral; and the motives for providing foreign aid are not considered: it could be to help the recipient, to help the donor, or to help both. This broad view of foreign aid would include resources to address humanitarian and development and poverty needs in the poorest of countries. But it would also comfortably embrace those (aid) resources provided to further the political and strategic interests of either the donor or recipient, or both, and would also include resources provided to help achieve military aims and objectives.

This catch-all description of foreign aid is rarely deployed by those who are directly engaged in the business of foreign aid. More narrow and restrictive definitions of foreign aid are far more common; these have usually been driven and shaped by those who have an interest in particular types and forms of foreign aid. Those concerned with world poverty are particularly interested in types and forms of foreign aid from rich countries to poor countries, and to poor people, which help to address acute human suffering and which contribute to human welfare, poverty reduction and development. These narrower types of foreign aid are often termed *development aid* or *development assistance*. But what, more precisely, is development aid? How might that part of foreign aid which contributes to human welfare and development be defined, and distinguished from other forms of foreign aid, such as foreign military aid?

Theoretically, there are a number of possible options. Most broadly, development aid could be defined in relation to those *receiving* it, with reference to its end-use. Or, it could be defined in relation to those *giving* it, with reference to the purpose for which it is given. Further refinements could be made. For instance, the definition of development aid could be based on the tangible effects it has on the beneficiaries: what its impact is, and whether it does any good. In this instance, it could be defined as that part of (overall) foreign aid which is successful in addressing the immediate humanitarian needs and reducing the poverty and vulnerability of poor people in poor countries. Or, it could be defined as those resources received from donors which contribute to the fulfilment of the basic rights and freedoms of poor and vulnerable people.

In contrast, the standard approach to defining development aid has focused predominantly on the *purpose* for which the aid is given. In practice, development aid has been defined (in general terms) as that part of foreign aid whose purpose is to contribute to human welfare and development in poor countries.[2] It is a definition based on intentions—the intentions of those giving the aid, the donors, rather than those using it, the recipients. Surprisingly, perhaps, there has been no systematic attempt across donor and recipient countries or among governmental and non-governmental organizations to debate the merits of, or formally agree, this way of defining development aid. The definition we have has largely been donor-driven; it is substantially based on agreements made by the leading donor countries more than 30 years ago, and has not really been contested.[3] Just as it has been the donors who have always decided how much to give, and the form in which it is to be given, it has also been the donors who have decided how development aid should be defined.

THE DAC DEFINITION OF AID

The most intense and substantial work undertaken to develop a set of operational definitions of what constitutes foreign aid—what counts as aid and what does not—has been led by the Development Assistance Committee (DAC) of the Organisation for Economic Cooperation and Development (OECD). This influential committee was formed in 1960 by the leading donor governments to coordinate and promote aid from donor governments.[4] The DAC's work on defining aid never set out to define aid in general, nor even all development aid. Rather, it sought merely to define that part of overall aid provided by donor governments to poor countries. This it named official development assistance (ODA), a term that has stuck with us ever since. However, it took almost ten years after the formation of the DAC for donors to agree on the definition of what it was they were providing. The core definition of ODA, first agreed by the DAC in 1969 and refined in 1972, is reproduced in Box 2.1.

As part of the process of defining aid, the DAC makes a distinction between two sorts of recipients, which it terms the Part I and Part II countries. Part II countries consist of the more advanced developing nations and 'countries and territories in transition'. Part I countries are the poorest developing countries as

---

BOX 2.1 THE DEFINITION OF OFFICIAL DEVELOPMENT ASSISTANCE (ODA)

ODA consists of flows to developing countries and multilateral institutions provided by official agencies, including state and local governments, or by their executive agencies, each transaction of which meets the following two criteria: (1) it is administered with the promotion of the economic development and welfare of developing countries as its main objective, and (2) it is concessional in character and contains a grant element of at least 25 per cent (calculated at a rate of discount of 10 per cent).

Source: Führer (1994: 25).

---

well as those countries termed lower and upper middle-income countries (with per capita gross national income in 2001 of up to $9,205). Only aid (as defined) going to Part I countries is classified as ODA. All official aid which meets the eligibility criteria (Box 2.1) and which goes to Part II countries is termed official aid (OA) rather than ODA. To this day, neither OA nor ODA includes any aid transferred from rich to poor countries that originates from non-governmental sources.

Since the original definition was agreed, a number of changes have been made, largely of interpretation rather than substance. From 1979, the costs of administering official aid have been included as part of ODA. After 1989, the poorest former Soviet Union countries, such as Tajikistan, were added to the list of Part I countries, from which they had previously been excluded, with the rest, including Russia, added to the Part II list. Periodically, as countries have become more developed, in per capita income terms, they have been moved from the Part I to the Part II list.[5] It is quite possible for countries which are recipients of ODA or OA also to be donors. For many decades, China has been a recipient of ODA and a major donor, while, more recently, India has become a significant provider of ODA. The Soviet Union was a major provider of ODA, but in recent years has become a larger recipient of OA, while still retaining a (much reduced) ODA programme.

More recently, certain costs of poor country nationals incurred within donor countries, covering education and refugees, have also been included as ODA. Some debt forgiveness has also been included as ODA, even when the original funds lent were not part of ODA: the issue of precisely what debt forgiveness figures do, or ought to, count as ODA still remains unclear and open to differing interpretation. From 2004 to 2005, the OECD recorded an increase in ODA of almost $27bn, a rise in aid levels of a third. Yet $23bn of this increase (85 per cent) was made up of debt forgiveness grants, and not new aid.[6]

As the DAC has not sought to define all development aid, the definitions of both ODA and OA exclude any aid funds raised and allocated by private organizations or foundations, NGOs or individuals.[7] Further confusion arises because 'development aid' and the technical term 'official development assistance' are also used interchangeably to describe concessional transfers which contribute to both development and humanitarian and emergency objectives.[8] To this day, there remains no internationally agreed definition of the aid provided by non-governmental development and humanitarian agencies, whether in terms of its purpose, its concessionality, or the type of recipient. Not even the largest international NGOs and humanitarian agencies provide a definition of their own aid on their own websites. The absence of an agreed definition of what constitutes NGO aid is likely to become an increasing problem, both because of the growing importance of NGOs, and because some NGO 'aid' activities would not qualify as aid under the DAC definitions. For instance, some NGO development projects include the payments of loans which, in the case of micro-credit projects, are often close to, or in some cases in excess of, commercial interest rates. Likewise, some international NGOs use their (aid) funds for projects within industrialized (donor) countries, and most use aid funds in advertising and fund-raising initiatives.

A key problem with purpose-based definitions is that purpose is a very slippery concept, the meaning of which is open to a wide variety of interpretations. Who is to judge whether a particular form or type of aid is intended to contribute to development, and what criteria should be used to judge whether the purpose-based criteria are met? If aid is provided in part to contribute to development and human welfare and in part to achieve other purposes—political, strategic or commercial—then how should these mixed-purpose transfers be treated?

The DAC definition seemingly addresses this problem by categorizing a transfer as development aid if the promotion of welfare and development is its 'main objective' (Box 2.1). But who decides whether the development objective is primary or not, and what criteria are to be used to inform such a decision? In practice, individual donors are usually the final arbiters, though the DAC deploys more rigorous, and objective, criteria when assessing the concessionality of transfers to determine ODA eligibility. Instead of ODA figures being lowered to exclude instances when aid has clearly been given principally for political, strategic and commercial purposes, providing some link to development could be made, for most donors all such aid is invariably included as ODA.[9]

If the definition of what constituted aid was based on it reaching the recipient, or—more substantially—on whether the recipient had the freedom to choose how it might be used, then data on levels of development aid would look radically different.[10] According to OECD/DAC data, out of total ODA of just over $60bn in 2002/3, only $17.4bn (less than a third) reached recipient country government budgets (OECD 2005a: 36). A recent study found that 60 per cent of all ODA to Mali recorded in the OECD/DAC statistics did not appear in any part of Mali's national accounting system. In the two-year period from 2001 to 2003, gross bilateral aid (ODA) to Africa rose by 25 per cent, yet the amount available to African governments fell by $400mn (ECA and OECD 2005).

Clearly, therefore, definitions of aid matter greatly. However, a lack of clarity persists. For example, a quick website search found that the term 'foreign aid' is used as a synonym for 'development aid' and 'development assistance' in over 80 per cent of the definitions of foreign aid given, while in other cases, 'foreign aid' was defined as both development and emergency aid. Further confusion is caused by those wishing to expand the definition of foreign aid. For instance, in the last few years, some have argued that the transfer of funds earned by migrant workers in rich countries and channelled back to their families in poor countries should be classified as part of foreign aid (see Adelman *et al.* 2005). If this were to occur, it would have a huge effect, because, from 1997, remittance income from workers to developing countries has exceeded flows of ODA to developing countries. By 2004/5 remittances were twice as large as the amount of aid flows recorded in official aid figures (World Bank 2006c: 3). For the past 30 years at least, campaigns to increase aid have ultimately been based on an assessment of the aid requirements of poor countries. Unless we are clear about how aid is defined, we will be unable accurately to assess how much aid poor countries need.

AID DEFINITIONS USED IN THIS BOOK

Defining precisely what is meant by 'foreign aid for development' is no easy matter. Against this backdrop, it is understandable why debates about what counts as aid remind us uneasily of Humpty Dumpty's notorious remark in *Through the Looking-Glass*: 'When *I* use a word, it means just what I choose it to mean—neither more nor less'. Yet, as discussed in Chapter 8, there is a strong moral case for foreign aid—providing it is the right sort of aid.

In this book, the terms 'foreign aid' and 'aid' are used to describe all aid from all sources, unless the context makes clear that it refers to a narrower form of aid. 'Development aid' will be used to refer to all aid provided or used for development purposes, the terms 'humanitarian aid' and 'emergency aid' for aid used, or intended for, humanitarian and emergency purposes. The term 'ODA' will be used in the sense that it has been given by the DAC, namely development and emergency aid provided by official donors.

A snapshot of the history of aid

For all its drawbacks, the long-term record of official development assistance remains the best initial indicator of trends in overall aid-giving. Figures 2.1 and 2.2 chart the levels of ODA provided by the leading OECD donors from the early 1950s (when records began) to the present day. They tell three key stories.

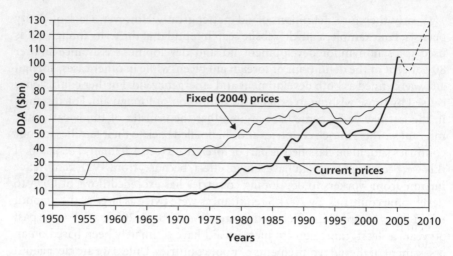

Figure 2.1 Official development assistance (ODA), 1950–2010.
Note: 2006–10 figures are OECD projections.
Source: OECD database.

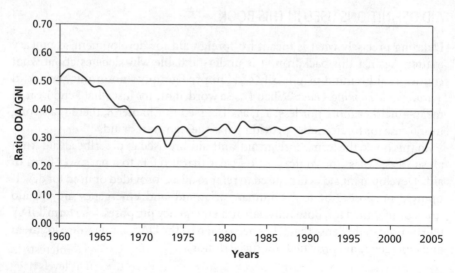

Figure 2.2 Ratio of ODA to GNI, 1960–2005.
Source: OECD database.

1. Not only has ODA continued to expand over the past 55 years, but it has grown to become a key part of the architecture of international relations, as more and more countries have become donors, and none has stopped providing aid. There have been short periods of stagnation of ODA (from the

mid-1960s to the mid-1970s), periods of rapid expansion (in the mid- to late 1970s, the mid- to late 1980s and the post-1997 period), and two small periods and one longer period of decline in aid levels (in the early 1970s and 1980s, and for much of the 1990s). Thus short-term volatility has provided the backdrop to long-term expansion as and when this has occurred.

2. One particular ratio—the share of gross national income (GNI) provided as official aid (ODA/GNI)—has provided a key indicator against which many have judged donor generosity (or the lack of it), especially since the late 1960s when donors agreed to the target figure of 0.7 per cent. Yet as Figure 2.2 shows, for the first 30 years after the target was set, the ratio steadily fell and has always been below half of 0.7 per cent, falling to its lowest levels at the start of the new century. Ironically, the ODA/GNI ratio was closest to the 0.7 per cent level in the early 1960s, more than five years *before* the United Nations formally endorsed the ratio as the target for donors to reach.

3. Notwithstanding the very short-term dip in ODA for 2006 and 2007, we are currently in the midst of one of the longest periods of revival and expansion of total ODA ever recorded, which, if current predictions are fulfilled, will lift the ODA/GNI ratio to its highest level for 50 years—though, at 0.36 per cent, it will still only be just over half the target set so many years ago.

What accounts for this varied record of aid-giving? There is no simple and single explanation. This is the key conclusion from the most detailed analysis, conducted by Dasgupta and Pezzini (1999), covering the period from 1970 to the late 1990s.[11] As the different chapters of this book will illustrate, ODA levels have been affected by a mix of factors, some having a more immediate impact on aid levels, some having taken longer to influence donors, some encouraging an expansion and others a contraction in levels of ODA. Thus, aggregate ODA levels have been influenced, directly and indirectly, by beliefs about the contribution and importance of aid to development, and beliefs about its impact. They have varied in response to the pattern, nature and extent of humanitarian disasters, and to the information available about, and the degree of publicity given to different emergencies. ODA levels have also been influenced by economic and financial conditions within individual donor and recipient countries, as well as the extent to which donors have allowed commercial interests to shape the way ODA funds are used. Of major importance, too, ODA levels have varied in relation to wider political and strategic influences within and across both donor and recipient countries. To add to these complexities, as ODA is a composite figure built up from the decisions of different donors, it has not been uncommon for some donors to provide more aid when other donors have provided less.

It is against this backdrop that we now look more closely at the very different ways that aid has been given and the very different ways that donors have thought about aid from when it was first provided to the present day.

The origins of aid: the pre-1949 era

The last few years of the 1940s are usually cited as the time when the modern era of aid giving is said to have begun. This is understandable because the events which occurred at that time informed and shaped aid-giving for the next 50 years. It was in the year 1948 that the US Secretary of State, George Marshall, spoke at Harvard University outlining his ambitious plan to aid the reconstruction of war-torn Europe. The aid initiative that followed was historically unprecedented. Marshall Aid, as it came to be known, was launched and over the course of just a few years totalled some $13bn. This is equivalent to over $85bn at current prices, an amount of ODA only surpassed for the first time very recently, in the year 2005. In 1949, in (Point Four of) his inaugural address, incoming US President Harry Truman gave the first speech by a national political leader outlining why and how it was necessary for governments to provide aid for the development of poor countries, heralding the way for a succession of other countries to make similar commitments. Yet to focus too much on these events is to distort the origins of aid, and particularly to eclipse the important role that other agents and actors played in the early days of aid and in the formation and institutionalization of the business of development aid.[12]

Aid was provided by governments long before the late 1940s. For instance, non-administrative aid was provided to British colonies through the 1929 Colonial Act, and the Colonial Development and Welfare Acts of 1940 and 1945, while French aid to its colonies expanded rapidly in the 1940s, and even included funding for universities prior to 1950. As early as the 1930s, the United States Department of Agriculture was funding and running agricultural research centres in parts of Latin America.

It was, however, within international organizations and at international fora that the notion of development aid as an institutional international activity was most clearly and strongly rooted. In the 1940s, the International Labour Office (ILO) had argued for aid funds to be provided in order to raise living standards in poor countries. Soon after it was established in 1943, the United Nations Relief and Rehabilitation Administration (UNRRA) was receiving funds from more than 40 countries in order to help it provide food, medicines and agricultural and industrial goods to recipients in almost 50 countries.

Of even greater significance to the development of the notion of a formalized international aid effort were the ideas contained in founding documents of the United Nations. The UN Charter, agreed in 1945, committed all countries to work for the promotion of higher living standards, full employment and economic and social progress and development (Article 57), and to do this by working together cooperatively. Complementing these ideas, the Universal Declaration of Human Rights, agreed in 1948, states that 'everyone has the right to a standard of living adequate for the health and well-being of himself and of his family, including food, clothing, housing and medical care' (Article 25), and that 'everyone is entitled to a social and international order in which the rights and freedoms set forth in this Declaration can be fully realised' (Article 28). Not only was the whole notion of international cooperation emerging from these UN foundation documents developed against the backdrop of war and global insecurity, but development and development cooperation were clearly understood not only as aiding the rise in living standards but, in so doing, as contributing to the furtherance of peace and security. It is also noteworthy that these early debates and discussions were far from being exclusively donor-led and donor-driven. Latin American and Asian countries were amongst the earliest to call, in effect, for the establishment of substantial programmes of development assistance. It was in the late 1940s that the Indian chair of the UN's Sub-Commission on Economic Development formally called for the UN to provide concessional loans to poor countries unable to obtain loans from commercial sources.

It is therefore within the context of these earlier, international discussions and initiatives that President Truman's 1949 speech needs to be placed. Indeed, in retrospect, perhaps the most important aspect of the Truman speech lay not so much in the appeal for aid for development, but in the long-forgotten recommendation of how it ought to be provided: by donors pooling their resources together, by coordinating their aid efforts, under the United Nations if possible; and by ensuring that the aid given would enable recipients to use it in ways they saw fit. This is how he put it (http://www.trumanlibrary. org/whistlestop/50yr_archive/inaugural20jan1949.htm):

... Our aim should be to help the free peoples of the world—through their own efforts—to produce more food, more clothing, more materials for housing and more mechanical power to lighten their burdens. We invite other countries to pool their technological resources in this undertaking ... This should be a cooperative enterprise in which all nations work together through the United Nations and its specialised agencies whenever practicable ... Such new economic developments must be devised and controlled to benefit the peoples of the areas in which they are established ... Only by helping the least fortunate of its members to help themselves can the human family achieve the decent, satisfying life that is the right of all people.

There is another reason why it is mistaken to mark the start of modern aid-giving at the late 1940s—this entirely ignores the earlier and major contribution to the overall 'aid effort made by voluntary agencies. During much of the colonial period, it was voluntary associations—often churches and church-based agencies—and not rich country governments which were the *main providers* of key services to poor people within and across most poor countries (Lumsdaine 1993: 193). Agnes Abuom, the African President of the World Council of Churches (WCC), with extensive knowledge of Eastern Africa, judges that between 40 and 60 per cent of health, education, water and food-security services during that period were provided by the churches in Africa.[13] They built and administered tens of thousands of schools and hospitals, most

---

BOX 2.2 THE CONTRIBUTION OF THE CHURCHES TO AFRICAN EDUCATION IN COLONIAL ZIMBABWE

The history of formal education for Africans in Zimbabwe is synonymous with the history of the Christian churches. 'Mission schools' were established over 30 years before the arrival of the white settlers to the country in the 1890s. By the year 1940, Christian mission and other aided schools totalled 1,392 compared with just two state schools serving the majority African population, with the state contributing less than $100,000 to African education in that year. It was only in 1947 that the settler-colonial government accepted responsibility for the payment of grants for African education for teachers' salaries and equipment. As recently as 1970, ten years before independence, the number of church and voluntary aided schools had swelled to 3,345, accounting for over 99 per cent of all African schools, though, by then, the state had accepted responsibility for paying the salaries of recognized teachers. By that date, no official aid donor had contributed any money directly to fund education in Zimbabwe.

Source: Dorsey (1975: 25ff.).

---

often with their own funds, usually raised by private donations. They also provided skills training, most notably to promote agricultural development. Though their efforts were often patchy rather than providing comprehensive services across many countries, in some places their efforts were of major national importance. Box 2.2 illustrates this, describing the role of the churches in providing education in settler-ruled Zimbabwe. And it was not only in development work that voluntary agencies were active: they also undertook relief work and distributed aid to the needy. Some of the largest relief and development agencies in North America and Europe, which have now become household names, such as Christian Aid, the Cooperative for Assistance and Relief Everywhere (CARE), Catholic Relief Services, the Oxford Committee for Famine Relief (after 1965 known simply as Oxfam), and Norwegian Church Aid, were founded and began work (initially in Europe) in the early to mid-1940s—some, like Danchurchaid and Save the Children, more than two decades earlier. All these (and others) were up and running before any official bilateral donor agency had even been created.

The 1950s to the 1960s

THE SLOW BEGINNINGS OF THE INSTITUTIONALIZATION OF ODA

President Truman's passionate speech and the deluge of aid given to Europe were not immediately followed by significant increases in aid to developing countries. Indeed, it was not until the mid-1950s that ODA began to expand significantly, and by the end of that decade, the United States still contributed in excess of half of all official aid.[14]

What was this early aid used for? Notwithstanding the Marshall Plan's focus on infrastructural development (to help reconstruct Europe), and the prominence given to infrastructural development for at least the next two decades in the aid given to poor countries, it is noteworthy that the earliest aid initiatives were dominated by technical assistance and technical cooperation programmes—because helping to ease skill shortages and to address weak institutional capacity in poor countries were seen as key catalysts for future development. It was these beliefs that had been the driving force behind the establishment, by the UN General Assembly in 1949, of the Expanded Programme of Technical Assistance (EPTA) and the Colombo (aid) Plan, signed by Britain and other wealthier members of the Commonwealth in 1950. In its first ever aid-pledging conference, also held in 1950, the United Nations raised some $20mn (about $175mn in current prices), primarily to fund technical cooperation programmes.

Yet even in these early days, development aid in the form of transfers of financial resources at concessional rates was also actively discussed. In 1951, in the first of many such initiatives, the UN Secretary General set up a group of experts to assess precisely how developing countries should be assisted. A key recommendation was for a large transfer of financial aid to be made, perhaps rising to $5bn a year, to enable poor country economies to accelerate their per capita growth to some 2 per cent per year, linked to the proposed establishment of an international finance corporation, and a Special UN Fund for Economic Development (Lumsdaine 1993: 236; Browne 1990: 45). However, by the end of the 1950s, with the contribution of funds provided by its member governments, the World Bank group was already emerging as a significant source of development finance. In 1960, the Bank's International Development Association (IDA) was set up. It grew to become probably the largest single channel for concessional aid to poor countries.

The 1950s saw the voluntary agencies switch their attention more firmly away from Europe to the developing world, notably to Asia and Sub-Saharan Africa. However, their early activities in poor countries were initially quite limited. They were hampered by a shortage of funds, as they were not yet able effectively to obtain official aid; by a shortage of skills, as many of their original post-war employees and volunteers migrated to other work; and by poor information about emergencies. In the early 1950s, emergency relief aid was initially dominated by the UN's Food and Agricultural Organisation (FAO), founded in 1945. But, as the 1950s progressed, following the 1954 Congressional decision to approve the distribution of surplus domestic wheat to developing countries under Public Law (PL) 480, the United States' influence was soon to become prominent in the emergency aid field, to be joined soon after by Canada. In 1960, the FAO launched its first 'freedom from hunger' campaign, created in part to mobilize support for its work among NGOs. In that year, active discussion to establish the World Food Programme (WFP) as the main channel for emergency food aid began. Up to then and into the early 1960s, NGO aid and development work remained dominated by small-scale relief and traditional service delivery activities.

PROVIDING THE EARLY INTELLECTUAL UNDERPINNINGS FOR ODA

The beginnings of the institutionalization of official aid in the 1950s were mirrored in the writings of the academic community on the constraints to development and the role that aid might play. A study by the influential West Indian economist Arthur Lewis (1954) identified capital shortages as a major impediment to development and necessary structural transformation. M. F. Millikan and Walt Rostow (1957) identified two specific roles for aid in order to achieve faster rates of economic growth: the first was as technical assistance, and the second as finance capital. They were careful, however, to caution against believing the impact of aid would be automatic, even if aid in these forms was provided, arguing that without an institutionally favourable environment, the anticipated beneficial effects of aid would not be forthcoming.

However, it was events in the 1960s rather than the 1950s which were to cement development aid as an enduring feature of modern international relations. This was the period which witnessed the establishment of a host of new multilateral aid organizations and institutions, and a rapid growth in the number of industrialized countries which formally established their own bilateral aid programmes. These were created in part to help administer the rapidly expanding volume of ODA (see Figure 2.1) which followed the achievement of political independence of scores of countries, especially in Africa, starting with the Gold Cost (Ghana) in 1957. Now attention could focus on efforts to achieve social and economic independence. The United Nations proclaimed the 1960s the (first) Development Decade, formally outlining a strategy for flows of capital to developing countries (both concessional and non-concessional) to reach a target of 1 per cent of the national income of all the industrialized countries. Aid targetry, so much a feature of the subsequent history of aid-giving, had begun.

On the intellectual front, the role of aid for development was refined and deepened. The period is particularly remembered for the seminal contributions of Hollis Chenery and Alan Strout (1966), building on earlier work by Paul Rosenstein-Rodan (1943). Rosenstein-Rodan has long been credited with creating and promoting the idea of the 'big push': providing massive amounts of aid to address different constraints which limit the ability of economies to raise investment levels. Chenery and Strout have been both acclaimed and criticized as providing the first rigorous presentation of what became known as the two-gap model. As commonly understood by students decades later, aid was needed to fill both a savings gap and a foreign exchange gap in poor countries, which would result in increased levels of investment and higher aggregate growth. However, none of these early aid theoreticians viewed the role of development aid so simplistically, or the relationship between aid and growth as something automatic or mechanistic. For aid to have a beneficial effect, they argued, it is critical to understand precisely how different poor economies function, in order to see how aid might contribute to their economic transformation. In the case of Chenery and Strout, this meant far more than financial assistance to fill savings and exchange gaps. It also required an improvement and expansion of human skills and, importantly, necessary institutional change. Likewise for Rosenstein-Rodan, perhaps the most critical factor determining the effective use of aid was identified as the efforts of the citizens of the recipient countries. Forty years later, a new generation of aid officials in donor agencies started to emphasize the importance of recipient ownership commitment and institutional change, many ignorant that it had all been said before.

FROM EARLY OPTIMISM TO DOUBTS AND UNCERTAINTIES

From the end of the 1950s towards the end of the late 1960s, not only did official aid levels rise steadily, but so did the rates of growth of poor country economies, including those in Sub-Saharan Africa. In retrospect, these were 'glory years' for development aid: support for aid was strong; more and more donors were providing aid in larger and larger quantities; there was broad agreement on the uses to be made of aid; and aid seemed to be working. In 1964, the DAC group of donors accepted a target of 1 per cent of external resources to be transferred to poor countries, but this did not tie them to providing any particular level of aid, as the target included foreign direct investment, over which they had little direct control. By the end of the decade, there were increasing calls (made first by developing countries meeting in Algiers in 1967) for official aid to be separated out from other flows and for a specific target for official development aid. However, rhetorical calls for more aid at the end of the 1960s were not matched by the sustained expansion of ODA, and by the end of the decade, the first wave of aid disillusion had set in. By 1970, aggregate official aid had fallen to 0.33 per cent of GNI, compared with over 0.5 per cent at the start of the 1960s, ODA expansion had come to a halt, and some large donors, such as the United States, had already begun to reduce aid levels, linked, in part, to the escalating costs of the Vietnam War, and to the growing political attention being focused on South-East Asia.

In the first of what turned out to be a number of subsequent attempts to revive interest in aid and development, the newly appointed President of the World Bank and former US Defense Secretary, Robert McNamara, set up the first-ever commission on international development, under the chairmanship of the former Canadian Prime Minister, Lester Pearson. Pearson's task was to conduct a 'grand assize', scrutinizing the first 20 years of official development aid, and his report, *Partners in Development*, was published as the decade came to an end. Many of its key messages, summarized in Box 2.3, remain as relevant today as they were when written more than 40 years ago.

BOX 2.3 THE PEARSON COMMISSION

The genre, style and approach of the Pearson Report (Pearson 1969) set the tone for subsequent international reports on aid and development. It stated that the world was at a turning point, and that this was a historic opportunity to make a difference to the prospects of the underdeveloped world. What was needed was a change in approach, and above all, a commitment by the rich countries to double aid levels within the space of the next five years, with rising aid levels linked to efforts to expand trade and investment, and to addressing the growing debt problems of developing countries.

The Commission explicitly called for official aid to reach the target of 0.7 per cent of GNI by 1975—some five years hence—but cautioned that increases in aid should only be forthcoming if efforts were made to enhance the efficiency of aid. Building on the insights of contemporary scholars, Pearson criticized those who claimed too much for aid, arguing that though aid can help, it cannot contribute to development—unless developing country governments take measures themselves to address the impediments to development. Aid, argued Pearson, needs to assist countries to develop in their own way, and thus it needs to be built on cooperation and a partnership between donor and recipient.

The Commission acknowledged that donors would (rightly) want to try to ensure that the aid they provide is used effectively. However, its Report warned that donor involvement in aid-recipient economies needed to be both carefully limited and institutionalized, or else it would create opportunities for friction, waste of energy, and mutual irritation, adding that 'the formation and execution of development policies must ultimately be the responsibility of the recipient alone' (Pearson 1969: 127). Harsh words, too, were written about some explicit failings of technical assistance (TA). Too often, the Commissioners said, TA was not adapted to the needs of the recipient country, and not sufficiently focused on helping to build sustainable institutions. They were also critical of the politicization of some bilateral aid, leading to the recommendation that there should be a clear separation of development aid from short-term political aid. They also warned about what they saw, even then, as the proliferation of aid agencies, which, they argued, reduced the overall effectiveness of the aid given.

Source: Pearson (1969).

3 Aid-giving from the 1970s to the present

The 1970s and 1980s

POVERTY TAKES CENTRE STAGE

In retrospect, it appears astonishing that up to the early 1970s, discourse about aid and development could take place without any explicit mention of poverty. At the close of the 1960s, when the Pearson Commission asked the question 'Why aid?, their answer did not even mention the words 'poverty alleviation' or 'eradication':

> Why aid? This is a basic question which . . . goes to the very root of the weakening of the will . . . to continue, yet alone strengthen, development co-operation. . . . It is not to close all gaps and eliminate all inequality. That would, in any case, be impossible. It is to reduce disparities and remove inequities. It is to help the poorer countries to move forward, in their own way, into the industrial and technological age so that the world will not become more starkly divided between the haves and the have-nots, the privileged and the less privileged. (Pearson 1969: 7–8)

One of the reasons why it took so long for the development profession and donors to focus directly on poverty is that while everyone knew about world poverty in general, little analysis had been undertaken focusing on poverty in particular: its incidence, its location, its causes and why it persisted. Indeed, to the early 1970s, there were not even any crude international estimates of the numbers of people living in poverty, either across the globe or within particular poor countries.

Poverty and unemployment had begun to be explicitly discussed in the DAC from the late 1960s, but their reduction was not directly linked to aid-giving until the early 1970s. The direct impetus for change came from two distinct, though partially linked, intellectual centres. One was the World Bank of Robert McNamara, the other, initially, was the International Labour Office (ILO) through its World Employment Programme, though the ILO's contribution was, in time, taken up by other UN agencies, most notably by the United Nations Development Programme (UNDP).[1] Both presented an approach to development based on the notion that to tackle poverty it was insufficient merely to try to raise growth rates and to try to stimulate structural and institutional changes to an economy which would—eventually and mostly indirectly—lead to a reduction in poverty. Poverty, it was argued, needed to be addressed directly, and new approaches were called for, in particular to address the problems of extreme or absolute poverty. The World Bank's approach was termed redistribution-with-growth (Chenery *et al.* 1974), the ILO's, the basic needs approach to development (Ghai *et al.* 1980). Both acknowledged that growth was important for poverty alleviation, but maintained (in slightly different ways) that it was insufficient, and that the direct targeting of the poor was both necessary and urgent.[2]

The impact of this thinking on aid-giving was quite dramatic, and neither aid-giving nor the discourse about aid for development were to be the same again. To the present day, donors have successively swung between the extreme views that development aid is best deployed to assist poor people directly, or that it is best deployed in accelerating and helping to shape the process of wealth creation, contributing to poverty alleviation more indirectly. As early as 1973, the prime purpose of United States aid was changed from growth to the satisfaction of 'basic human needs', and in 1975, the government of the United Kingdom produced a new White Paper on aid entitled *The Changing Emphasis in British Aid Policies: More Help for the Poorest* (Ministry for Overseas Development 1975). Under these new approaches to aid-giving, donors focused their aid far more on particular sectors and sub-sectors of aid-recipient economies and gave far greater prominence to aid provided in the form of discrete projects—in education, health and water—aimed at reaching down to and helping poor people directly. These changes did not make aid-giving any simpler. Indeed, the focus on the poorest and how to improve their well-being led donors to promote and fund complex development projects, some unwisely named 'integrated rural development projects'.[3] As aid diversified into a range of different projects, it required an expanded cadre of technical skills to create, implement and monitor these projects. So donors went in search of experts in education, health, agriculture and other disciplines to complement and add to the skills of their economists and administrators, swelling the numbers of people involved in the business of providing aid.

EXPANDING OFFICIAL AID LEVELS AND THE GROWING VISIBILITY OF NGOS

These changes were accompanied by a renewed expansion in aid levels. The 1970s opened with the General Assembly proclaiming the Second UN Decade for Development, and formally adopting the target of 0.7 per cent of GNI for ODA to be reached by mid-decade. Overseas Development Assistance from DAC donors quadrupled in current price terms, from $6.8bn in 1970 to over $27bn by 1980, rising 50 per cent in real terms, though, by mid-decade, the

ODA/GNI ratio was only half the 0.7 per cent target, and it failed to rise substantially thereafter for the next quarter-century.

Both aid-giving and donor country economies were deeply affected by the world oil crisis, but, following a slight downturn in aggregate ODA, levels rose again in the last part of the decade, in part to help address the consequences of the oil crisis. This increase was enhanced by the boost to aggregate official aid provided by leading oil exporting countries: at the start of the 1970s, aid from oil exporting countries amounted to about 5 per cent of ODA provided by DAC donors. By 1980, oil exporters had increased their aid nine-fold, and by then, their aid amounted to over one-third of all ODA provided by DAC donors.[4] The decade also saw the beginnings of what turned out to be a succession of initiatives focused on the lack of development of low-income (least developed) countries, soon to be joined by Sub-Saharan Africa (SSA), and their special needs for aid.

The decade of the 1970s was also a period when noticeable shifts were occurring in the role and approach of NGOs to development, as the range of their development activities began to extend well beyond traditional service sector provision. Part of this shift arose because the churches were simply not able to finance the running costs of many large schools and hospitals, which in a number of countries were 'handed back' to governments. Church-based agencies and independent NGOs then began to diversify and expand their activities, particularly into areas of rural development, credit and saving, as well as non-school-based skills training. Another impulse for change was the consequence of a particular initiative (funded by ODA) that had begun in the early 1960s, the Peace Corps, which sent young volunteers abroad to developing countries to use their skills (though many of the first batch were merely school-leavers) to contribute to the aid effort. Similar schemes were set up in most large donor countries, sending hundreds of young people from the rich world to work in poor countries. Often returning with a commitment to continue working in development, significant numbers of former volunteers sought longer-term employment in NGOs or formed their own, notably to set up projects with poor communities. As a result, this period saw a steady rise in NGO income. According to DAC statistics (known not to be comprehensive), NGO grants from voluntary income sources, which had totalled $860mn at the start of the 1970s, had risen almost threefold to over $2.3bn by the decade's end. Additionally and in a small way at first, growing numbers of official donors began to provide official aid money to NGOs as partial funding for their activities.[5]

THE 1980S AND THE ECLIPSING OF THE POVERTY FOCUS

In stark contrast to the start of the 1970s, when official donors suddenly "discovered" poverty, the start of the 1980s has been caricatured as a time when official donors just as promptly forgot about it. However, this is far too simplistic. Though official aid agencies did switch their main focus to what they perceived to be the core impediments to growth, they also continued to fund poverty projects. Many became more refined as donors learned more about the complexities of poverty. Gender and participatory dimensions of development were increasingly recognized as important, and donors responded by bringing in yet more technical skills—social development advisors became especially numerous—to accompany their widening portfolio of aid projects.

However, these initiatives certainly overshadowed changes happening at the macro-level. Stagflation (high inflation and recession) was gripping the industrialized economies, putting pressures on governments to implement deep cuts in public expenditure, to which no ministry was immune. These cuts were accompanied by the application of neo-liberal orthodoxies to the management of leading industrialized economies, most notably those of the United States and the United Kingdom. The solution to the ills of the richer economies which were advocated and promoted by policy-makers involved downsizing the public sector, cutting private sector regulations and reducing direct taxes, all to stimulate the more rapid expansion of the private sector. It was not long before these ideas began to influence official aid agencies, with the World Bank, in particular, taking the lead in persuading other donors to adopt an approach to aid-giving shaped by these views and perspectives. As big and interventionist government was believed to be a major cause of the economic woes of the industrialized world, it was a relatively short step to believe that these were also obstacles to the development of poor countries. Best then to seek to reduce the government's role and influence by reducing the aid funds which sustained it, and to give that aid which was provided only on condition that recipients pursue the neo-liberal policies that were being mainstreamed in the industrialized world. The results were dramatic: as the 1980s began, aggregate ODA fell sharply in current price terms, and over the course of the following years (though not all at the same time) all major bilateral donors cut their aid budgets.

FROM BRANDT TO THE HARSH WORLD OF ADJUSTMENT

This was the environment into which was propelled the second major international report on aid and development, issued by the Independent Commission on International Development Issues—threateningly entitled *North–South: A Programme for Survival*, but widely known as the Brandt Report after one chairman of the Commission, the former German Chancellor Willy Brandt (Brandt 1980).[6] Published in 1980, it was followed three years later by a sequel, entitled, even more starkly, *Common Crisis* (Brandt 1983). A key concept underpinning the two Brandt reports was that of global interdependence, and the assertion that the rich world had to assist the poor and disadvantaged, and would lose out if it didn't. In short, helping the poor was in the (self-)interest of the rich.

Though these two reports were wide-ranging, some of their key recommendations focused on aid issues. Indeed, reminiscent of Pearson ten years earlier, one of the main reasons why the Commission was set up was to try to address the growing criticism and scepticism about aid. While acknowledging that there had been aid failures, Brandt's perspective on aid was extremely bullish, contending that it had done much good, notably by relieving hardship in low-income countries, and that, for the poorest countries, it remained vital (1980: 226). Echoing Pearson, the first Brandt Report (Brandt I) called for a doubling of ODA by 1985 in order to reach the 0.7 per cent ODA/GNI target, but went on to propose that a higher ratio of 1 per cent should be fixed as a target to be achieved by 1990. Three years on, the second Brandt report (Brandt II) pushed the date for reaching the 0.7 per cent target on from 1985 to 1988 (Brandt 1983: 7). If an increase in ODA was the key indicator by which to judge the Brandt Commission, then history would have to judge it a failure: following the publication of Brandt I, ODA contracted.[7]

Surprisingly, Brandt I didn't even mention the neo-liberal paradigm that was already beginning to drive and shape donors' narratives about aid-giving—never mind debate its merits.[8] Brandt II was brief and dismissive: it referred to the new orthodoxy of the World Bank as 'alien views' and, rather lamely, appealed for poor country objectives and strategies to be 'respected' (Brandt 1983: 73–5). This was a far cry from Pearson, which had strongly asserted that if aid were to work, it needed to support and nurture policies and strategies owned, led and developed by the aid recipient.[9]

Away from the discourse about aid, in the real world of aid-giving of the 1980s, important changes were occurring in the way that official donors engaged with recipients. In strong contrast to Pearson, who had talked about partnership between donors and recipients, a dominant feature of aid-giving in the 1980s was the imposition of more and more complex conditions and linked 'policy advice' attached to ODA. A new word entered the aid and development lexicon—structural adjustment—though the notion that poor countries need to adjust, and transform, their economies in order to develop was prominent in development discourse in the 1970s and central to it in the 1950s. The key problem was now seen to be (low) growth, and the solution to be the addressing of constraints which donors believed were depressing potential growth, without which poverty could never be reduced, never mind eradicated.

According to the new conventional wisdom, for poor economies to resume growing, they needed to stabilize their economies and embark on a process of structural adjustment. Grant aid, adjustment loans and the conditions attached to them, it was believed, would achieve these objectives.[10] What was perhaps most notable, and explicitly new about the aid conditionalities of the

1980s, was the requirement that recipients adopt policies well beyond those that were thought to be needed explicitly to make *aid* effective. In line with neo-liberal orthodoxies, recipients were 'encouraged' to open up their markets, privatize state assets, adopt a more export-oriented, less protective trade regime as a *quid pro quo* for receiving aid, and reduce direct government expenditures, a condition from which key services, such as health and education, were not to be exempted.

RISING ODA AND A FIRMER FOOTING FOR NGOS AS AID-GIVERS

As the 1980s reached its halfway point, aid levels began to rise again, by the end of the decade quite sharply. Indeed, from 1980 to 1990, ODA in current prices had almost doubled from $27bn to $53bn, rising by almost one-third in real terms. Part of the reason for this change-around lay in the ending of the severe economic crisis of the main industrialized economies, and the return to an expansion in public expenditure. But part was attributable to worsening conditions in some of the poorest countries, and the growing view among some donors (led by the Scandinavians, Canada and the Netherlands) that the adjustment medicine wasn't working and that more aid was now urgently needed. Japan doubled its official aid from the mid-1980s to reach $11bn in the early 1990s, soon thereafter making it the largest official aid donor.

The 1980s saw the first of a succession of high-profile reports which focused on the problems and the plight of Sub-Saharan Africa. At the start of the decade, the World Bank produced *Accelerated Development in Sub-Saharan Africa* (World Bank 1981); at its end, *Sub-Saharan Africa: From Crisis to Sustainable Growth* (World Bank 1989). The second of these reports proposed a doubling of aid to Sub-Saharan Africa—to $22bn—as an essential component of efforts to stem the reduction in per capita income. Much of the aid was needed, the Bank argued, to boost human resources in Africa in order to strengthen both skills and institutions, and to make tangible progress in agricultural development and food security, education and health. Poverty, technical assistance and the role of institutions had returned to the aid agenda again. What is more, the Bank's 1989 report acknowledged that part of the continent's problems lay with donors and external advisors, and, reconfirming the early lessons of aid-giving to which Pearson had first drawn attention, it stressed that Africa's future could only be decided by Africans, and that external agencies (and their aid) could, at best, only play a supportive role (World Bank 1989: 2).

Another feature of the 1980s landscape was a significant increase across donor countries in public awareness of emergencies, and a rising share of aid (ODA) channelled to emergencies. There were a number of reasons for this. One was the growth in the number of major disasters—which rose from 16 in the 1960s to 29 in the 1970s, jumping to 70 in the 1980s.[11] Another reason was the way that the media began to give major prominence and coverage to particular emergencies, such as the drought in the Sahel in the early 1980s, and the Ethiopian famine of 1984. A third reason can be traced to the growing effects and influences of key changes, begun earlier, to the ways that donors approached and agencies responded to disasters. The early 1970s witnessed the beginning of the establishment of humanitarian agencies, such as Médecins sans frontières (MSF), committed to intervene even in complex emergencies, and to raise public awareness of particular disasters. At the same time, key official donors and multilateral institutions expanded the funds they channelled to emergencies through NGOs. Overall, the decade saw a significant increase in the amounts of emergency aid given by donors, rising six-fold from less than $400mn at the start of the 1980s to over $2.4bn by the early 1990s. Growing amounts of these funds were channelled through (largely international) NGOs, which expanded in both number and size. By the early 1990s, 75 per cent of British food aid was channelled through NGOs, 40 per cent of Swedish emergency spending through Swedish NGOs and the figure for the United States (excluding food aid) had risen to 65 per cent by the mid-1990s (Smillie 2000: 125).

The 1980s also saw a step-change in the engagement of NGOs in development work. A coincidence of the slowing down of ODA channelled directly into poverty projects, a growing literature that highlighted the complexities of such interventions, and expanding documentation from NGOs claiming both a commitment to and an ability to work with the 'poorest of the poor' boosted both the profile of NGOs in development and the income they received from state and voluntary contributions, and from private foundations (see Reimann 2006). Some of this new income was spent on more traditional, small-scale service delivery projects, a growing amount on a range of rural development and income-generating interventions. The influence of NGOs tended to vary considerably across countries. It was in 1985 that the government of India began formally to make use of NGOs to implement their own development programme with state funds. In Kenya in the late 1980s, the government judged that NGOs were then responsible for providing 40 per cent of all health facilities (Riddell 1997: 7). NGO poverty projects also grew in scale and size, as did the number of NGOs and community-based organizations within and across poor countries. NGO development work supported by aid funds also began to shift to different and, for most NGOs, new areas. Concerned especially about the effects of adjustment policies on the poor, some of the larger NGOs, especially, began to spend aid money on advocacy initiatives, aiming to influence the development and aid policies of official donors, and on trying to give a greater voice and greater power to poor people to influence policies, and the structures and institutions affecting them. In turn, these developments encouraged a noticeable and growing professionalization of NGOs. These changes were enhanced by the significant swelling of NGO coffers: in the decade from

1982 to 1992, NGO aid almost tripled from $2.3bn to top $6bn, while ODA funds channelled to NGOs more than doubled.[12]

From the 1990s to today

FROM GLOOM TO REVIVAL

The late 1980s and early 1990s were momentous years for international relations and for aid: the dismantling of the Berlin Wall symbolized the end of the East–West divide and hence, for some, the end of the need for aid. Certainly, the steep rises in ODA as the 1980s drew to a close were followed, notably post-1992, with falls in ODA even greater and more prolonged than those that occurred at the start of the 1980s (see Figure 2.1). At the start of the new century, ODA levels (in current price terms) were 10 per cent lower than in 1992. But, as in earlier periods, aid levels eventually recovered, and when they did, the rise in ODA turned out to be dramatic and more enduring.

Such was the extent and depth of the fall in ODA as the 1990s progressed that, from the early 1990s to well into the new century, a dominant theme in the aid literature was that we were witnessing the end of official development aid as we had known it. Understandably prominent among the explanations for this dramatic fall-off in aid-giving was the ending of the Cold War—assertions that we had reached 'the end of political aid' sat comfortably alongside those proclaiming 'the end of history'. Both proved to be mirages. But sharp falls in ODA were also linked to a (short) period of large fiscal deficits in leading donor countries (as they had been in earlier times), and to rising concerns about the environment, to which (falling) aid funds were additionally directed.[13]

There was one other similarity between the start of the 1980s and the start of the 1990s—in both periods a development-based rationale for falling aid levels was prominently aired in donor circles. In the 1990s, it was the notion of aid dependency: too much aid, it was argued, was detrimental to development as it encouraged recipients to depend continually on aid as a source of finance, thereby discouraging the expansion of domestically created revenue and self-sustaining development. But even after agencies had begun to switch their attention away from aid-dependency ideas, ODA continued to fall for a number of years, with the pessimistic mood fed by the public prominence given to the latest round of academic studies which concluded that aid 'didn't work'.[14]

The deep falls in overall ODA in the 1990s masked a trend of even greater magnitude for emergency and humanitarian aid—but in precisely the opposite direction. While ODA funds for development contracted, ODA funds for humanitarian assistance doubled. If emergency funds from non-governmental sources are included, the 1990s saw a four-fold expansion in overall emergency aid funds. There were two factors in particular driving these changes: the expanding numbers of people affected by natural disasters, and the expanding number of post-Cold War local conflicts in which civilians were increasingly caught up in growing numbers. The post-1990 period saw the introduction of the term 'humanitarian war', and the revival and growing importance of an old debate concerning the role of the military and civilians in emergencies, with donors and agencies alike trying to understand the role, purpose and function of humanitarian aid in our increasingly complex world.[15]

WHY AID? POVERTY TAKES CENTRE STAGE—AGAIN

Behind the headline falls and fluctuations in ODA in the 1990s, a lengthy period of intense debate and discussion about development aid and its role in the world was taking place, particularly within official aid agencies, aimed at reversing the early pessimism that aid no longer had a role to play in the post-Cold War era. The first outcome was that after a 20-year pause, poverty was 'rediscovered', and its direct alleviation reinstated as the primary purpose of development aid, soon to be followed by new commitments from leading official donors to provide more aid. As the new century began, major agreements had been reached and commitments made to expand ODA, as part of a wider set of initiatives to 'attack poverty'—as the new terminology put it.

However, the most rapid increases in ODA did not begin to materialize until after the terrorist attacks of 11 September 2001 on United States soil (subsequently referred to as 9/11), when aid-giving once again become more closely intertwined with wider political agendas. In spite of this new wave of more overtly politically driven aid, the renewed aid and poverty movement was by no means eclipsed. Indeed, most aid-donor attention and rhetoric has continued to be focused on the new poverty agenda.

The most recent refocussing of aid on poverty can be traced to two institutional sources: the UN, particularly the United Nations Children's Fund (UNICEF), the ILO and the United Nations Development Programme (UNDP), and the World Bank. Work in the late 1980s on the human dimensions of adjustment, supported by UNICEF and the ILO, fed directly into a UNDP initiative to emphasize and reflect upon the meaning of human development.[16] Starting in 1990, annual Human Development Reports (HDRs) have been produced by the UNDP which have grown in intellectual rigour and influence. These have included annual rankings and changes in development performance measured through the Human Development Index (HDI), consisting of life expectancy, knowledge and living standards. They have drawn attention to the scale, extent and complexity of poverty, as well as its human side, against the backdrop of indicators and indices of human development and human poverty.

Central to the HDRs' understanding of development are the need for poor people to be able to make choices about their lives and well-being, and for them to be empowered to make the choices that will make a difference to their lives.[17] The HDRs have advocated a range of initiatives—including more and better-targeted aid as well as debt relief—to rid the world of poverty. The UNDP-led initiative has also been associated with and has helped to heighten awareness and deepen understanding of the relationship between human rights (broadly understood to encompass economic, social and cultural as well as political and civil rights) and poverty. The UNDP, joined more recently by the Office of the Secretary General, have also given growing prominence to the links between human security, human development, basic human rights and peace, opening up a potential 'middle ground' and overlap between aid for poverty eradication and aid aimed at achieving wider political objectives, including security.

A second source of contemporary ideas and approaches to aid and development has been the World Bank. In its 2000/1 World Development Report, *Attacking Poverty* (World Bank 2000), the Bank placed poverty back at the heart of its approach to development, highlighting its complex nature, and advocating a comprehensive approach to address it, integrated at the local, national and global levels. According to the Bank, the three main 'drivers' of development are expanding economic opportunities, facilitating empowerment and enhancing security. Against this backdrop, the Bank's (not so new) view was that aid is needed to contribute to a comprehensive development strategy designed and implemented by poor countries themselves, not least through its contribution to building capacities, strengthening institutions and improving governance. Twenty years earlier, the state had been seen as a core part of the problem; now it was heralded as central to the solution. A steady outflow of major and minor World Bank studies was produced around the turn of the century to counter the pessimism surrounding aid-giving. These argued that aid does work, particularly when provided to recipients who are committed to using it well, supported by policies and institutions which facilitate its efficient use.[18]

RESHAPING THE DONOR RESPONSE FOR THE NEW MILLENNIUM

The intellectual debates and discussions about the role that aid should play, directly and indirectly, in contributing to development and poverty alleviation at the turn of the century ran in parallel with, and were often linked to, a succession of high-profile major international conferences devoted to a particular development issue, including education (for all), women, children and housing (habitat), most of which were organized by the United Nations. These tended to follow a similar pattern of outlining problems, highlighting solutions and eliciting pledges of support, including, especially, pledges of aid.[19] These events had their critics, who drew attention to the facts that they covered much the same ground, did not seem to lead to a clear and coordinated international response, and were expensive and time-consuming to organize and to run. There was much talk of aid fatigue at the start of the 1990s; by the end of the decade, there was growing talk of international conference fatigue.

It was against this background that the OECD/DAC embarked on a series of initiatives to regalvanize interest in aid. Particularly important was the work leading up to its 1996 publication—it reads more like a manifesto for the reinvention of aid—*Shaping the 21st Century: The Contribution of Development Co-operation* (OECD 1996). This pinpointed themes and used words and phrases which were to shape the language and rhetoric of the aid donors for the new century, mixing new with old (and perhaps forgotten) lessons of earlier periods of aid-giving. Among the most important were the following:

- The need for aid recipients to take control of the development process, for aid to be integrated into recipient-owned and-led policy frameworks, developed with the co-operation of local civil societies.
- The need for recipient countries to foster internal accountability for their activities.
- The need for strong and effective partnerships between donors and recipients.
- The need for donors to work more closely together by coordinating and harmonizing their aid activities, and by providing aid on a more reliable basis, including through direct support for public expenditure programmes.
- The need for all activities and policies of donors to be harmonized and consistent with their aid and development policies.
- The emphasis given to the building of institutions and capacities.
- The need to rethink how aid-giving is assessed, with a focus less on what is provided and more on results, and the wider impact of the aid provided.

Shaping the 21st Century highlighted the continuing gap between these (grand) intentions and the reality of declining aid levels in the mid-1990s. Indeed, an underlying purpose in producing and promoting the document was to contribute to shaming the donors into action.[20] It certainly contributed to shaping the thinking that informed the background inputs feeding into the Millennium Development Summit of Heads of State, convened by the United Nations, and held in September 2000.

The 2000 Summit was pivotal for the future of aid because it agreed the Millennium Declaration, pledging all nations to commit themselves to ridding the world of extreme poverty, and, in particular, to halve the proportion of the world's people whose income is less than one dollar a day by 2015. The Summit Declaration called especially on industrialized countries to raise levels of ODA, and, following the precedent set decades earlier, highlighted the particular plight of the least developed countries, and Sub-Saharan Africa.[21] In turn, the

---

BOX 3.1 THE MILLENNIUM DEVELOPMENT GOALS (KEY FEATURES)

Goal 1: Eradicate extreme poverty and hunger
- Between 1990 and 2015, halve the proportion of people whose income is less than $1 a day
- Between 1990 and 2015, halve the proportion of people who still suffer from hunger

Goal 2: Achieve universal primary education
- Ensure that by 2015 children will be able to complete a full course of primary education

Goal 3: Promote gender equality and empower women
- Eliminate gender disparity in primary and secondary education, preferably by 2015, and in all levels of education no later than 2015

Goal 4: Reduce child mortality
- Between 1990 and 2015, reduce by two-thirds the under-five mortality rate

Goal 5: Improve maternal health
- Between 1990 and 2015, reduce by three-quarters the maternal mortality ratio

Goal 6: Combat HIV/AIDS, malaria and other diseases
- By 2015, have halted and begun to reverse the spread of HIV/AIDS and the incidence of malaria and other diseases

Goal 7: Ensure environmental sustainability
- By 2015, halve the proportion of people without sustainable access to safe drinking water and basic sanitation

Goal 8: Develop a global partnership for development
- Address the special needs of the least developed countries, including more generous ODA for countries committed to poverty reduction

---

Summit and the Millennium Declaration led, in the following year, to the articulation of the more detailed Millennium Development Goals (MDGs), which all nations—aid recipients as well as aid donors—committed themselves to help achieve.[22] As is now well known, the MDGs quickly became a central yardstick against which most development and development-aid-giving efforts were subsequently to be judged. They are summarized in Box 3.1.

A NEW WAVE OF REPORTS

The International Development Goals (IDGs) agreed at the Millennium Summit and the MDGs provided the backdrop for the work of a United Nations panel chaired by Ernesto Zedillo, the former President of Mexico, set up to assess the funds needed and strategies required to mobilize funds to achieve the agreed IDGs. The panel reported to the Secretary General in June 2001.[23] It made estimates of the amount of development aid required to achieve the IDGs, concluding that an additional $50bn in ODA was required each year, 'almost double the ODA currently provided' (Zedillo 2002: 20), and urged the Forthcoming Conference on Financing for Development to 'obtain a commitment from the industrialised countries to implement the target of providing 0.7 per cent of GNP', suggesting this be reached by the year 2025 (Zedillo 2002: 8, 55). Harking back, in part, to the recommendations of the Brandt Commission 20 years earlier, it lamented the slow progress made in ensuring greater coherence and coordination of different aid agencies and institutions, and the fact that 'the international community has no commonly agreed instrument or procedure for deciding what it does' (Zedillo 2002: 23). It lauded the multilateral approach to resolving common human problems and specifically recommended that 'aid should be voluntarily and prudently shifted to a common pool basis that would finance the recipient's announced developed strategy'(Zedillo 2002: 8), adding that when countries are no longer poor, they, too, should become aid donors (Zedillo 2002: 61). As well as criticizing the low amounts of ODA, Zedillo was also very critical of the array of conditions that donors applied to their ODA, and of the continued tying of technical assistance to donor-country interests.

The Zedillo Report also introduced some new ideas and proposals. In particular, it drew attention to the shortfalls in (official) funding for humanitarian crises (estimating an adequate minimum standard of response would require 60 per cent more aid than prevailing ODA levels allocated to emergencies), and recommended that funds for emergencies be distinct and different from ODA for development. Building on the work done especially by the UNDP from the early 1990s, the Report also discussed the funding of global public goods and, as for humanitarian aid, recommended that such funds be provided separately from those required to address development and emergency needs. It warmed to the idea of developing new international tax sources to fund these important 'new needs' in order to provide both stable and contractual resources for these purposes. The Report added a further role for ODA, namely to confront and accelerate recovery from financial crises (Zedillo 2002: 5). It expressed the view that additional ODA in the amounts required was unlikely to be forthcoming unless pressure was brought to bear upon donors, and went on to recommend a public campaign to increase aggregate levels of ODA, aimed in particular at those who had fallen furthest behind in meeting internationally and domestically agreed aid targets.

In March 2002, in Monterrey, Mexico, heads of state of UN member countries met and produced the 'Monterrey consensus' on aid financing for the new millennium.[24] Monterrey has been acclaimed as a conference where rich countries pledged—yet again—to achieve the 0.7 per cent ODA/GNI target.

In fact, the declaration was far weaker than this: it merely urged 'developed countries that have not done so to make concrete efforts towards the target of 0.7 per cent of GNP to developing countries' (UN 2002: 9–10). Building on the work of the OECD/DAC and on the Zedillo Report, however, Monterrey placed ODA within the wider framework of an increase in all financial flows to developing countries, and urged all countries to work coherently towards removing trade restrictions and reducing unmanageable debt. On aid, it emphasized the role of donor–recipient partnerships as the basis for all aid-giving, and highlighted the role of aid recipients in contributing to aid effectiveness. It urged donors to harmonize their efforts, to work to reduce transaction costs, to untie their aid further, to enhance recipient-country ownership, and to improve ODA targeting to the poor (UN 2002: 10).[25] It spoke of the need to enhance coherence between the efforts of different donors, and was probably at its least bland in stating that 'greater co-operation among existing institutions is needed' (UN 2002: 15). Monterrey linked donor efforts to achieving the MDGs, and ended by calling on the UN to monitor performance against these goals, and to hold a further conference in 2005 to review implementation.

Following Monterrey, the United Nations set up an independent advisory body which became known as the Millennium Development Project. Originally conceived as an initiative to assess performance and progress, the Project commissioned an array of sectoral studies as background to a report produced in early 2005 as the key preparatory document for the September 2005 Summit. Termed by some a blueprint, the report, *Investing in Development: A Practical Plan to Achieve the Millennium Development Goals* (UN Millennium Project 2005), is more forward-than backward-looking. It fleshes out in detail precisely how the authors, most notably its lead author, Professor Jeffrey Sachs, believe the different MDGs might be achieved to halve poverty by the year 2015. A key recommendation is to call for a step change in aid-giving, in order to marry aid-giving more closely to aid needs, estimated in 2006 to be $135bn, double the prevailing levels of ODA. The Report not only calls for these aid gaps to be eliminated, but for a massive expansion in ODA to be sustained, in order to reach $195bn by 2015. The Report is highly critical of the way that ODA has been provided, arguing that the 'international system is ill-equipped to provide it [international support] because of a shortage of supportive rules, effective institutional arrangements and, above all, a lack of resolve to translate commitment to action' (ibid. 194). It argues that the aid-giving system needs to change by fine-tuning it to the core purpose of achieving the MDGs, requiring greater coordination, a longer-term framework, improved aid quality, and a commitment to linking ODA directly to achieving the MDGs.

Building on the central notion of recipient-country ownership, its 'core operational recommendation' (ibid. 56) is for each poor country to create its own development strategy, built on the MDGs, with development finance filling any unmet financing needs. It argues that aid is needed to help break out of what it calls the 'poverty trap', and that aid should be viewed more as contributing to self-sustaining growth (wealth creation) by enhancing the capital stock of a poor country (ibid. 50–2). But then the Report proceeds to detail precisely how aid ought to be spent to achieve the different MDGs, in many ways distancing itself from—if not contradicting—the earlier emphasis given to recipient ownership, and the need for donors to contribute to a recipient-driven development plan.

Quick on the heels of this UN-sponsored report, a few weeks later the report of the Commission for Africa—a group largely consisting of a select group of mostly African and UK leaders convened by the British Prime Minister, Tony Blair—was published (Commission for Africa 2005). Entitled *Our Common Interest*, this provided yet another blueprint, this time for Sub-Saharan Africa, written as an input to the 2005 annual meeting of the group of eight industrialized countries (the G8), hosted by the UK government. Like the UN Millennium Project Report and others before it, *Our Common Interest* calls for a big push on many fronts (aid, trade, debt relief) and a harmonization of all development policies in donor countries to resolve the continuing problems of African poverty. It focuses predominantly on what the 'world' must do, while acknowledging that many of the impediments to African development lie within the continent. It argues that a prerequisite for eliminating poverty in Africa is the achievement of good governance, peace and security (Commission for Africa 2005: 85). The Commission called for a doubling of aid (ODA) to Sub-Saharan Africa by 2010, from $25bn to $50bn a year, with a further increase to $75bn a year by 2015, which, the Commission added, would be well within the target of 0.7 per cent of GNI for aggregate ODA (ibid. 90).

The Commission's report highlights particular reforms to aid-giving which, it argues, are necessary to achieving greater impact. Many of these have been rehearsed in previous reports. They include ensuring that aid is aligned more closely with recipient priorities, channelling aid to where it is most needed and can be best used, radically reducing conditionalities attached to aid-giving and the tying of aid, ensuring aid is provided within a longer time frame, and using aid to poor countries to help protect them from external shocks (ibid. ch. 9). However, it also outlines some new ideas. It calls for a strengthening of aid accountability at the recipient end, and maintains strongly that it is African countries, and not donor countries, which must decide when and how they choose to promote external trade and what tariff regime to adopt. *Our Common Interest* emphasizes the need for accelerated growth to address poverty, and stresses that aid to Africa needs to be used to support the programmes and policies of the countries to which it is given. But then, like the UN Millennium Project Report, it proceeds to spell out in detail the many concrete ways (some 35) in which it believes aid ought to be used. Not surprisingly, the Report and all its recommendations were quickly and formally endorsed by the UK government. A year later, in mid-2006, it was announced that an independent Africa Progress Panel was to be set up, chaired by the UN Secretary General, to monitor progress, publishing an annual progress report for the G8 and the UN.[26]

Both the UN Millennium Project and the Commission for Africa reports have been used to press leading donors to increase their development aid spending and improve the quality of their aid, as have successive international aid conferences which took place in Rome in 2003, in Marrakech in 2004, and in Paris in 2005.

Led by the UN and the OECD/DAC, these conferences have focused particularly on increased donor cooperation and harmonization of aid efforts, and on aligning donor activities more closely with the policies and strategies of aid-recipient countries. The most important was the Paris conference, where donors (and some recipients) made concrete commitments to work more closely together, in what is now referred to as the Paris Declaration, (OECD 2005b).[27]

In the period leading up to and at the 2005 G8 meeting, a number of donors, including the 15 largest EU aid donors, committed themselves to reach the 0.7 per cent of GNI target by 2015, and 0.56 per cent by 2010, and most major donors agreed to double the aid they give to Africa. On this basis, in mid-2005, the OECD judged that ODA would increase by $50bn by 2010, including an additional $25bn for Africa.[28] However, not all the increased aid committed to Africa constitutes new aid and considerable confusion arose concerning the extent to which the forgiveness of debt arising from non-concessional funds should count as ODA.[29] Additionally, the history of aid has been replete with donor countries failing to commit aid funds that have been pledged, to budget aid in the quantities committed, and to disburse funds in the amounts budgeted.[30]

DIFFERENT WAYS OF PROVIDING AID

The world of aid has changed in many other ways since the early 1990s. An important cluster of changes involves the ways in which ODA is given, and the frameworks within which it is provided. Early on in the decade of the 1990s, the formal linkage between aid and structural adjustment was broken. Donors have sought to replace adjustment-linked aid by aid framework agreements which emphasize recipient-based development strategies, with a particular focus on poverty eradication. For a growing number of recipients, donors have encouraged the drafting of what were first called poverty reduction strategy papers (PRSPs)—now largely abbreviated to merely poverty reduction strategies (PRSes). Ideally, these provide medium-term expenditure frameworks which allocate resources according to agreed priorities, which are then reflected in annual budgets. They are meant to be produced by recipient countries themselves, based on consultations with, and inputs from, domestic interest groups, including, especially, civil society groups, notably those linked to, or representing, different groups of poor people. In practice, many of these documents have been criticized as being externally driven, and in some cases externally written, the similarity of many being cited as evidence of their Washington/World Bank origins.[31]

The past 15 years have also witnessed a marked expansion in the use of different aid modalities, including new ones. Many of these new approaches have been based on attempts to move away from the details of small discrete projects, replacing them with larger and less specifically targeted blocks of aid. For instance, some donors have been providing aid to sector-wide approaches (SWAps), which channel aid to whole sectors, such as health or education, or to defined sub-sectors, such as primary education.[32] More recently, and especially in countries where donors believe recipients are able to use aid funds well and account for them transparently, some donors have increasingly provided aid funds in the form of 'budget support'. This usually consists of a block grant to the recipient government, providing additional funds to boost and expand government expenditures, both recurrent expenditures to be spent in line with an overall 'plan' presented to and agreed by the donors, and agreed longer-term capital expenditures.

There are other ways in which official donor aid-giving has evolved and changed in recent years. First, and as noted above, official donors have also sought to expand and enhance the capacity of recipient governments, line ministries and related institutions, either by adding a capacity-building dimension to projects or, in growing numbers, by developing stand-alone capacity-building and -enhancing aid projects and programmes. Secondly, more and more donors have paid growing attention to the plight and the particular development problems of countries in conflict, countries emerging from conflict, and countries in which the risk of conflict is high, and many have channelled significant amounts of aid to such countries. There is sometimes a link between the two: instability and, at the extreme, war can undermine and erode the quality of institutions, eroding past development gains, and impeding future prospects. One consequence of donors channelling more and more 'development' aid (ODA) to conflict countries is that the distinction between development and emergency aid has become even more blurred.

There have been two other important recent developments. The first has been the growth in the number of extremely wealthy individual philanthropists, new private foundations (such as the Gates Foundation, the Open Society and Google.org) and corporations who are channelling significant amounts of money into development, swelling the amounts of private aid donations. The second has been the establishment of new development funds, targeted at particular development needs, such as the eradication of malaria, which have attracted massive funding from both official aid agencies as well as from philanthropists, foundations and private corporations.[33]

NGOS AS MAJOR PLAYERS

The post-1990 period has seen further changes and consolidation in the status and importance of NGOs as aid donors. The steep falls in ODA which marked the early 1990s were not mirrored in NGO income, which continued its steady increase throughout the decade, with the expansion of NGO activities in both emergency and development activities continuing in the post-1990s era. In the early years of this century, private donations from individuals and foundations to NGOs topped the $10bn mark, and, since then, the steady expansion of the previous ten years has been sustained. If one adds to this figure the funds that official donors provide to NGOs for them to use directly, and the funds official donors channel through NGOs for programmes and projects managed or run by NGOs, then in 2004 NGOs were responsible for some $23bn of aid money, equivalent to over 30 per cent of all ODA. A year later, with the inclusion of the private contributions for the Indian tsunamis, the total would have exceeded $30bn.[34]

More poor-country governments have also made greater use of NGOs, especially in service delivery projects and, in some cases, to encourage the take-up of programmes by more marginalized groups, as occurred, for instance, with the Indian government expanding four-fold the money allocated to NGOs to $50mn in a little over a decade (Thakur and Saxena 1999: 8). The role and importance of NGOs in providing emergency and humanitarian aid is even greater, with NGOs accounting for around one-third of ODA funds channelled to emergencies.

Changes have occurred in the way NGOs engage in development. Of particular significance has been the expansion of NGOs' utilizing official aid funds to implement donor-led aid activities. Official donors provide three times as much money for NGOs to carry out development and humanitarian projects and programmes on their behalf as they provide to support activities which NGOs themselves choose to implement. For many years, different UN agencies have made use of NGOs to help them implement their own programmes, and the amounts provided to NGOs through UN agencies has continued to increase (Reimann 2006). These developments, in turn, have led to the growth of large and complex NGO projects and programmes, a number in excess of $1mn, and often involving hundreds and thousands of beneficiaries. In some cases, NGOs directly compete with the private sector, and have become (with them) public service contractors, blurring the distinction between these NGOs and private sector agencies. Similarly, large official donors, such as the World Bank, have increasingly sought to involve NGOs in drawing up, and in some cases implementing, more and more of their own projects. This period has also seen the growth of a number of very large recipient-country-based NGOs, especially in South and East Asia, where local NGOs overseeing multi-million-dollar projects are becoming less and less exceptional. Another change has been the growing involvement of Evangelical churches in aid-giving, most notably in the United States, providing an added boost to private aid-giving.

There have also been changes in the way NGOs engage in development indirectly. Whereas the 1970s and 1980s saw NGOs use aid funds to move into advocacy and policy-influencing work, the most recent period has seen a number of NGOs (often working together in close or loose coalitions) use aid money to fund their direct engagement in campaigning activities, most often targeted at the aid policies of official donor agencies and the wider policies of their governments. At the same time, a growing number of NGOs have lobbied, or been invited to participate in discussions with, aid donors and aid recipients, to help shape the new and evolving aid agenda. Indeed from the early 1990s, NGOs have been active participants in all UN aid and development conferences and, more recently, have engaged in discussions with donors in OECD/DAC high-level conferences.[35] Similarly, some NGOs have been increasingly prominent in trying to expand the 'space' for civil society to operate within poor countries, often using funds from official agencies to support and expand their work in helping to strengthen civil society. Increasingly, the term 'civil society organisation' (CSO) is replacing the term NGO.

One consequence of this expansion of NGO activities has been to accelerate the growing divergence within and between NGOs: it is now far less easy to make generalizations about (all) NGOs as aid donors or as implementers of aid projects and programmes. They constitute a wide range of groups undertaking an extensive range of activities, with differing links to official donors and different perceptions of whether they are predominantly working with or challenging the efforts of official donors. Diversity and differences across NGOs and CSOs are now features of the growing complexity of the contemporary worlds of aid.

4 The growing web of bilateral aid donors

The world of aid is not a single unified system. There is not—and never has been—a master-plan, or even a rough blueprint for delivering aid, and ensuring it is used efficiently and effectively. Behind the big-picture stories of aggregate trends in aid lie the recipients and an ever-growing number of donors. Since aid-giving began, it has predominantly been the decisions of individual donors (and not recipients), and their own wishes on how to dispense their aid, which has shaped this 'whole'. Though some donors, and groups of official donors, have been more influential at different times, no single donor or recipient dominates. In the 1950s, the United States accounted for half of all Official Development Assistance (ODA), but since then its share of the total has fallen, and in 1993, Japan became the single largest official aid donor. From 2001, the United States regained its place as the single largest donor, but today only contributes around a quarter of total ODA.

This chapter and the next provide an overview of the approach of the major donors to aid-giving. Because of their dominance and greater importance, the main focus is on official aid donors, though attention is also focused, in this chapter, on the phenomenal growth in the numbers of non-governmental organizations (NGOs).

The ever-increasing number of donors

Official aid remains the most important component of aid, accounting today for over 70 per cent of all development and emergency aid. At its simplest, official aid is made up of two elements, bilateral and multilateral aid. Bilateral aid is provided directly by governments, through their official aid agencies, to an aid-recipient country. Multilateral aid is provided to the recipient by an international organization active in development. About three-quarters of ODA consists of bilateral aid. However, the significance of donor governments and their agencies extends beyond their share of either total aid or total ODA. This is because the largest and most important multilateral agencies are themselves funded by, the large donor countries, and because, as noted in Chapter 3, a growing amount of aid used by NGOs is also channelled through, and funded by bilateral donors. Thus, the decisions individually made by the largest donor governments about the role and use of aid are central in understanding the overall aid 'system'.

Reporting in 1969, more than 45 years ago, the Pearson Commission warned that there were already too many aid donors. Since then, the number of donors has continued to grow. In the last few years, Latvia, Lithuania, Estonia, Hungary and Iceland have all become aid donors. Today, there are about 100 major (large) official aid donors: bilateral agencies, international and regional financial institutions, and different United Nations organizations and agencies. When all the smaller agencies are added, the total number rises to almost 200 (Rogerson *et al.* 2004: 29ff.).[1] The bulk of bilateral ODA (over 95 per cent) is provided by the 23 members of the OECD's Development Assistance Committee (DAC), the rest by some 14 other countries; over 90 per cent of multilateral aid is provided by 15 agencies, the rest by some 150 others.[2] Official aid and ODA are predominantly provided to governments, and just over 180 countries are currently receiving official aid or ODA.[3] Of these, the poorest 50 are classified as least developed countries (LLDCs), a further 21 as other low-income countries, all of which have annual per capita income levels of less than $745. Forty-five countries are classified as lower middle-income countries, with per capita income ranging from $746 to $2,975 a year, and another 32 countries as upper middle-income countries, with per capita income ranging from $2,976 to $9,205.

On their own, these crude figures of official donors and recipients fail to lay bare a key characteristic of aid: the large and growing number of individual official donors with which each recipient individually has to interact. One hundred large official donors giving aid to 180 recipients would average out at fewer than two official donors per recipient. In practice, however, the world of aid is far more complex: each aid-recipient country receives aid (ODA) from an average of 26 different official donors. Only 13 per cent of recipients have fewer than nine donors, and a quarter of recipients have to interact with over 30 donors each (Acharya *et al.* 2004: 5). The problem of donor multiplicity has increased over time, as more and more bilateral donors have given aid to more and more recipients. In the 1960s, the 22 largest OECD donors each provided ODA (on average) to 37 recipients. But by 2002, this number had more than trebled to over 120 (Sagasti *et al.* 2005: 26).

Having more donors doesn't necessarily mean that recipients will receive more aid: there is no clear relationship between numbers of donors and the overall amount of aid provided. But it certainly does mean having to devote more resources to overseeing an ever more complex array of aid programmes and projects. Though the data are far from comprehensive, Roodman judges that the number of individual development projects of official aid agencies rose more than one and a half times in the eight-year period from 1995 to 2003, from just over 10,000 to over 27,000 (Roodman 2006: 7). But this figure is almost certainly an underestimate because, in 2007, the World Bank judged that the number rose from 20,000 in 1997 to 60,000 in 2004 (http://site resources.worldbank.org/IDA/Resources/Seminar%20PDFs/73449-1172 525976405/3492866-1172527584498/Aidarchitecture.pdf).

The sheer complexity of aid can be illustrated by some examples. The Ministry of Health in Mozambique recently had a portfolio of more than 400 official donor projects. In the early 1990s, Tanzania had a portfolio of more than 2,000 donor projects on its books, and in Ghana, over 60 ministries or quasi-government institutions were directly receiving ODA funds (Acharya *et al.* 2004: 4). Aid projects come with a string of administrative procedures, and donors tend to have distinct (and usually different) requirements for appraising, monitoring and reporting on the results of each discrete aid activity. Each donor needs to visit each recipient country at frequent intervals. A 2004 study by the OECD of 14 aid-recipient countries recorded, on average, almost 200 separate aid missions and visits initiated by donors or their consultants to each of these 14 countries. In the case of two countries, 400 donor missions took place, more than one a day; and the lowest number recorded was 30, still more than two a month (OECD 2005e: 44).

The explosion in the numbers of non-governmental organizations

Such complexities in the aid relationship are by no means confined to official aid. The rise in the importance and influence of NGOs in development and humanitarian work, discussed in Chapters 2 and 3, has led to an even faster rise in the numbers of NGOs.

No one really knows how many NGOs there are in the world. There are no accurate statistics recording the numbers of NGOs working in the development and humanitarian field, though no one disputes the rapid rise in numbers: indeed, as one specialist has observed, the 'proliferation of development NGOs has no parallel in other walks of life' (Smillie 1994: 21). Very broad definitions of what constitutes an NGO—including small community-based membership organizations and non-profit organizations undertaking welfare and development work—would put the number of NGOs today well in excess of one million worldwide.[4] However, the numbers of registered and more structured organizations formally receiving and using aid funds would be considerably smaller, probably numbering a few hundred thousand. United Nations estimates put the number of identifiable (and thus larger) NGOs at around 35,000 in the year 2000. In 2003, the Union of International Associations' *Yearbook of International Organizations* put the number of international NGOs at 21,000.[5] The London School of Economics' *Global Society Yearbook* estimated, also in the year 2003, that there were 59,000 international NGOs active in the world, with about 60 per cent (37,000) involved in social and economic development and advocacy work.[6] The number of 'international NGO secretariats' in each country has increased from just over 2,000 in 1993 to just over 3,000 by the year 2003, when 14 countries recorded the presence of more than 50 international NGOs, including four low-income countries: Kenya, India, Senegal and Nigeria (Anheier *et al.* 2004: 297–302). In the mid-1990s, the World Bank listed 8,000 NGOs on its registry, including both very large international NGOs (INGOs) and nationally based and some smaller NGOs (World Bank 1996c: 1–27).[7]

The last twenty years have seen the continued expansion of international NGOs into more and more poor countries, as well as the rapid growth (from a small base) of national NGOs, especially in countries with a longer history of civic involvement in development, such as India, Bangladesh, South Africa, Kenya and the Philippines. In India, some 15,000 organizations are registered to receive foreign funding; Bangladesh has over 1,000 registered NGOs, Kenya over 300. A few national NGOs are enormous: in 2004, the biggest in Bangladesh, the Bangladesh Rural Advancement Committee (BRAC), had a portfolio of hundreds of projects estimated at over $240mn, as well as a major programme in Afghanistan. Another large Bangladeshi NGO, Proshika, in receipt of over $80mn in grants from official and NGO donors, in turn was funding the activities of over 400 small Bangladeshi NGOs. Excluding the handful of aid-recipient countries in which more than a thousand NGOs are active in development and relief work, there are today probably, on average, upwards of 30 substantial local NGOs which use aid funds across almost all poor countries, with possibly 100 or more NGOs working in a third of poor countries. Together, they are implementing what must now amount to many hundreds of thousands of substantial aid-funded projects and programmes in the development and humanitarian fields. Many larger NGO activities are integrated within government or official aid structures within aid-recipient countries. However, both smaller aid-funded development activities of NGOs, and some large and even substantial projects taking place especially in more remote locations, or in countries with weak administrative structures, do so with little reference to any other development agency, official or voluntary. Indeed, a high proportion of NGOs undertake their work unaware of other agencies, and a number pride themselves on their independence of action, striving to preserve their freedom in choosing where and with whom to work.[8]

If the number of official aid transactions taking place in a year amounts to upwards of 60,000, the number of aid transactions taking place in the world beyond official aid must amount to more than ten times this number. As with official aid, no one NGO dominates. However, the rapid growth in the income of larger national and international NGOs means that in terms of overall NGO aid funds, a relatively small number of (big) NGOs dominate the expenditure of NGO development and humanitarian aid projects and programmes. An educated guess would be that the largest 500 national and international NGOs are probably responsible for over 90 per cent of total NGO aid expenditure.[9]

The main bilateral donors

In the year 2005, the 23 members of the Development Assistance Committee of the largest OECD countries provided some $106bn in ODA. These ranged from the smallest, Luxembourg, which provided $264mn, to the largest, the United States, which gave $27bn, over one hundred times as much. Japan, which had been the largest donor in the period from 1993 to 2000, was the second largest donor, providing $13bn in the year 2005. Next came the United Kingdom, providing $10.7bn in ODA, France, with just over $10bn, and Germany with $9.9bn. These top five accounted for 66 per cent of all ODA provided by the OECD/DAC donors, and, between them, they contributed almost 60 per cent of the official aid funds channelled to the main multilateral agencies. Table 4.1 summarizes trends in ODA by each OECD/DAC donor over the last 20 years, providing two-year averages to smooth out some of the volatility in annual aid figures.

The rest of this chapter provides, first, an overview of the approach to aid-giving of these top five donors, as well as the European Community. It ends with some briefer comments on key aspects of the approach of nine other leading official donors to aid-giving. Together, these donors accounted for over 90 per cent of all OECD bilateral aid in 2004/5.

THE UNITED STATES

Except for a short period in the 1990s, the United States has always been the single largest official aid donor. In the 1950s, it provided half of all ODA, though its share fell steadily to reach a low point of less than 20 per cent by the end of the 1990s. From the year 2000, the volume of US ODA began to expand again, increasingly rapidly from 2001 onwards. However, in terms of the ODA/GNI ratio, the United States has always performed well below both the 0.7 per cent target and the OECD/DAC average, reaching a low of 0.1 per cent at the end of the 1990s, though climbing back to over 0.2 per cent by 2005, for the first time for 20 years.

The core purpose of United States aid today is neither poverty eradication nor even the promotion of economic growth in poor countries. Rather, it is to 'protect America', using bilateral aid programmes to foster democracy and

Table 4.1 Official development assistance, 1984 to 2005 ($bn, two-year averages)

OECD/DAC donors	1984/5			1994/5			2004/5			Number of recipients, 2000/2
	ODA	% of DAC ODA	ODA/GNI	ODA	% of DAC ODA	ODA/GNI	ODA	% of DAC ODA	ODA/GNI	
Australia	763	2.7	0.47	1,142	1.9	0.35	1,563	1.7	0.25	104
Austria	215	0.8	0.33	711	1.2	0.33	1,115	1.2	0.37	127
Belgium	443	1.6	0.56	880	1.5	0.35	1,719	1.8	0.47	120
Canada	1,628	5.7	0.50	2,158	3.7	0.40	3,165	3.4	0.30	151
Denmark	444	1.6	0.83	1,534	2.6	0.99	2,072	2.2	0.83	75
Finland	194	0.7	0.38	339	0.6	0.32	788	0.8	0.42	104
France	3,080	10.8	0.62	8,454	14.4	0.59	9,266	10.0	0.44	167
Germany	2,862	10.1	0.46	7,171	12.2	0.32	8,724	9.4	0.32	166
Greece	—	—	—	137	0.2	0.15	500	0.5	0.23	77
Ireland	37	0.1	0.23	131	0.2	0.27	649	0.7	0.40	97
Italy	1,115	3.9	0.27	2,164	3.7	0.21	3,757	4.0	0.22	131
Japan	4,058	14.3	0.31	13,864	23.5	0.28	11,011	11.8	0.23	168
Luxembourg	8	0.0	0.16	62	0.1	0.38	250	0.3	0.85	76
Netherlands	1,202	4.2	0.97	2,872	4.9	0.79	4,668	5.0	0.78	139
New Zealand	54	0.2	0.25	116	0.2	0.23	243	0.3	0.25	100
Norway	557	2.0	1.02	1,190	2.0	0.95	2,487	2.7	0.90	122
Portugal	9	0.0	0.05	289	0.5	0.31	699	0.8	0.41	56
Spain	152	0.5	0.09	1,326	2.3	0.26	2,780	3.0	0.26	123
Sweden	790	2.8	0.83	1,761	3.0	0.86	3,001	3.2	0.85	120
Switzerland	294	1.0	0.30	1,033	1.8	0.35	1,658	1.8	0.43	118
United Kingdom	1,480	5.2	0.33	3,177	5.4	0.29	9,319	10.0	0.42	150
United States	9,057	31.8	0.24	8,647	14.7	0.12	23,581	25.4	0.20	158
Total ODA	28,442	100.0	0.33	58,880	100.0	0.27	93,015	100.0	0.29	
Memo item										
EC aid	1,493	5.2		4,396	7.5		9,166	9.9		

— = negligible.
Source: OECD statistical data-base and Sagasti *et al.* (2005: 26).

freedom. Nonetheless, a key goal is to stimulate economic growth and development, though only in those countries which are judged to be honouring basic human rights. A second goal is to bring 'poor countries out of poverty' but, in turn, this is linked to 'creating job opportunities for Americans by reducing barriers to free trade'. Another key goal is to support a compassionate society by funding programmes for HIV/AIDS, providing vulnerable people with food and humanitarian assistance, and promoting refugee programmes.[10] United States official aid is also influenced by commercial considerations. Under law, bilateral ODA implemented by the United States Agency for International Development (USAID), the main official agency, has to be tied to the procurement of goods and services from the United States, and aid goods and services have to be transported in United States-owned planes and ships.[11] In practice, about 70 per cent of all American ODA is tied. As a result, huge swathes of US ODA are channelled to US commercial, technical and consultancy firms, as well as US-registered NGOs, which tender for and are contracted to undertake development work. Most of these funds are not directly accessible to the recipient-country government.

In short, with the exception of humanitarian aid, the allocation of United States ODA is not directly based on, or shaped by, the poverty of the neediest recipients. Indeed, it was only in March 2002 that poverty became an explicit foreign policy priority. The most recent OECD/DAC report on the United States' official aid programme commented that the US does not 'explicitly target its ODA on poor countries or the poorest of the poor, nor does it focus on the achieving of the Millennium Development Goals (MDGs)' (OECD 2002c: 40). Similarly, the United States has never committed itself formally to a date for achieving the 0.7 per cent of GNI target for official aid, and has tried to ensure that international agreements on official aid targets remain consistent with its generally agnostic, and sometimes hostile, approach to aid targetry.[12]

Most United States ODA is distributed (bilaterally) by the government. In 2003, only 10 per cent of United States ODA was disbursed multilaterally, compared to the DAC average of just over 30 per cent, and far lower than the US average of 25 per cent achieved in the late 1990s. Nonetheless, the United States remains the largest contributor to the multilateral development banks. In 2000–1, only 57 per cent of bilateral US ODA went to low-income (including the least developed) countries, of which about a half went to Sub-Saharan Africa, though US ODA to Africa has risen sharply in recent years. The number of bilateral aid recipients of US ODA has always been large, rising from 100 in the late 1960s to around 160 today.

Harmonization and consistency in aid-giving is made difficult by the array of different agencies which provide aid and the complex ways that decisions about how to allocate aid are made. The United States has no single foreign aid budget, and over 50 official United States entities (agencies and departments) are responsible for delivering official aid. Most are small and, though all operate with considerable autonomy, their policies, including their allocation policies, are influenced not only by overall government policy, but also by the decisions of the United States Congress, where the passage of bills is shaped, to varying degrees, by different special interests. Congress has the ability to earmark funds to reflect those interests, and to influence allocations before they are signed into law by the President.

A number of recent changes have been made to the way the United States approaches the giving of development and humanitarian aid. These are set to influence not only its own bilateral programmes, but also its approach to funding multilateral aid organizations:

1. In early 2004 (though announced in 2002) a new institution, the Millennium Challenge Corporation (MCC), was created to administer a new aid fund, the Millennium Challenge Account (MCA). The MCA constitutes a novel way of aid-giving, whereby a core group of (eligible) countries that demonstrate responsibility for their own development by 'ruling justly, investing in people and encouraging economic freedom' can apply for MCA funds, and, if approved, will be given aid for projects which the recipient countries themselves put forward to the MCC for funding. However, the MCC has been slow to get started and in the first two years, there was a significant gap between the MCA funds voted by Congress and the drawing down of these funds by qualifying aid-recipient governments. For financial year (FY) 2007, the President requested total funding of $2bn, far less than the earlier $5bn annual target.[13] The 'ruling justly' approach has been adopted, in part, by USAID, historically the main provider of development aid.

2. A second change has been a massive increase in ODA, provided almost entirely through supplementary budgetary increases, to contribute to development and reconstruction efforts, particularly in Afghanistan and Iraq and to some other countries in the region. In FY 2004, United States supplementary aid expenditure of almost $16bn was approved, equivalent to more than the total official aid disbursed by the United States in 2003, though not all of this has been spent. These changes to aggregate ODA (expected to be short-term) exacerbate the volatility of US ODA levels, already a characteristic of official US aid-giving.[14]

3. A third and linked change has been the emphasis given by USAID to channelling ODA to what it terms failed and failing states: 'To prevent human suffering and protect our national security, we must devise bold, new approaches to arrest the slide of weak states towards failure. Such interventions will involve risk and their success is certainly not assured. But the greater risks to US national security associated with inaction in such nations can no longer be overlooked' (US Department of State and USAID 2004: n.p.). The Office for Transitional Initiatives was established within USAID to work in and to channel aid to these sorts of 'difficult environments'.[15]

4. A fourth change has been the increased focus on, and sizeable allocation of funds to contribute to, the global fight against HIV/AIDS, malaria and tuberculosis. In 2003, the President announced the establishment of a $15bn President's Emergency Plan for AIDS Relief (PEPFAR), consisting of an additional $10bn in ODA spread over a five-year period to address these concerns, with further substantial funding anticipated, to be overseen by the Office of the US Global AIDS Coordinator.[16] Most of the funds provided by the United States for AIDS work are to be allocated bilaterally, with only $1bn of the total to be allocated to the Global Fund over a period of five years, starting in 2004.

5. Finally, in early 2006, a major reorganization of US foreign aid was announced, making the Administrator of USAID also the Director of Foreign Assistance at the State Department, bringing the two even more closely together, though they formally remain separate agencies.[17]

JAPAN

Over a 40-year period, Japan's ODA expanded steadily, with the country growing from being one of the smallest aid donors to the largest single donor in 1993, when it contributed almost 20 per cent of all ODA from DAC donors, a position it held for eight years. But from 2000 to 2003, Japanese ODA fell by an average of 12 per cent a year, and, by 2005, Japan only accounted for 12 per cent of total ODA.

Like the United States, Japan's aid-giving has always been characterized by considerable volatility, in spite of the fact that disbursements are based on five-year planning horizons. The ratio of Japanese ODA to GNI fell below 0.19 per cent in 2004 for the first time since 1964, compared with an average of 0.25 per cent in the 1990s, and 0.3 per cent in the 1980s. Japan has not committed itself to reaching the 0.7 per cent target by any particular date. On the other hand, the number of recipients of Japanese aid has grown rapidly. In the early 1960s, Japan provided ODA to just over 20 different countries, but by 2002, the number had increased eightfold to almost 170, making Japan the donor with the largest number of recipients.

Similar to the United States, the core objective of Japanese aid—revised in 2003—is neither economic growth nor poverty eradication in poor countries. Rather, it is 'to contribute to the peace and development of the international community, and thereby help to ensure Japan's own security and prosperity' (Ministry of Foreign Affairs 2003: 2). Confirming the growing political nature of Japanese aid-giving, the Ministry of Foreign Affairs recently became the *de jure* coordinating body for the diverse institutions which manage its aid programme. However, the administration of Japan's official aid programme remains among the most complex of all leading donor countries: over ten institutions disperse ODA, though the bulk of Japan's official aid is administered by four.

Japan's ODA is framed within the context of five basic priorities: (1) supporting the self-help efforts of developing countries; (2) taking a human security perspective; (3) applying principles of fairness, noting the particular problems of vulnerable groups, differences between rich and poor, and regional differences; (4) making full use of Japanese experience and skills; and (5) working cooperatively with the international community. On the basis of these priorities, Japan has agreed four basic policies for allocating its ODA funds, none of which it particularly emphasizes: poverty reduction (focusing especially on education, health, water and sanitation, and agriculture); sustainable growth (emphasizing especially infrastructure, trade and investment); addressing global issues (environment, infectious diseases, population, food, energy, natural disaster, terrorism, drugs, organized crime); and peacebuilding (with an emphasis on conflict prevention).

Japan has still to develop a clear and consistent policy for allocating ODA on a country-by-country basis.[18] Some 30 per cent of Japanese ODA is channelled to multilateral organizations. Historically, and consistent with its broad purpose, the bulk of Japanese bilateral ODA (about 70 per cent) goes to Asian countries, and about 60 per cent goes to the least developed and low-income countries. The forms in which it provides aid have been shaped by its own development experience, with Japan believing that ODA is best applied in support of economic and infrastructural development. Consequently, some 30 per cent of its bilateral aid is channelled to infrastructure projects, particularly in the form of concessionary loans (rather than ODA grants), and in initiatives to promote foreign direct investment. Although Japan has stated that it places a high priority on humanitarian aid, historically the share of total ODA going to emergencies remains small, accounting for less than 1 per cent of total bilateral aid in the period 2001–3.

Recently, the government has signalled some changes in its approach to aid-giving. In mid-2005, Japan stated its intention to reverse recent declines in overall ODA, pledging to raise ODA by $10bn by 2010. Japan has also given greater prominence to the MDGs, although this has not led to its altering its core principles, which remain only loosely linked to a holistic approach to poverty reduction (OECD 2004a: 10). While the recent strengthening of the Japanese economy provides grounds for believing that the sharp contraction in Japanese ODA will be reversed, academic studies suggest there is little prospect in the short term of major changes to the way that Japan provides its official aid (see Cooray *et al.* 2005).

THE UNITED KINGDOM

The long-term steady expansion of UK ODA came to an abrupt halt in the late 1970s following the formation of the first Conservative government led by

Margaret Thatcher. In 1989, British ODA was 25 per cent lower in real terms than it had been ten years earlier. The following decade saw a small real increase, though the ratio of ODA to GNI continued to fall, and UK ODA did not reach the levels of the late 1970s until the year 2001. By 2005, the ratio of ODA to GNI stood at 0.48 per cent, still well below the peak of 0.59 per cent reached in the early 1960s. The first Labour government led by Tony Blair, which came to power in 1997, quickly reversed the contraction and stagnation of UK ODA. In the seven years to 2005, UK ODA doubled in real terms. For the future, the government has pledged to continue the rapid expansion of ODA in the years ahead, with budget figures indicating an annual rise of ODA in real terms of over 9 per cent to FY 2007/8, with the ultimate aim of reaching the ODA/GNI ratio of 0.7 per cent by the year 2013. With multi-year budget allocations from the Treasury, the Department for International Development (DFID) is able to set three-year budgets for overall aid expenditure (OECD 2006d: 12).

In tandem with the quantitative expansion of UK ODA, the two Blair governments introduced a succession of initiatives aimed at enhancing the quality of aid and its effectiveness. Its first White Paper in 1997, *Eliminating World Poverty: A Challenge for the 21st Century* (DFID 1997), placed poverty reduction at the centre of British aid policy, and committed the UK to contributing to the achievement of the 2015 international development targets. After the international airing of the MDGs, the UK quickly adopted them as the pivotal target for directing and shaping the British aid programme. Britain's approach to poverty eradication is multi-faceted, embracing direct assistance to poor people, wider efforts to stimulate economic growth and development, and increased attention on capacity-building and governance issues. The focus on poverty of Britain's official aid programme was confirmed in law with the passing in 2002 of the International Development Act, which requires ODA to be used solely for development and welfare purposes, provided the Secretary of State is satisfied that such assistance is likely to contribute to poverty reduction. By law, ODA cannot be tied to the purchase of British goods and services, and can only be used to benefit the UK commercially if this is clearly secondary to its core poverty-focused purpose. In July 2006, the UK produced its third White Paper, *Eliminating World Poverty: Making Governance Work for the Poor* (DFID 2006c). As its title suggests, this sees improvements in governance as a key to poverty eradication; consequently, support for governance will be at the centre of all DFID's work (2006c: p. xi).

In striving to ensure that the focus on poverty of UK ODA is achieved, Britain has given increased emphasis to the impact and results of its aid programmes, including tight monitoring (and publishing the results) of its performance against the different MDGs, and by engaging more formally with recipient governments in decisions about UK ODA programmes. Where possible, it has structured aid within the frameworks of poverty reduction strategy (PRS) mechanisms, and has encouraged aid managers to switch aid away from discrete stand-alone projects to programme aid, including both sector-wide approaches (SWAps) and budget support, working, where possible, with other donors, either informally or in cross-agency consortia. Technical assistance (TA) remains an important component of British bilateral aid, accounting for over one-third of all aid to Africa, though the share of TA to all bilateral aid has fallen in the past decade.[19] Britain has also greatly expanded its field presence, more than doubling the number of full-time staff working overseas, to 1,450 in the five years to 2004.[20]

The UK has introduced mechanisms to try to ensure a greater consistency between its aid policies and other government policies that affect, directly or indirectly, poor-country development. An early decision of the government was to replace the old Overseas Development Administration (oda) with the new DFID, giving the aid minister (the Secretary of State) full cabinet status and lead responsibility, working with the Treasury (Ministry of Finance) for ensuring consistency in policy across the main ministries. However, tensions and inconsistencies remain, not least in relation to trade policies and agricultural subsidies, many of which are linked to EU-wide issues and policies. Though DFID is responsible for some 84 per cent of total ODA disbursements (OECD 2006d: 10), the Treasury and Home Office still allocate some of the UK's official aid. Importantly, too, in recent years Britain has taken an increasingly pro-active role in trying to raise the overall level of ODA funds, and in encouraging other official donors to coordinate and harmonize their aid efforts, working particularly closely with the OECD/DAC and a small group of 'like-minded' donors, including the Netherlands, Sweden and Norway.[21] Britain has continued to channel part of its ODA through multilateral channels, and remains the single largest contributor to multilateral agencies after Japan, though the share of aid disbursed multilaterally fell from more than 40 per cent in the 1980s and 1990s to less than 35 per cent in 2002–3. With Denmark and Norway especially, the UK has been particularly active in analysing and trying to enhance the effectiveness of the multilateral aid agencies.

Britain has pledged to allocate up to 90 per cent of its bilateral aid to low-income countries, but only to those where it is judged that aid will 'make the most difference' (DFID 2005a: 4). By 2004, about three-quarters of UK ODA (net disbursements) had been allocated to low-income countries, up from just over 65 per cent ten years previously (OECD 2006a: 195). The bulk of the increase in British aid is destined for Africa and other low-income countries, following the decision in 2004 to limit the share of bilateral aid going to middle-income countries to 10 per cent. In 2002, the UK provided bilateral aid to 150 different recipients, 50 per cent more than in the mid-1960s, though lower than the peak of 168 reached in the 1990s. The UK's top ten recipients accounted for 58 per cent of the UK's bilateral aid, similar to the figure for the United States (56 per cent) but lower than that of Japan (68 per cent) (see Sagasti *et al.* 2005: 26.) The share of British ODA going to the top ten recipients has remained little changed from 20 years ago (see OECD 2006a: 239).

Britain remains committed to responding to emergencies and to humanitarian crises and, with the United Nations, has been active in trying to establish more effective international response mechanisms, confirmed in its 2006 policy paper, *Saving Lives, Relieving, Suffering, Protecting Dignity: DFID's Humanitarian Policy* (DFID 2006c). It has also played an active role, not least within the OECD/DAC, in assessing and developing approaches to aiding fragile states and countries in conflict. The share of UK bilateral aid (ODA) channelled to emergencies has fluctuated around the 10 to 15 per cent level over the past ten years (OECD 2006a: 193). For more than two decades, the DFID has provided a steady flow of funds to NGOs and civil society organizations (CSOs), both British and others. Almost 40 per cent of UK ODA used by NGOs supports humanitarian aid activities (OECD 2006d: 33).

FRANCE

France has always been a major aid donor and, until overtaken by the UK in 2005, had been Europe's largest donor. From the late 1980s to 1994, overall levels of French ODA expanded steadily; they then fell steeply, reaching a low point in the year 2000, when, in real terms, total ODA stood at half the level it had reached in 1994, falling almost $4bn at current prices from its peak. However, French ODA has begun to expand again, rising by over 12 per cent a year in the five years to 2005. It was against already expanding ODA that France committed itself (at the 2002 Monterrey conference) to raise ODA progressively (from the low point of 0.32 per cent of GNI in the year 2000) to 0.42 per cent of GNI in 2004, 0.5 per cent by 2007, and to the internationally agreed 0.7 per cent target by the year 2012. Yet even if these targets are reached, France's ODA will still be lower than it was 40 years ago. In 1961, the ratio of French ODA to GNI stood at 1.36 per cent, a record for all major donors at any time, and France exceeded the 0.7 per cent ratio in each of the first eight years of the 1960s.

Historically, there has never been a single comprehensive French aid budget or even a multi-year budget planning framework. In 2004, over ten different ministries were responsible (to different degrees) for allocating official aid funds, though two key ministries, the Ministry for Economic Affairs, Finance and Industry (MINEFI) and the Ministry of Foreign Affairs (MAE), had joint responsibility for the strategic management of ODA, and together were responsible for 90 per cent of all French ODA. Until recently, total annual ODA had been derived *ex post* rather than *ex ante*, by drawing together relevant expenditure items from different ministries and budget lines. However, from 2005 France began to shape an overall aid budget, and (for the first time) to develop country-specific budgets, linked to the introduction of new financial legislation, most notably the Institutional Act on Financial Legislation (LOLF), operative from 2006.

It was French bilateral aid which experienced the severest cuts in the 1994–2000 period, and French bilateral aid is now benefiting from the rapid expansion in overall ODA. About 65 per cent of French aid is currently disbursed bilaterally. A particularly important part of France's multilateral assistance is the support it gives to the aid budget of the European Union. In 2002, France provided ODA to almost 170 recipient countries, four times the number in the early 1960s. France's current portfolio of recipients is influenced by its colonial past, by the importance it places on *la francophonie*, and, most recently, by the growing importance it attaches to global issues and to its wider geopolitical and strategic interests.

France has committed itself not only to an expanding aid programme but also to a reorientation of its development and aid policy, including working with other donors, such as the United Kingdom, to raise aggregate aid levels. It has formally adopted the MDGs, and a reduction in inequality, as essential parts of its overall aid effort. Special emphasis has been placed on the need to ensure that the poor benefit from globalization, which has been an important motive for France's advocacy for new and innovative forms of development financing. Poverty reduction is now the 'main thrust' of both aid and development policy, and this commitment informs and shapes aid allocations. It is within this context that France has given particular priority and emphasis to selectivity in the choice of recipients, to Africa, and to sustainable development. However, the way that France interprets its commitment to poverty reduction is different from some other leading donors: its approach to poverty alleviation is centred on trying to integrate poor people into globalization, so that they benefit from it. This is why France is so supportive of global funds and the financing of global public goods, and why France (like Japan) has given priority in its aid programmes to the development and expansion of physical infrastructure.

In implementing its aid and development policies, France formally singles out for attention a group of countries to which it gives particular priority: the Zone de Solidarité Prioritaire (ZSP) countries. Since 2002, these have consisted of 54 countries, the vast majority of which are among the poorest, 40 in Sub-Saharan Africa. Within this context, France has signalled its intention of concentrating its bilateral aid on those countries 'most in need' (OECD 2004d: 36), including the poorest, and those it terms the most fragile states. While need is an important factor influencing policy on the allocation of French aid, so too is effectiveness, which has recently become 'upgraded to be a formal policy priority'. For France, democratic governance is at the heart of poverty reduction strategies (OECD 2004d: 24).

French ODA has been dominated by the following characteristics: a multiplicity of different instruments utilized by the many different agencies/ministries responsible for providing aid; an emphasis on sectoral and project aid; and the priority given to French technical assistance, often seen as crucial for the strengthening of institutions. This broad perspective informs France's approach to aiding 'problem' countries.

GERMANY

From the mid-1970s to the mid-1980s, Germany was the third largest aid donor until it was overtaken by France; it became the fifth largest donor in 2004, when it was surpassed by the United Kingdom. Partly because of the priority given to reunification and support to strategically important, former Eastern bloc countries, notably Poland, from the late 1980s, overall levels of German ODA (as opposed to official aid) fell markedly until 1998, when they began to rise again. In the early years of the present century, German ODA began to expand, though only slowly. By 2005, Germany's ODA/GNI ratio stood at only 0.35 per cent compared with almost 0.5 per cent in the early 1980s. About 60 per cent of German ODA is allocated bilaterally, below the DAC average of 67 per cent. With Japan and France, Germany has the largest number of individual aid recipients—166 in 2002, compared with fewer than 100 in the mid-1960s. In the decade from 1990/1 to 2000/1, the share of German ODA (bilateral and imputed multilateral ODA) going to all low-income countries fell from 60 per cent to 55 per cent, and the share going to Sub-Saharan Africa also fell, from 27 per cent in the period 1991/2 to 23.5 per cent in 2001/2. For the future, Germany has committed itself to expand ODA gradually to reach the 0.7 per cent of GNI target by 2015, with interim targets set at 0.33 per cent by 2006 (which it surpassed in 2005) and 0.5 per cent by 2010. However, as in the past, the aid levels that Germany achieves are likely to be critically influenced by the overall health of the federal budget and national economy, as well as the strength of the coalition government.

German development and aid policies are framed within the context of its overall foreign policy. The administration of German aid is complex, though key decisions about German aid are made by the Federal Ministry for Economic Cooperation and Development (BMZ), which is responsible for trying to ensure an overall consistency of approach among those agencies which provide ODA. However, the BMZ usually delegates the responsibility to implement the German contributions for individual measures to specialized agencies, the two main executing agencies being the Agency for Technical Cooperation (GTZ), the principal implementing agency for technical cooperation activities, and the German Bank for Reconstruction (KfW), the principal implementing agency for financial cooperation, set up in 1948 as part of the

Marshall Plan. Together with the Federal Foreign Office (AA), other federal ministries and agencies (such as Health and Agriculture) are responsible for administering about 20 per cent of the German aid budget. Beyond the federal government structures, the different German regional governments and states (*Länder*) administer and are responsible for about 10 per cent of total German bilateral aid. Outside governmental structures and institutions, NGOs and political foundations undertake a range of development activities, receiving about 6 per cent of total ODA.

The allocation of German bilateral aid is being increasingly shaped by and rooted in the April 2001 Cabinet-approved programme *Poverty Reduction—a Global Responsibility. Program of Action 2015*. This established poverty reduction as the overarching goal of German development aid. Important sub-goals include enhancing the global structural policy agenda (issues such as development finance and debt relief, reform of the international trade system, and peace and security), improving the coherence of policies relating to developing countries across all of the different ministries, and improving aid effectiveness through harmonization and coordination, in particular through EU development policy. The document is seen as Germany's contribution to halving the share of people living in extreme poverty by 2015, which will be made operational by an ongoing process of consultation and of defining the next implementation steps with key stakeholders. In late 2003, the BMZ established a task force to support and begin the process of putting the MDGs in the mainstream of all German aid instruments. This led to allocation policy benchmarks being established of 30 per cent of bilateral aid to go to Sub-Saharan African countries and a similar share to be channelled to the least developed countries.

The BMZ allocates German bilateral aid first by determining the countries to which aid should be given, and then deciding the amount of aid to be given to each. This is confirmed on an annual basis. Germany has decided to focus its aid on a particular group of what it terms 'priority partner countries' and 'partner countries'. This choice of countries, in turn, is shaped by the following criteria: needs (related to social, economic and ecological factors); an assessment of whether Germany can make a contribution/add value; a review of what other donors are doing or plan to do; and an assessment of the extent to which the general internal setting is conducive to aid effectiveness.[22] Additionally, there is the group of so-called 'transition countries', including countries in Central Asia and some other former Soviet Union countries, whose geographical proximity to Germany is considered important enough for them to qualify as potential aid recipients.

Five 'internal criteria' are generally applied to assess the overall 'framework conditions' within individual aid-recipient countries: respect for human rights; popular participation in the political process; the rule of law; market-friendly and socially oriented economic order; and development-oriented state action. The result of the assessment not only influences the allocation of aid across countries, but plays an important role in shaping the aid pro-grammes. On the basis of country-specific analysis, the BMZ is able to indicate which of the various instruments of German development cooperation (e.g. technical assistance, or assistance via non-governmental organizations) are most appropriate.

Germany is increasingly introducing results-based principles to guide state expenditures, and there has been a long history in Germany of trying to ensure that the aid provided is utilized in a transparent and result-oriented manner. This is likely only to confirm the historical importance Germany has attached to linking its aid to the provision of (German) technical assistance to ensure that the funds are used effectively. For Germany, a particularly important linkage is that between aid allocation and good governance. Indeed, Germany is one of the strongest proponents of good governance and considers 'good governance [to be] . . . a condition of co-operation' (OECD 2001b: 43). However, this does not rule out providing aid to countries with poor/weak governance where it would engage with policy dialogue to promote good democratic governance at all levels.

THE EUROPEAN COMMISSION

The European Community (Union) receives aid funds from its member states to implement its own aid programmes, which are overseen and administered by the European Commission.[23] As an intergovernmental agency, in most ways the Commission acts like a bilateral aid donor, even though its aid (ODA) is classified by the OECD/DAC as part of multilateral aid.[24] The Commission's own aid programme has grown steadily in recent years, with its share of all bilateral DAC ODA rising from 7.5 per cent to just over 10 per cent in the ten years to 2003, when it had become the second largest 'bilateral' donor after the United States. In the three years to 2005, EU aid (ODA) rose by an average of 20 per cent a year, exceeding \$9.5bn by the year 2005. The four largest contribu-tors to the EU aid budget are France, Germany, Italy and the United Kingdom, accounting for over 70 per cent of its aid budget.

The EU's own aid effort, managed by the Commission, consists of a number of different programmes, and is extremely complex. European aid is overseen by the EuropeAid Co-ordination Office, known more briefly as EuropeAid. This office's role and remit is to implement the external aid instruments of the European Commission, which are funded by the European Community budget and the European Development Fund (EDF). However, official aid consists of a number of different budget streams, overseen by two main directorates, linked to but dis-tinct from EuropeAid. The first is the Directorate-General for Development (DG DEV), whose mandate is to enhance development policies in all developing countries, but which oversees and has financial responsibility for the aid programme for the 77 Africa, Caribbean and Pacific (ACP) countries under the umbrella of the 20-year Cotonou Agreement, which came into force in 2003, replacing the former Lomé Convention. The second—and in terms of funds allocated, far more important—is the Directorate-General for External Relations (DG RELEX). This is responsible both for the overall external relations policies of the EU and for specific aid programmes, including separate ones for Asia and Latin America, the Balkans, the Mediterranean and Middle East, and Eastern Europe and Central Asia, as well as a growing number of thematic budget lines, covering areas such as reproductive health, the environment and NGOs.

Aid allocation decisions related to the (larger) External Action budget are formally taken by the General Affairs Relations Council, involving, as well, the European Parliament and the Council, with the Parliament having the final responsibility for the budget. In contrast, aid allocation decisions for the EDF are taken on an inter-governmental basis, involving EU and ACP member countries, with Parliament playing a relatively minor role (for details see Jones *et al.* 2004: 72ff.). The European Union also oversees a major humanitarian and emergency aid effort, functioning not as an operational agency but as a key donor. This is managed by a separate independent department, the Humanitarian Aid Department (ECHO), which consults with DG DEV and DG RELEX, but not with EuropeAid. In 2003, the Commission's overall development aid programme budget involved commitments for both ODA and OA. These totalled $14.2bn, of which 70 per cent originated in budget lines from DG RELEX and the remainder from DG DEV, dominated by the EDF. In that year, ECHO funded emergency projects valued at $678mn, making it the second largest disburser of bilateral humanitarian aid.

Historically, there has never been a single and uniform approach to aid policy across the entire EU. The sharpest divide has been between DG DEV and the different external actions budget lines. In brief, the EDF, managed by DG DEV, attempted to adopt a developmental approach, utilizing aid to further the development objectives of the ACP states, whereas the external action budgets were more directly placed within the wider political and foreign policy objectives of the EU. At least from the year 2000 onwards, EC development policy has been clearly focused on poverty eradication, with emphasis placed on low-income and least developed countries, and with particular attention paid to the results of aid interventions and to 'appropriate conditionality' (EC 2000b). A core problem is that this policy has not really been applied to aid administered and allocated outside the EDF framework. Partly to address this inconsistency, and as a result of pressure from member states who had been critical of the overall lack of coherence and consistency across the EU in relation to aid, in mid-2005 the Commission approved a proposal defining a new development policy for the entire EU, embracing both the member states and all the different aid instruments of the EU. The policy places poverty eradication at the core of EU development policy, aiming to contribute to reducing poverty in line with the MDGs. However, questions remain about the extent to which this new development (and aid) policy will lead to substantial changes in the approach to the Commission's different aid budgets, not least because, while the new policy of firms development 'as a key element of the EU's external action', development is placed alongside foreign, security and trade policy, where individual circumstances will determine the relative balance between each (Europa 2005).[25]

In practice, the EU continues to allocate a comparatively small share of its total ODA to the least developed and low-income countries. In the years 2003–4, the share of ODA going to these countries stood at 55 per cent, compared with over 70 per cent in the mid-1980s (OECD 2006a: 241). In the year 2003, it gave aid (ODA) to 160 different countries, compared with 137 recipients in the early 1990s. Under the ninth EDF, a fairly rigorous needs-and performance-based method of allocating ODA resources has been developed (see Jones *et al.* 2004: 73–5 for the details), but this approach is applicable to less than 50 per cent of all EU aid. A further problem is that the allocation of EU aid (ODA) historically has been tangential to what are traditionally considered poverty-focused end-uses: the latest OECD/DAC peer review notes that less than 10 per cent of all ODA within the EDF was channelled to education, health and water combined (OECD 2002a: 46–7). Additionally, the complexity of EU aid has created an array of different administration problems for recipients. For instance, in its 2002 report on EU aid, the OECD noted that Bangladesh was receiving aid for 21 projects under its main budget line, but a further 61 projects were being funded from other EU budget lines (OECD 2002a: 80).

In terms of aid modalities, the EU has actively expanded its support to SWAps and to budget support in an increasing number of recipient countries, as well as locating aid strategies within PRS frameworks. Far less headway has been made in developing consistency and coherence between the EU's work for development in-country and some of its broader policies. Particular problems remain in relation to its own agricultural, fisheries and external trade policies—including the high levels of subsidies paid to its farmers, the selling of surplus produce on world markets, which depresses prices, and quotas and escalating tariffs on high-value-added imports, which limit poor-country imports to the EU—notwithstanding the EU's history of granting trade preferences to ACP countries (see OECD 2002: 61ff.).

The smaller bilateral donors

Besides these six big donors, there is a growing array of comparatively smaller donors. However, they should not be dismissed lightly, the few paragraphs here not sufficiently reflecting either their relative or absolute importance. Taken together, in 2004 the other 29 donors whose aid levels are recorded by the OECD provided in excess of $30bn in ODA, more than three times the amount provided by the UK, France and Germany individually in that year. Twelve of these 'smaller' donors—Australia, Austria, Belgium, Canada, Finland, Italy, the Netherlands, New Zealand, Norway, Spain, Sweden and Switzerland—were providing ODA to upwards of 100 recipient countries in 2002/3; a further five—Denmark, Greece, Ireland, Luxembourg and Portugal—provided ODA to more than 50 recipient countries (Sagasti *et al.* 2005: 26). For some recipients, some of these 'smaller' donors are their largest. For example, in 2003 Australia was the single largest aid donor to Papua New Guinea, Italy the second largest donor to Mozambique, Belgium the third largest to the Democratic Republic of Congo (DRC), Spain the fifth largest to Bolivia, and Luxembourg one of Cape Verde's largest and most influential donors.

Seven of the 'smaller' donors each provided total ODA in excess of $2bn in 2005, their bilateral aid programmes together amounting to over $25bn in that year. These were the Netherlands and Italy (which both provided ODA in excess of $5bn), Sweden, Spain, Canada, Norway and Denmark. We shall briefly look at each of these.

NORWAY AND THE NETHERLANDS

Norway and the Netherlands have for many years consistently exceeded the 0.7 per cent of GNI for ODA target, and both have traditionally given prominence to poverty reduction as the principal and core objective of their official aid programmes. Norway has announced its intention of reaching an ODA/GNI ratio of 1 per cent soon. Since 2003, the Netherlands has linked its poverty-orientated focus explicitly to the achievement of the MDGs. Both donors emphasize the central role of poor-country governments' leading in the developing and implementing of poverty-reduction policies and see aid as a means to help strengthen the ability of partner countries to combat poverty. In common with the United Kingdom, the Dutch aid programme is overseen by a minister with full cabinet status. In recent years, both donors have viewed their development cooperation programmes through the lens of human rights.

Like the United Kingdom, the Netherlands uses an aid allocation model, based on need and performance and focused explicitly on the poorest countries, to inform and shape aid levels to particular countries. Both Norway and the Netherlands have taken the initiative in trying to encourage greater harmonization and coherence of policies and approach across donor countries, and in supporting multilateral and global approaches to development. They have both been in the forefront of donor efforts to expand the use of programme approaches, including SWAps and budget support.[26] Since the early 1990s, Norway has focused greater attention on security issues. For its part, the

Netherlands has tried to adopt a more sectoral approach to aid-giving (focusing on education, HIV/AIDS, water and the environment), and has tried to reduce substantially the number of recipients to which it gives aid. It, too, has given greater prominence to incorporating security issues into its wider global strategy, which has resulted in expanding cooperation to the Middle East, Sudan and Burundi.[27]

SWEDEN

Sweden is one of largest of the 'smaller' donors and, like the Netherlands and Norway, has already exceeded the 0.7 per cent ODA/GNI target, which it first reached in 1975. In 1968, it accepted for itself a 1 per cent ODA/GNI target, which it reached in 1982, and again in 1992. However, the ratio dipped in the 1980s and again in the 1990s, reaching a low point of 0.7 per cent in 1999, from which it has slowly begun to recover. Sweden recently stated its intention to reach the 1 per cent ratio again by the year 2006, and the 2006 budget allocations and growth estimates suggest that it has done so.

As far back as 1962, the core objective of Swedish assistance was to contribute to raising the living standards of the poor, while its long-standing commitment to solidarity with the poor helped to shape its recipient profile, linked especially to liberation movements and countries struggling to achieve political independence. In common with Norway, Denmark and Finland, Sweden's aid programme is administered by an official agency, in Sweden's case the renamed Swedish International Development Co-operation Agency (Sida), though development co-operation policy is led and overseen by their respective foreign affairs ministries. Sweden's broad approach to aid and development cooperation closely mirrors that of Norway and the Netherlands, with whom it has closely interacted historically, both formally and informally. Its 2003 policy statement, *Shared Responsibility*, articulates the core objectives of all its development cooperation, including its aid programme (Government of Sweden 2003: 18–21). These are to contribute to equitable global development, and to sustainable global development, by assisting in the fulfilment of the MDGs (which, like the United Kingdom, it monitors annually) through supporting activities aimed at strengthening poor people's efforts to improve their quality of life.[28] Like Norway and the Netherlands, it now views solutions to poverty through the lens of human rights, and seeks to support recipient-country programmes and policies by working more closely with other donors, and by raising the overall level of development assistance. Sweden, too, has tried to shift its focus towards helping to strengthen and build the capacity of recipients, and to channel aid increasingly through broader programmes rather than projects, including support to sectoral aid initiatives, particularly in the fields of education, health and trade.

Historically, Sweden has given high priority to support to civil society and to funding the development activities of (predominantly) Swedish NGOs, a policy and approach which is mirrored in the Netherlands, Norway, Finland and Denmark. Likewise, Sweden has a long history of support for emergencies, extending such assistance beyond the core countries on which it concentrates its development assistance. It has taken a leading role in working to create a sounder international framework for responding to emergencies.

SPAIN

As recently as 1979, Spain was still an aid recipient. It began to provide official aid in the 1980s, and in recent years has steadily expanded its aid programme. In 1991, Spain's ODA topped the $1bn mark, and in 2005 it exceeded $3bn. In 2004, Spain confirmed its intention of reaching the 0.7 per cent target by 2012, aiming to reach the 0.5 per cent ratio by 2008. More recently, Spain was party to the EU-wide agreement to reach 0.56 per cent of GNI by 2010 and the 0.7 per cent target by 2015. Since its official aid programme began, Spain has expanded the number of its individual recipients to 123. Until recently, its official aid programme consisted mostly of projects, with a high proportion of aid provided in loan credits linked to Spanish commercial interests, formally and informally, and a significant middle-income country bias.

A new approach to Spanish aid-giving was articulated in the 1998 Law on International Co-operation and Development, which established poverty reduction as the main objective of aid, though in practice little appeared to change (Alonso 2005: 513ff.). In 2005, after the 2004 election of the new socialist government, a Master Plan for Spanish Cooperation 2005–2008 was published. This confirmed the 1998 focus on poverty reduction, but framed it within the objectives of the Millennium Declaration and the MDGs. Relatedly, Spain has articulated its support for aligning its aid more closely with recipient-country strategies, including PRSes, and its earlier emphasis on capacity-building and institutional strengthening is set to continue. It has begun, in a small way, to participate in SWAps. In common with Italy, Germany and Switzerland, part of Spanish official aid is allocated by sub-national agencies and organizations, including regional and municipal authorities.

CANADA

Canada was one of the first donor countries to commit itself to achieving the 0.7 per cent ODA/GNI target by a particular date (the first target date being 1980), but this has never been achieved. In 2005, Canada refused to give a (new) date for achieving the target. Following major contractions in the 1990s, by 2005 the ratio still stood at less than 0.35 per cent. Historically, Canadian ODA has always held in tension three main objectives: humanitarian aid including poverty alleviation; security; and Canadian economic and commercial interests.[29] The government has now thrown its weight behind the MDGs as the basis for its official aid programme, emphasizing effectiveness and coherence between its development aid and wider policies, as well as its continuing commitment to humanitarian aid and to multilateralism. Its approach to aid is a mix of direct support to poverty projects and programmes, a growing emphasis on SWAps and budget support, and a continuing emphasis on private sector development. In that context, it has pledged to expand ODA by 8 per cent annually until the year 2010, doubling ODA to $5bn by 2010 from 2001 levels, as well as significantly reducing the number of countries to which it gives aid.[30]

ITALY

Italy's official aid programme has witnessed extreme volatility, expanding most rapidly in the 1980s. From its peak level in 1989 of $4.9bn (in 2003 prices), Italian ODA fell by over a third in real terms to $1.4bn in 1997, and notwithstanding some subsequent expansion, was still below its peak in 2005, even after a doubling of ODA to $5bn from $2.5bn in 2004. From the 1980s to the 1990s, when Italian ODA was contracting rapidly, the number of recipients increased, to reach over 140. In 2005, Italy's ODA/GNI ratio was 0.29 per cent. The government has not committed itself to reaching the 0.7 per cent target by any particular date, though it remains formally linked to the general targets adopted by the EU.

The administration of Italian aid is complex, involving scores of different agencies within regions, provinces and municipalities, all of which provide aid. Those with smaller amounts to disperse have frequently channelled their aid through NGOs, though all ODA to NGOs was (temporarily) suspended in 1995 following serious accountability failures. Like the United States, Italian law forbids the untying of aid. Italian ODA remains linked to both commercial interests and wider diplomatic interests though, since legislation introduced in 1987 (Law 49), poverty reduction has been the main objective of Italian ODA, with particular priority given to health interventions. Recent years have seen priority given to regional political issues, with an expansion of aid to Southern Europe and the Mediterranean region. Only 40 per cent of Italian aid is channelled to low-income countries. In early 2005, the OECD reported that though poverty reduction remains a main objective, Italy had not incorporated the MDGs into its overall approach to aid-giving and that there was little systematic attempt to coordinate aid with other government policies (OECD 2005a: 91; 2006a: 88).[31]

DENMARK

In 2005, Denmark was ranked the twelfth largest donor in terms of total ODA, but it was ranked fourth, after Norway, the Netherlands and Sweden, in terms of its share of ODA to GNI, which stood at 0.81 per cent. One thing that marks it out from other donors is that Danish official aid continued to expand in the early 1990s when other major donors were reducing it. However, official Danish aid contracted markedly at the end of the 1990s, when most other donors began to expand their official aid programmes again. Only in 2005 had Danish ODA levels surpassed that reached in 1997. From 2000 to 2004, when the government announced further cuts in its aid programme, Danish ODA fell by over 16 per cent in real terms. Uniquely, Denmark has announced that its ODA/GNI ratio will never fall below the 0.8 per cent level.

In terms of policies, Denmark's approach to ODA has closely followed those of its main Nordic partners, Sweden and Norway. Poverty reduction is at the heart of Danish development cooperation. Denmark has given priority to harmonization, coherence and consistency in its aid programmes, as well as recipient-country ownership, in order to achieve a more sustainable impact. In recent years, it has approached development cooperation increasingly through a human rights perspective. Denmark has always firmly advocated a stronger multilateral approach to development cooperation, and has been in the vanguard of donors expanding, and pressing other donors to expand, programme aid through the use of both SWAps and budget support. It has also been prominent among donors in urging a more effective international response to emergencies.

In recent years, and as outlined in its key 2000 policy document, *Partnership 2000* (Ministry of Foreign Affairs and Danida 2000), Denmark has emphasized the link between development, security and peace-keeping, and, since 1997, it has incorporated conflict prevention into the overall framework of development cooperation policy. Like its Nordic partners, Denmark has also seen support to NGOs, especially to Danish NGOs, as a key part of the overall aid effort, providing upwards of 15 per cent of ODA to and through NGOs. However, Danish NGOs have faced severe cuts in state funding as part of the overall reduction in Danish ODA. One difference with Sweden, especially, has been the way in which Danish ODA has been linked to the business community (see Olsen 2005a: 206ff.), and this has continued, notwithstanding new legislation introduced in 2004 to further formally untie Danish ODA. Denmark's most recent policy document, *A World of Difference*, outlines Denmark's approach to development cooperation from 2004 to 2008.[32] While broadly reinforcing earlier policy approaches, it places stronger emphasis on private sector development (education, health, water and sanitation), human rights, good governance, the environment, humanitarian assistance, and aid effectiveness. It explicitly advocates free trade as part of the solution to poverty. Though

Denmark's historical commitment to multilateralism is confirmed, this is presented in a more selective way, stressing expanding support to more effective agencies and to those working in Denmark's own priority areas. *A World of Difference* outlines initiatives for a further devolution of responsibility for aid decisions to Danish officials within particular aid-recipient countries. Denmark is committed to the achievement of the MDGs, though there is no direct link between Denmark's approach to its own development cooperation and the direct achievement of the MDGs.[33]

AUSTRALIA AND NEW ZEALAND

The largest Southern Hemisphere donors are Australia and New Zealand. Both countries started their official aid programmes in the 1960s, and both of these experienced their most rapid expansion in the 1970s. Reflecting the larger size of its economy, Australian ODA ($1.7bn in 2005) has always been six to eight times as great in absolute terms as that of New Zealand ($274mn in 2005). In real terms, Australian ODA was at the same level in 2004 as it was in the mid-1990s, which, in turn, was no higher than in the mid-1980s. Australia's ODA/GNI ratio peaked at 0.62 per cent in 1967, and has not exceeded 0.4 per cent since 1988, falling below 0.3 per cent in 1996. New Zealand ODA reached its highest level (in real terms) in 1975, when its ODA/GNI ratio reached 0.52 per cent, but it fell back to less than half that (0.21 per cent) in 1996. Since then, New Zealand's ODA has expanded more rapidly than Australia's, rising by almost 7 per cent a year in real terms to the year 2005.

For the future, New Zealand has not committed itself to increase its ODA to the 0.7 per cent level by any particular date, though it is planning to raise the ODA/GNI ratio to 0.28 per cent by 2008. For its part, too, the Australian government pledged in September 2005 to double ODA to around A$4bn a year by the year 2010, though, as explained in its 2006 White Paper, *Australian Aid: Promoting Growth and Stability*, the government is 'unequivocal' that such expansion needs to be based on assurances of its effectiveness, improved governance and reduced corruption (AusAID 2006: 2, 21).

Both Australia and New Zealand have participated in, and now broadly frame their aid programmes within, the context of the MDGs, with both placing strong emphasis on poverty reduction. However, as both New Zealand and Australia view their official aid programmes as a contribution to their wider foreign policy objectives, their bilateral programmes have been focused particularly on recipients in the Pacific and, to a lesser extent, on some Asian countries. Only around one-quarter of their ODA is channelled through multilateral agencies, and for Australia, this share has recently been falling. Less than 80 per cent of Australian bilateral aid goes to low-income countries; for New Zealand, the ratio is even lower (less than 60 per cent). Australia provides ODA to over 100 countries. With far less ODA, New Zealand also provides ODA to 100 countries in an even more dispersed programme.

The core objective of Australia's aid programme is to 'assist developing countries to reduce poverty and achieve sustainable development, in line with Australia's national interest' (AusAID 2006: 20). The main way this is to be achieved is through the contribution Australian aid can make to accelerating economic growth, supported by activities focused on fostering functioning states, investing in people, and promoting regional stability and cooperation. Particular emphasis is placed on the role of the private sector in helping recipients achieve higher levels of growth. Some 50 per cent of Australia's bilateral ODA is tied to Australian goods and services (OECD 2005c: 53), though the 2006 White Paper announced that in future Australian aid would be untied (AusAID 2006: 22). For Australia, too, security (including the fight against terrorism) is viewed as central to the aid effort, with poverty reduction in the region viewed as a key plank in achieving greater Australian security.

For its part, New Zealand places greater emphasis on assisting recipients to become more self-reliant and to address current vulnerabilities. Both countries have increased their share of humanitarian aid as a proportion of total ODA in recent years, and have begun to switch from project to programme aid. New Zealand, in particular, has been active in supporting SWAps, notably in the health and education sectors. They have also both played leading roles in supporting HIV/AIDS projects, especially in the Pacific region.[34] In line with OECD/DAC thinking, they have given increased emphasis to issues of harmonization and coherence in recent years, and to efforts aimed at trying to enhance the impact of their aid.

The complexities of multilateral aid

What is multilateral aid and how much of it is there?

At its simplest, multilateral aid is official development assistance (ODA) provided by multilateral organizations.[1] It has long been favoured over bilateral aid because it is widely viewed as less politically driven, and more likely to be channelled to recipients on the basis of need, and with fewer conditions attached. Many multilateral agencies are governed, in theory, by the collective decisions of both donors and recipients. In practice, however, multilateral agencies vary in the degree of independence they have. The greater the contribution one donor, or a small group of donors, makes to an agency, the more it is able to influence and shape the policies of that agency: the decisions made about the aid allocated, the form in which it is given, and the conditions under which it is provided. Additionally, some multilateral agencies are given funds which are explicitly tied or 'earmarked' for particular activities, reducing further the freedom of the agency to decide how best to deploy its resources. Confusingly, as discussed in Box 5.1, the Organisation for Economic Cooperation and Development (OECD) does not count this as multilateral aid. Hence the distinction between multilateral and bilateral aid and the benefits which the former theoretically brings are often not clear-cut.

There are more than twice as many major multilateral agencies which provide aid as there are major bilateral donors, and according to OECD statistics about one-third of all ODA is provided multilaterally (Rogerson *et al.* 2004: 29–31). In 2004, the total exceeded $21bn for the first time ever (OECD 2006a: 201). However, as Box 5.1 explains, official figures underreport the total funds that multilateral agencies have at their disposal.

The share of multilateral ODA in total ODA has stayed fairly constant for the past 30 years, following steep rises in the 1970s, when multilateral aid climbed from less than 10 per cent to over 25 per cent of all ODA. In recent years, it has fluctuated between 30 and 34 per cent. However, these figures include ODA provided by the European Commission, which is increasingly viewed both by European donors and by the European Commission as more akin to bilateral than multilateral aid. Indeed, it has now become an anomaly to continue to define EC ODA as multilateral aid.[2] Removing EU/EC ODA from multilateral

---

BOX 5.1 WHAT COUNTS AS MULTILATERAL AID AND WHO IS DOING THE COUNTING

Not all of the aid provided by multilateral agencies is included in the official data provided by the OECD. To be classified as multilateral, the ODA funds have to be available to be used freely by the agency: any aid which is provided to support particular activities earmarked by the official aid funder, or which is explicitly tied to specific projects and programmes, is deemed to be official bilateral aid. For some agencies, this constitutes a large share of total disbursements. For instance, in 2003, 80 per cent of donor funds provided to UN-Habitat was tied to particular projects. Additionally, while the voluntary income of multilateral agencies can theoretically be included in total disbursements of these agencies, the reporting by agencies to the OECD on this score is entirely voluntary, and the OECD acknowledges that there is underreporting.

It is for these reasons, and because some aid disbursements go to countries which do not qualify for ODA, that the total aid income and expenditure figures recorded by most multilateral agencies are (considerably and consistently) higher than the amount of ODA recorded in official statistics. The overall effect is to suggest that the expenditures of different multilateral agencies are far lower than they really are.

For instance, in 2003 the annual report of the United Nations Children's Fund (UNICEF) recorded worldwide expenditure of nearly $1.5bn. In contrast, the published OECD figures put the ODA (net) disbursements of UNICEF at only $629mn. Likewise, in the case of the United Nations Fund for Population Activities (UNFPA), the OECD recorded its net disbursements as $271mn, whereas the UNFPA's annual report recorded total expenditure of $380mn. More widely, in the year 2003, according to official (OECD) statistics, the largest UN agencies disbursed $3.5bn of ODA funds. Though many were involved in activities beyond simply providing aid, the total expenditures of these agencies as recorded in their annual reports amounted to more than $11bn (see Table 5.1).[a]

[a] The difference between the two figures is also explained in part by some double-counting. For instance, some ODA funds from bilateral donors to the UNDP are channelled to the specialized UN agencies, such as UNESCO: both agencies record these funds as income and (their use) as expenditures.

ODA, the proportion of multilateral ODA would fall markedly, from 30 per cent to a little less than 20 per cent.

There are three broad types of agencies which provide multilateral aid: an ever-expanding group of international financial institutions (IFIs), a larger number of United Nations agencies, and a small but growing collection of 'other' agencies. The most important grouping is the IFIs, which in 2004 accounted for 44 per cent of total net multilateral ODA disbursements (71 per cent if EC aid is excluded). Next come the United Nations' development and humanitarian agencies, accounting for a further 15 per cent of all multilateral aid (24 per cent excluding EC aid). Official statistics record the 'other agencies' accounting for some 40 per cent of all multilateral aid, but most of this is EC aid. Excluding the EC component, all other agencies accounted for less than 5 per cent of all multilateral aid. The details are provided in Table 5.1.

Even after the anomaly of the classification of EC aid is addressed, the breakdown of the share of aid (ODA) provided by different multilateral agencies

Table 5.1 Multilateral ODA disbursements, 1992/3 to 2004

Agencies	Net disbursements ($mn, current prices and exchange rates)					
	1992–3	%	2003	%	2004	%
International finance institutions (IFIs)						
ADB	938	7.4	826	7.6	694	5.3
AfDB	680	5.3	483	4.5	919	7.1
CDB	20	0.2	19	0.2	40	0.3
IDA	4,646	36.5	5,237	48.4	7,283	56.1
IDB	81	0.6	292	2.7	261	2.0
IFAD	80	0.6	155	1.4	165	1.3
IMF	461	3.6	9	0.1	−179	—
Other	—	—	260	2.4	124	1.0
Sub-total	6,906	54.2	7,126	65.9	9,307	71.7
United Nations Agencies						
UNDP	741	5.8	296	2.7	374	2.9
UNFPA	130	1.0	271	2.5	312	2.4
UNHCR	1,145	9.0	534	4.9	347	2.7
UNICEF	770	6.0	629	5.8	650	5.0
UNRWA	303	2.4	430	4.0	449	3.5
UNTA	288	2.3	504	4.7	434	3.3
WFP	1,531	12.0	319	3.0	268	2.1
Other	688	5.4	484	4.5	264	2.0
Sub-total	5,596	43.9	3,467	32.1	3,098	23.9
Other agencies						
GEF	—	—	107	1.0	138	1.1
MPF	—	—	66	0.6	59	0.5
Arab Funds	234	1.8	44	0.4	379	2.9
Sub-total	234	1.8	217	2.0	576	4.4
Total	12,736	100.0	10,810	100.0	12,981	100.0
EC	4,026		6,445		8,068	
Total with EC	16,762		17,256		21,049	

– = not available/negligible.
Source: OECD statistical data-base.

summarized in Table 5.1 still fails to provide an accurate reflection of the overall influence and importance of the different multilateral agencies. Self-evidently, aid statistics simply provide data on aid, and, whereas the UN development and humanitarian agencies channel their resources to developing countries largely in the form of aid (ODA and non-ODA), the IFIs do not. Far and away the largest element of resource transfer of the IFIs takes the form of non-concessional loans, which therefore falls outside the OECD definition of aid (ODA). However, a proportion of these non-concessionary funds is channelled to ODA-qualifying countries, and used to support a range of development projects and programmes, many similar to those funded with ODA monies. Similarly, many of the broader (non-financial) conditions under which the non-concessionary funds are provided are not very different from

---

BOX 5.2 NON-CONCESSIONAL FUNDS PROVIDED BY MULTILATERAL AGENCIES

In the year 2004, the IFIs together provided just over $9bn in aid (net disbursements of ODA) to ODA-qualifying countries. But their gross disbursements of both concessional and non-concessional funds to ODA-qualifying countries were nearly five times that figure, totalling just over $34bn—almost half of global ODA in that year (OECD 2006a: 200). Excluding EC aid, the IFIs accounted for almost 90 per cent of all gross concessional and non-concessional funds channelled to ODA-qualifying developing countries, the UN's development and humanitarian agencies accounting for only 8 per cent of the total.[a] And these differences have been widening over time: in the early 1990s, the UN agencies accounted for 17 percent of gross concessional and non-concessional flows to ODA-qualifying countries.

Set apart from other IFIs in terms of the scale of its activities, the most important IFI is the International Development Association (IDA) of the World Bank. In 2004, it alone provided $7.2bn in aid (net disbursements of ODA), more than half of all multilateral ODA (excluding EC/EU aid). Additionally, the Bank provided a total of $11.5bn in non-concessional loans through the International Bank for Reconstruction and Development (IBRD) and the International Finance Corporation (IFC). In total, and excluding EC aid, the World Bank group provided over 40 per cent of the total of multilateral concessional and non-concessional finance (gross disbursements) to all ODA-qualifying countries.

The final way in which the crude figures of net disbursements of multilateral aid (ODA) fail to provide a complete picture of multilateral aid is their omission of loan repayments. Not all ODA is provided in the form of grants, and when long-term loans are not forgiven, loans have to be repaid. While some bilateral donors (such as Japan and Spain) provide a relatively high proportion of their aid in the form of loans, the phenomenon is far more important in the case of multilateral agencies. In 2003, the difference between the gross and net disbursements of multilateral ODA was comparatively small, at $4.3bn.[b] However, the substantial gross transfer of some $26bn of non-concessional flows by the IFIs *to* ODA-qualifying countries in the year 2003 was wiped out by a reverse flow of over $33bn—$7.2bn more—*from* those countries, largely in the form of repayments of the interest and capital on former loans.[c]

[a] Whereas the IFIs provided twice as much aid (net disbursements of ODA) as all the aid provided by the UN agencies in 2003, their gross disbursements were ten times as large: $36.5bn compared to $3.5bn.

[b] These figures exclude EU aid. In 2003, net disbursements of multilateral aid were estimated to be $10.8bn (see Table 5.1). Gross disbursements were valued at $15.3bn.

[c] In recent years, the total new disbursements of non-concessional flows to ODA-qualifying countries have been negative. For example, in 2003, whereas new disbursements of multilateral aid (ODA) stood at $10.8bn (excluding EC aid; see Table 5.1), net non-concessional flows were negative, and totalled $7.2bn, reducing the combined net flow of concessional (OPA) and non-concessional (non-aid) flows to only $3.6bn.

---

those attached to concessionary aid funds. What this means is that the reach and influence of the IFIs is far greater than the official aid statistics would suggest. When non-concessional funds provided by the IFIs to ODA-qualifying countries are brought together with ODA figures, a very different picture emerges, as the discussion in Box 5.2 shows.

In short, the way in which multilateral aid is represented in official statistics conveys a confusing as well as inaccurate representation of the role and importance of the multilateral agencies as a whole, and of individual agencies.

The international financial institutions

The international financial institutions (IFIs) consist of the multilateral and regional banks and lending institutions. The two largest are the World Bank group and the International Monetary Fund (IMF). The IMF's remit is world-wide, principally focused on ensuring financial stability rather than on broader development issues. However, it has committed itself to help achieve the MDGs and has expanded its technical assistance programmes to poor countries. The IMF has increased its direct involvement in development in recent years and doubled its gross concessional lending from $570mn in the early 1990s to $1.2bn by 2004, when it accounted for nearly 10 per cent of gross ODA provided by all IFIs. It provides loans that qualify as ODA largely through the IMF Trust Fund and the Poverty Reduction and Growth Facility (PRGF), closely linked to the poverty-reduction strategy (PRS) process (OECD 2006a: 200). By 2005, the IMF was providing $5bn in concessional loans to low-income countries, though this accounted for only around 5 per cent of its total loan portfolio.

In contrast, the World Bank's whole mission and purpose is to fight poverty and improve living standards in developing countries, and its activities are now focused on the achievement of the MDGs. The World Bank group includes a number of different institutions, of which four play the most significant role in the development of poor countries: the International Bank for Reconstruction and Development (IBRD), the International Development Association (IDA), the International Finance Corporation (IFC) and the Multilateral Investment Guarantee Agency (MIGA). Together, the IBRD and IDA provided $17bn in gross disbursements to developing countries in the year 2004 ($14bn in net disbursements), with IBRD funds channelled mostly to middle-income developing countries, and IDA funds to the poorest. In 2004, the IDA disbursed $6.9bn (gross) and $5.5bn (net), compared with $7bn and $5.6bn respectively in 2003.[3] The IDA alone was responsible for 83 per cent of new ODA disbursements from all IFIs in 2004, and for more than half of all multilateral ODA (see Table 5.1). On the basis of 2004 figures, the IDA aid effort was roughly as large as the bilateral aid programmes of the fourth and fifth largest donors, Germany and the UK. World Bank lending encompasses almost all development themes and sectors, including agriculture, health, education, finance, transport, trade, urban and rural development and water, with well over $1bn of project lending in each area (for details see World Bank 2005m: 104).

Smaller, but still important, are the regional development banks, including the Asian Development Bank (ADB), the African Development Bank (AfDB), the Inter-American Development Bank (IDB) and the Caribbean Development Bank (CDB). Like the World Bank, most have set up concessional financial funds, such as the Asian Development Fund and the African

Development Fund, accounting for up to half of total funds disbursed. The exception is the IDB, whose concessional funding accounts for less than 10 per cent of its total portfolio. Many regional bank projects are similar to those of the larger IFIs, though they tend to have a larger number of small aid-funded projects in their overall portfolios. Together with the World Bank, most have become involved in sector-wide approaches, often joining consortia with bilateral donors, though larger stand-alone projects still dominate. The UN's International Fund for Agricultural Development (IFAD) is a financial institution focusing exclusively on providing (relatively small) loans and grants to address rural poverty. Working in 115 countries, its net ODA disbursements were valued at $148mn in 2003, out of $424mn of total grants and loans disbursed.[4]

The United Nations, development and aid

Though not as dominant as in the past, the different parts of the United Nations system remain a central component of today's multilateral aid system. Today, there are some 30 separate UN bodies or groupings involved in some sort of humanitarian or development work, all of which receive and utilize aid funds. The UN's aid system is complex, steeped in often obscure terminology, using different names for different bodies—notably 'agencies', 'funds' and 'programmes'—based on different remits, purposes and expectations. Figure 5.1 provides a diagrammatic representation of the UN and its constituent agencies, programmes and funds.

Different clusters of UN activities are overseen by various coordinating bodies, the most important being the Economic and Social Council (ECOSOC), which has a primary role in coordinating development and humanitarian aid and assistance programmes, in close liaison with the Department of Economic and Social Affairs, within the overall UN Secretariat. The UN's Office for the Coordination of Humanitarian Affairs (OCHA), also within the UN Secretariat, with a 2005 budget of $111mn and a presence across the world, is also responsible for coordinating the humanitarian aid of the UN and other agencies. The joint programme on HIV/AIDS, UNAIDS, founded in 1994, works to undertake and lead advocacy work on HIV/AIDS.[5] In 1997, a UN Development Group (UNDG) was formed, with 30 members, whose purpose remains to coordinate UN activities at the recipient-country level (see UNDG 2005a: annex 1).

Moving to specific organizations, the UN's development and humanitarian work is undertaken by two groupings. One group is termed the UN's specialized agencies, which have their own autonomy, their own governing bodies and their own budget frameworks. They are (legally) independent of the central UN, even

Figure 5.1

The United Nations system

PRINCIPAL ORGANS

Trusteeship Council	Security Council	General Assembly	Economic and Social Council	International Court of Justice	Secretariat

Subsidiary bodies
Military Staff Committee
Standing Committee and ad hoc bodies
International Criminal Tribunal for the Former Yugoslavia
International Criminal Tribunal for Rwanda
UN Monitoring, Verification and Inspection Commission (Iraq)
United Nations Compensation Commission
Peacekeeping Operations and Missions

Subsidiary bodies
Main committees
Other sessional committees
Standing committees and ad hoc bodies
Other subsidiary organs

Programmes and funds
UNCTAD United Nations Conference on Trade and Development
  ITC International Trade Centre (UNCTAD/WTO)
UNDCP United Nations Drug Control Programme[a]
UNEP United Nations Environment Programme
UNICEF United Nations Children's Fund
UNDP United Nations Development Programme
  UNIFEM United Nations Development Fund for Women
  UNV United Nations Volunteers
UNCDF United Nations Capital Development Fund
UNFPA United Nations Fund for Population Activities
UNHCR Office of the United Nations High Commissioner for Refugees
WFP World Food Programme
UNRWA[b] United Nations Relief and Works Agency for Palestine Refugees in the Near East
UN-Habitat United Nations Human Settlements Programme (UNHSP)

Research and training institutes
UNICRI United Nations Inter regional Crime and Justice Research Institute
UNITAR United Nations Institute for Training and Research
UNRISD United Nations Research Institute for Social Development
UNIDIR[b] United Nations Institute for Disarmament Research
INSTRAW International Research and Training Institute for the Advancement of Women

Other UN entities
OHCHR Office of the United Nations High Commissioner for Human Rights
UNOPS United Nations Office for Project Services
UNU United Nations University
UNSSC United Nations System Staff College
UNAIDS Joint United Nations Programme on HIV/AIDS

Functional commissions
Commissions on:
Human Rights
Narcotic Drugs
Crime Prevention and Criminal Justice
Science and Technology for Development
Sustainable Development
Status of Women
Population and Development
Commission for Social Development
Statistical Commission
Regional commissions
Economic Commission for Africa (ECA)
Economic Commission for Europe (ECE)
Economic Commission for Latin America and the Caribbean (ECLAC)
Economic and Social Commission for Asia and the Pacific (ESCAP)
Economic and Social Commission for Western Asia (ESCWA)
Other bodies
Permanent Forum on Indigenous Issues (PFII)
United Nations Forum on Forests
Sessional and standing committees
Expert, ad hoc and related bodies
Related organizations
WTO World Trade Organization[c]
IAEA International Atomic Energy Agency[d]
CTBTO PREP.COM PrepCom for the Nuclear-Test-Ban-Treaty Organization[e]
OPCW Organization for the Prohibition of Chemical Weapons[e]

Specialized agencies[f]
ILO International Labour Organisation
FAO Food and Agriculture Organisation of the United Nations
UNESCO United Nations Educational, Scientific and Cultural Organisation
WHO World Health Organisation
World Bank Group
IBRD International Bank for Reconstruction and Development
IDA International Development Association
IFC International Finance Corporation
MIGA Multilateral Investment Guarantee Agency
ICSID International Centre for Settlement of Investment Disputes
IMF International Monetary Fund
ICAO International Civil Aviation Organisation
IMO International Maritime Organization
ITU International Telecommunication Union
UPU Universal Postal Union
WMO World Meteorological Organization
WIPO World Intellectual Property Organization
IFAD International Fund for Agricultural Development
UNIDO United Nations Industrial Development Organization
WTO World Tourism Organization[c]

Departments and offices
OSG Office of the Secretary General
OIOS Office of Internal Oversight Services
OLA Office of Legal Affairs
DPA Department of Political Affairs
DDA Department for Disarmament Affairs
DPKO Department of Peace-keeping Operations
OCHA Office for the Coordination of Humanitarian Affairs
DESA Department of Economic and Social Affairs
DGACM Department for General Assembly and Conference Management
DPI Department of Public Information
DM Department of Management
OHRLLS Office of the High Representative for the Least Developed Countries, Landlocked Developing Countries and Small Island Developing States
UNSECOORD Office of the United Nations Security Coordinator
UNODC United Nations Office on Drugs and Crime
UNOG UN Office at Geneva
UNOV UN Office at Vienna
UNON UN Office at Nairobi

Source: UN Department of Public Information DPI/2342 (Mar. 2004).

Notes: Solid lines from a principal organ indicate a direct reporting relationship, broken lines indicate a non-subsidiary relationship. [a]The UN Drug Control Programme is part of the UN Office on Drugs and Crime. [b]UNRWA and UNIDIR report only to the General Assembly (GA). [c]The World Trade Organization and World Tourism Organization use the same abbreviation. [d]IAEA reports to the Security Council and the GA. [e]The CTBTO Prep.Com and CPCW report to the GA. [f]Specialized agencies are autonomous organizations working with the UN and each other through the coordinating machinery of the ECOSOC at the intergovernmental level, and through the Chief Executives Board for coordination (CEB) at the inter-secretariat level.

though their work is formally coordinated by the ECOSOC. Their boards or councils are the member states, including those who fund them. Besides the UN's financial institutions, the World Bank Group, the IMF and the IFAD, the specialized agencies include some of the major UN bodies that are involved in development and utilize official aid funds: the International Labour Office (ILO), the Food and Agricultural Organisation (FAO), the United Nations Industrial Development Organisation (UNIDO), the World Health Organisation (WHO), and the United Nations Educational, Scientific and Cultural Organisation (UNESCO). These specialized agencies cover key programme areas of employment, food and agriculture, health, industry, and education, as well as providing technical assistance and advice in their respective fields.

The second group of organizations involved in development and humanitarian work are called the UN's programmes and funds. Unlike the specialized agencies, these do not have independent boards and they fall directly under the General Assembly. They include the United Nations Development Programme (UNDP), the United Nations Children's Fund (UNICEF), the United Nations Fund for Population Activities (UNFPA), the Human Settlements Programme (UN-Habitat), the World Food Programme (WFP) and the United Nations High Commissioner for Refugees (UNHCR), thus covering core areas of development and technical assistance, as well as health and education, food, population and reproductive health, shelter, and emergency and humanitarian aid.

As providers and users of aid, the most important UN agencies are the UNDP, UNICEF, UNHCR, WFP, UNFPA, and the UN's Relief and Work Agency for Palestine Refugees in the Near East (UNRWA). Together, they accounted for three-quarters of all new disbursements of ODA spending by the UN in 2004 (see Table 5.1). Playing a pivotal role is the UNDP, which is present in over 160 countries. Formed in 1966 with the merging of the UN's arm for technical assistance and the pre-investment Special Fund, to the end of the 1980s one of the UNDP's initial and central roles was to channel the bulk of its programme resources (received from bilateral donors) to key specialized agencies, most notably the FAO, ILO, WHO, UNESCO and UNIDO. But with a steep fall in its core budget during the 1990s, this role diminished, and the UNDP has expanded its role as the principal UN in-country agency responsible for coordinating all UN activities. Most recently, it has had a lead role in trying to link and align UN aid activities more closely to the needs, policies and strategies of the host country. Since the early 1990s, its budget has expanded again, obtaining additional (voluntary) contributions, mostly from donor governments, to implement its aid programmes administered in-country. In the two-year period 2004–5, the UNDP was budgeting to spend $2.8bn a year, most for in-country projects and programmes. Its own budget averaged $283mn a year in the period 2002–3.[6]

Like the UNDP, UNICEF is one of the UN funds, and not a specialized agency. It is funded entirely from voluntary contributions (by governments, the private sector and individuals), and undertakes development and emergency work for children, encompassing education, health, including HIV/AIDS and immunization, as well as carrying out research and analysis, and advocacy for child rights. In 2004, UNICEF spent just short of $2bn, obtaining 65 per cent of its income from government or inter-governmental sources. It spent $1.6bn, mostly on projects and programmes across more than 180 countries, spending $256mn on administration and programme support.[7] Another large UN aid agency is UNFPA, which works on population issues, including reproductive health. It is active in both development and emergency contexts. Assisted with funds from over 166 governments and working in over 125 countries, UNFPA's income in 2004 was just over $500mn, of which 60 per cent was voluntary contributions from governments. Expenditure was $450mn, $241mn on country and inter-country projects.[8]

The UN's two main emergency and humanitarian organizations are UNHCR and the WFP. The funds provided to and spent by both UNHCR and the WFP are largely determined by the response of donors to different emergency appeals, based almost entirely on voluntary contributions.[9] As with the UNDP, the funds that go through these agencies considerably exceed the funds they use themselves on their own aid programmes. Their aid (ODA) funds have risen in recent years compared with the mid-1990s, totalling on average a combined $920mn a year between 2001 and 2003, compared with $650mn in 1996.[10] Like UNFPA, UNRWA provides both emergency and development assistance, spending a high proportion of its development aid funds on the provision of education and health facilities to Palestinian refugees across the Middle East, including Gaza and the West Bank. In 2004, UNRWA's general budget income and expenditure totalled approximately $340mn, most provided by government contributions. Emergency appeal funds received were a further $130mn a year in the three years to 2004.[11]

Other multilateral agencies

Outside the UN family are a number of multilateral aid funds and agencies. As shown in Table 5.1, these include two global environmental funds, the Global Environment Facility and the Montreal Protocol Fund (set up to help fund poor countries in order to enable them to comply with the protocol to reduce ozone gases), and different multilateral Arab/OPEC (Organisation for Petroleum Exporting Countries) funds.[12] However, major changes are occurring to the multilateral aid system which are substantially altering the total amounts of multilateral aid disbursed through IFIs, and the share of multilateral aid channelled, through different UN agencies. The biggest changes arise from the significant expansion of global funds for health, most notably disbursed by the Global Fund to Fight AIDS, Tuberculosis and Malaria (GFTAM), established in January 2002, and the Global Alliance for Vaccines and Immunisation (GAVI), launched in the year 2000, assisted by substantial funding from the Bill and Melinda Gates Foundation. The Gates Foundation has been providing GAVI with $75mn a year, as part of a ten-year commitment. By the end of 2005, GAVI had received $1.7bn, and following the establishment of the International Finance Facility for Immunization (IFFIm) in 2005, had received commitments of $4bn from donors for future spending. Even larger in scale is the GFTAM, which describes itself as a new financial instrument to attract, manage and disburse aid funds to fight these three diseases. On its board sit representatives of donors, recipients and NGOs. By mid-2006, the Fund had a portfolio of projects valued at $5.5bn and had disbursed $2.3bn of grant funds, with pledges of future funding amounting to over $9bn, most provided by ODA funds.[13]

Systemic issues

In theory, multilateral aid is preferable to bilateral aid, being less subject to political influence, likely to be more responsive to the development needs of recipients, more reliable in providing predictable aid flows, and less likely to be linked to conditions unrelated to the development purpose for which the aid is given. In practice, however, a series of systemic problems have arisen with multilateral aid, and these have tended to increase over time.[14]

The increasing rise in the number of multilateral agencies and multilateral aid funds has increased the overlap between different agencies. More than twenty years ago, the Brandt Commission warned that the growth of multilateral agencies had already 'led to fragmented and diffused activity, overlapping responsibilities and organisational rivalries; issues which ought to be dealt with in an integrated manner are continually shifted from one forum to another, each organisation seeking to preserve its status even if its original task has been achieved' (Brandt 1980: 260).

The establishment of each new multilateral fund or agency has usually occurred because of international pressure to address a particular need perceived to be inadequately addressed. However, the remit of many, if not most, new agencies and funds has inevitably encroached on those of existing agencies, adding to the overlap and complexity of the multilateral aid system. Even within the United Nations system, there is extensive overlap between and across organizations, with two, three, and sometimes four agencies supporting or directly implementing aid projects or programmes within the same sector. Thus, UNESCO, the World Bank, UNICEF and UNFPA are all directly involved in education. The FAO, IFAD, the World Bank and the WFP are all involved in agriculture. WHO, the World Bank, UNICEF and UNFPA are all involved with health, while UNCTAD, the World Bank and the World Trade Organization (WTO) are all involved in trade issues. The provision of humanitarian and emergency aid, and the grey areas between what constitutes development and emergency assistance in countries experiencing conflict, are two further areas where UN agencies overlap considerably, with the WFP, FAO, UNICEF, the World Bank, UNESCO, WHO, UN-Habitat, UNDP, UNHCR and UNFPA all actively involved. In the health sector, the problems created by the overlap between the work of WHO, UNFPA, the World Bank and UNICEF has in part been compounded by the expansion of other agencies (now more than ten) into HIV/AIDS work, including the WFP, UNDP and the ILO. Some 22 different UN agencies have some sort of involvement in delivering clean water.

A related problem concerns the role of those specialized agencies responsible for standard-setting in their particular area of expertise. The establishment of specialized agencies, covering different areas of expertise, might be thought to enable the respective agencies to exert some (minimal) quality control over the programmes of other agencies encroaching on its area of competence. In practice, however, this does not happen. What is more, a specialized agency's role in standard-setting in its own sphere of expertise can sit uncomfortably alongside efforts to expand its project and programme portfolios, competing with other agencies for scarce aid funds. This problem has become more prevalent in recent years because of sharp falls in the core funds provided by bilateral donors to specialized agencies. Today, most specialized agencies now have significant projects and programmes operating with non-core or off-budget funds.[15] A further consequence of this fall in core funding has been to stimulate agencies to extend their activities beyond their specialized areas, further exacerbating the overlap and duplication of activities across UN agencies, and, in some cases, further eroding their effectiveness.[16] A recent report for the UN referred to this phenomenon as 'donor-driven mission creep' (Dalton *et al.* 2003: 12).[17]

The changing fads and fashions of development have also encouraged agencies, particularly multilateral agencies, to put themselves forward as the 'agency of choice' to help implement new development ideas, creating further overlap between and across agencies. Twenty years ago the fashion was gender; more recently it has been governance and environmental management. Ironically, coordination itself is another area of overlap. The UNDP and the World Bank have both taken an active role in trying to coordinate aid activities within particular countries, but there often remains a lack of clarity over precisely which agency (if either) has the mandate to coordinate the activities of other aid agencies, and what such coordination entails, especially if this is perceived to challenge the authority of the host country itself.

All these problems are well known to, and readily acknowledged, not only by detractors of aid but by the United Nations itself. Indeed, the UN has led a succession of initiatives to try to address duplication and overlap of roles and activities, and to achieve greater coordination and collaboration, and a more efficient use of expertise and resources that tend to be replicated across very many agencies.[18] It is noteworthy that whereas one of the theoretical strengths of multilateral over bilateral aid lies in its better coordination of aid activities (Cassen 1997: 323), one of the reasons for the establishment of the UN Development Group (UNDG), in 1997, was to address weaknesses within the UN system of coordinating its own different aid activities, and to try to identify a single entity charged with overseeing the UN's entire development assistance effort (Jones and Colman 2005: 206). These efforts have certainly enhanced understanding within and across UN agencies, funds and programmes of the extent to which problems of overlap exist, and the adverse effects they have on the impact of development and humanitarian aid. Yet, many of the core problems remain.[19] It should also be noted that these sorts of problems extend well beyond the UN system. For instance, while some regional development finance institutions have developed specialized niches for particular types of project, there is also extensive duplication among the range of aid projects and programmes funded by multilateral and regional development banks (see UN 2005a: 121ff.).

The complexities of the multilateral aid system, with the overlapping remits of agencies, parallel systems and structures, and duplication of work and activities, might lead some to conclude that there should only be one aid agency or development finance organization exclusively expounding what is best practice, or implementing aid programmes or projects in one particular area or sector of development. But this would certainly be far too simplistic. There is a role for competition, not least in the arena of ideas. The world of aid has continually benefited from challenges to prevailing conventional views about development and how best to use aid funds, stimulating the drive to greater aid effectiveness and efficiencies in aid delivery. Perhaps the core problem with the present methods and structures of giving aid—seen most clearly in, but not by any means confined to, multilateral aid—is that they encourage the perpetuation and expansion of the agencies themselves, with their overlapping roles and activities, severe weaknesses, and under-performance.

These problems persist because there are no effective mechanisms and processes for ensuring that the agencies which have the funds are the ones most able to use them most effectively.[20] The world of official aid is still dominated by the discrete actions of different donors and agencies, driven predominantly by their own assessments of how to use aid and to whom to give it. Institutions strive and struggle to maintain their own survival, sometimes expanding into new areas or activities to ensure self-preservation, even when they have passed their sell-by date. Part IV of this book discusses how things might change.

Part II
Why is Aid Given?

6 The political and commercial dimensions of aid

Why governments give aid

There is no overarching system of allocating official aid: no organization, or group of organizations, marries the amounts of aid provided with the amounts different countries need. Official development assistance (ODA) is provided entirely voluntarily by different (donor) governments. In Western democracies, ODA funds are authorized by countries' parliaments most commonly on an annual basis, though, in some cases, within two-to four-year spending frameworks. What is more, until very recently, exceptionally few donors based their own aid allocation decisions on what aid other donors were giving, or planning to give, to particular recipient countries. Even today, for the vast majority of aid provided, separate decision-making by different donors remains the norm.[1]

Upon what basis do individual official donors allocate their aid? The discussion in Part I of the book would suggest that the core purpose of giving aid has not been in doubt—to save lives in emergencies and to contribute to development, growth and poverty eradication in poor countries. However, this provides a very incomplete picture, particularly of why governments provide aid. Official aid-giving is a political decision: it is provided by governments using public funds, and most is provided to recipient governments. The question is what informs this (political) decision. The following pages examine this question by looking first at what the main donors *say* are the reasons why they provide aid, and then by summarizing the evidence of how, in practice, donors have *actually* allocated their aid.

Six main clusters of motives have historically influenced donor decisions to allocate aid: These are (1) to help address emergency needs; (2) to assist recipients achieve their development (growth and poverty-reducing) goals; (3) to show solidarity; (4) to further their own national political and strategic interests; (5) to help promote donor-country commercial interests; and (6) because of historical ties. More recently two other motives have been added. In the last ten years, growing attention has been focused on (7) the contribution that aid funds can make to providing and strengthening global public goods, and reducing the ill effects of global evils (see Kaul *et al.* 2003). Additionally, (8) some donors have started more explicitly to base aid-giving decisions on the human rights records of recipient governments, in particular by reducing or halting completely the flow of aid to countries whose record on basic human rights they assess as seriously deficient. The vast majority of donors have allocated aid on the basis of a mix of these different factors, the particular mix differing, often sharply, between donors and over different time periods.

What influence have these different motives played in the allocation of aid, and the forms and manner in which it has been provided? At its broadest, the history of aid-giving has been one of competing pressures swinging the pendulum back and forth between the motivations of altruism, solidarity, poverty and need on the one hand, and the motivation of different forms of self-interest on the other.

A recent stocktaking of the history of foreign aid came to the view that if there has been one constant in the history of aid it is that 'the development objectives of aid programmes have been distorted by the use of aid for donor commercial and political advantage' (Tarp and Hjertholm 2000: 80). But by how much? There are two schools of thought, one that the effects have been profound, the other, that they have been less so. For instance, in a critique of aid, David Sogge judges that 'ideology and the pursuit of commercial advantage are the main determinants' of the allocation of foreign aid (2002: 43). More recently, a long-time scholar of aid, Stephen Browne, has written that the expansion of aid has been due primarily to geopolitical, commercial and other interests, not by altruism, adding that, when aid is allocated for the wrong reasons, it becomes largely a vain pursuit to measure its effectiveness (2006: 9). In contrast, in his book *Moral Vision in International Politics: The Foreign Aid Regime*, which surveys 40 years of aid-giving, David Lumsdaine concludes that 'foreign aid cannot be explained on the basis of the economic and political interests of the donor countries alone, and any satisfactory explanation must give a central place to the influence of humanitarian and egalitarian convictions upon aid donors' (1993: 29). In short, while no one seriously doubts that donor commercial pressures and national self-interest have been and continue to be important to the allocation of aid, the precise way in which this influence is manifested remains contested.

To what extent does this matter? The answer turns on how much aid is provided and how this relates to aid needs. If the overall amount of aid provided comfortably *exceeds* the aid needed to make an effective contribution to poor countries' development and welfare needs, it matters less that some aid in excess of the amounts required to address these needs is provided and used for non-developmental purposes. If, however, there is insufficient aid, then a case can be made either for increasing the overall amount provided, assuming the political and commercial 'diversions' of aid continue, or for trying to reduce the amount of aid provided but not used for humanitarian or developmental purposes.[2] The discussion in Chapter 18 will highlight the huge shortfall between the amount of humanitarian aid currently provided and that required adequately to address growing global humanitarian needs. The discussion in Chapter 8 will similarly conclude that the current amounts of development aid are insufficient. For the purposes of the present discussion, we shall assume (and not discuss further here) that there is a need to increase the overall amount of aid required for both development and humanitarian purposes and that it is therefore important to try to understand the basis upon which aid is currently allocated and how changes in aid allocation might influence the effectiveness of the aid provided.

A number of studies have tried to ascertain the relative importance of developmental and non-developmental ODA allocation decisions. The consensus emerging from these studies is that non-developmental factors have been and continue to be important, though varying between donors and over time. However, it has not been easy to pinpoint clearly the relative influence of different motives.

Over a period of more than 20 years, but using aid data for the 1960s and 1970s, and so less relevant to contemporary debate, a widely quoted study by Maizels and Nissanke concluded, with little qualification, that United States, British, French, German and Japanese aid allocations were made 'solely in support of donors' perceived foreign economic, political and security interests' (1984: 891). Fifteen years on, an influential study by Alesina and Dollar (2000), using aid distribution data a number of years before the events of 11th September, showed that political and strategic considerations were still remarkably important determinants of donor behaviour. In particular, they found that former colonies assessed as being 'non-democratic' and having 'closed' trade policies were found to receive on average twice as much aid from former powers as others. However, in a more recent review of the evidence, McGillivray (2003a) correctly pointed out that there can often be methodological problems in trying to separate out developmental from non-developmental allocations of aid, particularly when geopolitical factors lead countries to allocate more aid to very poor countries, as has clearly happened in recent years in the cases of Afghanistan and the Democratic Republic of the Congo.[3] Nonetheless, even he concludes that the allocation of aid on the basis of political, commercial and strategic interests is of concern and that 'in most instances, non-developmental criteria, especially trade promotion, remain a priority for many donors' (McGillivray 2003a: 27–8). Recent studies, by Berthélemy in particular (2004, 2005), confirm a strong link between donor aid allocations and their major trading partners, but they also suggest that the strong link between aid and former colonies appears to have weakened in the post-Cold War era. His analysis indicates that Switzerland, Ireland and the Nordic countries (except Finland) have been more altruistic in their aid-giving, while France, Japan and the United Kingdom have been driven more by self-interested motives (Berthélemy 2004: 20).

Following decades of aid-giving when political motives for allocating aid were of central concern, especially for the United States, the end of the Cold War heralded almost a decade when the pendulum swung more towards humanitarian and development concerns, and there was an expectation that this would represent a permanent shift in allocation priorities. Since 9/11, however, and subsequent terrorist attacks such as those in Madrid in 2004 and London in 2005, the pendulum has swung back again. We shall now look at what donors have said and what they have done in allocating and re-allocating aid, to try to draw some conclusions.

Politics and national self-interest in aid-giving

THE UNITED STATES

One-quarter of all ODA and almost 30 per cent of all official bilateral aid is provided by the United States. The way that the United States allocates its aid and the reasons it gives for providing it are probably even more significant than these figures suggest because of the way that its global leadership, as the only surviving superpower, has influenced other leading donors and the decisions they make about the role and allocation of aid.

The primary purpose of United States' aid has always been to further and promote its own interests, with foreign aid seen as an essential arm of foreign policy, playing 'a vital role in supporting US geo-strategic interests' (USAID 2004: 3). As a result, foreign aid allocations have always been critically influenced by national security priorities, with massive amounts of aid channelled to America's allies.[4] However, within this broad framework, development and humanitarian goals have also been important: since President Kennedy's Alliance for Progress, development has been an explicit aid priority, and in the early 1970s, Congress passed the New Directions legislation, which mandated an emphasis on recipient needs as a criterion for the allocation of US aid.

The end of the Cold War afforded the United States what turned out to be a relatively short break from the pressures to allocate aid according to clear geopolitical aims, but instead of refocusing aid to the poorest countries, deep cuts in the overall level of aid were made. In real terms, the total amount of United States official aid fell by half between 1990 and 1997. However, from the late 1990s, growing foreign policy concerns led not only to the start of a period of expansion of US aid, which is set to continue, but to a further refining of the relationship between aid and national security concerns. In the post-11 September period, this was articulated most clearly in the 2002 National Security

Strategy, which elevated development to become the third pillar of US foreign policy, on a par with defence and diplomacy, in the minds of many, blurring, rather than sharpening, the distinction between aid for development and aid for the national interest. A 'root of the national security threat to the United States and the broader international community is the lack of development, which can't be addressed by military and diplomatic means alone' (USAID 2005b: v).

In the aftermath of the events of 11th September, what the US Administration termed the 'global war on terror' has resulted in massive amounts of aid being deployed to countries perceived as critical to US geopolitical interests. Seen in isolation, such trends would suggest that US aid has swung back decisively to aid allocations being predominantly determined by security goals. However, there have also been significant increases in aid for development purposes, including billions of dollars of new funds allocated to the new Millennium Challenge Account (MCA), to the President's Emergency Plan for AIDS Relief (PEPFAR) to combat AIDS, tuberculosis and malaria, and increases in aid to assist 'fragile states'. What has been the overall trend? On the basis largely of data up to 2003, an analysis undertaken by Ngaire Woods (2005) judged that, in spite of a widely held perception of a diversion of existing aid to new security imperatives, existing aid flows had not been massively redeployed and diverted to counter-terrorism. Similar assessments were made in a recent study by Moss, Roodman and Standley which concluded that 'at this stage, concerns that there is a large and systematic diversion of US foreign aid from fighting poverty to fighting the global war on terror do not appear to have been realised' (2005: 14).[5] Post-2005 developments, more recent budget allocations, and budget proposals for the year 2007 would tend to confirm these analyses.[6] Box 6.1 summarizes trends in the allocation of United States ODA by country grouping.

For the future, the link between aid-giving and pursuing US national interests is set to continue. In 2006, the government published its Quadrennial Defense Review Report contrasting the Cold War period and the War on Terror

---

BOX 6.1 THE DISTRIBUTION OF UNITED STATES ODA TO POOR AND OTHER COUNTRIES

In aggregate, in the decade from 1993/4 to 2003/4, the share of United States aid going to the poorest (low-income) countries fell from 56 per cent to 50 per cent of total ODA. Likewise, on a different indicator, the share of US aid going to the 31 countries lowest in the UN's Human Development Index (HDI) fell from 31 per cent in 1992 to 19 per cent by 2002. However, in its first year, the Millennium Challenge Corporation (MCC) allocated aid funds (totalling $1.5bn) to eight countries, of which all but one were classified as low-income countries, though only two were in the lowest HDI category. In contrast, from the 1980s and until the mid-1990s, Egypt and Israel between them accounted for between 15 and 40 per cent of all US ODA. By 2004, reflecting different strategic priorities, six of the top seven recipients of US aid were countries of key strategic importance to the United States, accounting for a third of all aid: Iraq, Egypt, Jordan, Afghanistan, Pakistan and Colombia.

with what, in the Forthcoming period, it terms the Long War. Within this paradigm, not only are defence, humanitarian aid and development aid viewed as continuing to be provided in mutually reinforcing ways, but an increased emphasis has been placed on the United States working more collaboratively with its allies to achieve its goals—including doing so with aid funds:

Supporting the rule of law and building civil societies where they do not exist today, or where they are in their infancy, is fundamental to winning the long war. In this sense, today's environment resembles a challenge that is different in kind, but similar in scale to the Cold War—a challenge so immense that it requires major shifts in strategic concepts for national security and the role of military power. Therefore, the United States needs to develop new concepts and methods of interagency and international cooperation. (US Department of Defense 2006: 90)

OTHER DONORS AND THE WIDER PICTURE

For other leading donors, the influence of non-developmental motives in the allocation of aid has varied, but for most, it has always been, and continues today, to be important. In recent years, under the glare of publicity, repeated rounds of pledges and commitments by donor governments to increase aid levels to help achieve the Millennium Development Goals (MDGs) misleadingly conveyed the impression that development was now the only purpose for which aid was given. The fact that most donors (the United States being a major exception) underplay non-developmental, national interest, and foreign policy influences in most public statements about aid-giving reinforces this impression (Degnbol-Martinussen and Engberg-Pedersen 1999: 17).

Historically, Sweden, the Netherlands, Norway, Denmark and Finland have stood out as donors who have articulated solidarity and development as major factors influencing their allocation of aid. For most, their commitments to development and poverty reduction have, if anything, risen in recent years. By 2003–4, over two-thirds of their ODA was going to poorer (low-income) countries. However, it is important to note that over the past 15 to 20 years, most of these particular donors, as well as Ireland, have altered the way that their aid programmes are administered, placing aid policy decisions more clearly within their foreign affairs ministries, and leaving their aid agencies to focus more on the technical aspects of aid. Some have argued that this has enabled foreign policy decisions to be influenced more by the altruistic motives which have historically shaped their official aid programmes, others that these moves have aligned aid-giving more closely to ensuring broader consistency with wider strategic interests.[7]

In contrast, Japan, like the United States, provides aid explicitly to enhance its own security and prosperity, with poverty way down the list of priorities.

This was quite clearly expressed in 2006 by the Minister of Foreign Affairs: 'it must not be forgotten that in the end ODA is implemented for Japan's own sake. In other words, ODA is implemented to enhance the happiness and to raise the profile of Japan and its people in the world'.[8] This explains why Japan's aid is highly concentrated in Asia. Likewise, Australia and New Zealand view their aid programmes as a contribution to their wider foreign policy objectives, and, therefore unsurprisingly, their aid is heavily concentrated in Asia and the Pacific (see OECD 2005c, d).

For France and the United Kingdom in particular, as well as for Portugal, Spain, Belgium and the Netherlands, the allocation of aid has been profoundly influenced by their former colonial histories. However, like all other major donors, their aid-giving has balanced development interests on the one hand with political, strategic and also commercial interests on the other. How those tensions are resolved in practice has been documented in an in-depth history of Canadian aid, *Canadian International Development Assistance Policies: An Appraisal* (Pratt *et al.* 1996). Though written more than a decade years ago, this tells a story that could be repeated in many major donor countries, and still rings true today. Thus, the history of Canadian aid has been a continual 'battle between development, political and commercial interests', with different interests gaining or losing ground in different time periods. The factor which most crucially enabled these differing interests to influence aid allocations in different time periods was a simple one: the absence of any explicit criteria for country selection (Pratt *et al.* 1996: 3, 126–7).

In the 1990s, in line with all but the two largest donors (the United States and Japan), the view that the welfare and development criteria for providing aid should be its central purpose gained influence. This change in rhetoric, however, has only been reflected in a few cases by formal changes to the procedures for allocating aid. One country where tangible changes have been made is the United Kingdom. Thus, in recent years it has formally abandoned its commercial aid-funded window, the Aid and Trade Provision, it has enacted legislation explicitly requiring official aid solely to be used for development and welfare purposes, and it has committed itself to channelling no less than 90 per cent of bilateral aid to the poorest counties.[9]

However, in a recent survey of aid allocations among the leading OECD/DAC donors, Stephen Jones and colleagues could only find three out of the nine largest donors whose allocation of aid was 'specifically driven' by poverty considerations: Sweden, the United Kingdom and the Netherlands (Jones *et al.* 2005: 13). In practice, many donors have continued to be influenced (some profoundly) by the changes taking place in the United States' approach to aid-giving as a result of the 'global war on terror'. Indeed, despite the UK's explicit commitments to providing aid for poverty reduction, in the two-year period 2003–4, Iraq, Afghanistan and Pakistan appeared among the list of the UK's top 11 aid-recipient countries, though none had been listed among the top 15 recipients two years earlier. Moving beyond the UK, for the same years Iraq, Afghanistan or Pakistan appeared (in some cases as completely new aid recipients) in the list of the top ten recipients of aid of the following nine major donors: Australia, Canada, the European Union, France, Japan, New Zealand, Norway, Spain and Sweden.[10] This suggests that just as the United States has been successful in encouraging its main allies to continue to participate in key parts of the its 'global war on terror', not least by providing ODA funds to countries considered a security risk, so too it will be likely to convince them to support its Long War, and the continued linking of aid allocation to geopolitical interests.

The following provides a good overall summary of current approaches by the major donors to contemporary aid allocation. It confirms the continuing importance of non-developmental and especially political criteria in the allocation of aid today:

Current aggregate aid allocations are still significantly shaped and informed by other (non-developmental) criteria, of which the most significant relate to concerns about regional (Australia, EU, Japan) or global (US) security and political relations. Former colonial links remain significant in explaining the aid allocation patterns for France and the UK—but more in determining the countries with which there is a bilateral relationship rather than ensuring particularly high or stable levels of aid . . . . Aid from the largest bilateral donors is being provided for motives that are not purely based on poverty reduction objectives although the latter have been made more explicit in recent years and are formally the sole or major justification for development assistance for some donors. Security and regional relations are the most significant drivers of aid allocations for donors (cultural issues are particularly important in the case of France) with poorer and/or potentially unstable neighbours (Australia, Japan, and the EU) and for global superpowers (now just the USA, but in the past the Soviet Union) . . . Bilateral aid of EU member states appears to be becoming increasingly poverty-focused in its allocation, while aid provided through the European Commission is increasingly heavily focused on its Eastern and Southern neighbours and driven by considerations of economic, political and security relations.[11] (Jones *et al.* 2005: 25–6)

Commercial interests in aid-giving

Since aid was first provided, it has been linked with the commercial interests of donors. Most directly, this has occurred through the tying of aid to the purchases of goods and services from the donor country.[12] More indirectly, aid can be tied in a number of ways, such as through a variety of trade promotion activities, for example subsidizing export-credit schemes and providing aid to lower the costs of firms in bidding for tenders, and through more informal pressures on recipients to encourage them to purchase goods and services from donor-based commercial companies.[13] For decades, commercial interests in all major donor countries have lobbied to gain access to aid funds, usually based on a 'win–win' or mutual interest argument—that by tying aid to donor-based commercial interests, jobs and exports will be expanded at home at the same time as development is boosted abroad.

Against this backdrop, it is not surprising that the results of aid allocation studies have confirmed the links between aid and donor-based trade and commercial interests. However, their importance has varied between donors and over time. Recent reviews suggest that although there is evidence of donors giving more emphasis to development criteria, commercial interests of donors remain a 'significant feature' of contemporary aid relationships (see McGillivray 2003a: 28; Jones *et al.* 2005: 12).

THE TYING OF AID

The tying of aid is one dimension of the commercialization of aid that has been the subject of particular attention, and for some two decades, the OECD/DAC has led a number of initiatives to try to reduce aid tying among the leading OECD/DAC donors. One of the most important recent initiatives was the 2001 DAC Recommendations on Untying Official Development Assistance to the least developed countries (LLDCs).[14] This entered into force in January 2002, and is the subject of an annual progress report.[15] It would appear that significant progress has been made, with the ratio of untied to total aid to the LLDCs rising from 53 per cent in 1999–2001 to 70 per cent by 2003. On a related matter, the OECD/DAC reported in 2006 that just over 90 per cent of bilateral aid commitments to the LLDCs consisted of untied aid, with 100 per cent untied aid reported for three donors: Ireland, Norway and the United Kingdom (2006a: 209). However, these figures provide an extremely partial picture of aid tying, even to the LLDCs. The 90 per cent untied aid ratio distorts the degree to which aid to the poorest countries is untied, as it excludes technical assistance, and even the 70 per cent untied aid ratio excludes significant amounts of aid, including the areas of technical assistance and food aid.[16] Even then, more than 70 per cent of United States ODA to the LLDCs remains tied, and in recent years, Japan's aid has become more tied.

In terms of total ODA, more than half remains tied: data published in 2006 by the OECD/DAC showed that only 42 per cent of ODA was reported by donors as untied, not hugely different from the 48 per cent figure reported in the mid-1980s (see Jempa 1991: 23). For more than half of all ODA (54 per cent), donors have chosen not to report/declare the share of aid which is tied or untied. This is because, for most donors, commercial pressures to obtain benefits from their aid programmes remain important, and for a number of donors, business interests continue to exert influence, though most

---

BOX 6.2 AUSTRALIAN TIED AID

In 1997, a major review of Australia's aid programme was published, chaired by Paul Simons, former Executive Chairman of the private corporation Woolworths (Simons *et al*. 1997). The report noted that Australia tied more of its aid than any other country. It recommended that, 'as the minimum credible first steps in a process of completely untying all aid', all aid to the poorest countries should be totally untied and for other programmes recipient countries should be allowed to procure goods from domestic suppliers if cost-effective (Simons *et al*. 1997: 192).

Almost ten years later, 53 per cent of Australian ODA to LLDCs remains tied. The 2005 OECD peer review of Australia aid notes that although the country has committed itself to untying its aid to the LLDCs in line with the OECD/DAC recommendations, 'this decision has had limited impact on its programme because most of its ODA to LLDCs falls outside the coverage provisions' (OECD 2005c: 53).

Harking back to the Simons report nine years earlier, the 2006 White Paper announced that all Australian aid would in future be untied (AusAID 2006: 22). It will be interesting to see if history repeats itself.

Sources: Simons *et al*. 1997: ch. 10; AusAID 2006: 22.

---

donors are far more reluctant to admit this than they were 10 to 15 years ago. The case of Australia is instructive (see Box 6.2).

In the case of the United States, however, the tying of aid to US commercial interests remains particularly transparent: it is enshrined in law. Only three donors—Ireland, Norway and the United Kingdom—have formally agreed to untie all their aid, though for a further eight donors—Belgium, Finland, Netherlands, Portugal, Sweden and Switzerland—official aid is almost fully untied. However, the total aid provided by these donors accounts for less than 30 per cent of total OECD/DAC ODA. A 2004 study of European aid estimated that almost half the ODA provided bilaterally by European donors still consisted of tied or partially tied aid.[17]

THE COSTS OF AID TYING

Aid tying is thus extensive. But what is the cost? This is difficult to calculate, not least because of the reluctance of many donors to provide data on aid tying on which comparative costs might be accurately estimated. However, there have been no substantial challenges to the conclusions drawn in an OECD study whose findings were published in the early 1990s, which judged that the tying of aid inflated its cost to recipients by between 15 and 30 per cent. The study found that the costs of tying had steadily increased from the 1960s to the 1980s, so that by the early 1990s, an average figure of 20 per cent was judged to be a reasonable approximate average (Jepma 1991: 15).[18] Recent work for the

OECD estimates that the costs of the tying of food aid are even higher than this: in 2004, food aid from donor countries was 50 per cent more costly than local procurement, and 30 per cent higher than procurement in third countries (Clay 2005: 9). On the basis of these ratios, and the share of food aid in total ODA, the costs of the tying of bilateral aid (ODA) in 2004 is conservatively estimated to have amounted to $7.3bn—an amount higher than the total bilateral aid (ODA) given by any donor except the United States.[19] If all this aid had been provided untied, the effective amount of ODA provided by donors in 2004 would have been almost 10 per cent greater than the $79bn figure recorded.

There are, however, grounds for believing that the real costs of tied aid to recipients are even higher than this. First, the costs of some tied technical assistance are considerably higher than the 20 per cent premium assumed above (see Williams *et al.* 2003). For instance, a study of the costs to Uganda of providing long-term technical assistance found that the Commonwealth Secretariat was able to secure the necessary skills at the cost of £41,000, whereas the costs to bilateral agencies of providing long-term consultants ranged from 100 per cent to over 300 per cent more than this.[20] Secondly, though few country-based rather than donor-based studies have been carried out, a number of them indicate that the costs of tied aid to the recipient have been well in excess of the Jepma 20 per cent average. For example, a 2004 Ghanaian study for the years 1990 to 1997 found that the tying of aid raised the price of the importation of goods provided as aid from $40mn to $80mn a year (Osei 2004: 144).[21]

It would thus seem that the 'extra costs' of aid tying are likely to be significantly higher than the $7.3bn indicated above, and, though there have been no recent attempts to calculate them, the total costs of the commercialisation of aid higher still.

The overall impact of political and commercial influences on aid

A number of substantial, and influential, cross-country and longitudinal studies have been carried out which have compared prevailing allocations of aid against ideal or 'optimal' allocations. As we shall see, most show that a switch from prevailing to optimal allocations would have a major developmental impact. Before the numbers are presented, it is worth pausing for a reality check.

For those donors whose purpose in providing aid is integrally linked to the achievement of non-developmental (wider strategic and possibly commercial) objectives, it cannot be assumed either that they would agree to provide aid exclusively for development purposes, or that, if they were so persuaded, they would provide (exclusively development-focused) aid in the same amounts as current disbursements. To complicate matters further, as discussed above, the (theoretical) distinctions between developmental and non-developmental purposes for giving aid are repeatedly blurred when—as often happens—countries to which donors primarily give aid for geopolitical reasons would easily qualify for aid on poverty criteria. This blurring applies to all three main beneficiaries of recent 'geo-strategic' aid: Afghanistan, Pakistan and Iraq. Afghanistan is one of the poorest countries in the world—indeed, its under-five mortality rate is 40 per cent worse than the average for all 'low human development' countries. Pakistan is classified as a low-income country, and, on a key poverty/development indicator, Iraq would certainly qualify for development aid: its life expectancy at birth is estimated to be the same as that for the average of all low-income countries (UN 2005b: 253, 328).

There are further complexities. Many aid allocation studies compare actual allocations against 'ideal' allocations based on poverty criteria, most commonly determined by per capita income levels, rather than against aid need, thus sidestepping what is often a central issue: whether some poor countries (the over-aided ones) need more aid.[22] Another problem with using aid allocation studies to try to determine the influence of developmental and non-developmental criteria in the distribution of aid is that these are not the only variables which these studies examine and analyse. Many also incorporate into their analyses aid-effectiveness criteria, examining the allocation of aid on the basis both of need and whether it is likely to be used well. Indeed, a major purpose in undertaking a number of these studies has been to suggest that aid will be put to more productive and effective use if it is channelled toward those countries that use it effectively, and away from those which do not—even if the latter countries are extremely poor. The problem here is not that effectiveness is irrelevant: it is clearly a vital issue. What have been extremely controversial have been the criteria selected and used to judge whether aid will be used effectively, and the extent to which effectiveness criteria ought to 'trump' needs or poverty-based criteria as the basis for allocating aid. The impact and effectiveness of aid is discussed in full in Part II of this book, and in particular, the role and impact of policies prescribed by donors is discussed in Chapter 14. For the present, we will merely draw key findings from these studies which throw light on the more general question about the respective allocations of aid made on the basis of developmental versus non-developmental criteria.[23] Against the backdrop of these real-life complexities, what does the analysis of aid data and these studies tell us?

The distribution of official aid to countries at different levels of development reveals a considerable mismatch between aid provided and overall levels of poverty, as measured by average per capita income. In the year 2004, almost $9bn was provided in official aid (OA) to countries considered by the OECD/DAC as too rich to qualify for ODA, almost $1bn going to countries classified by the UN as 'high human development' countries. At the other end of the scale, in 2003/4, the total amount of aid (ODA) channelled by OECD/DAC donors to the 65 poorest countries and territories in the world amounted to only $31.4bn out of a total of $73.8bn.[24] This accounted for less than half of all the ODA (43 per cent) provided by the OECD/DAC donors, although the share of ODA to the 65 poorest countries was an improvement on the 38 per cent figure achieved ten years earlier, in 1993/4. While it is not being suggested that all aid should necessarily go to the 65 poorest countries, providing less than half of all ODA to this group of countries puts into critical perspective the verbal commitment of donors to use aid as a major tool in halving the numbers of people living in poverty.

The leading donors have committed themselves to the far less challenging target of providing ODA to the least developed countries (LLDCs) at least to the level of 0.14 per cent of their gross national income (GNI). However, by 2004, this ratio stood at 0.08 per cent for all OECD/DAC donors, about half the target level. Taken separately, only one-third of the major donors had managed to reach this target.[25] Table 6.1 presents trend data for the past 20 years of ODA going to LLDCs, both in aggregate and by donor. It shows that less than one-third of all ODA was channelled to the LLDCs by 2003/4. It also shows that although the amount of ODA per capita to the LLDCs increased over the 20-year period in current prices, in real terms it fell.

Even sharper disparities are apparent when one looks at the amounts of aid (ODA) provided at the country level. For instance in 2003, the average amount of aid (ODA) received per person in the Low Human Development countries was $27, ranging from $2 per head in Nigeria, $21 per head in Ethiopia, and $101 per head in the Democratic Republic of Congo. In contrast, some of the wealthier countries, such as Jordan, received on average $232 in ODA per capita in 2003.[26] Longer-term trends suggest that over the last two decades, the share of aid going to different groups of countries (low-income and middle-income) has remained fairly steady. However, these aggregate figures disguise huge differences between countries. For example, from 1969 to 1995, and with a mid-1970s GDP per capita of almost $4,000, higher than Ireland (now an OECD/DAC donor), Israel qualified as a recipient of ODA and was provided with a total of $24bn. In contrast, Sierra Leone received less than $2bn (McGillivray 2003a: 1). On the other hand, there has been a recent sharp increase in ODA going to Sub-Saharan Africa (SSA), with the total share rising from 28 to 35 per cent of total ODA in the ten years to 2003. Although this constituted a 20 per cent rise in real terms in ODA going to SSA, when set alongside the rise in the population, it tells a different story: in real terms, ODA per capita to SSA fell by 5 per cent, from an average of $38 per capita in 1993 to $36 in 2003 (OECD 2006a: 224).

All of the aid allocation studies look more closely at the distribution of aid over time within, between and across countries. Three broad conclusions

Table 6.1 Official development assistance to the least developed countries, 1983/4 to 2003/4 ($mn)

Donors	1983/4		1993/4		2003/4	
	ODA to LLDCs	% of total ODA	ODA to LLDCs	% of total ODA	ODA to LLDCs	% of total ODA
Australia	154	20	211	20	304	23
Austria	26	15	114	43	169	29
Belgium	205	44	255	33	867	52
Canada	447	31	556	24	668	29
Denmark	175	42	485	35	704	37
Finland	73	44	100	31	168	28
France	807	27	1,938	24	3,067	39
Germany	952	32	1,789	26	2,410	34
Greece	n/a	n/a	n/a	n/a	60	15
Ireland	16	32	38	40	294	53
Italy	461	47	625	22	946	39
Japan	1,003	25	2,276	19	1,803	20
Luxembourg	n/a	n/a	16	30	76	35
Netherlands	416	34	699	28	1,217	30
New Zealand	9	15	21	20	55	29
Norway	214	38	465	43	819	39
Portugal	n/a	n/a	178	66	541	40
Spain	n/a	n/a	119	9	383	17
Sweden	283	38	566	22	792	31
Switzerland	118	39	297	33	402	28
United Kingdom	497	33	906	26	2,630	37
United States	1,635	19	2,581	26	4,489	25
Total ODA to LLDCs	7,521	27	14,136	25	22,863	31
Total ODA to poorest 65 countries[a]	10,459	37	21,202	38	31,471	43
ODA per capita LLDCs, current prices	17.1		24.6		31.2	
ODA per capita to LLDCs, fixed (2003) prices	34.6		26.9		31.2	

n/a = not available

[a] Poorest countries are all LLDCs plus the following 15 countries or territories: the Republic of Congo, Ghana, India, Kenya, Kyrgyzstan, Moldova, Mongolia, Nigeria, the Occupied Palestinian Territories, Pakistan, Papua New Guinea, Tajikistan, Uzbekistan, Vietnam and Zimbabwe.

Sources: OECD and UN population data-bases.

emerge.[27] The first is that a significant share of aid goes to middle-income and not to the poorest countries. The second is that large poor countries have consistently received proportionately less aid per capita than have smaller poor countries, suggesting that, in relation to the distribution of aid, poor people in large countries are relatively disadvantaged. The third conclusion is that if aid allocations were based more closely on poverty criteria, the impact of aid on poverty reduction would not merely be greater, it would be very significantly greater.

Though the studies broadly agree that non-developmental factors influence prevailing allocations of aid, they differ in their estimates of the precise influence these have had, between donors and over time.[28] They all agree that in general, allocations should shift sharply away from richer and higher middle-income to poorer countries. However, they do not agree precisely which countries should receive more or less aid, and what the new levels of aid ought to be—differences that in some cases are as great as, and even eclipse, the differences in aid allocations due to geopolitical or commercial influences.[29] For instance, on the basis of aid allocations for the year 2000, one study recommends that the $1.5bn worth of aid (ODA) to India almost entirely cease, another that it should be increased to over $10bn (see McGillivray 2003b: 20). These differences are largely due to the different weights that are given to poverty, need and country size, on the one hand, and policy criteria, on the other; the factors that one judges ought to make up the 'best' policy package and how these are weighted; and whether aid allocations should (in part) be determined by the differing structural factors which can either facilitate or hinder poverty reduction.

For the present discussion, these distinctions are not so important. What matters most is the consensus across all studies which are in any way prescriptive: an allocation of aid funds based less on current criteria—which are a mix of developmental and self-interested—motives and influences and more narrowly based on development criteria (however precisely measured), would achieve huge poverty-reducing gains. Widely cited are the figures provided in the studies by Collier and Dollar. They suggest that, whereas under prevailing allocations of aid, some 30mn people a year can be 'lifted out of poverty', by reallocating current amounts of aid to different recipients, this figure could almost be trebled to 80mn people a year. This is a huge difference. Their calculations also suggest that to achieve these same poverty-reducing gains under present ways of allocating aid would require a threefold increase in the overall amount of aid provided (Collier and Dollar 2002, quoted in McGillivray 2003b: 18–22).[30] Other studies have produced even more startling results.[31]

Concluding comments

The clear conclusion of this chapter is that political, commercial and other criteria than the developmental and humanitarian motives for providing aid matter greatly. The ways that aid is allocated and the tying of aid have profound effects on the overall contribution of aid to development and welfare goals. Aid always has been, and still is, provided for non-developmental purposes, contributing to and shaping the way that it has been allocated, and the forms in which it is provided. Overall, the evidence forcibly shows, although not as rigorously as one might like, that these influences have reduced and continue to reduce aid's potential development and welfare effects. In many cases, political influences have also accentuated the volatility of aid-giving, reducing its potential impact still further. In a recent study, Collier, Goderis and Hoeffler (2006) find that political shocks are more damaging to poor countries than natural shocks. The politics of aid remains central to any discussion of whether and how aid works.

7 Public support for aid

Trends in public support

It is widely assumed that there is a strong link between the provision of aid by governments and public support for aid. Support for aid, wrote Robert Cassen, rests 'ultimately on public opinion which has to be convinced that aid is working well' (1986: 294). If this is true, then presumably, there is a link between the level and strength of support for aid and the amounts governments provide. The stronger the level of public support, the higher will be the amounts of aid given, and the stronger the support for aid provided for developmental and humanitarian purposes, the more this purpose will shape the way that aid is provided and who should receive it. David Lumsdaine's 40-year survey of aid-giving led him to conclude that rapid increases in aid have occurred in countries with high levels of support for aid and in those countries where the public said it wanted increases, but that aid levels declined where the public wanted declines (1993:142).

This chapter examines the evidence of the links between the views of the (voting) public on aid and the amounts of official aid governments have provided. We look, first, at trends in public support for aid, and the strengthening of that support, then discuss the reliability of public opinion data, and end by reviewing some evidence to assess the relationship between public support for aid and public perceptions of its effectiveness. A number of the conclusions are surprising, some counter-intuitive.

HIGH LEVELS OF AND PERSISTENT PUBLIC SUPPORT FOR AID

For many decades, across all leading donor countries, opinion polls have been conducted to ascertain the level and extent of public support for foreign aid. Although there have been fluctuations over time, the aggregate evidence from these polls provides remarkably clear and consistent findings across almost all donor countries. For over 20 years, successive opinion polls show an extremely high level of public support for foreign aid. These rebut the allegations that, at different times in recent years, the public has become disillusioned with aid and that 'aid fatigue' has set in, reducing public support for aid across the leading donor countries.

In the mid-1980s, an OECD/DAC review of 25 years of aid-giving judged that there was no evidence that public support for aid had been weakening (OECD 1985: 63). In the mid-1990s, a major cross-country review of the evidence similarly concluded that the level of support for development assistance 'has not changed significantly in recent years. Almost everywhere, a majority of citizens continues to favour development aid' (Foy and Helmich 1996: 11). A study synthesizing the evidence of all opinion polls, conducted at much the same time, reported that an average of 80 per cent of the public supported the provision of official development assistance (ODA), and that far from there being evidence of aid fatigue, support for aid had risen (by 2 per cent) over the previous 12 years (Stern 1998: 4). A 2003 review of polls conducted in 2001 reported that a similar majority of people in the main donor countries (81 per cent) were supportive of aid to developing countries (McDonnell *et al.* 2003b: 14), leading the authors to conclude that, on the basis of the most complete evidence to date, public support for development cooperation in OECD/DAC member countries has remained high for two decades (2003a: 12). Consistent though these findings have been, they do mask shifts in support across countries. For example, whereas the 1998 (Stern) study reported support ranging from a low of 45 per cent, in the United States, to a high of 95 per cent, in Spain, the lowest level of support in 2001, at 71 per cent, was in the United Kingdom and New Zealand, with Ireland recording the highest level of support, at 95 per cent (McDonnell *et al.* 2003: 12).

More recent cross-country evidence suggests even higher levels of public support for aid. The findings of a Eurobarometer survey conducted at the end of 2004 across 22 countries of the European Union reported that, from 2002 to 2004, there had been an increase from 83 per cent to 91 per cent of people who confirmed their belief in the importance of aid. The evidence from this particular survey showed levels of support among the main European OECD/DAC donors ranging from a low of 86 per cent, in Belgium, to 96 per cent in Sweden (EC 2005a: 25, 26). Studies conducted at much the same time in Canada and Japan confirm the continuing upward level of support for aid, while recent evidence from Australia and New Zealand also shows rising levels of public support for aid, to over 90 per cent in the case of Australia (OECD 2005d: 27; AusAID 2005: 16).

The overall level of public support for aid in the United States has consistently been reported as far lower than in all other major donor countries, with many surveys suggesting, and the widely held view being, that only between 40 to 50 per cent of the American public are broadly supportive of aid. Indeed, some survey evidence suggests that the level of public support for aid in the United States declined steadily from the 1950s to the mid-1980s (Lumsdaine 1993: 142). However, it is also clear that the level of recorded public support for aid among Americans is highly sensitive to the precise question asked by pollsters, and that with a slight turn of phrase, far more Americans appear to be in favour of aid than the data of these comparatively less supportive surveys would suggest. For example, while a significant minority of Americans have frequently expressed negative feelings about foreign aid—in 2001, 31 per cent viewed foreign aid negatively (PIPA 2001: 1)—a significant majority have consistently stated their support for foreign aid and for the Federal government providing it. From this perspective, the evidence suggests that support for aid has been rising over time. In the mid-1970s, almost 70 per cent of Americans were found to be favour of aid, rising to almost 80 per cent from the mid-1990s to 2001 (Lumsdaine 1993: 142). Indeed in 2005, 71 per cent of Americans were reported to be in favour of the United States increasing its aid, if other countries also did so (PIPA 2005: 2).

THE RELATIONSHIP BETWEEN PUBLIC SUPPORT AND THE AMOUNTS OF ODA PROVIDED

Public support for aid remains strong. But what is the relationship between level of support and the amounts of aid given? Studies from across donor countries provide a somewhat confusing picture.

Lumsdaine suggests that the strength of public support for aid roughly corresponded to the size of different donors' aid programmes (1993: 116). In particular, he was influenced by the contrasting evidence from the Scandinavian donors and the United States: in the case of the former, strong and consistently high levels of support for aid had been associated with high levels of aid (as measured by the ODA/GNI ratio), and in the latter, a low ODA/GNI ratio was associated with comparatively low levels of support for aid. However, as Stern's analysis makes clear, the relationship would appear to be far more complex. High levels of support for aid among many non-Scandinavian European donors have been associated with comparatively low levels of official aid (Stern 1998: 2–3). But a more substantive challenge to the Lumsdaine thesis comes from evidence concerning the relationship between changes in aid-giving and changes in public support across most if not all countries.

Not only is it difficult to find a clear relationship between levels of public support and levels of aid-giving, but there is a large amount of contrary evidence—a rise in ODA when public support was falling, and a fall in ODA when support was rising. For instance, in the ten years to 1997, the share of those in Norway wanting aid levels to be cut rose from 12 per cent to 30 per cent, yet Norway's ODA remained the highest of all donors, and in real terms, Norwegian ODA rose by 25 per cent from 1987 to 1997 (Stokke 2005: 483). Likewise, in the decade to 1999, Japanese ODA rose by 50 per cent, yet public support for aid fell quite sharply at the end of the decade (McDonnell *et al.* 2003b: 27). Similarly, public support for aid fell markedly in France in the 1980s while ODA rose significantly; French aid to Africa fell during the 1990s at a time when public support remained high (Olsen 2001: 650–1). In Canada in the 1990s, huge cuts in the ODA budget were associated with little evidence of a marked decline in support for aid (Noël *et al.* 2004). More recently, the United Kingdom has increased ODA rapidly in the period from 1998, with polling evidence indicating no major increase in overall public support for aid.[1]

Given this evidence, it is not surprising that cross-country analyses have drawn extremely cautious conclusions about the relationship between public opinion and aggregate aid levels. For instance, one study conducted for the OECD concluded that though it is widely taken as axiomatic that there is a close correlation between public opinion and aid levels, the evidence for this was, at best, 'shaky' (German 1996: 97). Likewise, an assessment of the influence of European public opinion on aid to Africa judged that aid to Africa is not driven by public opinion and is only influential in the case of some emergencies (Olsen 2001: 645, 647). In the case of the United States, a careful analysis of public influence on the legislature's decisions on foreign aid concluded that 'on the question of aid for development it would be hard to maintain that the views of the general public affected the actions of Congress' (Rice 1996: 6). Overall, the following assessment made more than a decade ago by the then Director of the OECD/DAC still rings true today: 'there is no immediate or necessary linkage between informed and supportive public opinion on the one hand and rising aid budgets on the other'.[2]

In recent years, growing prominence has been given to the Millennium Development Goals (MDGs), and to the increased aid needed to help achieve these goals, not least the ambition to halve the numbers of people living in poverty by the year 2015. To what extent have these efforts and initiatives led to changes in the public's perception of and support for aid? Here again, the evidence is somewhat contradictory.

The late 2004 Eurobarometer survey clearly shows a significant rise in overall public support for aid, from 76 per cent in the late 1990s to 91 per cent at the end of December 2004. However, the same survey found that almost the same number of people—88 per cent—had never heard of the MDGs (EC 2005a: 4, 25).[3] There is, nonetheless, strong evidence that in some countries support for increased aid has held firm, and even risen, after these countries began to expand their aid programmes significantly. For instance, a poll undertaken prior to the September 2005 UN Summit found, in contrast to earlier surveys, that a comparatively high number of people (78 per cent) supported the view that the United States should contribute with other countries to achieve faster reductions in world poverty, with 71 per cent supporting an increase in taxes to achieve a global increase in ODA of $60bn (PIPA 2005: 2). In contrast, 72 per cent of British people did not support the idea of the UK government raising taxes to help pay for effective malaria care for children. Likewise, at much the same time as Germany agreed to a significant expansion in ODA, 60 per cent of Germans believed that aid levels were either just right or too large (OECD

2006b: 26).[4] Finally, has the publicity surrounding the Asian tsunami and the massive outpouring of aid to support the victims led to increased support for aid, and in particular for long-term development aid? A mid-2005 poll from the United Kingdom would suggest not. Fifty-four per cent of people polled said that the tsunami had made no difference to their attitude to long-term assistance, and a further 10 per cent said they didn't know.[5]

THE STRENGTH OF PUBLIC SUPPORT

Part of the explanation for the lack of a consistent and strong link between public support for aid and the amounts of official aid given is found by looking at the nature and strength of public support for aid. While there is plenty of public support for aid, the bulk of that support would not appear to be particularly strong. What is more, public support for aid appears to be associated with an extremely high degree of ignorance about what it does: most turns out to be support for humanitarian and emergency aid to address immediate problems, rather than long-term development aid.

Simply stating that one is broadly in favour of governments providing aid leaves unanswered the crucial question of how important aid is, especially in relation to other government priorities. In general, surveys and studies confirm what one would expect—that for the vast majority of the population, development aid is not a particularly important issue when weighed against others, notably concerns about employment, job security, crime and the quality of key services such as health and education. For example, in the United States, 84 per cent of people believe that taking care of problems at home is more important than giving aid to foreign countries (PIPA 2001: 9). Similarly, as problems at home arise and appear more pressing, public support for aid falls (McDonnell *et al.* 2003a: 15).[6] 'In Australia, the late-1990s national review of aid judged that aid is something that most Australians tend not to think about, or think about very seriously' (Simons 1997: 292). These sorts of views and assessments appear to be applicable even in those countries where support for aid and knowledge about aid have been especially high. A recent overview of Danish aid concluded that aid simply did not feature on the list of priorities of people and was not on the political agenda of voters (Olsen 2005a: 193). In terms of global concerns, world peace and security and the environment are commonly seen as far more important than aid and development issues, which remain of principal concern to an active and growing, but still only small, minority of the population across all donor countries.

Further evidence of the relatively low priority given to official aid is provided by examining more closely the priorities given to different forms of assistance to poor countries. For example, the 2005 Eurobarometer survey asked people in the 22 EU member states what were the most important actions their

governments could take to help poor countries reduce poverty. Only
12 per cent of people thought that providing aid was the most important way
of helping, and when asked to assess the importance of aid relative to seven
other actions that governments could take, less than half (41 per cent) ranked
aid as one of the most important.[7] Consistently, too, public opinion surveys
have tended to rank support for, and aid to and through, NGOs as more
effective than official aid. Across donor countries, polls confirm that most
people believe that NGOs are more effective in reaching and helping poor
people, and, as discussed further in Chapter 18, from the 1990s onwards, public
donations to NGOs have steadily risen.

That high levels of support for aid are associated with a shallow understanding of aid-giving is confirmed by two indicators which reveal considerable
ignorance about official aid programmes. The first is a lack of knowledge about
levels of official aid. With few exceptions—Denmark being one—most people
do not know how much aid their own governments give or the main countries
in receipt of such aid. Survey results report that two-thirds of Europeans either
stated that they had no idea how much aid their governments gave, or assumed
levels of aid that vastly overstated the overall amounts given. This was the case
even in countries such as Sweden, with a long history of systematic public
awareness programmes (McDonnell *et al.* 2003b: 16). Outside Europe, the
extent of ignorance is even greater. For instance, in recent surveys, only
20 per cent of Canadians correctly stated that less than 2 per cent of the federal
budget was devoted to aid expenditure, and, on average, Canadians overestimated the aid budget by a factor of five (Noël *et al.* 2004: 34). Even more
erroneous are the perceptions of Americans. When asked how much (official)
aid is given by the Federal government, only 5 per cent stated that they believed
that the ODA/GNI ratio was less than 1 per cent—at a time when the actual ratio
was less than one-fifth of 1 per cent. The average response gave the figure for
United States ODA as twenty times that of the actual level (PIPA 2001: 6–7).[8]

The second 'ignorance indicator' relates to people's understanding of the
core purpose of ODA. As will be discussed in Chapter 18, a little less than
15 per cent of ODA is used for relief and emergency purposes, the rest (over
85 per cent) for longer-term development. In strong contrast, the survey data
show that 'most people in OECD/DAC member countries believe that ODA is
humanitarian assistance' (McDonnell *et al.* 2003a: 25). This is likely to be
because the reason most commonly given for supporting aid is in order to
address more immediate humanitarian problems. When asked what form of
aid they support, the vast majority of people—over 85 per cent in the United
States—favour 'giving food and medical assistance to people in needy countries' (PIPA 2001: 10).

Why then does the public support the notion of their governments providing
aid to developing countries? The polls suggest two principal motives: a
moral/humanitarian motive and a self-interested one. According to Lumsdaine,

for most people aid is supported because of 'our moral duty to help', based, variously, on the needs of those requiring assistance and our ability to assist, with the strongest supporters of aid for moral/humanitarian purposes being amongst the strongest critics of aid provided for the advancement of particular national interests (1993: 138, 149). This has been confirmed repeatedly by many country-based surveys. For instance, in Germany over 80 per cent of support is based on belief in humanitarian obligations or moral duty; in Canada, over 85 per cent of support is based on belief in humanitarian reasons, need or moral obligation (Stern 1998: 3, annexes). However, for many people both of these motives can be and often are the basis for supporting aid, where they are often seen as being complementary rather than mutually exclusive. According to Lumsdaine, 78 per cent of those who saw a national interest in helping poor countries said aid should go to the poorest countries rather than those of importance to the donor country (1993: 155). This has been confirmed by more recent evidence. For example, in a 2004 poll in the United Kingdom, almost 60 per cent of people agreed that poverty in developing countries could have effects which damage the interests of the UK (O'Brien 2004: 8).

Given the importance that successive United States governments have given to providing aid in order to promote US national interests, it is particularly significant that in the 1970s, 86 per cent of Americans polled agreed that helping to improve living standards of poor people should be an important part of overall foreign policy (Rice 1996: 73). Similarly, whereas 44 per cent of Americans polled in 1986 thought that United States aid should go to countries where there were links with US security interests, by 2001 support for this view had fallen by half to 23 per cent: 59 per cent thought that aid should go to the poorest countries regardless (PIPA 2001: 13).

The reliability of public opinion surveys

The discussion thus far has been based on the assumption that the view of the public—on aid or other issues—can be accurately obtained from opinion poll data. There is, however, some doubt about this. Indeed, it is widely agreed that the answers to opinion poll survey questions are particularly sensitive to the way that questions are posed. It would appear, for example, that people understand the term 'foreign aid' in many different ways, which makes it difficult to know how to interpret the answers given to specific questions. For example, in the United States, answers to questions such as 'Are you in favour of foreign aid?' consistently express significantly lower levels of support than replies to questions such as 'Should the United States be willing to share at least a small portion of its wealth with those in the world in greatest need?' (Foy and Helmich 1996: 33, 82; Rice 1996: 71–3).

Besides these more general problems, a number of major foreign aid polls commit the particularly serious error of failing to differentiate between supporting the notion of rich countries *helping* poorer countries and supporting the provision of *aid* from richer to poorer countries—an important distinction, as there are many different ways in which poor countries might be helped, of which aid-giving is only one. This problem has arisen most clearly in successive Eurobarometer surveys. At least since their 1991 polls, responses to the question of how important it is 'to help people in poor countries' have been interpreted as providing the key overall indicator of the level of public support for aid and of people's views on 'the importance of aid' (EC 2005a: 25). Not only are 'helping' and 'providing aid' different from each other, but, as noted above, when the 2005 Eurobarometer poll asked respondents to decide which out of a number of different ways of helping was the most important, 'increasing development aid' came well down the list. Increasing aid came in at 12 per cent, compared with 32 per cent support for 'reducing the possibility of conflict' and 15 per cent for 'cancelling debts', while 8 per cent of people believed that giving poorer countries fairer access to European markets was the most important way of helping (EC 2005a: 21).[9]

It is against the backdrop of some scepticism about the accuracy of public opinion surveys that some challenging and, in part, counter-intuitive views of the public on aid need to be highlighted.

Public support for aid and public perception of its effectiveness

The title of this book, *Does Foreign Aid Really Work?*, is based on the premise that the impact of aid is an issue of major importance: what aid achieves really matters. But what is the link between public support for aid and their views on the impact of aid? A widely shared assumption is that support for aid is closely correlated with its impact: support for aid rises to the extent it is known to work, and falls to the extent there is evidence that it doesn't. Opinion poll data frequently seem to confirm this. For instance, in a 2003 poll on aid to Africa, 33 per cent of Americans said they believed aid to the continent should be higher than it is. When asked whether they thought aid to Africa should increase if they had more confidence that it would really help those who needed it, support for increasing aid more than doubled to reach 80 per cent of those polled (PIPA 2003: 5–6).

Official donors and NGOs and many aid researchers take it as given that support for aid is not only based upon, but *needs* to be based upon, evidence of its success. Reflecting this view, in a major study of the political economy of aid,

Hopkins argues that 'a major condition for sustainability of future aid is the belief in its efficacy' (2000: 445). More controversially, this belief has all too often been used by donors as a motive for giving prominent publicity to stories of aid's successes, in the hope that this will boost support for aid, regardless of whether these stories are representative of all aid. The importance of the relationship between aid impact and support for aid was well expressed in the 1986 OECD/DAC annual report reviewing 25 years of aid-giving, which stated boldly, and without qualification, that 'maintaining and strengthening public support for aid can be facilitated by more effective communication of . . . the successes that . . . aid has achieved' (OECD 1986: 63). In contrast, as discussed at length in Part III of this book, the evidence of aid's impact is decidedly mixed: the impact of aid is usually dependent upon the context in which it is given and the commitment and ability of the recipient to use it effectively. In reality, while some aid does work, a significant proportion of aid does not achieve its objectives, and most aid is less effective than both donors and recipients would wish.

Against the reality of the impact of aid, donors could adopt three different approaches to providing information to the public:

1. Try to convince the public that some aid does indeed work.
2. Try to convince the public that steps are being taken to enhance the impact of aid, by trying to reduce the number of cases where it does not work well.
3. Try to nurture, extend and deepen support for aid, acknowledging that a significant part of it is clearly ineffective, and sharing knowledge about aid's failures as well as its evident successes.

In practice, both official donors and NGOs have focused their efforts overwhelmingly on the first two approaches. They have deliberately avoided addressing the third challenge almost entirely. Donors have never really thought about coming forward and providing the public with a rounded view of the evidence of its impact, presumably believing that evidence of failure will undermine public support for aid.[10]

What is therefore of particular interest is that one of the clear and consistent findings of public opinion polls on foreign aid across almost all donor countries is the high degree of support there is for foreign aid among people who believe that aid is failing to achieve its objectives. Contrary to the 'common-sense view' and some opinion poll data which suggest that support for aid is dependent on evidence that it works, there is a significant group of people who would appear to be supportive of aid even when they know, or believe, that it has not been working well. If the views expressed by these people and reflected in these polls accurately reflect wider public opinion, then aid failure is not the kiss of death to public support for aid that donors believe—and dread.

Table 7.1 presents evidence which shows this, summarizing recent poll data for the leading 22 OCED/DAC donor countries. It does this by placing the overall level of support for aid (column A) alongside the percentage of people

Table 7.1 Public support for aid and judgements about its failures

OECD/DAC donors	Percentage of those who support aid (A)	Percentage who judge aid a failure (B)	The Gap[a] (C)
Australia	91	17	8
Austria	86	17	3
Belgium	86	34	20
Canada	83	84	67
Denmark	91	23	14
Finland	91	20	11
France	88	33	21
Germany	91	25	16
Greece	95	31	26
Ireland	94	15	9
Italy	94	29	9
Japan	75	35	20
Luxembourg	93	15	7
Netherlands	93	14	7
New Zealand	76	24	0
Norway	88	n/a	n/a
Portugal	94	21	15
Spain	96	34	30
Sweden	96	16	12
United Kingdom	91	39	30
United States	79	60	39

n/a = not available

[a] The percentage of those who judge aid a failure minus the percentage who are not supportive of aid, i.e. C = [B − (100 − A)]

Sources: EC (2005); OECD (2005d); PIPA (2003, 2005); McDonnell (2006).

who do not believe that aid achieves its objectives (column B). The figures in column C are derived by subtracting the proportion of those who do not support aid at all (100 minus the figures in Column A) from the proportion of people who judge aid to be a failure (Column B).[11] This proportion of people who support aid but judge it a failure is termed 'the Gap'. As is clearly shown, in every donor country except New Zealand (comparable data for Norway could not be found), there is a greater percentage of people who believe aid is not effective than who are not in favour of foreign aid.[12] In eight countries— Belgium, Canada, Italy, Greece, Japan, Spain, the United Kingdom and the United States—more than 20 per cent of the population who are supportive of aid believe it is not effective; and in the case of four of these countries— Canada, Spain, the UK and the US—the figure is 30 per cent or higher.[13]

There is other evidence which not merely confirms this finding but suggests that these figures could well underestimate this phenomenon.[14] For instance, in Denmark, where public knowledge about aid issues is amongst the highest of all countries, polls suggest that almost 50 per cent of people believe that aid doesn't work yet, consistently over time, 75 per cent and more of the public remain supportive of aid (OECD 2001: 24–5). Likewise, in Norway in the 1980s, widespread publicity highly critical of Norwegian aid was spread across the Norwegian media but support for aid remained high (Bøås 2002: 4).

Most researchers who have commented on the phenomenon of people supporting aid when they believe it is ineffective have referred to it as an anomaly, a contradiction or a paradox, in some cases suggesting that it is an indicator of the shallowness of public understanding of foreign aid. But why should this be so? Why not take the findings at face value? Might it not be that a significant proportion of people do indeed support the giving of aid even when they know it is highly likely that it may not be effective?[15] Contrary to the mainstream view, some have suggested that this is the case. For example, in his review of support for aid in the United States, Rice observes that in spite of aid being widely perceived as ineffective and wasted, 'this opinion does not dissuade many Americans from supporting assistance efforts' (1996: 74).

If significant numbers of people do support aid-giving when they know much of it doesn't work, we need to try to understand why. It is likely that for many, this could have something to do with their understanding of the moral case for providing aid. It is to this issue that we now turn.

8 Charity or duty? The moral case for aid

There is a strong moral case for providing aid. This has been continually and repeatedly argued since aid was first given. Most non-governmental organizations (NGOs) believe that aid should be provided almost entirely for moral reasons, while practically all individuals, companies and foundations who give voluntarily to support the work of humanitarian and development charities do so because of some sense of responsibility or duty to help people suffering and in need. Perhaps not so widely known is that governments have also repeatedly stated that they provide aid for moral reasons. Consequently, ethics is central to any discussion of aid and why it is given.

The purpose of this chapter and the next is to look closely at the moral case for giving aid, by holding up to scrutiny the different elements which constitute the moral case for aid. What precisely is meant by the claim that aid should be provided for moral reasons? Does it mean that governments and people should give and respond to needs merely 'out of the kindness of their hearts'? In other words, should aid-giving be viewed solely as an act of charity, where the giver feels good in giving, but there is no particular requirement to give, and no link to any rights that those who receive aid might have? Or does it mean that there is a moral duty or obligation to provide aid? Further, if *governments*—in contrast to *individuals*—have obligations and responsibilities to provide aid, what precisely is the nature of these obligations? If individuals and governments have obligations to provide aid, how much needs to be provided to satisfy that obligation? How do government obligations to provide aid rank in relation to other obligations and responsibilities that governments have within their own countries? What moral obligations do NGOs have in providing aid? Perhaps most crucially and controversially, to what extent do the obligations or responsibilities of rich governments to provide aid require them to work together to ensure that sufficient aid is provided? What happens to the 'duty' to give if aid is not used for the purpose intended?

These are all important questions; a number are quite complex and have been given a range of different answers. They extend the discussion about aid to the disciplines of moral and political philosophy, and also to the field of international relations, where a number of answers to these questions are keenly debated and remain contested. Increasingly over the past 20 years, the ethical dimensions of aid-giving, and aid-receiving, have been the focus of attention of scholars working in the relatively new area of the ethics of development.[1] Against the backdrop of a large and growing literature, the ambitions of this chapter and the next are modest: more to provide an overview of the key issues involved in making the moral case for aid than to engage in an in-depth discussion of the merits of all the different arguments. That would require a book in itself. The next chapter looks at the reasons that governments and individuals give in arguing the moral case for providing aid, and hold these up to scrutiny. The present chapter prepares the ground for that discussion by examining the different elements which contribute to making the moral case for aid.

At the heart of the discourse about the moral basis for aid-giving lies the notion of obligation. However, most theories of, and approaches to, obligation skip over, take as read, or simply assume that aid is needed, and that it works. This chapter takes a more holistic approach. First, it discusses, briefly, the basic 'facts on the ground' upon which almost all theories of obligation to provide aid are based. It then looks at the different ethical theories, theories of justice, and perspectives based on a human-rights framework which have been used to argue the moral case for providing aid.

Facts on the ground

Three clusters of facts are central to building up the moral case for providing aid: (1) extreme poverty and human suffering, especially as it exists within the poorest countries of the world; (2) the enormous wealth contrasting with this poverty (especially within the richest countries of the world), which provides the means to assist; and (3) the ever-widening gap between the rich and poor. I discuss each of these in turn.

POVERTY AND HUMAN SUFFERING

The starting point of the moral case for providing aid is the human suffering and poverty experienced in the poor countries of the world, the extent and depth of which reduce and severely limit human capabilities, increase vulnerability to disease, and raise the number of deaths attributable to these factors. Whether these problems are viewed through the lens of unmet basic needs or unmet rights-claims, the overall judgement is much the same, namely, that there is an urgent need to reduce the number of deaths, and the numbers of people who have to live intolerable and unacceptable lives. Here we look briefly at some of the basic 'facts on the ground'.

Setting aside for now the important debates about precisely how poverty and deprivation ought to be assessed (which will be highlighted in Chapter 10), the broad message is clear: hundreds of millions of people across the globe are living in extreme poverty. Over 750mn people are 'chronically poor', one in five people in the world (over 1bn) live on $1 a day or less, and almost half the world's population (2.6bn) on $2 a day or less. Most very poor people (over 80 per cent) live in the poorest countries: almost half of Africa's population and 30 per cent of the population of South Asia live on less than $1 a day, with three-quarters of their populations living on less than $2 a day (World Bank 2006a: 9). Over 80 per cent of the population of the least developed countries (LLDCs) live on less than $2 a day, and almost 90 per cent of the population of the 31 African LLDCs.

The greater the depth and extent of poverty, the greater the vulnerability to disease—usually caused by a mix of insufficient food, poor water and sanitation, inadequate shelter or health care—all of which are major contributors to early, poverty-related deaths. Estimates by different UN agencies (FAO, UNICEF, WHO) suggest that each day upwards of 34,000 children and 16,000 adults die from hunger and preventable diseases which can be traced directly or indirectly to poverty-related causes. This amounts to around 18mn people a year. The vast majority of these deaths occur in the poorest 65 countries of the world, and are largely preventable. Though known, they pass largely unnoticed and are given little prominence in the media, partly because the numbers of poverty-related deaths are so large, and the scale of the problem so huge, that they are difficult to grasp, and partly because the regularity of these deaths means they are not considered to be 'news'. The annual number of deaths from poverty, predominantly taking place in poor countries, is equal to two and a half times the population of London. It is equivalent to 100 average-sized jumbo jets (each carrying 500 passengers) crashing each day, leaving no survivors. Two hundred and thirty thousand people are estimated to have died in the Asian tsunami and its aftermath; this number dies every five days from the extremes and diseases of poverty.

Besides poverty, natural disasters, war and conflict add to the toll of death and human suffering, much of which is also preventable. Over the past decade, disasters worldwide have caused an average of 90,000 deaths a year, and they are currently affecting the lives of some 250mn people a year. Most of these people live in the poorest countries of the world, and are already poor and vulnerable. Many long-running conflicts, in particular, dramatically increase the numbers of poverty-related deaths. As discussed in Chapter 18, nutritional surveys undertaken in the 2003–5 period suggest that the violence and instability in the Democratic Republic of Congo and Uganda were the main cause of 600,000 more deaths than had been recorded in these two countries alone before their respective conflicts began. Worldwide, the figure for such preventable conflict-and poverty-related deaths must be significantly in excess of more than one million a year—another five jumbo jet crashes a day of largely preventable deaths.

HUMAN SUFFERING, POVERTY AND THE NEED FOR AID

What role can aid play in addressing these problems of human suffering, extreme poverty and largely preventable deaths? This is by no means a simple question to answer. We can start, however, by focusing on emergencies and humanitarian disasters. There are very few people—and no donor governments—who would argue that aid is not able to address the problems caused by emergencies and humanitarian disasters. As discussed in Chapter 19, it can and does save lives. It is also widely recognized and understood that humanitarian aid has a role (an important role) to play beyond the immediate 'saving of lives'. The provision of food, medicine and shelter to those in desperate need is also effectively able to prevent more people from dying of malnutrition and disease. Equally, humanitarian aid directed at helping people rebuild their lives and restore their livelihoods has also contributed to saving lives, by equipping people with the means to raise their incomes above the poverty lines, below which disasters and emergencies have caused them to sink.

Similarly, some aid classified as development, as opposed to emergency and humanitarian aid, is used directly in 'saving lives', as it is used to address more immediate needs. Examples would include development food aid, the provision of bed-nets and medicines, and aid used to improve the quality of water and sanitation. Such aid will have immediate and tangible effects on poor people and contribute to reducing poverty-related deaths. Some development aid contributes to the reduction of poverty but does so less directly, though the long-term impact on poverty and poverty-related deaths can be even more important—for instance when donor governments provide aid to boost the budgets of health ministries to equip and rehabilitate clinics, and train nurses. Likewise, providing good education to those out of school or improving the quality of the country's infrastructure can have a significant impact on reducing poverty and saving lives, though many of the effects will be not be seen for many years.

More generally, development and poverty are inversely related: the more developed a country, the lower the incidence of poverty and the fewer the numbers of people who die from poverty-related illnesses. While specialists continue to disagree about what is the best development path to take, and what constitutes pro-poor growth, there is broad agreement that economic growth is necessary for poverty reduction.[2] The poorest countries in particular are usually characterized by low levels of investment, weak institutions, markets, and governance structures, and poorly developed physical and telecommunications infrastructures. In such a context, 'substantial and sustained poverty reduction requires the development of productive capacities so as to provide productive employment opportunities' (UN 2006: 283). Aid has the potential to contribute to accelerating growth and bringing about structural change, to produce a sustainable path of development in which further inroads against poverty can be achieved with, in time, proportionately less aid. The greater the urgency to reduce poverty more quickly, the greater will be the need for aid, both to help address immediate poverty problems and to hasten the process of achieving self-sustaining growth and development.[3]

Hence, if there is a moral case for aid to help reduce poverty and human suffering, then there is a moral case for aid to contribute both indirectly as well as directly, for either way aid will help contribute to the core end-goal. There is, then, no hard and fast division between humanitarian aid that is life-saving and development aid that is life-saving. Rather, there is a *continuum* from more immediate and direct to less immediate and more indirect ways of 'saving lives' by reducing human suffering and addressing the different factors which contribute to poverty, vulnerability and premature death. It is certainly possible to point to specific types of aid used exclusively in emergencies, such as the provision of winterized tents to shelter victims of earthquakes in the mountains of Pakistan. Likewise, it is possible to classify certain types of aid that will exclusively contribute to long-term development, such as aid to help build a power-station. But most aid either is or can be used in both 'emergency' and 'development' contexts. Even aid provided in the form of budget support or as part of a SWAp, considered in contemporary aid-giving to be mainstream forms of development aid, could easily be used to assist countries in times of emergency—funding the provision of emergency medicines, in the case of ministries of health, or supplying seeds and tools, in the case of ministries of agriculture.

Consequently, if aid is needed because it is able to reduce death and human suffering in times of emergency, aid is also needed because it is able to prevent deaths due to poverty, vulnerability, marginalization and discrimination. But, as noted above, in terms of numbers and the scale of the problem, poverty-related diseases and deaths far outweigh those caused by one-off emergencies. By its very nature, and when provided in response to need—as all emergency and development aid should be—aid should be viewed as something 'exceptional', not normal. It therefore does not particularly strain the definition to state that all aid, in a very real sense, is 'emergency' aid—something provided in exceptional circumstances.

HOW MUCH AID IS NEEDED?

If aid has the potential to help in the short term as well as in the longer term to reduce poverty and human suffering, how much is needed? Surprisingly, given the length of time that aid has been provided for both emergency and development purposes, the issue has not been addressed with much rigour. Historically, debates about aid-giving have been dominated by aid allocations based not on poor-country needs but on donor-country wealth: the ratio of official development assistance (ODA) to gross national income (GNI).[4] It has only been in the last 10 to 15 years that serious attempts have been made to estimate how much aid is needed globally, and even more recently that estimates have begun to be made to assess needs on a country-by-country basis.

In preparation for the 2002 World Summit on Financing for Development, a high-level UN team was charged with the task of assessing current and future aid needs. The panel was honest enough to admit that it had been unable to assess accurately how much development and emergency aid was needed by poor countries. However, it felt able to conclude that in order to reduce by half the proportion of people living in poverty, it would be necessary to double the amount of official aid currently provided and to increase the amount of humanitarian aid by at least 50 per cent (Zedillo 2001: 20). At about the same time, a World Bank study suggested that to achieve the MDGs including halving the proportion of people living in poverty, official aid levels would need to be doubled, rising by about $57bn from 1999–2001 levels, on the key assumption that increased aid would in future be used efficiently for development purposes, and not to address humanitarian needs (Devarajan *et al.* 2002).

Extrapolating these figures forward, and allowing for price changes, the total amount of aid (ODA) needed in 2004 would have been around $125bn, compared with the actual total of $79bn, a shortfall of some $46bn. A recent survey of studies suggests that the amount of aid required to achieve the MDGs could be as much as four times as much as current aid levels (Anderson and Waddington 2006: 32). What is more, both the Zedillo and the World Bank estimates were based not on the level of aid needed to address the overall problems of poverty by the year 2015, but merely to reduce *by half* the proportion of people living in poverty. Thus the *total* amount of aid needed would be far higher—perhaps close to twice the $125bn figure, or $250bn. Indeed, Thomas Pogge has argued that achieving the MDGs implies a far lower commitment to poverty reduction than is commonly and widely understood. In practice, even if the MDGs were achieved, the numbers of people living in poverty in 2015 would not be reduced by half: rather, only 19 per cent fewer people would be living in poverty than in the year 2000 (Pogge 2004b: 377–8).[5] Hence, if the objective were to tackle the whole of world poverty, aid levels would need to be considerably higher than this.

In 2005, the UN Millennium Project made a preliminary assessment of the aid needed by six countries—Bangladesh, Cambodia, Ghana, Tanzania and Uganda—not to solve the problems of poverty, but merely to enable them to achieve the MDGs by the year 2015. On the basis of these case studies, the Project extrapolated the results to derive a figure for overall aid needs. The study suggested that the total amounts of ODA required needed to rise to $135bn by 2006, $152bn by 2010 and $195bn by 2015 (all at fixed, 2003 prices) if the MDGs were to be achieved, and on the assumption that all increases in ODA would be used effectively and efficiently to achieve the goals. The study also assumed that a 50 per cent increase in humanitarian aid would be needed because of rising emergency needs.[6]

Although these three different calculations of the total amount of aid required to address effectively the problems of poverty in poor countries are acknowledged to be little more than crude assessments, they allow us to draw some quite firm conclusions. Current levels of official development aid fall well short of that needed effectively to address the problem of poverty in poor countries. Indeed, even doubling current aid levels would prove insufficient. Similarly, as discussed more fully in Chapter 18, there remains a significant gap between the levels of humanitarian aid currently provided and the amounts needed. This gap will grow even wider if the UN Millennium Project is correct in assuming that the problems caused by emergencies and disasters are set to rise in the coming years. This suggests that the amount of current humanitarian aid regularly given must at least be doubled if funds provided are more closely to address all emergency and humanitarian needs. In short, there remains a huge mismatch between the rhetoric of donors acknowledging their responsibility to respond to severe poverty and acute human suffering, and the amounts of aid they give and are planning to give.[7]

THE WEALTH OF DONORS AND WIDENING INEQUALITIES

Poverty and suffering in the poorest countries exist alongside the enormous wealth of the richest countries of the world, providing the grounds for arguing that the rich have the ability and resources to provide the necessary aid. The disproportionate way that increases in global wealth have accrued to rich and poor countries, resulting in widening even further the differences, and inequalities, between the two, provides an additional reason for aid to be given by those with the increasing means and ability to provide it. The following paragraphs summarize the key facts.

In the year 2003, the world produced goods and services to the value of $36 trillion. Of this total, 80 per cent accrued to the 52 richest (high-income) countries, in which 17 per cent of the world's population resided. Just 3 per cent of global wealth was produced in the 62 poorest (low-income) countries, which contained 37 per cent of the world's population. Thus in 2003, the per capita income of the poorest 62 countries stood at $477, that of the richest 52 countries at $30,182. For every $1 of wealth produced in the poorest countries, the richest countries produced $27, and in average per capita terms, the richest 52 countries of the world were 63 times as wealthy as the poorest 62 countries (World Bank 2005l).[8]

What has been happening to trends in the growth and distribution of wealth between rich and poor countries? On one measure, it would appear that the relative position of the poorest countries has improved over time: the share of global wealth produced by the highest-income countries fell from over 90 per cent of global wealth in the mid-1960s to around 85 per cent by the mid-1980s, and has remained around the 79–81 per cent level since then. However, the relative gains have been made by middle-income and not by the poorest countries, whose share of global wealth fell from 6 per cent in the mid-1960s to 2.8 per cent by the early 1990s, rising slightly (to 3 per cent) by 2003. When the trends in differences between per capita income are examined, the evidence clearly shows a massive widening of the 'wealth gap'. In 1965, the average income in the rich-country (high-income) economies stood at $2,305 a head, compared with an average income of $92 per head in the poor countries—$2,213 per head lower and 4 per cent of the rich-country average. Twenty years later, in 1985, average rich-country incomes had increased by $9,034 to reach $11,340 per head, with average incomes in the poorest countries rising by only $137 to reach $229, now accounting for only 2 per cent of average rich-country incomes. By the year 2003, average rich-country incomes had risen to $30,182 per head, an increase of $18,842 over 1985 levels, while the average income of the poorest countries had risen by only $248 a head to $477 per head, and accounting for only 1.5 per cent of average income per head in the richest countries. The widening gaps in average incomes are startling. They are shown pictorially in Figure 8.1.

The ratio of the average income in the poorest countries to the average income in the richest countries stood at 25:1 in 1965, widened to 50:1 by 1985 and, as noted above, stood at 63:1 by the year 2003.[9] One recent study suggests that when average incomes are compared using fixed rather than current prices, the gaps between the richest 20 countries and poorest 20 countries are diverging at an even faster rate.[10] In the 30-year period from the early 1970s to the late 1990s, the ratio of the average incomes per head of these sets of countries (at fixed 2000 prices) widened from 19:1 to 131:1.[11]

It is difficult to grasp fully the widening gaps in wealth creation between the richest and poorest countries. Another way of showing what has been happening is to look at how the overall share of total wealth created is shared between the richest (high-income) and poorest (low-income) countries. In the four years to 2003, global wealth rose from $31,492bn to $36,461bn, a rise of almost $5,000bn. Of this amount, $4,414bn accrued to the richest countries, whose wealth rose on average by $1,100bn a year, while only $213 accrued to the poorest countries, averaging $53bn a year. Perhaps even more startling is that in the year 2000, the *total* wealth of the poorest (low-income) countries amounted to

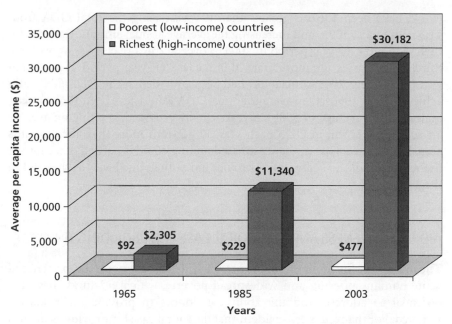

Figure 8.1 Average income per head, rich and poor countries, 1965–2003

Source: World Bank (2002 and 2005), *World Development Indicators* (Washington, DC: World Bank); World Bank (1990), and Penn World Tables, Version 6.1.

only $890bn, $200bn *less* than the *additional* amount of wealth created in the richest countries in only one year. During this four-year period, for every $100 of global wealth created, $88 went to the richest countries and just $4 to the poorest countries.

Against the backdrop of both rising global wealth and the unequal and widening distribution of the wealth created, one might have expected that the share of wealth which the rich countries have given to the poorest countries would either have risen or, at worst, remained at the same level. Yet, in sharp contrast, the figures reveal sharp declines in the share of wealth that rich countries have provided in official development assistance (ODA). In the ten-year period from 1965 to 1974, total aid (ODA) amounted to 0.35 per cent of the wealth rich countries created, the gross national income (GNI). In the following two decades, the share of wealth given over to aid (ODA) fell to 0.33 per cent and 0.32 per cent respectively, and, in the most recent ten-year period (1995–2004) was at an all-time low of 0.23 per cent, even though, most recently, it has begun to rise again.

Expressed in percentage terms, the falls look fairly small. But with the rapid rise in the wealth of the rich countries, the effects on overall aid levels have been extremely large. In the ten-year period to 1974, total ODA amounted to $75bn. If ODA had been provided in the subsequent three decades at the 0.35 per cent of GNI achieved in the period 1965 to 1974, then the total amount of ODA would have been $367bn greater than it was, raising the total ODA from $1,351bn to $1,730bn, and increasing the average annual amount from $33bn each year in the 40-year period to 2003 by over $12bn a year, a rise of over one third. These 'losses' are more marked in the last ten-year period. If in the ten years to the year 2004, official aid had been provided at the ODA/GNI ratio achieved in the 1960s, then average annual ODA would have been $86bn a year, instead of the average of $58bn a year actually provided, creating on average an additional $28bn in ODA each year, 50 per cent more than the amounts actually provided. One of the reasons a doubling of aid is needed is because of the repeated failure of donors to provide aid at the same levels as they did in the 1960s.

AID EFFECTIVENESS AND THE MORAL CASE FOR PROVIDING IT

The moral case for providing aid is not solely dependent upon the existence of acute human suffering and widespread poverty, which aid funds have the potential to address, and the ability of donors to provide the resources required. For many, it is self-evident that the moral case for providing aid also critically depends upon the ability of the aid provided to contribute effectively to the alleviation of human suffering and the reduction of poverty. However, the issue is more complex.

There are three slightly different questions that needed to be asked. First, does aid, as currently given, effectively contribute to the alleviation of human suffering and the reduction of poverty? Secondly, to the extent that some aid currently does not do so, is it possible for aid to be utilized more effectively to contribute to poverty reduction? Thirdly, if there is a need for more aid than is currently provided, what are the prospects for a substantial increase in aid being used effectively?

These central questions will be discussed in more detail in Parts III and IV of this book. One of the main conclusions from the discussion in Part III will be that aid does contribute to the reduction of poverty and human suffering, and that some of the gaps between what it does and what it can do have been narrowed. There is a potential problem of 'absorptive capacity', especially if aid were to be increased rapidly: it will take time to put in place mechanisms and processes to ensure it is used effectively. However, there is no fixed or binding constraint permanently preventing recipients from absorbing aid effectively, not least because aid itself can be used, and often is used, to help expand the capacity of the recipient to use it well.[12] Importantly too, however, there needs to be the (political) will to use additional aid effectively. This is likely to be influenced considerably, on the one hand, by government commitment to implementing a development strategy which gives priority to the eradication of human suffering and poverty reduction, and on the other, by the existence of mechanisms and processes to enhance the transparency and accountability of aid and development projects and programmes. All these issues will be discussed further in Part IV.

For the present, therefore, and on the basis of more substantive discussion in other parts of the book, we shall take as read that the evidence of what aid does and what it can do broadly support, and do not substantially undermine, the moral case for providing aid.

Ethical theories and approaches

We are now ready to focus on what, for many, constitutes the heart of the moral case for aid: the different approaches and theories which provide the basis for arguing that there is an obligation for governments and/or individuals to provide aid.[13]

To many people, there is no need for a theory to show there is an obligation to help and provide aid because, for them, the issue is clear-cut and self-evident. Put simply, those suffering and in need of help ought to be helped. 'Why is aid given? Because it is right to do so.' But why is it right? Upon what basis is this assertion made, and this conclusion drawn?

UTILITARIANISM

One particular ethical theory which has been closely associated with, and has lain behind, much development discourse is utilitarianism. Indeed, for some people, utilitarian theories are 'self-evident'. At its simplest, the basic notion of utilitarianism is that (moral) life should be guided by the objective of trying to achieve the maximum happiness and satisfaction for all (or for the greatest number of people). Hence, actions should be based upon, and judged, by this goal. It follows that if greater overall satisfaction can be obtained by providing assistance to those whose happiness and well-being are severely limited, then such help should be provided, as long as the reduction in happiness resulting from helping is less than the gain in happiness of those being helped. Peter Singer has applied this line of thinking directly to poor people in poor countries, asserting that if you have the ability to prevent something bad from happening without sacrificing anything of comparable moral importance (or, more mildly, anything morally significant), then you ought morally to do it. It 'makes no moral difference whether the person I help is a neighbour's child 10 yards from me or a Bengali whose name I shall never know, 10,000 miles away' (Singer 2004: 7, 11). Utilitarianism draws an especially close link between moral obligation and outcome: moral obligations are dependent upon what happens in practice—the consequences and results of particular actions.

Utilitarian arguments have long been used to justify the provision of aid, informing debates about aid and who should be helped. For instance, more than 25 years ago, the then Chair of the OECD/DAC stated, almost as if it were self-evident, that 'the core rationale of development assistance remains the profound intuition most people have that unrequited transfers from the averagely richer people of rich areas to the averagely poor people of poor areas usually add more utility to the latter than they inflict disutility on the former' (OECD 1980: 63). Likewise, utilitarian arguments have long been used to give a justification for the rich to respond to and to try to meet the basic needs of the poor. For example, in an article entitled 'Why development aid?', Paul Streeten, one of the earliest advocates of the basic-needs approach to development, suggested that the most common distributional arguments for aid can be justified on the basis of the utilitarian argument that 'a dollar redistributed from a rich man to a poor man detracts less utility than it adds, and therefore increases the sum total of utility' (1983: 380).

One can also see the powerful influence of utilitarianism in the increasing emphasis placed on the results and impact of aid interventions. Indeed, it has now become part of conventional thinking across many donor countries that more aid per head should be channelled to those countries at similar levels of poverty who are able to use it well than those not able to use it well (OECD 2006a: 19).[14]

LIBERAL THEORIES OF JUSTICE

To its critics, however, utilitarianism provides an unconvincing basis for moral action. They contend, for example, that there are major difficulties in measuring happiness and satisfaction, and in knowing what the consequences of our actions will be. Utilitarianism has also been criticized because it allocates no particular value, or importance, to the satisfaction of needs over any other moral action, and because it is not easily able to address the particular problems experienced by minorities or, more generally, to accord an absolute value to particular human rights.

In marked contrast to utilitarianism are a number of liberal theories of justice and approaches to obligation which differ sharply in the manner in which they treat duties, obligation and results. Notably, and in contrast to utilitarianism, where moral obligations are critically linked to outcomes and results, stand what are termed deontological approaches and theories of moral obligation—either to do or not to do something. These are based not so much on the results or outcomes of aid-giving, but on an understanding of how the prior duties that one has are to be matched with the rights that others have. From this perspective, while results certainly matter, they do not provide a sufficient account of morality. Hence, from a deontological perspective, if the anticipated results from which the (assumed) moral duty to act do not occur as intended, then the moral obligations of the duty-bearers remain as strong as ever they were, challenging them to work harder to achieve those results through the same means, or by different means. The relevance and importance of these different perspectives for the morality of giving aid should be immediately evident: a radical consequentialist would argue that if aid was shown not to work then the moral obligation to provide it falls away. However, from a deontological perspective, the moral obligation remains, driving those with the obligation to strive even harder to achieve the intended outcome.[15]

One of the best-known and most widely debated theories of justice has been John Rawls' contractual theory of justice, developed in *A Theory of Justice* (Rawls 1973). Framed within the wider social contract tradition, Rawls sets out ideas about the relationships and obligations between society and individuals. He argues that the correct principles of justice are those that would be chosen by a group of rational, self-interested individuals behind a hypothetical 'veil of ignorance'—that is, in complete ignorance of specific facts about themselves that 'put men at odds and tempt them to exploit natural and social circumstances to their own advantage' (1973: 136), because the knowledge of such facts would compromise the fairness of the process of choosing principles of justice. Among these would be the distinctive features of their own psychological make-up, and the actual position each would occupy in a particular society they might choose. In brief, Rawls argues that those individuals living behind the 'veil of ignorance' would unanimously agree that liberty, opportunity, income, wealth and the bases for self-respect (which he collectively terms primary social goods) should be distributed equally unless an unequal distribution of any or all of these is to the advantage of the least favoured in society; and therefore the state is obliged to take resources from some for the specific benefit of the least advantaged.[16]

More recently, but also from within the same broad tradition, Ronald Dworkin has produced an approach to justice (and virtue), termed the theory and practice of equality, which is based on the principle of 'equal concern' for all citizens. Though less well known, in many ways Dworkin's approach is more demanding than Rawls'. For Dworkin, an equal concern for all people requires an equal concern for poor people. For governments, this means having concerns for all the lives of those it governs, which, in practice, can lead them to countenance actions which can 'eliminate the liberty of some' if this is required to achieve an equal concern for all (2000: 130).

The rules of distributive justice contained in Rawls' *A Theory of Justice* have been widely used as a basis for arguing the moral case for providing aid. However, as Rawls makes clear in his more recent work, *The Law of Peoples*

(Rawls 2003), this is a misuse, as well as a misunderstanding, of his approach. According to Rawls, the moral imperatives presented in *A Theory of Justice* apply only to homogeneous societies, and not across societies to other countries. If one is to deploy Rawls' own arguments for constructing the moral case for governments to provide aid, this can only legitimately be done in reference to *The Law of Peoples*, where he presents explicit moral arguments for why some countries ought to provide aid to others.

Rawls starts by saying that peoples 'have a duty to assist other peoples living under unfavourable conditions that prevent their having a just or decent political and social regime' (2003: 37). On the basis of this general principle, Rawls believes that some countries have a duty to help others. But rather than referring to rich and poor countries, Rawls sees the world through the lens of what he terms well-ordered and burdened societies. It is his view that well-ordered societies have a moral obligation (a duty) to assist burdened societies. The near-term objectives of such assistance are to help them to manage their own affairs 'reasonably and rationally', with the ultimate purpose of enabling them, too, to become well-ordered societies. The sort of help provided is likely to vary, but it could include providing human capital or know-how, or material and technological resources (2003: 106). The more immediate aim is to help to realize and preserve just, or decent, institutions, in the same manner as the 'just savings' principle operates within well-ordered societies.[17] Strikingly for Rawls, the main aim of helping is not to provide resources to countries which are so poor that they do not have sufficient of their own to meet the needs of their populations. Indeed, it is his view that there 'is no society anywhere in the world . . . with resources so scarce that it could not, were it reasonably and rationally organised and governed, become well-ordered' (2003: 108). In short, for Rawls, widely cited on the basis of *A Theory of Justice* as providing a theoretical basis for the moral argument to provide aid, poverty and human suffering are not the motivations for well-ordered societies to help.

There are three fundamental problems with Rawls' approach as presented in *The Law of Peoples*, all related to the assumptions upon which his views are based. The first is that there is plenty of evidence to confirm that there are countries which are so poor that they do not have the necessary resources, human and otherwise, to meet the immediate needs of all their people. The second is that a comprehensive review of the evidence points to a complexity of causes of the development and perpetuation of poverty. The view that development will occur merely through the strengthening of institutions leading to a just and decent political and social regime is, at best, a partial truth.[18] Thirdly, and similarly, Rawls' view of the world as consisting of different societies (and economies) whose (well-ordered) progress or whose (burdened) brakes on progress are attributable to the way those societies are internally governed ignores many key real-world realities. For instance, the uneven distribution of power across societies influences and has the ability to influence market out-comes, which can have profound effects on patterns and forms of develop-ment. Space does not permit further discussion of these issues. However, it is likely that very few of those grappling with the problems of poverty and devel-opment would demur from concluding that Rawls' views on the moral basis for governments to provide aid, as articulated in *The Law of Peoples*, are very far removed from, and thus not particularly helpful in, resolving the moral dilemmas faced by governments in the real world.

In contrast to Rawls' perspective about states and morality, a cosmopolitan view of morality and justice takes *the world* as its core moral unit and focuses on people as the fundamental objects of justice and action. This perspective fits well with those (people and governments) who argue that the (moral) basis for providing aid is simply the solidarity or oneness we have with all of humankind, as the notion of human solidarity transcends national boundaries and extends to all people who inhabit our globe. From this perspective, if people are suffering or in need, or are deprived of their basic human rights, then, it is asserted, this provides the basis for helping, and thus for providing aid. From a cosmopolitan perspective, both individuals and governments have universal obligations to the whole of humankind; what is at issue is the nature and intensity of different obligations and precisely how those obligations should be met.

But why should governments have moral obligations (as opposed to self-interested or commercial reasons) to assist those outside their jurisdiction, and how can governments fulfil any obligations they might have if there are no clear global institutions to hold governments accountable for their actions or inactions? Moellendorf provides the following answer: 'it is no criticism of the claims of global justice to observe that institutions of redistribution do not exist, for it is precisely the fairness of existing international institutions and policies of distribution which are in question' (2002: 39).

THE CAPABILITIES APPROACH

With links to liberal traditions, but also shaped by notions of human well-being, Amartya Sen has developed a way of understanding development which views its pursuit through the eyes of freedom, and its promotion as a social commitment achieved through democratic means and processes. Sen's 'cap-abilities approach to development' focuses on what people require in order to live a full (and free) human life; it has provided some of the main building-blocks for the human development movement.

For Sen, it is a lack of substantive freedoms which has caused or contributed to the world's acute deprivations. To 'flourish', people need basic core freedoms, such as the freedom to be well nourished, the freedom to live a disease-free life, etc. (Sen 1980). The inability of people to function fully as human beings can be traced to the identification of particular 'capability deprivations' (Sen 1999: 87ff.). It is to these capability deprivations, or deficits, that action needs to be addressed. This can occur at two levels. Most immediately, actions can be directed to particular people to enable them to acquire particular freedoms. But probably more important are changes to political processes and appropriate institutions, and to the existing unequal distribution of substantive freedoms. What is needed is to set in motion (democratically based) actions and activities which will lead more systematically to the reduction, and eventually the elimination, of the deprivations and lack of capabilities of those currently deprived.

In contrast to the liberal approaches of Rawls and Dworkin, what is critical for Sen is to maximize substantive freedoms by extending opportunities and capacities. He maintains that his capabilities approach provides a more helpful tool than does Rawls to determine how the least advantaged members of society should be treated (Sen 2005: 156–7). However, as a number of commentators have argued, Sen himself has not (yet) developed a sufficiently clear link between the capability approach, a complete theory of the good to guide moral judgements, and the precise nature and articulation of the duties and obligations required (Gasper 2004: 178; Clark 2005: 6). In part this is deliberate, for Sen maintains that there is no overarching magic formula that can be applied in the (sometimes messy) interaction between democracy and technocracy (Sen 1999: 79).[19] Indeed, he is careful (many have argued over-careful) not to draw an explicit link between his capability approach and specific commodities that people might require to enhance and expand their freedoms, though others have done this—most notably Martha Nussbaum (2000).[20]

RIGHTS-BASED PERSPECTIVES

Human rights perspectives and approaches constitute another (important) framework through which questions of justice, rights and obligations increasingly have been viewed. From the 1990s onwards, extreme poverty has repeatedly been described in UN documents as 'a violation of human dignity and a denial of human rights', and extreme deprivation as 'gross and massive denials of economic, social and cultural rights'.

A human rights framework encompasses a range of different ways in which links are and can be drawn between rights and obligations. At its broadest, and as articulated in United Nations agreements, all human rights and fundamental freedoms are viewed as indivisible and interdependent, such that equal weight and attention should be given to their fulfilment. This perspective has clear intellectual appeal, because human rights constitute those rights people have by virtue of their very humanity. Human rights are 'rights possessed by all human beings (at all times and in all places) simply in virtue of their humanity . . . . [They] will have the properties of universality, independence (from social and legal recognition), naturalness, inalienability, non-forfeitability, and imprescriptibility. Only so understood will an account of human rights capture the central idea of rights that can always be claimed by any human being' (Simmons 2001: 185). Importantly, too, rights have a pre-emptory quality—they demand immediate satisfaction, not simply efforts to satisfy them at some future time (Beitz 2004: 201).

However, the broader and more inclusive one's perspective on rights, the more difficult it is to draw clear links between the fulfilment of these rights and the specific responsibilities and duties of those obliged to work to achieve their fulfilment.[21] As a result, and notwithstanding agreement—first in Vienna in 1993 and confirmed at the World Summit in September 2005—that all human rights are mutually interrelated and inseparable,[22] distinctions are commonly made between different sorts of rights, notably to isolate some (more basic) rights because they are deemed essential to the enjoyment of all other rights. These include minimum subsistence rights and security from arbitrary violence (Shue 1996) and the protection of people from chronic violations of at least these clusters of 'core' rights.

The process of narrowing down and focusing on a smaller number of 'key' rights makes it easier to draw the links between protection and fulfilment of the (specified) right and the identification of those deemed to be (morally) responsible for achieving these objectives and the realization of these rights. Indeed, placing duties and obligations within a human rights framework has

---

BOX 8.1 RIGHTS AND RESPONSIBILITIES IN TWO UNITED NATIONS DOCUMENTS

Article 22 of the Universal Declaration of Human Rights states that

Everyone, as a member of society, has the right to social security and is entitled to its realisation through national effort and international cooperation and in accordance with the organisation and resources of each State, of the economic, social and cultural rights indispensable for his dignity and the free development of his personality.

In contrast, Article 11 (2) of the International Covenant on Economic, Social and Cultural rights affirms

the right of everyone to an adequate standard of living for himself and his family including adequate food, clothing and housing and to the continuous improvement of living conditions [.]

Also in the Covenant, State Parties agree 'to take appropriate steps to ensure the realisation of this right, recognising to this effect the essential importance of international co-operation based on free consent' (Art. 11 (1)). Similarly, State Parties agree to take 'individually and through international co-operation relevant measures concerning the right to be free from hunger' (Art. 11 (2)).

Source: Alston and Quinn (1987).

the potential to move discussion on to the legal terrain: once one is able to identify who has the (moral) responsibility to ensure that certain rights are not violated, and that others are realized, one can then start to examine ways in which these (identified) obligations can become legally enforceable. This point is well illustrated in Box 8.1, which contrasts the very general way that rights and responsibilities are expressed in the Universal Declaration of Human Rights with the far sharper and more precise wording contained in the International Covenant on Economic, Social and Cultural Rights.[23] These issues will be discussed further below.

OBLIGATIONS BASED ON RESPONSIBILITIES FOR PERPETUATING POVERTY AND SUFFERING

Sitting alongside these more static theories and approaches are a number which look behind the existence of human suffering and poverty to examine those factors that are believed, either on their own or with others, to cause, or to contribute to, the existence and perpetuation of such suffering and poverty.

The history of aid-giving has always included assertions that the former colonial powers bear (some) historical and moral responsibility for current levels of poverty and underdevelopment in former colonial states. Although, as noted in Chapter 6, there is usually a strong link between former colonies and levels of aid given by donor governments, the longer countries have been independent, the more difficult it is to establish the degree of responsibility for poverty that might be attributed to colonial as opposed to domestic or other external factors. Consequently over the decades since countries received their political independence, there has been a sharp fall in the prominence in public debate of arguments that aid should be provided as reparation for past misdemeanours. In recent years, however, this has been replaced, or eclipsed, by growing claims that human suffering and poverty are caused, deepened and perpetuated not by past but by current policies, the practices of rich countries and rich-country interests, and by key international institutions whose actions are largely shaped by the power and influence of the rich world. The moral implications of contemporary international economic institutions and policies and their implications for the moral case in favour of governments providing aid have been clearly articulated, in particular, by Thomas Pogge.[24]

The moral debate about aid and development is usually cast in terms of the degree to which those in the rich world ought to assist those suffering abroad. For Pogge this is a seriously deficient approach because it entirely ignores any analysis of the possible causes of such suffering. The reason that an analysis of the causes of poverty is so central, argues Pogge, is, first, that the present global world order produces a 'stable' pattern of widespread malnutrition and starvation among the poor, and second, that there are likely to be feasible alternative regimes that would not produce similarly severe deprivations (2002: 176). In Pogge's view, actions by the rich countries are directly and over-whelmingly responsible for the continuation of poverty and suffering in poor countries. Indeed, he contends that individuals in rich-countries directly gain from rich country policies, structures and institutions which are primarily responsible for the disproportionate gains (affluence) and losses (poverty) arising from the way that wealth is created, and that, therefore, they 'participate in starving' poor people in poor countries, and are thus responsible for their destitution (2002: 214).

The root problem, for Pogge, lies in the economic ground rules upon which the regulation of property, commerce and exchange are based. These benefit the rich at the expense of the poor. For example, the overwhelming power of rich-country governments determines the rules of international trade and commerce, which result in disproportionate gains for themselves (2002: 19, 176). Likewise, the world's natural resources are not only used and consumed disproportionately by rich elites, but the global poor are systematically excluded from the benefits of the wealth created (2002: 202). In theory, the per-petuation of poverty could be attributed to a mix of internal (domestic) and external (international and cross-country) factors. Yet, in Pogge's view, it is external factors—the global economic order—which play a major role in the persistence of severe poverty worldwide. Indeed, he goes further to argue that non-indigenous factors are crucial in explaining 'the inability and especially the unwillingness of the poor countries' leaders to pursue more effective strat-egies of poverty eradication' (2002: 265).[25]

For Pogge, a core element of a just social order is the establishment of an international order in which each person would be able to meet his or her basic social and economic needs. For this to come about will require changes in the prevailing economic ground rules that regulate property, cooperation and exchange and which thereby condition production and distribution (2002: 176). Against this backdrop, he maintains that, as currently provided, inter-national aid should cease to exist. In its place, he proposes a distribution of resources from rich to poor based on a tax on global resource use, which he terms the Global Resources Dividend (GRD). The introduction of such a tax, he estimates, would raise about $312bn, some five times as much as prevailing levels of official aid (based on 2001 data). It would be used to ensure that 'all human beings can meet their own basic needs with dignity' (2002: 197, 205). The merits of the GRD are that, unlike aid, it 'avoids any appearance of arrogant generosity. It merely incorporates into our global institutional order the moral claim of the poor to partake in the benefits from the use of planetary resources' (2002: 207).

Pogge's view that extreme poverty and human suffering are caused predom-inantly by the global world order have, understandably, been the subject of criticism, some harsh (see Beitz 2004; Gilabert 2004; Crocker and Schwenke 2005; Risse 2005). So, too, have his (rather underdeveloped) ideas about precisely how the funds from the GRD would help meet core needs of poor people in ways very different from providing aid. Indeed, Pogge himself all but admits that it might not be out of place to view his detailed proposals as an exercise in polemics.[26] However, he has certainly contributed to drawing the link between the views—now quite widely shared even among the donor community in recent declarations—that international institutions and rich-country policies matter in resolving the problems of poverty, and that there is a moral dimension, indeed a (moral) urgency, to change the global order in order to make it more conducive to poverty alleviation.[27]

9 The moral case for governments, NGOs and individuals to provide aid

This chapter examines the ways that governments, individuals and non-governmental organisations (NGOs) explain why they believe there is a moral obligation for them to provide aid. The bulk of the chapter focuses on the moral case for governments to provide aid. It starts by summarizing the explanations that different governments have given to explain why they believe they have a moral obligation to provide aid. It then holds up these statements to scrutiny, assessing them both against the different theories and approaches discussed in Chapter 8 and against the changes taking place in the world. It discusses ways in which thinking about governments, aid and morality are shifting, and perhaps being fundamentally altered, as a result of changes in global politics and international relations, and of changes in approaches to human rights. The last section of the chapter moves the focus away from governments to look at the ethics of individual aid-giving and some of the new moral questions and dilemmas that voluntary agencies and NGOs are having to face.

Donor governments: current and evolving views

Most governments claim that there is a moral reason for them to provide aid. Many official donors have also explicitly stated that they have some sort of obligation or responsibility to provide aid, thus moving the discussion about aid and morality well beyond the narrower confines of charitable giving.[1] If there is a moral case for providing aid, there must be a moral problem, or set of moral problems, which the provision of aid is meant to address.[2] Contrary to what one might at first suppose, however, both among themselves and over time, donors have differed in their articulation of the core problems and sets of issues from which they conclude that they have a responsibility, duty or obligation to provide aid.

For Scandinavian donors, the notion of 'solidarity' has been a particularly important and prominent reason for providing aid. Some forty years ago, in 1962, when its parliament authorized Sweden to provide official aid, it needed 'no other motivation than moral duty and international solidarity' (Andersson 1986: 29).[3] These motives still have a strong resonance today. Recently, Denmark stated its acceptance of responsibility for supporting development, demonstrated in its 'solidarity with millions of people in the world whose lives are marked by poverty'.[4] For Finland, moral obligation is linked to distributive justice and based on a cosmopolitan view of the world, where rich countries have a particular responsibility for the well-being of citizens in poorer countries. Also for Finland, distribution issues are important: given the growing wealth of the world 'it would be morally indefensible to make no effort to tackle these inequalities, and for this reason rich countries give money to development co-operation'.[5]

Likewise for the Netherlands, a fair distribution of wealth, social justice, and non-discrimination are presented as important factors explaining why aid is given, while, for the Irish aid programme, absolute priority is given to the reduction of poverty, inequality and exclusion in developing countries. For the United Kingdom the objectives of international development are embraced by the government because it is 'right to do so': 'Every generation has a moral duty to reach out to the poor and needy and to try to create a more just world' (DFID 1997: 16). World poverty, says Tony Blair, 'is one of the greatest moral challenges we face' (DFID 2006c: ii).

Beyond the European Union, similar, sometimes strong assertions have also been made about the moral obligation to provide aid. These have also been explained in different ways. For Norway, development policy is 'not about charity': the fight for poverty is a fight for justice. As one of the richest nations, Norway accepts its moral responsibility not only to combat justice and promote development, but to make a difference, playing its role in speeding up reforms to reduce poverty, and allocating more resources to fulfil its obligations.[6] In North America, both Canada and the United States have continuously expressed the view that providing humanitarian aid, in particular, is a moral imperative.[7] In the case of the United States, the government has pledged to provide humanitarian assistance solely on the basis of urgent need, reflecting the concern 'for saving lives and alleviating suffering, regardless of the character of their governments' (USAID 2004: 20). The moral obligation to provide development aid was, perhaps, most clearly articulated by President Kennedy, whose words are still prominently displayed on the USAID website: 'Why, then, should the United States continue a foreign economic assistance program? The answer is that there is no escaping our obligations: our moral obligations as a wise leader and good neighbor in the interdependent community of free nations; our economic obligations as the wealthiest people in a world of largely poor people ... To fail to meet those obligations now would be disastrous'.[8]

Historically, extreme poverty, dire need and human suffering, contrasted with growing wealth, widening inequalities and the ability to help, have provided the main cluster of reasons for donors to suggest or assert that they have a moral obligation to assist, and provide aid. In recent years, these reasons have been linked to, and in some cases eclipsed or replaced by, an explicit focus on human rights, complementing and, in some ways, recasting the way that the moral case for providing aid is understood. The rights-based perspective in aid-giving has been particularly prominent in the justifications articulated by Switzerland, Finland, Germany, Norway and Sweden. For example, Germany has recently stated that all its development work, including its aid-giving, now takes place within a human rights framework, the core objective of which is the respect, protection and fulfilment of rights (of poor people), for which the international community, including Germany, is partly responsible. Indeed, Germany has asserted that human rights provide not only the moral, but also the legal basis for development. For Norway, the 'fight for justice' is, in essence, a human rights agenda, with Norway contributing to the realization of economic, social and cultural as well as civil and political rights. For Finland, a 'justice-based' approach to development implies that the fulfilment of rights defined in human rights agreements provides the starting point for its support. For Switzerland, aid-giving is part of a process of helping in the realization of basic rights, with human rights providing the framework through which its work on addressing problems of poverty is approached. Switzerland has committed itself to using binding human rights treaties and mechanisms as the basis for its work at both the bilateral and multilateral level.[9]

Box 9.1 summarizes the different reasons that donors have given to explain why they believe there are moral grounds for them to provide aid.

It is not only governments which have evoked morality as the basis for giving aid. In presenting the 'case for aid', and after posing the question why rich

---

BOX 9.1 MORAL EXPLANATIONS GIVEN BY DONOR GOVERNMENTS FOR PROVIDING AID

- On the basis of 'solidarity'.
- In response to human suffering: the humanitarian imperative.
- In response to extreme poverty, need, marginalization and exclusion.
- In order to enhance human freedoms, and to contribute to human development, and to the realization of capabilities.
- In order to extend and enhance the fulfilment of human rights, especially 'core' or 'basic' rights.
- Because of inequalities, notably wide and widening, or growing relative wealth compared with those living in extreme poverty.
- For reasons of distributive or social justice and fairness, to contribute to the fairer distribution of wealth.
- To secure a safer, more secure and peaceful world, including for the donor's own citizens.[a]

[a] It is sometimes claimed that the moral case for providing aid is different from that for providing aid for self-interested reasons. However, this is too narrow a view. There can (often) be strong moral reasons for countries to ensure the long-term interests of their citizens.

countries should provide aid, the World Bank's response was that human beings have a basic responsibility to alleviate suffering and to prevent the needless deaths of other human beings. They not only have a 'moral obligation to share their good fortune with others', but failure to take action is deemed to be 'morally reprehensible' (Stern 2002: 15–16). Similarly, in 2004, the Managing Director of the IMF asserted that the rich countries bear the 'greatest responsibilities' for achieving the goals of poverty reduction as encapsulated in the Millennium Development Goals (MDGs), by meeting their commitments to provide higher levels of aid (quoted in UN Millennium Project 2005: 197). In 2005, the 22 member states of the European Union signed the 'European Consensus on Development', agreeing not only that 'combating poverty is a moral obligation', but that progress in eradicating poverty will help to build a more interdependent world where we 'would not allow' one billion people to struggle on less than one dollar a day.[10]

Aid and the nature of governments' moral obligations

Governments say aid is a moral issue and say they provide aid because it is morally right to do so. But in what sense do governments have a moral obligation to provide aid? If governments do have an obligation to provide aid, what does that obligation entail: precisely how should they respond to the problems of extreme poverty against the backdrop of their large and growing wealth and the widening gulf between rich and poor sketched out in Chapter 8? If governments have moral obligations to provide aid, are these obligations which apply solely to individual donors, or are there wider obligations which extend beyond the confines of the choices that individual governments make in isolation? These are fundamentally important questions, but they remain insufficiently discussed and examined.

A key issue in determining whether governments have obligations to the distant needy revolves around the question of the 'moral unit' around which the discussion is cast. While to cosmopolitans it is clear and self-evident that the basic moral unit is the world, for many others, this is self-evidently wrong. Indeed, it would seem to be at variance with one of the most fundamental tenets of international relations and the way that governments have thought about issues of morality and obligation. For many people, that fact that we inhabit a world consisting of different nation states, and that there is no world government and no state wants one, means that moral obligations need to be framed within the prevailing state-based system. Consequently, it is the state which constitutes the core moral unit around which obligations and potential obligations revolve.[11] As governments view the world through the lens of states, we will begin the discussion on governments, morality and aid-giving by considering the core moral unit to be the state, and states, though the discussion will subsequently be broadened to the international 'system of states', not least because this is what states themselves increasingly have been doing.

Against this backdrop, we now look in turn at governments, aid and morality through three different lenses. The first, which we will call the 'narrow absolutist perspective', assumes that governments only have moral obligations to their own citizens. The second, called the 'mixed perspective', assumes that donor governments have some moral obligations to the poor beyond their borders but these obligations are weak and can usually be trumped by moral obligations at home. The third, called 'an evolving international perspective', assumes that the moral obligations of states are in part formed and shaped by factors and decisions beyond their borders which, in turn, influence the traditional mix of obligations between citizens and non-citizens.

THE NARROW ABSOLUTIST PERSPECTIVE

The core assumption of the narrow absolutist perspective is that governments only have moral obligations to their own citizens. From this perspective, governments do not have moral *obligations* or responsibilities to provide aid—and hence any particular amounts of aid—to help the 'distant needy'. This doesn't mean that governments may not provide aid. However, from this perspective, no assistance which governments might decide to give arises from any particular *duty* to act. Rather, if it is morally based (rather than based on furthering strategic or commercial interests), aid-giving should be judged to be merely an act of beneficence. Thus, while aid-giving might well be motivated by, and based in some way upon, a felt need to respond to human suffering or poverty, from the narrow absolutist perspective, governments which respond do so because they *want* to, rather than because they are *obliged* to. Their aid-giving is thus entirely voluntary, and there is no clear or enduring link between the overall amount of aid required and the amounts individual governments choose to provide.

How relevant is this perspective to contemporary donor practice and to what governments have said about the moral case for them to provide aid? Looking back to the statements made by different governments explaining how they understand their moral obligations, it is by no means clear that any major donor country would comfortably place itself within the narrow absolutist perspective. The clear majority of donor governments explicitly assert that they give aid because they believe that they have some sort of moral *obligation* to provide it. Those that would come closest to the narrow absolutist position would be the United States and Japan, for both of whom, as was discussed in

Chapter 6, national self-interest would appear to be so dominant as to swamp any moral obligation to assist citizens of foreign states. However, the case is far from clear-cut.

Take first the United States. As noted above, the US has always readily acknowledged that it has a (self-imposed) moral obligation to respond to need in time of emergencies. Indeed, for the United States, it is a fundamental principle not simply to provide humanitarian aid in general; the US believes, and has repeatedly stated, that it has a moral obligation to provide humanitarian aid to those in need regardless of the political hue of the government of the country in which emergencies occur. In practice, too, the United States has often been in the forefront of donor responses to emergencies, including countries in conflict. For the US, the moral obligation to provide humanitarian aid is based on its belief that it has an obligation to 'save lives'. But, as discussed above, there is no moral difference between saving the lives of people at immediate risk of death in times of emergency and saving the lives of people at immediate risk of death from, say, a lack of medication. Indeed, the recent (massive) expansion in official US aid to fund and support people in HIV/AIDS programmes suggests that such arguments play a far from insignificant role in contemporary US government aid-giving, extending well beyond the remit of humanitarian aid. What is more, as discussed in Chapter 4, since 2002 the alleviation of poverty has become an explicit priority for the government, forming an essential part of its goals in promoting its national interest. Hence to suggest that the United States does not provide aid on the basis of any moral *obligation* to do so cannot really be sustained. The case of Japan is more complex. Japan certainly provides aid to contribute to the reduction of poverty (and human suffering), but its view of obligation is based on the notion of self-help: its assistance is used to help those who help themselves (Nishigaki and Shimomura 1999: 152–3).[12]

The broad conclusion is that, in practice, none of the main donor countries, with the possible exception of Japan, would today classify itself as providing aid solely and exclusively on the basis of narrow self-interested motives. For almost all, and possibly all governments, aid-giving is seen by them as being driven, in some manner, by an obligation or duty to provide it.

THE MIXED PERSPECTIVE

The mixed perspective describes the situation where a government's moral obligations are almost entirely domestically and internally focused. Governments accept that they do have wider obligations but they are limited. In particular, these obligations do not *require* them to act on the basis of some externally based agreement, for which they can be held formally accountable. The basis for responding is entirely voluntary.

Applying this perspective to aid-giving would suggest that governments accept that they have some obligations to assist foreigners (with aid), but these would be small in number, relatively weak or 'imperfect' obligations. From this perspective, there is an acceptance by governments of some sort of a moral obligation to provide aid, but it remains less than fully developed, and crucially, there is no binding necessity to do so.[13]

What might a pattern of aid-giving based on this perspective look like? Broadly, it would be likely to include the following characteristics: higher amounts of aid given in aggregate than if the government did not accept that it had some sort of moral obligation to provide it; more aid for humanitarian and poverty-reducing purposes, and less to support domestic and strategic interests; forms of aid and ways of giving it based more on what recipients stated they wanted; less aid explicitly tied to their own commercial interests. Dynamically, one would expect aid levels to increase in relation to increases in human suffering and extreme poverty.

These criteria are quite broad and open-ended, and they are not particularly onerous. Indeed, they could be applied to most of the largest official donors today. That is precisely what is intended.

The way that most donors approach the notion of moral obligation in providing aid is that they acknowledge that they have a moral obligation either explicitly (by saying so), or implicitly by the way they explain why they give aid, selecting different moral arguments to support this assertion. They do this by drawing on different moral approaches and theories of justice or on a rights-based perspective, or, more commonly, by selecting elements of more complete theories, to help to explain why they give aid. The summary above (Box 9.1) of different explanations governments have given to explain why they believe there is a moral case for them to provide aid well illustrates this point. Over time, the basis on which they have argued that they do have a moral obligation to provide aid has tended to change, even though, in recent years for a growing number of governments, there has been a discernible shift towards directly linking the moral basis for providing aid to human rights criteria. In practice, donors have adopted what could be described—quite accurately—as a 'pick-and-mix' approach to aid, morality and the obligation to provide it.

It is important not to belittle these efforts, and this perspective. The pick-and-mix approach to the morality of aid-giving by official donors has certainly contributed to significant changes in aid-giving, including, in recent years, a rapid increase in overall levels of aid provided, and pledges made by more and more donors to increase overseas development assistance (ODA) to the 0.7 per cent of gross national income (GNI) target within a particular time-frame. Far-reaching pledges have also been made to channel aid more to those who need it most; to make aid flows more predictable and less volatile; to use aid (and other means) to halve the proportion of people living in poverty by the year 2015; to increase, substantially, the amounts of humanitarian aid;

to formalize a common funding pool; to provide a better match between humanitarian aid needs and the amounts of aid provided; and to align aid more closely with recipient needs and priorities. All these commitments are driven by the self-understanding of donor governments that they have a moral obligation to provide aid; indeed they are driven by a growing and shared perception that they have an obligation to provide more aid and to provide it in a more effective way.

But, equally, it is important to draw attention to what is missing in what we have termed the 'mixed perspective'. Most fundamentally, aid-giving within the mixed framework remains, in essence, a voluntary act. In donor countries, aid is allocated within the framework of annual appropriation legislation authorizing state spending programmes, which are usually approved annually, though in some countries they are placed within multi-year spending plans. State spending, including aid funds, can thus vary from year to year (OECD 2005i: 42ff.). While commitments and pledges are certainly made by donor governments to provide particular amounts of aid, if circumstances change, then these can be altered, even if in some instances the process of reducing aid might prove difficult. Above all, the moral basis for governments to provide aid within this perspective contains no explicit criteria or benchmarks against which to assess performance, from which obligations and responsibilities arise, and for which governments are held accountable, particularly in international or external fora.

The following checklist of key issues that are excluded from the mixed perspective of government aid-giving and morality highlights its limitations.

1. It provides no clear assessment of the relationship between the moral obligation of an individual state to provide resources to assist its own citizens and its obligation to those abroad who are experiencing acute human suffering and extreme poverty, nor any explicit criteria for determining the allocation of resources between the two.

2. It provides no binding rules, or even rough guidelines, for determining the relationship between rising wealth and growing inequalities between rich and poor, and the amount of aid that donors might be expected to give.

3. It provides no binding obligation on donors as a group to provide aid up to any particular level. Aid-giving remains, in essence, a voluntary act based on what each donor chooses to give. There are no penalties imposed on any donor who fails to provide aid to the amounts it pledges to give or commits itself to providing.

4. It does not base aid-giving on any rigorous assessment of the overall requirements for aid, based on adequately addressing acute human suffering and extreme poverty, and committing donors as a whole to provide the aid needed. The objectives of the MDG merely to halve the proportion of people living in poverty by the year 2015, and providing aid only to meet these objectives, remain remarkably unambitious compared with a moral imperative to provide aid in sufficient amounts effectively to contribute to addressing the problems of human suffering and extreme poverty, especially in poor countries.[14]

5. It does not commit any individual donor either to provide a particular proportion of the overall amount of aid needed, or to work with others to increase aid levels if an unpredicted shortfall develops, for instance as a result of increased emergency needs.

A likely initial response to this checklist is that it would be completely impractical and unrealistic to expect governments to agree, either individually or as a group, to adopt such criteria and benchmarks to assess and judge their moral commitments to provide aid. That is to misunderstand the reason for drawing up the list. The purpose is not so much to make criticisms as to lay bare what is missing or inadequately covered by the current 'pick-and-mix' approach of governments in giving aid within the context of claims that they are doing so because they have some sort of moral obligation to do so.

It is, however, important to note that we are already beginning to see signs of some government donors beginning to raise questions about the mixed approach to aid and morality and the nature of obligation, an approach which still in practice dominates the way governments approach the issue.

For instance, some years ago the government of Finland stated that in cases where poor countries were not able to realize their development goals without international assistance, they should be *entitled* to external aid provided either by individual states or by the international community as a whole (Tomaševski 1993: 49). More strongly still, the influential Netherlands Advisory Committee on Human Rights and Foreign Policy recently stated that, in its view, the combination of the UN Charter and Articles 12, 11, 22 and 23 of the International Covenant on Economic Social and Cultural Rights *already* implies an obligation to provide aid (of sufficient amounts) when (poor) states are not themselves capable of independently realizing the absolute minimum norms of these rights.[15] In a similar vein, in early 2006, Finland and Portugal stated that, in their view, the provision of international aid funds constitutes an essential element in the implementation of the Covenant, implying an obligation for aid to be provided to ensure the fulfilment of these rights.[16]

The implication is clear. Increasingly (some) governments are beginning to view the issue of state aid, morality and obligation within a wider international perspective, in which issues of obligation extend beyond what individual states decide to do in relative isolation from each other. We need to look more closely at what is involved in such an approach.

AN EVOLVING INTERNATIONAL PERSPECTIVE

One of the key starting points of 'an evolving international perspective' is that the process of developing some obligations to which states are willing to commit themselves is changing. They are being framed within an international context. Some agreements are negotiated and agreed by the international community (of states), obliging states to undertake specific actions, often including contributing funds, to achieve commonly agreed goals, for which each contributing state is held accountable. If aid-giving is cast within this perspective, the moral obligations that (rich/wealthy) countries accept they have to provide aid require them to contribute to the overall international aid-giving effort, the parameters of which they jointly agree, and for which they are held accountable. There are already signs of states beginning to move in this direction.

From the past to the present

The world of states in which we currently live is changing fast. In the distant past, it was more likely to have been possible for states to perceive their moral and legal obligations as principally applying only to internal and domestic matters. But as international relations have evolved, states increasingly have accepted the need to alter long-held rules and regulations for managing inter-state affairs, and to address inter-state problems. Over time, the distinction between how states address internal and external issues has tended to become blurred and more complex, stimulating the emergence of a distinctive dis-course which does not think of the issues of obligation as dividing naturally into domestic and international categories or compartments (Brown 2002: 3).

Over many decades, states have agreed methods, approaches and principles for determining how to conduct affairs between themselves. These have included the development of rules on not waging wars (except where the prin-ciples of self-determination and non-interference have been violated), on hon-ouring treaties, and on protecting their own citizens. Two long-standing pillars of inter-state relationships have been the principles of self-determination and non-interference. Yet, set alongside the working out of inter-state relations, there has also been 'a long tradition of interpretation that argues that individ-uals are the ultimate members of international society even if its immediate members are states' (Brown 2002: 115). It was from this tradition that the Universal Declaration of Human Rights (UDHR) was drawn up, agreed and formally ratified by (all) states, from which has proceeded a succession of inter-national treaties, conventions and protocols, to refine, to clarify and, in some circumstances, to develop the ideas contained in the original Declaration. What lay behind this movement was not merely the conviction that individ-uals, and in some cases, groups (such as indigenous peoples), have rights by virtue of their very humanity, but that if these (moral) rights are to be realizable, then they need to be legally enforceable.

While the fulfilment (and enforceability) of human rights has predom-inantly been viewed as a domestic issue, in recent years, growing attention has focused on the relationship between human rights violations and the roles and responsibilities of other states in protecting people, notably when extreme violations of human rights have occurred—the genocide in Rwanda providing a particularly important catalyst in shifting thinking on this issue. As a result, states have recently developed a consensus on, and have effectively agreed upon, two interrelated matters. The first is that there is a 'responsibility to protect' which all states share, and which they have a duty (to those whose rights have been violated) to follow through with concrete action. The second is that the principle of non-interference in the internal/domestic affairs of states can be challenged, and in some cases overridden, when the action (or inaction) of states causes, or fails to prevent, the extreme violations of the basic rights of citizens of that country. Indeed, when states fail to live up to their responsibility to protect their own citizens from mass atrocities, it is now accepted, almost universally, that this responsibility passes to the international community, which should stand ready to enforce it—even if the way that this should happen remains undefined and still rather unclear.[17]

In parallel with the evolution of these (new) ideas and approaches, since 1993 states have formally acknowledged and continued to affirm, most recently in the *2005 World Summit outcome*, that all human rights are universal, indivisible, interrelated and mutually reinforcing, and that all human rights must be treated in a fair and equitable manner, on the same footing and with the same emphasis (para. 121). If states are to commit themselves to protecting and promoting one set of rights, then it follows that they also need to commit themselves to 'actively protecting and promoting all human rights'. And states have now confirmed this (para. 119). The 2005 World Summit also confirmed that 'development, peace and security, and human rights are interlinked and mutually reinforcing', and that 'development also constitutes a central goal by itself' (paras. 9, 10). It reaffirmed the principle that each country had to take prime responsibility for its own development, but that there was an important role to be played by international cooperation (para. 25). In turn, these reaffirmations need to be seen alongside the International Covenant on Economic, Social and Cultural Rights (ICESCR), which, as noted above, makes specific mention of international cooperation, aid and technical assistance as having a role 'of central importance' in ensuring the realisation of the rights recognised in the Convention (Arts. 2(19) and 11(1)). In short, by the time of the 2005 World Summit, states had accepted (to use non-technical language) an acknowledgement of a general obligation for (rich) countries to provide assistance to poor countries.

In line with, and partly linked to, these general trends, the establishment of the Millennium Development Goals and the successive commitments that governments have made to cooperate actively to achieve the goals of poverty eradication have added new dimensions to the issues of international cooperation, and the obligations of governments to provide aid. Through the process of agreeing the MDGs, states have reaffirmed their commitment to eradicate poverty in two specific ways. First, they have agreed to support the efforts of developing countries to adopt and implement national development policies through, among other things, increased aid (development assistance). Secondly, they have agreed to 'support developing countries by providing a substantial increase in aid of sufficient quantity and arriving in a timely manner to assist them in achieving the internationally agreed development goals, including the Millennium Development Goals' (*2000 World Summit Outcome*, para. 22(c)). In the view of Special UN Advisor Philip Alston, the MDGs initiative is of 'major relevance for human rights' (2005: 757), including to our understanding of obligations.

Some have suggested that, because governments have reiterated their commitment to the MDGs so often, and on so many solemn occasions, these commitments *already* constitute the status of a binding obligation on governments with legal consequences, possibly having the status of international customary law. More cautiously, Alston's view is that at least the first six of the MDGs (see Box 3.1) reflect norms of international customary law. He acknowledges that the greatest resistance to agreeing that all the MDGs have the status of international customary law centres on the eighth goal, which calls for the 'development of a global partnership for development'. Opposition will come, he suggests, from some donors, who would 'be expected to resist strongly any suggestion that there are specific obligations enshrined in international law' on them to provide particular amounts of aid (2005: 775).

To what extent has the acceptance of responsibility for providing aid risen to the level of becoming an international obligation? According to Alston, at one level, it would appear that it might have done so already. If one accepts that at least some parts of the first seven MDGs have achieved this status, then, he suggests, the eighth would be a strong candidate. However, overall, he remains unconvinced that this stage has yet been reached. Consequently, it remains his view that the persistent rejection in all relevant UN documents that any given country is obligated to provide specific assistance to another country would 'present a major obstacle to any analysis seeking to demonstrate that such an obligation has already become part of customary law' (2005: 777). What might happen in the years ahead could be very different, and it is to the future that we now turn.

From the present to a different future

There are, broadly, two ways of looking ahead. The first is to see the future predominantly in terms of extensions to the current templates around which the discourse on obligation is cast. One possible future from this perspective, which seeks to extend and 'clarify' the specific obligations to which donors would be formally committed, has been presented by the UN's former Independent Expert on the Right to Development, Arjun Sengupta. He has proposed that poor countries draw up concrete 'development compacts' with groups of donors. These would specify what countries require to further the fulfilment of core rights in order to eradicate poverty—more precisely, these would specify details of the external resources needed to achieve concrete objectives, agreed with a group of specified donors. Then, if development-compact countries failed to achieve their objectives because of a lack of resources, they would be in a position to invoke 'callable commitments' from these donors to provide aid to meet the shortfalls in resources (Alston 2005: 777). Alston believes that, as we build on these sorts of initiatives, and against the backdrop of the persistent emphasis within the MDGs context on the mobilization of resources, the momentum will increase sufficiently to clinch the argument that some obligations to provide the additional resources necessary to enable countries to achieve the MDGs will have been crystallized into customary law (2005: 778). At this point, moral and legal obligations for governments to provide aid will have taken a further, important step forward.

But there is another way in which the debate about government obligations and aid-giving could develop: by extending ongoing initiatives on the right to protect people from extreme human rights abuses.[18] The following paragraphs explain how this might happen.

Three examples will illustrate how in tangible ways our understanding of international obligations has been evolving and changing. First, in 2000, the July 1998 treaty to establish a permanent International Criminal Court (ICC) was ratified by the requisite 60 countries. Secondly, through the Framework Convention on Climate Change, agreed in March 1994, and the 1997 Kyoto Protocol, which came into force in February 2005, the international community created regulations binding on states to address key problems created by environmental degradation. Thirdly, and of the greatest importance to the discussion about aid and international obligations to provide it, states have recently developed a consensus on actions needed to respond to the internationally accepted responsibility to protect. In particular, the International Commission on Intervention and State Sovereignty (ICISS) sought to shift attention away from an exclusive focus on the rights and prerogatives of states to focus, as well, on the victims: 'Our preferred terminology refocuses the international searchlight back to where it should always be: on the duty to protect communities from mass killing, women from systematic rape and children from starvation' (ICISS 2001: 17). The main argument of the Commission was that the international community has an obligation to intervene and to protect people whose rights are seriously violated when their own governments will not, or cannot, protect them. It would be a relatively small step for this principle to be extended and deployed to address effectively the problems of human suffering and extreme poverty and the denial of human rights which current arrangements perpetuate.

There is already widespread agreement that human suffering and extreme poverty are a violation of human dignity, and that they involve a major denial of a range of key human rights. Indeed, Mary Robinson has explained the problem more succinctly: 'I am often asked what is the most serious form of human rights violations in the world today, and my reply is consistent: extreme poverty' (quoted in Alston 2005: 786). Similarly, as noted above, since the signing of the Vienna Declaration in 1993, the international community has repeatedly affirmed that all human rights are interrelated, indivisible, inter-dependent and mutually reinforcing.[19] It is therefore an anomaly, and a contra-diction, that the human rights violations of millions of people living in extreme poverty are not addressed at an international level in an effective and compre-hensive way.

The crucial issue is whether—or perhaps when—the international commu-nity of nations will choose to pursue the linked issues of extreme poverty and human suffering in the same way that it has already addressed other forms of extreme human rights violations. There needs to be concerted, holistic and comprehensive international action, with appropriate legal backing, to supplement the present, essentially voluntary approach which does not bind any country to providing any specified amount of aid. Effective action has been hampered by three factors: first, the inability to accurately assess and agree upon the amounts of aid needed to address current problems of extreme poverty; secondly, a lack of consensus on a realistic timetable for doing so; and thirdly, the failure to enter into substantial discussion of how the necessary aid will be raised and distributed, including mechanisms to ensure that each (rich) country contributes on the basis of an agreed ability-to-pay formula.

The building-blocks of a new approach to the obligation to provide aid

Box 9.2 provides the key building-blocks for developing an approach to aid-giving based on an acceptance by the international community not merely that it has a (general and rather vague) obligation to address the problems of human suffering and extreme poverty, but that it also has an obligation to put in place mechanisms, processes and institutions to ensure this obligation is fleshed out in effective, internationally coordinated action, with concrete targets for aid-giving, and for which individual states would be held formally accountable. Consistent with the approaches to obligations of governments discussed earlier in this chapter (because this represents the way that the discourse on governments' obligations to provide aid takes place in the real world), these points are based on a 'pick-and-mix' use of different theories and approaches to obligation. However, they are particularly influenced by an assumed obligation to respond to needs and to human rights violations, and by the principle that aid should be provided on the basis of the ability to pay.[20]

BOX 9.2 BUILDING BLOCKS OF A NEW APPROACH TO THE OBLIGATION OF GOVERNMENTS TO
PROVIDE AID

---

1. Extreme poverty and the human suffering to which it gives rise constitute such a grave denial of key human rights that the international community agrees it has a fundamental responsibility to confront these problems and implement measures effectively to address them.

2. Responsibility for the protection, respect and fulfilment of all rights belongs primarily to those states whose people experience or are vulnerable to extreme poverty. It is they who need to adopt and implement development policies and strategies which give priority to reducing extreme poverty as quickly as possible, and with the aim of ultimately eliminating extreme poverty.[a]

3. However, the international community acknowledges that it also has a responsibility, especially in poor countries with insufficient and inadequate resources, skills, technologies, capacities and institutions, to take a range of measures to assist those countries to achieve their poverty-focused development objectives, including objectives in the areas of aid provision, international trade and debt. Particular and specific responsibilities fall on richer states.

4. More broadly, the international community acknowledges its responsibility to ensure that the structures and policies of international institutions give special priority to facilitating the achievement of poverty eradication.

5. In drawing up the development policies and strategies of each poor country, assessments should be made of the anticipated shortfalls in the resources, skills and technologies that poor countries have, or are able to obtain, without official aid funds, and of weaknesses in capacities and institutions required to achieve their poverty-focused development objectives within a mutually agreed time-frame.[b]

6. On the basis of these needs assessments, and while recognizing that such assessments will necessarily be subject to a degree of error, the international community as a whole commits itself to meeting these poor-country aid needs, and to raising the resources necessary to fill these gaps in domestic resources.

7. On the basis of the wealth of each country, and through an agreed formula, each nation state agrees to provide its share of the total external resources needed, with the international community as a whole ensuring that aid funds raised, on the basis of need, are channelled to recipients in order to contribute to meeting those needs.[c]

8. The international community believes that the obligation to assist those living in extreme poverty is not dependent on the nature of their government. In countries where the rule of law has broken down, and in instances where countries have failed to adopt appropriate national development policies and strategies, or where the international community believes there are fundamental problems in utilizing potential international funds sufficiently and effectively, discussions between the international community and key citizens of the country in question should take place to decide appropriate measures for utilizing the allocated aid funds as efficiently as possible.[d]

9. Needs assessments and aid contributions will be revised on a regular (possibly three-year) rolling basis.

10. The international community also acknowledges its responsibility to provide sufficient funds to enable countries to respond adequately to the suffering and needs that arise from humanitarian disasters and related emergencies.

11. On the basis of an analysis of the needs that have arisen in recent emergencies, and with a small cushion of reserve funding, the international community agrees to raise funds,

additional to those required to address the structural problems of extreme poverty, to enable humanitarian and other emergency needs to be adequately met.

12. On the basis of the wealth of each country, and through an agreed formula, each nation state agrees to provide its share of the total external resources needed for an effective international humanitarian response.

13. If substantially new emergency needs arise, the international community commits itself to providing additional funds on the basis of the agreed formula for regular contributions.

[a] There seems to be a disproportionately sharper focus by donors on the (moral) link between public spending and poverty alleviation in developing countries than in their own countries. It is common to hear rich-country donors arguing, for instance, that poor-country governments should ensure that extreme poverty is eliminated within their own borders prior to their spending taxpayers' money on other non-essential items, such as the arts, sport, or even defence. Donor governments appear to be far less (morally) concerned with the links between poverty and public spending allocations in their own countries. In winter months, it is not uncommon for thousands of elderly people to suffer premature deaths due to the cold. Indeed, in the winter of 2004/5, it is estimated that almost 30,000 elderly people died of preventable, cold-related illnesses in England and Wales (*The Tablet*, 11 March 2006, p. 11). Yet there was little sign of any debate from government ministers that these stark manifestations of poverty should lead them to switch to a more poverty-focused set of priorities.

[b] This is a huge task and, as suggested above, one that is really only beginning to be addressed at all comprehensively.

[c] This issue is discussed and developed further in Part IV.

[d] There is a view, quite widely and strongly held, that aid should only be given to those countries able to use it 'properly'. This argument was stated in forceful terms by the Commission for Africa, which suggested that if Africa failed to take the lead in development then 'the international community will find it even more difficult to discharge its responsibilities, act in solidarity with Africa and deliver effective support. The partnership we embrace therefore depends crucially on action in Africa. And the structure of the support must be tailored to Africa's action' (Commission for Africa 2005: 89). In contrast, the argument here is that while aid impact certainly matters, it should not be a necessary condition for the provision of aid. In particular, as the moral philosopher David Miller states, 'the more autocratic the community, the more hesitant we should be to hold back from helping people whose lives are less than decent on the grounds that they are responsible for their condition' (2004: 135).

What we have outlined here is little more than 'building blocks' for future debate and discussion. Some may say that all this is little more than 'pie in the sky'. A realistic future based on this approach to the obligations of governments to provide aid is highly unlikely to come about unless and until there is a sufficient groundswell of public support for these or similar sorts of proposals, and unless governments believe that this is how they ought to view their moral obligations to provide aid. Yet one way of advancing this debate is to begin to reflect on what a different final destination might look like, and this is one. Its importance lies in its being based on, and projecting forward, ideas and perspectives which are rooted in the way thinking on international relations and human rights debates are already moving.

Ethics, voluntary aid-giving and the world of NGOs

INDIVIDUAL MOTIVATIONS FOR GIVING AID

Individuals give a variety of reasons to explain why they personally contribute to organizations which help people in far-off countries. However, the main motives are strikingly similar to the accounts which governments give for why they believe that they have a moral obligation to provide aid: solidarity, need, duty, compassion, to contribute to the relief of suffering, and because 'I can afford it'. What is more, polls would seem to suggest that a majority of people in richer countries at some time have voluntarily donated to 'third world' charities, and for the past 20 years, contributions appear to have been firmly on the increase. There are, nonetheless, some differences in the way governments and individuals perceive their obligation to give aid.

Though a steady, and rising, number of individuals give money to help address the long-term problems of extreme poverty, most donations are given in support of emergency appeals. This is based on the public's understanding of the greatest need, which, in turn, is critically influenced by the media, whose prime-time coverage is dominated by pictures and reports which focus on (some) of the most visibly dramatic, quick-onset emergencies, rather than longer-term and more complex emergencies. As far more people die from the problems of extreme poverty than from natural disasters and the effects of quick-onset emergencies, public donations are based on an incomplete view of where the need is most urgent.

Why public perceptions and hence public donations have been so dominated by acute quick-onset emergencies has long been the subject of debate. Broadcasters argue that the public 'wants' to see images of rapid-onset emergencies, and that they have a moral responsibility to inform the public of such emergencies and the resulting human suffering. Aid agencies say that the public wants to respond to the suffering they see, and that they have a moral responsibility to establish effective appeal mechanisms to enable them to do so. Additionally, most voluntary aid agencies (NGOs) work hard, often with the assistance of broadcasters, to draw public attention to the needs of other, less immediately visible and more complex, emergencies, and many of these initiatives do well in terms of both awareness-raising and attracting funds to help. The problem is that by giving such prominence to emergencies, (distorted) public perceptions of acute need and human suffering are confirmed and reinforced, rather than challenged and corrected. A disproportionately small share of resources is allocated to efforts to create and deepen public awareness of the acute human suffering and deaths caused by extreme poverty.

The close association in the public mind between acute need and emergencies also helps to explain why public aid-giving is so little influenced by the argument that human suffering and extreme poverty are, in part, caused by the actions of rich countries. In spite of many decades of work by some NGOs, it remains the case that only a minority of people are motivated to give aid because they believe that the processes which result in the creation of their own individual wealth are a cause of human suffering and extreme poverty. However, a growing number of people (though still a minority) believe that the way they choose to spend their disposable income can contribute to poverty reduction—hence the rapidly expanding popularity of different 'fair trade' initiatives in many European donor countries.

Some of the central debates among moral and political philosophers about whether states have moral obligations to the distant needy appear to be of very little concern to individuals. Though most people would concur with the view that they have strong moral obligations at home, including, especially, to their immediate families and those within their own communities, they do not see the fulfilling of these obligations as creating any overriding constraint on their contributing to charities to help the distant needy. In other words, they tend, almost intuitively, to be committed to a more or less cosmopolitan view of moral standing (O'Neill 2000: 193ff.). Indeed, as the survey data summarized in Chapter 7 forcibly tends to suggest, there would seem to be a strong public perception that their governments' views on providing aid should also be informed by the same moral standpoint.

What views do people hold about the moral obligation to provide aid, the donations they choose to give to 'third world' charities, and the impact of the aid provided? There are two strongly held assumptions about individuals and aid-giving which are shared by many moral philosophers, such as Peter Singer (2004). The first is that most individuals believe that the aid given to charities goes predominantly to those who need it most; the second is that the aid is effective in alleviating the suffering and addressing the needs upon which the decision to give it (with the underlying moral assumptions that it ought to be given) are based.[21] However, even if these views are strongly held, it does not necessarily follow that those who donate would stop giving if there was evidence that the aid provided was not effective, or if a lack of hard evidence meant it was difficult to come to a firm conclusion about impact. Indeed, as discussed in Chapter 7 (see Table 7.1), it would appear that a significant number of people believe that the responsibility to provide aid is not wholly dependent upon its effectiveness. This could well mean that for a significant proportion of the public, the moral case for providing aid is not undermined by the failure of aid to make the difference intended: the obligation to provide aid remains as long as there are grounds for believing that it could be made to work, improving the lives and life-chances of the beneficiaries.

Yet there are two rather different ways that a looser link between aid provision and aid impact could be interpreted. For some, that link could be loose because, either explicitly or implicitly, they hold views about justice in which the obligation to donate to aid agencies is not entirely dependent upon the impact of the aid provided. For others, however, it could be that they are not really all that bothered about the good that the aid is intended to do. In this case, one explanation could be that aid-giving is linked to coping with feelings of guilt, the process of aid-giving being more inner-centred than outer- or other-directed. Here, its primary function is to reduce the dissonance felt between our fortunate selves and those whose plight and human suffering is 'beamed' into our sitting rooms, making us feel uncomfortable. Though this issue is rarely analysed in the literature on aid, it is likely that feelings of guilt abound in individual aid-giving to the distant needy, just as they do when one is confronted with a person begging for money on the street at home. Indeed, some aid agencies have used film and photographic images of human suffering deliberately to exploit feelings of guilt, with which many people remain burdened.

Overall, then, moral reasons constitute the core explanations for why people donate to agencies working with the distant needy, though this conceals a likely mix of different motivations.

MORAL OBLIGATIONS OF VOLUNTARY AID AGENCIES AND NGOS

We now shift attention from those who voluntarily give money to aid agencies, to the moral dimensions of the agencies which receive the aid donated. One important difference between official aid and the voluntary aid of NGOs is that most official aid goes to poor-country governments, ministries and agencies, whereas NGO aid either is, or has the potential to be, channelled directly to poor people and poor communities. It may seem, therefore, that the moral obligations of NGOs are fairly simple to articulate and explain—simply ensuring that the aid goes to those who need it most, and that it is put to the best possible use to relieve human suffering and to contribute to effective poverty reduction. This might be an appropriate way to assess the activities of NGOs if they themselves viewed their activities narrowly from a perspective in which aid-giving was solely based on beneficence. However, this is rarely the case today. Over time, more and more NGOs have viewed their work from a rights-based or justice-based perspective. Consequently, it would seem appropriate to assess the moral dimensions of their work with reference to these perspectives.

Who receives and uses NGO aid? From a welfarist, needs-based perspective, it would usually be assumed that aid—whether humanitarian or development aid—should be channelled to those who need it most. This is one of the most widespread assumptions of those who donate to NGOs, and, in turn, it is reinforced by much NGO publicity. However, this is not what NGOs necessarily believe, and is by no means consistent with how their aid money is spent. As will be discussed in Chapter 17, a growing number of NGOs identify the solutions to human suffering and extreme poverty as lying, in part, in the wider structures, processes and institutions that are believed to cause or perpetuate poverty. For these agencies, there is a crucial difference between 'responding to need' and 'channelling (all) aid to those who are in need'. Responding to need doesn't necessarily mean that all aid should go directly, and in its entirety, to those experiencing human suffering and extreme poverty. In practice, however, only a small proportion of aid (usually less than 20 per cent for large NGOs) is used to address human suffering and to tackle extreme poverty indirectly. The overwhelming majority of the aid funds donated is channelled directly to particular groups of poor people, mostly on the basis of need.

When NGOs channel aid directly to those suffering and in extreme poverty, what criteria do they use to determine who should receive it? If the moral basis for providing aid is needs-based, then it is widely assumed (not least by those donating to NGOs) that the allocation of aid will be determined by the scale of need. On this basis, the more needy people are, the more deserving they are, so more aid will go to the more needy, and the most aid to the most needy. Indeed, it is these assumptions which inform and shape much NGO publicity, which maintains, often explicitly, that the donations the agency receives are used to help 'the most needy', that the organization is driven by its commitment to help 'the poorest of the poor'. There are three quite different sorts of ethical issues raised by this perspective on helping the 'deserving poor'. We shall briefly consider each in turn.

The needy and the most needy, the poor and the poorest

Leaving to one side the aid which NGOs deliberately choose not to channel to poor people and poor communities, claims made by NGOs that, after general administrative costs have been paid, the remaining aid goes to the *most* needy and to the poorest of the poor are hard to sustain, even in rapid-onset emergencies, when it is relatively easy to identify those most seriously affected. A core problem lies in the ability of agencies to identify who are the poorest and most needy. Almost always, there is a lack of information with which to compare the scale of need between people and within particular communities. As discussed in Chapter 19, even if some organizations are given the task of undertaking an overall needs-assessment, invariably, gaps remain and some people in dire need will be overlooked. Additionally, although the larger NGOs increasingly make use of such overarching assessments, most decisions on whom to assist are taken by individual NGOs, on the basis of far more limited needs-assessments, which are usually critically dependent upon the reliability of the information coming from the networks of local organizations with whom the aid-delivering NGOs interact. Typically, the best that can be achieved is ensuring that within a particular locality, many of the most needy are identified, and NGOs are becoming more skilled in identifying potentially excluded groups, such as girls and women and members of ethnic minorities and other marginalized groups. However, there is another problem, identified in Chapter 19: increasingly, agencies are distributing goods such as food to whole communities, the more needy receiving levels of assistance similar to those of the less needy.

The least believable claims that their aid is reaching the most deserving come from small NGOs, with few resources, arriving new to an area, with little in-depth knowledge of the social, political, economic and power relations of the communities with whom they have chosen to work, working in regions where they do not know the language. More likely than not, a significant number of those being assisted by such groups will not be amongst the most needy. Possibly even greater problems arise in trying to identify those living in extreme poverty, those most vulnerable to the risk of death and disease beyond emergency situations. Here again, the identification of poor people and poor groups is often quite difficult. For many, a key characteristic of their poverty is that it will be hidden from view.

In practice, often the best that most NGOs are able accurately to claim with confidence is that they are coming to the aid of people, most of whom will be in acute need and living in poverty, and some of whom are likely to be amongst the poorest and most needy. How does this affect the overall thrust of the moral justification for providing aid? Possibly not much, if one's criteria for assisting are the overall needs of a population devastated by an emergency or by extreme poverty, for, set against average incomes, most would be considered poor and needy. The hard cases involve activities of NGOs which not merely fail to reach those most in need, but which, by assisting the 'not-so-deserving', cement further or widen inequalities and unequal power relations that already adversely affect the poorest, leaving the most deserving worse off in both an absolute and relative sense. Regrettably, insufficient data mean it is not possible to say whether this is a significant or a relatively minor problem.

Rights-based approaches, empowerment and judging how to help

Today, most NGOs use a needs-based discourse to explain the moral basis that determines and shapes how they work. However, a growing number of NGOs, both secular and religious, are now articulating the way they work, and how they interact with poor people and poor communities, through a rights-based perspective, with some additionally emphasizing the importance to their work of aiming to enhance human dignity.[22] Needs-based and rights-based approaches overlap and are interrelated. Many basic needs required for living a decent human life are 'claim rights': things which people have a right to claim from others, such as wealthy nations. However, there are a range of different ways in which a rights-based perspective alters the traditional needs-based approaches to those suffering and living in extreme poverty. Four are of particular relevance to the ethical dimensions of NGO work.

The first concerns how assessments are conducted of who needs help. From a rights-based perspective, responsibility for undertaking such assessments should start with the poor people and communities themselves: it is they who should decide who ought to be assisted, and in helping to clarify who are the 'poorest of the poor', not the (external) NGOs. The second change concerns decisions about the sort of help that should be provided. From a rights-based perspective, it is the poor people and poor communities themselves whose views are crucial in determining what sort of aid they need and the forms in which it is given—whether it is provided as food, shelter, housing, medicines, or in the form of cash or vouchers. Thirdly, from a rights-based (and capabilities) perspective, enhancing the power of poor people to gain more control over their lives and decisions affecting them is a key anticipated outcome. Consequently, the provision of aid needs strenuously to avoid creating or deepening the dependence of those being assisted on external agencies. As far as possible, the assistance which the communities choose to receive ought to be provided with a (central) eye on strengthening the independence and freedoms of those suffering and living in extreme poverty. Finally, from a rights-based perspective, NGOs remain accountable particularly to those poor people and communities to whom they give aid, providing opinions on whether the funds donated by supporters have been well spent.

In practice, there are still a sizeable number of NGOs claiming to use a rights-based perspective who have not yet changed their procedures to incorporate these new perspectives into their monitoring and assessment procedures, though many of the largest are trying to bridge these gaps.

NGOs and wider, more systemic, responsibilities

The (moral) legitimacy of NGO action in poor countries historically has been inextricably linked to the assistance that NGOs give to those suffering, at high risk and vulnerable to death. However, some recent changes have been occurring in NGO activities which alter this moral landscape and the assumptions upon which it is based.

A potential strength of NGO activities has been their ability to assist poor people and poor communities that cannot easily be reached by official aid. As the bulk of official aid is channelled to governments in aid-recipient countries, and increasingly provided to support and enhance the impact of their (poverty-focused) development strategies, much NGO aid has been channelled to a range of initiatives that remain outside the sphere and reach of recipient-country governments, even if NGO service-delivery activities often complement those of the recipient-country state. On the basis of these features of NGO emergency activities, and especially development activities, a growing number of official donors view NGOs not merely as different from, and as working in parallel to, recipient governments, but as a means of *bypassing* governments which they judge to be either not sufficiently committed to or unable to deliver the poverty-reducing impact required. This is not radically dissimilar to the long-held view that emergency aid is best channelled through international NGOs because many poor-country governments and domestic agencies are perceived as unable to deliver humanitarian aid quickly, efficiently and effectively to those who need it. Seeing the role of NGOs in this light is particularly attractive, as it seems to provide the solution to the (moral) dilemma many donors often feel they face—that they have a moral obligation to provide aid to countries experiencing extreme poverty, but they also believe that providing aid to and through a particular government will not have the poverty-reducing impact upon which the obligation to provide aid is based.

On the basis of this view of the role of NGOs, official donors have begun to expand the amounts of aid that they have provided to NGOs, while for their part, NGOs have expanded their activities in accepting often significant tranches of money. They have done this in three main ways: by running larger programmes (scaling up), by extending the reach of their programmes to include many more people as beneficiaries, and by extending the range of activities they are providing for particular communities. Consequently, it is now increasingly common (rather than a rare exception) for substantial NGO projects to cover large geographical areas, and to encompass numbers of beneficiaries stretching into the thousands, tens of thousands and even hundreds of thousands.

These trends have had two linked effects on NGOs, both of which have ethical implications. First, and especially where NGOs have been given responsibility for delivering services to large communities, such programme expansion has increased the likelihood that the beneficiaries of NGO projects will consist not only of the very poor, but also the less poor, and in some cases, people who, on any definition, are not poor at all. Secondly, and especially in those countries with particularly weak government institutions and agencies, it has become increasingly common for NGOs implementing very large projects to be the only agencies, governmental or non-governmental, responsible for providing services for entire population groups. In these circumstances, NGOs, in effect, assume the role of overall provider of services—a role usually reserved for governments. When this happens, it has profound implications for the moral basis upon which NGOs operate because being the sole or even the dominant provider of services carries with it the moral responsibilities that come with being a monopoly provider of services. In these instances, NGOs become, in the words of Onora O'Neill, primary agents of justice (2004: 253).

Two responsibilities are of particular importance. The first is that NGOs are required to provide those services in a fair and equitable manner to all. The second is that they are required to provide services to acceptable (minimum) standards, which, in turn, requires them to ensure that those who implement projects have the capacity, capability and technical skills to manage the quality and efficient delivery of those services. The first risks compromising NGOs' commitment to the poor and needy. The second requires NGOs to operate with a high degree of professional competence. When governments provide such services, they are morally and legally accountable for providing them in a fair, equitable and efficient manner. When NGOs undertake service delivery activities in the place of governments, the commitment and self-assumed obligations of NGOs to assist those in extreme poverty need to be fulfilled against the backdrop of an all-encompassing responsibility to the whole population within its *de facto* jurisdiction.

When NGOs provide these services, the circumstances in which they are often called upon to undertake these activities (weak government and governmental institutions) are often those in which it is difficult, if not impossible, for processes of legal accountability (even if they exist in theory) to be complied with in practice. This puts added pressure on NGOs to put in place transparent systems, processes and accountability mechanisms through which they can provide assurances that their activities conform to the responsibilities they have taken on. This is no small challenge.

The role of NGOs in providing aid and in contributing to development is changing. Their expansion into new areas and activities, and their adoption of human rights paradigms through which they approach their work, present them with a range of new and difficult ethical questions to add to those they have always had to address. Although many ethical questions that NGOs face are different from those faced by governments, the moral dimensions of NGO aid are fast becoming as complex as those of official aid.

Part III
Does Aid Really Work?

10 Assessing and measuring the impact of aid

Almost since its inception, the impact of official aid has been disputed. The mass media give great prominence to popular views on aid, which are usually briefly stated and polarized, with the critics of aid asserting simply that aid does not work and hence it is not needed, while its supporters contend that it does work, is necessary and should be increased. For instance, in the build-up to the Group of Eight (G8) Summit at Gleneagles in Scotland in mid-2005, where the issue of aid was a central item on the agenda, the British Sunday newspaper the *Sunday Telegraph* boldly asserted that 'aid can do harm as well as good . . . and the balance is on the side of harm' (5 June 2005: 19). In contrast, the international Catholic weekly *The Tablet* editorialized that there is 'a welter of evidence that much aid has been beneficial' and that more aid was vital (2 July 2005: 2).

These polarized views on the impact of aid are sometimes based on prejudice. More commonly, they draw on academic studies of aid's impact. But like their popular counterparts, academic studies about the impact of aid also fall along a wide range of views, some concluding that aid does not work, others that it does, with some drawing more qualified and nuanced conclusions. For instance, over the course of a few months in 2005, one academic review of the evidence of aid's impact uncompromisingly maintained that aid has neither increased welfare nor enhanced growth in poor countries, and thus it should be reduced rather than increased (Erixon 2005). One substantial book, *Overcoming Stagnation in Aid-Dependent Countries*, (van de Walle 2005) concluded that aid has had very little impact, while another, *The End of Poverty* (Sachs 2005), argued that aid should be increased because of compelling evidence (though not all the evidence) of its undoubted successes.

For their part, all those providing aid—official donors and NGOs alike—contend that, overall, the aid they provide themselves does indeed work, with most arguing that their aid works better now than it did in the past. Understandably, recipients are less forthcoming, reluctant to make any general comments on the impact of the aid they have received, but predominantly stating their wish to have more. It is against this backdrop that Part III of this book seeks to answer the fundamental question: does aid really work?

Most disputes about the impact of aid can be traced back to two sources: evidence and methods of assessment. As this chapter explains, there are significant gaps in the data, its coverage and reliability, and uncertainties in the methods used to track and assess the relationship between the aid provided and the outcomes achieved. These need to be borne in mind continually when drawing conclusions and making generalizations about aid's impact, though, in practice, many are forgotten or ignored.

Methodological challenges and data-gaps

DATA QUALITY AT THE NATIONAL AND INTERNATIONAL LEVEL

Assessments of the impact of aid are only as good as the information on which they are based.[1] Yet there are problems, many of them serious, with the accuracy of large amounts of data from which confident conclusions are drawn.

Does aid make a difference at the national level or, even more widely, at the international level? Tracing the overall relationship between aid and its impact at the national and international levels requires accurate, reliable and consistent data over time and across countries of both the amounts of aid provided and the different variables against which the relationship with aid is to be tracked, especially changes in poverty levels, and differences in overall economic growth rates. There are problems on both counts.

Take aid data first. As already discussed in Part I, there are serious questions about the accuracy of some official aid data, and usually significant differences between amounts of ODA recorded by donors and the amounts of aid that recipient governments receive. Similarly, conclusions about the overall impact of development aid remain open to question when, as is common, the aid figures used in most analyses do not include NGO activities funded by private donations (now in excess of $10bn a year), and ignore humanitarian and emergency aid.[2] Likewise, most aggregate studies assume that the impact of aid takes effect instantaneously, often at once, though sometimes two or three years after it has been provided. In reality, however, different forms of aid—supplying medicines, building schools, hospitals or roads, providing schooling or enhancing the capacity and efficiency of government departments—all take different time-periods to have an impact. Thus, any simple time-specific assumptions must necessarily result in inaccurate conclusions.[3]

It is not only the accuracy of aid data which creates problems for assessing relationships between aid and expected outcomes. If aid is meant to have a positive impact on the overall growth of a recipient economy, then data on growth need to be accurately assessed. Even in industrialized economies, national accounts data are known to be inaccurate.[4] They will be even less accurate in underdeveloped countries, one of the characteristics of most poor countries being the poor quality of their national accounts statistics (see Deaton 2005).

Even greater problems arise in relation to trying to pinpoint the numbers of people who are poor and trends in poverty over time. In spite of massive efforts to improve data-gathering in recent decades, we still do not know accurately across the poorest countries of the world the numbers of poor people, changes in the number of people living in poverty, those living in permanent or chronic poverty, and those for whom poverty is more of a temporary or transitory problem than a permanent feature of their lives. Much of the poverty data that are used, and widely quoted, are based on estimates—some extremely crude. For instance, World Bank statistics on the number of people in the world living on less than $1 or $2 a day are based on information from only 79 countries. According to the United Nations, for over 65 countries (mostly the poorest) there are no data on the numbers of people living in poverty; for almost 100 countries, no data which record changes in poverty over time; and for 115 countries, no data are collected which monitor changes in child malnutrition (as recorded by weight), a key indicator of poverty (UNDP 2005:336).

There are huge differences in the assessments made of the incidence of poverty, such differences arising from the different ways that poverty is defined. Measures of poverty using income or consumption data differ markedly from measures based, for instance, on capability approaches, which focus on out-comes linked to the quality of life, such as longevity, health and knowledge.[5] One study in Latin America found that the numbers of people living in poverty ranged between a small 17 per cent and a massive 77 per cent depending upon how poverty was defined.[6] Likewise, World Bank data on the number of people living in poverty at the turn of the century—2.8bn people living on less than $2 a day, 1.2bn on less than $1 a day—sit alongside far fewer (crudely) judged to be chronically poor, estimated to be between 300 and 420mn people.[7]

Against the backdrop of these sorts of data-gaps and data problems, we should be wary of studies which make bold assertions about aid's overall impact on growth and poverty, especially at the country and cross-country level.

PROJECT-LEVEL DATA-GAPS AND METHODOLOGICAL CHALLENGES

Moving down to the level of discrete aid projects, firm conclusions about impact require accurate information on performance and progress, which in turn must be based on accurate baseline data (gathered at the start of the project) and the systematic monitoring of performance over time until the project is completed, and even beyond. Without reliable data, it is not possible to record change accurately, and hence to assess impact. However, in a recent stocktaking of data quality and methods, the Washington-based Center for Global Development (CGD) has drawn attention to the significant gap between the quantity of material that is available purporting to assess the effectiveness of aid and the quality of the data, adding that systematic, rigorous and independent evaluations, even of aid projects, remain rare, and perhaps more worryingly, that few donors have developed systematic evaluations of their projects.[8]

Some donors have a longer history of evaluation than others, and among those acknowledged as having the greatest experience are the United Kingdom and Sweden. Yet for the UK, its *Development Effectiveness Report 2001* pointed to the clear gap between what DFID aspires to achieve and what it can confidently demonstrate it has achieved. It judged that until DFID gives a 'high priority to performance assessment and evaluation, this problem' will remain (Flint *et al.* 2002: 6).[9] Likewise, a review of a sample of Swedish human rights and democracy projects judged that due to data inadequacies, only 7 per cent could be evaluated properly (Poate *et al.* 2000).

Even if there were few data-gathering problems, the task of assessing the impact of aid still remains a methodological challenge. A moment's thought will confirm that it is simply not possible to compare the well-being of the same poor community before aid is given and after it is provided, as there is no identical 'control group' against which to make comparisons. As it is not possible to compare the same country or community 'with' and 'without' aid, assessments have to be made by comparing conditions 'before and after' aid has been provided. If aid is provided to build a road or a school or, in the case of emergencies, to provide food to those lacking it, then the (tangible) benefits of such aid-funded projects compared with the pre-aid situation are usually clear.[10] However, a significant proportion of aid is used to help achieve far less direct outcomes, such as providing health education in order to improve the health status of poor people, or giving agricultural training in order to improve crop yields. It is not a simple matter to try to disaggregate the changes that are attributable to the aid provided from those changes occurring as a result of other factors and influences.[11]

The more complex and wide-ranging the aid project or programme and the longer it takes to implement, the greater are the number of factors, internal and external, which will influence the outcome, and so the less sure one can be of the link between aid and the ultimate outcome. Indeed, the impact of external factors on communities receiving aid could be so great that they swamp the effects of particular aid projects, especially small ones. For instance, aid funds could provide a rural family with a goat which produces kids to be sold commercially when they grow up, but a drought ensues and all the goats die. In such cases, paradoxically, projects can achieve their immediate objectives, but the general well-being and living standards of the community decline.

Alternatively, projects might fail to achieve their immediate objectives, but overall the living standards of communities rise. It is not uncommon for aid agencies to highlight cases of a community's economic status starting to improve, and to claim that this has been due to the aid they have provided, without any analysis of the relationship between the aid provided and the improvements which occur.

A relatively new way of trying to address some of these methodological problems has been to undertake random-sampling evaluations. These compare the outcomes of aid projects on beneficiaries with a random sample of those who haven't participated in aid programmes. However, to date, relatively few randomized evaluations have been conducted, and the approaches have not been scaled up sufficiently to provide firm conclusions beyond the level of discrete projects. Neither can the methods used be applied easily beyond discrete project interventions.[12]

Another major problem arises in trying to draw more general conclusions about aid on the basis of the evidence we do have of the impact of individual projects. Only a small fraction of the hundreds of thousands of aid projects and programmes that have been carried out have ever been formally evaluated. This leads to the problem of aggregation. How representative of the 'whole' are those projects which have been subject to more rigorous impact evaluation? Does the set of existing evaluations provide a fair representation or a biased picture of the whole, either suggesting that aid more generally has achieved its objectives, or that it has not? In most cases, we simply don't know. When donors choose to undertake deeper assessments of discrete aid interventions, more attention is generally paid to the findings and conclusions of the projects studied than to understanding whether the findings are typical of all such aid interventions. Likewise, when the results of groups of assessments and evaluations are brought together and synthesized, we usually do not know whether, or the extent to which, these (meta-evaluations) are themselves generally representative.

Grappling with these sorts of issues and problems is light-years away from the popular-press pundits whose approach to aid effectiveness predominantly involves little more than searching for evidence of the direct impact of one or two aid interventions and then drawing generalized conclusions about all aid. Yet donors also commit aggregation errors in the publicity they produce on their work.[13] Quite understandably, they present information to the public which predominantly recounts their aid successes. Invariably, this is done without explaining that the examples chosen do not necessarily represent an unbiased cross-section of all aid interventions they have funded or promoted. Indeed, most information departments in official agencies do not have these data themselves. Where it exists, it is tucked away in evaluation or related departments. They do not see it as their role to explain just how representative of all aid are the examples they provide to show that their aid works.[14]

Judging the impact and performance of aid: what questions need to be asked?

There is a rich and growing array of information describing what aid is doing and has done. This includes hundreds of thousands of studies which record the performance of small discrete development and emergency interventions (providing food, building schools, building roads, providing schooling, shelter and health care to improve lives and livelihoods). It also includes hundreds of country and cross-country studies which have analysed the wider impact of aid on key longer-term variables, notably those which capture changes in poverty, growth and aggregate development. Some studies look at types and forms of aid whose purpose is to contribute to development and poverty alleviation less directly, either by empowering individuals and building their capacities and capabilities to enable them to live productive lives, or by helping to build and strengthen the capacity of institutions, and governments, to enable them to perform more effectively and efficiently. Other studies examine the impact that aid donors have had in shaping and enhancing the policies of recipients at the local or national level, and the extent to which, and the ways that, the different attitudes of different recipients have influenced the impact of discrete aid projects or more complex aid programmes.

Even this brief listing of the very different things that aid assessments have focused upon highlights the complexities involved in trying to answer the seemingly simple question: does aid really work? Aid no longer simply involves providing goods, services or financial resources to fulfil a short-term tangible objective. Consequently, the question 'Does aid work?' cannot be answered simply by trying to find out if a collection of individual projects have achieved their immediate near-term objectives. This is necessary, but by no means sufficient. As aid has attempted to do more, different and less tangible things, deeper and more complex questions have been asked, and need answers. The following list details some of the key questions which are increasingly asked when trying to understand if aid does indeed work.

- Should aid be deemed to have worked if it fulfils its objectives immediately after an aid project or programme has been completed, but the achievements wither away over time and are not sustained? Conversely, should an aid intervention ultimately be judged a failure or success if first, it is assessed as a failure, but over time is found to achieve its objectives?

- Should aid be judged a success if it is only channelled to those able to use it well, excluding the millions of people who need it, but for whom there is less likelihood of its being used well?

- To judge that aid is effective is it sufficient merely to show that people in need are reached and that some assistance is given them, or does it also require the form in which aid is provided (food, roads, education), and the amount of aid provided, to be more closely matched to the needs of those receiving it, involving the beneficiaries in decisions about how aid should be provided?

- Is it sufficient for aid to be deemed to have worked merely on the basis that it arrives and contributes to meeting the urgent needs of those assisted, or should it also be judged in relation to how efficiently and cost-effectively it is provided? If so, how should this be assessed?

- Growing amounts of aid are provided to achieve a purpose beyond the outputs of a particular aid project or programme. To what extent should aid be judged in relation to the outputs of the project or the anticipated outcome? For instance, if aid is used to send people on a course, receive training and receive a certificate, should aid be judged a success if all students pass but fewer than half find gainful employment?

- More and more aid is given to strengthen institutions and capacities and improve governance. Should aid be judged successful if the capacities of governments and their institutions are built and strengthened with aid monies, but their economies still fail to grow and poverty remains high?

- Is aid a success if it is provided to meet immediate poverty needs and does so, but in so doing diverts resources from uses which would have stimulated faster growth, thereby prolonging low levels of growth, and requiring even more aid than if it was used (successfully) to hasten the process of wealth creation?

- Is aid successful if small projects achieve both their short- and long-term objectives, and if aid at the national level contributes to overall poverty reduction and higher growth, but, as a result, particular poor ethnic groups, or women and girls, are absolutely or relatively disadvantaged, and become more marginalized as a consequence of the aid-giving process?

- Should aid be judged a success or failure if most discrete aid projects are successful but the country fails to reduce poverty or to grow, or conversely, if poverty levels fall and growth rates increase but most discrete aid projects do not appear to be sustainable?

- Is aid to be judged a success or a failure if the aid funds achieve their immediate objectives but the wider policies which donors promote as part of the 'aid package' are found to be misguided?

- Does a positive overall assessment of aid impact require all these issues to be examined or only some? Does it require that all aid provided by all donors 'works' in all aid-recipient countries, or only a particular proportion of aid? If aid provided by one donor to a particular aid recipient was found to have been largely effective, but this donor contributed less than half of the total aid given to this recipient, and all other aid is judged to have been relatively ineffective, what importance should be attached to the first donor's claim that 'its' aid had worked? Should aid be judged a success if, say, 5, 10, 15, 20 or 40 per cent of it was deemed to have been a failure? Where should the line be drawn? Or should overall judgements of aid be made in the way a football game is decided, where a side wins if it scores more goals than the opposition, no matter how many goals it concedes in the process? Who should make such a decision: donors, recipients, supporters of aid or its critics?

The history of aid and the evolution of aid-giving confirm that *all* these different questions and dilemmas are relevant to the enquiry into whether aid really works. Indeed, the process of asking increasingly challenging and difficult questions is probably an indicator of the maturation of the debates about aid effectiveness. In the early days of aid-giving, aid mostly consisted of discrete projects. Today, a growing share of development aid is provided as programme aid, sometimes to boost aggregate government expenditure, and often linked, directly and indirectly, to different forms of policy conditionality. Thus, the long-term and more systemic effects of aid—including project aid— increasingly need to be incorporated into the assessment of whether aid works. Likewise, before the Rwanda genocide, the impact and influence of aid on ethnicity was hardly considered relevant to an assessment of its impact. Now, few would challenge the need to incorporate an ethnic dimension into an overall assessment of aid to ensure that aid does no harm.[15] Similarly, as the adverse effects of gender-blind development and gender-blind aid interventions have been more clearly understood, the gender dimensions of aid interventions have, rightly, been seen as essential in both providing aid and in assessing its impact and effects. The implication of these trends for judging the impact of aid can be simply put. The question 'Does aid work?' is necessarily complex; it usually cannot be answered simply, with a yes or no.

Perversely, however, a more comprehensive approach to providing and assessing aid increases already existing data problems, making it even more difficult to know precisely what impact aid has had. Equally, adopting a more comprehensive approach to assessing and giving aid makes it increasingly necessary both to assess aid and to decide where and how it should be provided against the backdrop of our understanding of the process of how growth and development occur, and how they might be stimulated to reduce poverty more rapidly and in a sustained way. In turn, this means that aid donors (as well as those who assess the impact of aid) need to know what constitute the key ingredients of growth and development, what is most needed to enhance development and accelerate the process of poverty reduction and thus where aid should be concentrated and deployed. Unless aid is linked to and assessed in relation to the wider development process, it risks being judged as successful, or unsuccessful, but possibly irrelevant. Likewise, once the factors which constrain growth and development have been clearly identified, the role of aid in contributing to the processes of growth and development ought to be far clearer.

Understanding how aid contributes to growth and development

There is broad agreement today that economic growth and wealth creation are essential to development and poverty eradication, but few would now argue that they are sufficient.[16] There is far less agreement, however, about precisely what are the sources of growth and what are the key factors which contribute to development. This uncertainty is due, in part, to the growing recognition over successive decades of aid-giving that growth and development are extremely complex processes. The literature analysing the sources and causes of growth and development is substantial, and it continues to expand at an ever-increasing pace.[17] Not surprisingly, those factors believed to drive growth and development include many elements that have been of central concern in the provision of development aid.

As discussed in Chapters 2 and 3, initially, growth and development were seen to be constrained by skills gaps and shortages, infrastructural weaknesses, and a lack of capital, savings and foreign exchange. Later, impediments to growth and development were seen to be caused, in part, by low capacity and insufficient capabilities of people and communities: by poor health and education. The list then expanded further to include the following: patterns of distribution of wealth and power; market failures; weak and misguided macro-economic policies and distorted incentive systems and structures; and a lack of openness to the international economy. Increasingly, donors have also accepted that it was mistaken to focus on such a small number of largely economic and financial policy instruments to try to engineer higher growth rates, effectively downgrading aid's direct role in assisting poverty reduction. The focus has shifted back to what was seen as the pivotal role of the state in accelerating growth and enhancing the development process, and official development aid was increasingly focused on trying to enhance and strengthen this role. Most recently, conflict, weaknesses in government institutions and in governance, and a lack of commitment to pro-poor development strategies and policies by aid-recipient governments, have been identified by donors as major factors reducing the overall potential impact of aid.

Long though it is, this list of constraints is far from complete. Recent studies have drawn attention to other factors judged to be important to growth and development processes and to influencing efforts to reduce poverty. This list, too, is long. It includes technological change, innovation, entrepreneurship and productivity; the role of ethnicity, culture and religion; a country's geographical location, its environmental attributes and its climate; the influence of and perceptions of a country's history, including (where relevant) the inter-action between the present and the pre-colonial and colonial past; and the size and geographical distribution of the population. For many analysts, a central feature of development is that it is a dynamic process involving structural change and transformation. For development to occur requires a number of even more intangible attributes and competencies including flexibility, the ability to manage risk and cope with vulnerability and external shocks. It also requires the capability and capacity as well as the skills to manage change and the effects and consequences of adjustment, not least for those adversely affected by adjustment processes.[18]

In short, growth, development and poverty reduction are processes of political economy, tempering what is needed and wanted with what is possible. Policies and strategies are informed by theory and evidence, but are implemented against the backdrop of uncertainty and ignorance.[19] Growth and development are not merely very complex processes, but far more complex than the relatively narrow, even if increasingly extensive, range of interventions that official donors have chosen to fund to stimulate growth and development in order to help reduce poverty. Indeed, some of the most complex econometric models established to measure the different sources of growth (which is far narrower than development) acknowledge that a major part of growth still remains unexplained.[20] This suggests that there are no simple answers or simple approaches to growth and development likely to be applicable across all countries: there is no one-size-fits-all blueprint for development and poverty reduction. This is certainly the view of a number of specialists in economic growth. For instance, one of the most respected analysts of growth, Dani Rodrik, recently noted that 'the kind of certainty and consensus that existed 10 or 15 years ago about the appropriate policy framework for economic growth has almost disappeared' (2005: 1). Likewise, former senior World Bank economist William Easterly judges that the 'problem of making poor countries rich was much more difficult than we thought. It is much easier to describe the problems facing poor countries than it is to come up with workable solutions to their poverty' (2001a: 291).

There are important conclusions to draw from this overview of the complexities of development for the present discussion of the effectiveness of development aid and an assessment of how well it works. One is that if development processes are complex, then the ways in which aid interacts with and influences the development process are also exceedingly complex. A second is that if the most effective way to promote growth and development processes remains provisional, experimental and difficult to quantify, with no clear and simple template available across countries, then the way that aid might further these processes likewise remains imprecise, continually open to change across countries and within countries, at different periods of time. As Joseph Stiglitz recently put it, 'If there is a consensus today about what strategies are likely to help the development of the poorest countries it is this: there is no consensus' (2005: 1).

Against this backdrop, it would seem to be over-ambitious to believe it possible to quantify precisely the relationship between aid and growth, aid and development and aid and poverty reduction across countries and, possibly, even within a particular country. Even if aid were provided in very large quantities, on its own it could not be expected to make the crucial difference to overall development: there are too many other factors, some uncertain and unpredictable, which influence development performance. But in aggregate, its contribution remains comparatively small for almost all aid-recipient countries. In the year 2003, overseas development aid (ODA) accounted for less than 5 per cent of gross domestic product (GDP) and total capital investment in all developing countries, and for less than 20 per cent of GDP in both the least developed countries as a whole and across Sub-Saharan Africa. ODA per capita across all ODA-eligible countries has remained fairly constant over the last ten years, accounting, in 2003, for less than $10 per head per year, and less than $35 a head in the least developed countries overall and across sub-Saharan Africa. Amongst the 117 poorest countries ranked by the United Nations, only seven received ODA in excess of 20 per cent of their GDP in 2003, accounting for less than 10 per cent of all ODA disbursed and less than 2 per cent of the population of these countries.[21]

There is, however, a crucial difference between saying that it is difficult, if not impossible, accurately to assess the relationship between overall aid and growth and development processes at the national level, and arguing that aid is therefore unimportant or irrelevant to such processes. Potentially, aid could make a difference; indeed it could contribute significantly to accelerating growth, enhancing development and reducing poverty. It could do this by filling some crucial immediate gaps identified as constraining development and wealth creation at particular points of time, by helping to meet some key, immediate and urgent needs, by helping to fund initiatives to assist those adversely affected by structural changes, by contributing to knowledge about what growth and development strategies and policies to pursue and what capabilities and capacities are needed to implement them, and by contributing to a range of initiatives which more indirectly influence patterns of growth, such as by helping to strengthen the power of the excluded, and enhancing accountability and transparency in decision-making. At a project or sectoral level, aid's potential for making a difference could also be huge to the extent that it is able to help fill gaps, meet particular needs, and strengthen capabilities and capacities to enhance sustainability. It is in this role that aid has recently been called a potential catalyst for development (see Pronk *et al.* 2004). Our review of the evidence should help us judge the extent to which this potential has been realized.

Expectations about the impact of aid

Today, both donors and the public remain extremely sensitive to the findings of studies which conclude that it is not possible to show in general terms that at the aggregate level aid works, that it does indeed contribute to growth or to the reduction in poverty. A number of studies have been produced which conclude that the available data and methods do not permit us to judge whether or not there has been a positive, causal link in aggregate between the aid provided, and growth, investment, or poverty trends.[22] The reaction to these studies from within the aid community and among official aid donors, and to earlier ones, has not merely been adverse, but hostile. This seems to be because studies which are unable to point clearly to a direct and positive effect of aid on development in aggregate are not deemed to be neutral. They are perceived as providing support for those who assert that aid does not work, and an inability to prove that aid in aggregate has worked is viewed as a *sufficient* reason for not increasing aid in the future.[23]

Such a perspective appears particularly strange when one reflects for a moment on the nature of aid. As its name implies, aid is something which is added: it is something which increases and is additional to what the aid-recipient country currently has—providing an increase in resources, or an increase in knowledge, know-how or skills. Consequently, if it is difficult, or impossible, to provide the evidence to show precisely how these additions have benefited the recipient, there would seem to be a more compelling need to show how aid—perversely—has had a detrimental (subtracting) effect. The more reasonable default position on the impact of aid is that it should be viewed as helpful, unless it can be shown not to be beneficial, rather than (as frequently occurs at present) it is assumed to be detrimental unless proved to have been effective.

It is not difficult to suggest a variety of ways in which aid might have an adverse or neutral, rather than an additional, effect on the recipient. For instance, aid could be provided in such small amounts that it is incapable of making a difference, like drops of water sinking into the sand. Alternatively, aid could be provided in amounts sufficiently large, but be channelled into uses that are irrelevant, marginal to poverty reduction or unsustainable, including being diverted and used for personal gain. Likewise, aid could be judged harmful if it could be shown to feed or fuel corruption or if it sets off or stimulates other secondary adverse effects which are so pronounced as to eclipse its more immediate beneficial effects. For instance, instead of filling a resource gap, aid could be a disincentive to save or could even stimulate a fall in taxes, leading to an even larger domestic resource gap. Aid could induce a rise in the exchange rate (the so-called Dutch disease effect), making it more difficult to expand exports and thus constraining rather than enhancing overall wealth creation, or the release of foreign funds onto the domestic economy could stimulate a damaging rise in inflation. Similarly, donors could make a faulty analysis of the factors contributing to growth, development and poverty reduction, linking the aid they provide to policies which increase rather than reduce poverty. Aid could have any or all of these adverse effects on the aid recipient. What is important to this discussion of aid impact is that if these are the practical and concrete effects of aid—rather than the assertions of what consequences aid could or might have—then it is necessary to provide evidence to show these effects.

This requires evidence, in turn, not merely of an association of aid with perverse outcomes, but evidence that the detrimental outcomes have been caused by the aid provided and not by other factors. For instance, if aid is provided to a recipient when its economy is contracting, it does not necessarily follow that it is the provision of aid (or more aid) which is causing the economy to decline. Indeed, if donors are providing aid to a poor country and have become aware that the economy is in difficulty, a common first response might be to consider providing more aid to help cushion the adverse consequences of this decline.

Not only has our changing and increasingly complex understanding of the role of aid in contributing to development altered the way that aid is provided and assessed, it has also biased the assessment of aid's performance—in a negative direction. Many aid interventions, especially larger and more complex ones, can last many years, even decades—an average agricultural project can last for 15 years or more. When they have been completed and come to be evaluated, the assessments will be likely to incorporate some aspects or dimensions of development deemed to be important at the time of the evaluation, but not incorporated into the original design of the project. The result is not merely to build a critical (negative) bias into the evaluation of particular projects. The time-lagged nature of evaluation means that there is a wider systemic bias: current studies of aid effectiveness provide a better guide to the performance of yesterday's aid than they do of today's. Additionally, the setting in which aid is provided is likely to produce an additional negative bias when compared with projects in other contexts. Thus, aid is provided to countries whose core characteristics frequently include weak or non-functioning markets, skills shortages, an underdeveloped infrastructure, and fewer and less-developed institutions than in the industrialized world. These factors are likely to impede the efficient use of aid as well as the overall outcome, when compared with the use of such funds in a more developed country.

For instance, as the sustainability and gender dimensions of aid projects have been accorded growing importance, these dimensions increasingly have been included in the development of new projects, and in the assessment of *all* (past) projects. Unsurprisingly, assessments of projects which started before such emphasis was placed on gender and sustainability will likely highlight weaknesses of many older projects when judged against these (new) criteria. Similarly, many earlier aid projects were not directly linked to poverty reduction or carefully targeted on poor people, but today poverty usually provides the core purpose around which projects are chosen and shaped. For almost all current assessments of aid, poverty is a key criterion against which they are judged, including those drawn up and implemented before these changes occurred.

Finally, it has been argued by some aid practitioners that it is inappropriate to expect most aid to be successful, as this misconstrues a key purpose of development aid, namely its experimental nature. For example, on the basis of her experience administering aid to Africa for USAID, Carol Lancaster contends that a large proportion of aid (to Africa) remains predominantly experimental, and thus the default expectation is that such aid will result in a relatively high rate of failure (1999a, b). Providing that lessons are learnt from these failures and the experiments not repeated, the failures of particular projects should not be taken as sufficient grounds for concluding that aid will not work in the future.

Against the backdrop of this discussion of methodological challenges and data problems involved in assessing aid, the rest of Part III examines the evidence.

11 The impact of official development aid projects

It is twenty years since the last rigorous attempt was made, by Robert Cassen and Associates, to assess comprehensively the impact of official aid. In their publication, *Does Aid Work?* (Cassen and Associates 1986), they judged that the majority of aid had been successful in term of its developmental objectives, and that over a wide range of countries and sectors, aid had made a positive and valuable contribution. Nevertheless, they identified weaknesses and failures of official aid, including the low yield or complete failure of many aid projects in Africa, where livestock projects were identified as particularly prone to failure, as well as in other low-income countries. They indicated that aid had both helped and harmed the poor (without being drawn into stating which outcome was dominant), though most aid was not directly targeted at poor people. As for technical cooperation, accounting for a fifth of all ODA, most of this was judged to have been reasonably successful.

The study included a number of assessments of the impact of aid at the country level, including case studies of India, South Korea, Mali, Malawi and Kenya. With the exception of a few countries, such as South Korea, where the conclusion was that aid had worked, the study was reluctant to make generalizations on overall impact, focusing, instead, on particular successes such as aid to agriculture in India, and the contribution of aid to agricultural research and food production. The Cassen study looked at the evidence of impact from global (cross-country) studies and concluded that, overall, these did not show anything conclusive, either positive or negative, about the relationship between aid and overall economic growth.

In sum, the conclusions about the impact of official development aid were broadly positive—most aid does work—though the study pointed to significant data gaps, especially when moving beyond assessments of clearly defined projects, making it increasingly difficult to base broader judgements on firm data. As Cassen himself observed, the precise degree of the effectiveness of aid was judged ultimately to be unknowable (Cassen and Associates 1986: 8).

Twenty years on, do we know any more about the impact of official development aid (ODA)? What is the evidence of the impact of new and different forms of official development aid? Is the evidence upon which judgements might be made any firmer than it was then, and is there any evidence to challenge or contradict the conclusions of Cassen and his colleagues? This chapter and the next four lay out the answers. The current chapter focuses on the impact of official aid projects.

Project aid: an overview

In spite of recent changes discussed below, the majority of ODA still consists of specific projects. Project aid consists of a myriad of different activities, but it is still dominated by funds channelled to interventions in the following sectors: health, education, rural development including agriculture, transport and power, housing, and water supply and sanitation, with smaller amounts channelled to industrial, mining, trade, tourism and cultural projects, and more recently, to democracy, human rights and peace-related projects. The main purpose of most ODA-funded development projects is to achieve specific and concrete outputs, with many projects fulfilling some form of 'gap-filling' role: providing resources, skills and systems which the recipient country needs and lacks. Many of these have clear, tangible objectives—to build or supply such things as roads, school buildings, textbooks, clinics, hospitals and medicine, water tanks, building materials or houses, computers and different types of machinery. Some projects deliver skills, skill training or know-how, either linked to the provision of tangible goods or on their own. Other projects—though still a minority—have less specific objectives: the relationship between the project inputs (what is provided by the donor) and the expected outcome is often less direct and sometimes less clear, such as in some gender-awareness-raising initiatives or peace-accompaniment programmes.[1] Today, a large and growing number of aid projects include some form of capacity development as a constituent part of the project.

Against the backdrop of a significant strand of public scepticism about the benefits of aid, the evidence of much project aid tells a very different story. For almost all aid projects, project completion reports are written up which record the results achieved. Cumulatively over time, hundreds of thousands of project completion reports have been written. Though not all agencies publish aggregate reports on their results, the larger agencies do, and it is likely that these broadly reflect the performance of all official aid projects. They show that the vast majority of aid projects work: especially where the intended outputs are clearly specified (the majority of cases), most projects succeed in producing or delivering their intended outputs. The proportion of projects which achieve their immediate objectives (probably the most common general way of judging success) varies between donor and recipient country, but recorded success rates range from around 70 per cent to about 85 per cent, with most donors recording in excess of 75 per cent. Furthermore, the reported rate of success of projects across leading agencies, already high, has improved over time: more and more aid projects are succeeding in meeting their immediate objectives than in the past, notwithstanding data from some agencies, including the World Bank and the Asian Development Bank, for the period from the mid-1970s to the mid-1980s, when the success rate of projects deteriorated. The following paragraphs briefly summarize the individual evidence produced by key bilateral and multilateral donors.[2]

On the basis of a review of 1,400 post-1990 project reports and a sampling of project completion reports, the UK Department for International Development's (DFID) 2001 aid effectiveness report concluded that in the year 2000, about 85 per cent of projects (in terms of expenditure) and over 75 per cent (in terms of numbers of projects) had been successful, broadly similar to the published results achieved by other official aid agencies. This compares favourably with success rates of less than 70 per cent (in terms of expenditure) in the late 1990s and a low of 65 per cent (by numbers of projects) recorded in the mid-1990s (Flint *et al.* 2002). Three years later, in 2004, these broad findings were confirmed. Likewise, broadly consistent with previous annual reports, the 2004 report on the activities of the US Agency for International Development (USAID) reports overall project performance success rates of 84 per cent— 81 per cent for economic programmes and 84 per cent for social and environmental ones. The 2004 annual report on Australian ODA by the Australian Agency for International Development (AusAID) similarly reported that more than 75 per cent of activities had received a quality rating of satisfactory overall, or higher.

Comparable success rates have been recorded by multilateral agencies. For instance, in its 2003 annual aid effectiveness report, the United Nations Development Programme (UNDP) reported on the overall performance of some 400 projects in the period 1999–2002. Eighty-four percent of projects had been successful or partially successful, compared with 56 per cent in the period 1992–8. The Asian Development Bank's 2005 report, covering almost 1,000 projects, gave an overall project success rate of 71 per cent, and the African Development Bank's rate, covering 59 projects, produced an overall success rate of 69 per cent by numbers of projects and 85 per cent by value. Perhaps of greatest importance, given its overall share of ODA, is the performance of the World Bank. The Bank's 2004 review of development effectiveness records the outcome of all projects in the period 2000–2004, consisting of data on over 1,200 projects with an estimated value of $92bn, though not all of these will have been financed with concessionary (aid) funds. It reported that 76 per cent of projects (by number) and 78 per cent of projects (by value) achieved a satisfactory outcome over the period 2000–4. Long-term data indicate that the success rate of World Bank projects was at a low of just under 60 per cent in the mid-1980s before it began to rise, and the gains have largely been sustained.

An upward trend has also been recorded in the overall rate of return on World Bank projects. The rate of return is an estimated measure of the economic contribution of a project to the economy which compares the overall benefits achieved against the costs of providing the assistance. Traditionally, aid projects which achieve rates of return of 10 per cent and above have been judged as successful, with those above 15 per cent highly successful.[3] Rates of return on World Bank projects rose from an average of 16 per cent in the 1980s to 25 per cent in the late 1990s. The African Development Bank recorded an overall rate of return of 10 per cent, and for the Asian Development Bank, almost 60 per cent of projects achieved *ex post* rates of return of over 12 per cent, with only 14 per cent falling below the 6 per cent level.[4]

The evidence also shows that project performance varies, often markedly, across different sectors and countries, though it is not entirely consistent between and across agencies. The most comprehensive study, though not necessarily reflecting the performance of projects of other donors, is provided by the World Bank. In terms of sectoral performance, the Bank's 2004 review of development effectiveness records comparatively high rates of success (over 85 per cent) for transport, rural development and financial sector projects, and comparatively low rates of success (less than 70 per cent) for environmental projects. When comparing recent performance (2000–4) with project performance in the period 1995–9, World Bank data record a significant, though relatively small, improvement in education sector projects (from 74 to 81 per cent), and in health and nutrition sector projects (which rose from 76 to 83 per cent). However, over the same period, major changes are recorded for water supply and sanitation projects, with successes rising from 52 to 74 per cent, and for social protection projects, where successes fell from over 95 to less than 80 per cent (2005b: 59).

Both the Asian and African Development Banks also report on project performance by sector. For its part, the Asian Development Bank also scores transport and energy as the best performing sectors (a success rate of over 85 per cent), but, together with its financial sector projects, agricultural projects score the lowest—indeed the recorded success rate was less than 50 per cent. In sharp contrast, the African Development Bank reported project success for 75 per cent of agricultural projects, by number, rising to 94 per cent by value, though, like the Asian Development Bank, its financial sector projects scored comparatively poorly, achieving only a 46 per cent success rate by number of projects and 63 per cent by project value.

A number of other donors have tried to assess the impact of their aid interventions on a sectoral basis and to draw generalized conclusions about impact. For instance, in 2001, DFID undertook a synthesis of its health sector projects, reporting that technically, the bulk of projects were well designed and effective and achieved their immediate objectives (Cassells and Watson 2001). DFID's report on support to the agricultural sector since 1990 was more explicit in concluding that 80 per cent of projects had achieved their outputs (DFID 2002). However, these aggregate studies shed insufficient light on the differences in the types of aid projects within a particular sector between donors and over time. For instance, within the agricultural sector, there has been a general shift away from the promotion of complex, integrated rural development projects, and a focus and emphasis on projects linked more directly to rural livelihoods, though some donors, such as the Netherlands, Norway and a number of the development banks, continued to promote and fund these more complex projects well into the 1990s, in part because of the more positive assessments of the impact of these interventions.

World Bank data disaggregated by region record the highest level of project successes in East Asia and the Pacific (almost 90 per cent) and the lowest in Sub-Saharan Africa, at just under 70 per cent. Trends in performance over time record substantial increases in project success in South Asia, where the satisfactory rating rose from 68 per cent of projects in the period 1995–9 to over 85 per cent in the period 2000–4, and in the Middle East and North Africa, where the figures were, respectively, 68 per cent and 85 per cent. However, project performance fell in the Latin American and Caribbean region, from over 85 per cent to less than 80 per cent (World Bank 2005b: 58). Regional analysis from the Asian Development Bank and African Development Bank is not entirely consistent with the Bank's data. In the case of the Asian Development Bank, less than 50 per cent of projects were successful in the Philippines and Papua New Guinea, but high levels of success were recorded in Mongolia and the Central Asian Republics. For the African Development Bank, there was a clear link between project success and per capita income levels, as well as sharp regional differences, with no projects at all deemed successful in West Africa and none deemed as failures in Southern Africa.

Detailed project performance

PROJECT AID SUCCESSES

The aggregate picture of project success, and variations across sectors and regions of the world, are built on information on hundreds and thousands of different projects. Most aid-funded projects continue to fill gaps in poor countries, the majority of which either would not be met, or would be met far less adequately, without aid. Indeed, a notable feature of most official aid-funded projects is the high quality of resources generally provided. Roads are constructed and maintained, schools, hospitals, clean water and sewage plants are built, medicines and schoolbooks are supplied, the terracing of land to protect soil erosion takes place, credit agency personnel are given the necessary skills and credit is provided, teachers are trained, computer systems are installed and function, and telecommunications equipment is installed and rehabilitated. People receive the skills specified, plans for local councils are drawn up as expected, magistrates complete training courses, election monitors are trained. The scale, range and extent of the cumulative successes of aid projects, in terms of what they have produced and what they have achieved, is difficult to convey fully. Boxes 11.1 and 11.2 provide just three examples of the significance of

---

BOX 11.1 TWO SUCCESSFUL EXAMPLES OF AID TO HEALTH PROJECTS

In 1956, there were over 10mn cases of smallpox annually and over 1.5mn people died of the disease, most cases occurring in poor countries. The World Health Organization (WHO) led a global initiative to rid the world of smallpox. It worked. In 1977, the last endemic case of smallpox was recorded (in Somalia), and in 1980, the World Health Assembly declared that smallpox had been eradicated. The WHO programme was partially funded by official aid funds, amounting in total to $98mn.

Onchocerciasis, or river blindness, has historically been prevalent in western and central Africa. A control programme was launched in 1974 in 11 West African countries with support from the WHO, the World Bank, the Food and Agriculture Organization (FAO) and the United Nations; in 1995, this was extended to a total of 19 countries. By the year 2002, transmission had been halted in 11 countries. More than half a million cases of blindness had been prevented, 18mn children in the programme area are now free of river blindness and 25mn hectares of arable land have become available for resettlement, with the potential to provide food for 17mn people. The project would not have happened without the support of official aid donors who, together, provided a total of $560mn of official aid funds to support the project.

Source: Levine *et al*. (2004).

BOX 11.2 THE CONTRIBUTION OF AUSTRALIAN AID TO EDUCATION IN PAPUA NEW GUINEA

In the ten-year period from 1992 to 2002, Australian aid played a key role in expanding the quantity and quality of education in Papua New Guinea, where the number of children attending school doubled from 510,000 to one million.

Aid played the major role in providing education opportunities for about 270,000 children in 4,200 schools. At the beginning of the ten-year period there were no elementary schools.

Australian aid funds financed the upgrading of nine high schools, raising grade 11–12 enrolments from 1,000 to 5,000 per year, and provided essential textbooks to 272 secondary schools.

Australia led in expanding the number of teachers trained from 600 to 1,000 a year, and provided scholarships for 2,000 secondary and 150 tertiary-level students to study in Australia.

Aid played a key role in improving the quality of education through skills transfer, production and distribution of new learning materials, and support for the introduction of a life-skills-based curriculum to replace the previous academic Australian-based curriculum.

Source: Fallon *et al*. (2003).

some of the achievements of project aid, the first at the international level, the second at the national level. Thousands of other examples of aid projects meeting their immediate objectives could easily be given.

PROJECT AID FAILURES

Notwithstanding the high success rate of official aid projects, there have also been failures. Overall, donor data suggest that between 10 and 25 per cent of projects have failed to meet their immediate objectives, or have had extremely limited success, or else the data on the projects have been so poor that it has not been possible to form a judgement on project performance. As noted above, particular types of project, such as transport projects, are more likely to be successful, as are aid projects implemented in particular regions or countries. Dramatic and outright project failures, where there is nothing positive to show for the aid provided, are probably quite rare, and certainly rarer than in the past. However, there are demonstrable cases of failure, and in aggregate, these involve significant sums of money, almost certainly amounting to hundreds of millions of dollars a year. Likewise, there are cases (though too few have been documented) of project money and resources going astray, being channelled into uses other than those intended, including the lining of pockets, as well as cases of aid contractors inflating prices to reap unwarranted profits. Donor project-completion reports and evaluations increasingly record project failures, though they don't record the diversion of funds through corrupt practices, and a growing number of these are to be found on the websites of donor agencies and official auditors, even if they are often 'hidden' in the more technical evaluation-report pages of such sites.[5]

For instance, a recent report on the impact of official Swiss aid in Nepal judged that only a minority of projects to support occupational skills and enterprise development, good governance, and peace had even partially achieved their objectives. Most were assessed as having very limited impact, and one as having achieved no progress at all—coded language for varying degrees of aid failure (Gayfer *et al.* 2005).[6]

Particularly graphic and transparent in their recording and description of project failures are the periodic reports of the European Court of Auditors, who are responsible for reviewing and assessing the projects of the European Commission. For example, a 2003 review of 30 aid-funded infrastructure projects, which the Auditors broadly concluded had been carried out correctly, highlighted a range of specific problems and failures. These included design faults in building roads, such as the failure of contractors to lay the correct road surface material; using incorrect base material on some roads, which led to the roads collapsing; building roads of the wrong width; and faulty surveying, resulting in 'all-weather' roads having to be closed due to local flooding.

In Madagascar, the Auditors reported on a project to build and equip seven provincial slaughterhouses which at 'project-end' remained unfinished, with the 38 per cent of buildings that had been completed remaining unused. During the construction phase, no visits to the project took place, and at the end, amounts of 60 per cent in excess of budget were paid to contractors for work that had been less than half finished. For the 30 projects reviewed, 60 per cent required design changes or were subject to quantity or quality problems, leading to a 25 per cent increase in price, amounting to an additional £100mn having to be spent.[7]

Dramatic though these sorts of illustrations of aid project failure are, in light of the evidence of success provided in project completion reports these sorts of failure represent only a minority of completed official aid projects.

Data quality and the sustainability of official aid projects

The bulk of the evidence of project performance and the high share of projects deemed to be successful is drawn, almost exclusively, from the evidence of the agencies providing the aid and funding the projects. How reliable is this? Does it give a fair and accurate assessment of the success of official aid projects? The answer is that the data almost certainly give an over-inflated picture of project success, and this bias towards recording success is compounded when we introduce the issue of the sustainability of projects over time.[8]

There are three immediate reasons why donor project-completion reports are likely to overestimate the success rate of official aid projects. First, for some agencies, the reports do not encompass all of their projects. For example, the 2001 DFID study estimated that project completion reports account for less than one-third of total bilateral aid expenditure (Flint *et al.* 2002: 40). Secondly, for some donors, there are large data gaps which limit the ability to make firm judgements about project performance. For instance, two recent reports on EC aid by the European Court of Auditors—one assessing food aid, the other the Commission's whole programme in Asia—stated that the absence of information and the vagueness of the achievement targets made reliable judgements on performance and impact impossible.[9] Data gaps are particularly important to overall assessment profiles because it is likely that a significant share of projects with limited data are among those that have not been successful.[10] Thirdly, there is evidence of donor self-assessments over-inflating success rates. For instance, the 2001 DFID study ran a quality control test on the results of project completion reports, and found that one-quarter of all reports may have overscored project achievements (Flint *et al.* 2002: 33).[11]

Similarly, the Asian Development Bank found that following in-depth reviews, it had to downgrade almost a quarter of its project ratings in the period 1995–9; later reviews indicated that by 2005, only 9 per cent needed to be downgraded, still a significant number.[12] Taken together, it is evident that success rates are likely to have been exaggerated, possibly quite significantly.

When assessment is broadened to encompass a time frame beyond the immediate completion of projects, the number of favourable donor-based assessments falls considerably. Both donor data and independent evaluations consistently report far lower levels of project success when the time period is extended: the positive impact of a significant number of projects cannot be sustained. The good news is that most evidence suggests that a rising proportion of projects are achieving positive scores in sustainability. The bad news is that the numbers of projects that are not sustainable still remain stubbornly high. The UNDP judges that the sustainability of its projects rose from 48 per cent in 1992–8 to around 60 per cent in 1999–2002, 20 percentage points lower than the 'immediate' success score (2003: 20). The World Bank also reports an upward trend, from around the 56–64 per cent range from the early to mid-1990s to the 78–84 per cent range by 2002–4 (2005b: 57). However, in 2004, the African Development Bank judged 36 per cent of its projects were not sustainable, accounting for 78 percent of funds disbursed, while the 2005 European Court of Auditors review of all EC projects across Asia came to the equally harsh conclusion that the sustainability of *half* of all projects remained in doubt. Likewise, a substantial external evaluation of the International Fund for Agricultural Development (IFAD) found that for completed or nearly completed projects, less than half were judged to be sustainable (Poate 2005: ii, 141).

What bearing do these considerations have on the overall levels of project success provided by donors? It is not possible to give a firm answer. But a guess, generous to donors, would suggest that the project success rates provided by donors should be reduced by some 10 percentage points to allow for data inaccuracy and agency bias, and by at least a further 5–10 per cent for the share of official aid projects which are sustainable over time.[13]

The wider picture

Project completion reports and the aggregated assessment of their success rates look exclusively at individual projects. They tell us very little about how the projects fit into and respond to the important needs of recipients, and nothing about relationships between projects, or the wider systemic effects of project aid.[14] Clearly a project is a waste of (aid) resources if it fails to achieve its immediate objectives, or does so ineffectively. But it is also a waste if it is not relevant to the needs of the recipient, if it duplicates or overlaps with what is already being done by other donor projects, or if the benefits which the project brings are excessively costly to provide. In situations where aid is made up of scores of different projects provided by a large number of donors, it becomes increasingly important to examine the systemic effects of providing so much aid in so many discrete bundles.

Donors have become increasingly aware of the need to ensure that the project aid they provide is relevant to the needs of recipients, that it is sustainable, and that decisions about projects should be harmonized to avoid duplication and overlap. However, donor rhetoric still runs ahead of donor practice in regard to each of these objectives. Notwithstanding the rising share of aid being provided as programme aid, project aid still remains the dominant form in which aid is provided. The continuing drive of donors to ensure rapid disbursement of aid funds, the continued reluctance of most recipients to provide a list of specific priorities for project funding, and the continued willingness of most recipients to approve a multiplicity of projects, some of which are not formally linked to their own needs, mean that official donor aid continues to fund projects that are not particularly high priorities, increasing the risk of projects overlapping with other projects.[15] Studies confirm that there is often a 'herd instinct' among donors to try to fund projects in 'fashionable areas', HIV/AIDS being a current example. Aid funds for HIV/AIDS remain inadequate;[16] what is at issue is whether so many donors need to fund so many individual projects. Similarly, within and across donor agencies there remain few tangible incentives to encourage officials to work at enhancing the sustainability of project aid.[17]

There are negative systemic costs to a significant number of donors providing aid in the form of large numbers of discrete projects. Discrete projects have long been criticized as being 'islands of development', often providing successes which are isolated from the world outside the project. But this gives only a partial picture: the vast majority of official aid projects are not isolated from the community in which they are located or the world beyond them. Indeed, a feature of most projects (except the very small ones) is that they draw external resources *to* themselves, either directly, using scarce local skills to help implement projects, or indirectly, through the interaction with government ministries and departments required to establish the project and report on progress. The greater the number of projects the more these cumulative costs to the recipient grow: a major impetus in the donor drive to switch from project to programme aid has been the growing realization by donors that these costs are often extremely large.

Another important cluster of costs of project aid consists of costs paid by donors in providing the aid above and beyond the direct costs of implementing the project. For example, donors need to pay (usually consultants) to undertake feasibility and appraisal studies before projects begin, to monitor projects while they are running, to write completion reports when they are finished, and (often but not always) to carry out overall evaluations of their impact. Increasingly, as project portfolios have diversified, donors have had to employ or contract the services of an increasing range and number of people with specialized skills to accompany projects. In recent years, more and more bilateral donors have increased the numbers of staff in their 'main recipient' countries: it is not uncommon for donors each to employ their own specialist staff within particular disciplines to watch over their own particular cluster of projects. Some idea of the scale of the indirect costs of project aid can be gleaned from published World Bank data. Between 1996 and 2001, the Bank's administrative budget averaged $1.4bn a year. One estimate suggests that when these costs are factored in, the total rate of return on Bank projects would fall by almost one-third.[18]

THE AGGREGATE IMPACT OF PROJECT AID

Aid donors, and the wider public, certainly need to know if aid funds for projects to build a series of health clinics, schools or roads, to provide school-children with textbooks, or to provide skills and resources to farmers to enhance incomes, and so forth, have been successfully implemented in cost-effective ways to achieve these near-term objectives. But they also need to know whether the buildings, roads, textbooks and training contribute to improving the lives and well-being of the recipients of the aid in sustainable ways. If they do not, it is, in many respects, immaterial whether the projects were successful in achieving their near-term objectives—why go to the expense of giving people skills if there is no real chance of them being able to make use of the skills provided? Hence a key question for project aid is whether it contributes to the achievement of wider development objectives. This is clearly a more demanding question, as it not only requires data and information beyond the narrow confines of the project, linking the outputs of the project to the underlying purpose of the project, but also requires the ability to judge precisely how the immediate benefits of the project influence wider outcomes.

What does the evidence tell us about the success of aid projects to help fulfil these wider objectives? The answer is that there is remarkably little evidence available which enables us to form judgements at either the sectoral level or economy-wide. For decades donors never really thought it was necessary to assess the wider impact of their projects: it was simply assumed that if the project was successful so were the wider impacts. In recent years, some donors have sought to fill these information gaps by commissioning studies and evaluations which examine the systemic relationships between aid inputs and wider outcomes. However, the dominant conclusion emerging is that there is still insufficient evidence for sound judgements about the relationship between projects and wider outcomes, especially at the sectoral level and beyond.

These problems and data gaps can be illustrated by considering the evidence we have of the wider impact of project aid on poverty reduction. As discussed in Chapters 2 and 3, the 1990s were a period when, increasingly, official donors began to scrutinize more closely the extent to which their aid was contributing to poverty alleviation. However, by the late 1990s one of the most comprehensive attempts to study the impact of European donor projects on poverty found that only a tiny minority of donors—less than 5 per cent in Zambia, less than 10 per cent in Zimbabwe and only 20 per cent in India—were targeting their project aid directly towards the poor, and only one-third were intending to help the poor indirectly. And for the tiny minority of projects which were directly targeted on poor people, the study found little firm evidence with which to assess impact (Cox and Healey 2000: 78).[19] On the basis of a small sample and far from robust evidence, the study (heroically) tried to assess the wider impact of projects on poverty. It examined four dimensions of poverty impact: changes in livelihood status, changes in resources, changes in knowledge and changes in the rights of the poor. It found, respectively, that 60 per cent of projects had a large or moderate impact on livelihoods, 90 per cent had a large or moderate impact on resources, 80 per cent a large or moderate impact on knowledge and 68 per cent a large or moderate impact on rights (Cox and Healey 2000: 88). Overall, it concluded that 25 per cent had a large impact, 48 per cent a moderate impact, and 27 per cent a negligible impact on the poverty status of recipients.

What is notable about the Cox–Healey study was that it tried to draw some firm conclusions about project aid and the poverty status of the recipients. Far more typical have been studies of groups of projects which simply conclude that data gaps prevent solid conclusions about poverty impact. For instance, in 2002 a comprehensive review of the impact of the loans provided by IFAD on the living standards of poor people examined evaluation reports from ten countries but concluded that there was insufficient evidence of the effects of IFAD projects on production, income and consumption for reliable judgements (Dabelstein 2002: 9). Two broad reviews of EC aid drew similar conclusions. A 2002 synthesis study evaluating EC support to the education sector in African, Caribbean and Pacific (ACP) countries failed to draw any firm conclusions, positive or negative, about the overall and wider impact on poverty of the aid provided, largely, claimed its authors, because of data inadequacies (Mercer *et al.* 2002: viii–x, 3–5, 15). A year later, a comprehensive review of all EC food security projects reported that the information available was so poor that it was simply not possible to know if the poorest people had benefited, and by how much.[20] Likewise, a 2002 review of the evaluations of UNICEF's education activities from 1994 to 2000 failed to draw firm conclusions on the impact of UNICEF's education programmes, attributing this both to the failure of projects at design stage to clarify what the core purpose was and how this might be assessed, and to the wide range of approaches adopted. As one author notes, 'Relatively few evaluations actually assess the extent to which education activities achieve their broader goals or objectives. A number of evaluations report disappointing or no discernable outcomes or impacts' (Chapman 2002: 17).

One reason why it has been so difficult to assess the wider impact of project aid is because assessments and reviews of the wider impact of projects have successively used criteria to judge impact which is not centrally, and often not even peripherally, important to the purpose of the aid when first given. The problem is well illustrated in the assessment made of three decades of Swedish support to the Tanzanian forestry sector. Having reviewed 30 years of documentation on the project, the first conclusion of the study was that there was insufficient information with which to assess impact. In particular, it was not possible to assess the contribution of forestry aid to poverty reduction, because the project had no poverty focus for its first 20 years, or to judge the impact of the project on empowering the poor or building capacity, as these dimensions were added even more recently—though some modest contributions were noted. Likewise, as it was only relatively recently that the gender dimensions of forestry-sector aid were considered important, it was not possible to draw firm conclusions on gender impact (Katila *et al.* 2003: 3, 30). In a similar vein, the 2001 review of DFID support to the health sector criticized DFID for not providing evidence of the equity impact of its health projects, while noting that very few projects identified equity of service as an objective (Cassels and Watson 2001: 1, sects. 11, 15).

In spite of these data difficulties, evaluations at the project level have been carried out which have been able to draw conclusions about the impact of aid projects. Among the most rigorous and most reliable in the conclusions they have drawn have been the results of randomized evaluations, the most robust method of evaluation, in which results of aid to communities are compared against a (random) control group which did not receive aid. However, these are relatively few in number. Banarjee and He (forthcoming) report the results of a worldwide search of randomized evaluations and came up with only around 60, covering every category of micro-intervention subject to a randomized evaluation which had positive outcomes. They included water and sanitation, health, education, micro-finance and infrastructural projects, some recording dramatic improvements in the well-being of poor people. They judged that these interventions could be scaled up to successfully absorb $11bn in ODA funds.

There is also a growing, though still small, number of in-depth evaluations and more rigorous audits of discrete projects, a number of which have attempted to assess the wider impact of project aid. Not surprisingly, given the large number of criteria against which to judge impact, these evaluations record a far lower level of success than project completion results, which merely report on outputs provided. For instance, the 2001 DFID aid effectiveness study reported the findings of independent evaluations of projects assessed between 1993 and 1999, which showed that only 30 per cent had been effective, though the sample size was extremely small (Flint *et al.* 2002: 22). Likewise, the 2002 report on DFID's support to the agricultural sector, which concluded that 80 per cent of projects had scored highly in terms of outputs, judged that only 63 per cent had achieved their broader purpose (DFID 2002: 2). Similarly, when the Asian Development Bank conducted 18 project or programme performance audit studies in 2004, it failed to classify any projects as highly successful, concluding that 56 per cent were successful and a further 39 per cent were partially successful (ADB 2004: 80).

Unsurprisingly, as more and more donors have focused their aid efforts on the Millennium Development Goals (MDGs), we are now beginning to see the start of what is likely to become a new wave of studies assessing the impact on and contribution of aid, including project aid, to the different specific goals agreed—those for health, education, water, etc.—as part of the overall donor effort to reduce by half the number of people living in poverty by 2015. One major multi-donor study has been completed which reviews the progress and contributions of donors to basic education, focusing explicitly on achieving the goal of education for all (Freeman and Faure 2003). The report affirms that external support has helped to expand access to basic education, thereby directly contributing to the achieving of the MDG on education, notwithstanding huge problems encountered in determining the overall contribution of aid agencies to basic education. However, it points to a substantial gap between aid needs and the allocation of aid resources, and expresses concerns about whether and for how long external funding to education will be continued, raising doubts about whether the advances will be sustained. The overall conclusion is overwhelmingly, however, that aid for basic education can help, does help and is effective.

What is particularly important about this report is that it challenges donors, and others, on the relevance and appropriateness of the aid provided. One of its main conclusions is that the emphasis being given to the achievement of basic education risks undermining other aspects of education seen as essential for poverty reduction. Indeed, it notes that there is already evidence that the emphasis on basic education has resulted in insufficient attention being paid to secondary and tertiary education, widely acknowledged to be essential if poor countries are to achieve sustainable development. It also criticized donors for giving so much prominence to trying to achieve immediate poverty-reducing outcomes. It suggested that their attachment to 'blueprints, templates and pre-scribed solutions' was undermining the efforts of recipient governments to develop durable education strategies, which, they argued, needed to be tailor-made and locally rooted.[21]

Summing up

Most official aid is provided as discrete projects. The available evidence suggests, quite strongly, that the clear majority of official aid projects achieve their immediate objectives. However, the evidence is far from comprehensive and is likely to be biased in favour of a more flattering picture of the impact of project aid than is probably deserved. Additionally, a significant number of aid projects have problems in sustaining short-term successes over a longer time period. What is more, current ways of aid-giving, which involve scores of different donors establishing and funding thousands of individual projects, is a very costly method of providing aid.

For many, however, the key test of whether project aid is to be judged successful lies in its wider impact, and ultimately, the contribution it makes to overall aims of meeting development goals, accelerating wealth creation and achieving faster poverty reduction. To this day, there remains a lack of evidence with which to draw firm overall conclusions about the wider impact of project aid, or the cumulative effects of groups of projects across different sectors, even though, over the past 10 to 15 years, a growing number of donors have given priority to trying to answer these questions. These issues are examined further in Chapter 13, when the impact of aid at the country and cross-country level is discussed.

12 The impact of programme aid, technical assistance and aid for capacity development

For most aid-recipient countries, aid in the form of discrete projects has always been accompanied and complemented by three other forms of aid: as programme aid, as technical assistance, and as aid to help build and strengthen the capacity of recipient-country institutions and individuals. This chapter looks at the evidence of the impact of all three of these types of official aid.

Programme aid

At its broadest, programme aid is all aid that is not project aid.[1] In recent years, two forms of programme aid have become increasingly popular among official donors. The first is the sector-wide approach (SWAp), where a group of donors support a particular sector, such as health or education, with the aim of helping to achieve the goals and objectives of a government expenditure programme to which they contribute, sometimes through pooling their aid funds. SWAps have been particularly prominent in support of the health, education, water and agricultural sectors.[2] The second is budget support, where aid funds are provided to boost aggregate revenue and increase overall spending. These funds are usually channelled to or through ministries of finance (general budget support), though sometimes they are provided to particular sectors (sector budget support).[3]

Programme aid is set to expand significantly in the future, both in absolute terms and as a share of total aid provided. An increasing number of bilateral donors, including Canada, Finland, the Netherlands, Norway, Sweden and the United Kingdom, have indicated their intention to use programme-based approaches (PBAs) as their preferred mode of cooperation for their key aid-recipient countries, while the United Nations' development and specialised agencies have committed themselves to support the general trend towards an accelerated use of sector and budget support.[4] Even today, PBAs are the dominant form of aid for many of the larger donors in a growing—though, in aggregate, still a comparatively small—number of aid-recipient countries.[5]

SECTOR-WIDE APPROACHES

Sector-wide approaches (SWAps) are of recent origin. They began to be formally promoted and implemented in the mid-to late 1990s: by 2001, they amounted to some 20 separate programmes; by 2005, the total number was probably still less than 100. SWAps differ from project aid in a number of key ways, not least in their complexity. Box 12.1 provides the basic details.

These differing funding arrangements merely add to the complexities of assessing the impact of programme aid provided through SWAp mechanisms. Assessing the impact of SWAps is made difficult because the pooled aid funds make up only a part, and often less than half, of the total budget available for the given sector, diluting the link between the pooled aid funds and the impact on the recipient's sector programme. More fundamentally, however, aid donors are not directly responsible for ensuring that the aid is used effectively. It is the aid-recipient line ministry, such as the ministry of education, which implements the sectoral programme, even if most donors (but not all) perceive it as part of their role to discuss and possibly help to shape the sectoral programme (see Riddell 2003: table 1). One aspect of SWAps that has been highlighted as particularly beneficial, especially in contrast with project aid, is the claim that

---

BOX 12.1 WHAT IS A SWAp?

Strictly speaking, a SWAp is not in itself a form of aid. What characterizes a SWAp is the engagement of donor agencies in supporting a recipient-government-led, sector-wide strategy, as well as agreement between donors and the recipient government on the broad parameters for implementing and managing the sector strategy within a medium-term expenditure framework. In theory, most donors would wish to see a rising share of all aid which is channelled to a particular sector being pooled to enhance the overall sector budget. In practice, matters are often more complex. Although most SWAps entail agreed partnership arrangements, which include funding, not all SWAps include pooled funding. Furthermore, and confusingly, some donors have continued to fund projects in the given sector, remaining outside the SWAp mechanism entirely, while others have contributed to the funding pool whilst continuing to fund discrete projects.[a]

[a] A 2003 mapping of SWAps in health covering 11 countries found that in three cases (Burkina Faso, Cambodia and Malawi) no aid funds were pooled, project aid funds accounting for between 30 and 58 per cent of total external funds provided. For the four countries with complete data (Ghana, Tanzania, Mozambique and Bangladesh) pooled funds accounted for between 10 and 19 per cent of sector budget, but a further 12 per cent of aid was provided outside the pooled framework (Jeffreys and Walford 2003: 8–9).

providing aid as part of pooled funding within the framework of a SWAp is far more efficient (costs less) than providing aid in the form of a large number of discrete projects.

The impact of SWAps

What does the evidence tell us about the impact of SWAps, and most notably aid funds contributing to SWAps? Like the assessment of project aid, it is comparatively simple to review the different outputs that line ministry programmes produce, but far less easy to judge the wider impact of the additional outputs to which the pooled aid funds have contributed, or the extent to which sectoral policies or external factors have influenced outcomes.

Not surprisingly, given the relative newness of SWAps and the difficulties of tracing the relationship between the programme aid provided through SWAps and its wider impact, there is a reluctance to make sweeping generalizations about their impact. Nor is it surprising that where judgements have been made, the evidence of performance and impact is varied. In an early assessment, Jones (2000) judged that, overall, sector-wide approaches have been disappointing, but that against this backdrop, health, education and road sector development had been amongst the best-performing, with successes recorded in Ethiopia, Ghana, Mozambique, Uganda and Zambia. For their part, Foster and Mackintosh-Walker (2001) confirm that many SWAps have directly, and sometimes indirectly, stimulated an expansion of overall sectoral funding, but that the picture is mixed in terms of direct benefits to the poor, with some of the benefits accruing to poor people attributable to other influences beyond the SWAp.

Where SWAps have constituted a major part of a sector's activities, and have been well managed, and where governments have been committed to them and relationships with donors have been fairly good, the gains can be significant. A detailed study of the Uganda education SWAp attributes to the SWAp a succession of tangible advances, especially to the quantitative expansion of primary education (Eilor 2004). In contrast, in mid-2005, the Mozambique education SWAp was being funded by only nine out of the 26 donors active in the sector, contributing only 5 per cent of aid funds for education. It was difficult to trace the direct effect of this SWAp on the performance of the sector as a whole. One study suggested that there had been few distinct benefits (Killick *et al.* 2005: 48). More positively, the establishment of some SWAps has generated debate and tightened sectoral analysis, as well as sharpening the focus on poverty in certain countries, such as Ghana and Bangladesh, where mainstream sector programmes led to the greater inclusion of previously marginalized groups. There is also some evidence of efficiency gains within line ministries, thereby improving the productivity of all resources, including the pooled aid funds.

There is little evidence to suggest that aid provided through a SWAp frame-work has lowered the cost of providing aid. The expectation has been for trans-action costs to fall over the longer term, though possibly after a rise in short-term costs. General reviews of the different transaction costs involved in implementing SWAps have found little to no evidence that these costs are lower (see Killick 2004). A World Bank study concluded that more (donor) staff time was involved in monitoring and participating in SWAps, and a study of the Namibian education SWAp concluded that the workload of the ministry was higher than before the SWAp was implemented (West 2003). Likewise, the detailed Uganda education study concluded that transaction costs for civil servants had undoubtedly increased, in part because of demands made by donors for monitoring and evaluation to be expanded and for more reports to be produced. In many countries, there still remains a gap between theory about how donors might interact with each other and the host ministry to produce an effective SWAp, and what happens in practice.

There are also questions about the systemic and longer-term effects of SWAps. The tangible and immediate gains in terms of expanding school enrol-ments in Uganda have come at a price. The 2004 report highlighted a series of concerns about the quality of education, describing different ways in which the SWAp had taken over the sector, distorting and eclipsing other education priorities. It expressed concerns about the sustainability of the scheme when up to 60 per cent of the sectoral budget was funded by aid (Eilor 2004: 150ff.). Evidently, a number of the sustainability problems which project aid has faced have been 'writ large' in SWAps and other forms of programme aid.

Perhaps the key message of the review of these assessments is that the expected benefits of SWAps lie beyond the form in which the aid is given. The effective implementation of sector strategies is dependent on a commitment and a national consensus to use the resources well and the capacity to plan, implement and monitor the deployment of resources, and to learn from suc-cesses and failures. If aid is provided as partial funding of SWAps in a support-ive environment, in sufficient quantities and with funds committed over time, the impact will tend to be positive. If aid is provided to a SWAp in small and fluctuating amounts, by donors who differ among themselves and with the recipient government about how to use the funds, against the backdrop of a sectoral ministry which has limited capacity, and a fluctuating commitment to use the funds well, the impact will be in considerable doubt.

AID FOR BUDGET SUPPORT

Over the past ten years, there has been a revival of donor interest in and the provision of budget aid, with most activity and interest centred on general budget support (GBS), where non-earmarked aid is provided to the government to boost state expenditures. Most recently, donors have been increasingly involved in what has been termed partnership budget support, where the funds provided constitute a 'partnership' with the recipient government involving dialogue concerning the overall thrust of expenditure, and the provision of technical assistance, in the wider context of greater harmonization and alignment of policies and practices.[6] The focus of the discussion here is on the impact of this form of aid, and in particular whether it has led, in practice, to tangible gains for those receiving it.[7]

The impact of GBS is of growing importance because of its rising popularity among both bilateral and multilateral donors; it accounts for an increasing share of total aid provided by a growing number of aid donors. For instance, in 2004, the EC approved disbursements of 1.7bn in the form of budget support, and in the ninth European Development Fund (EDF) is planning to disburse 30 per cent of all its aid in this form, totalling over 4bn. In 2005, over 30 per cent of the UK's bilateral aid was provided as budget support and the share is planned to rise fast in future years. Budget aid is of particular importance to large aid recipients. It accounted for over 20 per cent of all official aid to Ethiopia in 2003–4, and provided 20 per cent of all public expenditure funds in Tanzania. In the same period, budget support made up 31 per cent of all aid to Uganda, 25 per cent to Burkina Faso and 19 per cent to Mozambique. Other African countries to which budget support has been provided include Rwanda, Uganda, Zambia, Malawi and Mali. Outside Africa, donors have budget support programmes as far from each other as Nicaragua and Vietnam.

Predominantly, GBS is provided where donors believe there has been sufficient understanding and agreement reached with the recipient, typically on development and poverty-alleviating strategies, and where there is sufficient capacity to utilize the funds effectively as well as sufficient transparency to be able to monitor expenditures. Additionally, GBS is favoured over project aid, as it is said to be less costly to provide, oversee and administer. Does the evidence confirm these beliefs, and what impact does aid given as GBS have on development and poverty reduction?

The impact of budget support

Only a few studies of the impact of GBS have been undertaken, the most important being a three-year study commissioned by a consortium of donors in 2003. This involved the development of rigorous methodologies to assess and evaluate GBS, followed by substantive case studies in seven countries: Burkina Faso, Malawi, Mozambique, Nicaragua, Rwanda, Uganda and Vietnam. The report of the evaluation, hereafter called the Synthesis Report (Lister 2006), was published in mid-2006. Its approach and findings were closely linked to a study of GBS in Tanzania (Lawson *et al.* 2005), and to earlier detailed work on developing methodologies for assessing this form of aid (Lawson *et al.* 2003; Lawson and Booth 2004).[8]

Against the backdrop of donors eager to show that this form of aid 'works', these studies, in particular, express considerable reluctance to make sweeping generalizations about the merits and impact of GBS. The core problem is that GBS is extremely complex: it is exceedingly difficult to trace through the effects on poverty and income levels of adding aid to overall budgetary resources. The problems of attribution and causality are compounded when GBS amounts to a relatively small share of all aid provided, as remains the case even in countries where donor activity in providing and monitoring the effects of GBS is intense, as in Mozambique and Tanzania. In both of these cases, project aid remains the dominant aid form, making it next to impossible to try to isolate the direct contribution of budget support to aggregate economic performance and to changes in the incidence of poverty. Additionally, since part of the GBS 'package', including some of the aid provided, is directed at enhancing the efficiency and effectiveness of the public finance management system itself, the time horizon for trying to assess wider outcomes will necessarily be long.

The Synthesis Report cautions against generalizing from its findings, both because they may not be representative and because the way GBS is provided is still evolving (p. S15). Because GBS 'is not a distinct project, programme or even settled strategy, it is not possible to isolate it for evaluation' (p. 117). This warning echoes earlier ones given in the 2003 Evaluability Study, which stressed that it was not possible accurately to assess the impact of GBS on broad aggregates such as changes in income and poverty levels (Lawson *et al.* 2003). Notwithstanding these reservations, the evaluations do comment on different aspects of the impact of GBS. What is their assessment of the impact of GBS?

In terms of poverty impact, the Synthesis Report makes four initial points. The first is that the data are not sufficiently accurate to enable firm conclusions to be drawn. The second is that, even if the data were better, it would still be exceedingly difficult to trace the causal links between the provision of aid in the form of GBS and changes in the poverty status of poor people, especially their income levels. Yet, thirdly, it does argue that there has been a marked expansion in the provision of key services in most countries, which is due, in large measure, to the additional aid provided, though in some countries at the cost of sharp falls in the quality of those services (p. 69). Similarly, the Tanzania study suggests that the emphasis on quantitative expansion may have contributed adversely to the sharp deterioration in the quality of some services which have occurred (Lawson *et al.* 2005: 7). However, fourthly, in terms of enhanced services and service delivery, it notes significant differences across the different countries: improvements in Burkina Faso and Uganda that were probably linked to GBS; improvements in Rwanda, the cause of which was difficult to discern; improvements in Vietnam not directly due to the additional aid provided under GBS, and no marked difference in Malawi or Nicaragua (pp. 71–2).

But what are perhaps of wider significance and longer-term importance are the more general comments about GBS and poverty reduction in the Synthesis Report. In particular, the Report raises questions about the appropriateness of donors pushing recipients hard (or harder than they would wish to be pushed) to adopt policies with such a strong focus on addressing immediate and short-term poverty problems. In some places (e.g. pp. 86–9), the report suggests that the aid might have been better spent helping to address the underlying structural problems causing and perpetuating poverty—a view which, it is suggested, is more strongly held by the recipients than by the donors (pp. S9–13).

On a number of other issues, the Synthesis Report voiced less tentative, even strong, views about impact. It concluded positively that GBS had helped strengthen recipient ownership of development strategies (p. S16), though this conclusion sits uneasily alongside the comment that the emphasis on poverty was overly donor-driven. It also concluded that the technical assistance linked to GBS had had some successes, notably in strengthening the budgetary process, but that overall the results had been disappointing, in part because of poor management and planning (p. 58). It judged that GBS had helped or been associated with greater donor harmonization and greater alignment between donor and recipient policies. This conclusion resonates with the USAID synthesis report, which covered GBS in Tanzania and Timor-Leste, among other countries reviewed (Beasley *et al.* 2005: x). However, the Synthesis Report added that there remained scope for considerable further harmonization (p. S4).

Finally, the Synthesis Report noted that GBS is not only a complex mechanism for providing aid, but one which involves the recipient having to accept a range of conditions. The evident risk is that the process of providing, and receiving, aid as GBS involves so many different tasks and objectives that 'there is a serious danger of overloading one instrument, and of expecting it to achieve too many things too quickly' (p. S10). Overall, the Report's preliminary judgement was that out of the seven country case studies, GBS had been successful in five, with the overall impact in Nicaragua and Malawi unclear (p. S3).[9] Ultimately, however, it noted that the impact and effectiveness of GBS relies less on what the donors do and more on what happens at the recipient end, a view which resonates strongly with the conclusions of the earlier Tanzanian study (Lawson *et al.* 2005: 8).

One of the motives driving the move away from project aid was to reduce (sharply) the costs of providing project aid. Most evidence to date suggests, however, that this has not (yet) happened.[10] For both donors and recipients, transaction costs seem to have risen, not fallen.[11] The Synthesis Report found little evidence to suggest that the direct costs of providing GBS were lower than providing aid in other forms, though it did expect transaction costs to fall over time, especially if donors reduced the share of aid going to projects (pp. 51–2). An early assessment of the Mozambique programme expressed alarm about the huge burden put on recipient government officials by the donors (Killick *et al.* 2005: 17, 35).

GBS is meant to enhance the predictability of aid inflows. To date this has not universally happened. But has the increase in aid provided as budget support reduced the efforts of governments to raise revenue themselves—a somewhat contentious issue in the wider aid literature? The evidence is consistent, and much of it quite robust, in concluding that expanding untied aid, including aid provided as GBS, has not led to a fall in government revenue receipts. On the contrary, aid rises have often been accompanied by a significant rise in government revenue.[12] The Synthesis Report found no evidence to suggest that the increase in aid had been associated with any lessening of the effort to raise taxes, and, more broadly, it concluded that overall macroeconomic stability had been enhanced (pp. 67–8). These are important findings, countering the (strongly held) view that providing aid for recurrent expenditure will lead to a fall in revenue from domestic sources. Yet, these are hardly surprising results, as one of the reasons behind donors agreeing to provide GBS has been on condition that the aid given is additional to those funds raised domestically, notably through taxation.

Technical assistance

Helping to address skill and know-how shortages was among the first reasons why official aid was initially provided more than 50 years ago. Technical assistance (TA)—the provision of skills, knowledge, know-how and advice—continues to be a major component of official development assistance (ODA). Indeed for many agencies, especially key UN agencies, technical assistance constitutes their *raison d'être*.

According to OECD statistics, technical cooperation expenditure accounted for over 36 per cent of the bilateral aid (ODA) provided by the leading OECD/DAC donors in 2004, amounting to almost $20bn, with the share of TA out of ODA hovering around the 36–40 per cent level for the past 25 years. However, this figure excludes the technical support provided for the implementation of capital projects.[13] If one adds together this component of assistance with the technical cooperation provided by the multilateral agencies (which the bulk of OECD statistics omit), the total amount of aid (ODA) provided as technical assistance would rise to at least $30bn, accounting for 40 per cent of total ODA.[14] For some aid-recipient countries, the importance of technical assistance has been far higher than these figures suggest. For instance, in Uganda, the ratio of TA to total ODA reached a peak of 73 per cent in the late 1990s, though the share has subsequently fallen (Williams *et al.* 2003: 66–7). The key question to be discussed here is whether technical assistance works.

THE IMPACT OF TECHNICAL ASSISTANCE

Twenty years ago, the Cassen study, *Does Aid Work?*, concluded that the greater proportion of technical assistance has been reasonably successful (Cassen and Associates 1986: 240). Is this a fair assessment? The answer hinges crucially on the basis upon which the impact of TA is assessed. This, in turn, is linked to what one judges to be the core purpose of providing TA. As we shall see, there is a growing consensus—not least among many leading official donors—that TA, as traditionally given, has largely been a failure.

In the early years of aid-giving, technical assistance was perceived as being required predominantly to fill skills and knowledge gaps, the assumption being that these skills and this knowledge resided largely within donor countries, and that these needed (simply) to be transferred to the aid-recipient countries. The TA provided was either linked to other aid projects, providing the (essential) technical component and know-how in preparing and 'delivering' project outputs, or constituted free-standing initiatives focusing on training and skills transfer. TA is still provided in both these ways. Did it work in the past, and does it work today?

If the question is whether those who were meant to ensure that aid projects achieved their immediate objectives effectively carried out these tasks, and if those transferring skills, imparting knowledge and providing training did so, then the answer is predominantly 'yes'. As discussed in Chapter 11, the bulk of aid projects *have* achieved their immediate objectives, so it can safely be concluded that the TA linked to the projects also 'worked'. It is also likely that in the minority of cases where aid projects failed, this failure would have occurred for a range of different reasons, and faulty TA is unlikely to have been the only cause. For many decades and for a number of large donors, such as France, a large part of stand-alone TA consisted of sending tens of thousands of teachers from donor countries to teach, train and impart skills to hundreds and thousands of children and students, especially in secondary and tertiary education. It has also included individuals or small groups of skilled people, including consultants from private sector firms, installed in government ministries to undertake specific jobs.

Surprisingly, though there is little aggregate evidence of studies which have assessed the results and impact of these activities, there are few who would question the broad success of this type of aid: hundreds of thousands of schoolchildren and students have benefited from skills training. Though today the numbers of foreign skills trainers are sharply lower than they were in the pre-colonial and immediate post-colonial eras, the smaller numbers of usually more specialized trainers perform skills training functions that continue to meet needs and to achieve their immediate objectives. For over 40 years the London-based Overseas Development Institute (ODI) has been running its Fellowship scheme for graduate economists, placing them in key ministries in developing countries. The scheme remains as popular among aid-recipient governments today as when it first started. Nonetheless, anecdotal evidence from almost anyone who knows the technical assistance world would confirm that it has attracted its share of incompetent, ineffective and inefficient people, in both long-term and short-term assignments, as occurs in other areas of human endeavour.[15]

Hundreds of thousands of people have gained skills from this form of TA, and there have often been wider systemic gains. One example would be the assistance given to the Indian Institutes of Technology, which began in the 1960s and were largely funded by TA funds. These institutes have gone on to produce a generation of graduates who have helped fuel the multi-billion-dollar Indian software industry. Some TA has helped to fill institutional gaps, and again, at least many, and probably most, of these achieved their immediate objectives, though again, there is little systemic evidence to confirm this. A recent example of this type of TA would be the British project to revamp the Mozambique customs service, using serving or recently retired UK customs officials. This resulted in goods being cleared 40 times faster and a rise in customs revenue of 38 per cent within the first two years of the commencement of the project.

However, this positive picture provides only part of the story. TA has suffered from a range of problems. First, the costs of providing TA have always been high, often very high. On one estimate, by the late 1980s some 100,000 foreigners were employed in Africa, costing in excess of $4bn (quoted in Van de Walle 2005: 72). In the early 1980s, the costs of employing a foreign consultant for a year amounted to about $150,000 (World Bank 1981: 132); today, the figure would be more than double this amount. In a study of UN agencies, Jones and Colman (2005) cite evaluations which judged that the quality of TA provided by UNESCO was deteriorating, and they comment on the higher-than-necessary costs of some of UNICEF's projects, attributable to a failure to pay sufficient attention to cost-effectiveness. Official bilateral donors traditionally sought to fill skill gaps by obtaining TA skills solely from their own countries, some because this was a legal requirement, when alternative sources would certainly have reduced costs considerably.[16] There were few, if any, pressures on donors to reduce costs by monitoring, analysing and trying to keep down the overall cost of providing TA, and donors rarely, if ever, saw the need to discuss with recipients decisions that donors alone made about allocating and spending 'their' aid on foreign consultants.

A second problem has arisen when expatriate TA personnel have been required to undertake two tasks simultaneously: do a skilled job, and train nationals so that they can eventually take over from the (high-cost) foreigner. While this dual-purpose form of TA has sometimes succeeded in achieving both objectives, it has been far more common for the training component to be eclipsed by the priority usually given to completing the (technical) task at hand. It is thus not surprising to find a World Bank review concluding that most TA experts were selected for their technical expertise, not their gifts as mentors or trainers; indeed in some cases, foreign experts had no wish to work themselves out of a job (1996b).

A third cluster of problems with TA has been a duplication of activities, which has arisen because donors have not consulted with each other in recruiting TA personnel for projects whose purposes are overlapping. It was not uncommon in the past, and still not unknown today, for long-term consultants, working in a ministry to discover other consultants, located even along the same corridor, funded by other donors to do work overlapping with their own. There is also evidence of some TA-providing agencies artificially creating a demand for their services (Williams *et al.* 2003: 38ff.). Indeed, the World Bank has admitted that some of the worst failures of TA have occurred as a result of transferring skills that were wholly inappropriate to the needs of the recipient, in other words providing skills that were not needed (1996b).

Harsh though these criticisms of TA are, they are by no means the severest made. These have come from perhaps a surprising source—from many of the donors who have been providing TA. From the late 1980s, a consensus emerged within and across the donor community that the most important failures of TA lay less in what it did, and more in what it had failed and was continuing to fail to do. The focus shifted away from an assessment of the short-term impact of discrete forms of technical assistance to wider systemic issues. What was seen as of growing, and eventually of major, importance was the contribution that TA was making to the enhancement, development and durability of national skills and the development and functioning of effective and efficient institutions. This led in turn to a focus on the role of the institutions receiving the aid and, more broadly, the role of recipient governments into whose institutions TA funds were being channelled. This was because of the growing belief that the long-term strengthening of institutions could not occur unless the process was owned, championed, led and overseen by those receiving the aid. From this perspective, the role of donors came to be understood less as one of transferring skills, or providing or funding training to fill short-term skill gaps, and more as one of helping to build and contribute to the development of local skills capacity, including through the use of technical assistance, where this was requested. Reflecting this change of focus, the terminology changed from providing technical assistance (TA) to participating in technical cooperation (TC).

Confirming this paradigm shift, and directly challenging the prevailing conventional wisdom, a senior UN official, Richard Jolly, boldly proclaimed in 1989 that the majority of programmes involving technical experts and expertise provided by the UN and donor system had outlived their usefulness (quoted in Williams *et al.* 2003: 6). Two years later, the OECD/DAC produced its own *Guidelines on Technical Cooperation*, which provided its own assessment that donor technical cooperation was too fragmented to create sustainable systemic capacity in developing countries, and may have contributed to preventing the emergence of sustained local capacities (see OECD 2002c: 51–61). Then in 1993, a UN report entitled *Rethinking Technical Cooperation* asserted, unequivocally, that technical cooperation was ineffective in what should be its major objective: the achievement of greater self-reliance in aid-recipient countries by building institutions and strengthening local capacities in national economic management (Berg 1993: 244). Harsher still were the words of the World Bank's Vice-President for Africa uttered in the early 1990s, that 'donors and African governments together have in effect undermined capacity in Africa; they are undermining it faster than they are building it' (quoted in World Bank 2005k: 7).

These qualitative assessments are substantially confirmed by a World Bank review of technical assistance programmes covering the period 1971–91. This concluded that although the outcomes of TA initiatives had varied considerably, overall, the efficacy and effectiveness of TA has been disappointing, especially in Sub-Saharan Africa. It reported that of 1,689 projects evaluated which had institutional development goals, only 29 per cent had a substantial impact on institutional development, with a further 45 per cent having only a modest impact. In other words, less than a third could be judged in any way successful (Denning 2002: 232). More sharply still, the World Bank admitted, in a 1996 review, that external interventions may have made matters worse on the capacity-building front, with donors behaving in a way that either had had no impact on local capacity or, at worst, had eroded it (1996c).[17] Tangible evidence of the impact and influence of this critique came from the Dutch government, which a few years ago closed down the department responsible for sending Dutch experts to the developing world. The message here was clear: when judged against the contribution that donors have made to developing and maintaining skills and building capacities, traditional TA appears to have failed massively.

This conclusion is reinforced by data on skills and migration. While, on the one hand, aid funds have been used to train skilled people, on the other hand, large numbers of skilled people have left home to work abroad, often in the same countries from where the skill trainers came. Increasingly over time across many aid-recipient countries, the numbers of skilled people leaving public institutions either to seek more lucrative employment in the private sector or to go abroad are on the rise. Tens of thousands of skilled people have left Africa. One study has suggested that the cumulative costs of this exodus have been at least $1.2bn, but could well be in excess of $10bn (Tettey 2002). In some countries in recent years, upwards of 30 per cent of the graduates of tertiary education and technical colleges go abroad after their training, with health and social work professions particularly badly affected.[18] Perversely, too, some donors sensitive to the criticism of using foreign consultants to help deliver their projects began to replace them with nationally recruited staff, but then lay themselves open to a new wave of (accurate) criticism that the high salaries paid by donors to locally recruited staff was further accelerating the exodus of skills from the very state institutions that they were also trying to strengthen.

The consequences of this new discourse on and assessment of the impact of technical assistance has not yet led to the radical changes on the ground that one might have expected from the rhetoric of failure. Though the numbers of those involved in stand-alone TA have fallen sharply,[19] the bulk of TA is still provided in the way it always has been, accompanying projects and as stand-alone skills training, with most of the leading providers of TC—the United States, Japan, Germany, France, the EU, Australia and Denmark—broadly maintaining this approach.[20] At one level, this is not surprising, as huge skill shortages persist, especially in low-income and poorest countries. Recipient governments continue to request donors to help fill these gaps, because, in our globalizing world, knowledge and skills are increasingly seen as key drivers of development.

Aid for capacity building

Though more traditional forms of TA and TC still dominate the portfolio of leading official donors, these are now taking place against the backdrop of an explosion of donor activities aimed to build, deepen and enhance the capacity of organizations and institutions in aid-recipient countries. Capacity building and development, and institutional strengthening, together with good governance, have become the latest philosopher's stone of official aid agencies.[21] The term 'capacity development' is now more commonly used than 'capacity building'. It is understood as 'the process whereby people, organisations and society as a whole unleash, strengthen, create, adapt and maintain capacity over time' (OECD 2006a: 9).[22] Increasingly over the past 10 to 15 years, a now-dominant, conventional wisdom is that the weaknesses of institutions constitute one of the key clusters of impediments to sustainable development. Consequently, not only have donors provided growing amounts of aid for discrete initiatives to help develop institutional capacities, but increasingly, they have added capacity-developing components to almost all other projects and programmes. Capacity development and institutional strengthening are now seen as a 'good thing'—and a good thing everywhere that aid donors are active. But what is the evidence of the impact of aid used for these purposes—does it work?

Perhaps the biggest problem that must be faced in trying to answer this question turns on what precisely is meant by, and what donors and those making assessments understand by, capacity development. This is because, in a fast-growing literature aimed at, used by and often written by donors and their advisers, capacity development is seen not so much as a new way of providing aid whose impact can be assessed like other forms of aid, but as a new way of understanding development.[23] From this perspective, capacity development initiatives are not short-term, discrete interventions whose impact can be measured, but something long-term and involving processes rather than events, the gains from which are not easy either to capture or to trace back to particular inputs. It is for these reasons that the latest synthesis of donor good practice deliberately avoids trying to provide a 'cookbook' approach to capacity development, arguing that there are no easy formulas for describing what capacity development is and how it might be promoted (OECD 2006c: 8). Some have argued that instead of assessing the *impact* of capacity building, one should try to assess the *contribution* it makes to these wider, long-term processes.[24] At its sharpest, such a perspective would lead one to be suspicious of studies which drew crystal-clear conclusions about the short-term impact of capacity building initiatives, thereby seeing them more as indicators of aid being provided within the template of 'old-style', discrete TA or TC approaches to institution building.

Against this backdrop, what does the information from project completion reports, studies and evaluations tell us about donor-funded capacity building initiatives? Not surprisingly, there appears to be a lack of hard information from which to draw generalized conclusions. As a recent World Bank study observes, 'determining just how much international donors are contributing to capacity development is a major problem' (2005l: 21). There are two main reasons. First, a number of studies which purport to be reporting on capacity building and development, and institutional strengthening, are merely reporting on traditional TA, explaining how many people went on courses or were trained. Secondly, most substantive studies which set out to assess whether institutional strengthening took place have concluded that there was an insufficient basis for firm conclusions.

Nevertheless some clear successes have been recorded. These would include: USAID's almost decade-long support to strengthen the juridical system in Costa Rica, Sida's support over 30 years to the National Bureau of Statistics in Tanzania,[25] and DFID's six-year support to the Rwanda Revenue Authority, as well as its support to the Budget Division in Zambia, the National Treasury in South Africa and the National Development Planning Commission in Ghana (Jones *et al.* 2006). In most cases, local ownership and commitment to institutional strengthening and to change—and, in some cases, a high degree of agreement on both priorities and approach—were identified as critical to the successes achieved. Clear goals and objectives appeared to contribute to success, as did a sensitive long-term interaction between external trainers and members of the respective organizations. For some interventions, their small scale and limited objectives for enhancing the capacity of discrete and fairly independent organizations were also important ingredients of success (see USAID 1996; Morgan *et al.* 2005). For the Rwandan and Costa Rican programmes, it was also apparent that the successes were cumulative, with earlier successes and changes in the institutions appreciated and internalized, providing the groundwork for further gains to be made.

Important though these examples of success have been, they do not seem to be particularly representative of the whole. The bulk of the reports on donor-funded efforts to help build capacities and to strengthen institutions have drawn attention to some major difficulties that these initiatives have faced, with few initiatives pointing to significant successes, and most being judged as having failed in a number of key areas and objectives. A 2006 study undertaken by a team from Oxford Policy Management (OPM) which examined TC in four African countries found that none of the activities reviewed in Ghana, Zambia or Kenya resulted in clear evidence of improved organizational capacity within government, except in agencies where there was both sufficient clarity about and government commitment to their role and objectives, and where, in addition, measures had been taken to address key constraints outside the framework of normal civil service rules (Jones *et al.* 2006: 3). More generally, a major ten-year review of the World Bank's efforts at supporting capacity building in Africa (World Bank 2005b) makes grim reading. Acknowledging the weaknesses and ineffectiveness of traditional TA approaches to capacity development, the Bank admits that its attempt to focus more directly on helping to strengthen public institutions in Africa continues to be a huge challenge, and that in its more recent efforts, a range of key weaknesses remain. It judges that its efforts are still fragmented and not based on clear needs-assessment, and that outcomes are poorly tracked. Capacity development efforts remain insufficiently led by the recipient countries, and based on insufficient knowledge about precisely what to do and how to do it.

More generally, the Bank notes that donor-wide efforts are impeded because donors understand capacity building and development in different ways. A major problem is that although capacity building is seen as a key to development, Bank efforts are not institutionally tracked and monitored: it found that for half of all projects, no prior assessments had been made of existing capacity needs, and for the same number of projects, capacity constraints had not been addressed. In a sample of projects which included a capacity-building component, less than a quarter had indicators in place to track performance. Perhaps the most telling observation was that the Bank's greatest successes in capacity building occurred when there was political support for them (2005c: xv). These findings are consistent with a 1999 review of World Bank assistance for civil service reform over the period 1980–97, which concluded that this had been too top-down and bureaucratic: 'rather than engaging civil services as dynamic systems that are influenced by multiple stakeholders, Bank operations relied on small groups of interlocutors within core ministries to design and implement one-size-fits-all civil service reform blueprints in diverse country settings'.[26] No wonder so many largely failed.

Other assessments of donor performance in institutional capacity building resonate with these findings. For instance, a synthesis of official donor assistance in the environmental sector for the OECD/DAC highlighted the lack of recipient-country ownership of initiatives as a key weakness, along with a failure to analyse the causes of institutional weaknesses and poor design of programmes. The study also added that donors were particularly poor at promoting these (new) sorts of initiatives, as they had such little experience themselves of work on process projects, which was partly why there were few if any indicators against which to assess performance (PEM Consult 2000: 18–19). Likewise, a synthesis study of the Netherlands' support to institutional development in the water sector across countries in the ten-year period from 1988 to 1998 described the overall effect of institutional support as disappointing (Bartelink *et al.* 2000). Among the reasons cited were the failure to formulate clear objectives and the setting of unrealistic objectives. But perhaps of most importance was that attempts had been made to achieve institutional change when recipients had been reluctant, or resistant, to change (Bartelink *et al.* 2000: 2).

The pivotal role of recipient commitment to the success of capacity development is well illustrated by an assessment of support given to the Ministry of Finance in Zambia, which, in terms of sustainability, was judged a complete failure. After the programme had trained 2,000 people, and the Ministry had been reorganized and restructured, the advisers were sidelined and not replaced, and the advice of senior policy-makers ignored, leading to the observation that attempts to provide technical assistance and training are largely futile when government commitment fades. The donor-country-based report writers ask rhetorically: 'why would the donor community wish to support projects that focus on policy advice and capacity building if the government will not take the necessary measures to sustain their impact?' (Hoover and McPherson 1999: 17) The problem is usually expressed rather differently from the recipient side. For instance, in noting that capacity building efforts have not achieved their desired objectives in terms of sustained improvements, the government of Uganda's Capacity Building Plan equally clearly observes that 'capacity building efforts have been primarily donor-driven, partly because the donors have the resources and usually select approaches that serve their own purposes, partly because the government and its institutions have not been assertive enough in taking control' (Government of Uganda 1994: 2).

The fundamental issue is that for capacity building and institutional strengthening to succeed and be sustained, it is recipient countries and not donors which need to lead, shape and adapt their own institutions in a process to which they are committed and which is internally driven, in order to meet the changing needs of their developing economies. The challenge for donors is whether they are willing and able to contribute by playing a supportive role, both by working together with other donors and by not expecting rapid successes. To do this effectively is likely to require donors to make a clearer separation between capacity development and the provision of technical cooperation. The recent OPM study suggested that donors will need to revisit the (still very strong) working assumption that TC ought to have a particularly privileged position as an input into capacity development, as some of the determinants of organizational capacity are not amenable to influence from TC interventions (Jones *et al.* 2006: 9). To the extent that these evolving insights do not influence future approaches and future assessments of TA and TC, aid in this form is likely to continue to produce disappointing results. It is against this backdrop that a major 2002 World Bank report was frank enough to admit that 'we do not understand fully how to help improve institutions and governance, especially in the poorest countries where the needs are greatest' (Goldin *et al.* 2002: 51).

To summarize, do these new approaches to TC and TA work? Though they are still relatively new, the emerging evidence is not particularly encouraging. As the OECD puts it, 'donor efforts in many countries have produced little to show in terms of sustainable country capacity' (2006c: 3). But this should not lead one to conclude that they cannot work. Indeed, we already know a great deal about when they are likely to work: when recipients perceive capacity and institutional development as important, and when they are committed to addressing current weaknesses; when donors work closely together with each other and with recipient-country governments and institutions to achieve clearly identified goals; and when donors are not driven to spend massive amounts of money when these preconditions are absent or weak. Above all, the time horizon for results to be achieved and for them to be sustainable needs to be far longer than the one that donors commonly use. Discouragement and frustration will arise when political setbacks happen and key trained staff move on. The challenge is to continue trying when these setbacks occur.

13 The impact of aid at the country and cross-country level

The impact of discrete aid projects, aid programmes and technical cooperation matters greatly, not least to the beneficiaries of such aid. For many, however, including donors and the wider public, the central question is whether aid works as a whole. Does development aid make a real, lasting and overall difference to poor people in poor countries, and to poor-country economies? This chapter examines and discusses the evidence. It starts by looking at the evidence at the country level, then broadens its focus to examine the impact of development aid across countries. It ends by drawing attention to the main factors which impede and enhance the wider impact of aid.

The country-level impact of aid

DONOR STUDIES OF COUNTRY IMPACT

What does the evidence tell us about the impact of aid at the country level? Until recently, comparatively few substantive assessments of aid at the national level were undertaken, the seven case-studies commissioned for the 1986 Cassen study (Cassen and Associates 1986) being a comparatively rare exception. Increasingly, however, from the mid-1990s onwards, many of the larger agencies—from Denmark, Sweden, Finland, Norway, the Netherlands, the United Kingdom and the EU, as well as the large multilateral agencies, such as the World Bank—have regularly commissioned and published evaluations, reviews and in-depth studies which have focused on the overall impact of their aid, and there has been a steady growth in the number of these country evaluations and assessments. Indeed, in 1999, the OECD/DAC ran a workshop on country programme evaluations which reported on 100 evaluations undertaken between 1994 and 1999. More recently, in September 2004, a World Bank trawl of country evaluations commissioned by 11 of the largest aid agencies produced a tally of 161 separate evaluations. In addition, the websites of many bilateral agencies regularly publish online reports of their own evaluations. For instance, by mid-2005, the EC had documentation on the findings of 23 evaluations of country programmes carried out after 1998. Likewise, Denmark produced a number of country evaluations in the early 2000s, and Japan has been producing a steady stream in recent years.[1]

What are the conclusions of these studies? While the quality of the information and data contained in these studies has certainly improved over time, with some notable exceptions (to be discussed below), the overwhelming majority of these studies provide insufficient information from which to draw firm conclusions about aid impact at the country level—as most authors readily and explicitly acknowledge.

Two types of information gaps have been identified. First, echoing the discussions in chapter II, there has often been insufficient data on the performance and impact of discrete projects and programmes, making it difficult to arrive at firm generalizations about overall performance at the country level.[2] Secondly, in the cases where project data have been available, evaluators have been reluctant to draw conclusions about the wider impact of these interventions. Many have been unwilling to comment on the wider sectoral impact of the aid provided—what difference one donor's education or health projects have made to the education or health sector overall. Almost all have been reluctant to link directly the overall contribution of a particular donor's aid programme to the country's aggregate growth performance, or to its poverty reduction achievements. Even for those (few) that have tried to trace these linkages, the 1999 OECD/DAC review of country evaluations noted that not a single evaluation had attempted to use econometric techniques to trace the influence of financial aid on country programme goals (1999a: 78). These problems persist. For instance, a 2004 synthesis review of DFID's country programmes concluded that assessment of programme-level performance was hampered by poor data, making it extremely difficult to assess DFID's contribution to wider development progress. Three studies of the impact of Danish aid to Burkina Faso, Vietnam and Nicaragua, and a study of Norwegian aid to Bangladesh, came to broadly the same conclusion, as did all the evaluations of EC country strategies and a 2004 review of Sida's performance.[3] To this day, individual bilateral donors, in particular, are still not able to produce clear evidence to document the wider contribution their aid is making to aggregate growth and poverty reduction.

This is not a particularly surprising conclusion. As discussed in Chapter 10, there are well-known methodological problems in trying to make assessments of the wider impact of aid. However, there are two more immediate reasons why the bulk of donor-country evaluations have produced such little information on the impact of aid at the country level. The first is that for many donors, until quite recently, the aid provided to particular countries was not really viewed by them as a unified country programme against which it might be judged. Instead, it was seen as a package of different projects and programmes loosely linked together, at best clustered around sectoral priorities. Secondly, and partly because of the absence of an overarching strategic framework, country evaluations have tended to focus on those criteria (not unimportant) against which it is far easier to assess performance: the relevance of the aid given to the country's needs and priorities, the efficiency with which it is provided, and its effectiveness in producing the intended immediate results. The predominant conclusion emerging from these studies was that you cannot assess the wider impact of aid if it has not been provided within a wider strategic context with clear indicators against which to judge performance and impact. However, there was one, more positive outcome: the failure of country-study evaluations to provide the evidence of wider impact provided an impetus for donors to think more strategically about their aid contributions.

So much for what the country evaluations do not tell us. What *do* they tell us? Any strong conclusions that have been drawn beyond the project level have focused on the impact of aid at the sectoral level. Most are consistent with the World Bank's sectoral impact assessments which, as we have seen, broadly judge infrastructural projects as having been more effective, and agricultural and rural development projects as less effective. However, there are some differences. Those individual bilateral country evaluations that have made judgements (the minority) have concluded that social sector projects and programmes, notably service delivery in health and education, have made a significant contribution to broader sectoral goals. Not unexpectedly, the country evaluations report differences between countries and donors: in some countries, health and education, or infrastructural projects, clearly contributed to wider sectoral goals and did so efficiently; in other countries they did not.

Perhaps the most important contribution that country evaluations make to our understanding of the wider impact of development aid is that they give us a clearer idea of why and when development aid beyond discrete projects and programmes is more or less likely to work. Not surprisingly, these resonate strongly with prevailing donor views about aid effectiveness, and there is a strong unanimity across all country evaluations about what is considered particularly important.

Above all else, the wider impact of development aid is judged to be crucially linked to the context into which it is provided. In particular, the degree to which recipients perceive themselves as owning and in control of the development agenda, the degree to which they are committed to pursuing a clear poverty-focused growth and development strategy, and the degree to which they are able to achieve basic macroeconomic stability are consistently cited across the country evaluations as fundamental prerequisites for aid to be effective at the country level.[4] In instances where donor aid is assessed as having failed to make a positive contribution at the sectoral level, and in some cases beyond, lack of recipient commitment and ownership are consistently highlighted as prime reasons for such outcomes. Additionally, while the present capacity of government and its institutions clearly influences the impact of current aid flows, the effectiveness of future aid flows, across all sectors, is seen to be dependent upon enhancing capacities and strengthening key institutions, which are dependent themselves upon recipient-country commitment to, and ownership of, the development process.

Two other factors identified as critical to the wider impact of aid are peace and political stability. All evaluations of donor aid in unstable countries and those experiencing varying degrees of violence and conflict unanimously conclude that these conditions limit, and in extreme cases prevent, aid from having a positive wider impact. Finally, many though not all country evaluations identify the way that donors act and behave as an important factor, either contributing to or limiting the positive, wider impact of aid. In particular, the failure of donors to coordinate, harmonize and align their individual efforts is highlighted as a particular impediment—for some evaluations, a major impediment—to greater and wider effectiveness. There would be few donors, aid recipients or even critics of aid today who would now challenge these broad conclusions.

The perspectives and conclusions of the growing number of bilateral donor evaluations provide the backdrop for focusing more directly on the findings of the most comprehensive and rigorous attempt to assess the overall impact of country programmes: the World Bank's country assistance evaluations, which explicitly and formally analyse the wider impact of the Bank's interventions in providing aid (loans) in recipient countries. Indeed, to this day, the World Bank remains the only aid and development agency which provides explicit ratings for its country programmes. In retrospect, it is astonishing to learn that it was only in 1995 that the World Bank first began to assess its aid at the country level, and only some five years later that it had developed a sufficiently standardized methodology to undertake country assessment reviews and country assessment evaluations (CAEs) and to have confidence in the results. The findings of the Bank's CAEs are important because, across many poor countries, the Bank is often the largest donor. But they are also important because of claims by the Bank that it has successfully overcome the most difficult problems with trying to make assessments of aid at the country level, namely the problem of attribution (drawing the link between the aid provided by the Bank and national development trends) and the problem of the counterfactual (what would have happened without the aid), though these claims have been strongly disputed.[5]

Leaving to one side these methodological problems, the results of the Bank's CAEs, and its assessments of the factors enhancing and inhibiting the wider impact of aid, are particularly instructive. In 2005, the Bank produced its (first) review of all CAEs for the years 2001–4, which confirmed that assessing aid projects from the country perspective provided a far more complete picture of impact than could be obtained merely by examining aid performance at the micro-level. The results of the review showed that one-third of projects that had been found to be effective in meeting their immediate objectives were judged to have been unsuccessful when assessed more broadly in terms of country programme outcomes. More specifically, the review found that in all those cases where the aggregate outcome of all project activities had been judged to be satisfactory, only 53 per cent of CAEs produced satisfactory outcomes, and 33 per cent were deemed unsatisfactory (2005c: 6). As noted in Chapter 11, recent evaluations from the Bank's Operations Evaluations Department (recently renamed the Independent Evaluation Group) have concluded that about 75 per cent of World Bank projects are successful (World Bank 2005a: 55–6). When these data are combined with the recent review of CAEs, the figures (though not strictly comparable) would suggest that less than half of all Bank projects would receive a satisfactory rating when assessed from a country-wide perspective.

In terms of different sectors, the CAE review confirmed the findings of bilateral country studies that outcomes of aid have been particularly good in the education and health sectors, but particularly poor for rural development and the private sector (2005c: 7). The Bank's 2005 review also makes some observations about the causes of differing impact. In particular, it isolates country ownership and commitment, and institutional reform and capacity building, as critical to aid impact, highlighting, in particular, a lack of recipient commitment as a primary cause of failures of adjustment lending (2000c: vi). It notes that when strong and sustained government commitment to institutional reform is absent, Bank assistance is not likely to be successful (2000c: 10–11). It also points to a direct link between in-depth knowledge of a country and successes at the country level, recommending that aid and assistance be provided within the context of a more substantive understanding of the country.

Finally, a few studies of long-term donor-commissioned country-wide impact have been produced by individual donors where the particular donor has been dominant. In general, these long-term studies confirm the key conclusions already summarized. One was a 50-year assessment produced in 1999 of official aid provided by the United States to Costa Rica, almost all from USAID. This showed the different ways in which US development assistance contributed to making a tangible difference to rural roads, public health, and the education and water sectors. But of perhaps greater importance was the policy conclusion drawn, namely, that it was not the aid which was the sole cause of the wider positive impact. The report noted that most aid interventions had only made an incremental contribution to activities already under way in the country (Fox 1999: 257). The study drew attention to the very different types of aid that had been provided at different periods of time, citing the efforts of USAID to engage in direct poverty reduction projects as having been the least successful because of its failure to appreciate, understand or integrate their efforts with the government's own efforts, and because of significant state financial constraints (Fox 1999: 253).

A more recent single-donor assessment was the 2003 study of the impact of 25 years of Australian aid (1975–2000) to Papua New Guinea (PNG), amounting to a massive $14bn, almost four times the country's current GDP. In terms of per capita income growth, PNG has been a development failure, but according to the assessment, this does not mean that Australian aid should be judged a failure (Fallon *et al.* 2003). Tangible gains in life expectancy, literacy rates and infant mortality have been achieved in PNG, though, like the Costa Rica assessment, the PNG report is clear that aid has only been one factor amongst many contributing to these gains. In some instances, the contribution of aid was judged to have been more one of helping to arrest further deterioration than adding to tangible improvements. The report unequivocally judges that much of the early discrete aid projects were ineffectual because they had been insufficiently linked to wider processes, having failed to contribute either to local ownership or capacity building. Indeed, its wider impact was merely to add to the burdens of already weak administrative structures. The report observes that it was only from the 1990s that Australia began to realize that the key to PNG's long-term development lay in helping to strengthen institutions and build capacity, as well as to encourage greater public debate and scrutiny of development performance. And the report notes that it will take a long time for the impact of this form of assistance to be felt, and that it will be difficult to assess the contribution that aid will make because of the complex relationship between aid and the wider context.

OTHER STUDIES OF THE IMPACT OF AID AT THE COUNTRY LEVEL

All of the country-wide studies discussed thus far are studies of the wider impact of the aid provided by only *one* donor. Clearly, this does not provide us with an assessment of *all* development aid provided to a particular country— for many, the *key* issue. What evidence is there of the impact of all aid to different aid-recipient countries? Surprisingly, no studies of the overall impact of all aid to particular countries have ever been undertaken jointly by either all donors or the leading donors to a particular country. It was only in the autumn of 2004 that the idea of undertaking a first pilot study to assess the development effectiveness of total ODA at the country level was formally discussed by the OECD/DAC's network on development evaluation. But by 2006, not even a first pilot study had been completed, so this crucial information gap remains effectively unfilled.[6]

However, there have been a number of attempts to step back and try to examine the overall long-term impact of all development aid to particular countries. The 1986 Cassen study commissioned assessments of aid to seven countries—Bangladesh, Colombia, India, Kenya, Malawi, Mali and South Korea—many of which were themselves book-length studies. A few years later, and on the basis of earlier work commissioned by USAID, a study was published which reported on the impact of aid in five countries: Côte d'Ivoire, Ghana, India, South Korea and Turkey(Krueger *et al.* 1989). Then in the early 1990s, the Swedish Ministry of Foreign Affairs funded a series of in-depth studies which looked at the impact of Swedish aid in four countries—Guinea-Bissau, Nicaragua, Tanzania and Zambia—but which included a substantial analysis of the wider effects of all aid in these countries. Additionally, a number of single-country impact reports have been produced, though most of these have not been in-depth or rigorous studies.[7] What do these studies tell us about the overall impact of aid to these countries?

Unsurprisingly, major parts of these country studies highlight the ways in which aid has had a positive impact at the sector level, with aid boosting resources to expand the ability of governments to increase recurrent and capital expenditure. Aid to India made a significant contribution to agricultural research, expanded the area of irrigated land and enhanced food security, contributed to urban development and had a positive impact on health. Aid enhanced the physical infrastructure in Kenya, Colombia and Malawi, and it contributed to the land reform process and water development in South Korea which underpinned most future development. Aid contributed to education sector gains in South Korea and Colombia; and its funding of family planning was successful in Bangladesh, as was post-war reconstruction aid. The case studies also point to sectoral weaknesses and failures. These included aid to rural development programmes in Malawi, water projects in Kenya, infrastructural projects in India, Turkey and Ghana, and capacity-building efforts in a number of countries in different time periods. The case studies suggest that aid had a positive influence on policies in Tanzania and South Korea, but the outcome was more ambiguous, or was negative, in most other countries.

How about the wider impact of aid on poverty and growth? Here the country evidence is far more circumspect, and most authors have been reluctant to come to firm conclusions. The case studies provide differing assessments. For instance, in Bangladesh, the analyses suggest that the impact of aid on poverty was disappointing, in Colombia it contributed to poverty reduction for long periods of time, and in India and Uganda, the evidence was mixed. Did aid contribute to growth? Again, the evidence is mixed. In Colombia, Uganda and Nicaragua (at particular times) it did; in Malawi, the combination of financial aid, technical assistance and institution building contributed to growth in the 1970s; in Kenya, it was not possible to say. The Tanzania case study illustrates the difficulty of making an overall judgement. It concluded that it is 'hard to argue that aid has had a very positive effect on economic growth', adding that growth mainly depended on factors other than aid, but concluding that the overall impact of the resource transfers was positive (Adam *et al.* 1994: 162). Likewise, trends in poverty and economic growth have been largely downwards in Zambia, even in times of rising aid inflows, but the case studies conclude that it is not easy either to attribute the prime cause of these changes to aid or, more particularly, to determine whether growth and poverty trends would have been better with less aid.

Thus the overall picture emerging from these country case studies is that in most countries, aid frequently has had a positive overall impact in some time periods, but a negative impact in others. In short, aid at the country level some-times worked and sometimes didn't. However, like the donor-funded country studies, one overriding conclusion to emerge from this set of case studies is a reluctance to make firm generalizations about the wider impact of aid on growth and poverty, not merely because impact tended to differ, but because it was judged impossible simply to trace firmly and unequivocally a *direct and causal* relationship between overall growth and aid inflows, or between overall aid inflows and changes in poverty. Three reasons predominate: because the aggregate data are too unreliable; because it is not possible to separate out the influence of aid from other factors; and because we cannot know what would have happened in the absence of aid. Howard White has summarized the overall country assessment problem succinctly. He says that the answer to the question of the relationship between aid and economic growth cannot be given, as 'we know surprisingly little about aid's macroeconomic impact . . . the combination of weak theory with poor econometric methodology makes it difficult to conclude anything about the relationship between . . . aid and growth' (1992: 121).

A recurrent theme in a number of case studies is the systemic effect of the provision of aid by different donors when uncoordinated with and provided independently from that of other donors. Until quite recently, this was the way in which aid was provided. The consequences were starkly illustrated by a com-ment from one of the early country case studies: 'If an aid programme means that the provision of resources is guided by an identifiable and coherent set of objectives, there is no aid programme in Kenya' (Cassen and Associates 1986: 174–5). The more recent case studies have drawn attention to the differing effects of donor harmonization and coordination on capacity building and institutional and policy development. At one extreme, aid can contribute to a virtuous circle of economic growth and poverty reduction through fostering desirable policy change, building effective institutions, relieving constraints on funds for investment and leveraging private resources. However, it can also contribute to a vicious circle whereby the provision of external finance serves to delay (essential) policy reform, undermining the (long-term) effectiveness of institutions and contributing to conflict over the distribution of economic rents (Mavrotas *et al.* 2003: 6).

COUNTRY-LEVEL IMPACT AND CHANGING APPROACHES TO PROVIDING OFFICIAL AID

The cumulative evidence of the constraints to wider aid impact that donor-sponsored and other studies have highlighted has stimulated a growing number of donors to approach the provision of development aid far more strategically than in the past.

For a number of years, donors such as Sweden, Norway, the Netherlands, Switzerland and the United Kingdom have been developing country assistance plans and strategies which assess their development aid against the backdrop of broader development goals, seeking to understand how the aid they give as a whole can contribute more effectively to recipient-country goals of higher growth and faster poverty reduction, both directly and through strengthening local institutions and capacities. Some large multilateral donors such as the UNDP, the Asian Development Bank and the World Bank have also signalled their intention of moving more systematically in this direction. In some countries small groups of donors have recently agreed formally to adopt a joint strategic approach and have begun to produce joint country aid and assistance plans, as they try to put flesh on their commitment to three of the contemporary buzzwords of development cooperation: partnership, harmonization and alignment.[8] The increased prominence of, and the growing donor commitment to, the Millennium Development Goals have given added impetus to these more strategic and cooperative ways of aid-giving. Together with the emphasis given to recipient ownership, this has spurred donor-led efforts to 'encourage' more and more aid-recipient countries to develop, own and implement their own development strategies, widely institutionalized in the production of concrete strategies under the umbrella term of 'poverty reduction strategies': PRSes and PRSPs.[9]

Growing donor cooperation and the growing emphasis given to the broader strategic issues involved in aid-giving should help considerably to increase knowledge of the overall and wider impact of aid at the country level as indicators are developed to monitor aid performance at the sectoral level and beyond. Indeed, some recent country studies are providing some far firmer conclusions about the aggregate effects of aid at the country level (see Arndt *et al.* 2006 for Mozambique), suggesting that aid has had a positive effect on growth or poverty reduction, or both, especially in more recent years, though these relationships should not be viewed as automatic.

Mozambique and Tanzania are two countries in which there has been growing cooperation among donors, and considerable interaction between donors and recipient governments (see Lipumba 2006). They are not necessarily typical. There remains a gap between the rhetoric of most donors about the need to work more closely and strategically together, and the still comparatively small number who have begun to do so effectively and comprehensively.

As the March 2005 Paris Declaration on Aid Effectiveness acknowledged, many donors (and partner countries) still need to undertake far-reaching and monitorable actions to reform the ways they deliver and manage aid (OECD 2005b: 1). By late 2005, less than 50 aid-recipient countries (well less than half the total) had developed PRSes, though a further 11 had produced interim strategies; far fewer were actively implementing these.[10] Even in many of these countries, significant disagreement persists about how best to promote a pro-poor growth strategy, with investment priorities often poorly defined and no clear link between medium-term objectives and short-term policies and strategies. Little headway has been made in working out precisely how to assess outcomes, with data-gathering problems compounded by considerable disagreement among official donors about precisely which indicators should be used to monitor performance (Driscoll *et al.* 2005).[11] A particularly telling indicator of the still large gap between donor rhetoric and reality comes from a recent OECD-commissioned sample survey of donors which found that 70 per cent of all donor projects were still being implemented outside national procedures (OECD 2005g: 19). Little wonder that in July 2006, 15 months after the Paris Declaration, the UK White Paper noted that donors needed to make far faster progress if they were to achieve the commitments they had made (DFID 2006c: 118).

In short, and in spite of a growing number of initiatives of different donors to try to work together more strategically, we are still a long way from having sufficient indicators and data with which to judge the wider impact of aid at the country level.

The impact of official development aid across countries

CROSS-COUNTRY STUDIES

We now shift our focus from one country to many countries. What is the overall impact of official development aid across recipient countries?

More money has probably been spent and more research time allocated to examining the impact of aid on different macroeconomic variables across different aid-recipient countries than on any other aspect of the aid relationship. The cross-country studies undertaken have grown in terms of their ambition and sophistication, often with the next wave of researchers decrying the simplicity of earlier efforts and techniques. The focus has changed over time, understandably mirroring prevailing debates and discussions about aid's overall impact. In earlier years, cross-country studies tried to trace the relationship between aid, savings and investment, and aid and foreign exchange, to assess whether aid did indeed plug the gaps that the theory suggested aid was needed to fill, and thereby contribute to overall growth. In later years, cross-country macro-studies of aid's impact were dominated by analysing whether—and if so, to what degree—aid contributed more directly to aggregate growth, examining, both separately and together, relationships between the main variables thought to influence growth. More recently, a new set of cross-country studies has begun to try to examine the relationship between aid and poverty, to assess whether aid has contributed to poverty reduction. Over the decades, hundreds of cross-country studies have been carried out. To this day, they are still commissioned, still undertaken and still use research money (including aid funds), developing ever more complex methods, usually involving sophisticated econometric models, to help shed light on the cross-country impact of aid.[12]

One reason why so many studies have been carried out is that the conclusions (and the results) have continually been contested. For over 40 years, successive cross-country studies concluding that aid's aggregate impact has been virtuous—that it has helped to fill key gaps, and to play a positive role in expanding investment and addressing skill shortages, that it has helped to raise growth levels and reduce poverty—have been challenged. A steady dribble of studies has concluded that the effects of aid have been anything but benign—that aid has not filled gaps, that it has not led to a rise in investment levels or enhanced human resource skills, that it has failed to boost aggregate growth or to contribute to poverty reduction—only to be superseded by the next round of studies challenging these conclusions. Some studies have concluded that it is not possible to show either a discernible positive or negative relationship between aid and key macroeconomic variables, or that a positive relationship in one set of countries over one time period contrasts with a negative relationship in another group of countries over other time periods.[13] Even these more agnostic conclusions have acted as a catalyst for further research to be commissioned, because, as noted earlier in this book, a major client of cross-country macroeconomic research has been the donor community, which has continually believed that its own work and legitimacy is crucially based on being able to show conclusively that aid's overall and cross-country impact is favourable. Thus, studies which challenge this perspective need to be refuted immediately.

One might expect that a book which is attempting to provide an overview of aid and inform debate about whether, in general, aid 'works' would devote considerable space to discussing, distilling, summarizing and reviewing this mass of studies focusing on the cross-country evidence of aid's impact. But to what purpose? A small but growing number of researchers and aid specialists are beginning to question the value of these studies in helping to inform discussion about whether aid works.[14] In the words of a recent review of the aid-effectiveness literature, subtitled 'The Sad Result of 40 Years of Research', the average effect of aid is positive, small but of dubious significance statistically, and as more data have become available, the results have grown gradually worse (Doucouliagos and Paldam 2005: 2).[15] Consequently, there is little merit in devoting much space to summarizing what these studies tell us about impact. Indeed, the point needs to be made in far stronger terms. It is time to call a halt to cross-country studies commissioned to *prove* that aid in general 'works', and to challenge the widely and deeply held assumption that such studies are necessary to confirm or validate the legitimacy of providing official development aid. The 'limits of cross-country regressions have become clear: they do not throw much light on the reality of aid' (Picciotto 2006: 1).

A growing number of influential voices have begun to challenge the usefulness of cross-country studies for confirming or challenging the virtuous, aggregate impact of development aid. Twenty years ago, the Cassen study was politely dismissive, but the force of its criticism was probably lost on many readers. It concluded that inter-country statistical analyses showed nothing conclusive about the impact of aid, adding that this was hardly surprising, and if one wanted to discern the impact of aid, one had best look elsewhere (Cassen and Associates 1986: 29, 227). More recently, a respected international scholar on aid effectiveness, Esther Duflo (2003), has argued that the question of whether development aid contributes to growth cannot really be answered, and so trying to look for a relationship (especially cross-country) is, in effect, a red herring. This view was reiterated in a recent review of the aid-effectiveness literature from the evaluation department of the Asian Development Bank, which suggested that because of data and methodological problems 'cross country growth regressions analysing aid effectiveness should be abandoned' (Quibria 2004: 17). Of perhaps even greater significance are the views of the former Chief Economist at the World Bank, Nicholas Stern. Since leaving the Bank, he has publicly acknowledged that cross-country regressions of the impact of aid are now 'running into sharply diminishing returns', as 'one cannot really disentangle with any confidence the direction of causation: aid to growth or poverty/decline to aid'.[16]

There are three reasons why cross-country studies of the relationship between aid and key macroeconomic indicators serve very little purpose in advancing our understanding of whether aid works. They all flow from discussions in earlier chapters. First, there is still not enough knowledge about what causes growth and reduces poverty to be able to trace the relationship through to aid's impact on key macroeconomic variables. As just noted, firm conclusions about aid's general impact cannot easily be drawn at the country level. Trying to draw conclusions at the cross-country level is even more dubious. Secondly, statistical relationships between aggregates tell us nothing about causality between variables, nor about whether the relationships observed are due to other (external) influences, or to the interrelationship between aid and other internal influences. At best, they merely capture and summarize regularities in the data used.[17]

Thirdly, perhaps the clearest and strongest conclusion to emerge from the individual country-based impact studies is that the influence and impact of aid is predominantly dependent upon, and determined by, a range of country-specific variables. Their influence changes over time, and a number are particularly difficult to quantify, such as the recipient's commitment to, and ownership of, the national and sectoral strategies into which aid funds are inserted. What this means is that even if it were possible to draw firm general conclusions about the *past* relationship between aid, growth and poverty (and this is all cross-country econometric studies are able to do), this would not necessarily provide any clear guide to the future. To use trends in aggregate (and dubious) quantitative data to attempt to prove that development aid works—or that it does not—is to fuel the false notion that aid's benign or adverse effects are automatic, divorced from the context in which it is provided, the forms in which it is given, and the conditions attached to its provision. On the contrary, the country-based evidence tells us that ownership, commitment, context and capacity all matter a great deal: indeed, they provide the only reliable backdrop against which to judge whether aid works or not.

It would be churlish, however, to end this particular discussion without drawing attention to the fact that the majority of cross-country studies have concluded that, overall, aid has contributed to growth. For instance, a substantial review of 131 cross-country studies, published in 2000 and elaborated in 2001, concluded that most of these reported a positive relation between aid and growth (Hansen and Tarp 2000, 2001). More recently, a 2005 survey of studies undertaken in the previous eight years reported that growth would have been lower without official aid, and thus that it 'worked'; criticisms of aid at the macroeconomic level—concluding that it is harmful, a failure or counterproductive—were simply not supported by the bulk of the research (Addison *et al.* 2005: 14), while the review of 40 years of studies by Doucouliagos and Paldam showed a 'positive but small' relationship between aid and growth (2005: 2). However, consistent with historical precedent, these most recent synthesis reviews were followed by two studies which concluded that the evidence showing a positive relationship between aid and growth remained unproven (Rajan and Subramanian 2005a, b). In mid-2006, Radelet's review of the evidence concluded that it did (2006: 11–12, 16). And so the circus continues.

KEY FACTORS ENHANCING AND LIMITING THE AGGREGATE IMPACT OF AID

Notwithstanding these criticisms, carefully undertaken country and cross-country studies of aid effectiveness continue to serve one extremely important function. They help to expand our knowledge and understanding about those factors which influence, enhance or inhibit the beneficial aggregate impact and effectiveness of ODA.

On the positive side, commitment to and ownership of a poverty-alleviating development strategy have been identified as centrally important for aid to be effective, at both the project level and more widely, as have the capacity and competence to utilize the available funds well. Likewise, commitment and ownership are now recognized as vital to the success of efforts to develop capacity and strengthen institutions, upon which the future effectiveness of aid and broader development strategies will critically depend. In contrast, macro-economic instability, external shocks, political unrest and overt conflict have been identified as influential factors constraining the effectiveness of aid, as have volatility and unpredictability in the amount of aid provided. More recently, the proliferation of donors, a number of whose aid programmes have been unconnected or only loosely linked to the efforts of other donors or to the central thrust of recipient government actions, has been identified as con-straining aid's potential impact. Recently, too, corruption and the misuse and diversion of aid have been highlighted as significant impediments to the effective utilization of aid funds, having adverse knock-on effects as they spread their contagion well beyond discrete aid interventions, exacerbating institutional dysfunction and further distorting markets.[18] What remains contested is the precise impact these influences have and are likely to have on the aid provided.

Additionally, the macroeconomic studies of aid at the country and cross-country level have drawn attention to different ways in which aid itself can, and does, lead to or induce perverse effects on recipient economies. Each, separately, has been shown to reduce, neutralize, or at the extreme, reverse the positive outcomes expected from the inflow of additional (aid) resources. When one or more of them interact, the overall cumulative adverse effects would be expected to be even greater.[19] We shall look at the main ones in turn.

Aid, taxes and fungibility

The first potential problem concerns the differing effects of aid on the public finances of aid-recipient economies. Macroeconomic studies of aid have high-lighted a number of ways in which the inflow of aid funds has not led to the expenditure gains and fiscal stimuli expected. For instance, it has been shown that aid money intended to boost investment expenditure has been used to expand consumption expenditure instead. Likewise, the inflow of aid funds and the assurance of more aid to come in the future have been shown to have resulted in recipient-country governments reducing commitments to raise taxes. And, at the extreme, aid flows have been associated with a fall in tax receipts. Studies have also shown perverse effects on the expenditure side. Donors give aid on the assumption that it provides additional resources to recipients—to build a hospital or road, to provide skills training and strengthen institutions, or to enable more children to attend school. But aid only creates additional money if the recipient government continues to allocate its own funds to those sectors and activities that it was funding prior to the inflow of aid funds. When donors provide significant aid funds, the temptation is for the recipient government to switch money away from the sectors which donors are funding to other consumption or capital expenditure priorities. This phenomenon is known as the 'fungibility' of aid: using the opportunity that the inflow of additional (aid) funds provides to reorder overall spending priorities and finance a range of non-developmental projects and programmes.

Aid and the exchange rate

A second way that aid inflows adversely and perversely affect recipient countries arises from the upward pressures on the exchange rate of the recipient's currency that the inflow of aid tends to induce. This is the so-called Dutch disease effect, so named because the upward movement of the exchange rate was first detected in the Dutch economy following the rise of foreign-exchange earnings from the sale of natural gas in the early 1980s.[20] It occurs when aid funds are used to enhance spending on domestic output, requiring production to be switched away from exports to import substitutes. When the exchange rate strengthens, the relative competitiveness of the economy falls, limiting export expansion and reducing the potential for further wealth creation. Consequently, when exchange rate movements are large, the medium-to long-term effects of providing aid are to reduce rather than enhance the capacity of the recipient economy to grow, to slow the wealth-creating processes, and thus to put a brake on poverty reduction. Theoretical studies show that this can happen, and there is significant country-based and cross-country evidence documenting the occurrence of Dutch disease in aid-recipient countries.

Aid and absorptive capacity

A large number of macroeconomic studies have shown that the more aid a recipient receives, the more likely it is that the additional amounts provided will be used less and less efficiently, and with decreasing effectiveness. More technically, as the volume of aid increases, its marginal utility declines, confirming that beyond a certain level, aid is subject to ever-falling or diminishing returns. Eventually the point will be reached—termed the absorptive capacity threshold—when providing more aid will be totally ineffective. Indeed the consequences could well be even more detrimental: providing aid in such large amounts that the recipient is unable to absorb it or to use it well may not merely lead to the inefficient use of the additional funds provided, it may also stimulate the aid already provided to be used less effectively.

Aid volatility

Finally, a number of studies have shown that the effectiveness of aid has been reduced (sometimes severely) as a consequence of its volatility. More specifically, it has been shown that aid inflows often fluctuate considerably year on year, and that the volatility of aid inflow is often marked in poor countries, which are particularly vulnerable to external shocks, and which plan expenditures on the basis of promised aid inflow commitments being honoured. When countries with a significant dependence on aid suffer external shocks, and when these shocks are accompanied by a sharp fall in aid funds—a not uncommon phenomenon—the overall effect has been shown to be highly damaging to growth and future growth prospects.

The counter-evidence

There are two types of response to the challenges to the effectiveness of aid arising from studies which provide evidence of the adverse macroeconomic effects of aid. The first is to point out that they provide only a partial picture. Sitting alongside these studies are others which show aid as not having caused these adverse or perverse effects; studies which show that where these adverse effects have occurred, they have been relatively minor and can be effectively managed; and studies which show how countries have successfully addressed the risks or overcome the constraints identified. For instance, a significant number of recent studies have shown that the effects of aid on public finances have been positive and that the diminishing returns problem can often be addressed by identifying and addressing key supply constraints. In some cases, recipient countries have increased taxes whilst large and even increasing amounts of aid have been provided. Likewise, aid has stimulated public investment, and even when aid has been used for consumption purposes, this has also been shown to have had a positive effect on aggregate growth. Similarly, aid fungibility has not been either a blanket or persistent problem, or even harmful. Evidence of aid's fungibility in one country (such as Pakistan) has sat alongside evidence of limited fungibility in others, such as Indonesia.[21]

The second type of response is to challenge the assumption that even when some or all of these adverse macroeconomic effects of aid have occurred in some countries in the past, they will necessarily and inevitably continue to occur in the future. Indeed, as noted above, it is now widely accepted that the aggregate impact of aid depends critically on the circumstances and context in which it is inserted and, in particular, on the attitude and commitment of recipients to use it well. Building on this perspective, there are studies which have shown the different ways in which different aid recipients have addressed or countered the various perverse aggregate effects that aid has had or might have had.[22]

One of the reasons why the fiscal and public expenditure response to aid inflows in recent years has been far more positive than in the past is that recipients have chosen (sometimes at the promptings of donors) to manage aid inflows in the context of supportive development-oriented public expenditure programmes (see, for instance, Fagernäs and Roberts 2004; Osei *et al.* 2005). Similarly, the Dutch disease phenomenon is by no means universal, and in some countries where it has been found, it has been quite effectively managed and therefore not a major problem (see Hjertholm *et al.* 2000: 361; Gomanee *et al.* 2003; Berg *et al.* 2006). Furthermore, it does not seem to have been relevant at all in the franc-zone countries (see Ouattara and Strobl 2004). But what is of even greater importance is that it is almost always within the capacity of aid-recipient countries to manage the Dutch disease problem if and when it occurs, particularly when it is of short-term duration (Barder 2006). Recent work by Adam and Bevan (2005) suggests that short-run, demand-side Dutch disease problems can be addressed to a considerable extent by focusing on identifying and addressing supply-side constraints. Indeed, when the focus is broadened out beyond mere issues of aid, it is clear there is a whole variety of factors influencing the exchange rate (upwards and downwards), as well as a range of different policies that can be deployed to address them.[23] Likewise, many of the worst effects of aid's volatility can be addressed; thus, aid volatility does not provide a sufficient condition for not providing aid (see Devarajan and Swaroop 2000). Indeed, studies have shown that aid is likely to be more effective if provided in a sustained manner to countries particularly vulnerable to external shocks (Chauvet and Guillaumont 2002; Collier *et al.* 2006).

Of perhaps greater immediate concern is the problem of aid absorption. The bulk of the literature predicts or confirms that as aid inflows rise, eventually a time will come when diminishing returns set in, though there remains considerable dispute about precisely when this might occur (ranging between an ODA-to-GNI ratio from as low as less than 10 to as high as 45 per cent). However, some studies have disputed or challenged this finding (see Gomanee *et al.* 2003; Rajan and Subramanian 2005b: 23; Guillaumont and Jeanneney 2006). Again, the central issue is not the static problem of aid absorption, but the dynamic response to the problem. The diminishing returns to aid (when they do exist) are only a problem if they have formed binding and immutable constraints. The main reason why diminishing returns set in is because recipient countries do not (currently) have the capacity to absorb more aid efficiently. The most effective way to address this problem is not to stop providing aid, but to identify where those constraints reside and work with the recipient country to help address them—most probably with aid (see Radelet *et al.* 2004; Addison *et al.* 2005: 4; Bevan 2006). There may well be instances where the prospects of enhancing the capacity of recipients to use aid more effectively are slim, but this is likely to remain a small minority of aid recipients.

The overall conclusion of this discussion is not that the potential and actual macroeconomic impediments to aid effectiveness do not exist or do not matter. To the extent that they do exist, they clearly need to be analysed and addressed. Many are capable of being addressed. To the extent that they are addressed, aid effectiveness will improve and the wider impact of aid is more likely to be achieved.

14 Assessing the impact of aid conditionality

This chapter discusses one of the most controversial issues in the debate about whether aid works: the relationship between the overall impact of development aid, the policy advice given by donors, and the policies pursued by aid-recipient governments. More often than not, donors have required recipients to pursue a given set of policies as a condition for providing aid. Has this been good advice?

Aggregate aid impact and the policy environment

In the late 1990s, a number of studies from the World Bank, most notably the publication *Assessing Aid: What Works, What Doesn't and Why* (1998), as well as studies authored by Craig Burnside and David Dollar (1997, 2000), became extremely influential in donor circles. In brief, these asserted that aid works (meaning it contributes significantly to aggregate growth) when targeted on countries with good fiscal, monetary and trade policies, and that aid does not work when targeted on countries with poor (fiscal, monetary and trade) policies. The studies went on to suggest that donor exhortations to recipients to alter policies made little difference, implying that if donors wished to ensure that their aid was effective, their only real option was to channel it to those countries with 'good' policies, and not to devote effort to trying to effect change in those with 'bad' policies. Ten years on, the donor community continues to be influenced by the broad thrust of these studies. Are these assertions about when and how aid works, and especially the primacy of (particular) policies, supported by the evidence?

At one level, the assertion that policies matter is not only uncontroversial but fairly self-evident. Indeed, it sounds almost tautological: aid is bound to work better when provided in contexts where it is likely to be more effective, and to work less well in more difficult or inhospitable environments. Similarly, you are not likely to influence someone who is not remotely interested in being influenced by you, as any parent of teenagers will tell you. Thus, to assert that policies 'matter' for aid to be effective is not particularly gripping news. However, the Bank studies were saying far more than this. They were arguing that aid only worked when a particular set of policies were being followed—and these just happened to coincide with the views of what constituted those good policies which were being advocated by the Bank at that time, in essence the package of liberalization measures that had became known as the Washington Consensus (WC), which are discussed later in this chapter. To some extent, arguments about the importance and effectiveness of the specific set of policies articulated in these particular mid-to late-1990s Bank studies are no longer relevant, because not even the Bank itself now promotes or advocates the narrow range of prescriptive policies linked to the early Washington Consensus, a number of which have been found to have been wrong, simplistic or inappropriately applied (see Lensink and White 2000). However, while the content of the Bank's policy package has changed, its views about the centrality of policy remain firmly in place. Hence it is important to know what the evidence tells us of the relationship between aggregate aid, policies and aggregate growth.

The Bank's views on the primacy of policy as the crucial determinant of aid impact have been widely and substantially challenged. A recent survey of the macroeconomic evidence by Addison *et al.* (2005) compared 23 independent studies which recorded a positive relationship between aid and growth regardless of the policy regime in place, with only six, all of which were World Bank studies, concluding that aid works better in countries with better policy regimes. In the larger group of (non-Bank) studies, influences other than policy variables were linked to a positive relationship between aid and higher rates of aggregate growth. These included, for instance, institutions, geography, climate, political stability, per capita income levels, and the extent of poverty within a country.[1] Some (non-Bank) studies found that aid worked even in instances where poor policies were being pursued (see Hansen and Tarp 2000, 2001). The dominant conclusion is that the Bank's assertions have not been substantiated by the bulk of the evidence. A particularly significant challenge to the Bank's views, and the links between aid policy and growth, comes from the study conducted by Easterly *et al.* (2003), which used exactly the same methods as the original Bank study, but fed in additional data from other countries. With this additional data, the link between aid, growth and policies was found to have disappeared. Perhaps the final nail in this particular coffin came from one of the two authors of the Bank's study. David Dollar has acknowledged the limitations in the measures of policy used in the study, admitting that some policy measurements and growth outcomes were linked, thus undermining some of the original findings (Collier and Dollar 2004: F254). Overall, therefore, it seems safe to conclude that the assertion that aid contributes to aggregate growth only when a preferred set of policies are followed has been effectively discounted—though, as noted above, this by no means leads to the conclusion that policies do not matter.

The debate has not ended, however. Rather, it has expanded and moved on. The World Bank has continued to give prominence to aid-effectiveness issues, but its more recent work has widened to encompass both policies and institutions. More specifically, its aid-effectiveness work is now focused more sharply on what it calls the Country Policy and Institutional Assessment (CPIA). The CPIA consists of 20 characteristics which cover macroeconomic and development policy, economic and public sector management, and institutional capacity and competence (World Bank 2003a). For every country, each of these 20 characteristics is assessed and given a score, and the scores are brought together to produce a single numerical CPIA index. Countries are then grouped together into five quintiles, the fifth quintile grouping together those countries with the lowest scores, the first those with the highest scores. Bank research has found a positive link between aid, a country's CPIA rating and aggregate growth: aid works best—it contributes to aggregate growth—when provided to countries with a high CPIA score (Collier and Dollar 2004: F244–F251).

As with the Bank's earlier work, at one level the results are unexciting, suggesting that aid is more effective when provided in a better and improving policy and institutional environment. But as before, the devil is in the detail, with the Bank suggesting that if donors are interested in the effectiveness of their aid, they would best channel it to those countries assessed as being able to use it well, that is, those with higher CPIA scores. What does the evidence tell us?

As before, there is considerable evidence to challenge the Bank's views. For instance, aid is positively linked to strong development outcomes—high growth and poverty reduction—in countries with weak institutions, and with policies that are not entirely consistent with the Bank's checklist of what is deemed either desirable or necessary, including countries which would rank low on CPIA scores, such as China, Vietnam, and, at different times, Ghana, Indonesia, Sierra Leone and Uganda. Addison *et al.* (2005) cite numerous macroeconomic studies which have found the aid–growth relationship influenced by factors other than the Bank's list of policies and institutions. Other recent cross-country studies have also called into question the veracity of the Bank's assertions about the overriding importance of policy and institutional variables. These show that while the policy environment and the quality of institutions, and governance more broadly, are undoubtedly important, other factors also contribute to positive development outcomes, suggesting that allocations of aid should not be confined merely to performance against a narrow set of indicators (see, for instance, Asra *et al.* 2005; Rajan and Subramanian 2005a, b; and Baliamoune-Lutz 2006). Additionally, work carried out by the Washington-based Center for Global Development, which separated out different types of aid, found a very strong relationship between 'short-impact' aid and growth, and while there appeared to be a relationship between strong institutions and growth, growth remained strongly positive even when institutions were weak (Clements *et al.* 2004: 37–9).[2]

It is not, however, only the country and cross-country study evidence which raises questions about the applicability of the Bank's approach to aid policies and growth. The whole CPIA process is riddled with methodological problems, raising further questions about its reliability. First, as the following comments by the Bank's leading experts on governance indicators explain, the CPIA process and the wider attempt to quantify governance indicators is open to wide margins of error:

While the addition of data has improved the precision of our governance indicators relative to previous years, the margins of error associated with estimates of governance remain large relative to the units in which governance is measured. This implies that cross country comparisons of levels of governance on this type of data should be made with caution. This is particularly the case for changes over time, which, in the vast majority of cases, are small relative to the margins of error associated with our estimates of governance. (Kaufmann *et al.* 2003: 1–2)

Even more fundamental questions are raised about the Bank's CPIA when the way in which the individual country ratings are scored and the quintile groupings derived are understood. Three linked issues are of particular importance. First, each year, the 20 different CPIA scores and the overall country index are derived from individual Bank staff who, on the basis of their own knowledge, assessments and judgements, produce the individual index scores for each country. The scores for all the different countries are then brought together, ranked and split into five groups (the quintiles). The country scores can, and do, vary from one year to the next, including movements of countries from one quintile to the next, making it difficult to trust the usefulness over time of studies which show links between aid, CPIA scores and aggregate growth. Secondly, the scoring of countries and their grouping into the five quintiles do not provide an absolute measure of policy performance and institutional capacity, but rather a relative ranking of countries. Consequently, it is quite possible for the position of countries to shift from one quintile to another from one year to the next, not because of what happens within a particular country, but as a result of changes in the scores of other countries. Again, this throws into question the usefulness of studies which conclude, say, that all those countries placed in the fifth quintile are necessarily less able to use aid effectively than those placed in the fourth quintile. Thirdly, until 2006, it was not possible to check the scores given to particular countries, as these remained secret and confidential to the Bank.[3] Though they have now been made public, there is no external scrutiny or independent verification of the scoring, so other donors and scholars have to accept the judgements of Bank staff entirely on trust.[4]

To point out these problems and to raise these questions is not to suggest that policies and institutions do not matter. They both matter a great deal to aid effectiveness: pro-poor policies need to be implemented by recipients committed to pro-poor growth and with institutions and capacity increasingly able to use aid funds well. But with the CPIA process, we seem to have entered a world of smoke and mirrors. We have been asked to believe that aid works best when provided to the best 20 per cent of all countries ranked on the basis of the personal and independently unverifiable judgement of Bank staff, derived from a comparatively small cluster of policy and institutional variables that are known to be subject to significant errors. Aid is least effective when provided to the worst 20 per cent when judged in the same way. When these concerns are placed alongside the conclusions of other Bank studies which explicitly acknowledge our continued ignorance about important dimensions of the content of policy and the nature of strong institutions and the need for development strategies to be home-grown and home-owned, it is difficult to understand how donors could be confident that allocating aid to countries on the basis of their CPIA scores will provide a reliable way of ensuring that their aid will be used effectively.

Official donor conditionality and recipient response

Since ODA was first given, it has always come with some sort of 'strings attached'. Historically, the World Bank and the IMF have been two of the leading donors and providers of development finance which have attached conditions to their aid and loans. Frequently, they have persuaded other donors to link their aid to the same cluster of conditions they applied.

What has been the impact of this policy advice? There are two linked questions that need to be distinguished. First, to what extent have recipients complied with, and implemented, the policies that donors have placed on the table along with the aid they have given? Secondly, have the conditions that the donors have sought to apply been the right ones? Have they led or significantly contributed to the strengthening of the recipient economy, its growth and development, and the reduction in poverty? These are substantive questions. We consider each of these in turn.

THE BACKGROUND

All aid donors, both official and non-governmental, have an obligation to ensure that the funds they provide are used for the purpose intended, and that they are utilized as efficiently and effectively as possible. Policy conditionality has been one means to try to ensure that this happens.

Donors could impose explicit conditions and requirements about how they believe the aid should be used, and then withhold or withdraw aid if these conditions are not met. Or they could merely satisfy themselves in general terms that recipients will use the aid funds for the broad purpose intended, and then wait to see the overall outcome. The history of official donor action over the past 25 years shows that in practice official aid-giving has tended to be more closely aligned to the former, input-based and conditionality-driven approach, though donors have only rarely, and then only temporarily, withheld aid when recipients have failed to comply with the attached conditions—the drive to spend aid commonly trumping concerns about effectiveness. In the last few years, however, some far-reaching changes have been occurring in relation to conditionality, or at least in relation to the rhetoric surrounding conditionality, with donors arguing that aid will only work effectively, not if conditions are attached to it, but if the aid provided supports a programme of action and activities that are owned, overseen and led by the recipient.

THE ERA OF STRUCTURAL ADJUSTMENT

Although, as already noted, official donors have always attached conditions to their aid, the start of the 1980s proved to be a watershed. It was then that the World Bank started to provide structural adjustment loans, joining the IMF, whose macroeconomic stabilization programmes had always come with specific conditions attached, but whose role in low-income countries intensified. Not only did both these institutions more formally and overtly attach policy conditions to their concessional and non-concessional lending, but most bilateral donors and other multilateral financial institutions followed suit, with leading bilateral aid agencies increasingly requiring recipients to be in compliance with the requirements of the Washington-based financial institutions, particularly the IMF, as an underlying precondition for their giving aid.

Having to attach *any* conditions to aid is an indicator of a difference in view, and thus of potential tension between donor and recipient—for if both were in agreement about what to do, and how to use the aid, conditionality would not be so necessary. The policy conditionality that began to be applied from the 1980s was so divisive because it was unilaterally required by the donors, it was predicated on the assumption that far-reaching reforms, including structural changes, were needed (to return poor economies to the growth paths from which most had so sharply strayed), because of the array of conditions demanded, and because many of the key conditions were different from those required in the past. The core policy conditions were grounded in the free-market, neo-classical macroeconomic orthodoxy that became known as the Washington Consensus (WC). This encompassed measures to tighten fiscal discipline, the reordering of public expenditure, tax and exchange rate reform, financial and trade liberalization, privatization and deregulation (Williamson 1994, 2004). According to the World Bank's own figures, in the early 1980s, on average, the Bank applied five conditions to their loans and used the same number of benchmarks against which to assess performance. By the end of the decade, the number of conditions had risen to over 30; they peaked at 45 by 1993 and by 1999 still numbered about 25. The average number of benchmarks trebled in the 1980s and averaged well over ten for the decade of the 1990s (World Bank 2005e: 7).[5] It was not only that the number of conditions rose, but the nature and degree of conditionality also tightened in the 1990s. By the mid-1990s, almost 120 countries had some form of adjustment programme (Killick *et al.* 1998).

The populist view is that the governments of aid-recipient countries universally, and strongly, disliked and were opposed to this form of aid conditionality. It is certainly (universally) true that trying to comply with the conditions placed huge and costly administrative burdens on recipients, and they were generally perceived as overly excessive and intrusive. Yet the response of aid recipients to this donor-driven policy conditionality differed both between recipients and over time. Some recipients, including many in Latin America, were receptive to the new conditionality; most others were cautious. For all, however, the first part of the conditionality package clearly 'worked'. There is no evidence of any recipients formally refusing to accept the policy conditions of the IMF or The World Bank—commonly referred to, in short, as the Bretton Woods Institutions' (BWIs)—and then being given aid: recipients did agree (some reluctantly) to comply with the policy conditions, most began to implement the required policies, and the aid flowed in.

But did aid recipients implement the policies prescribed? The evidence is mixed. Slippage occurred for a range of different reasons, including the lack of capacity across many poor countries to implement such a complex array of different policies. Some recipients continued to implement the required policies, but others—a growing number—did not. Some were unwilling to do so, perceiving the political and economic costs to be too high. In some countries, the response to policy conditionality was outright hostility, popular protest, and, in extreme cases, riots. However, the response was often more complex than it appeared. Some recipients were supportive of the policies donors were demanding but claimed they were implementing them only as this was required, using donor demands as a means of managing political opposition to help them implement difficult policy choices. The BWIs and bilateral donors failed to penalize recipients for not complying with many of the policy conditions they imposed, even if the flow of aid was in some cases temporarily halted, as occurred in Mozambique, Nicaragua, Tanzania, Vietnam, Zambia and Zimbabwe. New loans were provided with, in essence, the same conditions applied. This, in turn, provided a further stimulus for recipients reluctant to implement particular policy conditions to miss the next round of donor-set targets. From the late 1980s to the mid-1990s, only a quarter of World Bank programmes were completed on time (Killick *et al.* 1998: 30), and from

1992 to 1998 less than half the IMF's programmes were successfully completed (Wood 2004: 14).

A growing number of studies were undertaken, from the late 1980s onwards, to assess the impact and influence of donor conditionality. The broad conclusion of independent studies was stark, namely that this (new) form of conditionality didn't work, in the sense of having a very limited effect on policy change.[6] What is more, by the end of the 1980s, the World Bank concurred: 'conditionality as an instrument to promote reform has been a failure' (Devarajan et al. 2001). Yet Bank studies tended to nuance this assessment in an important way. Broadly, they concluded that recipients who did not wish to implement donor policies tended not to do so; those who agreed with them or who believed they would benefit from them tended to comply. Similarly, they argued that providing aid to 'non-reforming' governments often merely perpetuated the continuation of 'poor' policies. Taking their departure directly from the assessment that recipients will not implement reforms if they do not want to, and against the backdrop of a growing concern about the effectiveness of aid, some donors, most notably the World Bank, began more explicitly to channel more aid to those recipients deemed to be using it well—understood as those complying with donor policy conditionalities—and less aid to those who did not.

NEW APPROACHES

The assessment that policy reform could not be 'bought' dovetailed with the growing acceptance by donors of the view that aid effectiveness depended above all on the commitment and ownership of development (and aid) programmes by the aid-recipient country. As the 1990s progressed and the focus of donors shifted more explicitly to poverty reduction as the prime objective of development aid and the prime focus of development policy, 'policy conditionality' as we had known it was removed from the lexicon.

In 1999, the World Bank and the IMF abandoned the term 'adjustment lending' and put their weight behind different poverty reduction instruments and processes, most notably poverty reduction strategy papers (PRSPs) and the Poverty Reduction and Growth Facility (PRGF) as the formal instruments around which donors would provide aid.[7] Other donors supported these new initiatives. As its name suggested, the IMF's PRGF was to base lending on the contribution it made to poverty reduction and growth. PRSPs, as their name suggested, were to be developed through widespread participation within countries, comprehensive in their analysis of poverty, focused on outcomes directly benefiting the poor, and long-term in their perspective. This process was to lead to the creation of country-specific development strategies and policies, drawn up, 'owned' and led by recipient countries. Thus, the policy agenda was to be owned not by the donors, in particular by the BWIs, but by the aid recipients, with the PRSPs providing the principal instrument on which donor–recipient relationships were to be based. Gone were the externally driven, one-size-fits-all, blanket policy prescriptions in the former Bank-and Fund-led policy packages so widely criticized. If rhetoric were our guide, it would seem that this new recipient-led approach to development policy-making—universally accepted and supported by the aid-donor community—marked the removal of policy conditionality as we knew it from the real world of donor–recipient relationships.

In practice, however, this has not (yet) happened. Analyses of the content of PRSPs indicate that the vast majority retain most of the main policy components of the former donor-led and donor-driven policy conditionality, encompassing the core components of the Washington Consensus. They are all strikingly similar to each other, as the Bank itself in 2004 was candid enough to acknowledge (see Stewart and Wang 2003; Browne 2004: 7). Furthermore, even when PRSPs are authored within aid-recipient countries, this is no guarantee that they reflect the views and priorities of the recipients, and map out the development path that the recipient wants to pursue. For example, though the Bangladesh PRSPs were 'largely an indigenous effort', the Government 'felt compelled to genuflect to the structural adjustment reform agenda even though its relationship to poverty reduction . . . [was] at best tenuous' (Sobhan 2005: 63).

Likewise, the thrust of the IMF's PRGF and the conditions attached to these loans require countries to follow the same core macroeconomic stabilization package of conditions that applied to earlier Fund loans (see Bird 2005; Martin and Bargawi 2005). This is not surprising when one realizes that PRSPs and loan agreements made under the PRGF have to be formally endorsed and approved by their respective governing boards, and even many PRSPs have been largely written by Bank staff. It is true that the number of conditions attached to Bank lending has dropped sharply, as have those of the IMF following its post-1999 streamlining initiative: in the Bank's case falling from 30 in 1999 to 12 in 2005 according to Bank data, though the number of benchmarks against which programmes are assessed jumped from a low of four in 2000 to over 20 by 2005 (World Bank 2005e: 7). However, careful analysis suggests that it is the more peripheral conditions which have been removed and that at least for countries qualifying for debt forgiveness and those under IMF programmes, recipient governments are probably more constrained in terms of strategy and policy options now than was the case two or three years ago. According to one analyst, change means that recipient countries have first shout but little else (Wood 2004: 41). As Tony Killick puts it, in spite of widespread agreement that conditionality is a flawed instrument, it is still being relied on by the Bretton Woods institutions as well as by other donors (2004: 16).[8]

Additional confirmation of the reality of the persistence of much old-style conditionality comes from the UK government, which in March 2005 produced a policy paper entitled *Partnerships for Poverty Reduction: Rethinking Conditionality* (DFID 2005). This committed the UK government to provide aid without making it conditional on specific policy decisions demanded of recipient governments, including policy decisions 'in sensitive economic areas such as privatisation or trade liberalisation', stressing the need for donors to take a back seat to allow more space for recipients to draw up their own plans for poverty reduction (pp. 10, 18). If the PRSP process *had* ended old-style conditionality, it would not have been necessary to produce such a policy paper. Indeed, the paper observes that large aid-recipient countries still do not have genuine autonomy in determining their own policies (p. 18). In an oblique reference to the continuity of the IMF's approach to conditionality, the paper states that the UK will no longer require countries to have in place an IMF-agreed programme as a basis for its own aid support, and that it will work to ensure that the World Bank addresses the impact of its own conditionalities (pp. 16, 19).

The UK policy paper was followed by further waves of rhetoric emphasizing the primacy of recipient countries in leading on development strategies and policies. For instance, in July 2005, at their meeting in Gleneagles, the G8 leaders confirmed the need for recipient countries to 'decide, plan and sequence their economic policies to fit with their own economic strategies for which they should be accountable to their people'. Perhaps of greater importance have been the changes in rhetoric and some of the views of the World Bank on development policy approaches. In the same year, the Bank acknowledged that an important lesson of the 1990s was that generalized policy prescriptions have failed, that there is no single model for development and there are no generalized formulas, and that development depends on domestically owned strategies and not on universal policy prescriptions (World Bank, 2005j: xii). Building on this (new) perspective, the Bank has introduced a new operational policy framework which, it is claimed, no longer contains any policy prescription or presumptions for World Bank lending policy.[9] There still remains a significant gap, however, between the new rhetoric and the reality of the Bank's policy engagement. In practice, the Bank still works closely with the IMF, the broad thrust of whose macroeconomic and stabilization policies it endorses, and it has continued to apply privatization and trade liberalization conditions to its poverty support credits. This is confirmed by the views of 50 per cent of stakeholders polled in its 2005 conditionality review, who judged that the Bank was still introducing elements that were not part of the country's own development programmes (2005e: 12).[10]

One of the reasons for the continuing differences between the rhetoric and reality of policy conditionality of the BWIs is rooted in differences in the way ownership is understood. Predominantly for the IMF and (though to a lesser extent) the World Bank, ownership is understood as the process whereby recipient countries come round to accepting—that is, 'owning' not as possession, but in the sense of 'admitting as valid'—the respective financial institution's programmes, policies and approaches to development, growth and poverty reduction. Indeed, for the Fund, 'ownership does not require that an IMF-supported programme be a government's first choice, nor that it be the programme that officials would have preferred in the absence of IMF involvement' (Boughton 2003: 4; quoted in Wood 2004: 34). Likewise for the Bank, ownership is a concept that 'denotes a high probability that the policy and institutional changes associated with a lending operation will be adopted and implemented even if there is internal opposition' (World Bank 2001b: 73). Against this perspective, it is perhaps little wonder that so many recipient countries see the role of the Fund and the Bank as still centrally focused on ensuring that it is the policies of the BWIs which shape the course and pattern of development in their countries. It contrasts sharply with the far more common understanding of ownership, which sees the process of analysing problems and identifying appropriate solutions by the recipients themselves as essential components and the only way that recipients will find sustainable solutions to their problems.[11]

The debates about policy conditionality, ownership and reform will continue, and it is difficult to predict how events will unfold. However, it is likely that a number of other bilateral donors will follow the UK's lead and adopt the very different approach to conditionality that many believed the PRSP process and the IMF's new PRGF would usher in. What remains uncertain is whether such donors will adhere to the new principles they have articulated and whether this process will provide the necessary catalyst for the main international financial institutions (IFIs) to alter in practice the way they have traditionally done business.

Does policy conditionality produce the results intended?

It is one question to ask whether policy conditionality leads to the policy reforms intended. It is quite another to ask whether the policies upon which the conditionalities are based are the right ones. It is this latter question which is examined here. Have the policies which the donors have promoted and, in many cases, required recipients to implement as a condition for receiving aid led to the outcomes predicted? Have they resulted in higher growth and faster poverty reduction?

Of course, to assess the impact of policies implemented brings us back to the tricky methodological problems (discussed in Chapter 10) of trying to trace the link between policy inputs and development outcomes. If the expected development outcomes (higher growth and faster poverty reduction) do not occur, to what cause can one legitimately attribute this: implementing the right or wrong policies, implementing the right policies in a half-hearted way, or because the beneficial effects of implementing the policies have been overshadowed by other (unexpected and unintended) external influences? Conversely, if the expected outcomes do result, is it possible to attribute this directly to the application of the policies prescribed? These are crucial questions on which much ink has been spilt; they remain central to a complete understanding of the fundamental question of what constitutes the 'right' development strategy and the 'right' policies to pursue.

IGNORANCE AND ITS IMPLICATIONS

If there is one thing that policy advisers have in abundance it is confidence in the advice they give. When pressed, however, most advisers would readily admit that they are not able to predict what the outcome of their policies will be, given the uncertainties of the real world. What is of more interest—and of concern to those expected to act on the advice—is the lack of consensus in the research and academic communities about the links between policy, outcome and results concerning the central variables on which advice is based. Not even advisers know—for sure—that the policy advice they give is necessarily good advice. For example, as there is (still) no single, simple or agreed view on how best to promote growth, by definition there can be no best policies to take off the shelf to achieve higher growth, as the Bank has now publicly acknowledged. When it comes to understanding the central contemporary question of how to promote 'pro-poor' growth—how best to reduce poverty in a sustainable way—knowledge gaps are even wider because there is still no consensus on what 'pro-growth' is, never mind how to achieve it.

On the positive side, cumulative research findings have certainly increased our knowledge of what elements are necessary to stimulate growth and help to reduce poverty. Yet, we still remain ignorant about the relative importance of each of these, and even less clear about the correct sequencing of policies to implement. It is therefore sobering to note, and to their credit, that both of the leading agencies whose policy advice is so important, the World Bank and the IMF—at times, and almost certainly too rarely—have acknowledged the gaps in their policy knowledge. For instance, the IMF has admitted that 'knowledge of the links between policies and growth remains limited and knowledge of the links between policies and poverty reduction even less so' (quoted in Cabezas and Vos 2004: 18). Similarly, the authors of the large World Bank study of aid and reform in Africa were ready to concede that although there was 'a fair amount of knowledge about policies that promote growth and reduce poverty' there also remained 'policy areas about which we know less and about which there is ongoing debate' (Devarajan *et al.* 2001: 1–2).

There are two important conclusions to draw from these observations. The first is that as long as significant knowledge gaps remain, there clearly cannot be a single or simple one-size-fits-all cluster of policies that can or ought to be applied to all countries to promote their development. The second is not merely to urge that further research and analysis of the motors and impediments of pro-poor growth be undertaken. It is also to argue that, however much cross-country studies shed light on general trends, this is no substitute for, and can only complement and never replace, analysis of the specifics of the individual poor countries in which the aid and policy advice is to be channelled. Consequently, it is not possible to answer, or particularly helpful to ask, the question whether—in general—policy advice linked to aid-giving 'works'. We should remain sceptical of any donor or financial institution which suggests that it has found the Holy Grail.

THE IMPACT OF DONOR-DRIVEN POLICIES

Against this backdrop, what do the studies tell us of the impact of donor-driven policies? First, recapping a key conclusion from the previous chapter, the bulk of studies suggest that while certain policies often can and do contribute to economic growth, aggregate growth also occurs as a result of factors other than policy change or policy inputs. But far more can be said.

Though comparatively few rigorous and independent assessments of the impact of World Bank and IMF programmes and their linked conditionalities have been carried out, those that have been broadly confirm a positive correlation between programme implementation and economic performance.[12] Most notably, while IMF programmes have often led, directly, to a short-term contraction of economies, aggregate growth has generally increased and exports have expanded (Bird 2005: 39ff.). However, they do not seem to have had much effect on the *pace* of economic growth, and have also been associated with reduced levels of investment. Furthermore, where countries have experienced low growth and declining growth, this has been attributed to 'the way donors have applied conditionality' (Leandro *et al.* 1999: 285).

There is a strong popular belief, not least among many NGOs, that policy conditionality has had a clear detrimental effect on poor people 'in general' (see Lockwood 2005: 45ff.). This has not been confirmed by the more rigorous studies, though it is certainly true that during the 1980s and well into the 1990s, development strategies advocated by donors did not address the needs of poor people adversely affected by the policies promoted (Cassen 1994: 82). What is more, the World Bank was ready to acknowledge increasingly during the course of the 1990s that policy conditionality had a detrimental effect on many poor people, most notably the urban poor, across a large number of countries, and this was often associated with widening inequalities.[13] Additionally, the failure of policy conditionality to lead to sustained and significantly higher rates of growth has continued to be a key factor in the failure of policies, when implemented, to lead to a sharp *reduction* in poverty (Sobhan 2005: 174). IMF policies have been sharply criticized for constraining the expansion of public expenditure, thus limiting the ability of governments to expand, and some-times even to maintain, service provision to poor people (Rowden 2005). In mid-2005, in its submission to the World Bank's review on conditionality, the Nordic and Baltic donors (including Denmark, Sweden, Finland and Norway) judged that while conditionality had assisted some countries, it had harmed the development of other countries when applied in association with struc-tural reforms and in the absence of social protection.[14] For its part, the United Kingdom has admitted that even some recent policies, such as privatization and trade liberalization, have had detrimental effects on particular groups of poor people (DFID 2005b: 6–7).

These views on the impact of donor-driven policies sit rather uncomfortably alongside a significant strand, if not the majority, of research, which concludes that donor-driven policy conditionality doesn't work. As we have seen, one strand of World Bank thinking strongly believes that donors are not able to influence recipients to embark on a process of reform. Recipients will not imple-ment policies the donors claim to be necessary when they have no intention of doing so. It is best, argues the Bank, to focus funds (and advice) on these who are willing and able to use the money well and who are responsive to the advice proffered. At the extreme, if aid is provided to recipients not willing to imple-ment reform policies, this will contribute to the delay in implementing reform. However, if aid is provided 'as the level of policy improves', then the effect will likely to be positive: 'Thus money can help improve policies but the key is to dis-burse it as actual policy improvement is achieved' (Devarajan *et al.* 2001: 34).

Taken to its logical conclusion, this perspective would lead to the very odd result that donor conditionality can't really be blamed for any outcome at all, for a recipient would only do what a donor urges it to do if it wanted to do it in the first place. It would reject the advice, and the policies that go with it, if it strongly disagreed with what a donor was proposing. But this viewpoint can also be challenged by a careful review of the evidence, which suggests that the Bank's view about conditionality, reform and outcome is wrong, or at best mis-leading. This can be understood more easily if we ask the question about aid, policy and reform in a slightly different and less confrontational way. Thus, is there evidence to suggest that the process of aid-giving, when combined with interaction between donors and recipients, can contribute to recipients alter-ing their policies? Not only does the evidence suggest that the answer is 'yes', but there is growing evidence that donor–recipient action can not only lead to recipients changing their policies (in the direction donors believe to be desir-able), but can result in recipients *owning* those policies. There are three types of evidence which show this.

First, detailed, but older, studies suggest that long-term and long-established donor–recipient relationships can help (though not always) to build confidence and trust which, in turn, can lead to the adoption of policies that initially recipients were reluctant to implement (For examples, see Killick 1998: 116ff.). This is less likely to occur when the relationship remains at the technical level, and does not engender trust. It is more likely to occur with bilateral donors than with the multilateral financial institutions, who have often been viewed with greater suspicion. Perhaps this goes some way towards explaining why it has been World Bank studies and not evidence from bilateral donors which has tended to draw such stark conclusions about the aid–policy–reform mix.

Secondly, more recent analysis of donor–recipient interaction provides a wealth of evidence of the ways in which financial aid has influenced public spending in a pro-poor direction, including public spending in a number of countries which would have been judged to be poor candidates for expecting policy change—for instance, at different periods, in Ethiopia, Mozambique, Tanzania and Uganda (Mosley *et al.* 2004). But these outcomes are by no means automatic. What the recent case study evidence shows is that for policies to change, donors need to negotiate skilfully, coordinate their demands and be 'in it for the long haul', all of which often requires them to go through (long) processes of building up trust, being prepared for periods when they will constructively have to 'agree to disagree' with the recipient. As Mosley *et al.* explain, what seems to have happened is that when donors have adopted a new, more loose-reined, approach to conditionality that has been able to accommodate short-term deviations from targets as trust is built up, this can lead—and has led—not merely to policy changes being implemented but to shared, jointly agreed, and jointly owned targets. Their conclusion is clear: it 'contradicts the Collier–Dollar proposition of donors having no influence', revealing the considerable opportunities to turn potential into actual aid leverage (Mosley *et al.* 2005: F229).

Thirdly, and related to the previous point, the combined effects of the commitment of all United Nations member states to work towards the achievement of the Millennium Development Goals, and a growing and widening acceptance among aid-recipient countries of the importance of the need for macroeconomic stability (in its broadest sense) as a key ingredient not only for growth and poverty reduction, but as a means of enhancing political legitimacy, have helped substantially to extend, or in some cases to create, new common ground between donors and recipients. The result has been to narrow considerably the range of policies over which there are likely to be extremely divergent views. Consequently, while undoubtedly there remain some poor countries where there is little prospect of donors and recipients reaching agreement about policies in the short term, there are very few in which a long-term commitment by donors to policy dialogue will not lead to a sufficient narrowing of differences for most donors to be satisfied that the conditions can be created to expect development strategies to achieve higher levels of growth and faster reductions in poverty. In short, the strong assertions (made particularly by the World Bank) that policy change cannot take place in countries not currently committed to reform are both factually wrong and of diminishing relevance and importance to a growing number of key contemporary aid relationships.

HAVE THE POLICIES PROMOTED BEEN THE CORRECT ONES?

In the end, however, it matters far less who promotes policies, and the extent to which donors and recipients agree or disagree about them, than whether the policies being promoted and implemented are the correct ones. As noted above, the post-1980s wave of conditionality, to which aid-giving was crucially linked, was aimed at trying to ensure that aid recipients implemented pro-free-market macroeconomic policies that became known as the Washington Consensus. Were these the correct policies to promote and pursue?

The question has been vigorously contested. The debate has taken two, partly linked, forms. One part has focused on the substance of the policy recommendations and whether the theory on which they are based and the working-out of the theory in practice have been sufficiently sound to provide a firm enough basis for them to be promoted and implemented. A second part of the debate has concentrated on policies and linked constraints seen to be impairing growth and poverty reduction, which are ignored or downplayed in the approach promoted by the BWIs. The following paragraphs summarize the main clusters of the more measured criticisms which have been made by researchers and commentators. They have been complemented by far stronger populist statements and assessments, some of which have not considered a review of the evidence particularly relevant to the blanket assertions made. Taken as a whole, the substantive literature provides a robust challenge to the BWI approach, around which there is a growing consensus within the academic community and among a growing number of donors outside the main financial institutions.

The (changing) Washington Consensus

One of the problems of trying to analyse the BWI approach to policy-making is that, to some degree, one is dealing with a moving target. There is some dis-agreement about the precise content of the original 'Washington Consensus', though there is broad agreement that the group of policies that the BWIs have recently been advocating differ in a number of key respects from the group of policies promoted in the early 1980s.[15] The most substantial difference relates to the way the role of the state is perceived. The thrust of the early policies was to seek to reduce substantially direct state involvement in the productive economy, to shrink its size and its reach, and to highlight its role in providing the regulatory and legal framework for markets to operate freely and for private property rights to be enforced. The changes—from WC1 to WC2—have been to 'add on' and give strong emphasis to the strengthening of state structures and institutions, the weakness of which was identified as a major impediment to the implementation of a wide range of other, largely economic, policies.

Two features of the BWI approach to economic policy were promoted from the early 1980s onwards and differentiate it from earlier ones. The first was the (implicit) rejection of the notion that there is, or ought to be, a particular type of development economics and development theory applicable to poor, developing countries. From this perspective, what was needed was simply the application of the same set of policies to developing-country economies as were being applied to the industrialized, OECD economies. This led to the second feature of the post-1980s BWI approach to policy-making, namely its preoccupation with policies aimed at stabilizing the economy. These focused on restoring macroeconomic stability, downplaying the need to focus on detailed microeconomic policies. The assumption was that stabilizing the macroeconomy—getting prices right and providing the conditions for markets to operate more efficiently by removing key impediments—would not merely achieve short-term adjustment objectives but would be sufficient for (higher rates of) long-term growth to be sustained.

When these policies were first promoted, some questioned whether macroeconomic stability was necessary. In contrast, today there is almost unanimous agreement that macroeconomic instability, characterized by very high levels of inflation, price instability and volatility, large and rising fiscal deficits, overvalued (or severely undervalued) exchange rates and uncontrolled credit, are highly damaging to growth and poverty reduction—and thus that macroeconomic stability is necessary for development. What remains contested is how macroeconomic stability is defined and what quantitative targets, or range of targets, should be applied to monetary and fiscal indicators, and what wider conditions are required for macroeconomic stability to be created and sustained.

Doubts about the appropriateness of the WC approaches

For all the changes that have been made, there remains considerable doubt among many scholars about the appropriateness of applying WC policies to poor countries. These policies have been criticized for providing too narrow and restrictive a view of macroeconomic stability, which has contributed to low-growth regimes and the maintenance of macroeconomic policies in many aid-recipient countries which have failed to address a range of specific problems which additional policies are needed to address.

A first set of criticisms has focused on the appropriateness of the policies being promoted, both currently and over the entire period since the 1980s, to achieve the main purpose of stability, macroeconomic balance and the core conditions for longer-term growth. Taken together, they provide a formidable list.[16]

Thus, it is argued that the target rates set by the BWIs for inflation and for the reduction of the budget deficit are too low. Studies show that inflation rates well in excess of 5 per cent (though in most cases well under 20 per cent) and budget deficits of around 3.5 per cent (before grants) are both manageable in themselves and provide a sounder base for longer-term growth than the lower targets associated with BWI conditionalities. Indeed, there remains widespread support for the (largely Keynesian) view that deficit financing can and ought to be used as a pro-active policy instrument to stimulate the economy in times of recession, to reduce the adverse effects of economic contraction and to shorten the period of recession. Indeed, as volatility is far more common in poor-country economies, this approach is seen to be of even more relevance in low-income than in industrialized countries, and it is already widely used in the latter. Likewise, experience suggests that the (quite rigid) BWI policies on exchange rate management are too restrictive. Neither theory nor practice provides sufficient guidance to determine a priori how an economy's exchange rate should be determined, but experience suggests there is far more scope for exchange rate intervention, at least temporarily, to address and reduce volatility and uncertainty than that usually proposed by the BWIs. Similarly, there is widespread evidence that the financial, and especially capital account, liberalization advocated by the BWIs has frequently contributed to, and not reduced, widespread uncertainty and economic volatility, adversely affecting growth and growth prospects, seen most dramatically in the case of the liberalization of the capital account across a number of Asian and Latin American economies.[17]

A linked cluster of criticisms have focused on the adverse consequences of assumptions the BWIs have made about the expected effects of their policies. Overwhelmingly, BWI financial target assumptions have tended to overestimate future growth rates and underestimate the frequency and impact of external shocks on low-income economies. Most immediately, government revenue and government expenditure have frequently been far lower than projected, leading to greater economic contraction than anticipated, made worse by loan-fund inflows being based on over-optimistic domestic revenue levels (Martin and Bargawi 2005: 83ff.; Rowden 2005: 11). Over the longer term, this output gap has fuelled uncertainty and unpredictability, thereby contributing to low levels of investment, a major characteristic of so many poor-country economies pursuing BWI-prescribed policies (Ffrench-Davis 2004: 110ff.).

The final two policies promoted by the BWI that have been subject to criticism are trade liberalization and privatization. On their own, the evidence suggests that trade liberalization and privatization policies are unlikely to produce the virtuous outcomes intended, especially in poor countries characterized by weak institutions, structural rigidities and underdeveloped and distorted markets.

Concerning trade policies, there is a growing, and now quite extensive, consensus that trade expansion enhances growth and thus that export expansion should be encouraged. What remains in dispute are the best policies to promote in order to reap the potential benefits of expanded trade. There is a wealth of evidence, not least from the history of the development of industrialized countries and many of the more wealthy developing countries, which challenges the simplistic view that by lowering tariffs and removing trade restrictions, poor economies will necessarily grow and prosper. To reap the potential advantages requires not only an overall expansion in world trade, but market access and the ability of economies to address the range of supply constraints limiting expanded production and higher value-added. Importantly, too, there is a need to address the (multiple) needs of those adversely affected by the adjustment process.

In relation to privatization, the evidence provides a mixed picture, especially the privatization of public utilities. Some public utility privatizations have led to more efficient and cost-effective provision of services, with consumers paying less, more people gaining access to the services provided, and a significant spread of services to previously excluded poorer communities now able to access basic services (water, electricity, sanitation) through cost-effective methods of cross-subsidization. However, the majority have produced more ambiguous effects, with some providing services at higher cost, some increasing access to wealthier people, some reducing access to poor people because user charges are higher than poor people are able to afford and governments have not provided sufficient subsidies to those unable to pay. Where the privatization of public utilities has taken place in weak regulatory environments, these problems have often occurred together, with monopolistic private providers being more able to charge higher fees and obtain high profits. Both trade liberalization and privatization experiences confirm that initiatives need to be carefully appraised and managed if the anticipated rewards are to be achieved in practice.

Gaps and omissions in the BWI view of the policy world

A final cluster of criticisms focuses on gaps or omissions in the BWI policy package. The failure of the early policies (WC1) to incorporate the role of the state and institutions has been addressed in recent approaches (WC2). However, as discussed in Chapter 12, the ability of policies to strengthen institutions and build state sector capacities has been limited and disappointing. This calls into question the appropriateness of advocating the implementation of a core set of macroeconomic policies whose impact the BWIs themselves have acknowledged is in large part determined by the strength and competence of their core institutions.

More broadly, the BWI policy package has been criticized for failing to include policies to stimulate technological change and innovation, which have long been acknowledged as necessary for growth, structural change and industrial development (see Lall and Urata 2003). Likewise, there has been no attempt to address or incorporate into the policy framework differences in macroeconomic outcomes and changes arising from the different production structures of different economies. The very different outcomes of policies implemented in Poland, Russia, Ukraine and Vietnam, on the one hand, and China and other low-income countries on the other, confirms the importance of this point (Woo 2004: 25ff.).

On a related point, the thrust of the IMF's macroeconomic policies remains focused predominantly on addressing identified demand-side problems; little attention has been paid to identifying and implementing policies to address the range of supply-side constraints which continue to limit or constrain growth in many poor countries. This is doubly surprising because from the earliest days of aid-giving, physical infrastructural constraints have been identified as a key constraint to growth. Additionally, it is now widely acknowledged that the ability of poor-country economies to increase export levels, and—of greater long-term importance—to diversify their economies in order to add value to primary product exports, has been constrained by skill shortages, which are not part of the mainstream BWI lexicon, as John Williamson, one of the main architects of the World Bank's macroeconomic conditionality, has recently acknowledged (2004: 9).[18]

But perhaps of greatest concern has been that the BWI policies focus insufficiently on the particular problems of different groups of poor people. An early criticism was the failure of BWI policies explicitly to address the problems of poor people, both by failing to target poor groups explicitly and by assisting those adversely affected by the policies: Cornia, Jolly and Stewart's two-volume 1987 study, *Adjustment with a Human Face* (Cornia *et al.* 1998), was the first of many to argue the need for explicit pro-poor policies to be added to the policy package. While a range of present policies, most notably the expansion of health and education spending, are directed at enhancing some of the assets of poor people, far less attention has been focused on policies to assist those whose lives and livelihoods have been adversely affected by the adjustment process. It has also been increasingly recognized that implementing the macroeconomic policies has often resulted in disproportionate gains to some and losses to others. This has arisen, at least in part, because getting prices 'right' and making markets 'work' by removing constraints to their more efficient operation will not help those who either do not participate in, or are only peripherally engaged in, market transactions, including different ethnic groups.[19] By the end of the 1990s, the importance of empowerment and ensuring markets worked better for the poor were formally recognized by the World Bank in its 2000/1 World Development Report, *Attacking Poverty* (World Bank 2000). By 2005, in its *World Development Report 2006: Equity and Development* (World Bank 2005m), the Bank formally acknowledged that growing inequity and inequalities were impediments not only to poverty reduction but also to growth, requiring specific policies to enable poorer people to enhance their access to education, infrastructure and key assets such as land. However, clear and explicit policies, including redistributive policies, are still not part of the core macroeconomic growth and poverty reduction policy package promoted by the IMF.[20]

Summing up

Even this brief discussion should be sufficient to conclude that the package of macroeconomic policies advocated by the BWIs, with its focus on short-term stabilization policies, remains seriously deficient. Many of the weaknesses, problems, inadequacies and limitations of the policies identified in this chapter are increasingly being recognized and acknowledged. In part, the rhetoric has changed. Indeed, in September 2006, the President of the World Bank, Paul Wolfowitz, agreed that it was right for bilateral donor governments to question past Bank policies regarding conditionality, and stated that as a result of that questioning their policies have been revised.[21] Yet, the core policies of the leading IFIs remain rooted in and aligned to the traditional conditionalities of the past.[22] The major problems are well summarized by one of the most vigorous and prolific critics of countries blindly following narrow Washington Consensus policies, the former Chief Economist of the World Bank, Joseph Stiglitz (2002: 84):

(T)rade liberalisation accompanied by high interest rates is an almost certain recipe for job destruction and unemployment creation . . . Financial market liberalisation unaccompanied by an appropriate regulatory structure is an almost certain recipe for economic instability—and may well lead to higher, not lower interest rates, making it harder for poor farmers to buy seeds and fertiliser that can raise them above subsistence. Privatisation, unaccompanied by competition policies, and oversight to ensure that monopoly powers are not abused, can lead to higher, not lower prices for consumers. Fiscal austerity, pursued blindly, in the wrong circumstances, can lead to high unemployment and a shredding of the social contract.[23]

There are four broad conclusions arising from this discussion.

The first is that the process of achieving macroeconomic stability and of simulating higher levels of growth is more complex and is likely to take far more time than is currently assumed by the BWIs. Indeed, the problems of poor performance are in part directly linked to and caused by that over-optimistic assumption, not uncommonly compounded by the failure to provide sufficient resources (concessional and non-concessional) to enable targets to be met. The implication is that the time-frame for adjustment needs to be extended.

Secondly, the range of policies within the overall package needs to be widened considerably to encompass areas which either are not addressed at all, or are addressed insufficiently and inadequately. These include policies to address supply-side constraints, policies, including redistribution policies, directed at enhancing the ability of poor people to benefit from adjustment, and addressing the (multiple) needs of those adversely affected.

Thirdly, it is important to recognize that the policies proposed need to be related more closely to the specific characteristics (both constraints and opportunities) of particular countries, and adapted accordingly. The insights of macroeconomic theory and practice should not be ignored: indeed, they remain of fundamental importance. What is needed is the skill of understanding how they apply and how they ought to be applied to particular countries.

Finally, and similarly, changes need to be made to the 'epistemology' of policy advice, with due recognition explicitly given to the uncertainties surrounding the outcomes of any policy advice given. What is needed is a less assertive approach, one, instead, which is rooted in and attempts explicitly to build the confidence and capacity of poor countries to develop their own policies and, where necessary, to apply their own policy conditions. One way this might start to happen in practice is succinctly summed up by Graham Bird (2005: 44):

Mandatory conditions might be limited to policies that affect a country's ability to repay its debts to the Fund and to avoid falling into arrears; they should be based on the areas of broad economic consensus surrounding macroeconomic stabilisation. In the areas of economic growth and poverty, where there is much less economic consensus, governments should be granted as much discretion as possible. The Fund could make recommendations but should not impose these as performance criteria; at least not until reasonable alternative policies selected by governments had been shown not to work. . . . The Fund would still monitor performance and its support would remain conditional on governments pursuing the strategies agreed with the Fund. But structural conditionality would be more self-designed. This approach would also encourage poor countries to build up their own capacity to design long-term balance of payments strategies and to establish the necessary institutional arrangements for long-run economic success.

15 Does official development aid really work? A summing up

The wide-ranging discussion of the previous five chapters needs to be brought together. What general overarching conclusions can be drawn about the effectiveness of official development aid (ODA)? How does the review of the evidence inform discussion about whether it works or not?

Clearly, there is plenty of evidence of official development aid contributing positively and tangibly to improvements in aid-recipient countries: imparting skills, extending and improving the quality of services, developing and improving the physical infrastructure, contributing to improvements in production, incomes and well-being, and enhancing the reach and delivery of core services, including the provision of schoolbooks and bed-nets, drugs for inoculations and basic medicines. Some benefits have been less tangible, but nonetheless important, such as aid's indirect contribution to enhancing the efficiency and effectiveness of agriculture, improving the quality of key institutions, and strengthening the capacity of aid-recipient ministries to deliver education and health sector services. Development aid is given on the assumption that it provides additional resources to recipient countries. In many instances this has been the case, with the fears of enduring, negative impacts and outcomes outweighed by its potential positive benefits in practice. Programme aid has also had a positive effect, expanding the overall resource base of resource-poor countries and providing more funds for basic services.

If this were all that needed to be said, then the record would appear to be broadly positive—we could say, on balance, that official development aid largely 'works'. However, this is not the full story; indeed, it provides an extremely partial picture.

The search for sustainability

The benefits of much official aid have been predominantly due to its successes in addressing short-term, gap-filling needs. There have often been major difficulties in achieving longer-term sustainability for many aid-funded projects and programmes. Similarly, while a large number of projects and programmes have achieved their short-term objectives, far fewer have been successful in achieving or contributing to broader goals and outcomes in a lasting way. Some aid has clearly not worked, most notably by failing to achieve its immediate objectives. Some has had adverse systemic effects, and thus has been harmful.

Although aid has led or contributed to sustained growth and poverty reduction in some countries, the country-level impact has often been disappointing, sometimes because of the failures of aid but, more commonly, because the influence of other factors (external shocks, conflict, etc.) has reduced or eclipsed the good that aid has done, or might have done. Across many of the poorest countries, growth has remained stubbornly low and poverty stubbornly high, raising questions not merely about the impact of aid, but the appropriateness of the policy advice proffered. Many poor countries have been ill served by the rigidity and narrowness of much of the macro-level policy advice coming from the leading international financial institutions (IFIs), which have proved inadequate to address their complex, structural and long-term development problems. Much short-term technical assistance has had a tangible positive effect, but donors have been far less able to make lasting contributions to capacity development and institutional strengthening. While often valuable and important in the short term, much official development aid has not done much lasting good: there have been huge gaps between expectations and achievements.

But has *most* official development aid worked, or failed? The honest answer is that we still don't know—not for lack of trying, but due to the inherent difficulties of tracing its contribution. After more than five decades of aid-giving, the bulk of the most reliable and accessible information on impact relates to discrete projects, supplemented in the last decade by some assessments of the contribution made by individual donors in particular countries. Cross-country studies seeking to find the answer to the question 'Does aid work?' do not provide a reliable guide on the overall and explicit contribution of aid to development and poverty reduction. They never will.

It has only been in the last five to ten years that donors have seriously acknowledged the need to begin to work more closely together, by coordinating and harmonizing their individual aid efforts, and aligning their support with aid-recipient strategies and their institutional development needs. It will still be some years before more rigorous, long-term, time-series data will be available at the country level with which to assess the overall impact of these continuing, discrete aid interventions and the aid which donors have pooled together and provided en bloc. Even then, firm conclusions may still remain elusive. Continual changes to the ways that aid is provided make it even more difficult to assess its wider impact, not least comparing the impact from one time period to the next, as does our still incomplete knowledge about the contribution of the different array of factors which drive the complex engines of growth and development. They will differ both across different countries and within different time periods.

This environment of uncertainty and searching has left the discourse on aid impact particularly open to bias, distortion and even propaganda. Against the backdrop of major data gaps on the precise relationship between aid, growth and poverty, as well as considerable uncertainty about precisely how aid might best contribute to poverty reduction, it is not surprising that interest groups with widely differing views about aid's impact remain influential in their claims about the workings of development aid. Space is given to aid's critics, who both claim and provide evidence that aid is ineffective, as well as to aid's supporters, who also provide evidence to show that it works. As there is no authoritative, overarching evidence to clinch the argument about aid's enduring impact, the lure of using partial evidence to 'prove' aid's virtuous or destructive influence becomes particularly attractive. It is far more attention-grabbing to assert, sweepingly, that aid either works, or that it doesn't, than it is to conclude—with more accuracy and more honesty—that the evidence is mixed, or that we are not able to provide a definitive general answer. The discourse about the impact of official aid takes place on the mistaken assumption that there is sufficient evidence of sufficient quality 'out there' to prove that it works or that it doesn't. As a result, far too much discourse about aid effectiveness is little more than a game of chasing shadows.

One of the main reasons why so much energy is devoted to trying to prove that official development aid works (or that it doesn't) is the strong belief that the answer to this question provides the core justification for providing (or not providing) it. Most donor agencies, and those working in these agencies, appear to believe that the basic justification for providing ODA is that it is needed and that it works. Clearly, if a central part of the reason for giving aid is evidence that it works, then it is vital to provide, or to go in search of, evidence which shows that it does. Likewise, if a central part of the reason for not giving aid is evidence of its failure, then it is vital to provide, or to go in search of, evidence which shows that it doesn't work.

One way in which the necessity of aid has been understood is that 'aid is necessary for development'—meaning that without aid, there can be no development. One of the main conclusions to be drawn from a dispassionate review of the evidence is that this is not true: it cannot be sustained as a general proposition. Development, growth and poverty reduction do take place without recourse to aid.

Does that mean that the claim that development aid is needed cannot be justified? No, it can be made, but the argument is more complex. First, it has to be shown that development aid is required by the recipient. Secondly, it has to be shown that the funds and resources which make up the aggregate aid flow are capable of contributing to development and poverty reduction.[1] For very poor countries with large numbers of poor people, insufficient resources to provide for core services, high levels of debt, ineffective institutions and little prospect of being able to achieve substantive structural changes in the short term, aid would appear to have an important gap-filling role to help meet the immediate basic needs of poor people. What is more, the evidence presented here confirms that in helping to address these short-term needs, much aid has been successful (between 75 and 90 per cent) when it has provided tangible goods needed and used directly by poor people—medicines, bed-nets, seeds to plant, improved water supplies to prevent cholera. What is not so clear is whether this sort of short-term, practical, gap-filling, consumption-focused and often 'ring-fenced' aid sufficiently contributes to longer-term sustainable development for it to be included under the nomenclature of 'development' aid. Many would argue that such aid is better viewed as 'life-saving', and thus closer to humanitarian than to development aid.

Are the (usually still far larger) quantities of development aid which play a more indirect and less immediate role in contributing to growth and poverty alleviation necessary? The claim that this sort of aid is essential can be sustained if it can be shown that such aid is able to contribute (directly and/or indirectly) to the enhancement of (pro-poor) growth and development and to a sustained decline in poverty levels, notably by helping to create a favourable environment through strengthening capacities, institutions and infrastructure, and that it is *urgent* to achieve these higher rates of development and faster declines in poverty. If such aid can hasten the achievement of such outcomes, then the justification for providing development aid is compelling. However, this constitutes more of an ethical than an economic argument because it involves moral value judgements. It is based on one's views about the value of human life and what is needed for human lives to flourish. It is about the value one places on striving to ensure as many people as possible are able to have all their basic human rights fulfilled. These issues were discussed more fully in Part II.

For the present, it merely needs to be accepted that there is an urgency, and that long-term development aid can contribute to these outcomes. At the extreme, and even if there were great urgency, there would be no justification for providing development aid if there were insurmountable obstacles to its ever being used effectively. However, if it can be shown that development aid can help to reduce poverty, create wealth and contribute to development faster than if it were not provided, this would be ample justification for providing it.

Effectiveness does matter

This should not be interpreted as suggesting that overall aid effectiveness does not matter—that providing aid is justified as long as some of it works. Overall aid effectiveness matters greatly, and the justification for providing development aid will be considerably enhanced if it is used as effectively as possible. The more effectively aid is utilized, the more quickly it can contribute to long-term development outcomes. Hence, whenever aid is provided in contexts where its impact is less than optimal, one must analyse and isolate those factors which constrain its greater impact, and apply those lessons as quickly as possible to all future aid-giving to enhance its future impact. The crucial question then is not whether, overall, development aid works, but whether, when it is urgently needed, there is evidence that it can make a positive contribution to development and poverty reduction.[2] If it can be shown that it cannot—ever—make a difference, then it should not be provided. However, if it can be shown to be doing some good, then whether 20 per cent, 50 per cent or 80 per cent of development aid is currently judged to be 'working', or whether we have insufficient evidence to judge how much aid is effective, becomes a secondary issue. The onus is *always* on trying to improve its impact and effectiveness, whether most of it currently 'works' or most of it currently does not.

If official development aid can be shown to be needed, then attention needs to focus far less on worries about whether in general it 'works', and far more on working out and implementing policies to make it work better. Over the past 20 to 30 years, the evidence suggests that the aggregate impact of aid provided by individual donors has increased, though from a fairly low base. But it also shows that significant gaps still remain between what we know about how the impact of aid can be enhanced and the prevailing methods and ways donors provide it. If the sceptics are to be convinced that aid works, the gap between the claims that aid is urgently needed and its effective and efficient use continually needs to be narrowed.

Thus, the central question in aid discourse is not 'Does aid work?', but rather 'How can aid to poor countries be made more effective?' Ironically, the more donors are dominated by the felt need to reassure their supporters that the aid they provide works, the less able they will be to explain that the real challenge they face lies in making aid work better, notably in countries and contexts where it is desperately needed but most of it (currently) may not be working. If enhancing the effectiveness of aid were to become the central question in aid discourse, then a good aid agency would not be judged in relation to its ability to show that all its aid works. Rather, it would be judged by showing that, in circumstances where the prospects for success are exceptionally poor, and, at the extreme, where aid has predominantly failed, the agency has worked with other donors and with poor people to make some tangible differences to the lives of those who really need external assistance.

16 NGOs in development and the impact of discrete NGO development interventions

NGOs: an overview

The discussion now shifts from official aid to that provided by non-governmental organizations (NGOs). The last 25 years have witnessed a phenomenal growth in the contribution of NGOs to the overall aid effort. NGOs run many times more development projects and programmes than those funded by official aid agencies, and by 2004, the total value of NGO aid-funded activities was almost $24bn, equivalent to over 30 per cent of overseas development aid (ODA). In some poor countries, NGOs (including church-based agencies) are responsible for 10 per cent of health and education services—in a few countries, such as Haiti, probably in excess of 50 per cent. In Bangladesh, one NGO on its own, the Bangladesh Rural Advancement Committee (BRAC), provides basic curative and preventive health services to more than 97mn people, out of a total population of 143mn.

WHAT ARE NGOs?

The term 'non-governmental organizations' covers many different agencies from locally based to global, those based in the industrialized donor countries usually called northern NGOs (oddly, as they include Australian and New Zealand-based organizations), and those based in developing countries, called southern NGOs. They include direct implementers of projects with grassroots communities, intermediary support organizations and different sorts of umbrella organizations. Those of concern to us here all share three common characteristics: direct or indirect involvement in humanitarian and development work; the not-for-profit nature of their activities; and, as their name suggests, the fact that they are distinct and separate from both governments and from private for-profit organizations.¹ Box 16.1 provides a summary sketch of the different sorts of organizations which are usually included under the umbrella term NGO.²

Especially since the early 1990s, NGOs have been viewed as a part of what has been termed 'civil society'. At its most general level, civil society refers to all people, activities, relationships, and formal and informal groups that are not part of the process of government. It includes an array of civil society organizations (CSOs) of which NGOs involved in development and humanitarian work constitute a subgroup, together with all other non-governmental groups and associations, including trades unions, business associations and looser groupings such as social movements, networks and even virtual groups.

Though some NGOs derive part of their income from commercial, usually trading, activities, almost all NGO development projects and programmes are funded by aid money. The three main sources of NGO aid are private donations, governments, and private foundations. All these income sources have expanded rapidly in recent years. Foundation funding comes from long-standing household names such as Ford and Rockefeller, new organizations such as the Bill and Melinda Gates Foundation in the United States, and

---

BOX 16.1 THE WORLD OF NGOs

The term NGO encompasses a wide range of organizations ranging from very large to tiny. The term International NGO (INGO) refers to organizations whose work extends across sometimes scores of different countries. The work of national NGOs is predominantly focused on activities related to one country. Many national NGOs are extremely small, focused on activities related to a province or an even smaller locality in a particular country. However, some larger national NGOs as well as INGOs engage in advocacy, lobbying and campaigning at both the national and international levels. In the United States, the term private voluntary organization (PVO) broadly equates with what is known elsewhere as a non-governmental organization.

NGOs can engage in development either directly or indirectly. Those that are not directly involved in implementing projects are often called intermediary organizations, which provide funds, advice or other forms of support to implementing agencies. Both INGOs and national NGOs implement projects and programmes with poor communities, but some INGOs and some national NGOs (though far fewer) choose not to be direct implementers. Confusingly, some INGOs implement projects in some countries and act solely in an intermediary capacity in others. Where implementing agencies work exclusively in and among poor communities they are often termed grassroots organizations (GROs). A membership-based organization (MBO) is a particular type of GRO which represents and is accountable to the community of members, who are likely to be the prime beneficiaries of its activities.

Ambiguously, the term non-governmental development organization (NGDO) is also used to refer to NGOs involved in both development and humanitarian and emergency works. The term will be avoided here. Some NGOs are involved in activities not principally concerned with development and poverty alleviation, including environmental NGOs and some human rights NGOs. These NGOs, though important, are not the focus of discussion in this book.

hundreds of smaller ones such as the Gatsby Foundation in the United Kingdom. Together, these sources provide hundreds of millions of dollars each year to support NGO activities. Most private donations are made by citizens of industrialized countries, though in some middle-income developing countries, such as South Africa, Chile and Brazil, a (relatively small) share of income received by locally based NGOs is raised domestically. In China, it is estimated that about 1 per cent of NGO income comes from private donations (Cotterrell and Harmer 2005: 21). Though there has been plenty of talk of 'aid fatigue', the private funding of NGOs has risen steadily, and at times rapidly, over the past 15 years, and in some donor countries, such as the UK, short-run economic downturns have had little or no impact on the long-term expansion in private donations. The sources of official funding of NGOs are more varied than is commonly thought. It is not only rich-country governments which fund NGO activities, though this expanding source of funding still remains the most significant. A growing number of poor-country governments are now supporting and providing funds for NGO activities, their ability to do so boosted by the increase in official donor funds channelled to budget support and SWAps. In some poor countries, however, government support to NGOs has a far longer history. For instance, since the early 1980s the growth of many Indian NGOs has been linked to expanding government funding, which quadrupled in the five years to the year 2000 to more than Rs2bn ($50mn) (Thakur and Saxena 1999).

Equipped with these aid funds, NGOs undertake their emergency and development work. Chapter 19 discusses the impact of their activities in the emergency and humanitarian fields. In this chapter and the next, we focus on the development side of their work, examining the evidence in order to assess the impact of NGO development activities, and thereby answering the question: 'Does NGO development aid work?' This question is not easy to answer, which is probably why, to this day, no book has been produced or study undertaken which attempts rigorously to answer it.

NGOS' UNDERSTANDING OF THEIR ROLE IN DEVELOPMENT

In trying to answer the question 'Does NGO development aid work?', it is necessary to understand the nature and range of NGO development activities. At one level, this is a relatively easy task, which involves listing and describing the different activities that different NGOs undertake in the name of development. But even this exercise can be seen as controversial, because NGOs are far from united in their analysis of development and how best to eradicate poverty. Indeed, there are some NGOs who contend that poor people don't want to be 'developed' at all, and others who contend that poor people have no wish to be drawn into the process of modernization upon which mainstream NGO development activities are based. From such perspectives, the very provision of aid is likely to be viewed as damaging rather than beneficial: the more aid that is given the more damage that is done.[3]

For others, debate is centred on the legitimacy of NGOs engaging in certain types of activity. No one seriously challenges the view that NGOs ought to work with poor, grassroots communities. But should they do more than this? For over three decades, one strand of opinion has argued that (development) NGOs should only be involved in a narrow group of 'hands-on' activities centred on service delivery, or on income-generating activities. All other types of activities, such as advocacy and lobbying work, are deemed illegitimate because they move NGOs into the political realm, an arena into which NGOs, the critics contend, ought not to venture. From such a perspective, if NGOs fail in their lobbying and advocacy work, this would be deemed beneficial, for it would encourage NGOs to shift resources back to their more narrow service delivery and linked activities, giving greater priority to enhancing the impact of these activities.

Space does not permit further discussion of these more extreme dissenting voices, though they do illustrate an important feature of NGO development work, namely that its boundaries have always been contested. The present discussion is focused on what might be termed the 'centre-ground' views of NGO development activity. As understood here, the centre ground encompasses a large space, indeed, one occupied by the vast majority of NGOs which are actively involved in development work, and which use the aid funds provided to them. They broadly share a common view about development and their role in helping to promote it, which, in principle at least, is largely shared by the majority of governments who support and fund their development activities. In brief, the centre-ground view is that poverty and deprivation are intricately linked to a lack of power, voice and influence. Poverty is caused not merely by a shortage of assets, skills and basic services, but by structures, institutions, policies and processes which marginalize poor people, particularly women and girls, and which maintain or increase vulnerabilities and limit opportunities of both individuals and communities, restricting the development and expansion of core capabilities.[4] It is against this multi-dimensional backdrop of the causes of poverty that NGOs use their aid funds to undertake a wide array of activities that they consider essential for long-term poverty eradication.

Both historically and today, the bulk of development work undertaken by NGOs has involved the support or implementation of specific projects and programmes for particular groups of (poor) people and (poor) communities, encompassing service delivery activities (providing schooling, health, housing, water and sanitation) and activities aimed at raising the incomes and enhancing the livelihoods of these communities. However, the centre-ground view is that this work should not be seen in isolation. One of the core, though less tangible, purposes of the majority of NGO projects and programmes involving poor people and communities is to seek to further the objective of 'empowering' poor people and poor communities, assisting them to gain a louder 'voice' and greater influence to enable them to take greater control of their lives, not least by helping to alter policies and key decisions affecting them.[5] One way that NGOs have increasingly tried to pursue this objective has been by helping to strengthen and build the capacity of poor communities. This is why service delivery and income-enhancing projects have increasingly been undertaken in conjunction with efforts aimed at strengthening those community-based and grassroots organizations which represent their views and aspirations.

The centre-ground view of poverty and its causes also provides the backdrop for understanding why NGOs have used aid funds to support a range of different purposes *beyond* activities targeted at particular people and communities. If poverty is, in part, caused and perpetuated by structures, institutions, policies and processes that directly or indirectly impinge upon the lives of poor people and (poor) communities, then a lasting solution requires these to be identified and efforts directed at addressing them, no matter where they are found—not merely in the locality where poor people live, but at the regional, national and international level. Likewise, to the extent that poverty is caused or perpetuated by political structures or processes and by the actions and activities of powerful political and economic interest groups, then the centre-ground view is that these are also legitimate targets to influence and change.[6] It is these perspectives which have led NGOs to utilize aid funds to support a range of activities beyond discrete projects and programmes for (poor) people and (poor) communities. The activities funded, supported and promoted have included advocacy, lobbying and campaigning activities, awareness-raising, and development education work. They have taken place at the local, regional and national, as well as international, levels.

Some NGOs have undertaken other types of activities. For instance, NGOs have taken it upon themselves to review and monitor the activities of other agents of development: governments, other aid agencies and private sector providers. This work has consisted of three elements: examining the reach of basic services provided by these agencies, ensuring that poorer and more marginalized communities are included; monitoring the quality of services to ensure that it meets minimum standards; and ensuring that they are affordable. Increasingly, too, NGOs have linked up with other NGOs to establish formal and informal networks to make a greater impact, most recently taking advantage of modern communications, not least the World Wide Web, to expand and strengthen their influence, voice and impact. Today, few medium-sized or large NGOs undertake development work on their own and in isolation: most belong to at least one cluster, grouping, network or umbrella group (and often a number of these), some on a permanent but many on a temporary basis.

The result is that a growing number of NGOs, especially medium-sized and larger ones, are now using aid funds to undertake some or all of these 'beyond-the-project' activities. Some NGOs have been established exclusively to work on advocacy, lobbying and campaigning issues, and many of these do not fund, implement or directly support *any* projects with poor communities. However, for the vast majority of bigger NGOs, these types of activities typically consti-tute a small part of their overall activities, absorbing considerably less than a quarter of their expenditure budget. There is no accurate aggregate breakdown of the share of directly targeted and other activities of NGOs, largely because many NGOs, including the largest ones, do not provide a clear breakdown of types of expenditure: many lump together all expenditures under what is euphemistically called 'programme support'. In some cases, this is deliberate, as even some large NGOs fear that members, supporters and private donors are wary, and some even hostile, to the marked swing to advocacy, lobbying and campaigning work which has taken place in practice.

But there is another explanation. There has been a very rapid rise in the funds channelled to capacity building and institutional strengthening, where it is often difficult to distinguish clearly between support to enhance the impact of discrete poverty-focused projects and beyond-the-project activities. In turn, expanding support for strengthening the capacity and capabilities of NGOs has been taking place at a time when growing emphasis has been given to the role of civil society in development. Especially over the past 15 years, the concept of civil society has emerged to take a central place in discourse about develop-ment, and in assisting the achievement of the Millennium Development Goals (MDGs) in particular. Not surprisingly, a growing number of NGOs have relabelled major areas of their work as contributing to the 'strengthening of civil society'. This catch-all phrase includes capacity building and institutional strengthening, but it also includes initiatives aimed at creating new NGOs and expansion of the activities of NGOs beyond their narrower, project-based work. These changes are now reflected in the way NGOs report how they are spending aid funds. For instance, in its 2005 annual report, the large Dutch church-based NGO, the Interchurch Organisation for Development Co-operation (ICCO), recorded total annual spending of 125mn in 2004, of which 48 per cent consisted of direct poverty-alleviation activities, 17 per cent policy influencing activities, and 31 per cent civil society-strengthening projects and programmes.[7]

Though there are no aggregate figures which show accurately the share of NGO aid going to direct project versus beyond-the-project activities, a rough (best-guess) estimate would be that beyond-the-project activities, including advocacy, lobbying, campaigning and linked information and publicity work, are now absorbing upwards of 15 per cent of all NGO expenditure on development activities, rising to perhaps 25–35 per cent if capacity building and strengthening civil society are included. Consequently, an assessment of the impact of NGO development activities can no longer omit an assessment of these activities. It needs to include an assessment of the impact of aid funds used to support and implement discrete projects and programmes with particular communities, aid funds used for advocacy, lobbying and campaigning, aid funds used to build the capacity of development-oriented NGOs, and aid funds used, most generally, to help strengthen and build civil society. This is a very tall order. The impact of these types of NGO activities is discussed in Chapter 17. The rest of this chapter discusses the impact of NGO projects and programmes on particular poor people and communities within poor countries.

Methodological challenges

DATA GAPS

The gaps in data and information which limit our ability to form judgements about the impact of official aid are even more severe in the case of NGO aid-funded development initiatives than in the case of ODA. Part of the problem can be traced back to the formation and the very nature of NGO activities. Most long-established NGOs were inspired by and still give the highest priority to action and 'doing'; they have devoted far less attention and priority to analysing carefully not only the wider but often the immediate impact of their activities. While large and medium-sized NGOs have always been fairly rigorous in terms of financial reporting and accounting, it has only been in the last 15–20 years that, with some exceptions, even the largest NGOs have formally begun to produce systematic project-based information.[8] However, the bulk of this growing and now large data-bank of information remains largely descriptive, focusing on the recording of the inputs provided (medicines, school-books, goats, training) and the outputs achieved (patients in hospital, children receiving books, people trained). Notwithstanding these advances made by many larger NGOs, many small NGOs still remain hard-put to provide even basic project information in any comprehensive fashion.[9] What is more, most NGO project reports do not even try to assess the impact of their projects on the lives and living standards of the beneficiaries.

Things are changing, however. Over the past 15–20 years, there has been a growing interest in impact evaluation, especially among the larger and medium-sized NGOs, a number of which, like BRAC, Oxfam and Save the Children, have produced their own evaluation manuals. Most have now internalized the need to try to assess the impact of their work and there has been a steady growth of NGO impact assessments of discrete NGO projects and programmes. But, just as with official aid projects, the ability to draw firm and unambiguous conclusions about impact has been seriously impeded by

the absence of baseline data, as well as the difficulties of determining attribution (see Chapter 10). Additionally, because the number of more rigorous
evaluations has been comparatively small—and tiny in comparison with the
total number of NGO projects—there is no reliable way of knowing how far
the results of these evaluations are representative of the wider whole. One of
the most evaluated NGO projects is the multi-million-dollar Aga Khan Rural
Support Program (AKRSP) in Pakistan, involving around 900,000 beneficiaries. Over an 18-year period, the World Bank has conducted four comprehensive in-depth evaluations of this project. But even in its fourth attempt, the
Bank still found it difficult to judge the extent to which changes in living
standards and income were due to the NGO project itself rather than to other
factors and influences (2002b: 5–17).

There are other methodological challenges involved in trying to assess the
impact of NGO development interventions. For many NGOs, it is insufficient
merely to assess the impact of aid-funded projects in terms of whether, in the
short term, basic services, or water, education and health, have been adequately
provided, and poor people's incomes have been enhanced in an efficient, effective and sustainable way. What matters most to many NGOs is whether poor
people have greater control over their lives—greater power and more voice—to
influence future patterns of development. Yet these issues fit uneasily into the
priorities of the orthodox aid evaluation toolbox. Additionally, as just noted,
the majority of discrete NGO projects now contain a capacity-building
component, creating a more complex intervention and making it even more
difficult to judge the relative contribution of the different components of what
are increasingly becoming multi-layered aid interventions.

As with official aid, the more interesting, and ultimately more important,
question about NGO development interventions concerns their wider impact.
What is the overall impact of NGO development activity in particular countries? Regrettably, there has always been and remains to this day an almost
complete absence of data and information with which to assess the wider and
systemic impact of NGO development interventions and activities. Compared
to the amount of money spent and ink spilt trying to analyse the impact of
official aid at the country level and beyond, it is surprising that no rigorous
attempt has been made to try to assess the overall effect of NGO activities in
any aid-recipient country. Indeed, neither has there been an attempt to aggregate the combined effects of all the major NGO interventions in a particular
country, or even of a particular sub-sector where NGO contributions play a
major role in the delivery of services, in order to try to develop a sense of the
overall effect of all the different interventions in different sectors.[10] This remains
a major gap in our understanding of the overall impact of NGO development
activities because in a growing number of countries, these activities are of
national importance. For instance, it has recently been estimated that NGOs
and CSOs provide around 40 per cent of all health care in Ghana, Zimbabwe

and Kenya (Court *et al.* 2006: 1), while a study of aid to Mozambique judged that NGO aid amounted to $50–80mn, accounting for 2 per cent of GDP (Arndt *et al.* 2006: 27). However, it remains a gap that is unlikely to be bridged quickly. It is not easy to assess the overall impact of official aid in a country (see Bigsten *et al.* 2006). It is far harder to assess the impact of all NGO development activities. Perhaps the best that can be hoped for in the short term is for overall assessments of aid at the country level to try to include all types of aid, and thus to shift away from the historically narrow exclusive focus on official aid.[11]

A trawl through the literature on the impact of NGOs shows that a number of studies have been carried out which purport to be assessments of NGO activities in particular aid-recipient countries. Studies of NGOs in Bangladesh, Kenya, Uganda and Zimbabwe have been particularly prominent. Yet, none of these have attempted to provide a rigorous assessment of the overall impact of NGO activities in these countries. Rather, they are limited to providing a descriptive overview of the number, type and range of NGO interventions, in some cases providing data on the share of aid used by NGOs. This provides the backdrop against which to introduce a review of the more detailed impact of a number of discrete NGO interventions.[12]

DIFFICULTIES OF OBTAINING INFORMATION ON PROJECT PERFORMANCE

The absence of information is only one problem. Trying to obtain existing information constitutes a second major hurdle. With very few exceptions, the information which NGOs put forward to the public on their projects and programmes does not provide a representative picture of the performance of their activities. It is heavily biased towards showing success, dominated by examples of projects illustrating the areas in which they believe they are making a significant difference to the lives of those people their projects are trying to assist. This does not mean that agencies are deliberately trying to deceive their different publics.[13] The purpose of distributing this information is not to provide a rounded picture of performance. It is to elicit support for the agency, which, it is assumed, will grow more by highlighting its successes.

NGOs themselves do not have information to enable them to judge their overall performance. Key staff in most NGOs will have some idea of difficult and under-performing projects and of those which are failing, but only a very few NGOs collate this information systematically or even distribute it regularly within their own agencies or to their governing boards. Most NGOs themselves do not know enough about how well they are performing.

In recent years, wider debates across many industrialized countries about the accountability and transparency of public and private sector organizations have begun to be extended to the not-for-profit sector, including NGOs. Over time, this is likely to lead to changes in the way that larger NGOs, in particular, manage their project information and public access to it. Already, it is having an impact, stimulating the work that agencies are doing to expand, upgrade and enhance their own work on impact assessment. Yet most of the details of the outcome of this work remain confined to the technical departments of the larger NGOs, and it is difficult to access. There are only a handful of NGOs today which put information into the public domain which draws attention to failures and problems as well as successes. Among these are the Cooperative for Assistance and Relief Everywhere (CARE) USA, which every two years, since 2001, has published the results of the findings of all its evaluations, and Oxfam (GB), which now produces annually a programme impact report which provides examples of problems, failures and weaknesses in its projects and programmes as well as its successes (Goldenberg 2001, 2003; Oxfam 2005). One of the earliest examples of an NGO putting critical evaluation material into the public domain is the largest Bangladesh-based NGO, BRAC. Since its establishment in 1975, BRAC's research and evaluation department has presented to the public critical evaluations of the impact of the agency's different development projects and programmes.[14]

The most accessible body of data and information available on the impact of NGO development initiatives consists of evaluations which have been commissioned by official aid agencies. In the case of USAID, there is quite a large body of material stretching back as far as the 1970s (see Barclay *et al.* 1979). For other countries, donor-led evaluations began to be commissioned in growing numbers from the mid-1980s. In the mid-1990s, the OECD/DAC commissioned a study which, ambitiously, attempted to gather and synthesize the results of all evaluations of the impact of NGO development projects and programmes undertaken up to the year 1997. The study synthesized the findings of 23 donor-sponsored studies, commissioned 13 country case studies and drew on the wider literature (see Riddell, Kruse *et al.* 1997). Since then, there has been a steady stream of further donor-funded evaluation studies, and a number of donor-funded studies undertaken by NGO staff and consultants. These studies have focused predominantly on the impact of discrete NGO projects and programmes using orthodox evaluation approaches. As a result, they have given relatively little prominence to the empowerment dimension of project work, and have provided only limited information on the impact of capacity and institutional initiatives, and next to no information on advocacy, lobbying and campaigning work. For their part, NGOs have expanded their own capacity to undertake impact studies and evaluations. Most NGO-based assessments have been undertaken in order to learn lessons for the future, usually using participatory approaches, involving the implementing NGOs and, in some instances, the ultimate beneficiaries.

The impact of NGO development projects and programmes

THE REACH OF NGO DEVELOPMENT ACTIVITIES

One dimension of the impact and influence of the projects and programmes implemented by NGOs is their 'reach': the numbers of people whom their activities aim to assist. Various 'guesstimates' of the numbers reached have been made. In the early 1990s, a UN study judged that whereas in the early 1980s, NGO development activities 'touched' 100mn people, this had risen to around 250mn by the early 1990s (UNDP 2003: 93). Ten years on, the numbers will have increased even further. It is not possible to say with any certainty how many people are being assisted by direct NGO development projects, but if the claims made by the larger NGOs provide anything like a reliable guide, and allowing for some double-counting, then today probably well in excess of 600mn people in the developing world have some sort of direct contact with NGO projects and programmes.[15] When the indirect effects of NGO advocacy work and the monitoring done by NGOs and other CSOs of government and official aid projects, there can be no doubt that the development activities undertaken by NGOs reach hundreds of millions more poor people. The most recent expansion of NGO aid-funded activities has coincided with a significant shift of official aid away from projects that are directly targeted at poor people. It is thus likely that more people in poor countries are now directly assisted by projects and programmes run or overseen by NGOs than by projects funded directly by official aid.

THE ACHIEVEMENT OF IMMEDIATE PROJECT OBJECTIVES

What has been the impact of the tens of thousands of discrete NGO projects and programmes aimed at providing basic services, raising incomes and enhancing livelihoods?

The results from published evaluation material, encompassing donor-led studies and syntheses undertaken and published by individual NGOs and by NGO umbrella organizations, provide a broadly consistent picture: a large majority of NGO projects would appear to be successful in achieving their immediate objectives.[16] Studies undertaken in the late 1980s and early 1990s judged that around 85 per cent of NGO projects which had been the subject of an evaluation had fulfilled their immediate objectives. Most studies also suggested that performance had improved over time. More recent studies confirm both these conclusions. The 1997 OECD synthesis study concluded that 90 per cent of all NGO projects achieved their immediate objectives

(Riddell *et al.* 1997: 18), while the Danish impact study, published two years later, was unable to find any evidence of project failure, reporting that all projects examined were able to deliver a significant proportion of expected outputs (Oakley *et al.* 1999a: 10). Likewise, a 25-year review of EU support to over 8,000 NGO projects in 132 countries, involving detailed country-based research, concluded that 60 per cent of projects scored from 'satisfactory to excellent' in relation to the stated objectives achieved (South Research 2000: 39). The 2003 mega-evaluation of CARE's projects concluded that 82 per cent had achieved their immediate objectives, 18 per cent had 'mixed results' and none had 'no substantial results' (Goldenberg 2003: 5).

What precisely do these results tell us? To what extent does the high success score merely reflect the selection of a biased sample of more successful projects which have been the subject of more rigorous scrutiny? In some though not all cases, the projects examined have been selected by the NGOs, suggesting a bias towards those assessed as better-performing (see Riddell and Robinson 1995: 53ff.). However, most donor-commissioned studies addressed this question, and the general conclusion was that although there probably was some bias in project selection, it would not have made a major difference to the overall thrust of the conclusions.[17] Consequently, the evidence does seem to be sufficiently robust to enable us to conclude that a huge number of projects implemented by NGOs have delivered the key intended outputs. Health sector NGO projects have provided medicines, run clinics and hospitals and undertaken a range of preventive services. Education and training projects have built schools, enrolled pupils, trained teachers, taught pupils and run higher-level skill courses for students. Agricultural development projects have provided seeds, tools, training and access to credit. Water projects have provided communities with clean water, and infrastructural projects have built and upgraded roads and footpaths, installed irrigation, and provided people with housing. The results are certainly on a par with those reported for official aid projects.

The following constitutes some of the explicit findings of the recent batch of studies which have examined the impact of discrete NGO projects. Generalist NGOs (those willing to turn their hand to anything) appear to have had more success in social sector activities, supporting health and education projects, but less success in implementing more technical and complex projects. In contrast, specialist NGOs with trained staff tend to have had far greater success with more specialized interventions. For instance, United States-funded child survival projects have had a major effect on reducing child mortality across a number of countries (Mansfield 1997), while a number of the projects run by non-specialist NGOs aimed at increasing the incomes of productive cooperatives have produced minimal benefits to the members (Riddell *et al.* 1997: 21). A number of specialist NGOs focusing, for instance, on activities in the water and sanitation sector, on livestock projects and agricultural technology, have produced some impressive results. These have often been linked to the following attributes: clarity about the project purpose, sufficient funding, extensive engagement with and participation of the beneficiaries, technical competence, institutional capacity and adequate management.

THE EFFECTS OF NGO PROJECTS ON THE LIVES OF BENEFICIARIES

As with official aid projects, the fact that most projects achieve their immediate objectives is clearly important, and comforting. Yet on their own, these findings do not tell us nearly enough. What effects have these projects had on the lives of the beneficiaries: have they led to improvements in well-being, increases in income and enhanced lives and livelihoods? As with official aid projects, the evaluations and synthesis studies draw attention to the paucity of reliable data and information for reaching firm conclusions, but most are drawn to making some judgements, and they report quite a wide spread of impact results. Some are judged to be extremely successful, while some appear to have had very little impact on incomes and livelihoods. But in a very large number of cases, the studies either point to the difficultly in drawing firm conclusions, or suggest (often on the basis of minimal hard evidence) that the overall impact appears to have been small.

Given these extremes, one should be extremely wary of generalizing about the 'average' impact of NGO projects on lives and livelihoods. But there are other reasons to be cautious. A number of studies of NGO projects plead for caution in making judgements about the impact of NGO development efforts solely on the basis of the available impact results. For instance, the OECD synthesis study explains that paying too much attention to impact data runs the risk of the (very thin) available evidence being 'misused and having the perverse but unintended effect of downplaying NGOs' apparent strengths' (Riddell *et al.* 1997: xiv). Three points are made in support of this conclusion. First, impact assessments tend to ignore or give insufficient prominence to the empowerment dimensions of NGO development projects, which, for many, constitute a core purpose of NGO development interventions. As one experienced NGO researcher puts it, one of the most important things an NGO can give a local group is confidence to engage with outsiders (Carroll 1992: 116).[18] Secondly, and a related point, changes that appear marginal to the outside observer can often provide a crucial catalyst to galvanize poor people and poor communities, not least women and other excluded groups, into future longer-term action. Thirdly, if NGOs are right in their analysis that isolated projects are limited in the extent to which they are able, on their own, to change and improve the lives of communities, then the impact of discrete projects needs to be viewed alongside and not in isolation from changes occurring in the world beyond the project. The importance of this point is made in the OECD synthesis study, which argues that the external links between discrete projects and the world outside are critical in determining the wider impact of projects (Riddell *et al.* 1997: xiii).

Against this backdrop the following points have been made in the different evaluation studies about the wider impact of NGO projects. A minority have concluded that discrete NGO projects have made a major difference to the lives and potential of poor people. Most have concluded that they have made a positive impact, and in a few cases, a major impact. The majority of NGO projects have probably delivered tangible benefits, but many have probably made only a small contribution to improving the lives and enhancing the well-being of the beneficiaries. To most people, not least to the NGOs implementing NGO projects, this is not a particularly startling conclusion, for the purpose of the vast majority of NGO projects is to try to make a significant, but usually small, difference to the lives of the beneficiaries, as the discrete projects focus on one, or at most, a few dimensions of the manifestation and causes of poverty. Yet more needs to be said. An underlying objective of many discrete NGO projects is to try to provide a catalyst for poor people and poor communities, empowering them or providing them with added confidence to face the future. The extent to which this has happened has been insufficiently researched, though discussions between implementing NGOs and project beneficiaries often confirm that it has.

Almost 30 years ago an attempt was made to assess the wider impact of NGO projects in Kenya and Niger. The findings of this study provide a fairly accurate summary of what we know today about such impact. It concluded that in broad terms the participating population received at least some benefit in almost every case, judging that 18 per cent of projects had had a high impact, 47 per cent a moderate impact and 35 per cent a low impact. However, it commented that even in the case of successful projects, these were 'likely to represent the thin edge of the wedge, introducing a process of developmental change that will require other, complementary inputs from both inside and outside the beneficiary community' to make a long-term and sustainable difference to the lives of these poor people (Barclay *et al.* 1979: 87ff.).

SUCCESSES AND FAILURES

Box 16.2 gives the flavour of a handful of more successful NGO discrete project interventions. They illustrate the sorts of development outcomes that NGOs are able to achieve, though they are not necessarily representative of the wider picture.

Though more difficult to find, there is some documentation on NGO project failures. For instance, a joint evaluation of development projects in Kenya supported by two UK church-based NGO, the Catholic Agency for Overseas Development (CAFOD), assessed its two livestock projects as failures,

---

BOX 16.2 ILLUSTRATIONS OF SUCCESSFUL NGO DEVELOPMENT PROJECTS

In Zimbabwe by the early 1980s, a church-based NGO, Silveira House, working with farmers' groups, had assisted over 3,000 farmers to achieve a sevenfold increase in yields of maize on small-scale plots, enabling them to move out of subsistence farming into the cash economy.

The Van Gujjar community in northern India spend six months of the year travelling the Himalayas with their herds, which effectively exclude them from formal schooling and perpetuate high rates of adult illiteracy. The Indian NGO Rural Litigation and Entitlement Kendra (RLEK) devised adult literacy classes, established mobile schools and teachers and developed a curriculum adapted to the Van Gujjar's nomadic way of life. Their efforts resulted in the achievement of high rates of literacy among both young and old. In recognition of its work, RLEK won the UNESCO literacy award in 1988.

In 1985, in Bangladesh, BRAC began a programme of education for deprived children not being served by the formal school system. By 2004, almost 50,000 non-formal schools had been established, teaching the same competencies as formal schools, but in a shorter period of time, providing education to a far higher number of girls than in the formal sector and retaining a significantly higher proportion of harder-to-teach students.

In the Philippines, the Mindanao Baptist Rural Life Centre (MBRLC) worked with local farmers to develop a technology that enabled them to grow crops on degraded sloping land, resulting in considerably improved crop yields. The NGO then began to teach government agricultural extension officers how to use the same techniques, replicating the impact far more widely.

Farm Africa's management of the Maendeleo Agricultural Technology Fund in East Africa brings farmers' groups and NGOs together to make use of relevant agricultural technologies. The introduction of drought-resistant varieties of cassava has led to farm yields rising by 400 per cent.

Oxfam's 2005 programme impact study reports 37,000 women and men farmers achieving 200 per cent increases in their maize yields as a consequence of their participation in livelihood programmes, and a producers' cooperative in Ghana which had managed to increase sales by 35 per cent.

The following—also from the 2005 Oxfam report—is typical of hundreds of stories recounted each year by many medium-sized and large NGOs of the impact of their development projects on the lives of poor people:

Before, we were sitting in our houses with only a skirt without a top waiting till cooking time for what might be provided by our husbands. My first child did not go to school because of school fees. I now have an acre of rice and another plot planted with tomatoes, and I am able to sustain myself, pay my other children's school fees and eat well.

Sources: UNDP (1993); BRAC, RLEK and Farm Africa's websites; Lewis (2001); Muir (1992); Oxfam (2005).

---

achieving very limited achievement of objectives and few significant benefits in relation to costs.[19] The evaluation of an agricultural cooperative in Zimbabwe found it cost over $5,000 per participant, produced minimal benefits and was not viable (Muir 1992). Some NGO projects fail because of a lack of managerial and technical skills with which to implement projects. For example, the UNDP cited the case of income-generating projects in Africa supported by the Ford Foundation, and concluded that there were 'very few successes to talk about' (UNDP 1993: 94).

Some NGO projects fail because of the diversion of funds and corrupt practices. The following three examples illustrate these sorts of problems. In India, the Central Social Welfare Board blacklisted over 3,000 NGOs for failing to submit accounts on projects funded by the Board. In some instances it was apparent that funds had been misappropriated (Samuel 2000: 117). One study of NGOs in Dehradun revealed that out of 221 NGOs surveyed, 139 (over 60 per cent) were found to be fraudulent or existing only on paper (Saxena, 2003: 22). A World Bank study reported corrupt practices in a number of micro-enterprise NGOs in Togo, including one in the town of Kloto which convinced villagers to save money to build a pivotal base for future credit services; once the funds had reached a significant level, the NGO simply disappeared with the villagers' savings (2005e: 17). How typical are these examples? As with official aid, there are no accurate data on which to base generalizations. My own experience, overseeing the international work of the church-based agency Christian Aid, channelling over $35mn a year to support over 600 projects and programmes run by southern NGOs, was of a very small number of cases, amounting to one or two instances coming to light every four or five months, where problems arose in the accounting of project funds, not all of which were due to corrupt practices. In the overwhelming majority of cases, these involved relatively small amounts of money (under $20,000), accounting in aggregate for far less than 1 per cent of all project funds.[20]

THE WORLD OF MICRO-FINANCE

Micro-finance is one group of NGO project activities which has received extensive publicity as making a significant impact on the lives of poor people, with major successes claimed in raising their incomes and living standards. In its resolution 52/194 of 18 December 1997, the United Nations General Assembly noted that in many countries micro-credit programmes have proved to be an effective tool in freeing people from poverty and have helped to increase their participation in the economic and political processes of society.

Millions of dollars of aid, much of it provided by official donors, have poured into NGOs to provide small loans to tens of millions of individuals, often channelled through small-group mechanisms. By the end of 2005, it was estimated that some 100 mn people were involved in micro-credit schemes in poor countries. Much of the pioneering work in the field was led by the Grameen Bank in Bangladesh which, by the end of 2005, had provided credit to over five million clients, over 95 per cent women, in schemes characterized by low interest payments and very high rates of repayment. The Grameen 'model' has been replicated across poor countries on three continents, sometimes linked to other ways of giving poorer people access to credit.

There is an extensive and growing literature on the effect and impact of micro-finance projects. Here we can do little more than summarize some of the key findings on their impact. A small number of NGO schemes have failed to provide the funds promised, and some have had to wind up as clients have failed to repay their loans. But micro-finance schemes have attracted attention because, overwhelmingly, they do seem to have been successful. In particular, many schemes, including those run by NGOs with staff having the financial and management skills, have enabled those who would not otherwise have had access to cheap loans to obtain funds, and in the process, achieving high rates of return of outlaid loan funds.

However, unsurprisingly, many schemes have been costly to operate and have incurred high transaction costs, and a significant number have failed even to cover the more direct running costs of operating the schemes. Worryingly, too, there has often been an inverse relationship between the financial viability of NGOs providing micro-credit and the ability of organizations to reach poor borrowers in a sustainable manner. Additionally, some village-level studies reveal considerable overlap of different NGOs working in the micro-finance field (Jayasinghe and Wickramasinghe 2005). Some NGO schemes have foundered as they have grown and expanded operations, though some of the more successful have discarded their NGO status and become fully fledged banks (Hulme and Mosley 1996).

Of wider concern has been evidence of a number of micro-credit schemes failing to reach down to and benefit some of the poorest people in particular communities—one of the main reasons why micro-finance schemes have attracted such attention. In recent years, BRAC in Bangladesh acknowledged that this had been a weakness of its own extensive micro-credit schemes, leading it, in 2002, to launch two new pilot/experimental programmes for the 'ultra-poor'. These have smaller micro-credit components than their regular programmes, and are deliberately linked to other initiatives directed at the ultra-poor, including the provision of subsidized food and skills training. This evolving experience reinforces the findings of earlier studies which have suggested that the poorer the clients, the less likely it will be that credit on its own will provide a quick route out of poverty.

What has been the overall impact of micro-credit schemes on the lives of poor people? Though there are plenty of studies confirming that loan funds have been plentiful, there have been relatively few rigorous studies assessing the wider impact of credit on the lives of poor people. One of the most rigorous was a longitudinal study completed in 2002 which compared clients and non-clients, assessing impact in Zimbabwe, Peru and India (Snodgrass and Sebsted 2002). Its findings were mixed: in India, the incomes of those receiving funds rose, in Zimbabwe they did not, and in Peru the income gains were limited. However, even when income gains occurred, they were modest, with most clients continuing to move in and out of poverty. These broad findings are confirmed by a recent World Bank study of micro-finance and poverty in Bangladesh, which judged that only about 5 per cent of borrowers were able to 'lift themselves out of poverty' solely through micro-credit funds (Khandker 2003).

The Snodgrass and Sebsted study found that in all three countries, extremely poor people were reached, though they often used the funds provided to help meet immediate needs and to protect themselves against risk rather than as a means of raising income or expanding employment opportunities. In Peru during the period of analysis, both clients and non-clients had to reduce the limited assets they had in times of crisis, confirming the wider finding of NGO projects that successes and failures are (often) linked to what is happening in the world beyond the project. However, challenging the findings of some other studies, Snodgrass and Sebsted found that married women were empowered by the schemes, enabling them to engage actively in decisions with their husbands, and that micro-credit which targeted women did not exacerbate intra-household conflict (see Otero and Rhyne 1994).

Cost-effectiveness, quality, innovation and replication

NGO projects are widely assumed to provide excellent value for money. Most NGOs certainly pride themselves in keeping down administrative overheads, and the publicity of many large and medium-sized NGOs gives prominence to the very high share of total funds raised which go to projects for poor people, and are not channelled into administration and management, nor used for fund-raising activities. For instance, CARE US asserts that 92 per cent of its funds are spent on programme activities, only 8 per cent on support services and fund-raising.

COST-EFFECTIVENESS OF NGO PROJECTS AND SOME COMPARISONS WITH OTHER PROVIDERS

Assessing the cost-effectiveness of NGO aid projects is difficult. The OECD synthesis study reported that of the 28 studies reviewed, only one provided detailed data linking costs and benefits. For the vast majority of the many hundreds of NGO projects examined in almost 30 major donor studies, the data were insufficient to form firm judgements about cost-effectiveness (Riddell *et al.* 1997: 25). The little evidence there is encompasses the extremes. Some evaluations reveal projects that have received hundreds of thousands of dollars, equivalent to thousands of dollars per beneficiary, but which have produced little evidence of any positive outcome at all (Muir 1995: 261–2). Other NGO initiatives, such as the use and distribution of oral rehydration kits to treat cases of diarrhoea, pioneered by UNICEF, provide effective treatment to hundreds of thousands of people at the cost of a few cents. Are NGO projects, in general, cost-effective? Though most NGOs would argue they are, there is insufficient detailed evidence to make confident generalizations one way or the other.

A few studies have compared NGO projects with similar projects undertaken by poor-country governments and with projects implemented by official agencies, including USAID, the World Bank, DFID and Danida. Those studies comparing NGO with official aid projects have come up with mixed results, providing evidence of both higher and lower rates of cost-effectiveness (Huntingdon 1987: 24–5). Those comparing NGO and government interventions have also produced sharply divergent evidence. For example, a study of the Orangi Pilot Project in Karachi in Pakistan, which provided 28,000 families with water and sanitation, suggested that these services were provided at one-quarter the cost of similar projects built under the auspices of the local government (UNDP 1993: 86). Likewise, thousands of family wells and toilets constructed by the Mvuramwanzi Trust in Zimbabwe were erected at one-tenth the cost of government projects (Riddell and Robinson 1995: 54). In contrast, a study of rural clinics in Mozambique in the mid-1990s found that health services run by NGOs were up to ten times as expensive as those run by the government (Bond 2000). A study comparing NGO and government population projects in Kenya found that NGOs were more cost-effective in expanding demand for family planning services but not in providing services, though NGO services were found to be of higher quality (World Bank 1999b: 33).

Simple cost comparisons can be deceptive, however, as they do not always compare like with like. The Orangi and Mvuramwanzi projects were both less costly in part because beneficiaries provided their own labour at minimal cost, whereas government projects used paid labour. However, both these examples illustrate an important attribute that has characterized a number of NGO projects, namely their innovativeness. There are scores of examples of NGOs pioneering new and different ways of addressing particular problems, in many instances at lower cost, as well as examples of these approaches being replicated more widely (see Box 16.2; Carroll 1992: 120; Lewis 2001: 130). An illustrative example would be the water projects implemented by the NGO Dushtha Shasthya Kendra (DSK) in Dhaka, Bangladesh, supported by WaterAid. From the mid-1990s, DSK developed a model for those living in squatter settlements to secure access to clean water, negotiating installation agreements between communities and the water authorities, and supply agreements that included the payment of services by very poor households. Initial successes led to scaling up, extending and replicating this model, with DSK working with others, including UNICEF, Plan, UNDP and the World Bank (Ahmed 2003).

There are also thousands of examples of NGOs which have not necessarily introduced completely new methods and models, but have successfully adapted approaches from elsewhere. One of these is the (very simple) strategic positioning of bricks and stones on the edges of agricultural plots in West Africa, promoted by dozens of NGOs, which have enabled hundreds of thousands of hectares of marginal land to be used for growing crops. Much NGO project work is neither innovative nor replicable. But equally clearly, some has been, confirming the (cost-effective) benefits of blending together knowledge transfer and the addressing of need, which has characterized many discrete NGO projects and programmes, especially those that have been rooted in understanding the specific problems of particular communities.[21]

One simple but powerful indicator of the success of NGO projects is consumer choice. When people have had a choice, there is plenty of evidence to show that they often prefer to use non-governmental rather than government clinics, hospitals or schools, as the quality of service is judged to be better. Frequently this is because NGO projects have more resources (Carroll 1992: 120; Oakley 1999a). Regrettably, free state-run education has often meant classrooms with no textbooks and no teachers, due to a high level of teacher absenteeism, while many state-run clinics sometimes offer little more than free advice because they do not have regular supplies of even basic drugs.[22] Judged against such low standards, it has not been difficult for even minimally funded and not very efficiently run NGO projects to be favoured, and for the more efficient and effective NGO services to be in very high demand.

HOW MUCH DO NGO DEVELOPMENT PROJECTS REALLY COST?

As noted above, most northern-based NGOs, in particular, pride themselves on the very large share of total expenditure which is channelled into project and programme work directly for the benefit of specific poor communities. Similarly, many (probably most) individuals in donor countries who support and contribute financially to the work of NGOs believe that there is a close relationship between the funds NGOs allocate to projects and programmes in poor countries and the amount of money which the ultimate beneficiaries receive. In a number of ways, these claims and beliefs are misleading, if not erroneous, as the following paragraphs explain.

It is a common accounting practice in many countries to distinguish between 'general' agency-wide costs incurred in running the overall organization, and the costs incurred in implementing particular projects and programmes. When NGOs refer to the proportion of funds going into administration, it is only the former set of costs that they 'count' as administrative expenses, and it is on the basis of this assumption that the share of administrative costs to total programme and project expenditure usually appear to be so low.

Consistent with this convention, all administrative, management and support costs that are associated with or traceably linked to the implementation of specific projects and programmes in poor countries are classified as part of programme costs, not as (general) administrative costs. For large INGOs these costs would include the salaries of northern project staff, and the salaries of those administering projects and programmes in locally based NGOs. By convention, all these costs are included in (and count as) programme costs, not as administrative costs. Likewise, all transport and subsistence costs related to visits by programme and support staff from northern NGOs to southern NGOs and to the specific project location are also, by convention, classified as project or programme costs and not as administrative costs. In some cases a high proportion, if not all, of the costs incurred by a local NGO in a poor country which oversees, manages and administers particular projects are also included in overall programme costs of northern NGOs who support them. These would include all the running costs of southern NGO offices: transport, rent, computer purchases, utility bills, fuel, and the salaries of ancillary staff. In cases where a field project office is sited out of the main city centre, in the locality where the community lives, all costs directly or indirectly associated with the running of this field office are also classified as programme, not administrative costs. Taken together, all these programme and project support costs are considerable. Indeed, except in the case of large projects, they are likely to amount to a significant share of total project costs, often in excess of 20 per cent. In the case of small projects, they can, in exceptional cases, absorb half or more of total development project costs.

When all these 'support' costs are subtracted, how much is left to be spent on or used by the ultimate beneficiaries? Most NGOs are not able to answer this question with any accuracy because they have never actively sought to gather and analyse financial information in this way. Most NGO staff would be hard put to provide the answer.[23] In 2003, Christian Aid undertook an internal study to try to estimate the amount of money allocated to the agency's international development work which was ultimately used by—rather than provided for projects designed to help—the ultimate beneficiaries. The results suggested that less than 30 per cent of the overall international development budget reached the ultimate beneficiaries. However, by no means all the rest was spent on support costs. Much was absorbed in a range of capacity-building and institutional strengthening activities aimed at enhancing the capabilities of local organizations and their employees to undertake more effective development work. It is likely that other industrialized-country NGOs would have fairly similar programme cost figures, some even higher.

One reason for the high level of support costs is simply explained: most NGO projects, including service delivery projects, are expensive to oversee, manage and run: the more isolated the communities that NGOs work with, the more costly it is to reach and assist them.[24] It is not possible for NGOs to undertake or oversee projects which make a difference and to ensure that the funds provided are used for the purpose intended without spending considerable amounts on project management, staff skill training, and transport. What is of most concern are not the high costs, but the widespread public belief, fuelled by the way NGOs explain how they spend their money, that things are different, and by the 'powerful myth that development should be cheap' (Smillie 1995: 151).[25]

HOW MUCH NGO PROJECT AID REACHES THE BENEFICIARIES?

It is also widely believed that one of the key attributes of NGO development projects is their ability to reach down to and assist the poorest people. Indeed, many NGOs refer to the 'poorest of the poor' to describe the beneficiaries of their projects and programmes. What does the evidence tell us?

Little aggregate analysis has been done on this matter, and the studies that have been done are based on such flimsy data or questionable methods that their conclusions are neither robust nor reliable.[26] However, there are numerous examples from NGO project documents of NGO activities taking place among poor and marginalized communities, in both rural areas and in the slums and squatter settlements where populations are growing rapidly in many developing-country cities. Many NGOs, including larger ones such as BRAC, Oxfam and ActionAid, not only deliberately target marginalized communities but regularly undertake 'needs assessments' to analyse the social and economic stratification of societies in order to try to target those in more urgent need of assistance.[27] For example, BRAC's very large and successful project establishing informal schools deliberately targets those excluded from the formal school system, especially girls.

However, most donor-funded evaluations which have examined NGO projects suggest that it is far more common for NGOs to presume that they are working with the poorest than it is for them to undertake an assessment to confirm, or challenge, this assumption. Because the *very* poorest are difficult to reach, and even difficult to locate, increasing evidence suggests that it is unlikely that they will be included in NGO projects unless deliberate steps are taken to include and target them.[28] This does not mean that NGO projects are not targeted at poor people. Most beneficiaries of NGO projects would certainly be classed as poor, probably very poor, commanding income levels of less than $2 a day, and vulnerable to falling even below this level at certain times of the year. It is probably also true that the beneficiaries of most NGO projects are poorer than the beneficiaries of many official aid projects. But this is very different from the claim that a key characteristic of NGO projects is that they are explicitly focused (solely) on the poorest of the poor. That claim comes trippingly off the tongue, but in many cases, there is little evidence to support it, and considerable evidence to challenge it. Hence when CARE US asserts, as it does in its 2004 annual report, that its projects reached 45mn people with 870 'poverty-fighting' projects, it would be wrong to assume that all these beneficiaries are at the very bottom of the social and economic pile. It should also be noted that a number of church-run schools and hospitals across Africa, the Caribbean and Latin America, some of which are classified as NGOs, have historically served and still continue to serve—out of choice—middle-class and even wealthy clients, and are not targeted on poor clients.

LONG-TERM SUSTAINABILITY

The long-term financial sustainability of NGO projects has received growing attention in recent years, especially as both official donors and larger NGOs have been giving growing priority to results, impact and cost-effectiveness. The bulk of the NGO evaluation material which looks into the issue of sustainability has concluded that most NGO projects are not financially sustainable without the continued injection of external funds. Nor is it surprising that the poorer the beneficiaries, the less likely they are to be able to pay for the services, training or goods provided to them. Indeed, the prospects for financial sustainability of projects examined in the donor-funded study of Finnish NGO-supported projects were judged to be so poor that it was suggested that many development projects would be more aptly called welfare projects, as they consisted predominantly of helping poor people gain access to goods and services that they were unable to pay for themselves (Riddell *et al.* 1994: 139).

Exceptionally few studies have provided a long-term view of NGO projects and programmes. Most views on the sustainability of NGO projects are based on forward extrapolation of short-term assessments. In contrast, as noted above, the AKRSP in Pakistan has been the focus of successive studies extending for almost 20 years. The most recent evaluation of the project, in 2002, included the observation that the early objective of the Aga Khan Foundation, 'working itself out of a job', had proved unrealistic; the strong view was emerging that a continuing financial injection into the project remained critical for future viability (World Bank 2002b: 11–13). Similarly, even some examples of the highly successful NGO projects in Box 16.2 have had problems with sustaining these successes. For instance, many of the initially highly successful Silveira House farming projects subsequently collapsed. Especially when the environment beyond the project does not provide the context in which narrower project gains can be exploited, it has proven exceptionally difficult for discrete NGO projects on their own to enable poor people to build up a sufficiently large and sustainable asset or skill base permanently to live free from poverty (Oakley *et al.* 1999b: 40).

It is the existence of these sorts of problems which have led more and more NGOs to focus increasingly on activities beyond the project which are judged to be causing, contributing to or perpetuating poverty. The extent to which they are successful in these different endeavours is the subject of the next chapter.

Capacity development and institutional strengthening

THE IMPORTANCE OF CAPACITY DEVELOPMENT AND INSTITUTIONAL STRENGTHENING

Studies of the impact of NGO projects and programmes confirm that impact and effectiveness depend critically upon the capacities and capabilities of the organization implementing these projects and programmes (as well as the size and duration of the funds available) (Riddell *et al.* 1997: 97). It is thus not surprising that as attention has focused increasingly on results and the impact of NGO activities, capacity and capacity building have grown to take a central place in NGO activities and NGO discourse about development. Today, almost all medium-sized and all large NGOs are involved in some sort of capacity-building and institution-strengthening activities, and growing amounts of aid funds are used by NGOs for these activities.

However, there exist neither accurate nor even rough figures recording the amount of aid funds NGOs utilize to support this particular set of activities, though a conservative guess would be that many hundreds of millions of dollars are spent each year on building and strengthening the capacity and capabilities of NGOs. These funds are predominantly used either to help enhance the ability of NGOs to undertake their current tasks more effectively, or to assist them to expand into new areas of activity. In contrast to much of the literature on official aid, NGOs often do not distinguish clearly between skills training for particular individuals and assistance which is aimed at enhancing and building the capacity of the organization: it is generally all lumped together and called capacity building.

Not only are large amounts of money spent on capacity building, but these amounts are growing. There are a number of factors driving this growth:

• The first lies in the increase in both the number of NGOs and the scale of their activities: as NGOs have grown, so the need has increased to develop new and different organizational structures to enable them to undertake larger and more complex activities efficiently and effectively.

- Secondly, the movement of NGOs to undertake activities beyond the project has meant a growing need to have a wider range of skills within different organizations.
- A third factor has been the growing demands made on NGOs, initially by official donors and by other NGOs, but also by NGOs' own boards and governing bodies, to provide more rigorous data and information in the areas of financial management, appraisal, monitoring and evaluation.
- A fourth factor has been the wish of many developing-country NGOs to become more self-sufficient and less dependent upon the funds, skills and resources of donor-based NGOs.[29]

THE IMPACT OF NGO CAPACITY BUILDING AND INSTITUTIONAL DEVELOPMENT ACTIVITIES

Has the aid spent by and on NGOs on capacity building and institutional strengthening been well spent—has this form of aid spending 'worked'? It is not possible to provide a firm and reliable answer to this question. Indeed, of all the different ways that NGO aid is allocated and spent, least is known about the overall impact of capacity-building initiatives, even though, ironically, some sort of capacity-building activity is undertaken by more NGOs than any other activity, and many undertake some form of capacity building on an almost continuous basis.

Only a tiny number of NGOs publish data on the aggregate amount of money spent on capacity-building projects and programmes, and these tend to be the NGOs whose main function is capacity building (often of other NGOs). It is still extremely rare for NGOs separately to assess even the direct impact of such activities, never mind the wider effects on the lives of beneficiaries.[30] Most projects in which donor-country NGOs provide funds to developing-country NGOs contain some element of what is termed capacity building or institutional strengthening, but it is often difficult to separate this out from other project costs, and impact reviews suggest that the capacity-building dimensions of project impact are often excluded from the assessment (Madsen 1999: 32).

Older and narrower approaches

Some initiatives which are included under the 'catch-all' term of 'capacity building' constitute little more than the training and skills upgrading of particular members of staff. Some of this takes place on site, though sometimes NGO staff are sent away on training courses. Much training is informal in nature, learned on the job from other colleagues or, in the case of local NGOs with links to large donor country-based NGOs, when foreign NGO staff come to visit. There is very little comprehensive data to indicate how successful such training of individual NGO personnel has been. Anecdotal evidence suggests that the record is mixed, with some successes and some failures, but probably, over time, a rising level of success as larger and most medium-sized NGOs have realized the importance of training, and have addressed skill shortages in a more systematic way using more skilled trainers. Generally speaking, if particular skills are taught by those adequately trained to provide skill training, then most skill training is likely to be successful. For more than two decades, many large donor-country-based NGOs have successfully provided training to large and medium-sized developing-country-based NGOs in the area of finance, book keeping and accountancy. However, in more recent years, most poor countries have had access to skilled trainers in both the areas of finance and in appraisal and monitoring from within their own country or region. Ironically, a proportion of failures have occurred because those giving the training have not themselves had the necessary skills to impart.

The correct assessment that capacities and skills need to be enhanced and upgraded have sometimes led northern NGOs wrongly (and paternalistically) to assume that their own staff have the necessary skills, even if they have had no formal training and limited on-the-job experience. Likewise, some interaction which goes by the catch-all name of capacity building can directly or indirectly contribute to the undermining of an NGO's capacity. One example would be when small and relatively inexperienced poor-country-based NGOs become involved in significant donor-funded projects, but do not have the capacity to undertake appraisal, monitoring and evaluation or to provide reports of sufficient quality in a timely manner. In such cases, it has not been uncommon for northern NGO staff (or consultants) to undertake this work themselves. The more this happens, the more likely it will be not merely that the current capacity weaknesses of the (southern) NGO will remain, but at the extreme, overall capacity can deteriorate over time as the more skilled staff become frustrated and leave.

Newer and more systemic approaches

Important though discrete one-to-one or small-group skill training has been, such activities have a limited impact. As NGOs have grown in number and size, the sorts of capacity building that have become of wider significance are those which have focused on NGOs as institutions, and involved different forms of institutional strengthening. For many decades, United States NGOs and consultants have been heavily engaged in helping to build and strengthen the institutional capacities and basic competencies of NGOs across the world. More recently, a growing number of NGOs have had to face a range of challenges as they have 'scaled up'—moving from small single-issue agencies to medium-sized, multi-purpose and more complex organizations, and in some cases growing to become significant NGOs on the national and international arena. As this has occurred, a whole range of new institutional and organizational strengthening capacities and capabilities have been required, including the development of a range of new managerial and technical skills.

How successful have these broader and more systemic capacity-building and institutional-strengthening initiatives been? Two initial proxy indicators provide grounds for thinking that they have experienced a considerable degree of success. First, the steady overall growth and expansion in the number of NGOs—with failures and closures of NGOs being considerably outstripped by their growth and expansion—would suggest that as a whole NGOs are thought to be doing a worthwhile job by those who fund them. Secondly, the earlier discussion in this chapter confirmed the tangible gains made by NGOs in a wide cross-section of activities, directly and indirectly enhancing the lives of poor people.[31] Beyond this, however, the evidence is too thin and patchy to be able to form firm judgements on the impact of institution-strengthening initiatives, in part because building and strengthening the capacity of organizations is widely recognized to be a complex and often ill-defined process: some initiatives have clearly worked (see below), but there have also been failures, even if it has been more difficult to gain information on these.[32] The 25-year review of the impact of European NGO projects funded by the European Commission concluded that (northern NGOs) were not very good at institutional strengthening (South Research *et al.* 2000: 39–40).

There is no single, simple or agreed method of building such capacities (Buzzard and Webb 2004: 6). Firm baseline data against which to measure progress are often difficult to pinpoint, and, as studies have confirmed, successful outcomes have often resulted from identifying and addressing new constraints as they arise (see Hailey *et al.* 2005). Indeed, one of the characteristics of NGO approaches to capacity development, clearly identified as a strength, has been the development of customized, endogenous approaches rather than the use of blunt, one-size-fits-all measures more similar to those of official aid (Bebbington and Mitlin 1996: 10–11; Watson 2006) It could be that the emphasis on these factors, as well as the confirmation that to be successful, institutional strengthening usually needs to be viewed as a long-term process, provide the basis for suggesting that there have been more instances of successful NGO capacity building and institutional strengthening than of successful efforts by official donors to strengthen public sector institutions in developing countries.[33]

Evidence of some successes

In-depth studies of institutional development and strengthening of NGOs are still comparatively rare. One recent study traced the successes of St Mary's Hospital in the Gulu district of northern Uganda, which began as a small, isolated church-based hospital, but evolved to become the second largest medical centre in the whole country, acclaimed as a centre of medical excellence, as a result of systemic staff training, adaptability as growth and expansion occurred, effective but flexible management, and networking, which was critically important in maintaining and enhancing the technical quality of care (see Hauck 2004). A second example, mentioned previously, is the Aga Khan Rural Support Program in Pakistan, the most recent evaluation of which concludes that the institutional development undertaken by the Programme constitutes its *most* notable achievement (World Bank 2002b).

More impressive has been the impact and quality of work undertaken by an NGO named Pact, founded in the United States in 1971 to provide support, especially capacity building and institutional strengthening, to NGOs across the world, working with both individual NGOs and different groups of NGOs. By 2004, its budget had expanded to $40mn, and by then Pact was working with over 500 local groups in more than 60 countries. Building on the potential offered by the Internet, Pact was a founder member of the Impact Alliance, described as a 'global market place for capacity building service providers and those seeking its services', and it has won at least five international awards for its work on women's empowerment and literacy.[34] The impact of Pact's work has long been recognized by donors, such as USAID and the World Bank, which have continued to fund its capacity-building and institution-strengthening activities.[35] For Pact, the key test of its effectiveness lies in the ability of NGOs and CSOs with whom it has interacted to achieve tangible change for beneficiaries.

In Madagascar, Pact supported the creation of a regional federation of neighbourhood associations, which has tackled difficult political issues, such as access to safe drinking water and land tenure, and has become fully integrated into the municipal decision-making apparatus of the region. In Zambia, a coalition of membership organizations supported by Pact led a public campaign that galvanized citizens across the country to demand greater participation in revising the country's constitution. In Cambodia, Pact has worked with a coalition of civil society leaders, donors, the media and government to gain passage in the National Assembly of a Freedom of Information Act, and has supported stakeholders in anti-corruption efforts. In Zimbabwe, the Ministry of Education removed 171 teachers in the Lake Kariba area because they refused to enforce children's attendance at the highly unpopular, government-run militia camps. Empowered by a local NGO trained by Pact in advocacy, families withdrew their children from school until the government reinstated the teachers.

Almost certainly, these examples do not reflect the more general impact of efforts to strengthen the capacity of NGOs to undertake their work more effectively. But they do suggest that claims that NGO capacity building and institutional development do not work are very wide of the mark.

17 The wider impact of non-governmental and civil society organizations

Increasingly over the past 20 years, growing amounts of the aid money received by NGOs have been channelled into advocacy, lobbying, awareness-raising and campaigning initiatives, so that, today, it is exceptional for any sizeable NGO not to involve itself in at least one of these activities. These beyond-the-project activities vary greatly: they can be small-scale or substantial, involving short-term, discrete and concrete initiatives; or they can be longer-term activities with more 'open' agendas. Advocacy, lobbying and campaigning takes place at the local level, the national level, regionally, internationally and globally, usually targeting particular policies, particular institutions and particular interest groups. This sometimes can mean NGOs working with official aid agencies and governments or with international institutions. More commonly, it involves challenging governments and lower-level authorities to change their policies and approaches, as well as challenging key international institutions, whose policies and governance are determined by member governments. It can involve NGOs working both on their own or together with other NGOs or other civil society organizations (CSOs), in formal or informal networks or alliances. Indeed, some NGO alliances have been formed to undertake advocacy, lobbying and campaigning with no prearranged agenda of precisely what to do, as happened in 2002 with the formation of the Ecumenical Advocacy Alliance (EAA) established by major Roman Catholic and Protestant agencies and their partners.[1]

Do these closely linked groups of beyond-the-project activities undertaken by NGOs, and funded with aid money, work? To what extent do the advocacy, lobbying and campaigning activities succeed in achieving their objectives? What evidence is there to show that as a result of these activities, policies, interest groups or institutions have changed? And if change has occurred, what evidence is there to show that it has been been due to NGOs, and not others, and that, in turn, NGOs have helped to enhance the lives of poor people, on whose behalf they have been working, and for whom the expenditure of aid monies has been justified? These are substantive questions, many of them difficult to answer.

NGO advocacy, lobbying, awareness-raising and campaigning

METHODOLOGICAL CHALLENGES

Some researchers believe that it is premature to try to find answers. For example, a keynote paper to a recent international conference on NGOs judged that the effectiveness of NGO advocacy has 'yet to be determined' (Mitlin *et al.* 2005: 17). The key problem is not so much a lack of evidence of the results of such activities, as the difficulty of tracing through the relationship between cause and effect, linked to a lack of consensus about how the evidence should best be judged. As with other types of NGO development interventions, the impact of advocacy, lobbying and campaigning work remains a highly contested area.

The first methodological problem in assessing impact is our old friend 'attribution'. Advocacy, lobbying and campaigning objectives might be achieved, but there are many agents and agencies that can and often have influenced the outcome. How does one determine the relationship between the outcomes desired and the particular actions and activities undertaken by NGOs? For example, when apartheid ended in South Africa, many organizations, including NGOs, were quick to make a direct link between their activities, the release of Nelson Mandela and the ending of apartheid. In the Netherlands, a study was commissioned to assess the role of NGOs in the building of a just and democratic South Africa. The study (correctly) laid out the complexity of the issue and pointed to a range of influences, internal and external, which together contributed to the ending of apartheid. Nonetheless, it felt able to jump to the conclusion, strongly stated but with very little hard evidence to support it, that 'NGOs have undoubtedly played a particularly important role in the struggle against apartheid. Their success is a justified reason for pride. It contributes to a feeling of self-respect and to a positive image. It gives courage to go on' (Flinterman *et al.* 1992: 38). These problems are compounded when trying to assess impact at the international level. The closer to a particular community and the more concrete and specific the identified change required, the easier it is to see the gains made, and to link these to the advocacy, lobbying and campaigning efforts made. The more distant from particular communities is the initiative and the more all-encompassing the change demanded, the less easy it is for a particular organization to confirm or even reliably claim success.

Another problem in judging effectiveness concerns the relative weights that should be given to short-term and long-term outcomes of advocacy, lobbying and campaigning. In some of the most rigorous attempts to assess how one might judge the impact of advocacy work, both Covey and Miller argue that it is often mistaken to judge effectiveness solely in relation to short-term successes. They suggest that advocacy needs to be viewed from a long-term perspective. They point to two criteria for assessment in addition to achieving immediate goals and objectives. The first is the contribution made to expanding the 'political space' within which NGOs (and other CSOs) are able to undertake future advocacy work, enhancing their legitimacy to undertake advocacy in the months and years ahead. The second is the contribution that short-term advocacy initiatives make to strengthening and building the confidence and ability of affected communities to undertake future advocacy work themselves (Covey 1994; Miller 1994). Approaching advocacy assessment through a longer-term perspective means that a short-term failure to achieve particular policy-change objectives could well be viewed as a success if it is judged that the process of undertaking short-term advocacy has significantly contributed either to one or both of these longer-term objectives being fulfilled.

Another problem is that, especially in campaigning, evidence itself can become a campaigning 'tool'. It is a commonplace in campaigning for different interest-groups to give different weights and attention to particular sorts of data and information. Success in campaigning is often dependent on the number, commitment and staying-power of campaigners, and one of the best ways to sustain these, and to widen the campaign, is to claim that the actions and activities of campaigners are already achieving the core goals, even before they have done so. Consequently, assessing the results of campaigns, as well as some advocacy and lobbying work, needs to be able to discern and trace through the causal links between effort expended and the outcome achieved in a context likely to be replete with claims of dramatic successes, and counter-claims of dramatic failures.

Against this backdrop of these dilemmas and challenges, what does the evidence tell us? We start by stepping back from the details of particular initiatives to take a brief look at the big picture.

'BEING THERE'

At least since the 1940s, NGOs have been involved in and invited to attend and engage in discussion with policy-makers at the international level concerning matters 'within their competence', interaction with the United Nations and its different agencies providing some of the earliest fora for such interaction (see Reimann 2006). Over subsequent decades, NGO engagement with policy-makers has expanded hugely: more and more NGOs have been accredited to different international agencies and international processes, NGOs have been increasingly consulted, both formally and informally, on a range of development policy issues, and NGOs have been directly involved in key international conferences where major policy issues have been on the agenda. Organizations and networks of NGOs and other CSOs, such as Social Watch, have been set up to monitor compliance with agreements made.² Related in part to their enhanced status and importance at the international level, NGOs have been well positioned to engage in debates and discussions at the national level, though this has not led to such a 'formalization' of their role as has occurred internationally.

Hence, the first—and notable—success of NGOs lies simply in their 'being there'. NGOs have become a part of what Reimann (2006) calls 'political globalization': space has opened up for NGOs to engage in policy debate at the international level, and NGOs have ably filled that space—often, she argues, because states have allowed this space to be opened up rather than solely because of the efforts of NGOs. Similarly, NGOs have contributed to an increase in awareness, within the media and the public, of some of the key development issues that face the world and its governments.³

It is evident, however, that success extends well beyond merely being there, providing 'noise' and raising the level of awareness of issues through the information provided. Perhaps the best indicator that NGOs matter in international and some national fora comes from the growing criticisms made of NGOs by key interest groups who have been the target of their advocacy, lobbying and campaigning initiatives. Especially since the mid-1990s, business groups, especially, and also some politicians have grown louder in their complaints that NGOs should not be given the prominence (and influence) that they have because, it is asserted, they are not elected and it is not clear for whom they speak and to whom they are accountable. If NGOs were having no influence, there would be little need for these groups to articulate these criticisms so often and so loudly.

In most cases, effective policy change requires those advocating for change to link with a range of different interest groups to ensure sufficient political support for a switch in policies. The closer or more clearly linked the proposed changes to the prevailing policies, the more likely they are to be accepted, which is why it is more common for more modest objectives to be implemented more easily and more quickly. If more far-reaching changes are to be engineered, this is likely to require a long time-frame, considerable expertise in understanding the technical details of alternative policies, and the forging of link with other interest groups with political influence (Bratton 1990: 93). Simply 'being there and making noise' is usually insufficient to bring about effective change away from policies from which powerful domestic groups currently benefit.

The creation and expansion of international space for NGOs to influence debate and policies has had some impact at the national level. In particular, in states where their role in influencing and monitoring policies and policy-making has been challenged by politicians, political parties and the political establishment, NGOs have used a variety of methods to attempt to create space for activities beyond service delivery. Their efforts have often been supported (morally and financially) by the governments of the industrialized countries committed to 'the spread of democracy'. These efforts have met with a variety of responses, ranging from stubborn resistance to varying degrees of success— the more repressive the regime the less willing it has been to provide NGOs with the legal and regulatory space publicly to undertake advocacy, lobbying and campaigning.

MORE DETAILED EVIDENCE OF IMPACT

Beyond these more systemic contributions made by NGOs, what evidence is there of the success of individual advocacy, lobbying and campaigning initiatives undertaken by NGOs? Far less than has often been claimed by many, but, almost certainly, far more than NGOs' harshest critics maintain. Many studies of the impact of NGO initiatives beyond the project concur that it is not uncommon for NGOs to claim credit for policy changes when they constitute only one sub-group of agencies or interest groups that been involved in advocating, lobbying or campaigning for change.[4]

A number of studies suggest that in many successful campaigns with which NGOs have been associated, it has not been NGOs which have been the initiators of policy change: as Black succinctly puts it, NGOs have been particularly good at riding waves, but far less good at making them (Black 1992, quoted in Pitt *et al.* 2005: 18). In some cases, NGOs have prematurely proclaimed success—heralding victory when governments and key agencies have stated they will change policies consistent with NGO advocacy goals—reducing their efforts at the crucial time when monitoring what happens in practice is vital to ensuring the policy changes deliver the results intended. A recent in-depth study of Ghana, Uganda and South Africa concluded that groups other than NGOs—such as trades unions and trade associations—were more effective in bringing about substantial policy changes. NGO impact was weakened by the lack of, or a failure to provide, a sustained engagement with the policy process, and because of insufficient links to key policy-makers. To be successful, NGOs required substantial (domestic and not foreign) funding, and sustained organizational skills (Robinson and Friedman 2005).

Impact at the local level

It has been claimed by researchers that NGOs and CSOs are not very effective at influencing policies within developing countries. For instance, in their 2006 survey, Julius Court and colleagues argue that 'CSOs are having a surprisingly limited impact on policy and the lives of poor people' (Court *et al.* 2006: 14). Yet there is plenty of evidence to counter such a view.[5]

There are numerous examples of NGOs and other CSOs contributing to achieving tangible gains for particular poor and marginalized communities as a result of advocacy, lobbying and campaigning efforts. Some of the most fundamental have involved defending the very right, especially of marginalized people and peoples, to exist and be recognized, often involving, first, recognition of the seemingly abstract but essential notion that aggrieved people or peoples have individual or group rights, as the basis for defending those rights and protecting them against abuses. The work of human rights organizations has often resulted in changes in the law to protect land rights or to win compensation when land has been appropriated (Roche 1999: 195ff.; Landman and Abraham 2004).

More widely, surveys from the more specialized literature provide long lists of other positive outcomes. For example, Blair lists numerous successes of women's, farmers' and *dalit* groups in India in winning tangible benefits to improve their lives (2000: 111), Chapman records the successes of NGOs in Ghana in promoting breastfeeding in the face of commercial milk powder promotion (2002: 142ff.), Carroll describes how the Colombian NGO FUNCOL successfully worked for the achievement of land rights for indigenous people (1992: 56), and Covey (1994: 4–5, 9, 13–15) records the success of the Urban Land Reform Task Force (ULRTF) in the Philippines, which was working in alliances with others to achieve changes in urban legislation to protect the rights of the urban poor. Some of these authors (such as Covey) also cite examples of the failures or the limitations of NGO advocacy and campaigning work in achieving tangible short-term gains for poor people.

What the examples in the specialized literature do not provide is sufficient understanding or appreciation of the numerous successes of locally based advocacy and campaigning work: much remains undocumented and often unknown to outsiders. It remains still very difficult to find information about small-scale advocacy and campaigning successes. The in-country information most readily available about NGO advocacy and campaigning tends to be dominated by the 'big-time' advocacy and campaigning initiatives. Discrete, and especially small-scale, successes of NGO advocacy work carried out in 'far-away' countries are neither newsworthy nor usually of sufficient interest on their own to the editors of academic journals. Box 17.1 provides one example of the hundreds of successful but little-known small-scale advocacy and campaigning initiatives occurring each year across the developing world, achieving tangible gains for poor people and poor communities. Ignorance of these successes fuels the inaccurate and distorted view that it is only big-time international advocacy which matters.

Are most locally based advocacy and campaigning initiatives successful in achieving tangible gains for those most directly affected? The paucity of documented information at both the local and country level means it is still impossible to say. However, as just suggested, it is evident that there are plenty of

---

BOX 17.1 ACCESS TO FREE MEDICINES BY POOR PEOPLE IN ICA, PERU

A small Peruvian NGO, Casas de salud (literally 'health houses') works in the poor urban areas and among the families of poorly paid agro-industrial workers in and around Ica, 250 kilometres south of Lima. In mid-2002, Casas de salud discovered that the state-run clinics were not providing a free course of medicine to families with tuberculosis, which they were required to do. Discussions with the health authorities failed to persuade them to distribute the free medicines. Consequently, Casas de salud initiated publicity and lobbying campaigns involving writing articles in the (national) media and making contacts with local politicians, drawing attention to the problem. This was successful. The action undertaken exclusively by this NGO led directly to the distribution of free medicines at government clinics, which the NGO continued to monitor, benefiting in particular the very poorest families, who were most vulnerable to TB and least able to afford the medicine they needed.

Source: Personal notes on visit to Ica, October 2002.

---

examples of success, which provides an important counterweight to a widely held view prevalent in the early 1990s, influenced by a literature based more on large-scale than small-scale advocacy efforts, that concluded that most NGO advocacy and campaign initiatives did not really work.[6] What is more, there has been a growth of cumulative knowledge and understanding of when and where locally based advocacy is likely to work and when it is not: in most cases tangible gains are likely to require clear and realistic strategies, advocacy skills, sufficient resources and the securing of linkages and alliances with groups able to influence key decision-makers. In many cases, too, locally based and small-scale advocacy and lobbying work requires considerable personal courage. Trying to change laws and regulations which discriminate against poor people, monitoring and publicizing human rights abuses, seeking to protect those who are vulnerable, and launching campaigns which expose the unscrupulous actions of elites and powerful oligarchs who often dominate rural and urban society, frequently involves challenging long-held norms, and powerful interest groups, and this can often be dangerous. The numbers of people involved in advocacy, lobbying and campaigning at the local level who undertake their work courageously, at times risking their own lives, is insufficiently known, and when known, often too quickly forgotten, in the donor countries. One example is given in Box 17.2.[7]

In recent years, growing emphasis has been placed on the role of NGOs and other CSOs as monitors of the activities of other agents of development, most notably governments, at the national and local level. Monitoring can involve a range of different activities, but most attention has been focused on efforts to ensure that the quality of services meets minimum standards and that the funds allocated, especially to poor communities and to localities where poor people live, do indeed reach the intended beneficiaries.[8] Have locally based NGOs and CSOs been successful in their various monitoring roles?

BOX 17.2 THE WORK AND DEATH OF PASCAL KIBEMI

On 31 July 2005, Pascal Kibembi, the Executive Secretary of a small development and human rights NGO, Héritiers de la Justice (heirs of justice), whose work is focused on the monitoring and documentation of human rights abuses and lootings, particularly those perpetrated by the political and military authorities in and around the town of Bukavu, in the east of the Democratic Republic of Congo, was gunned down in his home and killed. Two years earlier he had received death threats for his efforts, and, for a time, he went into hiding before emerging again to lead the work of the NGO, until he was murdered. Others have taken over the work and leadership of Héritiers de la Justice, which continues to this day.

Sources: Personal communication; personal notes from visit to Héritiers de la Justice, Nov. 2003. See also their website, <www.heritiers.org>.

One of the biggest clusters of initiatives is the International Budget Project (IBP), which was set up in 1996 for the purpose of assisting NGOs and CSOs to analyse, monitor and generally influence the budget process in favour of the poor and marginalized. A recent review suggests that while there has been a rapid escalation of activities across many countries, there is far less evidence of impact, and where impact has been identified, such as in Kenya, the results have been only modest. It appears that, in common with advocacy initiatives more generally, effectiveness is crucially related to the development of links with influential interest groups, which was missing in and helped to explain the limited impact of a substantial initiative in São Paulo (Pollard and Court 2005: 17). This assessment is confirmed in a study by Bräutigam (2004) which concludes that NGOs', CSOs' and peoples' participation in budgetary processes is no guarantee of effective change resulting. What is crucial is engagement at the political level with those who wield power. In cases where pro-poor political parties have gained power, such as in Porto Alegre in Brazil, effective change can be negotiated; in others the impact is likely to be minimal, though demands for more information and greater transparency of budgetary processes can sometimes lead to some (limited) changes in budgetary processes even in cases where governments are not 'pro-poor'.

Impact at the national and international level

How effective have NGO advocacy, lobbying and campaigning efforts been at the international level and at the national level within donor countries? The literature cites numerous examples of tangible successes. These would include efforts to establish a baby-milk marketing code, the campaign to ban landmines, the campaign against sex tourism, the coalition to establish the International Criminal Court (ICC), a number of initiatives of environmental NGOs to prevent the construction of dams, to preserve the rainforest and to stop illegal logging of hardwood timber, and, more recently, the introduction of laws making it illegal for companies to engage in corrupt practices when operating abroad.[9] Some achievements have been less easy to pinpoint, though often of major importance. For instance, the work of NGOs has been credited as providing one of the main, if not the main, catalyst in influencing official donors and the international financial institutions (IFIs) to incorporate a gender, and more recently a human rights, dimension to their approach to development, in bringing into the mainstream the notion of sustainable development, and in gaining acceptance of the views that participation and empowerment are central to an understanding of effective and sustainable development.[10]

The late 1980s and early 1990s saw NGOs focusing their attention on the problems arising from implementing structural adjustment policies, most notably their documenting the adverse effects on particular groups of poor people and poor communities. The last half of the 1990s saw international and national NGOs involved in a succession of (linked) campaigns, such as Jubilee 2000, aimed at forgiving the (unsustainable) debts of the poorest countries. More recently, international and cross-national NGO advocacy and campaigning has focused on trade issues (linked to the Doha trade round), and on the governance of major international financial institutions and the World Trade Organisation (WTO). Their activities have also focused on trying to ensure the achievement of the Millennium Development Goals (MDGs), including more specific and targeted efforts to raise aggregate levels of ODA to the 0.7 per cent of gross national income (GNI) target, and a series of different (aid, debt and trade) initiatives aimed at the all-embracing and more distant goal to Make Poverty History. Linked to some of these more specific initiatives, NGOs have highlighted the differing, adverse effects of globalization on poor people and poor communities. Human rights and development NGOs have also continued to campaign against the corporate sector, most recently attempting to muster support for the introduction of binding international legal obligations on companies to ensure compliance and conformity with international agreements (see ICHRP 2002).[11] What impact have these different advocacy, lobbying and campaigning initiatives had?

The first area of impact concerns enhanced knowledge and information about these issues. As with successive international conferences since the early 1990s, all major advocacy, lobbying and campaigning work which international and national NGOs have either led or been a part of has made a significant impact in terms of the publicity and information they have provided or spawned. The issues of debt, aid, trade, globalization and poverty, and corruption are more widely known than they were 15 to 20 years ago, when interest was limited to a fairly small group of people concerned with development. Against the backdrop of a growing understanding of today's globalized world, key development problems, such as third world debt, have become household words.

Beyond information, there is evidence of tangible achievements in relation to some of the key advocacy and campaign goals, and a shift in perceptions of key policy-makers in relation to others. For instance, adjustment policies promoted by the World Bank have changed significantly since evidence was produced (in part) by NGOs of their adverse effects on some poor communities. Likewise, from the late 1990s onwards, significant amounts of sovereign debt have been forgiven in some 20 countries in successive agreements under the highly indebted poor countries (HIPC) initiatives. More and more countries have introduced anti-bribery legislation. Major changes in official aid-giving have been taking place. From 2004 onwards, as discussed in earlier chapters, a number of countries have significantly increased the amounts of ODA they provide and have committed themselves to reaching the 0.7 per cent ODA/GNI target by a specified date. Shifts in traditional positions on trade have also been occurring. For instance, some industrialized countries, including many in the European Union and among the Nordic countries, have come to accept that the sequencing of trade liberalization needs to take place in a more balanced manner, with poor countries not being required to reduce trade barriers when industrialized countries continue to maintain a range of trade-distorting and linked (farm subsidy) policies. Similarly, there is a growing sense among many industrialized countries that, within the framework of developing a more effective international trading regime, poorer countries should be able to play a stronger role in adopting a trade and tariff regime which enables them to manage the adjustment process necessary to create more diversified and competitive economies, in part by extending the (already accepted) principle of being able temporarily to protect emergent industries.

However, the literature has been cautious about confirming the claims made by NGOs that it is their contribution which has made the crucial difference. A number of studies and evaluations have suggested that where advocacy and campaign goals have largely been achieved, this has often been due, at least in part, to the efforts and influences of groups other than NGOs, a conclusion with which many NGOs often concur (see Edwards 1993, 2005; Lewis 2001: 124ff.; Landman and Abraham 2004). It is evident that not all campaigns and advocacy initiatives of NGOs have been successful. Structural adjustment programmes have been altered, not abandoned, as some of the more radical NGOs had campaigned for. The ODA/GNI ratio for the three leading donors continues to fall well short of campaign objectives, and the governance of the IFIs and the WTO remains little changed. Acclaiming—and judging—success is more difficult when, as is quite common, different NGOs, broadly aligned under blander banner to which all are able to subscribe, work to achieve different concrete goals. For instance, some debt campaigners called and campaigned for the cancellation of all debts of all poor countries with no conditions attached; others focused on campaigning to have cancelled only the 'unpayable debts' of the poorest countries (see Keet 2002).[12] As noted above, it has been the less radical and more reformist goals that have tended to 'work'. In many ways this is understandable, providing the parameters around which campaigning is more likely to succeed. However valid the criticisms of prevailing policies, NGOs with more radical goals, who are not willing to engage in substantive discussion with those responsible for creating and changing policies, and who are unable to put forward credible alternatives to prevailing policies, in many ways set themselves up for failure.

Yet these critical comments also need to be placed in a wider perspective. There are four reasons for concluding that international donor-country-based NGO advocacy, lobbying and campaigning has, broadly, had a more positive impact than many of the critics have suggested.

1. The first relates to the information provided and the publicity generated by recent major initiatives. The greater awareness of key issues, to which the major NGO advocacy and campaign initiatives have (largely) contributed, has not merely provided more 'noise'. In many instances, it has contributed to preventing key decision-makers from avoiding or indefinitely postponing confronting the issues raised and has stimulated them to seek ways of resolving them. Additionally, the evidence suggests that where NGOs have persisted in highlighting particular issues over an extended period of time—the effects of structural adjustment and the need to expand aid levels—some (though not all) substantial outcomes have been achieved. In short, NGOs have influenced debate on key issues, and contributed to shortening the time before policies closer to those for which they have campaigned have been introduced.

2. Even in the short term, there is clear evidence of the influence that NGO actions have had on policy-makers. For instance, a recent study of the history of aid-giving in Luxembourg concludes that the role of NGOs proved to be the critical factor that influenced that country to expand its official aid programme (Hoebink 2005). Likewise in the United Kingdom, the persistence of NGO lobbying and the cumulative evidence of the damage that the rapid reduction of import tariffs was having on poor farmers in some developing countries contributed to influencing the government to change its stance on advocating a one-size-fits-all approach to trade policy, and its acceptance, in 2005, of the view that poor-country governments should be allowed far greater freedom to determine their own development, including trade and tariff policies.[13]

3. There are a number of instances where organizations which have been the target of NGO advocacy, lobbying and campaigning work have specifically confirmed that NGOs did indeed influence them to change their policies and approaches. For instance, in its 2005 review of relationships with CSOs, the World Bank is explicit in acknowledging the role that environmental NGOs had in 'greening' the Bank in the 1980s and 1990s. It also confirmed that advocacy NGOs had played a 'critical role' in getting Bank member governments to adopt the HIPC debt relief programme in 1996, in winning agreement for the 1999 enhancement of the HIPC, and in ensuring that the funds released were directly linked to poverty reduction goals and strategies (2005h: 26).[14]

4. Similarly, UN insiders have recently confirmed the influence and impact of NGOs and CSOs within the United Nations system and through the UN to the wider world (Jolly *et al.* 2005: 51–3):

Almost every volume in our United Nations Intellectual History Project series and the vast majority of those interviewed for the oral history highlight the crucial role in international affairs and the distinct perspective of civil society. . . . Over the years, there has been a slow and dramatic growth in the role and influence by NGOs in UN corridors and elsewhere . . . The role of civil society has been important in all areas of UN activity. But it has been most crucial in the case of women and children, the environment and human rights[.]

In sum, international and national advocacy and campaigning by NGOs has often been effective. It has influenced and led to changes in policy, as well as changes in the way official donors provide aid. Clearly, however, not all initiatives have worked, and even in cases where advocacy successes can be attributed and traced to the actions and activities of NGOs, it is evident that the goals achieved have often fallen well short of many initial hopes and expectations. NGOs are especially able to influence policies when they work together, either formally or in loose networks, when they gather and effectively make use of evidence to put forward clear alternatives to prevailing policies, when they communicate well, win over groups with the political power to influence change, and engage with policy-makers (Oxfam 2005: p. xii; Court *et al.* 2006: 25–41).[15]

There is, however, much we still do not know. There remains a significant gap between the growing numbers of advocacy, lobbying and campaigning initiatives undertaken by NGOs and the number of rigorous assessments of their results. Major gaps also remain in understanding how best to influence policy, including the best mix of different forms of engagement, from dialogue, quiet diplomacy and mass campaigning to shaming, demonstrations and protests.[16] At both the national and international levels, NGO advocacy, lobbying and campaigning activities are often driven more by the desire for change and the sense of urgency which this spawns than by a carefully crafted strategy of what to do and how to do it. More dispassionate assessments of the impact of recent and ongoing initiatives are needed so that the activism and passion for which NGOs have long been known may be channelled into processes most likely to result in effective and lasting change. Recent years have seen a significant growth in the number of campaigns that NGOs have initiated: too many campaigns are likely at some point to create campaign fatigue and hence to reduce their effectiveness.

THE SUBSTANCE OF NGO POLICY DEMANDS

Many NGO advocacy, lobbying and campaigning initiatives have led to policy changes. But have NGO demands—both those that have been pursued by policy-makers and those that have not—proposed the right policies? This is an important question, but one that is not easy to answer. It is often difficult to know the extent to which poor outcomes are due to poor policies and faulty analysis, or to quite unexpected external influences. Policies can turn out to be right or wrong without NGOs and other lobbyists telling governments either to continue implementing them, or to change them.

Unequivocal answers to the question of whether the policies that NGOs articulate are the correct ones are sometimes constrained by the fact that NGOs have often been far better at articulating what they are against than they have been at spelling out clear alternatives to the policies they wish to see changed. To take a contemporary example, 'free trade' has been criticized by NGO campaigners (in part because it is not free), but it is not entirely clear what the alternative—encapsulated by the equally anodyne term 'fair trade'—would entail in practice. Against the backdrop of these uncertainties, it seems safe to conclude that some policies which NGOs have advocated may well not have proved to have been as beneficial as it had been assumed they would be. Yet this is by no means the end of the discussion.

What NGOs, at their best, bring to policy debates is the viewpoint of poor people, and the impact that prevailing policies are having on them. This perspective ought to make a major contribution to debates about policy. Indeed, it merits far more attention than debates about policy alternatives based on and driven by a priori ideological perspectives. In turn, it raises a question increasingly asked of NGOs—on whose behalf do you speak? This is a pivotal question because the legitimacy of NGOs to enter into and engage in policy debate in a privileged way hinges crucially upon how this question is answered.[17]

That a significant number of policies and approaches to development championed by NGOs *have* been adopted is one quite powerful indicator of the broad merits of these policies, as it is unlikely that governments and major institutions would adopt policies which they knew to be wrong or misguided. Indeed, to the extent that positive development outcomes are dependent on their being accepted and internalized by the people on whose behalf they are being implemented, and NGO advocacy accurately represents the views and perspectives of these people, one would expect a growing match between NGO advocacy and policy prescriptions. However, it is possible to overplay this argument. That policies are adopted is, in itself, no guarantee that they are the right policies: neither NGOs nor poor people have a monopoly on the truth. Indeed, the fact that it is quite common for NGOs to disagree among themselves about what constitutes the best policies to be pursued and lobbied for confirms the point. There is evidence to suggest that in some cases policies advocated by NGOs and adopted by policy-makers have been the wrong policies. For example, Robert Wade, a leading critic of key areas of Bank policy, has argued (2001) that as a result of pressure from NGOs the World Bank has had to adopt standards for the environment and for resettlement projects that are both unworkable and higher than those prevailing in industrialized countries, to the ultimate detriment of poor people and poor communities (quoted in Clark 2004: 199).

NGO policy approaches, especially as articulated in international advocacy and campaigning, and linked lobbying within industrialized countries, are vulnerable to two sets of potential distortions.

The first concerns the identification of the main causes of poverty. Advocacy, lobbying and campaigning initiatives conducted at the international level and directed at industrialized countries focus (quite rightly) on those policies influencing development which such advocacy, lobbying and campaigning are best able to target, namely those that have their origins *outside* poor countries. It is against this backdrop that attention has been focused on such issues as international trade, aid and financial flows (including debt payments and repayments), the conduct and activities in poor countries of those private transnational corporations which have their home base in the industrialized countries, and the policies which the donor-country-based IFIs require poor countries to implement.

There is no disputing that these issues, organizations and policies are of profound importance to the development prospects of poor countries. However, they do not constitute the *only* factors which influence those prospects. A range of internal and domestic factors, policies, practices and constraints influence, and some impede, development, poverty eradication and wealth creation, as do the conduct and activities of private transnational corporations whose home bases are in the (wealthier) developing countries. More effective and supportive external policies will certainly help, but on their own they will not solve the problems of poverty. In some cases, poor domestic policies and domestic constraints prove to be more important than the external constraints. However, the bulk of international and northern-country-based NGO advocacy and campaigning fails to draw attention to such (domestic) policy and constraints. Hence in practice, even if by default, NGOs lay themselves vulnerable to claims that the picture they paint of the 'policy map' is often a very partial one.[18]

A second group of problems arises when, as happens quite frequently, NGOs claim that the policies they wish to change are 'bad for the poor'. Such a claim assumes that 'the poor' comprise a single homogeneous group, that policies affect all poor people in the same way, and (usually) that only the immediate impact of policies is of relevance. They also assume that the (external) policies that affect poor people can be simply identified. In practice, however, the issues are far more complex. 'The poor' invariably consist of different groups who are affected by different policies in different ways over different time periods. Indeed in most cases, some poor people will tend to benefit, either relatively or absolutely, from the consequences of changes in the external policy regime, and some will tend to be adversely affected. For instance, in the short term, while the urban poor will tend to benefit from a fall in the prices of basic commodities, poor farmers trying to sell crops will benefit from a rise in the prices of commodities or livestock they bring to market. Those without access to land and living in urban areas are likely to benefit more from policies aimed at providing incentives that expand non-farm employment. It is also quite possible for those initially adversely affected (farmers receiving lower returns for traditional crops whose prices fall) to gain in the longer term—for instance, by switching to growing higher-priced crops, and possible even for short-term losses to be addressed by providing for their basic needs in the process of adjustment.

Consequently, claims that particular policies either help or hinder 'the poor' often obscure the expected detailed outcome of policies, and oversimplify the difficult decisions which poor-country governments need to weigh in deciding what course of action to follow. Likewise, pursuing policies which are aimed at preserving current ways of earning a living and current income levels are usually not what most poor people want. Most poor people are looking for ways to raise income levels, expand employment opportunities, reduce risk and expand their levels of consumption.

Strengthening NGOs and strengthening civil society

BACKGROUND AND DEFINITIONS

There is common agreement between NGOs and official donors who fund them that NGOs have a contribution to make that is more extensive than any single organization can achieve. NGOs and CSOs are part of the wider civil society, and, as such, are perceived to have a critical role to play in influencing institutions, policies and processes that are central to and underpin civic life, enhancing the governance of poor countries, which is increasingly seen as central to development and poverty eradication (see DFID 2006c). More particularly, donor governments see NGOs and CSOs as key players in helping to advance democracy and the rule of law, and in enhancing the transparency and accountability of institutions as part of a more general strategy of 'strengthening civil society'. What concerns us here is the impact of these efforts to strengthen NGOs *as a whole*. What effects have the growing amounts of aid directed at strengthening NGOs and CSOs had? Has this use of aid funds been effective: has the overall strength of NGOs and CSOs increased, and has this led to the positive knock-on effects expected?

Civil society is a slippery concept for which there remains no definitional agreement. However, broadly speaking, civil society is understood as the arena, conceptually distinct from the state, market and individual households, in which people come together in formal and informal groups to promote their shared interests, either alone or through interaction with others, with the state, with markets and with individuals. NGOs are part of the wider civil society.[19]

Donor interest in the wider role of NGOs and CSOs is not new, but it has been changing. In the UK in the early 1990s, a government working group recommended that support to NGOs should be considerably expanded, in part because of the perceived ability of NGOs to promote participatory democracy and because of their potential to apply pressure to enhance good government and pluralism (Hodges 1992: sect. 1.25). It was against the backdrop of these broader goals that the UK and other official donors followed far earlier initiatives of the United States government to support a range of different NGOs. Many donors opened up new funding windows to expand the numbers of NGOs and other CSOs in receipt of donor funding, in a clear shift away from the practice prevalent up to the mid-1990s of predominantly funding donor-based NGOs. For example, USAID and the United Kingdom's Foreign and Commonwealth Office created funding windows explicitly to promote the growth, expansion and even creation of new NGOs and CSOs as part of broader goals to support the advance of democracy.[20]

For some donors, strengthening civil society now underpins much of the support given to individual NGOs and CSOs. For example, in Sweden, the whole approach of the Swedish International Cooperation Development Agency (Sida) to the support it gives to civil society organizations is now based on the notion that regardless of the primary aim of specific interventions it funds, every programme of cooperation with NGOs and CSOs needs also to be viewed in relation to 'the development of a vibrant and democratic civil society in which people have the opportunity to act together in order to influence the development of society and/or improve their living conditions' (2004: 6). By the end of the 1990s many larger NGOs, too, had also begun to use the term 'strengthening civil society' to articulate what for them was also becoming a central activity.

ASSESSMENTS OF IMPACT

What has been the overall impact of these initiatives aimed at strengthening NGOs? To what extent have these efforts enabled the NGO sector to flourish and become more influential as part of the wider process of strengthening the whole of civil society?

One indicator that might be used to answer this question would simply be data on the numbers of NGOs. On this basis, we would convincingly conclude that, as a whole, NGOs have been strengthened for, as we have already seen, the trend data reveal a massive expansion in funding and in the growth of NGO numbers (Anheier *et al.* 2004). Indeed, a major thrust of the United States programmes across the countries of the former Soviet Union has involved efforts simply to assist in the creation of new CSOs, many of which are involved in activities focusing on the areas of governance and the promotion of social, economic, cultural, political or civil rights.

However, this is a very crude and ultimately unsatisfactory indicator with which to judge the strengthening of civil society, as there is no necessary relationship between numbers, influence and impact. Clearly, at the extreme, numbers matter: if there were no NGOs or CSOs they would, self-evidently, have no influence. But influence and numbers are not necessarily virtuously linked. Indeed, the overall capabilities of NGOs for influence will almost certainly be increased more by enhancing the quality, strength and reach of carefully selected existing NGOs than by trying to create as many new NGOs as possible, as existing organizations are likely to be far more firmly rooted in or have developed links with key communities and constituencies who under-stand the potential dynamics of change. Thus, numbers matter most once the potential importance of different NGOs and CSOs, and different types of NGOs and CSOs, have been assessed, and it is known how these organizations are likely to influence different sorts of processes to achieve different outcomes.

Apart from counting the numbers of NGOs and CSOs, what do the assess-ments of the efforts of official donors and NGOs to strengthen NGOs as a whole tell us about the overall impact of these initiatives? This question is difficult to answer because of the lack of overall substantive assessments. Beyond crude observations, anecdotes and disparate pieces of information, little of significance has been placed in the public domain, which would enable us to form judgements about the effectiveness of the strengthening of NGOs and CSOs *as a whole*. We know what support has been given, but we do not know much about its overall impact at the country level, or beyond.[21] However, the following provides a hint of some worries and concerns that are beginning to emerge: assistance to civil society 'may have done little to encour-age genuine pluralism or to support broader democratic objectives' (Unsworth 2005b: 6). Individual NGOs have not seen it as important either to address this question individually, or to come together to build up the aggregate picture of their individual NGO-strengthening efforts.

What is of far greater concern, given the amounts of official aid that have been channelled to NGOs under the general-purpose umbrella of strengthen-ing civil society, is that there is very little evidence of official donors trying to search for answers to this central question. Individually, donors have not tried to gauge the overall impact of their efforts to strengthen civil society and NGOs, and only now are some donors even beginning to *ask* such questions, never mind beginning to search for answers.

Donors certainly choose which NGOs to fund; many have quite complex criteria, rules and regulations for this purpose. However, these decisions are not made on the basis of rigorous or comprehensive assessments of why the particular NGOs selected are those best able to contribute to furthering the broad objectives meant to be achieved by the strengthening of civil society. Indeed, many donors base their funding decisions on the evidence of past project performance, rather than on an assessment of their ability to exert influence within the wider civil society and of the resources and types of support that might be needed to enhance their power to influence. The result is that with little evidence feeding back into future funding decisions, most official donors remain content to continue to provide broad support to CSO- and NGO-strengthening efforts on the (unproven) assumption that it is 'a good thing', with support to NGOs based on narrow performance-impact criteria assumed to be sufficient to create a more vibrant, effective and influential civil society.

Where NGOs have had limited success in contributing to the wider impact of civil society, has this been due to some inherent weaknesses of NGOs, to supporting the wrong NGOs, to failure of efforts to strengthen them, or to external factors which eclipsed potential successes? These are critical questions, the answers to which would likely suggest very different NGO-strengthening strategies. But there remains a paucity of information about the ability of NGOs to influence policy in different contexts. Likewise, assessments have not been made to enable donors (and NGOs) to know what mix of technical, human and financial resources are needed in particular contexts to enhance their influence. Without this detailed information, it is likely that the efforts made to strengthen NGOs as a whole will remain sub-optimal.

Further doubts and questions

If NGOs are to play a part in strengthening civil society, there needs to be sufficient legal and regulatory space for them to operate, and they need sufficient (human, technical and financial) resources to enable them to play their influencing roles effectively. Not surprisingly, NGOs have come together, sometimes with donor support, to lobby and campaign for their recognition, and to preserve or expand the regulatory space without which they would not be able to play their influencing roles. There are many examples of governments which, at different times, have sought to restrict or limit the influencing role of NGOs, from Eritrea to Russia, and from Zimbabwe to Orissa in India, as well as of the efforts by individual NGOs and umbrella groups of NGOs to counter these restrictions. For its part, the Civic Engagement Group of the World Bank has developed an analytic tool to understand the constraints to civic engagement, including assessment of the freedom to associate, the ability to mobilize resources, the scope for furthering agency objectives and for formulating and expressing voice, and the space and rules for engagement (see World Bank

2005h: 11). What has usually been missing has been assessments of the impact of these measures.

Questions have also been raised about precisely how civil society can bring about effective change once NGOs and CSOs have been strengthened. For instance, a recent study by Robinson and Friedman notes that in spite of high donor expectation of the potential of CSOs to promote democratization, there is still no consensus on the precise role that civil society is expected to play in strengthening democracy (2005: 2). Their case study research suggests that donors have often lacked an understanding of the environment in which they are supporting organizations, and they often simply do not know which organizations to support (2005: 43). Similar concerns have been raised by Edwards (2001: 95ff.) and by Howell and Pearce (2000: 81ff.), all of whom argue that without a rigorous analysis of the context in which the strengthening of civil society takes place, support for CSOs and NGOs risks merely promoting and developing partnerships with some organizations over others on the basis of insufficient, or more worryingly, preconceived notions of what civil society should look like.

Another concern voiced in the literature is that support to strengthen NGOs risks undermining rather than enhancing democratic processes because, it is argued, most NGOs are appendages to, and not part of, mainstream democratic processes. Such a view suggests that NGOs, instead of empowering the voiceless and enhancing their influence, are more interested in promoting themselves. A recent study in India by Harriss (2005) would tend to support this view, but one from Brazil concluded that the result of CSO strengthening was to reinforce and contribute to enhancing the voice of poor people through traditional political channels (Lavelle *et al.* 2005), suggesting, not unexpectedly, that neither result is inevitable.

A further concern, expressed about external support to developing-country NGOs, whether provided by official donors or NGOs, is that it risks creating an overdependence on funders, resulting, perversely, in a weakening rather than strengthening of local NGOs, exacerbated by the funds doing little more than augmenting the service-delivery role and capacity of NGOs. Such a risk would clearly be reduced if the funds were deployed to develop a local funding base, though the opportunities for this are clearly limited in very poor countries.

These questions and doubts appear to have had little effect on current practice. Too few donor or NGO voices have articulated concerns that 'strengthening civil society' might produce adverse effects. However, this situation might have begun to change. The UK's Department for International Development (DFID) recently warned that support to civil society has the potential to support 'uncivil' society—weakening the state, strengthening existing systems of patronage, neutralizing radical voices, distancing civil society groups from their clients and fuelling divisions leading to rising levels of violence.[22] Likewise, Sida has stated that cooperation with CSOs should *always* be based on a detailed contextual analysis to avoid support which reinforces existing conflicts or those that could arise as a result of the support given (2004: 32). The World Bank has been even more clear and outspoken in a rare analysis of the overall role of NGOs and CSOs in conflict-affected states, an analysis whose conclusions have far wider applicability. Its study pointed to an approach to civil society characterized by overlap, confusion and inconsistency vis-à-vis the efforts of different donors, challenging donors to rethink their approaches. It called for a far more rigorous and systematic analysis prior to engagement, and the need to place individual efforts more explicitly within a clear overall framework (World Bank 2005e: 21).

Only when clearer baseline benchmarks are developed will it be possible to know the extent to which initiatives supporting the broad purpose of strengthening NGOs and CSOs are, or are not, achieving their assumed objectives. For now, since both NGOs and donors view current approaches to strengthening NGOs as overwhelmingly beneficial, few strong voices are heard which question whether the overall thrust of this approach is both beneficial and effective. However, some are now beginning to raise fundamental questions. For instance, Sue Unsworth has argued there is a 'need to *think differently about civil society*—not as an autonomous space which should be "strengthened" to put pressure on the state, but as a collection of interest groups that are themselves reliant on having state institutions in place and which form and re-form in response to state action' (2005a: 46). What the impact of these differing views will be on future allocations of aid channelled to strengthening civil society as a whole is difficult to predict. Strengthening civil society remains very much still 'work in progress'.

The contribution of NGOs to development: a summing up

The wide range of development interventions that NGOs undertake with the aid funds they have at their disposal, and the paucity of hard data from which to draw firm conclusions, go a long way towards explaining why views differ quite sharply about the impact of NGO development activities.

On the one hand, NGOs, and those who work for them, remain convinced that what they do is valuable, indeed vital, and most use evidence of discrete-project successes to convince supporters that these examples reflect the overall impact of what they do with the aid funds they receive. On the other hand, sceptics, including many of those targeted by NGO lobbying and campaigning activities, claim that the impact of aid-funded NGO activities is wildly exaggerated. They assert that NGO projects make little difference to the lives of those they assist, that NGOs are not transparent in what they do, and that their views represent no one but themselves, and consequently that NGOs should be 'reined in'. Between these extremes, evaluators and academics search for evidence, ask hard questions for which there are no easy answers, and try to form judgements about the extent to which NGO development activities 'work'.

Some have drawn uncomfortable conclusions. For instance, David Lewis judges that the overall contribution of NGOs to reducing global poverty through service delivery and advocacy remains small and largely unproven (2001: 134). Alan Fowler, more harshly, concludes that there is little evidence to counter the assertion that the role of NGOs as agents of structural change for people who are poor and marginalized is more an aspirational self-image than an on-the-ground reality (2005: 16). Likewise, David Lewis and Tina Wallace believe that NGO rhetoric on gender issues lulls them into a sense of achievement, whereas their own practices fall far short of achieving real changes in the status and condition of women (2000: xii).

These judgements are probably too harsh. The identification of weaknesses and failures needs to be placed in its proper, wider context. As Edwards (2005) persuasively argues, if one pitches the bar deliberately low and asks if the world of development would be a better place without the development efforts of NGOs, the answer would certainly be 'no'. Likewise, the absence of detailed information on the overall impact of NGOs within and across countries, and the contribution they make to particular sectors of an economy, such as health and education, should not be taken as the basis for advancing the extreme and overly simplistic view that we don't really know whether any of these activities do any good. Clearly, the aggregate impact of the activities of NGOs which, for example, provide up to 40 per cent of the health services of a country have to be both positive and extremely significant, or else their services would not continue to be in high demand What we do not know accurately, at the national level, is how effective, and especially how cost-effective, the aggregate contribution of NGOs is, though, as discussed in Chapter 16, services provided by NGOs are often far better than those provided by the state. Additionally, as Ian Smillie points out, many of the major insights that have now become part of mainstream thinking across the development and aid community have been due to NGOs, even if many NGOs involved in development education and policy issues have been ineffective (1994: 32, 2000: 128).

The review of the evidence presented in this chapter, and the previous one, should caution us against drawing overall, general conclusions about the impact of different NGO development initiatives. Indeed, trying to draw simple, all-embracing conclusions that apply across the board probably adds to the confusion.[23] Against the current backdrop of a substantial lack of information on impact, assessing the impact of NGO activities remains more an art than a science. The ever-present risk is to make generalizations either without any hard evidence, or without any reliable assurance that the evidence one is able to find is broadly representative. People with substantial experience of NGO activity in one country often boldly, but mistakenly, assume that this in-depth local knowledge provides the basis for worldwide generalizations. Much of the literature on which many journalists rely for their comments about the impact of NGO aid is based on this partial data, which only adds to the confusion.

NGOs comprise a very wide range of different organizations. Some are able to record impressive achievements, but some are, frankly, hopeless. Even among the more successful 'front-runners', confusion about effectiveness and impact is aggravated by the mixed messages that the public is asked to believe. For instance, it is difficult to reconcile the claims made by the majority of NGOs that they do make a major difference to the lives of poor people with the assertions, frequently heard, that poverty is increasing across the globe.

The evidence summarized in this chapter and the previous one suggests that in terms of discrete projects and programmes aimed to assist particular communities, NGO interventions yield a very wide mix of different results. At one extreme are NGO projects which are highly efficient and cost-effective, involving beneficiary participation, making a tangible difference to their lives, often replicable and involving new and different approaches. Most will not solve the problems of poverty, but the best provide both tangible benefits in the areas of importance to poor people and the necessary confidence and skills to make a difference to their own lives with less external assistance—one of the key (but largely unmeasurable) differences such projects can make. At the other extreme are NGO projects which are top-down, high-cost activities, implemented by organizations without the necessary skills, which have little lasting impact and which, because they have made the community dependent on the NGO, may well leave some people worse off, and even more disempowered. In contrast, many NGO interventions empower poor people and poor communities, putting them in stronger positions to negotiate and advocate further improvements for themselves, reducing the risks they face and making their futures less uncertain.

Many NGO projects probably do not reach the very poorest, though some clearly do. The more complex the projects, the greater the potential impact on poverty, but the more expensive they are likely to be. Many NGO projects, except the simplest, are expensive to implement: those that manage to reach and make a difference to poorer strata of the community are even more expensive. Some unsuccessful project outcomes are caused by the failures, weaknesses and ignorance of NGOs, some by external pressures and influences, most by a mixture of different causes. Consequently, it often happens that one NGO which has contributed to successful outcomes in one context achieves little in another. How many discrete NGO projects are successful and how many are failures? We simply don't know. Most probably make a positive difference to the lives of the beneficiaries, even if that difference is often small, though the vast majority of projects for the very poor are unlikely to be financially sustainable.

Beyond this largely static perspective, the assessment is encouraging. Although there still remains a significant gulf between the impact of most discrete NGOs and what is still needed to enable people and communities to live a life permanently free from poverty, the evidence clearly points to a growing and greater impact of discrete NGO activities. This arises, first, from an overall expansion of the number of NGO projects, but, secondly, and more importantly, from an overall improvement in the quality of projects. Large and most medium-sized NGOs are accumulating knowledge about impact— knowing more about what works and what doesn't, and why—from the greater priority given to evaluation, analysis and learning, and they are applying those lessons to particular contexts. However, it is important not to exaggerate. While tangible progress is being made, even among the better NGOs, there still remains a considerable gap between knowing more about what works and applying those lessons on the ground. The rhetoric still runs ahead of the reality. For the future, the more NGOs that are confident enough to acknowledge publicly that they have made mistakes in the past, that they have much to learn and, above all, that development is difficult, the greater is the likelihood that the gap between aspiration and reality will continue to narrow and further gains will be made.

NGOs have made an impact in their advocacy, lobbying and compaigning work. Some of the most tangible gains to poor people and poor communities have arisen from the numerous local, small-scale initiatives rarely reported outside the locality. To the outsider, they may seem small victories, but many are valued both for their immediate effects, and for the confidence they bring that change is possible and injustices can be addressed. At the national and international level, NGOs have had their mix of successes and failures. They have commonly claimed more successes than those for which they alone have been responsible, and they have been reticent both about admitting failure and about the influence and impact their activities have had. NGOs have made a significant impact simply by placing critical issues on the political agenda, supported by a largely supportive press and media, and, sometimes but not always, by their ability and agility in keeping public interest alive and focused.

In terms of policy changes, their influence has been far greater in drawing attention to the failures, weaknesses and injustices of prevailing policies and approaches, most notably when they have been able to show when policies adversely affect particular groups of poor people. They have been less influential in providing, or working with others to provide, workable alternatives. Divisions within and between NGOs about the content of alternative policies, and sometimes insufficient research to support alternatives, have limited their ability to influence policy change. Over time, as NGOs have focused on more substantive policy issues, passion and 'noise' have become increasingly insufficient tools with which to produce effective change. Building alliances with those more able directly to influence policy changes has become of even greater importance.

There is certainly evidence that many capacity-building and institution-strengthening initiatives targeted at or undertaken by NGOs have achieved tangible results. However, there is simply not enough evidence to be able to judge how much capacity building and institutional strengthening has worked, although there is certainly a strong sense that overall efforts have met with greater success in the NGO than the official aid sector.

Where the jury is still out is in relation to the impact that NGOs and CSOs have played in terms of that nebulous concept 'strengthening civil society'. There is broad agreement that civil society needs to be strengthened and that CSOs and NGOs have an important role to play as part of this wider process. What is largely missing is an understanding—in different contexts—of the precise role that NGOs and CSOs can and ought to play *en bloc* to contribute to the (ultimate) goal of permanently and tangibly influencing policies to make them more pro-poor. Until this becomes clearer, the present scattergun approach to strengthening civil society will reduce the potential impact, as well as limiting our ability to assess the impact of such efforts on the poor and marginalized.

18 The growth of emergencies and the humanitarian response

Emergencies and disasters: an overview

This chapter moves away from development aid to focus on aid provided to help those whose lives are profoundly affected by, and whose livelihoods are immediately at risk as a result of, natural or man-made disasters. Disasters and emergencies occur in many different forms. Some are sudden and unexpected events, such as earthquakes, floods, hurricanes and tsunamis, while others develop more slowly and are more predictable, even if not easily prevented. These would include droughts, food shortages, famines, wars and severe political, economic and social breakdowns. Disasters and emergencies can be big or small; they can be confined to a small locality or extend across countries, and, exceptionally, even continents. They can result in a few or in hundreds and thousands of deaths, to scores, hundreds or even millions left homeless, some temporarily and some for generations. Some disasters cause immediate loss of life and rapid displacements of population; in others, a slow or inappropriate response can result in massive loss of life over time if the basic needs of food, health care, water, sanitation and shelter for those whose lives have been disrupted are not adequately met. The impact of many, though not all, disasters can be reduced if prior actions are taken and preparations are made.

The assistance provided to help people when disasters strike is known technically as humanitarian aid, though it is more widely referred to as emergency aid, or sometimes simply as relief aid. Those directly providing such aid are referred to as humanitarian (aid) agencies. One of the best known is the Red Cross. Other humanitarian agencies consist of three groups: official donors, different United Nations agencies, and scores of big, and hundreds of small to tiny, non-governmental organizations (NGOs).[1] The core purpose of humanitarian aid is to save lives, alleviate suffering and enable those suffering to maintain (or retain) their human dignity during and in the aftermath of natural disasters and man-made crises.[2] The basis for providing humanitarian aid (as its name suggests) is our shared humanity. Flowing from this, a number of humanitarian principles have been developed:

- The most important is the principle of impartiality: humanitarian aid should be provided solely on the basis of need, and thus without discrimination on the grounds of race, religion, gender, age, nationality, ethnicity, or political affiliation.
- Flowing from this is the view that humanitarian aid should, in principle, be neutral, with assistance channelled to all needy civilians, and not favouring those caught up in one side or the other in wars or conflict.[3]
- To ensure this happens, it is broadly accepted that aid should be provided independently.
- A further universally accepted principle of humanitarian aid is that it should be given unconditionally: provided on the basis of need, there is no obligation of those receiving humanitarian aid to give anything back.

Based on this understanding of what humanitarian aid is and what it is intended to do, it would seem to be a relatively simple exercise to assess whether the overall humanitarian enterprise and the response to particular emergencies and disasters are effective, in short whether humanitarian aid 'works'. To the extent that lives are saved, preventable deaths avoided, and the basic needs of those affected by disasters are met, then it would seem safe to conclude that humanitarian aid does indeed work. To the extent that this does not happen, humanitarian aid falls short or, at the extreme, is judged a failure. However, as this chapter and the next show, the issues involved in assessing the impact of humanitarian actions are far less clear and far more complex than they might seem at first sight. There are two main reasons for this.

First, in spite of some major advances in understanding how best to assess humanitarian aid interventions, and a growth in the number of evaluations undertaken and placed in the public domain in the last ten years, the data and information upon which to judge the impact of humanitarian aid remains extremely crude and sketchy. Independent annual reviews of the best evaluations produced each year judge that only about half are of satisfactory quality.[4] There remains a large gulf between the predominantly upbeat claims made by most agencies providing emergency aid about the successes of their own particular interventions and the paucity of reliable data to assess the overall effectiveness of emergency aid, and the extent to which the needs of all those requiring assistance have been met. It is usually fairly simple to demonstrate the effects of humanitarian action in the saving of lives through the provision of food, shelter and medical care. But precisely how many lives have been saved, and how many deaths have been prevented, and what role did aid play? Most often, we still simply do not know.

Secondly, while the broad purpose of humanitarian action is agreed—to save lives, alleviate suffering and maintain human dignity—there are very different views about how this purpose should be achieved in practice, leading to sharply different perspectives on the nature of the humanitarian response and how it ought to be assessed. Most agencies providing assistance now believe that especially for large and complex emergencies, help should be provided over a number of years, in contrast to much public opinion, which believes that humanitarian response should by judged by how well and how rapidly agencies meet immediate (relief) needs. Should the effectiveness of humanitarian aid be assessed on the basis of how the agencies spend the funds, or on the basis of how much of the public—who contribute to appeals for donations—believe their funds should have been spent?[5] The complexities do not stop there. There is a growing view among many humanitarian agencies, influenced by some of their harshest critics, that it is wholly inadequate to assess humanitarian activities solely on the basis of what the aid has achieved. This view has been informed, in part, by evidence that in some circumstances—Biafra in the 1960s is commonly cited—providing humanitarian aid has, at times, prolonged emergencies and (inadvertently) led to greater hardship, more suffering, and more deaths.[6]

Consequently, it is argued, humanitarian action needs to be judged not merely in terms of how best it is able to help those clearly and most visibly affected by emergencies, but also in relation to the contribution it makes, or fails to make, to preventing emergencies from arising, reducing their effects and ending them more quickly. From such a perspective, humanitarian action is far more than merely saving the lives of the victims of disasters. It needs also to include advocacy and lobbying to influence policies that create or perpetuate complex emergencies, and to ensure that those suffering from, or who are vulnerable to, the effects of emergencies are adequately protected. The crucial question is not whether such actions are needed—as confirmed by the universal reaction to the horrific events that have unfolded and persisted in the Darfur region of Sudan from 2003 onwards—but whether humanitarian action *needs* to venture into the world of politics, and thus be judged (in part) in relation to its success in influencing political processes and outcomes. It is against the backdrop of these debates about the role and purpose of the humanitarian response that the discussion in this chapter and the next is placed.

THE NUMBERS OF DISASTERS AND PEOPLE AFFECTED

The world has always had to face emergencies and disasters, some man-made and some rooted in the patterns of nature. While statistics on the numbers affected have never been more than rather crude approximations, the available trend data reveal that over the past 50 years, in particular, the world has experienced a sharp rise in the numbers of reported disasters, the numbers killed, and the numbers of people whose lives have been affected.

The total number of disasters reported since the mid-1950s rose from fewer than 80 in the mid-1960s to more than 200 by the end of the 1970s. This number rose further, to 300, by the start of the 1990s, to over 700 by the turn of the century, and to almost 850 by 2005.[7] Though the number of deaths from disasters fell dramatically in the 30 years to the late 1960s, thereafter, with some dips, the trend has been progressively upwards. In the decade to 2004, over 900,000 people are estimated to have died in disasters, a 40 per cent rise over the 640,000 killed in the previous decade (IFRC 2005: annex 1, table 13). The numbers of people affected by disasters has expanded even more rapidly from the 1960s onwards: from 100mn in the early 1980s, to 200mn by the early 1990s, and to over 250mn people by the early decades of this century. There is also evidence of growing numbers of people requiring emergency food supplies, especially in Africa. In early 2006, the World Food Programme (WFP) estimated that it was trying to provide food for 40mn people compared with 20mn ten years earlier.

However, the rise in the number of emergencies has not been mirrored by a similar rise in the worldwide refugee population. The number of refugees doubled during the decade of the 1970s, from some four million to eight million, and more than doubled again to reach 19mn by the late 1990s. Since then, however, the number has remained fairly stable around the 19–20mn mark (UNHCR 2005). In marked contrast, and reflecting changes in the nature of man-made disasters, there has been a sharp rise in the number of people displaced by war and conflict but remaining in their own home country. The number of these internally displaced persons (IDPs) increased five-fold from the 1970s, and was estimated to have totalled some 25mn by 2005, now far exceeding the number of refugees. Not surprisingly, the rise in the number of disasters and the numbers of people affected has led to a rise in the estimated consequent damage. From the 1950s to the 1990s, the cost of disasters to global insurers rose fifteen-fold, and in the year 2004, disasters were estimated to have caused damage of over $123bn.[8]

The numbers killed in and affected by different disasters vary markedly, and there is no necessary correlation between the media attention given to disasters and the numbers who die. For instance, at the turn of the century the world's media was dominated by floods in Mozambique, which claimed the lives of a few hundred people. In December 2004 and early 2005, the Asian earthquake and linked tsunamis are estimated to have killed about 230,000 people. These contrast with food shortages in North Korea which are estimated to have led to the deaths of some 270,000 in the last four years of the 1990s, the 1976 Tangshan earthquake in China, estimated to have killed at least 245,000 people, and floods in Bangladesh in the 1970s, in which between 300,000 and 500,000 people were killed almost overnight.[9] These far larger emergencies, in terms of the numbers of lives lost, are now long forgotten by the outside world.

While the aggregate figures probably fairly accurately portray the overall crude trends in the rise in the number and extent of disasters worldwide, country-specific and detailed studies of changes in morbidity and mortality rates (a key indicator of a crisis) provide a dramatically different picture of the impact, especially of complex emergencies. For instance, mortality studies conducted in the eastern part of the Democratic Republic of Congo (DRC) suggest that between August 1998 (when the most recent war started) and the end of 2004, almost four million more people died than in the period before the conflict began—over 30,000 more a month. Similar surveys conducted in the first half of 2005 in northern Uganda suggested that 26,000 more people were then dying each month as a result of the conflict in that region.[10] Comparing these death rates with the overall death rate in the Asian earthquakes and linked tsunamis suggests that the DRC and northern Uganda between them have been experiencing the equivalent of two 2004 Asian tsunamis a year in the early years of this century as a result of the ongoing emergencies they have been facing.

The humanitarian aid response

THE ORGANIZATION OF HUMANITARIAN AID

As mentioned earlier, humanitarian aid is provided by four main types of agency: government donors, multilateral agencies, particularly different United Nations agencies, NGOs and the Red Cross Movement. However, the humanitarian system is more complex than it might at first appear, because of the range of cross-linkages that have been developed between and across all groups. While some official donors distribute emergency aid themselves, the majority channel substantial funds to NGOs, the Red Cross and to different UN agencies, which in turn undertake emergency work. The largest official government providers of humanitarian aid are the United States (alone responsible for about a third of all official bilateral humanitarian aid), the European Community Humanitarian Aid Department (ECHO), the United Kingdom, France, Sweden, Norway, the Netherlands, Germany and Canada.[11]

Some of the UN agencies involved in humanitarian aid are operational, the largest being the Office of the United Nations High Commissioner for Refugees (UNHCR) and the World Food Programme (WFP). Overseeing the work of the UN humanitarian agencies is the Office for the Coordination of Humanitarian Affairs (OCHA), which also plays a wider role in humanitarian aid coordination, through the Emergency Relief Coordinator, through its chairing of the Inter-Agency Standing Committee (IASC), which brings together humanitarian agencies from each grouping, and through its central role in raising emergency funds, notably through the Consolidated Appeals Process (CAP), discussed below.[12] Other UN agencies, such as the Food and Agriculture Organization (FAO), the World Health Organization (WHO) and the United

Nations Children's Fund (UNICEF), play both a direct and indirect role in distributing humanitarian assistance. As with their government counterparts, UN agencies also make use of NGOs to distribute humanitarian assistance.

For their part, NGOs obtain their funds from government donors and different United Nations agencies, as well as raising funds themselves to undertake their own humanitarian work. Thousands of different NGOs are involved in providing humanitarian assistance. These include large international NGOs, such as CARE, Oxfam, World Vision, Save the Children, Médecins Sans Frontières (MSF), Lutheran World Relief, Catholic Relief Services, the International Rescue Committee (IRC), Mercy Corps, and members of faith-based networks such as Caritas (Catholic) and Action by Churches Together International (ACT) (Protestant and Orthodox), local NGOs. The International Red Cross and Red Crescent Movement consists of the International Committee of the Red Cross (ICRC), the International Federation of Red Cross and Red Crescent Societies, and some 185 member societies spread across the globe.[13] Figure 18.1 represents diagrammatically the ways that the current humanitarian aid system is structured.

HOW MUCH HUMANITARIAN AID IS PROVIDED?

How has the international community responded to this rise in the number of disasters? It is difficult to answer this question with much precision, on two

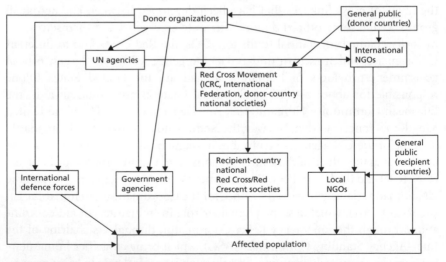

Figure 18.1 The structure of the global humanitarian response mechanism.

Note: The arrows represent the flow of funds and/or the establishment of discrete projects from one agency, group or population to another.

Source: Adapted from Macrae (2002b: 12).

counts. First, comprehensive aggregate data on the total amount of humanitarian aid provided worldwide are still not collected and collated. Secondly, while (as we shall see) formal appeals are made to fund some of the larger disasters and emergencies, the estimates made of the funds required to address the needs that arise from different emergencies are known to be only crude estimates.

The most accurate trend data on overall humanitarian aid are provided by the OECD/DAC. However, these only record official aid which is channelled into what is termed 'emergency and distress relief', with published data recording only the amount of humanitarian aid disbursed bilaterally, though these figures do include humanitarian aid funds used by NGOs that are provided to them by official aid donors—by far the largest source of humanitarian funds used by NGOs.[14] The best attempt to incorporate these data into estimates of the global amount of official aid disbursed by multilateral agencies and come up with an overall figure for humanitarian aid has been made by the UK-based Development Initiatives (DI). The DI data-base provides estimates for all humanitarian aid.[15] It includes estimates of the humanitarian aid provided by non-DAC donors, who, between the years 2001 and 2004, have contributed on average about $330mn a year in humanitarian aid (Harmer and Cotterrell 2005: 16), and makes an estimate for private donations, adding a further 10 to 15 per cent to official humanitarian aid figures (Randel and German 2000: 20). On the basis of these data and assumptions, in 2004 total humanitarian aid amounted to no less than $12.4bn, with official humanitarian aid for OECD/DAC donors accounting for some $11bn, almost 14 per cent of all ODA. However, on different (and arguably more accurate) assumptions concerning private donations, the figure may have been closer to $15bn, equivalent to over 18 per cent of total ODA in that year.[16]

Over time, both the amount and the share of total ODA channelled as emergency aid has increased. Thus, just over ten years ago, in the two-year period 1994–5, official emergency aid accounted for less than 5 per cent of total aid. The steepest increases in official emergency aid occurred in the early 1990s, doubling in real terms in the two years to 1992, and in the post-2002 period, when annual rises of over 30 per cent have been recorded. In the 25 years since 1980, there has been an almost four-fold expansion in official humanitarian assistance in real terms, and a 50 per cent rise over the past 12 years (Development Initiatives 2005: 5).

Over the past ten years, there has been a marked increase in the share of official humanitarian aid that has been channelled bilaterally and a shift away from the relative importance of the UN agencies: whereas in the mid-1990s, about one-quarter of all humanitarian assistance went to or through UN agencies, by 2003 this share had fallen to just 15 per cent of the total. Another important, though more gradual, change has been the rise in the importance of NGOs in implementing humanitarian aid programmes. By 2004, the two largest government donors, the United States and ECHO, reported that at least

60 per cent of their humanitarian aid was channelled through NGOs; in the case of the United States only 20 per cent went through the United Nations agencies, in the case of ECHO the figure was only a little higher, at 28 per cent.[17] Also, out of a total contribution made to the ICRC of $688mn in the year 2004, 90 per cent was provided by governments and by the European Commission.[18]

RESPONSES TO APPEALS

There has been a rise in the number of disasters and a rise in the amount of humanitarian aid given, but has the rise in donations matched the rise in the needs of those affected? There is no direct and accurate way of knowing this, so it is necessary to make use of the best available proxy data. One indicator, albeit quite crude, is the response made to the appeals sent out by the United Nations. It is the responsibility of the UN's Office for the Coordination of Humanitarian Affairs (OCHA) to mobilize international assistance for both complex emergencies and for natural disasters. It does this by means of the Consolidated Appeals Process (CAP), through which it raises funds for complex emergencies, and by means of Flash Appeals, through which it raises (additional) funds for sudden-onset natural disasters. As some appeals extend over a number of years, it is difficult to analyse the response to these appeals at any particular point in time. However, one clear message is apparent from an examination of responses to appeals over time: the funds made available by different donors consistently fall well short of the funds required, as the following paragraphs explain.

As Figure 18.2 shows, in the five years to 2005, overall funding of appeals has almost consistently raised under 60 per cent of the amounts required. Additionally, funds committed have also been very volatile year on year, making the planning of responses even more difficult than the overall shortfall in funds would indicate. Furthermore, there is no guarantee that all funds pledged will be committed, and that all funds committed will be disbursed, or that disbursements will be made on time. Again, the record reveals gaps, often quite large, between what donors say they will provide and what happens on the ground to meet the needs of those affected. For instance, an analysis of the appeal funding received during the three years from 2002 to 2005 for 17 major flash flood appeals revealed that one month after the appeal was launched, 50 per cent or more of the funds required had been received in less than 20 per cent of cases (OCHA 2006: 10). Figure 18.2 also indicates the very wide range of funding commitments made by donors to individual appeals, which the average figures conceal. In each year, numerous appeals fail to secure even a quarter of funds required. For instance, in 2004, Côte d'Ivoire received only 35 per cent of the relief funds it needed, and the following year, the proportion of the requirements funded had fallen to 10 per cent.

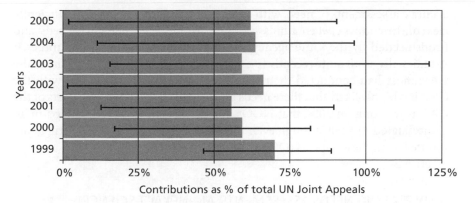

Figure 18.2 United Nations Flash and Consolidated Appeals, 1999–2005

Note: The solid bars show overall contributions as a percentage of all UN joint appeals for each year. The lines show the range between the best- and worst-supported appeals for the year.

Source: OCHA (2005), reproduced from Cosgrave (2005: 10).

Overall, the evidence suggests that donors tend to support the one or two largest appeals, usually those with significant publicity, and provide proportionately lower contributions to all other appeals (Porter 2002: 32). One of the consequences of the variable response is to widen further the gaps between the amounts that each recipient needs and the amounts, on average, that each receives. For example, the 2003 UN appeal for Chechnya was 91 per cent funded, resulting in an average of $40 per beneficiary. In contrast, the 2003 UN appeal for Mozambique was 15 per cent funded, resulting in an average of approximately 40 cents per person.[19] The United Kingdom's National Audit Office's 2003 report on British official emergency aid judged that in responding to emergencies since 1997, the Department for International Development (DFID) had provided five time as much per capita assistance in response to European emergencies as to those in Africa, and that this could not be explained by costs of delivery and associated security (NAO 2003: 4). To add to these complexities and differences, there is evidence to suggest that on occasions, even when appeals are fully funded, the amounts provided still fail adequately to meet the needs of those requiring emergency assistance.[20]

This analysis of responses to UN appeals provides only one set of indicators of the response to humanitarian crises—and confirms a major gap between need and response—because the CAP itself encompasses only a part of the overall humanitarian response. In the ten years to 2002, the CAP accounted for only about a third of all recorded (official) humanitarian assistance, and in recent years, this share has fallen to even lower levels (Porter 2002: 27–8). Indeed, donors openly acknowledge that the funding decisions they make are only indirectly influenced by these appeals. One reason has been a strong perception of a lack of rigour by some UN agencies in compiling accurate assessments of need, with some agencies failing to make a sufficiently clear distinction between funds required to address emergency needs and funds needed by the same agency to support their ongoing programmes.[21] Additionally, until quite recently (post-2004), NGOs had never been part of the CAP: most had conducted their own needs assessments in parallel with the CAP. It is highly likely that these needs assessments overlapped with parts of the CAP. It was only in 2006 that NGOs, for the first time, were included in all Consolidated Appeals, though even then major NGO projects were still being omitted from these appeals (OCHA 2006: 9).[22]

UNDERTAKING NEEDS ASSESSMENTS: AN INEXACT SCIENCE

Problems of disaster funding are not confined solely to the inadequate and varied response to the appeals which are launched. Concerns have also been raised about the quality of the information and data upon which aggregate appeals for funds are made. For instance, informed observers believe that the amount of funds requested in an appeal reflects estimates not so much of the overall needs but of the needs which are likely to be funded (Smillie and Minear 2004: 3; Cosgrave 2005: 10).

As those undertaking needs assessments are often the first to acknowledge, it is difficult accurately to assess both the precise numbers of those affected by an emergency and the precise nature of their needs. For all the advances made and technical training undertaken, needs assessment remains today a very inexact science: at bottom, in many, probably most emergencies, even after needs assessments have been carried out, we only have a very crude idea of the needs of those affected, and hence of the funds required to help meet those needs. As the WFP put it in a communication brief launching its new assessment handbook in mid-2005, the 'difficulties of obtaining precise estimates of emergency needs in crisis situations cannot be underestimated'.[23] Access and coverage are usually major problems. Clearly, numbers affected can be either over- or underestimated, and there is evidence of both occurring. But in either case, dramatically revising figures, either upwards or downwards, undermines faith in the needs-assessment process. Successive studies show that many of those in greatest need (including women and minority groups) often come from the more marginalized and hidden parts of the wider society; locating them and searching them out requires special skills, time and additional funds. Additionally, the accurate assessment of needs normally requires an understanding of people's mechanisms for coping with calamity, including knowledge of the extent to which those directly affected have links, such as family ties, to the world beyond the emergency. Perhaps above all else, accurate needs assessments require close interaction with the people affected by the particular emergency. In sharp contrast, the evidence suggests, repeatedly, that needs assessments are often made without sufficient consultation with those directly affected (see Darcy and Hoffman 2003: 7).

Once needs have been identified, it is by no means simple to ascertain how these can best be met.[24] For instance, assessments of the cost of meeting housing needs can vary as much as twenty-fold depending on whether temporary or permanent housing is being considered. What is judged to be necessary is often derived from a confusing mix of what people had in the past, agreed standards and cultural norms. Importantly, too, there is often a lack of clarity as to where the line should be drawn between merely providing relief and addressing immediate needs, and expanding assessments to cover needs in what is now termed the continuum from relief through to rehabilitation, restoring livelihoods and eventually to development. In recent years, most agencies have extended their assessments to include resources well beyond meeting immediate relief needs, and this has profound effects on both the assessment of needs, and on the costs of responding adequately. However, this has inadvertently aggravated the problems because today there is even less agreement about what should and should not be included in an overall needs assesment.[25] Costs, in turn, are sensitive to assumptions about the source of the goods. Generally speaking, costs escalate if goods have to be brought in from outside the disaster area, markedly if they have to be brought in by air. A key conundrum arises here because some donors tie their aid to the purchase of goods in their own country, and others do not, but the initial headline estimates are undertaken prior to launching an appeal, so it is not known what proportion of appeal funds will be met from tied and earmarked, as opposed to untied, sources.

Another cluster of problems concerns more systemic issues. One relates to funding expectations. Needs assessments are often undertaken by agencies which are, or intend to form, part of the emergency response. Each comes to an assessment with the knowledge of how it has fared in the distribution of funds raised in earlier emergencies. If that experience is one of marked shortfalls, then they will (understandably) tend to inflate their requirements, in order to narrow the gap between what they require and what they expect to receive. It is claimed that inflating requirements is common practice among a number of NGOs, and it is not unknown among larger agencies.[26] Similarly, if needs assessments are to be accurate, they ought to include some assessment of 'leakage': the proportion of the goods arriving in the emergency location which they believe will be misplaced, either through inefficiencies or the deliberate pilfering of goods. As discussed below, in some emergencies a significant proportion of goods never reach those for whom they are intended. Almost all needs assessments are silent on this issue, so it is difficult to know the extent to which inefficiencies and corrupt practices are incorporated into needs assessments and linked estimates of costs.

Many needs assessments are undertaken by international agencies; many are too prone to assume that the best agencies to provide relief and emergency assistance are external, usually international ones, even though substantial evidence exists which strongly points to the critical and usually dominant role that local communities play in saving lives and assisting those most desperately and most immediately in need (see Telford and Cosgrave 2006: 40ff. for recent evidence). The result is that costs of providing assistance (largely through international channels) are likely to be considerably inflated. Though current UN guidelines make provision for local inputs into needs assessments, too often local voices remain largely unheard and their views unheeded.

NEEDS ASSESSMENT AND THE RESPONSE TO THE DECEMBER 2005 EARTHQUAKE AND LINKED TSUNAMIS

Over the past 30 years, there has been a huge response by donors and the donating public to a few large emergencies, such as Ethiopia in the mid-1980s, the former Yugoslavia in 1993–5, the Great Lakes in 1995 and Kosovo in 1999. But these responses pale into relative insignificance when placed alongside the global response to the 2005 Indian Ocean earthquake and tsunamis. Mid-2006 estimates suggest that over $18bn in aid money was pledged for this single disaster, $13.5bn from international and $5.5bn from national sources (Telford and Cosgrove 2006: 81). The smaller figure ($13.5bn) is 70 per cent more than the total amount of official humanitarian assistance provided globally for the year 2004, and comes close to the total estimated figure ($15bn) for all humanitarian aid (including private donations) provided in that year. Of this $13.5bn total, $5.9 bn was pledged by donor governments, and an even larger amount, $7.6bn, was provided by the general public through private and corporate donations.[27] One year after the disaster, almost $4bn of government donations had been formally committed, of which just over half had been disbursed (one-third of the $5.9bn pledged). By that time, just over 35 per cent of the £350mn raised in the main public appeal made in the United Kingdom by the leading UK NGOs had been spent (Vaux *et al.* 2005: 1).

On the other hand, the (revised) UN Consolidated Appeal for the Indian Ocean tsunami totalled $1.3bn (OCHA 2006: 64). Comparing this with the contributions made (or at least committed) would suggest either that there was a massive (twelve-fold) surplus of funds over estimated needs, or that the appeal process is even less of an accurate indicator of need than the discussion above has suggested.[28] How much humanitarian aid was needed to address the needs of the 1.8mn people displaced by the tsunami? We simply do not know. What we do know is that the UN's CAP appeal was aiming to raise on average 73 cents per affected person, and that in the year to October 2005, an average of $3.47 per person (almost five times the appeal average) was spent, compared with an average of $9 per person in funds raised.[29] The impact of the funds provided to the tsunami is discussed in Chapter 19.

NEW INITIATIVES

Increasingly over the past decade, a growing number of humanitarian agencies and the majority of major donors have stated publicly what they all know privately—that there are major problems with the way the humanitarian aid system has evolved and that in many respects it is no longer fit for purpose. Among the problems that have been articulated are: continuing and large gaps between the amounts of aid needed and the amounts provided, major inadequacies in the way emergency aid is allocated, and fundamental weaknesses in the coordination of the humanitarian response. However, it has proved far easier to agree that there are (major) problems than it has been to resolve them.

One impetus for change has been the Good Humanitarian Donorship (GHD) initiative, launched by a number of donor governments, the International Red Cross and Red Crescent Movement, and other humanitarian actors in Stockholm in mid-2003 to improve the international response to humanitarian crises. A core element of the GHD initiative involved establishing a set of 23 core norms and principles, the Principles and Good Practice of Humanitarian Donorship, to guide donors in the decisions they make about humanitarian aid, and in particular, to address (far better than current efforts) the common international goal of meeting the entirety of global humanitarian needs.[30] Since its inception, a growing number of official donors as well as UN agencies have participated in the GHD initiative. It now has strong support from the United Nations and major NGOs. In April 2006, the Principles and Good Practice was formally endorsed by all OECD/DAC donors. However, progress in achieving tangible results has been slower than anticipated. Two concrete outcomes have been achieved, wholly or partly linked to the GHD initiative. The first has been the piloting, in Burundi and the DRC, of a new and more comprehensive way of carrying out needs assessments, undertaken by government donors, major NGOs and ten UN agencies. The second has been to provide crucial political support to the creation of a new and substantial global humanitarian funding facility.[31]

Following commitments made by leaders at the World Summit in September 2005 to improve the timeliness and predictability of the provision of humanitarian aid, a new resolution of the UN General Assembly was passed in December 2005, to establish the Central Emergency Response Fund (CERF), replacing the smaller and far narrower Central Emergency Revolving Fund. The purpose of the (new) CERF is to have in place a global emergency fund sufficiently large and flexible for monies to be allocated quickly to specific emergencies as and when they arise. CERF funds are to be raised by donors contributing annually to the general fund. The establishment of the CERF aims to remove two of the main problems of the prevailing system—the discretionary funding of emergencies on a case-by-case basis and the growing practice of donors earmarking their funds to specific agencies and purposes to create a cumbersome, and at times almost unworkable, bureaucratic system.

The CERF was launched in March 2006. The initial funding target was put at $500mn, but by mid-2006 the sums pledged amounted to only a little over half this figure, at $263mn. Though the $500mn target is ten times as large as the old revolving fund it replaced, and consists predominantly of untied grant money, it is far less than the $1bn figure for which some donors had been lobbying, and constitutes less than 10 per cent of all humanitarian aid provided in 2005. The initial 18 grants made during the first few months after it was established were small, averaging less than $1mn each, with most funds allocated for projects run by the WHO, WFP and UNICEF, largely in the Horn of Africa.

While these new initiatives are clearly important steps forward, they do not address three other major linked problems of the current system of allocating humanitarian aid: that humanitarian aid is still given on a voluntary basis, that the amounts provided are highly volatile, and that global amounts of humanitarian aid continue to fall well short of what even conservative estimates suggest is needed. Importantly, too, while the Principles and Good Practice state that humanitarian action includes the protection of civilians (no. 3), they provide little guidance as to how, in practice, such protection can be achieved. It remains to be seen whether the GHD and CERF initiatives will herald the start of a more comprehensive attempt to address prevailing problems or simply remain an important, but partial and limited, response to these problems.[32]

19 The impact of emergency and humanitarian aid

This chapter looks at what humanitarian aid has achieved. It examines the extent to which this aid has succeeded in meeting its core objective of saving lives, reducing suffering and maintaining human dignity. It starts by looking at the different ways that the impact of humanitarian aid is assessed, highlighting some of the key problems that arise and with which evaluators have to grapple. The bulk of the chapter reviews the evidence of the impact of humanitarian aid on the ground. This is followed by a short discussion of the impact of advocacy in the humanitarian sphere. The chapter ends with a brief summary of the overall impact of humanitarian aid.

Assessing humanitarian aid

OVERVIEW

The process of assessing the impact of humanitarian aid with any degree of rigour shares many of the same methodological problems faced by those assessing the impact of development aid. It requires establishing baseline data, monitoring carefully what happens after the aid has been provided, and attempting, as far as possible, to draw a link between the outcomes achieved and the aid provided.

It is probably even more important in examining the impact of humanitarian aid to be sure of the relationship between what agencies provide and the outcomes achieved, given the claims regularly made by humanitarian agencies about how successful they are in saving lives, and in reaching those in distress and meeting their most urgent needs. It is also important to take a holistic view of impact, going beyond an examination of the impact of what particular agencies do to provide a more systemic assessment of the combined impact of all who are involved in the humanitarian response to a particular emergency. Saving the lives or reducing the suffering of thousands, or even a dozen people, is clearly important, but these successes will look very different if dozens or thousands of others died or were left to suffer because they were located in areas away from where the relief efforts were concentrated.

IMPACT ASSESSMENT AND ITS LINKS TO UNDERSTANDING WHAT HUMANITARIAN ACTION COMPRISES

A key problem facing the assessment of humanitarian aid is that, surprisingly, there is still no universally agreed definition of what humanitarian action comprises, beyond the very general purpose of saving lives, reducing suffering and maintaining human dignity. As Joanna Macrae, an experienced and reliable researcher on humanitarianism, recently observed, the 'very meaning of humanitarianism has become elusive' (2002b: 5). Clearly, the less clarity there is about what constitutes humanitarian action, the more difficult it is to reach agreement about its impact and how to assess it.

There is no dispute about the need to provide food, shelter, health care, and water and sanitation. What has been particularly controversial is whether humanitarian action includes providing other, less tangible things, most notably protection, especially physical and legal protection against human rights violations. It remains an unresolved question whether, especially in complex emergencies, it is part of the core purpose of humanitarian action, and hence a core role of humanitarian agencies, to seek to address, or contribute to addressing, the underlying as well as the immediate causes of conflicts, the solution of which will usually have a profound impact on lives, suffering and human dignity. The problem—for some agencies—is that if they are to engage in effective protection, this may require them to enter into the political sphere, which is seen—by some agencies—as potentially compromising their commitment to the principles of independence, impartiality and neutrality.

Obtaining clarity on the demarcation between political and humanitarian action has become an even more important issue in recent years as non-humanitarian actors and agencies have entered the terrain previously occupied by traditional humanitarian actors and agencies, claiming that their actions should also be termed 'humanitarian'. This has led to the coining of the term 'the new humanitarianism'.[1] One reason for these growing complexities has been the changing role of the United Nations. One part of the UN has taken on more peace-keeping and 'peace-making' roles at the same time as other parts have expanded their relief and emergency activities.[2] Another is that in recent years governments—and their armies—have intervened in some conflicts and claimed that their actions have been based, primarily or in part, on humanitarian motives. This has occurred, for example, in the former Yugoslavia, Sierra Leone, Somalia and (at least in retrospect) Rwanda.

More challenging still, following the terrorist attacks on the United States in September 2001, have been the activities which the military have taken on in our 'post-9/11' world, most notably in Iraq and Afghanistan. Here military personnel have been involved not merely in distributing humanitarian aid in dangerous locations (an action which humanitarian agencies have recognized is sometimes necessary *in extremis*), but also in making assessments of the humanitarian needs of civilian populations. Not only does this violate principles of independence in humanitarian action, but, in turn, it has increased the vulnerability of traditional humanitarian agencies and their staff, even those deliberately distancing themselves from military-led relief work. In such contexts, it is difficult for any humanitarian agency not to be seen as part of the 'new humanitarian' effort, as illustrated by the killing of UN staff in Baghdad in 2003 and scores of other humanitarian workers in Iraq, Afghanistan and beyond. The blurring of roles has been further increased by the emergence of new agencies and organizations undertaking relief work under contract with governments and under the supervision of the military, a number of whom are less familiar with, and in some cases have little interest in, the distinct role that independent humanitarian action has played in the past. It is against the backdrop of these developments that it becomes clearer why governments in particular—political actors *par excellence*—continue to find it difficult to agree among themselves on what, in practice, humanitarian action is.[3]

Though seemingly new, questions and debates about the nature, content and form of humanitarian action have a long history. Many can be traced back to different traditions of humanitarian action, with their differing views about what constitutes the very essence of humanitarianism and humanitarian action, including the extent to which, and the manner in which, the principle of neutrality is understood and given prominence. On the one side are those who maintain that a failure to speak out against and attempt to dissuade those perpetrating inhumane activities for fear that it prevents the delivery of relief items to those who desperately need it—as happens in extreme cases of genocide—compromises or even distorts the humanitarian imperative. Those who hold this view take what has been termed a 'solidarity approach' to humanitarianism. This involves undertaking a political analysis of each emergency and, where necessary, taking a particular political stand in order to push for the implementation of policies which will reduce deaths and life-threatening suffering and protect human rights, especially in situations of violent conflict. Such a perspective has been associated perhaps most strongly with the agency Médecins Sans Frontières (MSF) (see Brubacher 2004).[4]

On the other side stand those who argue, equally vociferously, that the essence of humanitarianism and humanitarian action requires agencies strenuously to avoid 'taking sides'. Here it is asserted that there need to be agencies who are willing and able to provide relief activities in the harshest of environments and whose legitimacy is protected by an unequivocal commitment to not taking sides in highly charged and dangerous situations. Unless there are agencies who are 'non-political', it is argued, the provision of relief items to those caught up in conflict and unable to survive without external assistance can never be assured. Greater good will result, it is submitted (more lives will be saved and more suffering alleviated), by upholding and acting on this principle, notwithstanding individual (exceptional) instances where such action has self-evidently led to perverse outcomes. This is the traditional neutralist, or 'Dunanist', view, which gives pre-eminence to the saving of life.[5] It is upheld and articulated by the ICRC, but has been associated with the approach of other leading agencies such as the European Community Humanitarian Aid Department (ECHO) and the Office of US Foreign Disaster Assistance (OFDA).[6] However, partly influenced by the findings of the four-volume assessment of the Rwandan genocide and the humanitarian response, the International Committee of the Red Cross (ICRC) has spoken out, calling for international action to be taken in the case of genocide (Borton *et al.* 1996).[7]

GROWING AREAS OF AGREEMENT

In practice, there has been a narrowing of differences between many of the largest agencies about the different components that ought to compose humanitarian action, as a result of two prime and partly interlinked factors. The first has been work undertaken on developing and debating the principles of humanitarian action, itself influenced by the growing attention being paid to the issue of human rights. Ongoing reflection and debates on the nature and content of what is termed international humanitarian law (IHL) has led to growing prominence being given to, and a growing acceptance of the need for, protection, leading to confirmation that 'the need to protect' ought to be a constituent part of humanitarian action.[8] This was manifested most prominently in the agreement reached at the World Summit in September 2005 when the 'responsibility to protect' was universally accepted by world leaders. Under para. 139, member states agree

to take collective action, in a timely and decisive manner . . . on a case by case basis, and in cooperation with relevant regional organizations as appropriate, should peaceful means be inadequate and national authorities manifestly failing to protect their populations from genocide, war crimes, ethnic cleansing and crimes against humanity. We stress the need for the General Assembly to continue consideration of the responsibility to protect populations from genocide, war crimes, ethnic cleansing and crimes against humanity and its implications, bearing in mind the principles of the [United Nations] Charter and international law.[9]

Additionally, there has been a growing focus on, and a growing acceptance that, humanitarian action ought to be based on the observance of (quality) standards, with agreement reached on some specific standards. The most significant development here has been the production of the Humanitarian Charter and Minimum Standards in Disaster Response, produced by the Sphere Project (now widely referred to as the Sphere Standards), which lays out the principle that those receiving humanitarian aid have the right to receive assistance which achieves or surpasses minimum standards. The Project has begun to develop specific standards in core areas against which humanitarian action is to be judged, notably food, water, shelter and health care (Sphere 2004). A more recent initiative has been the development of and agreement on norms and minimum standards for education in emergencies (INEE 2004).[10] The emphasis on protecting the basic rights of those affected by emergencies has given prominence to the need for agencies to consult closely with those affected by emergencies, as a core part of any needs assessment.[11] Additionally, it is now almost universally accepted that humanitarian aid can (or ought to) be used to help prevent or reduce the costs of future disasters, under the umbrella of what is termed 'disaster preparedness', aiming, in part, to build (local) capacities to enhance the impact of work in future disasters or emergencies.

A number of these dimensions of humanitarian action have been brought together and agreed by most of the major agencies in a Code of Conduct (see Box 19.1) established to guide the work of agencies, to which all the major international NGOs agree to adhere. Together with the Sphere Standards, and notwithstanding the vagueness of some parts of the Code, these documents provide some core criteria against which most agencies would agree that humanitarian action can and ought to be judged.[12]

One activity not explicitly mentioned in this list is advocacy. This is not surprising given the ICRC's views about how speaking out risks compromising

---

BOX 19.1 CODE OF CONDUCT FOR THE INTERNATIONAL RED CROSS AND RED CRESCENT MOVEMENT AND NGOS ENGAGED IN HUMANITARIAN AID ACTIVITIES

1. The humanitarian imperative comes first.
2. Aid is given regardless of the race, creed or nationality of the recipients and without adverse distinction of any kind. Aid priorities are calculated on the basis of need alone.
3. Aid will not be used to further a particular political or religious standpoint.
4. We shall endeavour not to act as instruments of government foreign policy.
5. We shall respect culture and custom.
6. We shall attempt to build disaster response on local capacities.
7. Ways shall be found to involve programme beneficiaries in the management of relief programmes.
8. Relief aid must strive to reduce future vulnerabilities to disaster as well as meeting basic needs.
9. We hold ourselves accountable to both those we seek to assist and those from whom we accept resources.
10. In our information, publicity and advertising activities, we shall recognise disaster victims as dignified human beings, not hopeless objects.

neutrality. However, not only do the majority of the large NGOs undertake advocacy in times of emergency, but advocacy is also undertaken by the leading UN agencies involved in humanitarian activities as well as by leading donor governments involved in the Good Humanitarian Donorship (GHD) initiative. They believe advocacy constitutes an essential part of overall humanitarian action—because of the potentially crucial role it can play in contributing to the protection of those affected by emergencies, in helping prevent emergencies from arising, and in helping to reduce the impact of those affected. Indeed, the official Swiss aid agency has produced its own guidelines on humanitarian advocacy (SDC 2004).

One implication of these changes and developments has been a growing acceptance of the view, especially in complex emergencies, that politics does matter, and thus that it is (usually) necessary to undertake a political assessment to understand the respective roles that (independent) humanitarian actors and political actors play, and need to play.[13] However, agencies continue to disagree sharply about what that means for each of them in practice.

One area on which there still remains a lack of clarity and on which there is no agreement is where the boundaries should be drawn between humanitarian action and development activities. On the positive side, it is now widely acknowledged by all the large agencies and by governments that humanitarian action needs to include not only the supply of relief items, but assistance which is focused beyond the immediate saving of life to rehabilitating communities, reconstructing destroyed lives and contributing to rebuilding livelihoods. For instance, the UNHCR–WFP needs-assessment guidelines require an analysis and identification of opportunities for self-reliance to be improved, and an assessment of the measures needed to increase self-reliance (UNHCR and WFP 2004: 111). However, there is considerable confusion between and across agencies over what constitutes humanitarian and what constitutes development work, reflected in the word 'continuum', which is now used to describe the process of moving from the one form of engagement to the other.[14] Clearly, the further an agency moves on this continuum from relief and recovery to rehabilitation, reconstruction and restoring livelihoods, and even to improving livelihoods, which is frequently a specific objective when pre-emergency standards are used—say for housing, health care and education—the greater the potential overlap between emergency and development work and the greater the blurring of the distinction between what the different types of aid are meant to do.[15]

EVALUATING HUMANITARIAN AID IN PRACTICE

Though the provision of humanitarian aid precedes the provision of development aid, far greater advances have been made in constructing methods of assessing development aid. It was only from the mid-1990s that donors began seriously and systematically to address how humanitarian aid might be rigorously assessed, and only in 1999 that the OECD/DAC produced its *Guidance for Evaluating Humanitarian Assistance in Complex Emergencies* (OECD 1999b).[16] While these guidelines recommend the use of traditional criteria to assess humanitarian aid activities—relevance, efficiency, effectiveness, impact and sustainability—their importance lies in the far broader array of factors considered necessary in undertaking a complete assessment of humanitarian aid. They state that humanitarian evaluations need 'to assess the "humanitarian space", the security situation and the protection needs of the affected populations', even though they acknowledge that this will be more difficult than evaluating development aid because far less basic data and information are likely to be available, and what data and information there may be are less easy to obtain. (OECD 1999b: 14, 16).

The guidelines also propose that the attempt should be made to undertake a 'total system' evaluation which places discrete interventions in a wider context and which also focuses on such crucial issues as the coordination of the activities of different agencies, and which seeks to understand how and why the emergency occurred.[17] Importantly, too, even in cases where particular agencies do not themselves focus on protection, the guidelines recommend that evaluations should still assess the extent to which protection needs have been addressed, and whether the agency in question is 'correct in its assumption that this was somebody else's responsibility and whether it might have done more to enhance protection', including lobbying for international action or providing witnesses to atrocities (OECD 1999b: 21).[18] Likewise, in regard to the assessment of humanitarian space, it is pointed out that agencies sometimes need to take the initiative in creating or expanding such space, and may sometimes need to refuse to supply relief inputs 'where an unacceptably high proportion of these are being diverted by combatants to fuel the war' (OECD 1999b: 22). In short, the remit of the evaluation is seen to cover not merely an assessment of what was done, but also of what was not done and why, using prevailing norms or standards, including IHL, codes of conduct and the Sphere Standards, against which to assess activities undertaken or not undertaken. In essence, the guidelines view humanitarian aid evaluation not merely as an assessment of the impact of the aid provided, but as an assessment of the whole humanitarian effort.

Building in part on the OECD/DAC guidelines, and taking more specifically as its basis the principles of the GHD, in 2004 the OECD/DAC introduced, for the first time, an assessment framework for incorporating humanitarian activities into its peer review process for assessing the performance of each DAC donor (OECD 2004c). Additionally, some of the key approaches contained in the DAC guidelines have been used in the growing practice of undertaking 'real-time evaluations'. As their name suggests, these involve assessing humanitarian actions and activities as they are taking place.[19] Their purpose is to appraise, but more importantly to recommend, changes to ongoing activities, not only if these are deemed to have weaknesses, but also if other types of action are judged necessary to achieve more effectively the core objectives of humanitarian interventions.

In spite of these advances in developing approaches to evaluating humanitarian action, gaps and questions remain. For instance, there remain uncertainties about when a complex man-made emergency starts and when it is deemed to have ended, although ongoing work on monitoring morbidity and mortality rates in areas of high risk can certainly help in pinpointing when significant changes to these key indicators take place.[20] Likewise, norms have yet to be developed for assessing the extent to which assistance has contributed to disaster prevention or capacity building has worked (see OECD 2004c: 13). Additionally, as noted above, uncertainties still abound in deciding which aid-funded activities beyond the relief stage of assistance should be classified as humanitarian and which as development.

But perhaps the most difficult and controversial issue concerns where the line can or ought to be drawn between military and humanitarian activities. A core problem arises when military activity aimed at addressing humanitarian needs is undertaken in a manner which contravenes internationally accepted norms and principles of humanitarian action. Donors disagree among themselves, as do their own military forces. For instance, the United Kingdom Department of Defence distinguishes between humanitarian-like activities, which are presented as tools for 'influencing', 'hearts and minds' activities aimed at encouraging local acceptance of the military presence, and humanitarian assistance, which is defined as 'support provided to humanitarian agencies in an insecure environment'. However, the United States Department of Defense defines humanitarian assistance from the US military simply as 'assistance to the local populace provided predominantly by US forces in conjunction with military operations and exercises' (McHugh and Gostelow 2004: 8). The greater the role the military plays in allocating relief in a partisan manner, in contracting agencies to distribute relief supplies in conformity with these norms, or in preventing the establishment of independent humanitarian space, the larger will be the amount of 'relief' assistance that does not qualify as impartial and independent humanitarian assistance. These problems and dilemmas remain unresolved.

THE EXTENT AND QUALITY OF THE INFORMATION DATA-BASE

Surprising as it may now seem, for the first 40 of the 60 years that emergency aid has been provided—at least until the start of the 1980s—there was very little demand for accurate data for rigorous assessment of the impact of emergency aid, and few internal demands among agencies to produce such data, which explains why very little detailed information on impact was produced. The large UN agencies, the ICRC, and those governments which provided aid certainly reported on how the funds they disbursed were spent, and even medium-sized NGOs produced financial reports, most of which went through formal auditing processes. However, these tended to be largely internal documents.

Beyond formal annual reports, most agencies did not perceive themselves as needing to furnish a detailed account of the impact of their different activities, still less to assess critically whether they could have done more with the funds they had available, or could have implemented their activities more effectively. Glossy magazines and brochures were produced by some organizations, recording the successes of those particular agencies—people saved from floods and earthquakes, refugees fed and clothed, health care and shelter provided. Few people questioned whether the portrayal of these discrete successes accurately reflected the overall aid effort, whether all those in need were reached, and whether their needs were adequately met. The main focus was on raising funds to help those in immediate danger; governments and individuals donated funds to emergency appeals, and the largely unchallenged assumption was that by and large the aid 'worked'. Compared with development aid, which for decades has had its harsh critics, emergency aid was subject to very few hard-hitting or sustained assaults. Most attention was focused on the supply and delivery of emergency assistance, based on accounts that insufficient amounts of aid were being provided too slowly. The solution was seen less in terms of reflecting on the effectiveness of what was provided, and almost entirely in terms of supplying more aid and speeding up its delivery to those who clearly needed it. To many people today these remain the key issues surrounding emergency aid: the public contribute to emergencies because they are aware of specific needs (largely through the media), and they respond, predominantly, by supporting agencies which, through their own publicity, assert that they have the ability to reach those in greatest need, and provide them with the support they (urgently) require.

But behind the ongoing rhythm of governments and the public continuing to respond to appeals for discrete emergencies, changes have been occurring in the way that many agencies, especially the larger ones, assess their emergency work. Starting in a small way in the 1980s, many began to realize that the absence of rigorous data with which to show their effectiveness left them vulnerable even to mild probing. However, external pressures to provide a more systematic and rigorous account of their activities remained weak because, in marked contrast with development aid, which fell sharply for most of the decade of the 1990s, emergency aid funds continued to expand rapidly. The result, however, was simply to delay, not to remove, the momentum towards greater accountability.

Today, it is accepted by all major agencies that monitoring, evaluation and impact assessments should form a necessary part of their humanitarian work. All major government and UN agencies undertake, or commission others to undertake, impact assessments, as do most of the large international NGOs. Scores of evaluations of humanitarian actions are now carried out each year. However, very few government agencies and very few NGOs, even large ones, undertake comprehensive assessments of all their humanitarian work, though all the larger agencies certainly provide detailed financial reports of all their different emergency interventions, usually on a project-by-project basis. Those humanitarian agencies which most systematically plan, implement or commission evaluations of their humanitarian work are ECHO and the leading UN agencies, most notably UNHCR, WFP and UNICEF.[21] A growing number of the very large NGOs, such as CARE, Catholic Relief Services, World Vision and Save the Children, and some smaller ones such as Tearfund, also undertake or commission a growing number of one-off evaluations and place a number of these in the public domain. However, at the time of writing, no large humanitarian NGO website has a portal where regular studies of the impact of their emergency projects and programmes can be accessed and downloaded.[22] Exceptionally, a UK umbrella organization, the Disasters Emergency Committee (DEC), whose membership consists of the 13 largest UK humanitarian NGOs, agreed some years ago to commission a formal external evaluation of all emergencies for which it raised funds, and, until recently, these evaluations were placed in the public domain.[23] However, there is still no requirement for individual DEC member agencies to conduct or commission regular evaluations of their own humanitarian activities, and the majority still do not do so on a regular basis.[24]

The ALNAP data-base

Since 1999, a London-based but global humanitarian group, the Active Learning Network for Accountability and Performance (ALNAP), has conducted an annual synthesis of all humanitarian evaluations sent to it by the members of its comprehensive network. From 1999 to the end of 2005, it had received and reviewed just over 250 different evaluations of humanitarian activities, an average of around 40 a year. This constitutes the largest and most detailed collection of reviews and assessments of humanitarian evaluations to date, and has informed and influenced the discussion in this chapter.[25] It is not known what proportion of all evaluations this collection represents. Nor, more importantly, is it known what share of all emergency projects or programmes are now regularly subjected to a formal evaluation process, though the proportion is likely still to be lower than 10 per cent even if smaller NGO interventions are to be excluded. However, as the ALNAP cluster of evaluations are submitted for scrutiny voluntarily, it seems safe to assume that these are likely to be biased towards the more successful humanitarian interventions. A number of agencies still refuse to place some evaluations of their activities in the public domain, presumably because of their critical content. For instance, in the flurry of reports and studies which were produced one year after the Indian Ocean tsunami, the International Federation of Red Cross and Red Crescent Societies (IFRC) and one British NGO held back on publishing complete evaluations that had been undertaken to assess the impact of their work.

Those humanitarian evaluations which have been carried out and published are overwhelmingly studies and assessments of the work undertaken by individual agencies, or else, in a few cases, evaluations of the joint activities of a very small number of agencies. What we still lack are assessments of humanitarian assistance that extend beyond particular agencies to assess the overall response to a particular emergency. The very few that have been carried out include Rwanda (1996), the Indian Ocean tsunami (2006), and, though far less rigorous and comprehensive, Ethiopia (2004). However, ALNAP has studied and attempted to draw out emergency-wide conclusions for which a significant number of evaluations have been carried out. These include Kosovo (1999–2000), Hurricane Mitch in Central America (2000–1), Afghanistan (2003–4) and Darfur (2003–5).

The growth in the number of evaluations is clearly welcome. But what is of equal if not greater importance is to know the quality of the evaluation material that is increasingly being placed in the public domain. To what extent does this material provide a reliable source for conclusions about the impact of humanitarian assistance? Fortunately, it is one of the main purposes of the ALNAP review of evaluations to assess the quality of the material submitted to it. Unfortunately, their quality assessments make fairly grim reading.

Every year since they were first produced, the ALNAP reviews have expressed concern at the poor quality of the evaluations of humanitarian aid reviewed. The 2005 report is typical: it noted some improvements, but overall, the quality of evaluations were judged to be 'unimpressive', with only just under half rated as satisfactory or better, and only 40 per cent judged as having satisfactorily assessed the overall impact of the humanitarian activities of the agency concerned. Only a single report out of more than 40 received a 'good' quality-rating assessment (ALNAP 2005: 131, 156, 157). Donor agencies were rated slightly better than NGOs, followed by the UN agencies (ALNAP 2005: 131). The ALNAP assessments of quality have been confirmed by the conclusions of another recent stocktaking of the quality of evaluations of humanitarian aid, which were judged to be 'consistently poor' (Hofmann *et al.* 2004: 2).

The sharpest criticisms were directed at the terms of reference given to the evaluators, which were often too narrowly based for reliable conclusions about impact. Additionally, the reviews criticized agencies for not sufficiently seeking out the views of beneficiaries, even if some improvements over earlier years were noted (ALNAP 2005: 170). This is clearly a fundamental issue. If the people affected by emergencies are not being consulted, it is very difficult to know whether their needs are being met. While the 2005 report welcomed the rise in the number of individual evaluations undertaken, it criticized the continuing failure to provide overall assessments of an entire emergency. It also referred to what it termed a 'culture of defensiveness' which still pervaded the whole process of humanitarian evaluation. As recently as 2003, ALNAP reported that some 70 per cent of all evaluations submitted to it for assessment were marked by agencies as 'for ALNAP members only', NGOs and a number of UN agencies being among those most reluctant to place their evaluations in the public domain, with two exceptions, UNHCR and ECHO (ALNAP 2003: 164).

The impact of humanitarian action and humanitarian aid

OVERVIEW

Accepting that the quality of the data remains poor, what does the available evidence tell us about the impact of humanitarian aid? At one level, the news would appear to be good. In terms of saving lives, providing food to those who are hungry, health care and medicines to those vulnerable to acute disease in emergencies, water, sanitation and shelter to those whose homes have been destroyed, the evidence from five annual ALNAP reviews since 2001 convincingly shows that 'humanitarian action is a resounding success'. Indeed, in terms of tangible goals achieved, it is judged that humanitarian aid constitutes 'perhaps one of the main successes of the aid world' (ALNAP 2004: 30). Additionally, there is evidence of substantial gains arising from agency learning: good judgement from health and food aid officials, and the pre-positioning of emergency resources, have helped to save more lives today than would have been possible ten or twenty years ago (ALNAP 2005: 63). From this perspective, it can be said that humanitarian aid undoubtedly 'works'. Each year, on average, tens of thousands, and in exceptional years hundreds of thousands, directly affected by disasters and emergencies have had their lives saved by the actions of humanitarian agencies. Not only are these important concrete and tangible achievements, but for much of the general public, they provide sufficient evidence that humanitarian aid is a success. Box 19.2, based on a UN evaluation of the response to the 2002–3 Ethiopian emergency, provides a concrete and compelling illustration of success in providing humanitarian aid.

Similar stories of the overall effectiveness of humanitarian interventions in saving lives and preventing disease have also been told. Syntheses of recent evaluations suggest that these would include the provision of food aid and

---

BOX 19.2 THE HUMANITARIAN RESPONSE TO THE 2002/3 ETHIOPIAN DROUGHT

In the mid-1980s, Ethiopia was struck by an appalling famine in which around one million people are estimated to have died and a further eight million people were directly affected. Less than two decades later, and following harvest failures, the largest-ever internationally supported emergency operation ever undertaken in Ethiopia began. In spite of fears of inadequate infrastructural capacities, a staggering 1.5mn tonnes of donated food aid came into the country, providing sustenance for more than 12mn people, which was distributed through 1,200 centres managed by the government and NGOs. Additionally, over 21mn children received vitamin A and measles vaccinations, successfully preventing the measles epidemic which took the lives of over 2,000 in the previous crisis in the year 2000. Almost two million people received improved water and sanitation facilities and 800,000 farming households received seed for sowing. Though the response was at first a bit slow, the donor community provided sufficient aid, the emergency food reserve system and the early warning systems set in place after the 1983/4 famine successfully alerted the international community to the gravity of the situation, with the support of NGO advocacy efforts, and the whole aid and relief operation was successfully coordinated by the Ethiopian authorities. A massive potential loss of life was avoided, as were related potential deaths from disease.

Source: Simkin *et al.* (2004).

---

medical care in southern Africa in 2003, where 14mn people were estimated to have been in need of humanitarian assistance, and the evidence of similar life-saving successes in Afghanistan at much the same time (ALNAP 2004: ch. 3).

However, this good news provides only a partial and, many would argue, a much-distorted picture of the humanitarian aid effort. For some, the facts that Ethiopia had to face an acute food shortage at all in 2002, after the massive response to the mid-1980s famine, and that each year over seven million people still remain vulnerable and in need of food aid, are indicators of failure. It is argued that humanitarian aid ought to be judged (increasingly) not merely by what it has done, but in relation to its performance in protecting lives and in preventing emergencies, notably man-made disasters, from occurring or continuing. From such a viewpoint, a number of emergencies are judged to have been failures, some huge failures—Biafra in the 1960s, Uganda in the late 1970s, Rwanda in 1994/5 and Sierra Leone in the late 1990s. Partial successes in protecting people have occurred in instances where what is termed 'negotiated access' (approval from the authorities to reach and address the needs of civilians) has been achieved, as occurred in Sudan, Angola and Tigray, but, it is argued, these 'successes' remain limited (see de Waal 2002: 145ff.).

In terms of the resources deployed, and the numbers of humanitarian agencies involved, the (post-1999) Kosovo crisis elicited one of the largest emergency responses ever. The recent synthesis by ALNAP of the evaluations of humanitarian action undertaken in Kosovo broadly concluded that this—one of the largest humanitarian initiatives ever—constituted a major humanitarian failure. The assessment of needs and the response to need were judged to have been inadequate, as at best only one-third of those affected, those in refugee camps, received assistance. Much of the aid provided was not required, as the needs assessment which had been carried out had failed accurately to appreciate the extent of local mechanisms for coping, and a serious lack of coordination meant that too many agencies provided similar types of assistance in a highly inefficient way. Likewise, many agency staff did not have the skills necessary to carry out the work required: staff in five of the 12 UK DEC member organizations implementing aid projects were not aware that their agencies had signed up to the codes and standards requiring them to achieve minimum standards in aid delivery, by which they were to be assessed. No one knows whether lives were saved or morbidity rates fell as a result of humanitarian activities, because there was no overall attempt to assess performance trends accurately. ALNAP's review confirmed numerous tangible immediate benefits of the assistance given, but judges that these were eclipsed by the withdrawal of the agencies at a key moment, leading to the failure to provide and sustain humanitarian space, which resulted in a 'collective failure to protect'. Lives were saved, but how many more lives could have been saved if agencies had seriously addressed the issue of protection? What was particularly worrying was that agencies could have prevented further loss of life. The ALNAP review is highly critical of the failure to implement lessons learned from previous emergencies, commenting that 'It is a damning indictment of the humanitarian system that the findings and recommendations synthesised here are neither new nor Kosovo-specific' (ALNAP 2002: sect. 3.3.5).[26]

The overall impact of humanitarian activities lies somewhere between the extremes of the 'success' of Ethiopia and the 'failure' of Kosovo. But quite where is difficult to judge. The ability to form accurate judgements on impact is severely impaired by data inadequacies. That ability is also influenced by the importance given to the issue of protection, and thus by the framework within which an assessment of saving lives is made. Heroically, and somewhat at variance with its usual reticence in making generalizations about impact, the 2005 ALNAP report judges that in the three years to 2005, only about half of all evaluations reviewed achieved ratings of satisfactory or better in relation to a central criterion for judging humanitarian action: reaching population groups facing life-threatening suffering wherever they are, providing them with assistance and protection proportionate to their need and devoid of extraneous political agendas (ALNAP 2005: 158).[27]

The synthesis studies provide sufficiently strong and consistent data to enable us to highlight three key weaknesses which, directly or indirectly, adversely influence impact, reducing the effectiveness of the aid provided and the overall humanitarian response.

1. The first is that the coordination of humanitarian activity remains extremely weak, and this has a detrimental effect on performance. The case of

Ethiopia—where there is some capacity of the country affected to take a lead in coordinating the response, and the donor community allows the competent authorities to do so—is judged to be an exception. There is plenty of rhetoric about coordination, but in practice agencies undertake humanitarian activities relatively independently, and most fight to preserve their independence—notwithstanding the lead recently taken by OCHA to try to address this problem, the efforts of the GHD initiative, and growing examples of NGOs working closely together in some countries. As a recent ALNAP annual review puts it,

The central finding from the evaluations over the last four years . . . is that the priorities of individual donors take precedence over a co-ordinated response, with subsequent loss of effectiveness. Thus the overall situation is little improved since 1994. (ALNAP 2004: 2)

Consistently over the past five years, ALNAP's reviews have drawn attention to the inefficiencies caused by the sheer numbers of agencies involving themselves in disaster and emergency response, especially those that receive high-profile media attention. Against the backdrop of ineffective coordinating mechanisms, there is often an influx from abroad of inexperienced agencies, whose activities risk overlapping with and duplicating those of others. Rwanda (1994/5), Kosovo (1999) and, most recently, the Asian tsunami (2004/5) are all cited as examples either where humanitarian aid was a failure, or where effectiveness was adversely affected in a significant way because of coordination failures. Improved coordination would also help to address another common weakness of many emergency interventions—slowness of response—which is particularly prevalent when the larger international agencies are involved. At the extreme—though this is not common—emergencies have ended before the aid has reached the affected areas. One place where this happened was in Albania in 1999: most of the 15mn worth of items for refugees only arrived, or were still in storage, after the refugees had left and gone home (Court of Auditors 2001: 12).

2. A second weakness of humanitarian response concerns the whole issue of protection. Repeatedly and consistently, evaluations and syntheses of evaluations point to numerous instances where there has been insufficient action to protect vulnerable populations, the positive actions of some agencies often impeded or frustrated by the failure of others to take action, especially in a coordinated fashion.[28] In 2004, the UN Secretary General judged that a staggering 10mn people worldwide were denied humanitarian access (DFID 2006b: 10). These problems persist in spite of the growing awareness across almost all agencies of the importance of protection, and the willingness of some to attempt to address the problem. Particularly highlighted has been the growing plight of internally displaced persons (IDPs); indeed, one review

recently argued that some large agencies even fail to acknowledge the necessity of assessing the needs of IDPs (Borton *et al.* 2005: 11).[29]

3. A third general weakness highlighted in the evaluation reviews has been the failure of humanitarian activities effectively to contribute to building local capacities—the example of Ethiopia, illustrated in Box 19.1, appears to be a notable exception. A core problem is that in practice most humanitarian interventions are launched in the belief that effective action requires not only an international response, but a response which is dominated by external agencies, notwithstanding compelling and repeated evidence that usually most lives are saved by the actions of local people and organizations.

NEEDS ASSESSMENT AND THE QUALITY OF RESOURCES PROVIDED

In this section, we look a little more closely at the different resources and items that make up large parts of the content of humanitarian aid—food, shelter, water and sanitation, etc. Have the items provided been appropriate and adequate, and have they met minimum standards? Have they sufficiently addressed the needs of those who require them, and have they been delivered efficiently and effectively, and on time?

Most humanitarian aid is still delivered in the form of food aid, which is why most needs assessments are dominated by food issues. One consequence is that not uncommonly the needs for other resources are often insufficiently assessed, leading to major gaps between the resources required and those provided. In terms of what is provided, including the quality of those resources, the evidence suggests that provision is often best in areas of high population density. But herein lies a major dilemma. It is certainly easier, cheaper and more efficient to provide humanitarian aid to people who move into specially provided settlements, or camps, and easier to locate those in greater need within such settings. However, the social and economic ruptures caused by moving from home (even if this is sometimes necessary for purposes of protection) are almost always likely to be worse than staying put because it is much more difficult for people to rebuild their lives and livelihoods if they have had to leave their home areas.

As so often happens with humanitarian aid, the television footage fed to the public frequently conveys an entirely misleading picture of how needs are and ought to be addressed. Pictures of people streaming into camps to be fed and housed within settlements usually convey a false picture that 'now all is well'. Likewise, pictures of soldiers freely distributing food from the backs of lorries tend to convey to the public a view that the aid is 'getting through at last', when all the evidence shows that this is precisely the wrong way of distributing aid because those who need it most (marginalized social groups, the elderly and the sick) are the ones least likely to be strong enough to be able to come anywhere near the lorries—and the cameras.[30]

Another misleading image of the seeming virtues of the humanitarian response is conveyed by pictures of concerned citizens putting into boxes an array of different provisions contributed by those eager to help, to be channelled (often quickly and by air) to those desperately and urgently in need in far-off places. Again, the bulk of the evidence suggests that this is one of the least effective ways of meeting needs, because there is usually a large mismatch between what is sent and what is needed, resulting in huge amounts of aid being sent but never used, and because the funds used to air-freight such goods could have been used far more effectively to purchase needed goods within the disaster region. There is a role for goods to be flown in, or sometimes shipped in, to disaster areas from distant lands, and much has been learned in recent years about pre-positioning goods and stockpiling emergency supplies. Indeed, there is a persuasive case to be made for increasing the use of strategic stockpiles. However, even those agencies with long experience in these issues have made costly mistakes. For instance, in response to the 2000 earthquake in Gujarat, Oxfam and Concern International were criticized for flying out pumps, pipes, buckets and other items at a cost of £100,000 per flight, both because many of the items remained unused months later, and because most could have been purchased locally for a fraction of the cost. This particular evaluation concluded, sharply, that rather than responding to need, such action constituted a 'violation of the humanitarian imperative' (ALNAP 2004: 98).

Over the past five to ten years, the development of and conformity to minimum standards for the delivery of humanitarian assistance has become a central issue. How do agencies perform against such standards? A major problem in answering this question is that a majority of evaluations (over 75 per cent between 2002 and 2004) are still failing to assess performance against agreed standards (ALNAP 2005: 162). Those that do so tend to show that water and sanitation and health provision usually score high in terms of meeting minimum (Sphere) standards. The evaluations suggest that significant problems have occurred in relation to accommodation, with many drawing attention to the failure of agencies to provide adequate housing, a number citing the failure of agencies to provide housing to agreed minimum standards, and some highlighting long delays in providing both temporary and more permanent housing. Notwithstanding these overall weaknesses, some evaluations provide examples of good or better practice, such as ECHO-funded housing in East Timor, and work undertaken by Save the Children after the Gujarat earthquake (ALNAP 2003: 25, 84). Similarly, a growing number of UN agencies and NGOs, including Oxfam, Save the Children and MSF, now regularly assess their own activities against the relevant Sphere standards. To many, it will be surprising that more do not do so.

HUMANITARIAN FOOD AID

For decades, food aid has formed a significant component of official development assistance, though its relative importance has progressively declined to less
than 5 per cent from over 20 per cent 40 years ago. Since 1994, OECD/DAC statistics have separated out that part of food aid which is used in emergencies from
'developmental' food aid. Since donors first provided food aid in the early 1950s,
the merits of this type of aid have been keenly debated. These issues are complex
and cannot be addressed here in any depth: food aid remains controversial.[31]

A number of concerns about food aid relate to procurement. For some, the
key questions centre on the costs of providing food and the costs of alternative
sources of food aid. For others, the key questions revolve around the influence
and impact on domestic food production and food prices of the importation of
significant amounts of food aid. A recent study synthesizing a mass of evidence
confirms the importance of food aid in emergencies, though it notes a succession of problems caused by delays in the aid arriving and inappropriate food
being provided (Clay 2005). The study concludes that the impact of food aid on
agricultural production and food prices will vary depending on the context,
sometimes deflating prices and adversely affecting local production, but sometimes causing minimal adverse effects.

A major, and persistent, problem with food is the high cost of tied aid. A rigorous analysis undertaken in the Clay study showed that purchasing food locally
was estimated on average to be some 46 per cent cheaper than the cost of using
tied food aid (2005: 161). In some cases, the differences can be even greater. For
example, in 2005, United States food aid was delivered to northern Uganda at a
cost of $447 a ton when it could have been purchased from the south of the
country for $180 a ton.[32] The 2005 ALNAP review suggested that NGOs pro-
vided food aid at a higher unit price than the main UN agency, WFP, though it
suggested that this was at least in part due to the fact that NGOs delivered
smaller quantities of aid—often to more remote areas (ALNAP 2005: 178).

The delivery of food to those who need it constitutes one of the most important areas of humanitarian assistance, and it is also the area where large gaps
between the needs of those affected by disasters and emergencies and the
humanitarian aid provided are likely to be most keenly felt. Indeed, detailed
evaluations tend to suggest that in larger and more complex emergencies, as
well as those emergencies where there is a significant shortfall in funds, coverage is rarely comprehensive, resulting in significant numbers of people either
receiving inadequate amounts of food, or being left out entirely. Broadly
speaking, those easier to reach tend to have their needs more adequately met
than those living away from camps, in scattered homesteads or in more distant
locations, as the Kosovo evaluations confirmed. Self-evidently, the food needs
of those never reached will never be clearly assessed. The bulk of evaluation
studies merely report on the extent to which the often self-selected group of

people a particular agency chooses to assist receives sufficient food. However, it must not be assumed that food needs are therefore always underestimated. They seem to have been overestimated in southern Africa in 2002 (ALNAP 2003: 87).

The ALNAP reviews suggest that food aid is provided less effectively than aid targeted at water and sanitation and health needs. Two particular problems are highlighted: insufficient quantities of food provided and failing to understand the needs of particular recipients. On the positive side, one of the main messages of the reviews is that food aid interventions mainly succeed in their primary objective of feeding the hungry (ALNAP 2004: 49). However, the way that these interventions are commonly assessed may raise concerns in some quarters.[33]

Ask anyone in the street who should be the first to receive food aid and the answer will invariably be 'the most needy'. Consequently, one would expect assessments of humanitarian aid to examine carefully whether the beneficiaries who received aid were the most vulnerable and most needy. Partly in response to this expectation, the major agencies, such as WFP, have been developing methods to assess need and to try to isolate those groups or individuals who are most vulnerable, in order to channel food to these, the most deserving. However, the evidence strongly suggests that there is often a trade-off between providing the food quickly and ensuring that those most in need are tracked down and specifically targeted. Even agencies such as the FAO and WFP sometimes find that those responsible for undertaking assessments do not have the time to pinpoint the most needy (ALNAP 2004: 68).

Also, there is often a potential tension between targeting the most needy and cultural norms and practices. In practice, many agencies have found that the process of trying to differentiate between various groups of people (the needy and more vulnerable, and those more able to cope) within particular communities can prove self-defeating when, as often happens, custom and cultural norms dictate that food is to be shared across all members of a particular community in a way that is not necessarily consistent with needs. Consequently in such contexts, the best way of ensuring that the most needy receive the food they require, and potential social tensions are minimized, may often be to carry out a general food distribution. It is against the backdrop of these situations that this seemingly counter-intuitive comment can be understood: 'the notion of providing a full monthly ration to a limited number of the most needy households may not be appropriate in the context of widespread need' (ALNAP 2004: 95).

HUMANITARIAN AID AND CORRUPTION

One of ways that the effectiveness of humanitarian aid can be reduced is when the goods provided do not reach those for whom they are intended. What do the detailed evaluations tell us about corruption in the world of humanitarian aid: what proportion of the aid ends up in the wrong hands?

Understandably, there is no detailed comprehensive evidence. However, a number of evaluations either make explicit mention of corruption, or indicate (predominantly without providing detailed evidence) that it is likely to have been present. The discussion of corruption in humanitarian aid broadly confirms what one would expect—that the likelihood of resources being siphoned off (and often sold) for personal gain increases to the extent that humanitarian aid funds are channelled into contexts where accountability is low, or accountability chains are broken, particularly when aid delivery is placed in the hands of organizations with inadequate monitoring systems. The risks of aid diversion are particularly high where law and order has broken down, where governments are weak, and where civil society organizations have little capacity or are not allowed to monitor deliveries. Some studies have suggested that the risk of corruption exists within and across international agencies as much as it does across national agencies.[34]

There, is, though, some counter-intuitive evidence. For instance, at first sight it might be thought that stories of people in receipt of food selling it rather than eating it—a practice not uncommon in many refugee camps—is clear evidence of a mismatch between need and what is provided, confirming that people are receiving too much aid.[35] But this practice can often be due to two other causes. One is the unpopularity, and at the extreme, the unacceptability, of the particular food handed out, rather than because food is not needed. Recent examples include agencies providing split peas to people in central Africa who never eat such food, and yellow maize to people in southern Africa who use this solely as cattle feed (ALNAP 2003: 63). A far more common reason for selling food is because inadequacies in the overall needs assessments have failed to pinpoint pressing needs beyond that of food. When non-food needs are not adequately met in the package of goods provided, people will sell or barter food to obtain other essentials, and not uncommonly when there is also an overall shortage of food.

In some contexts, the diversion of humanitarian aid as a result of corrupt practices has been assessed as very significant. One example of extensive corruption in food delivery was in Somalia in the early 1990s, where it has been estimated that between 50 and 85 per cent of the aid provided went directly into the hands of powerful politicians, even if much did eventually reach those who needed it, but for a premium (Addison 2000: 394; de Waal 2002: 169–70). More worrying is the evidence of relief aid distributions fuelling corruption. One example where this appeared to happen was in the Democratic Republic of Congo. An evaluation of US humanitarian aid provided to the DRC suggested not merely that food aid was diverted through corrupt practices, but that the existence of large amounts of humanitarian food aid acted as a catalyst to extend and deepen corrupt activities, especially in the east of the country, where many soldiers of different militias received neither cash wages nor food:

> The presence of international resources offered elite groups an opportunity to benefit in a situation where there were few other sources of material wealth. In some areas, the result has been the development of a predatory system by local authorities and elites, and some international staff as well, to manipulate assistance inputs at the expense of affected people. Known locally as *operation retour*, common practices included 'taxing' food and non-food items before or after receipt, skimming by police and military, and infiltrating IDP camps and hijacking the camp committees ... Community members reported giving a percentage of their relief allocations, both food and non-food items, to local authorities or military groups. This ... seemed to be viewed as an expected outcome of receipt of material goods. (Reed *et al.* 2004: 38)[36]

Clearly, there is corruption in the distribution of humanitarian aid funds, though the rarity with which extreme examples are documented suggests that huge diversions of humanitarian aid funds or goods are likely to be exceptional.[37] Nonetheless, many evaluations of humanitarian activity point to major weaknesses in reporting and monitoring the use of emergency funds in both big and small agencies alike, which must increase the risk of corruption. Weak systems of accountability provide a context in which cases of small-scale, petty corruption are likely to remain unnoticed and undetected. If they are honest, most humanitarian agencies would acknowledge awareness of corrupt practices in the field. As a result, and especially over the past five years, many of the larger agencies have begun to put in place more rigorous monitoring procedures to try to address these problems.

In the short term, it needs to be acknowledged that while the problems of petty corruption can certainly be reduced, it is unrealistic to expect them to be completely eliminated. However, it should be stressed that corruption is by no means a problem unique to the provision of humanitarian aid in poor-country settings. The United States Government Accounting Office estimated that some 16 per cent of the funds provided to survivors of Hurricanes Rita and Katrina in New Orleans in August 2005 were lost to fraud, amounting to between $600mn and $1.4bn.[38]

THE IMPACT OF HUMANITARIAN AID FOR THE 2004 ASIAN EARTHQUAKE AND LINKED TSUNAMIS

At the end of 2005 and the beginning of 2006, around the time of the first anniversary of the Asian tsunami, an initial clutch of reports and preliminary assessments of what the humanitarian aid had began to achieve were beginning to appear. Dozens of agencies produced reports on their own websites of the different ways that the aid they provided had assisted particular people or groups of people. However, these consisted predominantly of selective and partial descriptions of activities, with a strong emphasis on their achievements, rather than careful assessments of overall results and impact. To their credit, some agencies, including Oxfam, World Vision, CARE and the WFP, did publish early independent evaluations of their efforts, some of which were more critical.

More important in understanding impact was the establishment, a few months after the tsunami struck, of the Tsunami Evaluation Coalition (TEC), set up with support from all the major governments, the UN and the larger NGO agencies involved, and the OECD/DAC, and with the cooperation of ALNAP. The Coalition's tasks included undertaking its own independent evaluations, and monitoring and synthesizing the evaluations produced by individual agencies and clusters of agencies.[39] In July 2006, the TEC published its first substantial assessment, a 175-page Joint Evaluation Synthesis Report, which summarized the findings of five specially commissioned thematic reports, and distilled and incorporated the findings of a further 140 studies, evaluations and assessments (Telford and Cosgrave 2006). It provided the first rigorous, overall, independent assessments of the humanitarian response to the disaster, building on the preliminary conclusions of its Initial Findings Report, published in late 2005 (Cosgrave 2005).

In broad terms, the findings of more substantive evaluations of the response to the tsunami, including the Synthesis Report, are largely consistent with those of other recent evaluations of especially large natural disasters. On the positive side, the broad conclusion was that the aid given for the tsunami had made a significant contribution in helping those affected by the disaster, providing them with many of the basic necessities required for survival. Additionally, the aid made a significant contribution to assisting many on the road to recovery through major rehabilitation, reconstruction and rebuilding work, and through a range of activities that were contributing to the restoration of livelihoods, including the provision of equipment, agricultural implements, credit facilities and some capacity-building initiatives.[40] There were examples of effective use of cash grants, the food provided was found to be appropriate and adequately targeted, and no cases of malnutrition were recorded. Indeed some agencies, such as CARE and World Vision, were praised for the manner in which they successfully ensured that marginalized people, minorities and women had their needs assessed, and were included in the distributions. A number of agencies were commended for achievements in helping to protect people in both camps and temporary shelters (Vaux *et al.* 2005: 3). Many of the evaluations spoke positively of the scale of the response.

But alongside these positive conclusions was set some extremely strong criti- cism, not only of inefficiencies and mistakes, but of the repetition of mistakes made in earlier major disasters, the lessons of which do not appear to have been learnt, or acted upon effectively. The Synthesis Report drew a number of overarching negative conclusions, among them the following three. One was that the 'impact of the "aid tsunami" on affected communities has on balance not been overwhelmingly positive' (Telford and Cosgrave 2006: 77). A second was that the international response failed to live up to its commitment to allocate funds in proportion to needs and on the basis of needs assessments (pp. 95–6). A third was the failure to understand how the mass of funds left over after the relief and initial recovery might be effectively used: 'only a small proportion of international personnel demonstrated a deep understanding of what kind of interventions might eventually prove sustainable with respect to livelihoods, market relations, community development and natural resource management' (p. 103).

Some extremely harsh criticisms were made of a number of both specific and more systemic failures. The following are among the most important.

1. First, and most fundamental, was the failure to provide a comprehensive assessment of need, either across the region, country-wide, or even in many different localities. A 'profusion of assessments' was undertaken, but these were dominated by individual agencies undertaking their own assessments for their own needs: 'At no stage in any country was a single reliable common census register or database of the affected populations established during the emergency phase'. Even UN data-bases were fragmented and duplicative (Telford and Cosgrave 2006: 21, 48).

However, the general view was that very few people in need were excluded, though more rigorous assessment might add to the worrying evidence from Thailand that those who failed to register for assistance were automatically excluded from receiving it, and a study by ActionAid which documented evidence of systemic discrimination against *dalits*, Thai Mokens and other marginal groups (p. 51).

2. Second was the failure of coordination: like other high-profile emergencies, the tsunami led to a massive influx of hundreds of foreign agencies entering countries to help. There were simply too many agencies, notably in Sri Lanka and Indonesia. In some places, tourists and well-wishers with little or no experience of emergency work set about helping those with whom they came into contact. There was also evidence of agencies displacing able local staff with poorly prepared internationals (p. 18). The result was not merely the 'usual' lack of coordination, but far less coordination among even the larger agencies than had been taking place in other recent large emergencies. In other words, not only were earlier lessons not learned and acted upon, but previous lessons seemed to have been unlearned. Coordination failures led to a considerable duplication of effort, reduced cost-effectiveness and even 'waste' (Cosgrave 2005: 13). A linked failure was a marked mismatch between the funds flowing to particular countries and the comparative scale of the problems that needed to be addressed, with proportionately less aid going to

Indonesia, which was estimated to have suffered 60 per cent of the damage, and with Somalia being particularly marginalized (Vaux *et al.* 2005: 3).

3. A third criticism was the evident lack of preparedness for such an emergency. The major agencies in particular were criticized not only for being inadequately prepared, but also for not giving priority to the funding of disaster-preparedness activities in the affected countries. Many admitted privately to being overwhelmed by the emergency, of having to recruit extra staff when skilled staff were in short supply, and reducing coverage of other ongoing emergencies. In response, it has been suggested that it is not possible to be adequately prepared for such complex and large emergencies. But as some evaluators pointed out, this sort of assertion had been made before, notably after Hurricane Mitch, which hit Central America in a disaster that affected more than five times as many people as the tsunami and which destroyed livelihoods across a very wide region.

4. A fourth criticism made in the evaluations was the failure of many agencies sufficiently to consult with the beneficiaries. The Synthesis Report judged that there was not merely a huge failure of agencies to provide people with information about programmes but that 'not many international agencies lived up to their own standards with regard to respect and support for local and national ownership' (Telford and Cosgrave 2006: 17, 18). In some cases, agencies made promises that they would provide assistance and then never returned to deliver it. Linked to this was the criticism that the way the emergency was portrayed in the media—and which most of the major agencies did little, if anything, to challenge. The overwhelming impression conveyed was that what was most urgently needed was an international aid response. In contrast, and in common with other emergencies, the evidence confirmed that many of the resources and skills that made the critical difference to saving lives lay within the countries and communities where the disaster struck. Far more could have been done, more effectively and at lower cost, by working with and though local organizations, channelling aid funds to and through them and helping to build their capacities.

5. A fifth criticism was the failure of agencies to provide assistance consistent with the principles to which they agreed. There was a general failure of agencies to meet their formal commitments to either the Sphere or GHD principles, throwing doubt on the value of such voluntary quality initiatives (Telford and Cosgrave 2006: 22). Particularly sharp criticisms were made about the response to housing needs. Promises were made, but a year after the disaster struck, hundreds of thousands of people were still only housed in temporary accommodation, much of it, as well as some of the more permanent housing, not meeting minimum (Sphere) standards. Twenty-five agencies promised to build 50,000 houses, 21,000 in Aceh, yet only 500 of the 50,000 had been built (Telford and Cosgrave 2006: 56). One evaluation was critical of the

appropriateness and the prolonged use of food aid in parts of Indonesia (Goyder *et al.* 2005: 58).

6. Additionally, there seemed to be evidence of some confusion among agencies about the relative shares of funds that would be allocated to immediate relief, to longer-term reconstruction, and to efforts to restore livelihoods. Agencies were also criticized in both evaluation reports and in the press for the inability of many to show the share of funds disbursed which had gone directly to those who needed it and the share that had been spent on administering the delivery of emergency aid.[41]

Further detailed assessments of the response to the tsunami are to be expected over the coming years, as substantial spending is planned to continue for much of the current decade. Only then will it be possible to have a more complete assessment of the overall impact of the response, and how effectively and efficiently it will have been implemented. Given the worldwide interest in the tsunami, it is likely that calls for deeper, more rigorous and more independent overall assessment of the response will be heeded. However, the prospects of such an assessment producing an accurate account of impact and effectiveness are not good, as a key finding of the early evaluations was that there was even less rigorous monitoring and collection of baseline data than for most other recent emergencies.[42] Consequently, as with so many emergency aid efforts over the past 15 years, we will probably have to conclude that we will never accurately know how effective the humanitarian response to the tsunami really was.

Finally, serious questions have been raised about the numbers of people that some key agencies claim to have been assisting, and about their failure to coordinate their activities, illustrated by an analysis of the assertions made by key agencies on their websites of the numbers of people that their aid reached and helped. A year after the tsunami work had begun, the majority of the leading British NGOs involved in the DEC appeal specified on their respective websites the numbers of people they had each assisted, or were in the process of planning to assist. Adding up these numbers produced the astounding figure of 5.6mn people assisted, three times the total number of those affected by the tsunami. As no agency made any mention of their working with any other DEC agency, one has to conclude that the numbers of people the agencies claimed they were assisting were vastly exaggerated.

Advocacy in humanitarian action

There is a growing consensus among all major operational agencies (except the Red Cross/ICRC, for reasons already explained) that advocacy ought to be a key component of humanitarian activities. Indeed, not only do a growing number of large NGOs and UN agencies undertake humanitarian advocacy on a regular basis, but so do some governments—themselves the targets of much development aid advocacy. Aid funds used for advocacy constitute only a comparatively small amount of total humanitarian aid spending—probably less than 10 per cent for even those operational NGOs for which advocacy is a high priority. Nonetheless, a complete assessment of humanitarian action needs to ask about the impact of such activities.

The underlying basis for all advocacy in the humanitarian sphere is to save lives, alleviate suffering and contribute to the effective protection of vulnerable populations. There are, broadly, four main types of advocacy that agencies undertake:

1. Advocacy aimed at drawing attention to, and raising awareness of, emergencies.
2. Advocacy aimed at improving the quality, range and effectiveness of the humanitarian response.
3. Advocacy that gives voice to those affected by emergencies and disasters.
4. Advocacy, often includes campaigning, which is aimed at changing actions and policies of those able to influence the humanitarian consequences of existing complex emergencies, and to prevent others from ever occurring.

The first type—awareness-raising advocacy—has a long history. It has been undertaken for many decades and one of its core purposes is to raise funds for emergencies. Therein often lies a core problem. It is common practice among agencies to 'launch' appeals for forgotten (and thus by definition underfunded) emergencies when there has been a lull in emergency aid-giving. It is not that forgotten emergencies are suddenly 'remembered'; it is more a case of fund-raisers believing the time is ripe to tap potential supporters for additional funds by drawing attention to particular forgotten and underfunded emergencies. Inevitably, some forgotten emergencies remain permanently forgotten. To add to the confusion, some agencies, such as UNICEF, now launch regular annual appeals for general funds (those to be used for development and humanitarian purposes) by focusing (largely) on emergency needs which UNICEF is able to help address.

What impact does this awareness-raising/fund-raising have? In terms of direct impact, the evidence is mixed. Some agencies have been quite successful in drawing attention to particular forgotten (underfunded) emergencies, alerting the public to emergencies about which little is widely known. For instance, Save the Children has been credited with drawing public attention to the 2002/3 food crisis in southern Africa, which led to a substantial and largely effective response. However, more widely, awareness-raising advocacy has substantially failed to bridge the large overall global gap between humanitarian need and the prevailing levels of humanitarian aid provided.

In contrast, as the discussion in this chapter and the previous one confirms, significant advances have been made and continue to be made in expanding the number of agencies which understand the need for core standards and principles when undertaking humanitarian work, and the importance of advocacy 'to protect'. Nonetheless, significant gaps remain. The first concerns compliance with core standards. Verbal agreements to implement activities based on such standards need to be matched by more extensive good practice on the ground. Operational agencies still fall well short of the standards they claim to wish to be judged by, while governments are still failing, individually and together, effectively to protect civilians they have committed themselves in principle to protect. The second gap concerns the failure of agencies sufficiently to inform the general public about the centrality of standards in humanitarian work. This is not so much a failure of advocacy as a failure to undertake and give priority to advocacy in this area. The public do not challenge the agencies (and governments) to produce evidence that their humanitarian activities conform to minimum standards and to international humanitarian law (IHL), largely because they are not aware that such standards and laws exist. In practice, advocacy geared to fund-raising still dominates the advocacy agenda of agencies, eclipsing the (more half-hearted and less well-financed) advocacy aimed at public education and changing public perceptions about standards.

On a related point, humanitarian principles, IHL and codes of conduct stress the central role to be played by those directly affected by disasters, including the need to ensure that humanitarian action is informed, shaped and even managed by those affected and that the voices of those affected are effectively heard. In marked contrast, the voices and views of those directly affected are seldom heard. Again, agencies would be less likely to be criticized in evaluations for their repeated failures to consult sufficiently with beneficiaries about their needs if they gave greater priority to informing the public that they are required to do so.

The most challenging area of advocacy is the fourth listed above—advocacy aimed at protecting the victims of violence and those at risk from complex emergencies. A growing number of agencies are not only speaking out against, but effectively bringing to the public eye, cases of atrocities, killings, abuse and the manipulation of humanitarian aid for political purposes. Indeed there are few examples of large, complex emergencies where agencies as a whole remain silent, as occurred in Biafra and Uganda more than 25 years ago. What remains in doubt is not so much the amount of 'noise' produced, but the effectiveness of these advocacy initiatives. For instance, from 2003 onwards, many agencies have launched a series of wide-ranging and high-level advocacy initiatives to draw attention to the humanitarian and linked human-rights problems in Darfur; but effective solutions remain elusive.[43] The fundamental problem is that while governments have verbally acknowledged their obligations (under humanitarian law) to protect the vulnerable, the mechanisms, procedures and processes required to ensure compliance remain wholly inadequate. This dimension of humanitarian advocacy work requires continued and urgent attention, not least from the international community, if it is to be effectively addressed.

Emergency and humanitarian aid: a summing up

Humanitarian aid is successful in saving lives and in contributing to restoring livelihoods. It continues to be needed; indeed, as the number of people affected by disasters continues to rise, so does the need for such assistance. Yet humanitarian action has changed substantially in the past few decades, not merely in terms of the scale of the needs that it has been required to address, but, perhaps more importantly, in relation to understanding its core purpose and role in the contemporary world. An assessment of the impact of humanitarian action depends crucially on two factors. The first is the quality of the data and information available, the second is the basis on which one judges its precise role. Though humanitarian aid continues to save lives and alleviate suffering and helps people and communities rebuild their lives, many hundreds of thousands of people in need of life-saving protection remain unprotected and vulnerable to human rights abuses. Consequently—depending on one's assumptions concerning humanitarian action—one could either be broadly happy with, or appalled by, the overall impact of humanitarian action.

Lying behind this crude polarization of views is a paucity of reliable data and information on which to form firm judgements about the impact of humanitarian action in particular emergencies, in spite of a growing commitment of most agencies to undertake more rigorous assessments and to monitor impact against reliable baseline data. Assessments and evaluations continue to be made, but evaluators continue to chide agencies for failing to have in place the basic data and information which rigorous assessments require. A root cause of this problem is that the (understandable) impulse to respond, especially to high-profile emergencies, repeatedly eclipses the commitment to balance immediate response with reflection and assessment. Another cause is the still dominant place that fund-raising plays in shaping the way that individual agencies choose to portray their roles to the public. A third cause can be traced back to the voluntary nature of humanitarian action and the lack of any effective mechanisms to coordinate and ensure the complementarity of the often disparate activities of individual agencies. For almost all large emergencies, we are still largely ignorant of whether needs are being effectively assessed, how much aid is needed, and who can best provide it. We know even less about how much aid never reaches those who need it, and the extent to which those who receive the aid are satisfied with the scale, nature and quality of the response. The general sense conveyed by almost all substantial evaluations, however, is that behind and beyond the common headline good news that lives continue to be saved, far more could be done to improve the quality of the response.

At the level of individual agencies, there is a richer data-source and a growing commitment to inter- and intra-agency learning. Among the best of these agencies, needs assessments, consultation with beneficiaries, close monitoring of expenditure against planned spending, and regular reporting of results against agreed standards are now taking place, and independent assessments of impact are growing. However, too many agencies still do not undertake or commission rigorous evaluations of their work, and only a handful regularly provide public access to the independent assessments of their humanitarian activities. Until this changes, the forming of accurate assessments about the impact of the delivery of humanitarian aid will continue to be frustrated. But change is not likely to come about until humanitarian agencies as a whole give greater priority to informing the general public and the media about the norms and standards that they have already agreed their activities ought to be judged by, and the public and media make greater use of these standards to call these agencies to account.

Part IV
Towards a Different Future for Aid

Does aid really work? Earlier parts of this book have reviewed the best available evidence to conclude that large amounts of development and emergency aid have saved lives, both directly and indirectly. They have led to tangible benefits for millions of poor people, and made some positive wider contributions to poor-country economies and societies. Some aid interventions, however, have been failures, and large amounts of development aid have not had a significant, long-term, systemic or sustainable impact. Emergency aid has succeeded in saving many lives, but many lives have been lost because of a shortage of funds. The failure to coordinate the humanitarian response effectively has meant that much aid was been wasted, while large numbers of those caught up in emergencies and disasters remain inadequately protected.

Today, some 60 years since aid was first provided, our ability to judge its overall impact still remains severely hampered by limited and inadequate data, not least by the partial nature of the information put out by the main providers of aid, governmental and non-governmental alike. What information that is available tends to be biased towards discrete interventions at the project level whose success is often attributed disproportionately to the resources and efforts of the agency involved. Most of the information placed in the public domain gives little prominence to (and often completely ignores) the wider contextual factors which often seriously impede the ability of aid to make a lasting difference. It also usually fails to highlight two of the most crucial determinants of aid's impact, namely the commitment and the ability of the recipient to make effective use of the funds provided.

Aid has made a difference, but it could make a far greater difference. Lives have been saved, livelihoods improved and poverty reduced with the direct or indirect help of aid resources. But much more could have been done, and much more can be done, with aid funds, and by the hundreds of thousands of people who work professionally and as volunteers in the different worlds of aid-giving and aid-receiving. There has always been, and there still remains today, a significant gap between what aid could do-the expectations, still strong, of what it *ought* to achieve—in alleviating human suffering and contributing to the reduction of poverty, and what happens in practice.

The main purpose of this final part of the book is to look forward, and examine ways in which the impact of aid might be enhanced, improved and increased to make a greater difference to the lives of more people still having to live in extreme poverty and vulnerable to emergencies and disasters in the poorest countries of the world. Chapter 20, 'Why aid isn't working', focuses on the main factors which have reduced, and continue to reduce, the impact of development and emergency aid to the present day. It distinguishes between those problems which are endemic to the aid relationship, because donors and recipients have to live with them, and those which can more easily be addressed. The analysis suggests that there is far more scope for improving aid effectiveness than much contemporary debate about aid policy is ready to acknowledge. This provides the entry point for the final two chapters of the book. The first, Chapter 21, 'Making aid work better by implementing agreed reforms', discusses the prospects for aid in the context of the current reform programmes to which donors and recipients have committed themselves. It suggests that gains will continue to be made, but they risk producing only comparatively small improvements. The second, Chapter 22, 'Making aid work better by recasting aid relationships', discusses the prospects for aid if the most important, overarching systemic problems which continue to limit the impact of aid were to be addressed. If this were to happen, aid could be a far more effective instrument in helping to relieve human suffering and reduce global poverty than it has been, or is today. Yet for this to become a reality, rather than remain the vision of a distant future, will require fundamental changes to be made to key contemporary aid relationships, and the political will to implement them.

20 Why aid isn't working

What's the matter with aid? Plenty. In their recent assessment, Clark Gibson, Elinor Ostrom and colleagues judge that over the last four decades, 'hundreds of researchers have identified hundreds of problems' (2005: 3). This chapter does not attempt to list and discuss all of them. Rather, it focuses on the more fundamental problems which impede or limit the effectiveness of aid.

Many problems with aid arise because of poor decision-making. Some problems with aid are specific to particular projects and programmes, and arise from the wrong decisions made by individuals and agencies as to the type of aid that should be provided to particular recipients, often as a result of insufficient understanding of what is needed, and how aid may help. Some problems with aid arise because of individuals and agencies making over-optimistic assumptions about the capacity of organizations receiving aid to use it effectively. Other problems arise because donors or recipients either fail to undertake risk assessments or make assumptions about the external environment which turn out to be wrong, and the unexpected effects of these errors undermine or eclipse the expected beneficial outcomes intended.

However, many problems with aid are caused or exacerbated by wider systemic or institutional factors. Some of these originate with the donors, some can be traced to the recipients, and some can be traced to the overall aid relationship across and between donors and recipients. It is these more systemic problems of aid which are the focus of the discussion in the present chapter.

The first part of the chapter looks predominantly at problems that occur at the donor end of the aid relationship. It brings together and summarizes the main systemic or institutional factors constraining aid's impact discussed in earlier chapters, but also focuses on constraints caused by weaknesses in the incentive systems of organizations which give (and use) the aid. This is followed by a discussion of the problems of aid predominantly from the recipient side of the aid relationship. It highlights the structural and institutional constraints which impede aid's effectiveness and the dilemmas these constraints pose for donors.

The chapter then turns to what many now consider the central challenge of aid, namely the political and governance dimensions of the aid relationship. Though donors—quite rightly—wish to channel their aid to countries, programmes and projects with the capacity, ability and commitment to put the aid to good use, the reality is that for those poor countries with the greatest need for development (and often emergency) aid, these conditions rarely apply.

Large amounts of aid are needed by, and given to, countries which have weak institutions and capacities, and weak governance, which constrains their ability to use it effectively—even when there is strong political commitment to do so.

Systemic impediments to aid effectiveness: problems caused by donors

DISTORTIONS CAUSED BY THE POLITICAL, STRATEGIC AND COMMERCIAL INTERESTS OF DONORS

From a humanitarian and development perspective, aid should be provided to those who need it. The greater the inability of those suffering and in poverty to address their own core needs and the more those responsible for them (usually their governments) are unable to help, the greater the need for external assistance. However, as discussed in Chapters 6 and 18, there has always been, and to this day continues to be, a major mismatch between the way aid is allocated and humanitarian and development needs, though for some donors the distortions are more pronounced than they are for others. The overall allocation of aid is not only influenced by humanitarian and development considerations, it is also determined and shaped by the political, commercial and strategic interests of donors. The impact is considerable: less than half of all official aid is channelled to the 65 poorest countries (over $50bn of total ODA in 2005), and well over 10 per cent of official aid goes to countries too rich to qualify as recipients of ODA (over $11bn of total ODA in 2005). If ODA was allocated on the basis of need, studies suggest that at least three times as many people could be lifted out of poverty.

The commercial, political and strategic interests of donors in providing aid are also responsible for the inflated costs of aid due to tying—the requirement by donors that aid be used solely for the purchase of goods and services, including technical assistance and consultancy services, originating in the donor country. Almost 60 per cent of all ODA remains tied, or partially tied. Tying directly increases the costs of aid by upwards of 20 per cent: on this basis and in aggregate, the overall costs of tying currently reduce the purchasing power of ODA by well over $15bn. Additionally, aid tying dramatically increases the likelihood of recipients having to accept resources which are not a high priority for development, eroding further the development potential of aid funds.

In short, the overall effects of the political, strategic and commercial influences on aid significantly reduce the potential development impact of ODA— by at least a third, or possibly more.[1] These problems are due entirely to decisions taken by donors, and their impact is largely (if understandably) ignored in most studies of aid effectiveness.

AID VOLUMES, VOLATILITY AND VOLUNTARISM IN AID-GIVING

These problems would not be so severe if the total amounts of aid provided comfortably met the humanitarian and development needs of poor countries. How much aid is necessary to meet these needs, and how does this compare with the total amounts currently provided? Surprisingly, there are no accurate figures with which comparisons can be made. Only recently have assessments been made of development aid needs on a country-level basis, and these are acknowledged to be incomplete and crudely calculated. Nor do they estimate total development aid needs, but only the far lower amounts required to meet the Millennium Development Goals (MDGs). And no donor agency or group of agencies accurately assesses the total amount of emergency aid needed. However, best estimates suggest that the total amount of ODA required to meet the development aid needs of the poorest countries and emergency aid needs worldwide is more than twice, and possibly more than three times, as high as currently provided, notwithstanding the significant increases in aid achieved in the past few years. It is safe to say, therefore, that another major problem with aid, which is at least a potential cause of its reduced impact, is that insufficient amounts are provided by the international community.[2]

Another major problem with the provision of aid is its volatility: the amounts of official aid vary from year to year, often markedly. Studies suggest that the volatility of aid is increasing rather than decreasing (Hudson and Mosley 2006), and that volatility in the allocation of aid is particularly marked in countries emerging from conflict, with aid levels often falling sharply at precisely the time when aid could be utilized more effectively (Collier and Hoeffler 2004). The more volatile and unpredictable the amounts of aid which recipients receive, the less able they are to plan ahead. To minimize risk, aid recipients are likely to draw up spending plans on the assumption that they will receive lower quantities of aid, reducing their ability to absorb higher amounts if these happen to be provided.

A key factor underlying the insufficient amounts of aid and its volatility is the voluntary nature of aid-giving. Donors provide official aid, for both development and humanitarian purposes, on an entirely *voluntary* basis. Though parliaments in donor countries formally approve particular levels of aid expenditures, usually on an annual basis, individual donors remain free to provide as much or as little aid as they wish, and there is no procedure or mechanism either to enhance the overall level of aid when one or more donors provides less (or fail to increase aid at a steady rate), or to put pressure on donors who are considering reducing the amounts of aid they intend to give.[3]

There is no aggregate planned giving related to the needs of each recipient. Recipient countries receive official aid predominantly on the basis of the cumulative decisions of those individual donors who choose (individually) to provide them with aid. It is certainly true that international aid-pledging conferences and similar processes do provide an important, but loose, framework within which some attempt is made (for some countries) to marry requests for aid with aggregate donations. However, even in such conferences, most donors do not formally consider the amounts of aid other donors give or are planning to give when they decide how much aid they will allocate to a particular country. The main parameters for aid-giving are usually decided at home before country delegates attend such conferences. Likewise, there is no mechanism to ensure that countries are not penalized with less aid when one donor chooses to switch aid to a different recipient, perhaps for political, strategic or commercial reasons. In short, the current methods of allocating aid for both emergency and development purposes, either in aggregate or to particular countries, are not based on any system which effectively matches needs with the aid funds provided, or which even tries to do so.

THE MULTIPLICITY OF DONORS AND AID FUNDS, PROGRAMMES AND PROJECTS

The number of official donors and agencies is close approaching the 200 mark, as new aid donors, funds and mechanisms are established, almost on an annual basis, to channel different forms of aid to different destinations. The largely independent and voluntary decisions donors make about how much aid overall they will give to which country (and to which multilateral agency) are largely mirrored in the decisions they make about how that aid will be provided. It is individual donors who choose for themselves whether to provide aid in the form of discrete projects or as programme aid, and how much aid will be divided up into how many different aid projects and aid programmes.

The result is a web of aid transactions so numerous and so complex that it is hard to envisage. Each year, over 35,000 separate official aid transactions take place and, on average, each aid recipient has to deal with more than 25 different official donors. The world of NGO aid-giving adds a further dimension of multiple aid transactions, with more than 50 large NGOs working in most aid-recipient countries, in some more than ten times that number, many providing identical skills and services. Donors often compete with each other to fund projects and programmes; they employ an army of administrators and contract consultants with similar skills and specialities, creating parallel systems, structures and processes, often to oversee similar sorts of projects and programmes, and to create, manage, monitor and evaluate their own projects and programmes. Different donors require recipients to comply with different regulations and procedures, and they attach an array of different conditions to the aid they give (Birdsall *et al.* 2005: 143). For their part, recipients have to allocate valuable time and scarce human resources to interact with these different donors and their projects, although the majority of the tens of thousands of official aid projects implemented in aid-recipient countries are managed by different project-implementation units of the donor agencies, many remaining outside the formal planning mechanisms of the aid-recipient country.

To their credit, many leading official donors have been among the first to acknowledge the range of problems which this multiplicity of donors, projects and programmes creates—no one disputes that it seriously undermines and reduces the overall potential impact of official aid. A number of official donors have begun to work more closely together, both with each other and with recipient governments, to attempt to rationalize their individual aid efforts, and to cooperate together more formally through new aid modalities such as sector-wide approaches (SWAps) and the provision of budget support. Additionally, there has been some pooling of aid funds, and what are termed 'silent partnerships'—where one donor provides aid to a recipient but another aid agency oversees its use, management and impact.[4] For its part, the United Nations has also begun to try to provide aid in a more unified and consistent manner, matching agency expertise with recipient priorities. In Rome, in 2003, and in Paris, in 2005, all major donors pledged to work hard to coordinate and to harmonize their different aid activities, and align them more closely to the plans and programmes of aid-recipient countries. These initiatives have been extremely important in challenging major donor agencies to rethink long-standing practices in aid-giving, and in catalysing donors to commit themselves to working more closely together. However, when set against the enormous problems caused or exacerbated by multiple agencies who continue to implement their own aid programmes still relatively independently, progress appears more modest. One year on from the Paris Declaration, the 2006 (annual) Global Monitoring Report (GMR), responsible in part for reviewing progress against donor commitments, commented in relation to harmonization and alignment objectives that 'the gap between the baseline and the targets' still remained 'wide' (World Bank 2006c: 7).[5]

AID AGENCIES, IMPACT AND INCENTIVE SYSTEMS

The impact of aid is not only related to the fulfilment of pledges and commitments made at the macro-level. It is also dependent on decisions made at the micro-level within and across donor agencies and institutions, which, in turn, are related to internal systems and processes, including the incentive and reward systems of those who manage and oversee aid programmes. At the level of rhetoric, donors and aid agencies are unequivocally committed to ensuring that aid funds are used to maximize impact, just as influential policy-makers and senior managers within agencies are committed to achieving the core mandates of their agencies. However, some substantial research which has examined the internal dynamics of how aid agencies function reveals a marked disjuncture between the rhetoric of commitment to improving aid effectiveness and the incentive systems which drive and reward agency staff, and influence the front-line decisions which ultimately determine aid effectiveness.

Most notably, a substantial four-year study based on the experiences of one of the most forward-looking donor countries, Sweden, examined the internal workings of the Swedish International Development Cooperation Agency (Sida) (Ostrom *et al.* 2002). It concluded that the ways that key staff are assessed and judged are not geared to rewarding them for the contribution they make to achieving the core purpose of the Agency—enhanced aid impact and long-lasting and sustainable aid programmes and projects.[6] Similarly, they found that there are few incentives to staff to learn from current and past aid projects and programmes, and to use the knowledge that exists within the Agency to inform decisions about future aid projects and programmes. They also found that aid quality is adversely affected by (informal) pressures put on staff to disburse funds quickly and, surprisingly, that too few resources are allocated to designing and monitoring aid projects and programmes, which also adversely affects the quality of aid and its ultimate impact.[7]

Similar institutional and incentive weaknesses have been noted in other studies of other agencies. For instance, work by Eyben (2005) suggests not merely that aid agencies fail to learn, but the methods of learning how to improve the impact of aid interventions which aid agencies do use are wholly inappropriate to the complex nature of aid relationships. Similarly, in their study of aid to Africa, Conyers and Mellors (2005) argue that aid decisions are frequently made with insufficient knowledge of the policy environment, and that one of the consequences of the growing practice of agencies to contract technical work out to consultants has been to reduce further the institutional knowledge of agencies, which is so critical in informing decisions about how aid funds can best be utilized.

Other studies have expressed doubts about the ability of most aid agencies to change their internal institutional practices in order effectively to achieve their commitments to harmonize and coordinate their aid activities with other donors. For instance, a comprehensive study of donor practices by the Overseas Development Institute (ODI) concluded that agency plans look more like 'reports designed to comply with specific commitments made at international fora' than operational internal management tools. In most agencies 'there is a perceived lack of clear policies and guidelines for staff to follow to decide if, when and how to engage in harmonisation activities' (de Renzio *et al.* 2005: 14, 23). Likewise, van de Walle's analysis of donor practice, especially in Africa, leads him to conclude that remarkably little progress has been made on donor coordination issues in the past decade: the 'failure of donor coordination is almost entirely due to bureaucratic resistance within donor agencies' (2005: 75).

The recent publication *The Samaritan's Dilemma* (Gibson *et al.* 2005) draws attention to two different types of institutional problem which adversely influence the impact of aid: those it is possible to address and those that are more endemic. The term 'the Samaritan's Dilemma' applies to the latter, and refers to the inclination of the Samaritan to help and to the reaction of the recipient. For his/her part, the Samaritan wishes to help, and so is 'better off' no matter what the recipient does. However, once the recipient recognizes that the Samaritan will always help, and exert 'high effort', s/he only has to respond by exerting 'low effort' (Gibson *et al.* 2005: 38–9). In short, the best outcome for the donor of wishing to disburse aid quickly and with *high effort* is not matched by an equal response from the recipient.[8] Rather, the 'best outcome' for the recipient will be achieved by accepting the aid, but utilizing the aid funds provided with *low effort*. Gibson, Ostrom and colleagues suggest that the (quite common) phenomenon of aid-funded infrastructural projects breaking down far earlier than similar non-aid-funded projects because of the lack of attention to planned maintenance is illustrative of the Samaritan's Dilemma operating in practice: the recipient relies on the donor coming back to provide additional aid to repair the faulty plant (Gibson *et al.* 2005: 38–40). However, while the authors contend that this problem 'pervades development aid' (p. 38), they do not provide evidence to show how extensive the problem is, nor, importantly, the extent to which it reduces the potential impact of the aid provided.

AID, POLICY ADVICE AND THE WIDER CONTEXT

Critics of aid often cite the stagnation of many aid-recipient economies and persistently high levels of poverty as clear evidence of the failures of aid. Aid could well be a *cause* of economic stagnation, if it could be shown that the potential benefits which donors expect to occur as a result of aid are reduced or, at the extreme, eclipsed by perverse effects caused, directly or indirectly, by the aid provided. This is, in part, the problem raised by the Samaritan's Dilemma. But there could be other reasons for such stagnation.

One cause of economic stagnation could be aid-related: the advice that donors give, and especially the conditions they attach to the aid they provide, requiring aid recipients to implement a particular set of economic policies as the *quid pro quo* for the aid given. To the extent that aid donors provide poor advice and it is followed through, donors could then be blamed for detrimental outcomes.

Another cause of stagnation and the perpetuation of poverty could be traced to the influence and impact of factors external to, and seemingly far removed from, the aid relationship. If these are mild, they could certainly reduce the intended positive impact of the aid provided. If they are significant and severe, they could eclipse it entirely. Most aid-recipient economies are fairly 'open' and are thus significantly influenced by movements in key regional and international financial and economic indicators. These would include changes in external aggregate demand; movements in prices, notably exchange rates; commodity price changes; and trade rules and regulations. Indeed, these wider influences are of such importance that for the whole period during which aid has been provided, many have argued that it is not aid that matters to poor countries but other, more important, drivers of development, especially trade. What is the link between aid, aid donors, and these usually extremely important influences that are seemingly not directly related to the aid relationship?

Is donor advice an impediment to better aid impact?

As discussed in detail in Chapter 14, most aid-recipient governments have expressed a dislike of both policy advice and conditions attached to aid-giving. Especially in the 1980s to early 1990s, the heyday of policy conditionality, those that disagreed with the policies put forward by donors tended in effect to disregard them, and most of those who agreed with the broad thrust of what was proposed would have implemented them anyway. If this were the only basis on which to judge the influence of policy advice, then it would seem, ironically, that donors cannot really be blamed for any failures in the impact of aid that might have arisen from the policy advice they gave. However, this provides a very partial picture of the history and influence of the policy advice given by donors, and especially the advice provided by the most influential international institutions, the World Bank and the IMF. For many, the crucial question is whether the orthodox package of stabilization and adjustment policies advocated by the Bank and the Fund constituted the best policies for poor countries to adopt. On both theoretical grounds and on the basis of the evidence, the (narrow/orthodox) macroeconomic policy package of measures propounded by the Bank and the Fund was deficient in a number of respects—in relation both to what was advocated, and to what was omitted (see Chapter 14 for the details). Consequently, it did not (and could not have had) the beneficial outcomes that their promoters had hoped for. To the extent that it was adopted, it almost certainly contributed to the failures of many aid-recipient countries to make greater headway in raising growth levels, and in achieving faster reductions in poverty—though by how much it is really not possible to say. In short, the lack of effectiveness of aid at the national level has been due, in part, to deficiencies in the policy advice given by donors.

However, changes have occurred, and continue to occur, which make it less easy to draw such unequivocal conclusions about the impact of contemporary policy advice on aid-recipient economies. There is far less unanimity across the donor community about the role that donors should play in influencing policies, and a degree of ambiguity in precisely what policies donors are proposing that aid recipients should pursue. Even the World Bank has stated that what matters most is for aid-recipient countries to develop and 'own' their own development strategies and policies, and for donors to move away from providing policy advice as a condition for providing aid, acknowledging and accepting that there is no general one-size-fits-all template of policies that are applicable to, and which ought to be applied willy-nilly by all aid recipients (World Bank 2005j: xiii). On this basis, one might be drawn to conclude that pressures on aid recipients to accept a particular policy package as a condition for receiving aid is a thing of the past. Yet Bank and Fund staff continue to 'encourage' aid recipients to adopt and implement a number of macroeconomic policies strikingly similar to, and as restrictive as, many of those advocated and promoted in the past. However, growing amounts of official aid are being provided outside this narrow macroeconomic policy framework, and many believe that the gap between what the Bank says and what it does will continue to narrow.

The wider policies of donors: supportive of aid or not?

Moving on to the second issue, do donor-government policies and actions beyond the aid relationship which shape and help determine international economic activity support or undermine the expansion, diversification and strengthening of aid-recipient economies, thereby enhancing or reducing the wider impact of the aid they provide? This is clearly a substantial and complex question and it is not possible to provide a complete answer here. However, four important summary points can be made.

The first is that whereas until recently donors largely ignored the issue of consistency between their aid and other policies, in the last decade, more and more donor governments have acknowledged that the issue is important, and a growing number of donor governments (though by no means all) have explicitly stated that they need to ensure that there is consistency between their aid policies and objectives and all other actions, activities and policies which impinge directly or indirectly on the health of, and prospects, for aid-recipient economies. Secondly, however, only a minority of donors have undertaken systematic reviews and begun to implement policies to ensure effective compliance with these normative statements. For example, only in 2006 did DFID and the Department of Health in the United Kingdom begin implementing a policy to stop recruiting ('poaching') nurses and doctors from a list of poor countries such as Ghana and South Africa (in conjunction with a code of practice for private sector providers of health care to follow the same norms).[9]

Thirdly, there is very little evidence to suggest that donor governments actively engage in international negotiation to promote, enhance and strengthen aid-recipient economies. The most commonly articulated 'default position' in international negotiations is for donor governments merely to try to ensure that in aiming to secure maximum benefits for themselves, aid-recipient countries are not worse off. But at the start of the new millennium, donor governments stated their wish actively to help promote development. Nowhere was this more clearly stated than in the build-up and beginning of what turned out to be the long and drawn-out Doha trade negotiations, termed a 'development round'. However, as occurred in the earlier Uruguay Round, donor governments have been ambiguous at best in how they have interpreted this position in practice. Though the issue remains contested, the industrialized countries have been sharply criticized by poor aid-recipient countries and trade specialists for using these fora and processes to continue to promote their own interests, even if and when this adversely affects the prospects for poor-country development. In the view of Stiglitz and Charlton in their recent study, in many respects the rest of the world has tilted the playing field against the developing world (2005: xii). And the 'fears of the developing countries that the Doha round of negotiations would disadvantage them . . . were in fact justified' (p. 6). By mid-2006, the talks had effectively collapsed.[10]

However, fourthly, the extent to which donor governments implement policies consistent with the thrust and orientation of the goals and objectives of their aid policies varies enormously from issue to issue, sector to sector and donor to donor. Donor governments and agencies have taken major steps, mostly acting together, to address the debt problems of many highly indebted countries, though campaigners continue to encourage them to do more. Likewise, significant steps have been taken to create effective mechanisms to discourage trade in 'conflict diamonds', the effects of which are to encourage and prolong debilitating war and unrest in a number of aid-recipient countries. However, little has been done to halt or limit the sales of arms to many more aid-recipient countries where unrest and conflict impede the effectiveness of the development aid provided.

In sum, therefore, while some actions have been taken by donor governments to ensure greater consistency between the development objectives of their aid policies and other, wider activities, there still remains a significant gap between what has been done and what could be done to reduce the adverse effects of their wider policies on aid-recipient economies. Indeed, it remains the rare exception when donor governments systematically implement policies to strengthen aid-recipient economies, especially if these are expected to harm their own interests, however small those interests are, or appear to be.

NGOS IN DEVELOPMENT: WEAKNESSES AND GAPS
IN OUR KNOWLEDGE

Some of the problems with official aid are paralleled within and across the NGO development world—not least the paucity of accurate and comprehensive information about the impact of NGO development projects and programmes. Other problems include the massive escalation in the numbers of NGOs engaging in development work, many offering identical services and frequently operating in an uncoordinated fashion, thereby increasing the risk of duplicating of activities with other NGOs, and, in some cases, with government and official aid projects. Larger NGOs have tended increasingly to dominate the sector in most countries, often bringing skills and professionalism, but sometimes using their dominance to eclipse the activities and mute the voices of smaller grassroots membership organizations. The quality of NGO development programmes and projects remains mixed: some make a major difference to poor people and are highly cost-effective, others are run or managed by agencies and individuals with insufficient skills, providing few tangible gains to the beneficiaries, some of whom wrongly assume that the NGOs are able to provide them with what they need, even though they often have little choice in accepting their help. NGO interventions which fail or fall well short of their potential often do so because of an incomplete analysis, and not infrequently the absence of any analysis, of the main causes of poverty. Surprising, too, given the way many NGOs market themselves, is the lack of rigour with which some NGOs seek out the views of the beneficiaries to understand what the priority needs are and how these might best be met. As with official aid, the sustainability of NGO projects remains a major difficulty. NGOs have been criticized, sometimes justifiably, for their own failures to provide an accurate account of the impact of their activities, to funders and to beneficiaries, and for not providing a transparent account of the costs of reaching and providing acceptable services to poor people in distant locations.

A number of these problems occur because of the lack of an effective regulatory framework or system. In many countries, NGO activity is subject to no or very little regulation or monitoring, though, in some countries, vital NGO development activity has been crushed, or severely constrained, because of excessively restrictive legislation. When large NGOs become the exclusive provider of services to large numbers of people in a particular area or locality, the need to ensure quality of service and fair access to it becomes a central regulatory and accountability issue.

The activities of NGOs and civil society organizations (CSOs) extend well beyond their engagement with and their promotion of discrete projects and programmes. They now engage in a range of activities aimed at monitoring, influencing, challenging and changing the policies of donors and other agencies, and ensuring that the voice and perspective of poor people helps to shape policies and the allocation of resources. Identifiable and tangible gains have been made in this often vitally important area of work, though probably fewer are attributable to NGOs than those for which they have claimed credit. The rapid expansion in the number, range and influence of NGOs in many aid-recipient countries has been an important factor in the process of strengthening civil society. However, the 'scatter-gun' approach, whereby donors fund a whole range of NGOs and CSOs willy-nilly, has been costly, and there remain significant gaps in our understanding of the role, function and comparative advantage of NGOs and CSOs in contributing to extending and deepening the transparency and accountability of agencies and institutions in aid-recipient countries.[11]

EMERGENCY AID: PROBLEMS IN FUNDING AND ADEQUATELY RESPONDING TO SUDDEN-ONSET AND COMPLEX EMERGENCIES

The evident ability of humanitarian aid to save lives and to contribute to restoring livelihoods conceals a number of fundamental problems with the whole humanitarian system. Dependent on the voluntary giving of governments and individuals, the volume of official aid channelled into humanitarian activities, though rising, remains seriously inadequate, unpredictable and volatile. Notwithstanding some recent successes in expanding the UN's Central Emergency Response Fund (CERF), the aid which is provided is distributed unevenly in relation to need, in part because of weaknesses and gaps in needs-assessment systems and processes, in part because too often there is insufficient consultation with beneficiaries, and in part because some of the key (UN) agencies are compelled to attempt to raise funds for ongoing work under the umbrella of emergency appeals. Though serious problems of coordination among agencies, including UN agencies, have been well known for many years, they remain largely unaddressed, resulting in increased costs and reduced efficiencies of response. For many major emergencies, we still don't know whether needs are being effectively assessed, how much aid is needed and who can best provide it. In many countries vulnerable to emergencies, especially in poorer and often higher-risk countries, the resources and logistical capacity to respond even to predictable emergencies remain inadequate, in part because of insufficient priority given to disaster preparedness and to skills training, perpetuating the high level of dependence on external, high-cost responses.

It is increasingly—though still not universally—recognized that a complete humanitarian response, especially in complex emergencies, needs to encompass activities to protect the population at risk. However, in a large number of emergencies there is still a failure to protect the vulnerable, as well as a failure to initiate programmes aimed at addressing, in more than piecemeal fashion, potential fundamental human rights abuses before they occur, even if their occurrence is clearly predictable.

In spite of some significant improvements in recent years, the quality of assessments of the impact of emergency assistance remains poor. There are many agencies, including many NGOs, frequently forming a major part of many emergency response efforts, who respond effectively, quickly and effi-ciently, and who provide aid to the standards of quality to which agencies have accepted they need to be held accountable. Nonetheless, the available evidence frequently points to the same cluster of common weaknesses and failures of the overall response:

- Insufficient consultation with the affected population.
- Weak coordination within and across agencies.
- Often a surfeit of agencies, and a surfeit of inexperienced agencies, some acting too slowly, and providing sub-standard forms of assistance.
- A concentration of effort and resources on a few high-profile emergencies and the relative neglect of, and insufficient resources channelled to, 'silent' emergencies, including many long-running emergencies across Africa.
- Concerns about the relevance and appropriateness of some of the aid-in-kind provided.
- The (high) costs of tied aid, including, perhaps most notably, emergency food aid.

Problems at the recipient end: aid dilemmas

This chapter has so far omitted discussion of one of the most serious aid impact problems identified in earlier chapters of the book: the persistent failure of so much aid to help build the capacity of, and strengthen institutions in, aid-recipient countries. The omission was deliberate, as the causes of these failures go to the heart of some of the most fundamental problems and dilemmas of the aid relationship, those at the recipient end. They require a more wide-ranging discussion.

COMMITMENT, CAPACITY, OWNERSHIP AND GOVERNANCE

The immediate reasons identified for the failure of aid to help build capacities and strengthen institutions in aid-recipient countries centre around the degree of commitment of aid-recipient governments to, and 'ownership' of, these activities and processes. In a nutshell, if governments do not own these programmes and are not committed to them, then—it is now almost universally agreed—they are almost bound to fail. (The same is also true for aid given by NGOs.) This assessment constitutes part of a wider view of aid impact which has become so influential among both donors and aid researchers over the past 10 to 15 years that it is now the conventional wisdom, and has almost become an article of faith. Without recipient ownership and commitment, it is not possible to form the partnership between donors and recipients on which, according to the donors at least, the very basis for the aid relationship is dependent (OECD 2003a: 15–19). It is ironic that rising donor rhetoric about the importance of *their* achieving tangible results with aid has occurred at precisely the same time as donors have become increasingly convinced that the impact of aid lies predominantly in the hands of the recipients.

This trio of commitment, ownership and capacity is closely linked to another central concept of the contemporary aid lexicon, also increasingly, and now widely, believed by donors and aid specialists alike to be crucially linked to the impact of aid, namely *governance*—the art and practice of governing.[12] It is now increasingly asserted that poor governance, and a weak commitment to better governance on the part of aid-recipient countries, explain the failure of aid to strengthen and contribute to building the capacities of state institutions. But the reach and importance of governance is far more extensive than this. Indeed, governance, and the commitment to governance, are now regarded as the central concepts which account for all, or almost all, of the performance of aid—both successes and failures. From such a perspective, good and better governance is seen to hold the key to greater aid impact. Illustrative of this perspective is the view of the Australian government that 'good governance is the basic building block for development. It is the most effective investment that Australia can make in promoting sustained growth, improving living standards and reducing poverty' (AusAID 2000: introd.). More recently, the British government argued in its 2006 White Paper, entitled *Eliminating World Poverty: Making Governance Work for the Poor*, that good governance was 'essential to reduce poverty' (2006c: 19). For some, promoting good governance and development are seen as one and the same thing (Hyden *et al.* 2004: 198): for example, the 'UNDP is convinced that governance and sustainable human development are indivisible' (UNDP 1999: ch. 8, sect. 3).

DIFFICULTIES IN ADDRESSING THE CORE PROBLEMS THAT IMPEDE THE IMPACT OF AID

Identifying the core problems which limit the impact of aid is clearly important. But there remains a crucial difference between identifying problems and working out how to address them. Aid works best if given to countries and governments with strong commitments and capacities to use it well, with transparent and accountable institutions, and with policies and strategies geared to poverty reduction and even better governance that have been developed in a participatory way and are owned by the country's government and citizens—though even here, as noted above, external factors can still profoundly affect and indeed eclipse the contributions which aid has made and can make. The problem is that these—ideal—conditions are very different from those that prevail in most aid-recipient countries. Development aid is provided, and required, because of a country's poverty. Yet poverty is manifested not merely in low and inadequate incomes, low growth and limited job opportunities, but also in precisely those areas most crucial to aid effectiveness: weak commitments, capacities and capabilities of governments; weak institutions, systems and processes of governance and weak accountability; and limited abilities to draw up home-grown plans and programmes and to implement them. The challenge is how to provide aid when the context is not just marginally sub-optimal, but when countries face a range of deep-seated, and often interlinked, systemic problems.

In recent years, donors have begun to face this problem head on by focusing attention on a group of countries in which the context for providing aid have been particularly challenging. These countries have been successively referred to by different names, some less complimentary than others: 'Low Income Countries Under Stress' or LICUS (World Bank); 'difficult partnerships' (OECD/DAC), 'difficult environments' (DFID), 'failed states' (United States) and, lastly, 'fragile states', which is, since 2006, the preferred and now most widely used nomenclature. Though the countries falling into these groups have been classified in slightly different ways, there is considerable overlap between them, all of them sharing weaknesses in the areas of commitment, capacity, ownership and governance. Additionally, however, fragile states have also included countries which are either in conflict, emerging from conflict or vulnerable to conflict, a further significant factor impeding or limiting the impact of development aid.[13] The common thread running through this group of countries is that they are characterized by an environment in which it is particularly difficult for aid to be effective (Torres and Anderson 2004).

However defined, this group consists of a comparatively large number of poor aid-recipient countries—at least 50 of the poorest countries on most assessments, and accounting for well over 50 per cent of people in all developing countries living on less than $2 a day. Over half of all African countries appear on most lists of fragile states. Yet it is also recognized that the classification of states into 'fragile' and 'non-fragile' is both rather arbitrary and subject to change over time, with countries moving in and out of those deemed 'hard to help'. It is by no means easy to distinguish clearly between good and poor performers. Indeed, an increasing number of donors would agree with the view of the UK's Department for International Development (DFID) that most if not all low-income nations and many middle-income ones are fragile and that countries move in and out of fragility (DFID 2005c: 7). According to one comprehensive review, exceptionally few countries remain permanently classified as no-hopers (Macrae *et al.* 2004: 18ff.).

Much donor rhetoric would tend to suggest that the main challenge for aid donors is to channel aid into those countries where the conditions are most conducive to its being used well.[14] The reality, however, is that in most recipient counties the environment is such that, to a greater or lesser extent, the potential impact of aid is likely to be constrained by one or more serious structural or systemic weaknesses. Only a few poor countries, and even fewer of the poorest ones, have provided a long-term environment that has been particularly conducive to aid working effectively. The surprise is the length of time it has taken donors publicly to acknowledge the extent and seriousness of this problem, even though aid officials have had to confront these problems for successive generations. Confronted with the problems of fragile states in particular, donors are faced with a stark choice: either withdraw and provide no aid at all, or stay engaged and try to address the problems identified as impeding the effectiveness of aid. In practice, donors have overwhelmingly chosen the path of continuing engagement, increasingly trying to address the main problems impeding aid's greater impact. Indeed, the OECD/DAC's *Principles for Good International Engagement in Fragile States* do not merely state that *all* fragile states 'require substantial international engagement', but that 'given low capacity and the extent of the challenges facing fragile states, investments in development, diplomatic and security engagement may need to be of *longer duration* than in other low-income countries' (OECD 2005j: 2, 4; emphasis added).

Governance

In trying to address the main problems which limit the impact of aid, donors, in particular, have encountered another difficulty: knowing precisely *how* to help. The ways donors have engaged with the issues of governance well illustrate these difficulties.

As noted above, over the past 10–15 years, donors have come to believe that good governance is central to understanding why aid is effective, and why it is therefore important to help address problems of weak or poor governance. It is thus important to understand precisely what governance is, and how providing aid to address governance problems could help. Loosely, governance is the activities, institutions, and processes involved in effectively managing and running a country's affairs in all its different spheres, economic, political and administrative, including the relationships between the state and the wider society. The problem is that this is such an all-embracing concept, deployed to encompass anything or everything that is good or bad with the state and society (and everything in between). Hence, labelling problems as elements of bad or weak governance does not get us very far in identifying what precisely the main problems are, how they might be addressed, and in what sort of order. Consequently, governance is a very slippery concept, which, not surprisingly, has been used to mean different things.

Donors disagree among themselves about how to define governance, and these disagreements are mirrored in the different ways that governance is understood within the academic community (See Box 20.1, p. 374.). Not surprisingly, donors also disagree about how to improve governance in aid-recipient countries, and indeed, on the priority that they should give to governance, though they agree that their engagement in fragile states should 'do no harm' (OECD 2005j: 3). At one level, these differences can be traced to disagreements about the relationship between governance and development. Thus 'there remain a number of unanswered questions about which institutions matter most and which kinds of governance interventions are most likely to promote development' (Grindle 2005: 2). Yet donors also disagree—even more sharply—about what constitutes the essence of 'good governance', and how best to promote it. For instance, for some donors a move towards democracy is an essential part of good governance, for others it is not.[15] In an attempt to narrow down these differences, one initiative has tried to isolate and focus on a smaller cluster of more important issues, under the nomenclature of 'good enough governance' (Grindle 2004). However, this remains still very much 'work in progress', with donors divided over what ought to be included even in this shortlist (Grindle 2005). Box 20.1 traces some of these differences to their roots by providing a number of different definitions of governance used by key agencies and influential academics.[16]

Some of the disagreements about governance and how to approach it are rooted in the different ways that governance, policy and administration are understood, and the role that donors believe they should play, directly or indirectly, in influencing politics and political relationships. For some, governance is concerned principally with rules and institutions. For others, it is primarily concerned with the way that policy is put into practice (Hyden and Court 2002: 7).

There is no doubt that governance is important to aid effectiveness and that there is a relationship between the ineffectiveness of (some) aid and the quality of governance. What remains far less clear is precisely which dimensions of poor governance contribute to which aspects of the poor performance of aid, and thus how the problems of weak governance ought to be addressed, and the precise role that aid can play in addressing these problems. Donors have steered well clear of trying to assess the overall impact of their aid-funded governance projects and programmes on the quality of governance, not least because existing indicators provide poor measures of key governance processes (ODI 2006: 2).[17] Most donors and many recipients are still searching for answers.

BOX 20.1 GOVERNANCE: DIFFERENT VIEWS AND DEFINITIONS

World Bank

The process and institutions through which decisions are made and authority in a country is exercised.

UNDP

The exercise of economic, political and administrative authority to manage a country's affairs at all levels.

DFID

How the institutions, rules and system of the state—the executive, legislature, judiciary and military—operate at central and local level, and how the state relates to individual citizens, civil society and the private sector.

USAID

The ability of government to develop an efficient, effective and accountable public management process that is open to citizen participation and that strengthens rather than weakens a democratic system of government.

Hyden, Court and Mease

The formation and stewardship of the formal and informal rules that regulate the public realm, the arena in which state as well as economic and societal actors interact to make decisions.

Kaufmann

The traditions and institutions by which authority in a country is exercised for the common good. This includes the process by which those in authority are selected, monitored and replaced; the government's capacity to effectively manage its resources and implement sound policies; and the respect of citizens and the state for the country's institutions.

Sources: Hyden *et al.* (2004: 16); Grindle (2005: 14–15); Kaufmann (2005: 41–3).

BRINGING BACK THE POLITICAL DIMENSION

The problems of aid ineffectiveness in aid-recipient countries do not arise in a vacuum. As the discussion on governance has illustrated, they occur within a particular context, including, importantly, the wider political setting. Increasingly over the past ten years, donors have begun—again—to look more closely at the way that politics influences the impact of aid.[18] A number have commissioned their own studies to shed light on this question, while most donors have searched through the wider literature on political economy to try to understand better the links between some of the main weaknesses impeding the greater impact of aid and the different political forces and processes operating within aid-recipient countries. Donor-initiated studies include a series of studies commissioned by the DFID in the UK, called 'drivers of change' analyses, conducted in more than a dozen aid-recipient countries.[19]

A consistent—if hardly surprising—cluster of conclusions from these studies is that context and politics matter, often a great deal. For example, Booth suggests that the 'root cause' of Africa's governance problems lies in the nature of its political systems (Booth 2005: 494).[20] However, this (rather obvious) point assumes greater importance when set against mounting evidence that donors have often provided aid without sufficiently understanding, or seeing it as relevant to try to understand, the political context within which the aid they provided was meant to work (Unsworth 2005: 1). Donor knowledge of country contexts and history has often been found to be exceptionally shallow, with donor staff who are responsible for making key decisions on the allocation of aid and the form in which it should be provided ignorant even of relevant studies undertaken by their own agency in the same recipient country (Booth *et al.* 2006: 29ff.).

A number of studies have focused on the problems in a particular group of countries in which the state is characterized as neo-patrimonial (individual rulers, and often their relatives, hold disproportionate power) or clientelistic (access to basic services and the use and allocation of state funds are significantly influenced by patronage). These include a significant number of countries in Africa. Perversely, one of the prominent conclusions emerging from studies of weak clientelistic states is that aid provided with the aim of strengthening institutions and promoting good governance in such countries not only risks failing to achieve its objectives, but can have the (unintended) effect of reinforcing some of the very problems that it was intended to ease, such as patronage (Bräutigam and Knack 2004).[21]

The failures of governance initiatives to achieve their core objectives have been attributed (by donors, amongst others) to weak commitment and ownership. Both donor-commissioned and wider studies of the political economy of aid shed further light on understanding these relationships. The 'new' conventional wisdom on aid effectiveness suggests that aid will only be effective if the recipient is committed to using it well. Yet these studies suggest that commitment is a complex concept. Particularly in clientelistic states, political leaders can pledge, with all sincerity, to use aid effectively, but they are not able to deliver on their promises because they do not have effective power and the necessary means to follow through on their commitments (Booth *et al.* 2005: 2). Likewise, current conventional wisdom amongst donors suggests that aid will work if it is integrated into development plans and strategies which are 'owned' by aid recipients. The discussion in Chapter 14 drew attention to the setting up of consultations, including consultations with representatives of civil society, to achieve local ownership of poverty reduction strategies (PRSes), a core assumption being that local ownership is something fairly easy to achieve. Yet, as the studies suggest, developing and achieving ownership of a development strategy is extremely complex, encompassing far more than merely achieving formal agreement on a finite time-bound document. Ownership needs to be seen more as a long-term process which involves negotiations, difficult at times, with different, often competing, interest groups. It evolves, with different twists and turns involving the strengthening and loosening of alliances with different groups. Like commitment, the test of ownership lies not merely in what is formally agreed (though this is an important first step), but in the outcome of the interplay of agreement and action. Again, in clientelistic states, the gaps between the two are likely to be large. But in all aid-recipient countries, ownership, like commitment, is best seen in terms of processes which require a considerable period of time to become embedded.

Transparency and accountability are two governance indicators widely assumed to be important in influencing the impact of aid across recipient countries. The studies shed light on these issues in two ways.[22] First, they point to the importance of taxation as a major influence in calling governments to account. In particular, they show that rising taxes paid by citizens are particularly influential in increasing demands for governments to be more accountable and transparent in their management of public resources. What this suggests is that the provision of aid, and rising amounts of aid inflows, need to take place within a framework which encompasses the wider governance relationships of revenue raising and resource spending. Secondly, the studies challenge the overly simplistic notion that the accountability of government (and by implication, accountability for how aid funds are used) can be enhanced by 'strengthening civil society'. They point to cases where civil society as a whole is 'strengthened', but the voice and influence of the views of poor people are no stronger than they were before. In many contexts, it is suggested that if civil society organizations (CSOs) are to make an effective difference to state accountability then it may be necessary not merely for CSOs to work to enhance their capacities in isolation, but to do so in conjunction with efforts directed at strengthening the effectiveness of the state itself and its institutions, including action to strengthen parliamentary representation.

In short, the studies suggest not merely that an understanding of the complexities of the political context into which aid is inserted is vital to understanding the prospects of its impact, but that it is also likely to require a far longer time-frame than donors are accustomed to before tangible and sustainable gains might be detected.

Even in the most difficult settings, however, achieving positive outcomes is by no means impossible, though it is probably far more difficult than donors have been willing to acknowledge publicly. There is evidence of tangible gains on the road to good governance being achieved in some of the most inhospitable settings, such as in Afghanistan in the days of Taliban rule (OECD 2006c: 31). Possibilities for effective action can arise not least because the lack of effective control at the centre can open up opportunities for good-governance initiatives in a range of institutions and areas outside the control of, and often of little interest to, the central government authorities. They can also arise well beyond formal institutions, whose impact is often decisively shaped and influenced by a range of agencies, associations and processes beyond the state whose role in contributing to the wider 'rules of the game' is often critically important (Heymans and Pycroft 2005: 6). Only if donors stay engaged in difficult circumstances, employing highly skilled staff, will they be able to know if and when such opportunities arise. Clearly, too, not all fragile states exhibit the extremes of patrimonialism and clientelism, and not all aid recipients are, or remain, fragile states. Indeed, as noted above, one of the features of aid-recipient economies and states is the way in which positive change, sometimes dramatic and unexpected, can occur (Hyden *et al.* 2004: 196; Kaufmann 2005: 42–3).

Particularly challenging for donors are the conclusions which suggest that there are far fewer pre-packaged answers to improving governance in aid-recipient countries than donors have been willing to assume. Not infrequently, too, the paths to good governance may look very different from those experienced in donor countries (Unsworth 2005: 45). What this suggests is that if donors wish to address the problems of aid in particularly difficult environments, they need to spend less time developing and commissioning studies aimed to producing general 'how-to' manuals and templates for dispensing different types of aid in different forms, to be applied willy-nilly across aid-recipient countries. Rather, they need to devote resources to understanding better the political economy of each country to which they provide aid, focusing especially on trying to isolate and understand the nature and effects of the constraints which limit the ability of aid to work more effectively.

ADDITIONAL DILEMMAS OF AID

The overarching dilemma of aid is that it is needed most in those countries in which the prospects for its being most effective are the poorest—countries in which commitment and ownership tend to be amongst the most fragile, and the problems of capacity and governance tend to be amongst the most severe. But donors face an additional dilemma. The more they channel their aid to where they believe it can make a more immediate, and often direct, impact on the lives of those in need, the less aid is available to be used to address many of the wider, less immediate and more systemic constraints which impede or hold back faster long-term development. This will mean prolonging the day when the recipient will no longer need aid; and it will probably result in donors having to provide more aid over time than if aid had been deployed differently. Indeed, as discussed below, focusing aid on meeting immediate needs can even undermine the efforts of recipients to accelerate the process of wealth creation. The recent emphasis on, and prominence given to, the Millennium Development Goals (MDGs) has put this particular dilemma into even sharper relief.

The more extensive and deep-seated are the problems of commitment, ownership, capacity and governance within aid-recipient countries, the less likely it will be that channelling more aid to and through governments unconditionally will result in the MDGs being achieved. Thus, especially in such contexts, donors find it particularly attractive to try to 'ring-fence' their aid, isolating it in stand-alone projects which they manage and implement themselves, or bypassing the government perceived as the problem, using other channels and agencies—the private sector, NGOs, and other civil society organizations—to try to achieve these tangible and immediate gains for poor people encapsulated in the MDGs: universal education, better health, clean water, etc. However, these anticipated short-term gains need to be set against a number of perverse effects which are likely to result.

First, as the evidence discussed in Part III shows, stand-alone projects, especially those which are either not integrated into or only loosely grafted onto governments' plans, are likely to face problems of long-term sustainability, because of weak ownership of and commitment to these projects. More systemically, the higher the levels of aid provided to fund the recurrent costs of the major service delivery ministries, such as the payment of salaries and the purchase of books and medicines, the less aid is available to help boost long-term development—for instance, to help expand and enhance the quality of the basic infrastructure, to strengthen institutions and capacities, and to help create a more favourable environment for more sustainable wealth creation. Without more rapid wealth creation, recipients will need to continue to depend upon aid funds, rather than domestic revenue resources, to continue to meet recurrent government expenditures.

Similar sorts of problems arise when donors choose to circumvent weak, ineffective and corrupt states by channelling aid to and through non-governmental agencies. Though many of these agencies are able to provide the services required, recurrent cost problems similar to those that occur when official donors themselves run or fund service delivery initiatives will arise. Over time, both official donors and NGOs have made increasing use of locally recruited staff to implement their projects. As many of these are drawn from the public sector, their departure from state agencies and institutions not only adds to the existing, and often severe, short-term skill shortages in the public sector, but makes it even more difficult for the state to provide the support necessary to enhance the longer-term wealth-creating capacity of the economy.

For many supporters and advocates of aid, these problems constitute not so much a dilemma but a necessary cost. Thus, it is asserted that there is a pressing moral imperative to provide aid now, deploying it in ways which will help meet the immediate and urgent needs of poor people—at the extreme, in order to reduce the numbers of needless deaths arising from failures to tackle extreme poverty. Yet, it is quite possible that more deaths could be prevented by targeting aid to address and help ease the systemic problems constraining the pace of long-term development, thereby accelerating the pace of poverty reduction. Indeed, we are beginning to see a number of agencies explicitly saying this. For instance, the main thrust of the UN's 2006 edition of its Least Developed Countries Report calls for a. complete 'paradigm shift' based on the recognition that the best way to achieve substantial and sustained poverty reduction lies in directing assistance to help accelerate the development of the productive capacities of the poorest countries, which, it argues, neither national nor international policies are adequately promoting (UN 2006: 283). Against this backdrop, the central moral challenge lies less in pondering whether it is better to use aid to save lives now or in the future (for all lives are of equal worth), but in ensuring that sufficient (aid) resources are provided to contribute to the reduction in the numbers of all deaths from poverty, whether this takes place today or in the future.

Conclusion

As the purpose of this chapter has been to bring together and summarize some of the main problems with aid, it would be understandable if readers were drawn to conclude not merely that aid faces a myriad of substantial problems, but that it never works. This would be mistaken. The chapter has drawn attention to a succession of specific problems which limit the potential impact of aid, indicating, too, that when, in some countries at particular points of time, a number of these problems are present, they provide an extremely difficult environment for aid. But this is a far cry from presenting systematic country-based and cross-country evidence to prove that aid overall, in aggregate and overwhelmingly, doesn't work. As the discussion in Part III of the book showed, much of the data on aid impact remains partial and of poor quality, making it very difficult to defend firm and overarching generalizations about the impact of aid. If the overall evidence is too poor to prove, in general, that aid works, it is also too poor to assert, in general, that it doesn't. Indeed, when the evidence presented and examples given in Part III of effective aid is set alongside the problems of aid presented in this chapter, the evident successes that some aid has had can be seen in a quite different light—given the substantial and systemic problems which exist in many aid-recipient countries, what is particularly noteworthy is that major successes have been achieved at all.

In recent years, donors have focused their attention more carefully on the problems which impede the greater impact of aid—a major step forward from the decades when impact, assessment and results were not central concerns of most donors. Knowing more about what doesn't work, and why, provides a better context for learning and for understanding what changes can or might be made to improve the overall impact of aid. The last two chapters, in particular Chapter 22, look at ways in which tangible progress could be made to reduce significantly some key gaps between the potential of aid and what, in practice, it currently achieves.

21 Making aid work better by implementing agreed reforms

Aid works, but not nearly as well as it could. Though the list of problems summarized in the previous chapter is long, few individual constraints are absolute. It is also extremely rare for a combination of impediments to last for a prolonged period of time, preventing aid in some form from achieving significant benefits. In most countries, there are opportunities for aid to be used effectively, even if the process of locating them requires careful analysis of the political economy and governance of each recipient country, and it may not always be possible to marry the achievement of immediate gains with sustainable and lasting benefits.

We now turn to the future. This chapter discusses the prospects for aid if we do better what is already being done: if donors individually take to heart the lessons learned, and if donors and recipients pursue the goals of the current reform programme for aid which culminated in the agreements made in Paris in 2005 under the banner of greater harmonization, coordination and alignment. The conclusions are broadly positive. Changes are likely to continue to be made in the way aid is given, received and used, and aid impact will continue to improve.

Working to enhance the impact of aid has grown into a multi-million-dollar business. Each year, thousands of reports are written by aid officials and consultants which, directly or indirectly, focus on how to make aid work better. These contain numerous recommendations for enhancing the impact of the particular project, programme, sector or country examined. If acted upon, they would enhance the impact of aid, most in small ways, but some more profoundly. Our interest here is not so much on the small-print details, though these are clearly important building blocks to improving the overall impact of aid. Rather, it is on the wider, more aggregate impact that these recommendations would make.

Stepping back from the detail, two broad though increasingly interrelated approaches are used to try to enhance the effectiveness of aid. We shall term these the *discrete individual-donor approach* and the *step-change international cooperative approach*, and shall look at each in turn.

The discrete individual-donor approach

The discrete individual-donor approach to improving the impact of aid is the one that aid agencies, official and non-governmental, have traditionally used since the foundations of official aid some 60 years ago. It involves each donor agency focusing narrowly on its own aid programme, and making up its own mind about how to improve the effectiveness of its own aid funds. Two ways in which donors have done this have been particularly important.

The first has involved the allocation of aid and linked conditionalities. Improvements to the effectiveness of aid have been dominated by decisions about how aid is allocated—to whom and in what particular form—and how to interact with recipients, determining the range and intensity of conditions attached to the provision of aid. The second has involved donors applying different 'blueprints' to their aid—changing the forms in which it has been given, influenced especially by the latest insights from the development profession. This method has been particularly important: over successive decades, donors have been profoundly influenced by the latest fads and fashions of development discourse—with aid successively deployed to fill foreign exchange, savings or skills gaps, to help meet basic needs, promote growth, and now, to 'make governance work'. Taken together, these two ways of approaching aid and aid relationships have been so dominant that, in practice, donor governments have historically given little priority to the evidence of aid impact when making core decisions about how to improve the quality of the aid they provide.

In recent years, however, the traditional, discrete individual-donor approach has changed quite markedly. As the discussion in earlier chapters of this book has shown, donors have become far more reflective, giving more priority to issues of impact and trying to understand better what works and why. It has led them to realize more clearly that the impact of aid depends on the context in which it is given, and on the capacity and commitment of recipients to use it well. More recently still, donors have become increasingly aware that the impact of the aid they provide is critically dependent on the quality, competence, skills and incentive structures prevailing among their own staff and within their own agencies. However, most have not yet thought through how they ought to address the constraints within their own agencies, some of them institutional and systemic, which impede aid's greater impact.

It is against these changes and this more complex backdrop that decisions about allocating aid—for instance, in what form, and for how long—are now made. However, this narrower donor-specific approach is no longer the only game in town.

The step-change international cooperative approach

For many decades, official donors have known that the impact of their aid and the decisions they make about where and how it is allocated are related to decisions made by other donors. Likewise, NGOs have known about, and worked for changes to be made to, the way official aid is provided and used, urging greater international cooperation among donors, advocating a greater voice for, and the participation of, recipients in aid decisions, and campaigning for an overall increase in the total amount of official aid provided.

Yet it was really only from the early 1990s that official donors began to take significant and concrete steps to begin to work more closely together in order to improve the effectiveness of their own aid funds, the cumulative effect of which enhances the aggregate effectiveness of all aid. And it has really only been in the past ten years that donors have begun to engage together more formally with recipients, both individually and in groups, to focus on ways to improve the overall impact of aid, especially at the country level. The donors' club, the OECD/DAC, joined more recently by the United Nations, has played a pivotal role in initiating, helping to formalize, and implementing this 'step-change' in the way donors provide and think about official development aid. The essence of this new approach is inter-donor and donor–recipient cooperation, with donors providing more aid in a more integrated and mutually consistent fashion against the backdrop of pledges to implement these changes urgently.

Since its formation over 45 years ago, the OECD/DAC has continually sought to try to enhance the impact of official aid. But for the first 30 years of its existence, its work was dominated by trying to alter donor practice largely through the power of persuasion, notably by 'naming and shaming' donors deviating from agreed norms of 'best practice', and through 'peer pressure'. Increasingly, however, since the mid-1990s it has worked with key official donors (now more receptive to its greater tendency to take the initiative) to adopt an approach to aid-giving based on agreement of more formal mechanisms and processes to work together in more cooperative ways. The publication *Shaping the 21st Century: The Contribution of Development Co-operation* (OECD 1996) laid out some of the early guidelines. It led to agreements made by donors (with some recipients) at the Millennium Summit (2000), Monterrey (2002), Rome (2003), Marrakech (2004) and the World Summit (2005). Most important was the conference in Paris (2005), where donors agreed on specific targets for joint action and cooperation.

The cynics suggest that all this is little more than window-dressing, that 'we have seen it all before' and that it will make little to no difference to the delivery and effectiveness of aid. This view is singularly uninformed. Anyone who has been involved in aid implementation efforts for the past 20 or 30 years cannot help but notice the tangible differences these events and processes have had on the rhythm of aid work. They have significantly influenced the approach to aid-giving, and the way aid is provided on the ground. Official donors are devoting enormous resources, at a scale unprecedented a decade ago, to thinking about and analysing those factors which constrain development and how aid might be used more effectively, experimenting with and trying out new ways of cooperating and new ways of giving aid. For their part, recipient governments are being involved more directly than ever in discussions and decisions made on the deployment and use of aid, both individually and together.

This step-change in cooperation has been manifested in a variety of different ways: undertaking joint aid-programmes (SWAps and direct budget support); pooling aid funds together; harmonizing aid procedures; aligning aid more closely with developing-country plans and strategies; and undertaking joint programming, monitoring and evaluation missions. It has also involved a range of new initiatives within and across UN agencies, programmes and funds to coordinate their work more effectively, both to bring their individual aid efforts into a more unified structure and to link them more closely and more formally to recipient-country plans and priorities. Parallel initiatives have been under way to work more cooperatively in providing emergency assistance, including the creation and expansion of the new international emergency fund, CERF, increased cooperation among groups of large NGOs working on emergencies, and the piloting of joint assessment missions. Additionally, inter-national action has played an important role in encouraging donors to expand overall aid levels, and some are committing themselves to providing aid within frameworks beyond a single year to begin to address the problems of aid volatility.

Notwithstanding the gains already made in inter-donor and donor-recipient cooperation, far more could be done. By no means all donors have actively participated in this international cooperative approach to aid-giving, and there remain significant gaps across the donor community between pledges and commitments made to harmonize and align their aid and what has so far been achieved in practice. As discussed in Chapter 20, some of the cooperative goals set and agreed remain relatively unambitious, with almost all falling well short of full cooperation (see note 5 for the details). A growing number of donors realize that significant changes need to take place in the way that technical cooperation funds are provided, realigning support to recipient-country needs and priorities, pooling funds together, and radically untying this form of aid. Likewise, overall aid levels still fall well short of targets set, aid volatility remains a major problem, and commercial and political interests still dilute and, at times, directly conflict with the development goals for poor countries which underpin their aid-giving.

Importantly, however, the momentum created by the initial step-change is likely to be maintained, and possibly even increase, leading (probably) to more ambitious targets being set, increasing the likelihood that further tangible gains in the overall impact of aid will be made. However, further progress will depend crucially on the interest in and support for aid among leading donor governments and across the different UN agencies being sustained, which, in turn, will be influenced by the priority given to aid by campaigners, and by their understanding of what constitute the main factors impeding the greater effectiveness of aid.

Taking stock

A continuing focus on the (changing) traditional individual-donor approach and on more cooperative international approaches to aid hold out the prospect for a future of further improvements in the impact of aid. Donors, consultants and researchers are likely to continue to analyse the factors which facilitate and constrain the greater impact of aid in different settings, and to continue to learn from detailed studies of the impact and effectiveness of new forms of aid-giving and of cooperation.

In the near future, it is likely that the emphasis already being given to the problems of how to provide aid more effectively in difficult environments and in fragile and clientelistic states will grow, increasing knowledge about how political structures, institutions and processes influence and constrain development processes in different ways in a large number of aid-recipient countries. The results of these studies should shed much-needed further light on how aid might legitimately be used more effectively to support the political change necessary to deepen commitment, enhance capacities and strengthen recipient economies.[1] They should also assist efforts to increase the power of organizations within aid-recipient countries to demand greater domestic accountability of how aid funds are used. Greater attention is also likely to be given to the issue of corruption, as knowledge about the complex relationships between corruption and aid is still insufficient. This heightened attention should help to ensure, minimally, that aid does not contribute to a worsening of the problems of corruption in aid-recipient countries, and, more significantly, should deepen understanding of how aid funds might more effectively be used to help reduce it. The expectation is that increased knowledge will, in turn, not only inform the next round of discussions between donors and recipients on aid effectiveness, but will act as a further catalyst to stimulate changes in policies and practice, resulting in even closer collaboration of donors and the increased impact of aid. Tangible gains have been made in the past five years. These are likely to be mirrored by similar if not greater gains in the next five, with a growing number of donors likely to work more closely together to provide aid in programme rather than project form, most likely including the more extensive use of general budget support.

These expected developments will certainly improve the effectiveness of aid, enabling more aid to 'work', but by how much? Certainly far less than might be achieved. This is because current initiatives either fail adequately to resolve, or do not even begin to address, some of the most fundamental problems which continue to impede the greater impact of aid. The following five groups of problems constitute some of the most important of these. Each, on its own, has a significant adverse effect on the potential impact of aid; cumulatively the effects are even greater.

1. Aid is still not provided in sufficient overall quantities to meet the differing needs of poor countries and the key gaps and deficiencies in resources that they are themselves unable to bridge. The major cause of this problem is that official aid-giving remains based on the voluntary decisions of each donor government, resulting in an extremely loose and tenuous link between the amounts of official development aid provided and the aid needs of either individual poor countries, or of all poor countries as a whole.

2. The aid which is provided is not allocated in any systematic, rational or efficient way to those who need it most. The amount of aid each country receives is determined by the individual decisions of scores of different donors. While these decisions are certainly informed by development needs, they are also profoundly influenced by the political, strategic, commercial and historically rooted interests of most of the major donors. The result is a massive mismatch between aid provided and aid requirements. Severe distortions in the allocation of aid play a major role in reducing its overall potential impact.

3. The aggregate amounts of aid provided to recipient countries are volatile and unpredictable, subject to significant change from one year to the next, and from one country to another, with no recipient country able to undertake efficient resource planning based on a knowledge of what quantities of aid will be provided one, two or three years hence. Political, strategic and commercial factors, including the tying of aid and particularly the tying of technical assistance, continue profoundly to shape and influence the way aid is allocated and for how long it is provided. Decisions made by individual donors can, and do, result in the immediate suspension or cessation of aid that has been promised, pledged and committed, or to the unilateral decision by donors suddenly to switch aid to different uses.[2] The overall effect of these practices is to reduce further the overall potential development impact of aid provided.

4. Development aid relationships are still dominated by recipients having to interact with scores, and, at the extreme, hundreds of different official donors and donor agencies in order to agree arrangements for the many hundreds and, at the extreme, many thousands of individual projects and programmes, most of which are only loosely linked to each other, with many not integrated into a common development framework. Donors have different requirements for the planning, monitoring and assessment of their projects, and they still compete

with each other to fund the 'best' projects. The overall effect is to increase considerably the costs of providing aid, and to reduce further its potential impact through overlap, duplication and inconsistency across aid projects and programmes. As noted above, these problems *have* begun to be addressed. Yet, in spite of further progress expected in the years ahead, the overall impact of these efforts will be limited in relation to the scale and extent of the problems that will remain unaddressed.

5. While donors regularly articulate the centrality of recipient ownership and of partnership between donors and recipients as critical for aid to have a positive impact, in practice the overall aid relationship remains extremely lopsided, with donors remaining almost wholly in control. It is donors who determine how much aid will be allocated, the type of aid that will be provided, the conditions under which it will be given, and the time period for which it will be given. Even recipients who are committed to using aid effectively are not equal partners. They remain junior partners who have to struggle to make use of funds over which they have and retain limited control.[3]

How these problems can be addressed is the subject of the next, and final, chapter.

22 Making aid work better by recasting aid relationships

Current efforts to enhance the impact of aid take place within parameters which fail even to engage with some of the most pivotal and fundamental problems which continue to constrain, and in some cases undermine, the potential beneficial impact of aid. Many of these arise directly out of, or can be linked to, the way that contemporary aid relationships are currently cast.

Confronting the fundamental problems of prevailing aid relationships presents the international community with its greatest challenge. Yet working to address these problems opens up the prospect of achieving even greater improvements in the impact and effectiveness of aid than can be achieved within prevailing paradigms, resulting in a far more significant contribution to the overall goal of ending extreme poverty and vulnerability in the poorest countries. With donors today pledged and firmly committed to make their aid more effective, and against the backdrop of some of the most far-reaching changes in aid-giving and aid-receiving countries having taken place and currently under way, there has probably not been a more auspicious time to confront these fundamental problems, and to stimulate wider debate about how they might best be tackled. What has for so long been dismissed as wishful thinking needs to be pondered anew.

This chapter discusses and lays out a number of concrete proposals for addressing many of these core problems. It starts with a discussion of politics because the prospects for the sorts of changes discussed in this chapter relate to issues that are fundamentally political in nature: without the political momentum for far-reaching change, it will not take place. Against this backdrop, the chapter outlines some of the core building-blocks of a new type of aid relationship, one more suited to the needs and values of the twenty-first century than the present one, which was established in a very different context. The chapter then considers how the world might more effectively resolve a number of central contemporary aid issues which remain insufficiently addressed under current arrangements and proposed reforms. It ends by returning to the central issue of politics to consider how the divide between ideas and implementation might be bridged.

Confronting the politics of aid-giving

It is politics which created the way governments give and receive aid, and it is the decisions of today's politicians which determine contemporary aid relationships and the array of public institutions which provide aid. It is the primacy of politics which explains why aid is still provided by individual donors who continue to make almost all of the crucial decisions about aid, and why individual donors remain unwilling to lose control of how it is allocated and how it is spent. Consequently, the key to addressing many fundamental problems which continue to constrain the potential impact of aid lies in prising official aid away from the overarching political influence of the main donor governments who provide and control it.

For many commentators, the primacy of politics, and the continued use of official aid agencies to dispense and control aid, and determine the terms under which it is provided, are immutable 'givens', and cannot be challenged. They constitute the foundation of the official aid system, the bedrock on which all recommendations to improve aid effectiveness have to be based. In contrast, the discussion that follows considers how aid and aid effectiveness might look if these supposedly immutable 'givens' are set aside, and the direct link between politics and official aid-giving is broken.

Some will dismiss this discussion as academic, unrealistic and politically naïve. That may have been true in the past, but it is not easy to be so dismissive today. The current system of aid-giving is moving further and further away from the norms on which contemporary international relationships are increasingly being shaped. It would appear to have long passed its sell-by date. As the discussion in Chapters 6 and 20 suggested, there is a growing inconsistency between donor claims that they are committed to making substantial inroads into poverty eradication and achieving the Millennium Development Goals (MDGs) by providing more aid in a timely fashion, and the current system of raising aid funds and making use of them. Likewise, a human rights approach to development, which all major donor countries claim to have embraced, and which gives prominence to the involvement and participation of recipients in decisions about how aid should be used, sits increasingly uncomfortably alongside existing aid relationships, where the donor is still king.

Discussions about recasting aid relationships have been part of international debate about aid and aid effectiveness for more than four decades. They appear, however, either to have been ignored or forgotten by most. This is because they have been overwhelmed by discussions of aid reform which do not raise fundamental questions about the existing political architecture of aid-giving. And the reason for this is that governments have repeatedly approached aid reform on the basis that it is better to move slowly, and for all governments to agree, than even to begin substantially to air the systemic weaknesses and inconsistencies of aid, for fear that this will expose disagreements to public gaze, and undermine public support for aid. The consequence has not merely been that aid's systemic problems remain unaddressed, but that they have become progressively worse.

More than four decades ago, when aid was far less important and influential than it is today, the Pearson Commission—the first international body to examine in detail aid and development on a global scale—judged that the international aid system with its profusion of agencies 'lacks direction and coherence' (Pearson 1969: 22). It went on to argue that aid should be separated from, and should have a separate identity from, short-term political consider-ations (p. 128), and that, though donors understandably have a keen interest in ensuring that the aid they provide is well spent, their interests should be 'care-fully limited and institutionalised' (p. 127). It was more than 25 years ago that the Brandt Commission judged that the time had already passed when the world ought to be raising aid funds through some sort of automatic mechanism, and dispersing aid without the repeated interventions of governments (Brandt 1980: 244). More recently, in its mid-decade analysis of international aid, the United Nations Development Programme (UNDP) expressed the view that 'fixing the international aid system is one of the most urgent priorities facing governments' (UNDP 2005: 75). It called for a recasting of the current approach to aid (p. 108), though it stopped short of challenging the core politi-cal 'givens' of the current aid system.

It is not only commissions and institutions who have been calling for far-reaching change. There are now senior politicians who are ready to acknow-ledge publicly that long-held assumptions about politics and international agencies ought to be challenged. For instance, at the 2006 spring meetings of the IMF and the World Bank, the British finance minister, Gordon Brown, made a path-breaking plea for the operational work of the IMF to be made 'independent of political influence and wholly transparent' to make its work 'more credible, authoritative and effective' ('Crisis Prevention in the New Global Economy', *Financial Times*, 27 April 2006).

If world political leaders are beginning to call for the removal of the direct influence of politics and governments from the work of the IMF, it would not seem premature to begin to look more seriously at what official aid relationships would look like unencumbered by the distortions which politics has imposed on them since aid emerged onto the international stage some 60 years ago.

Recasting aid relationships

OVERVIEW

What would aid relationships look like if they were freed from the yoke of short-term political interests, and were shaped by a disinterested view aimed at addressing aid's fundamental problems? A number of scholars have grappled with these issues over the last few decades, and a variety of different recommendations have been made, differing considerably in the small-print details. Largely on the basis of this work, but in resonance with changes over the past decade, the following paragraphs lay out five clusters of ideas about how, in concrete terms, current aid relationships might be radically altered.[1] The focus here is explicitly on recasting development aid relationships with the poorest countries. Some of the ideas presented here will be new to many readers, and for most readers they will raise immediate questions of 'when', 'where' and 'how'. Answers to many of these questions can be found in the discussion following the presentation of the core ideas.

1. A new International Aid Office (IAO) for development aid should be established, whose roles and responsibilities would include overseeing and ensuring the effective functioning of a new International Development Aid Fund (IDAF) for the poorest countries.

2. Thus, a new International Development Aid Fund (IDAF) for the poorest countries should be established. The monies to be raised for the operation of the Fund would equal the total amount of official development aid (ODA) required by all qualifying poor countries. The Fund would be financed by compulsory contributions from each of the world's wealthiest countries, with the amounts each would contribute and channel to the Fund determined by the relative wealth (gross national income) of each qualifying rich country.

3. Development aid funds for each qualifying aid-recipient country would be earmarked for, but not initially allocated to, each qualifying recipient country. On the basis of consultations with each recipient country and with key donors, the IAO would determine which of two possible ways these earmarked funds would be disbursed. If the IAO was satisfied that a qualifying poor-country government had the commitment, competence and capacity to use the aid funds effectively, it would allocate the earmarked funds directly to the recipient government. If, however, the IAO was not satisfied that the qualifying poor-country government had sufficient commitment, competence or capacity to use the aid funds effectively, the earmarked funds would pass to the country's National Aid Implementation Agency (NAIA). NAIAs would be set up in each (relevant) country for the purpose of, and with the responsibility for, allocating its aid funds as it deemed appropriate.[2]

The IAO would be responsible for ensuring that reviews of the status of each recipient country take place, and would be open to representations from parliamentary, civil society or other groups from recipient countries, and from donors, who have substantive concerns that aid funds are not being used as effectively as they might.

Recipient countries would be expected to spend the aid funds provided to them. However, future earmarked contributions would neither be reduced nor held back if aid funds already disbursed to the country had not yet been spent. All unspent aid funds would remain committed to the recipient country, to be disbursed at a later date.

4. Both recipient-country governments and, where applicable, the different NAIAs established in aid-recipient countries would not merely be free to, but would be encouraged to, make use of and draw directly upon the skills and experience currently residing in existing aid agencies, international financial institutions and aid consultancy firms to assist in ensuring that aid funds are effectively used. Any supportive technical assistance would normally be con-tracted on the basis of a transparent tendering process. Both recipient govern-ments and NAIAs would be at liberty to contract one, or a number of, donor agencies to manage and oversee the use of all or part of a recipient country's aid programme, provided the agency was willing to sign such aid contracts and accept the conditions laid down by the recipient-country government or NAIA.[3]

5. If individual donors or UN agencies wanted to provide aid to recipient countries additional to that provided through the auspices of the IDAF, they would be at liberty to do so, provided recipients were willing to accept such aid, and any conditions attached to its provision. It would be up to the relevant donors and recipients themselves, and no one else, to determine how to make use of the aid funds offered.

BACKGROUND AND REALITY CHECK

To understand the thrust of these ideas and how they represent a radical departure from current institutional arrangements, it is necessary to go into some detail to explain how these ideas would work in practice. This is done in the rest of this section.

But before embarking on this discussion, it is important to stress that these proposals represent only one set of ideas. They are far from immutable, and they probably need to be amended, perhaps radically, in the light of further discussion and analysis. This is no major drawback. The main purpose in presenting these proposals is not so much to outline the 'perfect' alternative system, but rather to provoke people into thinking about a very different future. The ideas presented here provide merely an example of what a different system—but one which addresses the core weaknesses of the existing one—would look like. Each of these five proposals could, and indeed ought to be, challenged, changed and refined, in whole or in part. At this stage, it is not possible to provide a 'right answer' to the question of how aid relationships could or might be recast. Indeed, the 'right answer' will be based on a blend of what is technically desirable and politically possible. What is critical is for substantial discussion and debate about recasting these relationships to take place and for them to be taken seriously and inserted into high-level discussions about aid effectiveness.

Establishing an International Aid Office

The proposal to establish a new International Aid Office is linked explicitly to the proposal to set up an International Development Aid Fund, as clearly there would be a need for some body to oversee and manage the fund. It is a proposal of basic principle and, deliberately at this stage, does not go into details about its location, size on relationships to other agencies or institutions.

For some time, there have been calls for recipient governments to have their interests represented in an organization which complements and provides a counterweight to the donors' club, the OECD/DAC (see, for example, Browne 2006: 146). Calls have also been made for there to be an 'aid ombudsman' to adjudicate on aid matters, or an 'aid czar' located within the United Nations, perhaps with roles and responsibilities similar to those of the UN's different special rapporteurs (see, for example, ActionAid 2005: 46–8). The November 2006 report of the High-Level Panel on UN reform, *Delivering as One*, recommended a single UN Sustainable Development Board to oversee all UN programmes, and a single UN funding mechanism (Aziz *et al.* 2006). All these ideas are relevant to how this proposal might develop. For many people, the institutional home of an international aid office would appear to lie most naturally within the United Nations. However, the question of its institutional location has been left open here because it touches upon the central issue of such an office's legitimacy, which, in turn, will be dependent upon its political acceptability, not least to the donors. It could well be that establishing an International Aid Office, initially with closer links to the OECD/DAC, rather than to the UN, and to the international finance institutions (IFIs), could determine whether such a proposal would 'fly' in donor circles, or not. If this were the cost of establishing an International Development Aid Fund, it would probably be a cost worth incurring.

Setting up and operating an International Development Aid Fund

There are two initial issues to address concerning the establishment of an International Development Aid Fund: the criteria for raising the money for the Fund, and the criteria for disbursing the funds to aid recipients. Least difficult is devising a formula for rich countries to contribute to the proposed fund. Considerable work on this has already been undertaken, notably by Griffin and McKinley (1996).[4]

More difficult is to decide which countries would qualify to receive aid from the proposed fund, the principles upon which the assessment of need would be based, and how, in practice, those needs would be determined. In deciding which countries would qualify for aid funds, a simple cut-off criterion would be easiest, using either the current official classification of least developed countries (LLDCs), low-income or low human development countries. However, using the LLDC classification would exclude a number of deserving countries, like Tajikistan, which are extremely poor and vulnerable but which are still not classified as least developed, their historical exclusion having undoubtedly been influenced by their being part of the Soviet Union—suggesting that further discussion is needed.[5]

Assessing the aid needs of recipient countries is a far more difficult challenge than is widely believed, not least because the link between aid needs and the 0.7 per cent gross national income (GNI) for ODA target was tenuous when it was devised some 50 years ago, and does not really provide today even a crude indicator of the aid needs of individual countries. However, the World Bank, the United Nations and some bilateral donors have begun to undertake studies to assess aid needs at the country level (see Chapter 20 for details). On the basis of this ongoing work, it should be possible to draw up a common template to undertake country-wide aid needs-assessments, suitably flexible to incorporate country-specific characteristics, and apply this across each country.[6] The results will never be as accurate as the purists would like, but if they are based on transparent criteria, a workable solution should easily be within the grasp of donors and recipients alike.

The allocation of aid

The proposed IAFD would disburse aid to each aid recipient, but how and under what conditions? Deciding how to allocate aid to recipients, and under what conditions, goes to the heart of one of aid's central dilemmas. There are two sharply differing views. First, from the donor viewpoint, aid always has to come with some conditions attached, not least because donor governments are accountable to their taxpayers to ensure that aid funds are spent well—so aid ought to have a complex and detailed array of different conditions. The more difficult the environment, the stronger are the conditions likely to be necessary to ensure the funds are used for the purpose intended. In sharp contrast, Griffin and McKinley argue that all aid due to recipient governments should be given directly to them. They acknowledge that some aid will go astray, but as much aid goes astray anyway, they argue that the overall effect would not be large and it is a price worth paying (1996: 25). The South Centre also argues for aid without conditions (1999: 81). Similarly, in the two-tiered aid system he outlines, Matthew Lockwood proposes that basic assistance should be channelled to recipients with minimal conditions, with donors offering additional aid only if specific (outcome) conditions are met (2005: 126).[7]

The position taken here steers a path between these extremes, but assumes that some conditions will most likely be necessary. It is based on the conviction that it is necessary to focus on impact and results, and the belief that there is no prospect of donors agreeing to a system of aid allocation which does not contain some mechanism which is able to provide, transparently and clearly, some basic assurances that aid will be used as effectively as possible, and for the purpose intended.

The solution offered to the dilemma is to transfer the responsibility for ensuring that aid is used effectively from the donor to the recipient, with some clear provisos and limitations. In all instances where there are grounds for believing that the recipient government does not have the capacity or will to use the aid effectively, the oversight of a recipient country's aid programme should pass to a national agency, the NAIA, whose integrity, capacity, commitment, competence and 'good standing' with the donor community would constitute a key part of the process of its creation.

More specifically, what is envisaged is a national aid implementation agency unique to each country in which it is deemed necessary to establish such a body (for details, see below), but one which is internationally recognized as competent. It would be an autonomous body managed and run by professional/technical staff (nationals but also foreigners if that was thought desirable). It would be distinct and separate from, but also clearly linked to, the state and its institutions, but would also have institutional links to the wider civil society—the weaker the government, the stronger the links—which would help to ensure and cement its national legitimacy.[8] Aid conditionality would exist, but it would be applied and monitored by each national aid agency. A major advantage of wresting the control of aid from the hands of donors is that aid flows and the use of aid would no longer be determined by the (political) decisions of individual donors.[9] One of the prime functions of the NAIA would be to work (with others) to ensure that aid is allocated to high-priority projects and programmes and used effectively. In working to achieve this objective, it would clearly need to have, or to coopt and make use of, macroeconomic competencies, working with relevant ministries to ensure that potential perverse effects of additional aid inflows are minimized, including monitoring the relationship between aid and fiscal policy, ensuring that the inflow of aid funds does not unduly delay the raising of additional resources domestically through increased taxation.[10]

Why would the government of a poor country accept the legitimacy of such a body? For two reasons. First, because without it, no aid could be used, and secondly, because it is highly likely that one of the main recipients of the aid to which the Agency would choose to disburse its funds would be key state agencies and ministries. Why would a donor have faith in such an agency? Because each NAIA would need to be approved by the (proposed) International Aid Office before it could start disbursing funds, and, as noted above, the IAO would itself only be established if the donors were satisfied, in turn, that it had the competence to carry out its roles and responsibilities.[11]

But why would either donors or recipients agree to creating a whole new layer of potentially quite large aid agencies and organizations across what are likely to be many of the poorest countries when all are agreed that one of the main problems with aid is that there already too many aid organizations, and too many bureaucrats, administering aid programmes? There are three answers.

First, once the NAIAs are up and running, it would no longer be necessary for the almost 200 official aid agencies to continue to employ as many people as they now do, and to retain such large numbers of technical staff. Indeed, the creation of NAIAs should not only lead to a dramatic fall in the numbers of technical staff currently employed by official aid agencies, but a wave of competitive recruitments of technical staff to NAIAs should create a smaller and far more qualified cadre of aid professionals. This would provide a major and much-needed catalyst to accelerate the process of removing the accumulated deadwood of earlier eras still present in many aid agencies. So, it might be asked, why set up a completely new set of agencies if all that is going to happen is that large numbers of people who were formerly working for the donors now work for the new agencies? This is precisely why. The skills of aid and development professionals would remain as vital as they are today; the crucial difference contained within these proposals is that these professionals would no longer be working for the donors but either for the recipient directly or, more likely, under the auspices of the NAIAs.

Secondly, having a recipient-based aid agency with adequate resources, whose understanding of the local context would be one of its major strengths, should help to plug one of the major weaknesses identified as undermining the effectiveness of aid, namely the ignorance of so many key decision-makers in donor agencies of the complexities of the political economy of aid recipient countries.

Thirdly, as official aid agencies would no longer need to establish their own aid programmes (though the best would likely be inundated with requests from aid-recipient governments and NAIAs to help manage and oversee programmes and spend *their* aid funds), the IFIs and the specialized agencies in particular and those with sectoral expertise—UNESCO, WHO, FAO, IFAD, etc.—would be able to focus their efforts and activities more sharply on undertaking, commissioning and keeping abreast of research to enable them to stand ready to share insights and 'best practice' with aid-recipient countries. For their part, recipient countries would be able to choose which agency to work with on a particular technical or sectoral issue, creating a much-needed competitive environment for aid and development work.

These brief paragraphs can only begin to scratch the surface of what the fundamentally recast aid relationship might begin to look like. Experience from other fields suggests that the final outcome is likely to be different from these initial proposals, even if they are drawn from the ideas of many serious scholars mulled over for many decades. What is important at this stage is to lay out the first markers upon which subsequent serious discussion might be based.

Making aid work better: addressing five key problem areas

Clearly, even on the most optimistic scenarios, it would take some time before the sorts of far-reaching changes outlined here could come to pass. In the interim, there are a number of systemic problems with aid which can begin to be addressed more easily and more quickly. It is clearly not practical to attempt to discuss each of these here. Rather, to make the discussion more manageable, this section focuses on a small number, selected, in part, because they are of central concern to enhancing the impact of different forms of aid to the poorest countries, or because they concern issues that have not been sufficiently aired in contemporary debates on the future of aid.

Consequently, a number of issues on the future of aid that are the subject of considerable debate will not be discussed further here. These include the following: the expanded use of aid to enhance the provision of international and regional public goods;[12] the ideal mix of bilateral and multilateral aid (see Maxwell 2005); how aid might more effectively help to stimulate the development and expansion of markets and the private sector (see Sagasti *et al.* 2005; Browne 2006; and Lancaster *et al.* 2006); how aid might contribute more effectively to the reduction of conflict (Browne 2006); and the use of aid to help stimulate trade.[13] Likewise, this discussion does not examine or comment upon the various proposals for, and initiatives under way, to address the problems of governance of the major international finance institutions (see Woods 2006), or the re-organization of the UN development agencies. All of these issues remain important.

AN INTERNATIONAL COMMISSION ON AID AND DEVELOPMENT TO HIGHLIGHT THE SYSTEMIC PROBLEMS OF AID

Many of the most fundamental problems of aid are systemic in nature. For example, over successive decades of aid-giving, the number of official agencies and funds providing aid has continued to increase to produce a myriad of different agencies, many offering identical, parallel or overlapping competencies, each requiring different reporting requirements, many linked to a long list of different conditions, and some offering recipients contradictory advice. Recipient governments have long experienced the range of problems associated with having to face a multiplicity of donors. Donors, too, have recognized them. However, the ways that the donor community, in particular, has sought to address these problems—by focusing on greater coordination and harmonization of their efforts, and trying to align their efforts more closely to the plans and policies of the recipients—have been based almost exclusively on trying to make the current range of official donors, agencies and funds work better together. Only extremely rarely have these initiatives sought to raise questions about the range of systemic problems caused by having a multiplicity of donors. Consequently, not only do the current problems arising from multiple donors remain unresolved, but no effective mechanism has yet been put in place to prevent the creation of ever more official agencies and funds.[14]

In order to address these problems, what—at first sight—would seem to be needed is an analysis of the different impediments to aid effectiveness that are caused by the multiplicity of donors, leading to proposals for how these problems might be addressed. But this provides only a partial answer, because it does not sufficiently address the most fundamental problem: the will and drive to bring about substantial change. Indeed, a number of studies by independent scholars have already recently been conducted (see Sagasti *et al.* 2005), and the United Nations itself has commissioned or undertaken a succession of reviews, which have pinpointed the problems arising from the overlap and duplication of agencies within the overall aid system. Not surprisingly, a key conclusion emerging from these studies is the need for a 'rationalization' of (i.e. a reduction in) the overall number of official agencies and funds, including a number of different United Nations agencies whose work overlaps and duplicates those of other UN agencies. However, the impact of such studies has been minimal because they have not contained the necessary ingredients to stimulate effective change in current practice.

What is needed is not so much more studies, but a different sort of initiative, with three ingredients: first, a perspective with sufficient breadth to clearly lay bare the main systemic problems with aid; secondly, sufficient sensitivity to political possibilities to develop a set of a carefully crafted recommendations for progressive and effective change; and thirdly, a sufficiently high international profile to create greater public awareness of the most fundamental systemic problems with aid, and with sufficient *gravitas* to shame donors who might otherwise ignore its findings. In short, what is needed is an independent international commission on aid and development consisting of well-known and respected commissioners whose ongoing work and final report are prominently reported and profiled in the international press and media. To some, this suggestion will sound very odd. Surely the last 10 to 15 years have been characterized by commission and summit overkill? However, not since the Brandt Commission—convened more than a generation ago, ten years before the fall of the Berlin Wall—has there been an independent international commission focusing on the overall issues of aid and development and with a remit which includes an examination of the systemic problems of aid and the political factors which underlie so many of them.

Since Brandt, as is well known, successive major international initiatives focussing on aid and development issues at the global level have taken place, at fairly regular intervals. Long and detailed reports have been produced, linked to international conferences, world summits and a succession of agreements on the way forward, including, perhaps most notably, those focused on the MDGs. Yet, especially in recent years, these have not provided an independent stocktaking of the increasingly complex worlds of aid and development. Rather, most have either been undertaken by or intricately linked to the donor community, even those initiated under the auspices of the United Nations. Their core aim has been to map out a way forward, but one which has always been based on the political status quo. Consequently, recent international public discourse on aid and the solutions which have been reached have been built overwhelmingly on achieving the agreement of the most reluctant of the more powerful donors. It has been a 'least common denominator' approach. International discourse and discussion on aid has thus not been based on trying to create the optimal, or even the second-best, way forward, or been driven by trying to make the *most* effective use of aid—only the most effective use of aid within fixed, politically based, and highly restrictive parameters.

Hence, rather than being an unnecessary diversion, the establishment of an independent international commission on aid and development which has the freedom to address the systemic problems caused by the multiplicity of donors—and the other systemic problems of contemporary aid relationships discussed in other parts of this chapter—is long overdue. As Fransisco Sagasti and his colleagues correctly point out (though their focus is on the financing of aid), 'current institutional arrangements and instruments . . . are woefully inadequate and require major restructuring' (Sagasti *et al.* 2005: 128).

Hence, it is proposed that:

An international commission on aid and development, independent of the donor community and of the (important) discussions taking place about UN reform, should be established.[15] Its remit should include a review and analysis of the strengths and weaknesses of contemporary official and non-governmental aid relationships, including the inadequacy of aid funding, and the systemic effects of the multiplicity of donors, agencies and funds. It should assess whether the way that aid funds are raised, allocated and utilized are adequate to address the current and future problems of poverty and human suffering, especially in the poorest countries, and to provide for the future needs for global and regional public goods, especially those required to address the problems and threats arising from our globalizing world. On the basis of wide consultation with donors and donor organizations, the UN, recipients, civil society organizations (CSOs), non-governmental organizations (NGOs) active in development and emergency work, and the wider academic community, the commission should make recommendations for mapping out and managing aid relationships appropriate to the needs of the twenty-first century.

EFFECTING SYSTEMIC STEP-CHANGES IN EMERGENCY AID RESPONSES

In many ways, the efforts currently under way to address the problems imped-ing the more effective use of emergency aid would appear to mirror the world of development aid. On the one hand, a series of important incremental changes are being made by individual agencies to improve their impact, new initiatives to coordinate better the efforts of different clusters of agencies (especially the UN, Red Cross and NGO providers) are under way, and all these will lead to an improvement in the overall impact of the emergency response in the years ahead. For instance, the newly expanded emergency fund, the Central Emergency Response Fund (CERF), provides a greatly improved way of deploying more funds quickly to where they are needed. The Good Humanitarian Donorship (GHD) initiative has been formally endorsed by the OECD/DAC. It has been providing, and should continue to provide, leadership to improve impact through its efforts to enhance the quality of response, learning and accountability. And the initiatives led by the UN's Emergency Relief Coordinator (ERC) with important support from the Secretary General, most notably those around the *Humanitarian Response Review* (Adinolfi *et al.* 2005), are making significant step-changes to improve coordination and collaboration among different humanitarian agencies.[16]

On the other hand, a number of underlying systemic problems which reduce the effectiveness of the overall response remain largely untouched. What is different from development aid, however, is that there is a far wider acknow-ledgement across agencies and donor governments that systemic problems surrounding emergency aid are fundamentally important to its impact and have to be addressed. In particular, there is broad and growing, and in some cases universal, agreement on the following issues:

• The way that emergency funds are raised, allocated and earmarked to particular agencies is inadequate and needs to be changed.
• The ways in which responses to emergencies are coordinated are wholly inadequate.

- Humanitarianism is changing. It is now understood and defined in a number of different ways. There is a need to agree on its core nature and purpose in today's world.
- Though there is almost universal agreement that the responsibility to protect is an essential part of the humanitarian response, in practice, civilians are repeatedly left unprotected in precisely those situations where rights violations are most serious and extensive.
- Far more needs to be done to enhance the capacity of countries to prepare for emergencies.
- In spite of work undertaken in agreeing standards in the provision of humanitarian aid, in practice the quality of the emergency work undertaken by different agencies today remains extremely variable.

The growing consensus among donors around these issues and the initiatives under way to address them are clearly important. However, mainstream debates about these problems and efforts to address them fall well short of confronting some of the more fundamental and systemic problems of the global response to emergencies which prevent their being adequately addressed. The sorts of changes that could be made, and which do attempt to come to grips with and address these fundamental problems, are illustrated by the following four sets of proposals. These are largely based on discussions taking place among humanitarian aid scholars and informed commentators. Most are far-reaching, and if followed through, would significantly enhance the impact of humanitarian aid.

1. To address funding gaps and problems, the current system of voluntary contributions to discrete emergencies and different agencies needs to be substantially replaced by a comprehensive, and very much enlarged, Global Emergency Fund to which governments are required to contribute, with funds provided on the basis of far more rigorous (annual) overall needs assessments, and a cushion for the unexpected.[17] This would mean overhauling the Consolidated Appeals Process (CAP).[18]

2. Today's global emergency response is built on a coordination-by-consensus mode of operation. Both the allocation of funds from such a revamped Global Emergency Fund and the global response to emergencies needs to be managed, coordinated and led far more effectively by an organization/agency with far greater power than is currently vested in the Emergency Relief Coordinator (ERC), the Office for the Coordination of Humanitarian Affairs (OCHA) and the Inter-Agency Standing Committee (IASC).[19] Such an agency needs to have a remit wide enough to cover all major humanitarian agencies, expertise which is rooted in field knowledge, and the ability to make decisions to ensure effective coordination among key operational agencies. This requires the overall responsibility for overseeing global emergencies to be clearly distinct from the ongoing

work of any particular operational agencies or groups of agencies, not least UN agencies. The powers vested in such an agency need to enable it to ensure overall assessments of need are rigorously undertaken, and the duplication of activities by competing agencies is sharply reduced.

3. Governments need to create a consensus on a strategic vision for, and agree the core purpose of, humanitarian action in today's world, based on the fundamental principles of humanitarianism (independence, impartiality, neutrality). From this starting point, mechanisms need to be agreed and put in place to ensure compliance of actions and activities with these norms and principles. This would probably require oversight by an internationally recognized ombudsman. Within this overall framework, agreement needs urgently to be reached on the implementation of clear and effective processes to ensure that those whose fundamental rights are violated and those in need of protection are, in practice, effectively protected.

4. While there is a continuing need to have an effective international response to emergencies and for some considerable time internationally led coordination of emergencies will still be needed,[20] a step-change in current practice and in perception is required to establish as the default position that responses to emergencies should be led and coordinated by the country in which the emergency occurs.[21] This requires far greater priority to be given to, and resources deployed in, building local capacities. International agencies and the UN should work with countries to develop codes of practice which ensure that only recognized international agencies undertake emergency work, and that their work is driven and shaped by effective consultation and participation with those requiring emergency assistance. For now, where local leadership and coordination is weak and inadequate, and as part of overall emergency preparedness, the UN (through OCHA and/or IASC) should have in place mechanisms to ensure the rapid deployment of an experienced coordinator, equipped with sufficient authority and qualified staff to manage an effective emergency response and to coordinate the work of the major operational agencies.[22]

One practical way in which these and other core proposals for change could be more prominently aired and brought into mainstream debate would be for them to be addressed by the international commission on aid and development proposed above. What this suggests is that such a commission should extend its remit beyond aid and development to include an in-depth review of humanitarian aid and the global response to emergencies, assessing the extent to which current approaches are sufficiently fit for purpose. An added advantage would be that the commission would also be able to address the important but difficult issue of how and where to draw the line between emergency and humanitarian assistance, and what this would mean for current donor practice.

NGOS AND DEVELOPMENT ACTIVITIES AMONG POOR COMMUNITIES: THE GROWING NEED FOR AN OPERATIONAL CODE

Especially over the past two decades, there has been an explosion in the number of NGOs undertaking development work with poor communities in poor countries, resulting in a rapid expansion in the reach and scale of NGO activities. Consequently, NGOs now constitute a major part of the world of development aid. Yet the expansion of NGO engagement in development initiatives with poor communities has not kept pace with the development of processes and systems to monitor and ensure that NGOs make effective use of the growing amount of aid funds made available to them—even though more and more NGOs today readily acknowledge that the more significant their presence in poor countries, the more important it is for them to know— indeed, to help shape—the basic ground-rules within which their development work takes place.

Many NGOs, including all large, many medium-sized, and a growing number of small organizations, are undertaking systematic and increasingly rigorous appraisal, monitoring and impact assessments of their development interventions, specifically to improve impact and effectiveness. Yet significant gaps remain. Similarly, in many countries and localities in which NGO development work takes place, the ability of external agencies to oversee and monitor NGO activities, or sometimes even their knowledge of where they are working and what they do, remains limited. Indeed, NGO development activities have expanded most rapidly in those countries in which legislation, regulation and the ability of the authorities to approve and monitor the quality of NGO development interventions is weakest. This growth has often been facilitated by greater access to official aid funds provided by donors trying to circumvent government agencies deemed to lack the competence or commitment to use funds effectively. At the extreme, NGO development activities take place completely unsupervised, and in localities where there is no effective state or non-state alternative provider. Donors are increasingly funding NGOs to provide and deliver services to whole communities over large geographical areas, where no one monitors whether principles of equal access or minimal quality standards are met.

There is often, too, a paucity of information readily explaining how and why local communities agree to work with particular NGOs and not with others. Equally, there is often a lack of information concerning the methods used by NGOs to engage with communities in order to decide how the funds which they have allocated for development work with these communities are to be spent, and priorities agreed, and what mechanisms exist for those who feel the need to be able, without fear, to file complaints and, at the extreme, seek redress. At a time when more and more NGOs are adopting a rights-based approach to their work, which attaches fundamental importance to the engagement with and participation of beneficiaries in all the crucial decisions about their development, these issues are central to the development approach of most NGOs. Similarly, as noted in Chapter 16, the advances that have undoubtedly been made in undertaking more rigorous appraisal and monitoring and assessment of projects have not been matched by efforts to place impact assessment reports in the public domain. In short, there is a large, and almost certainly a growing, gap between the increasing responsibilities which NGOs readily undertake and the quality and flow of information to provide assurances that aid funds are being used effectively.

The vast majority of NGOs recognize the need to be increasingly transparent and accountable for their development work to their funders and supporters but, importantly too, to their beneficiaries. The crucial question is how. Part of the answer lies in undertaking, commissioning and placing in the public domain evidence of the impact of their work. But, especially when working in environments in which there is usually no effective external agency able to monitor their work, NGOs are increasingly acknowledging the need to do far more than this. More and more NGOs recognize:

- the need to provide assurances of their competence and capability to undertake development work, often in a privileged context where no alternative agency exists.
- the need to provide assurances—not least to the beneficiaries—of their ability to provide services to an acceptable standard and, where there is no other provider, to supply those services to all in an equitable manner.
- the need to provide assurances that the methods and approaches they use to engage with poor people and communities are informed, shaped and consistent with the core principles of beneficiary participation, the bedrock of all their development work, and that there are mechanisms and processes in place for those aggrieved to seek redress.

To strive to provide these assurances is far more demanding than merely producing a documented historical record of projects after they have been completed. It requires adopting a more comprehensive approach to accountability, but one which, in the absence of effective external verification, has to be internally driven rather than externally imposed. One tangible way forward is for NGOs to complement more general initiatives aimed at enhancing their accountability and transparency by developing for themselves specific standards for their development work among poor people and poor communities which would provide the basis for them to account publicly for these activities, especially those undertaken in environments with little or no external surveillance or monitoring of their activities.[23] A growing number of NGOs recognize that changes along these lines are needed, indeed that they are long overdue.[24]

Against this backdrop, and more specifically, it is proposed that:

NGOs, particularly those undertaking development work in environments with little to no external surveillance or monitoring of their activities, should draw up specific standards and norms for undertaking and assessing their development project work among poor people and poor communities. These would be brought together in simplified but concrete 'operational codes of conduct'. These codes of conduct would be 'live' working documents, which would provide the key benchmarks against which to monitor their own performance on the ground, and to review the progress and performance of their interventions against the norms set.[25] The reviews would also provide the basis for giving a public account of their development project activities. Over time, and on the basis of lessons learned, these operational codes would be revised.

Clearly the details would need to be worked out. What is envisaged here is not a single operational code for all NGOs, externally imposed upon them, but rather the evolution and development of different practicable codes applicable to different types of NGOs working in different contexts and environments. Larger and more complex projects (run and managed by bigger NGOs) would require operational codes of conduct covering more details of performance against more key indicators; smaller projects (run by locally based NGOs) would be far simpler and 'lighter' ones.

Why would NGOs adopt this type of approach to accountability? A major attraction is that it would be developed by the NGOs themselves, using the core norms and principles on which their work is based, and to which they are themselves committed. Its strength as a tool of accountability would be built on the views of NGOs' key stakeholders, on the fact that it encompasses the main dimensions of NGO development work, and on the integrity of the assessments of performance against the standards and norms adopted. Additionally, the approach is not new. Indeed, as discussed in Chapter 18, a growing number of larger NGOs involved in emergency work have already drawn up, agreed and adopted norms and standards in emergency work under the Sphere initiative, against which they have begun to be judged and held accountable. Similarly, in a growing number of aid-recipient countries, NGOs are required to sign general codes of conduct as a requirement for affiliation to national representative bodies.[26] What this proposal does is to extend to NGO development work the principles which have already been accepted in NGO emergency work though what is envisaged here is, operationally, a far more hands-on and less complex tool.[27]

'JUST GIVE CASH TO THOSE WHO NEED THE AID'

Most poor people and poor communities have no knowledge of how development aid provided to help them is used, and even when development aid is directly targeted to poor people and poor communities, it has often been personnel within aid agencies and not the poor people themselves who have decided how aid should best be given—in the form of goods, services, information, awareness-raising and skills training. In recent years, most aid agencies have recognized the importance of consulting beneficiaries in decisions about aid provided directly to assist them. However, today, only a tiny amount of aid (almost certainly less than 10 per cent) is given directly to poor people and poor communities for them to choose how to use it.

For many years, humanitarian agencies have handed out goods free to those in need during emergencies, especially food. More recently, both humanitarian and other aid agencies have given food aid in return for work, and, more recently, cash for work. However, very little aid has been provided to those in need simply as 'free' cash, enabling people to spend it as they think fit. Though increasingly wishing to make a tangible difference to very poor people, donors have shied away from providing cash for extreme poverty. Historically, a reluctance to give cash directly to poor people has often been based on the belief that they will 'only spend it on immediate consumption goods' (and thus that it will be 'wasted'), and on the linked paternalistic, and condescending, view that poor people do not know how best to use it. These beliefs sit uncomfortably alongside the increasingly mainstream view that beneficiary choice and participation are fundamental to the aid relationship.

Especially over the past five to ten years, both research and some examples of donor practice have begun to challenge past practices and these historical perceptions and prejudices. Unsurprisingly, recent studies in poor countries confirm decades of research in the industrialized world that transfers to poor people, families and households, in the form of cash, vouchers for services, and in-kind benefits, can contribute significantly and directly to poverty reduction, as well as stimulating production and employment opportunities in local economies.[28] In some cases, cash transfers have been very effective in raising incomes and improving the health status of poor people; in others, providing vouchers tied to the 'purchase' of services has proved effective; while in some countries, the regular payment of targeted pension payments has been of major benefit to poor people.[29] Additionally, providing aid in this way is usually a far cheaper way of administering and distributing aid funds.

On the basis of this evidence, the case for significantly enhancing the impact of aid by giving it directly to poor people would seem to be compelling. However, the issue is more complex. A key question is whether aid agencies should try to channel the money to the poor, or whether the funds should be given to governments to boost their own social protection schemes. Unsurprisingly, the success of government schemes tends to be related to the availability of adequate and sustained financing, the capacity and capability of governments to manage programmes effectively, and their political commitment. Where these conditions do not obtain, as in many fragile states, the best alternative would be for aid agencies themselves to provide or oversee the distribution of 'cash aid'. However, there is no guarantee that aid agencies will be able effectively to provide adequate and sustained financing. Most official aid agencies have very little experience of working directly with poor communities. NGO experience is certainly more extensive, but even NGOs admit that they still have much to learn about what works and why, and, especially, how to scale up and extend what have often been small projects assisting only a relatively small number of beneficiaries (Devereux *et al.* 2005: vi, 51–4). Additionally, even NGOs find it difficult to identify the neediest in some contexts, and to ensure that those receiving funds, especially women, are able to use them as they wish. In many poor communities, poverty is manifested in indebtedness to rich and powerful elites, restricting the ability of poor people to spend money on their own priorities.

Notwithstanding these complexities and difficulties, there is almost certainly considerable scope for providing more aid directly to poor people and poor communities, informed by further research to expand our (still limited) understanding of the effectiveness of cash and voucher schemes. But perhaps of even greater importance is the need to challenge the historical reluctance of donors, official and non-governmental alike, seriously to provide aid in this form in a major way. Against this backdrop the following proposal is made:

The OECD/DAC should initiate a new work programme further to understand, encourage and promote donor 'best practice' in providing more aid in the form of cash payments or other social transfer schemes to poor people and poor communities. The proposed work programme would include a review of current knowledge of the impact and cost-effectiveness of both emergency and development aid provided through social transfer schemes, including direct cash payments, by official aid agencies, NGOs and other providers. It should also examine why donors have been reluctant to provide aid in these forms, and provide guidance for donors seeking to expand these aid modalities.[30]

AN INTERNATIONAL TASK FORCE ON PUBLIC INFORMATION AND AID

Debates about the impact of aid are influenced by the information available about its effects, and particularly by the nature and quality of that information. Though there is a vast—indeed, an exploding—literature on aid, informed judgements about aid are hampered by two factors. The first, as discussed in Part III, is that there are still relatively few rigorous assessments of aid's impact, particularly those which examine the impact and influence of aid beyond the level of discrete projects. The second, as discussed in Chapter 7, is the biased nature of the information on aid's impact placed in the public domain.

Most information reaching the public is put out by the agencies, official and non-governmental, which provide the aid. This kind of presentation does not attempt to give a rounded picture of the impact of the aid which each agency provides, because this is not its purpose. Its purpose is to show that the aid which the agency provides does indeed 'work'. For example, in mid-2006, the UK's Department For International Development (DFID) published a booklet entitled *Development Aid Works 52 Weeks a Year*. Its purpose was to 'show the range of work DFID supports and the real impact it is making ... [providing] a convincing collection of stories to prove that real change is possible' (DFID 2006a: i). As this example illustrates, the information provided by aid agencies is dominated by positive examples of aid working, illustrated by highlighting the short-term impact of discrete aid projects. In emergencies in particular, the reporting of aid successes is frequently dominated by 'easy win' stories and examples. Official donors and NGOs alike consistently tell us how many people have been helped, how many lives they have helped save, how many people they have helped feed. The vast majority of agencies provide no information to tell us the extent to which they achieved the standards in aid delivery that they have pledged to meet.

Do these gaps and distortions in our knowledge about aid matter? In three different ways they do. First, there is the question of integrity. For many, it is a basic axiom, of both scholarship and public life, that the truth should always be pursued and told. Giving a distorted picture of what aid achieves self-evidently violates this principle. Secondly, the less that is known about the impact of aid, the more likely it is that aid will be provided in ways that are ineffective. It is for this reason that official aid agencies have increased the priority they attach, and the resources they are allocating to, assessing the more systemic impact of aid. Similarly, in recent years, influential aid think-tanks have called for more assessments of the impact of aid to be undertaken by independent scholars and agencies, as, in their view, there are serious questions to be answered about the integrity of the results of evaluations undertaken by or under the control of the agencies whose aid is being assessed.[31]

The third reason why distortions in the information about aid matter concerns public support for aid. Put briefly (the issue is discussed more fully in Chapters 7 and 18), over many years, public support for aid has remained strong, and, believing that support for aid needs to be based on good-news about its impact, agencies continually provide a stream of good news stories about what aid has achieved. This creates both an immediate risk and a long-term problem. The short-term risk is that support for aid is likely to fall sharply when (or if) the public is provided with a more rounded picture of what we know about aid's impact: namely, that far less is known about the over-all impact of aid than agencies are ready to admit, and from the evidence that we have, it is far less effective than the bulk of the information provided by aid agencies would suggest. The long-term problem is that by continually drip-feeding information on aid which is biased towards aid's successes, aid agencies reinforce the view that support for aid *has* to be based on evidence of its success, and that *donors* have the power and ability to make aid 'work'. In sharp contrast, as this book has shown, for development aid to achieve consistent positive results is not merely difficult—even more difficult in countries in which it is needed most—but whether aid works or not is largely out of the hands of donors. Consequently, while no one is suggesting that aid should be provided to recipients when it is known that it won't work, support for aid needs to be based less on believing and convincing the public that it necessarily will work, or does work, and more on appreciating that it often doesn't, and that efforts continually have to be focused on understanding how to improve its impact.

The conclusion, then, is that the distortions in the way information about aid is provided do matter—possibly greatly. The more difficult question to answer is how they might be effectively addressed. The core problem is that information distortions are largely systemic. It is difficult to attribute blame to any aid agency, official or NGO, for wanting to put its own aid efforts in the best possible light. Indeed, an individual agency would risk inducing a fall in support, and in funding streams, were it unilaterally to provide a more rounded (and accurate) assessment of its achievements when other agencies did not do the same. Yet, the cumulative effect of each agency continuing to feed the public with repeated positive images of its activities and impact is to create and perpetuate a distorted (false) picture of aid's overall impact. What is needed is a way of providing the public with a more balanced view of aid's impact and the factors constraining its effectiveness. If the public were to be provided with a more informed and accurate picture of aid's overall impact and potential, the evidence of aid's failures would provide insufficient grounds for reaching the misguided conclusion that aid should not be provided because it doesn't work. The outcome would be that public support would likely be less fickle and fragile, and more concerned with ensuring that lessons are learned to try to make aid work more effectively.

Yet how this might come about is very difficult to envisage. The problem is that no aid agency or group of aid agencies is responsible for providing 'overall' information about the impact of aid. Neither the OECD/DAC nor umbrella organizations of NGOs have acknowledged that they have a role to play in correcting the systemic distortions in the information provided by their members. The following proposal provides one way of trying to advance discussion on how to address distortions in the way information about aid is provided and presented. It clearly does not provide a complete answer.

An independent High-Level Task Force on Public Information on Aid should be established (possibly under the umbrella of the United Nations) with a remit to appraise and review the ways that information about aid and aid impact is presented to the public, and its effects on support for aid. The Task Force would take evidence from both official aid agencies and NGOs, as well as from the media. It would consider ways in which the gap between the actual impact of aid and the mainstream information provided about the impact of aid might be narrowed, and realistic expectations of aid's potential impact might be better conveyed, and the role that existing or new agencies might play in achieving these objectives.[32]

Bridging the divide between ideas and implementation

In varying forms, nearly all the proposals and recommendations to address the systemic problems with aid presented in this chapter have been made before. Many of the most challenging ones have been dismissed with faint praise: nice ideas, but impractical or unworkable, or else unlikely to be taken seriously by those who matter.[33] Here we consider the mix of ingredients necessary to enable them to 'fly'.

To start with, they need to be more widely noticed, their importance to aid impact more clearly appreciated, and debate about them injected more centrally into current mainstream discussions of aid effectiveness. Unless this happens, they will remain what they are: merely nice ideas about how to enhance the impact of aid, but little more than that. Individuals and researchers, with their books and articles, can make a contribution, not least by challenging unsound conventional wisdoms, and by drawing attention to the opportunities lost by avoiding substantive discussions about core problems and how they might be resolved. But, on their own, these contributions have an extremely limited direct impact on achieving effective change.

In contrast, the networks of organizations which advocate, lobby and campaign on aid issues, and which have become increasingly influential in the past 10–15 years, have a major role to play—first, by getting new and different ideas on aid noticed, and secondly, by their proven ability to elicit responses from aid agencies and political leaders to the challenges they make. But for such agencies to 'take up and run with' these fundamental systemic issues in a major way will require them to shift their attention away from the 'easy' messages and targets that have dominated their activities over recent years. The campaigning, lobbying and advocacy initiatives undertaken by large organizations based in the industrialized countries have been dominated by the following: for the 0.7 per cent ODA–GNI ratio to be reached, for an end to the tying of aid, and for the link between donors' commercial interests and the development and humanitarian purposes of aid to be severed. These are not unimportant issues, but they are marginal to some of the core underlying problems with aid. Some agencies, such as ActionAid International in its study *Real Aid: An Agenda for Making Aid Really Work* (AAI 2005: 53), have begun to call for action to address some of the systemic issues which impede aid's impact. It is these sorts of initiatives—which are taking a fresh look at, and are beginning to challenge, the failures of governments and aid agencies to address some of aid's more fundamental problems arising from contemporary aid relationships—which provide some ground for optimism that debates about aid are beginning to shift.

However, far more needs to be done by more lobby and campaign groups if these core issues are to be more widely noticed. This is not as easy as one might think because most of the larger NGOs that lobby and campaign on aid issues are also operational agencies, running themselves, or overseeing, development and emergency programmes in poor countries. It is far from easy for them to raise searching questions about, to challenge and to call for fundamental change to, a system of which they are a part, and from which they benefit, both directly and indirectly. Not surprisingly, therefore, within most of these agencies internal tensions are evident between those who believe their role is to confront, lobby and campaign for these core systemic problems to be effectively addressed, and those who believe that to take on these challenges in a major way would risk damaging their operational role and the funds which lubricate it.[34] As noted above, NGOs have often been as guilty as official aid agencies in suggesting, in their informational literature, a far greater lasting impact of their own aid projects and programmes than the evidence would support.

Getting these ideas into the mainstream and having them aired, debated and placed centrally on the agendas of international and intergovernmental conferences is a necessary first step, but far from sufficient. To achieve substantial and effective change requires political action, and this will only come about if world statesmen and stateswomen can be convinced of both the need for, and the desirability of, such change. Hard and persistent advocacy, lobbying and campaign work will help to create a different vision of aid relationships. But it will not itself create a new international consensus across donor and recipient nations on the need to create a more effective and efficient way of raising and using aid funds. This will require, above all, key political leaders to believe that a different future is possible and to persuade others to help create it. The problem is that most 'serious' contemporary discourse about improving aid remains predominantly focused on marginal change, because incremental steps forward are believed to be the only ones achievable.[35] All else is politely, and often impolitely, dismissed as pie in the sky. However, political change is not only based on successive small incremental changes. It is also based on politicians, often led by one or two leaders and governments, having the vision and conviction to do things substantially differently, spurred on by the knowledge that systemic and far-reaching political changes can and do occur.[36]

Far-reaching changes to the international system, of which aid is a part, can and do take place, so radical change should not be dismissed as a non-starter. Towards the end of the 1980s, I was invited to a closed and confidential meeting in London in which the former United States National Security Advisor, Zbigniew Brzezinski, explained to a growingly incredulous audience that communism was about to end, that the Soviet Union would soon crumble, and that the Berlin Wall would eventually be dismantled. What was even more surprising was that what almost everyone in the room believed to be impossible occurred even more rapidly than the speaker had predicted. These momentous events set in motion political changes that the generation brought up in the post-war era had been led to believe were impossible. The unfolding of these events could have provided the catalyst necessary to confront the anomalies in prevailing aid relationships. Indeed, altering some of the fundamentals in contemporary aid relationships would have involved a far less radical change to post-war international relations. But the opportunity was lost, not least because the world was focused on what were judged, in the short term, to be more pressing issues.

Cumulatively over the past ten years, events, processes and decisions have been taking place in international relations and in international relations discourse to create a new window of opportunity to confront these anomalies. There is a greater and growing realization that the issues of extreme poverty and acute human suffering are central issues for international relations, and a growing belief that these can only be solved by rich and poor nations confronting them and trying to address them together. What is more, a formal commitment (though not a contract) to do this in the framework of the Millennium Declaration has now been made. In parallel with these changes, and with growing frequency over the past decade, almost all major donor governments have repeatedly confirmed their belief that providing aid to the poorest countries is, for them, a moral issue.

If there is a compelling moral case for governments to provide aid to the poorest, then most would agree that there is an equally strong case for analysing what constrains and impedes the ability of aid to make a greater difference to extreme poverty and acute human suffering. And if some of these key constraints to making a crucial difference lie in some of the long-standing ways aid has been delivered and received, then there is a strong moral and political case for changing these and doing things differently. Compared with many other contemporary international problems, and the sizeable shifts in political relationships which have been brokered, the changes required would be small, but the potential rewards would be enormous. What is needed are more people, agencies and institutions, influential newspapers and media outlets, who have the vision, believe such change is possible, and who will work, ideally together, to make it happen.[37]

■ NOTES

1 'A good thing'?

1. In the mid-1980s, especially, a number of books focused explicitly on the impact and effectiveness of foreign aid, most notably Cassen 1986. Some ten years later, a new wave of influential books on aid and development were produced, including World Bank 1998, Tarp and Hjerhelm 2000 and Degnbol-Martinussen and Engberg-Pedersen 2003. (This last volume was the English edition of a Danish book originally written and published in 1999).

2. This list omits one major area of contemporary discourse on aid's possible different future, namely the role of aid in supplying international and regional public goods. Though this issue is of importance, and is referred to in a number of places in this volume, the book contains no in-depth discussion of the use of aid beyond 'conventional' uses to its potential role in helping to supply international public goods and to address international public 'bads'. Chapter 22, note 12, refers readers to key literature and a website which discuss ways in which aid might be used in this new way.

3. The first part of Chapter 2 discusses the definitions of aid in more detail.

4. This total includes about $10bn provided by governments, which is thus included in the overall ODA figure. Chapters 2, 4 and 16 discuss how these different figures have been estimated.

2 The origins and early decades of aid-giving

1. The term 'foreign assistance' has been more commonly used in the United States, but increasingly, US-based literature has also used the term 'foreign aid'.

2. Some scholars and specialists using a 'purpose-based' definition have focused less sharply on the poverty and welfare dimensions of aid. For instance Krueger, Michalopoulos and Ruttan (1989: 1) define (foreign) aid as 'an instrument used by a government to strengthen the economy of another country'.

3. However, there has been some intense debate in recent years about whether official aid data, in particular, accurately reflect the 'true' value of the aid provided. See, for instance, AAI (2005) and Roodman (2004a, b).

4. The DAC was initially called the Development Assistance Group (DAG), formed as an organ of the Organisation for European Economic Co-operation (OEEC), reconstituted as the OECD in December 1960. See Führer (1994: 11–12).

5. For details see OECD (2005b: 236–44.)

6. For details see <www.oecd.org/document/40/0,2340,en_2649_33721_36418344_1_1_1_1,00.html> (accessed 22 June 2006).

7. As discussed later in the chapter, however, the definitions of ODA and OA do include official aid funds provided directly to or channelled through NGOs. In recent years a growing amount of official aid has been provided directly to or channelled through NGOs.

8. In the case of ODA, this would only include humanitarian aid resources provided by official donors, not those provided by NGOs raised from private and corporate donations.

9. There are some exceptions, however, such as the United States, where some distinction is made between overall assistance and aid funds. In recent years, the United States Congress has regularly approved as aid funds some $3bn more than the amounts the OECD/DAC records for US ODA, even though a significant proportion of funds which are deemed to be ODA by the OECD/DAC are provided principally for strategic purposes.

10. These issues are discussed again in different parts of the book, especially in Chapters 6, 8 and 9.

11. Their study of the aid of the seven largest donors concluded that different factors were responsible for different trends in aid levels in different donor countries.

12. For a more detailed discussion of the early days of post-1949 aid, see OECD (1985), Krueger *et al.* (1989), Browne (1990), Lumsdaine (1993), and Dichter (2003), from which material in these paragraphs has been drawn.

13. See Eunice, K. Y. 'African Churches' Effort in Africa's Revival Widely Recognised', *Christian Today*, 22 Nov. 2004, available at <www.christiantoday.com/news/africa/african.churches. effort.in.africas.revival.widely.recognised/136.htm> (accessed 19 July 2005).

14. Official aid statistics for the 1950s are known to be inaccurate. Estimates for this period are based upon the OECD's statistical data-base, and Pearson (1969: 379–82).

3 Aid-giving from the 1970s to the present

1. The UNDP was officially constituted in 1965 as a new organization, formed from the merger of the UN's Special Fund and the Expanded Programme of Technical Assistance (EPTA), created in 1949.

2. The redistribution-with-growth approach additionally encompassed proposals for narrowing income and wealth differentials, and for enhancing the assets of poor people in order to expand opportunities.

3. One of the main reasons for disillusion with these complex rural projects was precisely because of their failure to integrate their different constituent parts.

4. Replenishments to the World Bank's IDA during the decade affirmed the secular rise in aid-giving: funds provided by IDA were doubled in 1972 to $2.5bn at the third replenishment, increased to $4.5bn in the mid-1970s, and then rose to $7.7bn for the fifth replenishment, for disbursement to the year 1980.

5. Germany had begun to do this in the 1960s.

6. The Commission was independent and began its work in 1977 with a remit 'to study the grave global issues arising from the economic and social disparities of the world community'. It promised to 'suggest ways of promoting adequate solutions to the problems involved in development and in attacking absolute poverty' (Brandt 1980: 8).

7. British ODA began to fall in 1979.

8. The Brandt Reports were not wholly disconnected from donor discourse. For instance, in September 1981, at the UN conference on the least developed countries, 'most' donor countries committed themselves to reach a target of 0.15 per cent of GNI for ODA to the least developed (within the overall 0.7 per cent target), with 'others' agreeing to double their aid to these countries, so that, overall by 1985, they should receive twice the aid received in 1981.

9. The Brandt Commission was not the only one to appeal for large increases in aid which failed to materialize. In 1981, the World Bank called for a fourfold increase in aid (ODA) to Africa, from $4.9bn in 1980 to $17.8bn in 1990, a doubling of ODA in real terms (World Bank 1981: 123).

10. The World Bank led in formally providing structural adjustment aid and loans which came with a raft of conditions, with the International Monetary Fund (only marginally involved in providing highly concessional loans, thus ODA) demanding equally harsh conditions as a prerequisite for access to its shorter-term stabilization loans. In practice, most bilateral donors eventually fell in line with the main tenets of such approaches and conditionalities.

11. Figures from the United Nations, Food and Agriculture Organisation (FAO), available at <www.fao.org/documents/show_cdr.asp?url_file=/docrep/W6020E/w6020e01.htm> (accessed 21 July 2005).

12. As discussed later in this chapter, aggregate international statistics on income and income sources of NGOs are known to be inaccurate.

13. The Global Environmental Facility (GEF), established in 1991, provided over $4bn to poor countries in the years 1991 to 2003. Fiscal deficits declined from 4.3 per cent of GDP in 1993 to a far smaller 1.3 per cent by 1977.

14. Widely quoted in the media were studies by Boone (1994, 1996).

15. These themes and issues are discussed in detail in Chapters 18 and 19.

16. An early contribution was the book by Cornia, Jolly and Stewart (1998).

17. This approach, in turn, has been particularly influenced by the writings of Amartya Sen, most notably his work on freedoms and capabilities. These are discussed further in Chapter 8.

18. These include, most notably, World Bank (1998) and World Bank (2002a).

19. These included the Education for All Summit (1990), the World Summit for Children (1990), and the World Summits on the Environment and Development (1992), Human Rights (1993), Population and Development (1994), the Social Summit (1995), Women (1995) and Habitat for Humanity (1996). See Jones and Colman (2005: 42).

20. The following is one example: 'It is . . . clear that an effort to build stronger compacts with developing countries on a foundation of shrinking resources and declining commitment will lack credibility. Therefore it is necessary to express, once again, our deep concern that domestic preoccupations and budgetary pressures in some Member countries seriously jeopardise the international co-operation effort at a critical juncture' (OECD 1996: 16–17).

21. For the full text see <www.un.org/millennium/declaration/ares552e.htm> (accessed 22 July 2005).

22. The full details of the MDGs can be found at <www.un.org/documents/ga/docs/56/a56326. pdf> (accessed 22 July 2005).

23. Its report, *Financing for Development* (Zedillo 2001), is available at <www.un.org/reports/ financing/full_report.pdf> (accessed 27 July 2005).

24. The agreed consensus document can be found at <www.un.org/esa/ffd/0302-finalMonterreyConsensus.pdf> (accessed 25 July 2005).

25. 'Transaction costs' refers to the costs of providing, appraising, monitoring, assessing the impact of, and in general administering aid programmes and projects. 'Tied aid' is the practice of donors restricting the ability of recipients to choose how they can use aid allocated to them, often by requiring them to purchase goods or services from the donor country. These issues are discussed further in Chapter 6.

26. The Africa Partnership Forum had been set up earlier to monitor progress within Africa. The Africa Progress Panel will also report to this body.

27. By the year 2010, the aim is for at least 75 per cent of aid-recipient countries to have in place operational national development strategies, for 85 per cent of aid flows to be aligned to national priorities, for at least 75 per cent of aid monies to be disbursed in a medium-term

and more predictable time frame, and for at least 25 per cent of ODA to be provided in the form of programme aid (predominantly SWAps or budget support). The details are discussed more fully in later chapters of the book.

28. See the Appendix to the Gleneagles Agreement, available at <http://news.bbc.co.uk/1/shared/bsp/hi/pdfs/g8_gleneagles_communique.pdf> (accessed 25 July 2005).

29. At the Gleneagles G8 Summit, President Bush stated that US aid to Africa had tripled since 2000, and he pledged to double aid to Africa. However, in a detailed study of trends in US ODA, Radelet and Siddiqi (2005) concluded that US ODA to Africa had only doubled, and that the pledge to double aid in the future was a recommitment to previous pledges rather than an announcement of anything new.

30. However, one indicator of more tangible progress is provided by the most recent Replenishment of IDA resources (IDA 13), finalized in April 2005. Donors agreed to contribute $18bn of new funds to the $34bn that will be available for the period July 2005 to the end of June 2008; this represents a 25 per cent increase over IDA 13 and the largest expansion of IDA funds for two decades.

31. Part of this concern is linked to history: in the 1980s, the World Bank introduced Country Assistance Strategies (CAS), which were based on the country's own vision of its development but which also included the Bank's own diagnosis of the countries' problems and proposed ways forward.

32. SWAps and budget support are discussed more fully in Chapter 12.

33. Details of the main funds are provided in Chapter 5.

34. The 2004 figure of $23bn is built up as follows. The OECD data-base records total grants (private flows) made by NGOs as $14.9bn and total ODA given by donors to NGOs as $1.8bn (OECD 2006a: 168, 178). Additionally, in early 2005, OECD/DAC officials estimated that as well as the funds governments provide to NGOs ($1.8bn in 2004), approximately $4bn more was used by NGOs to implement official aid projects (termed funds 'through NGOs'). The $4bn estimate was based on an amount of $1.7bn channelled through NGOs by the United States government (OEDC/DAC source, personal communication). However, figures published in 2006 by USAID showed that in 2004, $2.7bn went to NGOs from USAID (USAID 2006: 154, 176), suggesting that the total passing through NGOs in 2004 would have been closer to $5bn. Finally, it is estimated that at least $1.5bn is used by NGOs in the form of in-kind contributions (for all US voluntary agencies registered with USAID, a third of their total private income of $15bn consists of the estimated value of in-kind contributions, though the totals given here include funds used both within the United States and abroad). Adding up all these figures gives a total of $23.2bn. This estimate is low, both because only half of OCED/DAC donors report the amounts of aid they channel through NGOs, and because the figures exclude any income raised by national NGOs in developing countries, which is at present probably well in excess of $500mn. A few years ago, American Foundations provided NGOs with more than $1bn for their international activities (Reimann 2006: 54). Today the amounts are far higher than this.

35. In March 2005, of the organizations which participated in the Paris High-Level Forum on Aid Effectiveness, 14 out of 45 organizations (35 per cent) were NGOs and civil society groups.

4 The growing web of bilateral aid donors

1. The OECD/DAC lists 166 multilateral (international) agencies who report ODA receipts or disbursements, available at <www.oecd.org/dataoecd/36/16/31724727.pdf> (accessed 21 Sept. 2005).

2. DAC membership consists of the 22 countries listed in Table 4.1, plus the European Commission. Non-DAC OECD donors include the Czech Republic, Hungary, Iceland, South Korea, Poland, the Slovak Republic and Turkey. Non-OECD donors include Kuwait, Saudi Arabia, the United Arab Emirates, Israel and China. Among these, Saudi Arabia, South Korea and China are the three largest donors. The OECD produces no aid statistics for China. The data on multilateral ODA are discussed further in Chapter 5.

3. From the late 1980s, some bilateral donors expanded their funding of NGOs to include recipient-country NGOs. However, outside particular countries, such as Bangladesh, these funds have remained far lower than the ODA funds provided to NGOs from donor countries.

4. For India alone, Thakur and Saxena (1999: 14) estimate that there are one million non-profit organizations, of which about half were considered active.

5. Figure quoted in Reimann (2006: 45).

6. See Anheier *et al.* (2004: 320).

7. At that time, the government of Bangladesh registered 13,000 NGOs, of which 843 were Bangladeshi NGOs engaged in development work, as well as 150 foreign development NGOs (Ojanperä 1997: 1).

8. Ian Smillie draws attention to comments by one of the most respected writers on NGOs, David Korten, about the difficulty NGOs have often had in working seriously with one another (Smillie 1994: 23). Though writing some years ago, Korten (1987) observed that 'Jealousies among them are often intense . . . [paralysing] efforts to work together towards achievement of shared purposes'. However, the past decade has seen major efforts by groups of NGOs, especially those in the humanitarian aid field, to work more closely together.

9. Obtaining an accurate figure of the share of overall NGO funds used by NGOs of different sizes is particularly difficult, as many of the larger NGOs are themselves funders of smaller NGOs.

10. These are drawn from the 2006 Federal Budget; see <www.house.gov/budget/prezbudget. htm> (accessed 3 Aug. 2005). For an historical perspective see Lancaster: 2006: 62–109.

11. Some exceptions, for instance in case of emergency, are allowed. Since early 2002, a waiver to US law permits the United States to implement the OECD/DAC recommendation to untie ODA to the least developed countries. However, food aid and free-standing technical cooperation, consisting of major components of US ODA, are, by mutual agreement, excluded from the recommendation's coverage.

12. For an informative and accessible discussion of the origins of the 0.7 per cent target and the United States' attitude to it see Clemens and Moss (2005).

13. For up to date information on the MCA see the following webpages: <www.mcc.gov/ about_us/congressional_reports/index.shtml> and <www.cgdev.org/section/initiatives/ _active/mcamonitor>.

14. See Woods (2005). The impact and influence of the political and strategic interests of donors on aid allocations is discussed in Chapter 6.

15. For a recent review and assessment of the way the US Administration approaches poorly performing states see Birdsall *et al.* (2006).

16. For FY 2006/7, expenditure of $6.5bn on US HIV/AIDS work was planned, but with only $600mn allocated to the Global Fund, available at <www.stat.gov/s/gac/coop/gfund/ index.htm> (accessed 1 Feb. 2006). The 2007 aid budget provides for $3.4bn in total assistance for HIV/AIDS.

17. According to a former senior US aid official, Carol Lancaster, the changes are unlikely to address the 'organisational chaos' that has been a feature of US ODA, though it is likely to

increase the influence of short-term political factors on the development programmes of USAID: 'Bush's Foreign Aid Reforms Do Not Go Far Enough', *Financial Times*, 19 Jan. 2006.

18. The most recent OECD/DAC study of Japan (2004) highlights the continuing lack of coherence among and within different official agencies as a major weakness, resulting in ODA continuing to be used to promote Japanese rather than recipient-country goals (OECD 2004a: 12).

19. See Morrissey (2005) for details and for a review of other trends and changes in British official aid since 1997.

20. However, in line with the rest of the civil service, DFID is having to cut staff numbers (by 10 per cent to 2008), which, as noted by the 2006 DAC Peer Review, sits uncomfortably with an expanded aid budget and a commitment to increasing aid quality (OECD 2006d: 11).

21. Under the leadership of Secretary of State Clare Short, Britain became an active member of the Utstein Group of like-minded donors, including Germany, the Netherlands, Sweden, committed to increasing aid levels internationally, achieving greater harmonization and co-ordination of ODA, and achieving higher levels of debt relief. For further details see <www.u4.no/projects/utstein/utsteinprinciples.cfm> (accessed 31 July 2005).

22. Priority partner countries are those for which all development instruments may be deployed and for which country strategy papers are to be drawn up, whereas in partner countries, aid is generally to be focused on only one priority area. Outside this primary grouping is a more fluid cluster of 'potential cooperation countries', with which Germany might in future like to cooperate but for which, at present, the context remains unsuitable.

23. In November 2003, the former European Community (EC) changed its name to the European Union (EU), a union at present of 25 independent European states. However, official development assistance provided by the EU is still termed EC ODA by the OECD.

24. How EU aid is and ought to be classified is discussed further in Chapter 5.

25. The extent of these problems is well illustrated by the comments made by the former Development Commissioner Poul Nielsen, shortly after taking up his post in the year 2000: 'the Commission machine was never constructed to deliver development assistance. It was designed for producing directives, regulations, trade negotiations, to facilitate political relations between EU states. For development assistance it doesn't work' (quoted in Olsen 2005b: 598).

26. In Norway's case, this is well summarized in its 2003–4 report (no. 35) to the Störting (parliament), entitled *Fighting Poverty Together: A Comprehensive Development Policy*; available at <odin. dep.no/filarkiv/226164/1_Introduction_and_summary.pdf> (accessed 9 Sept. 2005).

27. For recent overviews of Norwegian and Dutch official aid, see Jones *et al.* (2004), Schulpen (2005) and Stokke (2005).

28. The early years and evolution of Swedish development cooperation are well described in Frühling (1986). For a more recent study of Swedish aid see Danielson and Wohlgemuth (2005), which concludes that notwithstanding decades of intensive debate and discussion, Swedish aid remains today little changed from earlier decades (p. 543).

29. For a historical review of Canadian aid see Pratt (1996) and Freedman (2000).

30. Canada's most recent approach to aid is contained in the government's 2005 policy statement, *A Role of Pride and Influence in the World: Development*; available at <www.acdi-cida.gc.ca/ INET/IMAGES.NSF/vLUImages/IPS_PDF_EN/$file/IPS-EN.pdf> (accessed 9 Sept. 2005).

31. For a discussion of the recent history and development of Italian ODA see Rhi-Sausi and Zupi (2005).

32. Available at <www.um.dk/Publikationer/Danida/English/DanishDevelopmentCooperation/ AWorldOfDifference/index.asp> (accessed 9 Sept. 2005).

33. A more detailed review and assessment of Danish aid is contained in Degnbol-Martinussen and Engberg-Pedersen (2003).

34. For the most recent OECD/DAC peer reviews of Australian and New Zealand ODA, see OECD (2005c, d).

5 The complexities of multilateral aid

1. The OECD/DAC used to define multilateral aid as that channelled through a multilateral organization whose policies and practices are governed by the collective decisions of net contributors and net recipients (Browne 1990: 91). Now, multilateral agencies are defined by the OECD/DAC as 'those international institutions with government membership which conduct all or a significant part of their activities in favour of development and aid recipient countries' (OECD 2005a: 238). However, this definition fails to embrace all United Nations agencies, especially those, such as the Office for the Coordination of Humanitarian Affairs (OCHA), which are part of the UN Secretariat and thus lack autonomous governance.

2. Even the OECD has historically recognized that EU/EC aid provides a classification problem, which is why the OECD/DAC used to treat it separately from both bilateral and multilateral aid and termed it a 'collective bilateral' arrangement—at a time when the definition of multilateral aid required the aid provided to be governed by the collective decisions of contributors and recipients (Browne 1990: 73). Today, the annual OECD/DAC reports present the EU's aid programme under a chapter titled 'Policies and Efforts of Bilateral Donors', but then include EU aid in the official statistics of multilateral ODA (see OECD 2005a: 84). In their study of multilateral organizations, Degnbol-Martinussen and Engberg-Pedersen (2003: 142) concur that the EU should be recognized as a 'regional body with clear politico-economic interests rather than as a multilateral agency'.

3. Figures for fiscal years are taken from the World Bank's Annual Report for 2004. IDA replenishments for disbursements in 2005–8 of an additional $18bn sit alongside $24bn of outstanding credits.

4. See the IFAD 2004 Annual Report, available at <www.ifad.org/pub/ar/2004/e/index.htm> (accessed 16 Sept. 2005).

5. UNAIDS is co-sponsored by ten different UN agencies. In its own words, 'The UNAIDS Secretariat operates as a catalyst and coordinator of action on AIDS, rather than as a direct funding or implementing agency. It serves the entire programme, with headquarters in Geneva and staff posted in over 60 countries', available at <www.unaids.org/en/about+unaids/what+is+unaids/ unaids+secretariat.asp> (accessed 16 Sept. 2005).

6. Figures from UNDP budget estimates for the biennium 2004–5 and Annual Reports of the Administrator (DP/200311 and 28).

7. See the UNICEF *Annual Report 2004*, available at <www.unicef.org/publications/files/UNICEFAnnualReport2004_eng.pdf> (accessed 14 Sept. 2005).

8. Figures from the UNFPA's *Annual Report 2004*, available at <www.unfpa.org/upload/lib_pub_file/434_filename_annual_report_04.pdf1> (accessed 15 Sept. 2005).

9. Further details are provided in Chapter 18.

10. OECD/DAC statistics for these two agencies are not comparable prior to 1995, as they then included non-core activities. In 2004, the WFP delivered $2.9bn worth of food aid. 2004 figures are from the WFP's Annual Performance Report for 2004, available at <www.wfp.org/eb/docs/2005/wfp050750~6.pdf> (accessed 14 Sept. 2005).

11. Figures from UNRWA's website at <www.un.org/unrwa/finances/index.html> (accessed 14 Sept. 2005).

12. These include the Arab Fund for Economic and Social Development (AFESD) and the OPEC Fund for International Development. In the late 1970s, these provided upwards of $270mn annually in ODA.

13. See <www.theglobalfund.org/en/files/pledges&contributions.xls> and the Global Fund's *Annual Report 2005*, available at <www.theglobalfund.org/en/files/publications/annualreport/2005/2005_Annual_Report_lowres.pdf> (accessed 23 June 2006).

14. These problems are discussed further in Chapter 20.

15. For instance, UNESCO's budget appropriations for 2002–3 totalled $544mn, but its extra-budgetary resources amounted to $334mn. The extra-budgetary resources for UNESCO's education-sector work were almost 40 per cent higher than its regular education-sector budget of $94mn. See UNESCO's approved programme and budget, at<portal.unesco.org/en/ev.php-URL_ID=6376&URL_DO=DO_TOPIC&URL_SECTION=201.html> (accessed 16 Sept. 2005).

16. It is not just that official donors have reduced their commitments to core funding of key multilateral agencies; they have not matched the commitments they have made to the funds they have provided. Thus, at the end of 2003, member countries owed the UN $1.6bn in assessed contributions (Sagasti *et al.* 2005: 52).

17. The following remarks on UN humanitarian financing, though focused on humanitarian assistance, have wider applicability: 'The erosion of core resources . . . coupled with ear-marked funds predicated on an operational presence pushes UN agencies to secure donor funds through the continuation of field programmes. The temptation has been to respond to donor funds with an "I-can-do-that-too" approach in order to secure funding. This has often led agencies to over-extend themselves and contributes to situations whereby they claim to have core competencies in various donor-determined areas. Inevitably this leads to turf battles and results in negative forms of overlap and duplication' (Sagasti *et al.* 2005: 10).

18. One of the earliest of these initiatives took place more than 40 years ago, in 1969. (See Browne 1990: 267). The most recent was *Delivering as One* produced by the Secretary-General's High-Level Panel in November 2006 (Aziz *et al.* 2006).

19. In its assessment of progress on harmonization and reform, the UNDG's 2005 report acknowledged that 'Efforts need to be strengthened to ensure that the principles of "better working together" and the tools and procedures developed are accompanied by a continued commitment of all UN staff to engage in further attitudinal and behavioral change . . . . There is now a wide consensus that the UN's impact on the lives of the poor and vulnerable can only be optimized when the entire UN family bring together its vast knowledge and expertise in co-operation with other partners' (UNDG 2005: 13).

20. The points raised here are directly related to the issues of aid impact, which are addressed in Part II.

6 The political and commercial dimensions of aid

1. In those recipient countries for which donors provide aid in the form of budget support or as part of sector-wide approaches (SWAps), some donors do consider the aid other donors are planning to provide when determining their own contributions to these mechanisms. But even in these countries, most donors still provide aid outside such frameworks.

2. As discussed later in the chapter, considerable amounts of aid tied to commercial interests are more costly to recipients than when provided untied. Thus, loosening the commercial tying of aid should lead to a more effective use of aid, provided—and this is clearly crucial—the amounts of aid do not fall markedly once donor-country commercial interests are reduced or eliminated.

3. OECD/DAC statistics show that in the years 2003 and 2004, Afghanistan and the DRC together received a total of $11bn in ODA, more than ten times the amounts received in the years 2000 and 2001, which, together, came to less than $1bn.

4. In 1951, the Mutual Security Act initiated economic aid programmes specifically designed to support United States security and political interests. From 1978, this became known as the Economic Support Fund (ESF), which exists to this day.

5. However, this study was only based on allocations from USAID.

6. The President's budget request for 2007 proposed a foreign aid budget similar to 2006. Twenty per cent cuts in traditional development and disaster assistance programmes were more than matched by significant increases in funding to the MCA and the PEPFAR. Thus, overall, development-focused funds were not cut. See <www.whitehouse.gov/omb/budget/fy2007/> (accessed 10 Feb. 2006).

7. The OECD/DAC 2005 peer review of Swedish aid drew attention to continuing tension between Sida's wish to focus its aid more on poverty alleviation in a relatively small number of countries and the Ministry of Foreign Affairs' wish to spread the funds more widely, because of failures to coordinate approaches effectively between the two (OECD 2005h:14–15).

8. Speech by Mr. Taro Aso, Japan National Press Club, 19 Jan. 2006; available at <www.mofa.go.jp/announce/fm/aso/speech0601–2.html> (accessed 18 Feb. 2006).

9. In 2006, the International Development (Reporting and Transparency) Bill was tabled, requiring the government annually to report to parliament on progress in achieving the 0.7 per cent of gross national income target as well as tracking progress on achieving the MDGs. See <www.publications.parliament.uk/pa/cm200506/cmbills/019/2006019.htm> (accessed 28 Feb. 2006).

10. In the year 2004, these nine donors, plus the United States and the United Kingdom between them, accounted for 60 per cent of all the aid (ODA) provided by all major OECD/DAC donors.

11. In 2004, the top eight recipients of aid (ODA and OA) from the European Commission were European countries plus Turkey. Together they accounted for 30 per cent of all the aid provided (OECD 2006a: 81).

12. A distinction is made by the OECD/DAC between 'tied aid' and 'partially tied aid'. Tied aid is official aid whose procurement is tied to the donor country, or a restricted group of countries, the latter being particularly important for ODA coming from the European Union. To be defined as 'partially tied', procurement is extended to all recipient countries, but not to all countries worldwide.

13. For a good overview of the way that aid and trade policies are mixed together see Morrissey (1993).

14. The term 'LLDC' is applied to a group of very poor countries, classified (by the United Nations) on the basis of three criteria: low income (defined in 2006 as less than $750 per capita), weak human assets, and economic vulnerability, with no one category predetermining membership. Every three years, the UN General Assembly approves the list of LLDCs. The 2006 classification was based on data for the years 2002–4. It is well known that the LLDC

grouping has consistently excluded a number of 'large and poor' countries with low per capita income levels, and other poor countries and territories (see UN 2006: iii).

15. The 2005 report was published at the end of the year. See <www.oecd.org/dataoecd/ 15/22/35029066.pdf> (accessed 14 Feb. 2006).

16. Free-standing technical cooperation is excluded from the coverage of the Recommendations, as are some elements of food aid.

17. See <www.europarl.eu.int/meetdocs/2004_2009/documents/pr/559/559598/559598en.pdf> (accessed 14 Feb. 2006).

18. Although Jepma noted that some multilateral aid was tied, he judged that the problem was predominantly one of bilateral aid.

19. My estimates, calculated as follows. Total bilateral ODA in 2004 was $57.3bn, of which 41.7 per cent was untied, leaving $33.42bn. Of this, $8.5bn was development food aid and emergency aid. Assuming (generously) that 70 per cent of food aid and emergency aid was tied at a rate of 30 per cent and all other united aid was tied at a rate of 20 per cent, the total additional costs of tying would come to $7.3bn (aid figures from OECD data-base).

20. The costs were, £80,000 for Denmark, £73,000 for consultants recruited by the European Commission, £108,000 for Germany, and some £130,000 for the United States (see Riddell and Stevens 1997: 70).

21. The Osei study quotes an analysis of aid to Sudan which reported the prices of tied-aid commodities as 74 per cent higher than from alternative sources—considerably higher than the Jepma average figure. It is not known to what extent these studies are representative of the experience of other recipients of tied aid.

22. The terms 'aid darlings' and 'aid orphans' have been coined for countries assessed as receiving respectively more or less aid than would be predicted (see Levin and Dollar 2005).

23. Particularly since the seminal studies produced in the late 1990s (especially World Bank 1998), it has been argued not only that policies matter to aid effectiveness but that, consequently, aid should be channelled to those countries able to use it better. More recently, concern has grown about what that means for countries that are poor and need aid but are judged less able to use aid effectively. This has led to the commissioning of a massive wave of studies on what have been termed variously 'fragile states', 'difficult partnerships', 'forgotten states' and 'poorly performing countries'. Important though it clearly is to understand better what factors contribute to making aid more effective, recent studies on how donors have been allocating their aid funds provides very little evidence to suggest that donors have switched funds away from these countries. In practice, while donors continually articulate the priority they give to supporting countries with good policies, the large donors have neither pronounced that they will give less aid to 'difficult partner' countries (Australia is the only country to have developed a formal policy on the issue), nor have they done so. On the contrary, most donors have been developing polices for greater engagement with fragile states, and the aggregate evidence suggests that, in recent years, aid to such countries has been rising, not falling (see Jones *et al.* 2005: 20–5).

24. These 65 countries and territories consist of the 50 countries classified (in 2006) by the United Nations as the least developed countries (LLDCs), plus an additional 15 of the poorest countries and territories. These additional 15 countries and territories consist of countries with per capita incomes (in 2000) lower than $600. They are: the Democratic Republic of Congo, Ghana, India, Kenya, Kyrgyzstan, Moldova, Mongolia, Nigeria, the Occupied Palestinian Territories, Pakistan, Papua New Guinea, Tajikistan, Uzbekistan, Vietnam and Zimbabwe. The aid figures used here were calculated from OECD (2006a) and from the on-

line OECD/DAC statistical data-base, available at <www.oecd.org/dataoecd/50/17/ 5037721.htm> (accessed 16 Feb. 2006).

25. These were Belgium, Denmark, France, Ireland, Luxembourg, the Netherlands, Norway and Sweden. However, some of these had pledged to reach a higher target ratio of 0.20 per cent (OECD 2006: 171).

26. Figures in this paragraph come largely from UNDP (2006) and OECD (2006a).

27. These include the following: McGillivray and White (1994); Collier and Dollar (1999, 2001); Llavador and Roemer (2001); Berthélemy and Tichit (2002); McGillivray (2003b); Berthélemy (2005); and Cogneau and Naudet (2006).

28. The variables against which the allocation of aid have been assessed include trade patterns, colonial roots, extent of civil liberties and freedom, and even voting patterns at the UN.

29. Different authors have drawn up different lists of which recipients should receive more or less aid on the basis of need—defined differently but including income-related measures, including for some the Human Development Index (HDI). Collier and Dollar (1999, 2001) use a growth-dominated poverty-reduction approach; Llavador and Roemer (2001) and Cogneau and Naudet (2006) adopt approaches which use equal opportunity, utility and equality of opportunity functions which also incorporate a 'risk of poverty' variable, while McGillivray and White (1994) use need and absorptive capacity criteria with an unbiased weighting for population size. The lists of which countries should receive more or less aid, and how much, differ sharply, though, as McGillivray explains, a dominant feature of these results is that most countries would receive less aid than they actually receive, and a relatively small number of countries would receive significantly more aid—there would be many losers and few winners. According to Collier and Dollar (2002, quoted in McGillivray 2003b: 18–21), Honduras, Lesotho and Uganda would receive far more aid, China, Indonesia, Poland and Russia far less. According to the McGillivray and White approach, Ethiopia, India, Nigeria and Pakistan would receive more aid and China, Colombia, Malaysia, Poland and Russia would receive much less (McGillivray 2003b: 13–14).

30. For an accessible critique of some technical weaknesses in the Collier–Dollar methodology see Beynon (2003) and McGillivray (2005).

31. For instance, on the basis of equality of opportunity and an aid allocation model which switches aid from countries that are poor but have sufficient aid, Cogneau and Naudet are able to reduce to 30 per cent the proportion of people living in poverty in a key group of poor countries by the year 2015, whereas under the Collier–Dollar model over 60 per cent of people in this group would still be living in poverty (Cogneau and Naudet 2004: 21).

7 Public support for aid

1. Official aid levels in the UK fell (dramatically) in the late 1980s while public support was increasing sharply, and ODA has risen from 1998 onwards even though surveys show a long period of declining support for aid which continued as ODA levels began to rise again (McDonnell *et al.* 2003a: 218–19). In the year 2005, a majority of the United Kingdom population (55 per cent) thought the government provided either the right amount of aid or too much, compared with 37 per cent who thought it gave too little. See YouGov Survey 2005: 2; available at <www.yougov.com/archives/pdf/OMI050101006_1.pdf> (accessed 21 Feb. 2006).

2. Comments by Bernard Wood in Foy and Helmich (1996: 21).

3. In a few countries, awareness of the MDGs was far higher—highest in Sweden, where 27 per cent of the population were aware of them.

4. The focus of this discussion is on the influence of public opinion on aid levels. To the extent that public opinion has played a relatively minor role in contributing to the massive increases in official aid-giving which have characterized the past few years, the question is, what did? Besides the influence of strategic interests (discussed in Chapter 6), a number of authors suggest that the most critical factors determining the amounts of aid that particular countries decide to give, and particularly the decision markedly to increase aid levels, are political leadership, the conviction of the most senior politicians to increase aid, and the linked influence of peer pressure (see German 1996; Round and Odedokun 2003).

5. See YouGov Survey 2005: 2; available at webpage cited in n. 1.

6. This is in part why the OECD's mid-1990s stocktaking review concluded not merely that development aid was low in the overall priorities of electorates but that its relative importance was in decline (Foy and Helmich 1996: 12).

7. The questions were explicitly linked to achieving the MDGs and referred to 'increase in development aid to countries committed to poverty reduction to meet internationally agreed aid targets' (EC 2005a: 21). However, 14 per cent listed 'providing training and technical expertise to developing countries' as the most important (EC 2005a: 21), which, as this is a form of aid, would raise the share to 26 per cent.

8. There has been some discussion whether these wildly inaccurate assessments have been due to Americans confusing development aid with defence spending. However, when respondents were told the differences between the two, these huge inaccuracies remained.

9. The questions were asked in relation to possible actions which governments could undertake to help developing countries achieve the MDGs. Clearly support for 'increasing aid' is different from 'support for aid in general'. The point being made here is that it is quite evident that the public are able to distinguish between support for 'helping' and support for 'aid', and thus it cannot be assumed that support for helping and support for aid are one and the same.

10. One exception might be Denmark. See OECD (2001a: 24–5).

11. This assumes, of course, that the numbers of respondents who are neither supportive of, nor opposed to, aid (the 'Don't know's) constitute a small minority. In fact, the Eurobarometer survey tends to confirm this (see EC 2005a: 26).

12. We are concerned here with the beliefs people have about aid, which may not necessarily reflect reality accurately. Some authors have argued that by stressing that poor people need to be helped, aid agencies contribute to the perception that poor people are 'helpless' and unable to develop without external assistance. For Americans, with a strong sense of independence, the belief runs very deep that development can best occur by peoples' own efforts, which perhaps explains, in part, why support for aid has tended to be lower in the United States than across most of Europe.

13. For the United States, the 60 per cent figure represents the proportion of those who believed the aid provided ended up in the hands of corrupt officials (PIPA 2003: 6).

14. On the basis of data from the mid-1990s, Stern records far higher percentages for those who do not believe aid is successful in reducing poverty: Spain, 59 per cent; Sweden, 56 per cent; the Netherlands, 52 per cent; and Finland, 67 per cent (1998: 12).

15. Some have suggested that it is not that people support aid when they know it doesn't work, but that their core values remain sympathetic to the goals of development assistance (see Yankelovich 1996). My own reading of the evidence is that in most cases, people are genuinely expressing support for aid actually provided, not merely support for the 'idea' of providing aid. The distinction is between support for aid knowing that the aid one supports doesn't work, and support for aid knowing that some of the aid (possibly most of it) doesn't work. These issues will be discussed further in the next two chapters.

8 Charity or duty? The moral case for aid

1. The International Development Ethics Association (IDEA) was established in 1984. The home page of its website is <www.development-ethics.org/default.asp>. Two of the most accessible texts on the ethics of development—which encompass but extend well beyond the narrower questions of ethics and aid—are Dower (1998) and Gasper (2004).

2. This does not necessarily mean that the wealthier a country the less poverty there is. Poverty is related to both growth processes and the distribution of wealth and income.

3. The discussion here is focused on whether aid has the potential to reduce poverty, not whether there are other ways besides giving aid which could also reduce poverty and accelerate the development process—which there undoubtedly are. These wider issues are discussed in Chapters 13 and 20.

4. The original 0.7 per cent ratio of ODA to GNI was established over 40 years ago. When originally conceived, it was loosely linked to an assessment of poor-country needs, but discussion between the author and the late Hans Singer, who was directly involved in the creation of this ratio, confirmed that this was literally a quick 'back of the envelope' calculation made hurriedly before a UN meeting, and not based on a rigorous assessment of aid needs.

5. This is his argument. In the year 2000, when the commitment was made, 18 per cent of the world's population were living in poverty: 1,094mn people. If the commitment had been to halve the *number* of people living in poverty then, if achieved by 2015, that number would have been reduced to 547mn. In contrast, halving the *proportion* living in poverty means that by 2015, the proportion living in poverty would fall from 18 per cent to 9 per cent. With projected increases in total world population of 18.6 per cent, the target number of those living in poverty would then be 883mn, only 19 per cent fewer than the 1,094mn living in poverty in the year 2000.

6. The study did not assess whether current levels of humanitarian aid were sufficient.

7. This point was spelt out clearly at a public meeting held in London in the spring of 2006, in which the British Secretary of State for International Development, Hilary Benn, laid out his ideas for the ways that the international aid system needs to change in the twenty-first Century. In answering a question about how the political and commercial influences on the allocation of aid might be reduced, he observed simply that 'we need to be responsible for what we do, other donors need to be responsible for what they do' (author's notes, 14 March 2006). For the full speech see <www.dfid.gov.uk/news/files/Speeches/wp2006-speeches/architecture140306.asp> (accessed 15 March 2006).

8. For the 2005 edition of the *World Development Indicators* (World Bank 2005l), low-income countries were defined as those with per capita incomes of less than $650, high-income countries, those with per capita incomes in excess of $9,386.

9. Figures calculated from World Bank *World Development Indicators*, 2002 and 2005, World Bank (1990), and Penn World Tables Version 6.1 (for 1965 population data). In order to iron out major distortions, these figures omit China, which, by 2003, was no longer classified as a low-income country.

10. See Global Policy Forum, 'Average GDP Per Capita in 20 High and 20 Low Income Countries, 1970–2000', available at <www.globalpolicy.org/socecon/tables/gdpdeftab.htm> (accessed 15 Mar. 2006).

11. In ongoing work, the preliminary results of which were made available in late 2005, Milanovic compares the incomes of people rather than countries. His analysis suggests that the ratio of the richest 5 per cent to the poorest 5 per cent of people in the world is 165 : 1, the richest group earning in 48 hours what the poorest earn in a year. The top 10 per cent of

people earn half the total world income, the bottom 10 per cent, a mere 0.7 per cent of world income (Milanovic 2005: 14).

12. The question of whether increasing amounts of aid can be used effectively has been the subject of substantial recent debate. See, for example, Foster and Killick (2006) and Guillaumont and Jeanneney (2006). The macroeconomic effects of increasing aid flows are discussed later in the text, especially in Chapters 10, 14 and 15.

13. While this chapter and the next address some of the arguments of those who claim that there is no moral obligation for governments to provide aid, the primary focus is on the strength of the arguments of those who claim that there is such an obligation. In an earlier study, I looked in some detail at the arguments of those who claimed that governments had no moral obligation to provide aid, which included a detailed assessment of the views of Peter Bauer and those who based their views on the writings of moral philosophers like Robert Nozick (see Riddell 1987).

14. One can see the influence of radical utilitarian thinking in those scholars and aid agencies who suggest that if aid is found not to be effective in one country then it is better to redeploy it to countries where it has a better chance of achieving its objectives.

15. Of course, it is quite possible for those who adopt a utilitarian perspective to think through (practical) ways in which aid might be made more effective. The point being made here is that many of those who believe that there is some moral obligation to provide aid also believe that this obligation is removed if it can be shown that aid, as currently provided, is ineffective.

16. Rawls' theory has its roots in the Kantian view that all principles adopted (including those of morality and justice) should be able to be adopted by everyone, that one should treat humanity never simply as a means but always as an end as well, and that one should refrain from actions that could not be acted upon by others (O'Neill 1986: 121ff.).

17. The just savings principle specifies the (minimum) 'suitable amount of real capital accumulation' that one generation needs to put aside for the next generation (Rawls 1973: 285ff.).

18. In recent years, others, such as Risse (2005), have followed Rawls in arguing the moral case for aid on the assumption that development is driven predominantly by a single cause, focused on institutions. For a balanced discussion of why this view is wrong see Rodrik (2005).

19. It is Dworkin's view that Sen misunderstands his own approach to the equality of resources, and that their approaches are very close to each other, if not identical (2000: 299–303). See Moellendorf (2002: 83–6) for a discussion of the closeness of Sen's and Rawls' approaches.

20. For an overview of the issues discussed here, see Clark (2005).

21. Another weakness of rights-based discourses is that they give no place to beneficence or help outside the rights-framework. As O'Neill puts it (1986: 102), 'A world in which rights discourse is thought the appropriate idiom for ethical deliberation is one in which a powerful theoretical wedge is driven between questions of justice and matters of help and benefit. Justice is seen as consisting of assignable, claimable and enforceable rights which only the claimant can waive. Beneficence is seen as unassignable, unclaimable and unenforceable . . . . Once the discourse of rights is established, generosity, beneficence and help are likely to seem less important, especially in public affairs.'

22. The details are contained in the Vienna Declaration and Programme of Action agreed by 171 states at the World Conference on Human Rights, available at <www.unhchr.ch/huridocda/huridoca.nsf/(Symbol)/A.CONF.157.23.En?OpenDocument> (accessed 20 Mar. 2006).

23. Additionally, the 1986 Declaration on the Right to Development declares that 'states have a duty to cooperate with each other in ensuring development and removing obstacles to development, and to take steps individually and collectively to formulate international

development policies with a view to facilitating the full realization of the right to develop-ment'. However, though adopted by a majority of the General Assembly, the declaration is not legally binding and has not been supported by key donor countries. Hence it does not carry the weight of the international covenants. Peter Uvin, a respected commentator on the sub-ject, calls it simply 'verbiage' (2004: 43).

24. Pogge's ethical approach has been termed institutional cosmopolitanism (ICHRP 2003: 73ff.).

25. Pogge contrasts this situation with the normative statement set out in Article 28 of the Universal Declaration of Human Rights that 'Everyone is entitled to a social and international order in which the rights and freedoms set forth in this Declaration can be fully realised'.

26. Pogge writes that even if his hope of mobilizing support for the proposed GDR 'is not realis-tic, it is still important to insist that present global poverty manifests a grievous injustice according to Western normative political thought' (2002: 211).

27. Pogge's work has also helped gain wider acceptance for the view that there is a moral obliga-tion to avoid systematic and avoidable injury.

9 The moral case for governments and individuals to provide aid

1. The veracity of this statement is supported by the presentation of donors' own views summa-rized in subsequent paragraphs in the text. However, it is not universally accepted. For instance, Gasper contends that 'rather than obligation, rich country donors have largely taken self-interest and charity as their bases for giving' (1999: 23). Lumsdaine takes the opposite view, arguing that humanitarian values and the response to dire human need worldwide became a principle acknowledged by almost all powerful states, significantly influencing their cash outlays, that humanitarian and egalitarian convictions have played a central role in offi-cial aid-giving, and that the creation and operation of the OECD/DAC 'represented an acknowledgement by all the industrialised democracies of an obligation to assist the less developed countries in their development' (1994: 239, 290–1).

2. Keenly debated in moral philosophy has been the question whether an identified problem can successfully lead to the robust claim that (moral) actions should be taken to address (resolve) the problem—whether you can derive an 'ought' from an 'is'. The present discussion is differ-ent because in this case donors are claiming that there is a moral obligation (the 'ought' is the starting point). Hence, the thrust of this discussion is to determine precisely why donors claim that they have a moral duty to provide aid.

3. The word 'solidarity' refers not merely to sympathies but to common bonds with those to whom aid is given. It implies working to achieve common goals, sharing the risks and suffer-ing with them, and taking concrete action to support those with whom one is in solidarity—in short, a substantive agenda of action. Solidarity has been defined as 'a willingness to tie one's fate to that of others and . . . to share a sense of group identity' (Lumsdaine 1993: 185).

4. See Ministry of Foreign Affairs and Danida (2000), available at <www.um.dk/Publikationer/ Danida/English/DanishDevelopmentCooperation/DenmarksDevelopmentPolicyStrategy/ index. asp> (accessed 9 Mar. 2006).

5. 'Finland's Development Co-operation' (2005), available at <http://global.finland.fi/julka-isut/pdf/ perusesite_en.pdf> (accessed 9 Mar. 2006).

6. Report no. 35 to the Störting (2003/4), 'Fighting Poverty Together: A Comprehensive Development Policy' (summary), available at <www.dep.no/ud/english/doc/white_paper/ 032131– 030005/ind-bn.html> (accessed 10 Mar. 2006).

7. In Canada's case this has been articulated in Canada's *International Policy Statement* (2005), available at <www.acdi-cida.gc.ca/INET/IMAGES.NSF/vLUImages/IPS_PDF_EN/$file/IPS-EN.pdf> (accessed 10 Mar. 2006).

8. See <www.usaid.gov/about_usaid/usaidhist.html> (accessed 10 Mar. 2006).

9. For Germany, see *Development Policy Action Plan on Human Rights 2004–2007* (2004), available at <www.bmz.de/en/service/infothek/fach/konzepte/konzept128engl.pdf>, and for Switzerland, SDC's *Human Rights Policy: Towards a Life in Dignity. Realising rights for poor people* (Feb. 2006), available at <http://162.23.39.120/dezaweb/ressources/resource_en_25225.pdf> (accessed 10 Mar. 2006).

10. See 'The European Consensus on Development', available at <http://europa.eu.int/comm/development/body/development_policy_statement/docs/edp_declaration_signed_2 0_12_2005_en.pdf> (accessed 21 July 2006).

11. Thomas Nagel terms this perspective 'the political conception of justice', the prime focus being on the individual state, upon which and around which the norms of justice are applied (Nagel 2005: 120).

12. I am grateful to Howard Lehman for drawing my attention to this study (Lehman 2006: 4).

13. In part, this perspective could be considered quite close to what Gasper terms an obligation of 'contributive justice', which requires states to 'provide some aid but not an obligation to support each and every individual case of need' (1999: 39).

14. This is increasingly recognized and acknowledged even in donor countries providing the highest amount of official aid. For instance in Norway, whose ODA-to-GNI ratio has for decades exceeded the 0.7 per cent figure, leading NGOs, such as Norwegian Church Aid (NCA), have recently begun calling for ODA levels to be more than doubled to reach 2 per cent of GNI.

15. I am grateful to Wouter Vandenhole for this point. See his (undated) paper 'An Optional Protocol to the International Covenant on Economic, Social and Cultural Rights', available at <www.escr-net.org/GeneralDocs/Leuven%20HR%20Institute.doc> (accessed 23 Mar. 2006).

16. See the February 2006 report on the third session of the Working Group to consider options regarding the Optional Protocol to the Covenant, available at <www.ishr.ch/About%20UN/Reports%20and%20Analysis/CHRWG/WGOPICESCR/WGOPICESCR-3rdSessionFI.pdf> (accessed 23 Mar. 2006).

17. The consensus reached on these views and principles have been summarized on a number of occasions by the UN Secretary General. See, for instance, Annan (2005). States have agreed that this responsibility should normally be achieved through diplomatic, humanitarian or other peaceful means but that collective action 'in a timely and decisive manner' should be taken in cases 'when peaceful means are inadequate and national authorities manifestly fail to protect their populations from genocide, war crimes, ethnic cleansing and crimes against humanity'. See *2005 World Summit Outcome*, UN General Assembly A/60/L.1, para. 139; available at <www.un-ngls.org/un-summit-FINAL-DOC.pdf> (accessed 24 Mar. 2006).

18. A number of the ideas contained in this paragraph are drawn from ICHRP (2003: 51ff.).

19. For the text of the Vienna Declaration, see UN General Assembly, *The Vienna Declaration and Programme of Action*, A/CONF. 157/23 (New York: United Nations, 1993).

20. As discussed earlier in the chapter, a key issue concerns the potentially competing duties to assist those at home and abroad. This is most easily answered by those who adopt a cosmopolitan (worldwide) perspective. From this perspective, Moellendorf argues that 'since we may not say that, in general, claims of one group override the claims of the other, it is impossible to

give an account of the duties owed to members of one of the two groups, in cases of conflicting claims, without considering the claims of members of the other'. Consequently, 'if expending resources on behalf of the cause of justice in other states is required by justice, then whatever the content of a statesperson's special duties to the constituency, it does not necessarily trump general duties to expend those resources' (2002: 43, 124).

21. The liveliest debates concern the share of aid that goes to those who need it, and the amounts used in administering these aid flows—not whether the bulk of aid is directed to those who need it.

22. The stress on human dignity is contained in, for instance, 'Together for a Just World', produced by NCA; available at <http://english.nca.no/article/view/4562/1/450> (accessed 24 July 2006).

10 Assessing and measuring the impact of aid

1. For further and, in part, more technical discussion of some key methodological challenges involved in assessing aid, see, for instance, Degnbol-Martinussen and Engberg-Pedersen (2003); Stewart (2003); Clemens *et al.* (2004); and White (2005a).

2. Some more recent studies have distinguished between development and emergency aid. See, for example, Clemens *et al.* (2004).

3. These methodological problems are discussed in Clemens *et al.* (2004).

4. It has long been recognized that national accounts data in industrialized countries are subject to a significant degree of error (of 10 per cent or more). See Oscar Morgenstern's classic text (Morgenstern 1963).

5. Capability approaches are discussed further in Chapter 8.

6. Szekely *et al.* (2000), quoted in a discussion paper on the different definitions of poverty and how and why these matter (Ruggeri Laderchi *et al.* 2003: 12).

7. The chronically poor are those who remain in poverty for five years or more. See McKay and Baulch (2004) for estimates of chronic poverty and a discussion of the inaccuracies and implausibility of some World Bank poverty estimates of income poverty.

8. See Birdsall (2004: 14) and Savedoff *et al.* (2006).

9. Three years later, a synthesis report of DFID's country programmes concluded that there remained insufficient information with which to judge the overall performance of DFID's aid programmes at the country level, pointing to the need to improve the quality of project-and programme-level monitoring and evaluation (Flint *et al.* 2004: viii).

10. I recall, however, undertaking an assessment of water and sanitation projects in Zimbabwe some years ago and was proudly shown a gleaming new borehole which was then providing clean water for a group of villagers. When I asked my hosts about a second new borehole less than 20 yards away and supplying water to the same village, I was told that that had been provided by the local council and had nothing to do with the one which this particular NGO had built, and which I had come to see.

11. This problem is known technically as the problem of the counterfactual or the attribution problem.

12. For a discussion of random-sampling approaches see Duflo and Kremer (2003), and the website <www.povertyactionlab.com>.

13. Some have suggested that the bias to present a positive picture of aid's performance extends to those undertaking evaluations for aid agencies. For instance, Degnbol-Martinussen and

Engberg-Pedersen contend that 'there is an aid industry with vested interests in assuming and claiming impact, often documented through instrumental project cycle analyses . . . and anecdotal success stories' (2003: 264).

14. This point was confirmed at an OECD meeting of senior information staff from member donor countries to which the author gave a presentation.

15. See Uvin (1998) for a challenging assessment of the role that aid and aid agencies played in contributing (though often unwittingly) to the Rwandan genocide, and Anderson (1999) for a review of the way aid, including emergency aid, can (again unwittingly) do harm.

16. The central theme of the 2006 edition of the World Bank's *World Development Report* is that equity (as well as growth) is a core part of development (World Bank 2005a).

17. For a recent summary of this literature see Szirmai (2005) as well as Easterley (2001a).

18. The problems are well summarized in Stiglitz (1998).

19. For further discussion of these points see, for instance, North (1990); Killick (1993, 1995, 1998); Easterley (2001a); Rodrik (2005); and Szirmai (2005).

20. In their 2002 study, Rodrik and colleagues developed a complex growth model, but this only managed to 'account' for about half the variance in incomes across their country sample (2002: 6).

21. Over 90 per cent of this was accounted for by the Democratic Republic of Congo, whose ODA receipts jumped from \$1.1bn in 2002 to \$5.4bn in 2003, largely due to inflows of emergency aid.

22. These include studies by Easterly (2001a) and Rajan and Subramanian (2005a, b).

23. The headline in the leader in the London-based *Financial Times* commenting on the findings of the two studies by Rajan and Subramanian was entitled 'Time to prove that aid works' (1 July 2005: 18).

11 The impact of official development aid projects

1. For instance, the Swedish International Cooperation Development Agency (Sida) has recently supported the latter type of programme in El Salvador. For a discussion of this Sida programme and others like it, see Poate *et al.* (2000: annex 6).

2. For the complete reports upon which this summary data is based see Flint *et al.* (2002, 2004); UNDP (2003); World Bank (2002, 2005b, c, d); AusAID (2004); ADB (2005); and AfDB (2004).

3. A rate of return of 10 per cent means that for every dollar invested, annual net economic benefits of 10 cents arise. It is not possible to assess the rate of return on all projects and a range of assumptions have to be made to assess the rates of return of non-economic projects. For a discussion of rate-of-return analysis see, for instance, Isham and Kaufmann (1995).

4. See Dalgard and Hansen (2005) for a discussion of rates of return on investment funded by aid and non-aid sources, and recent assessments at both the macro-and micro-levels.

5. The Cassen study noted that donor agencies conspire consciously or unconsciously in an unsatisfactory state of affairs in which failures are not openly discussed (1986: 13). Today, it remains true that donors remain reluctant to take the initiative in publicising and discussing their aid failures in public fora.

6. It is not being suggested here that this is in any way typical of Swiss official aid more generally. In 2003, an independent evaluation painted an extremely positive picture of 12 years of Swiss aid to former Eastern Bloc countries. See <www.deza.ch/ressources/deza_product_de_868. pdf> (accessed 7 Oct. 2005).

7. The details are contained in Court of Auditors Special Report no. 8 of 2003, *Official Journal of the European Union Information and Notices*, 46: C181 (31 July 2003); available at <www.eca.eu.int/audit_reports/special_reports/docs/2003/rs08_03en.pdf> (accessed 5 Oct. 2005).

8. The part of the World Bank responsible for providing evidence on the impact of the Bank's projects and programmes used to be called the Operations Evaluation Department. Its name was recently changed to the Independent Evaluation Group (IEG). However, few outside the Bank believe that the IEG is sufficiently independent to eliminate the in-built bias in its reports, for which it continues to be criticized. See Easterley (2006).

9. A 2003 EC evaluation of Bangladesh could not find a complete list of all EC interventions, never mind project reports (MWH Consultants 2003: 1). See Court of Auditors Special Report no 4. of 2005, *Official Journal of the European Union Information and Notices*, 260/01 (19 Oct. 2005), available at <www.eca.eu.int/audit_reports/special_reports/docs/2005/rs04_05en.pdf>, and Court of Auditors Special Report no. 2 of 2003, *Official Journal of the European Union Information and Notices*, 46: C93 (17 Apr. 2003), available at <www.eca.eu.int/audit_reports/special_reports/docs/2003/rs02_03en.pdf> (both accessed 5 Oct. 2005).

10. This view is supported by the Asian Development Bank's 2005 annual evaluation review, which suggested that problems in the design stage of projects and inadequate or insufficient monitoring data was associated with poor project performance (ADB 2005: 6).

11. On a related manner, it is difficult to believe that whereas in the period 1992–8, the UNDP was unable to assess the effectiveness of 35 per cent of its projects, by 1999–2003, this ratio had fallen dramatically to less than 5 per cent, leading to a rise in non-effective projects from 9 per cent to only 14 per cent of the total (UNDP 2003: 20).

12. The share of project ratings which did not need to change rose from 69 per cent to 82 per cent over the period. Interestingly, in the latter period, 8 per cent of projects were assessed as needing to be upgraded (ADB 2005: 48).

13. Project impact and sustainability are discussed further in Chapter 12, when evidence of the impact of technical assistance and capacity development is considered.

14. Most project assessments now ask whether projects were 'relevant', but the term encompasses a broad set of issues, including global priorities; and relevance to the recipient is frequently based merely on donor judgements. For this and other OECD/DAC-agreed definitions see <www.oecd.org/dataoecd/29/21/2754804.pdf> (accessed 8 Oct. 2005).

15. This problem was specifically highlighted in the EU Report on the Millennium Development Goals 2000–2004, which noted that progress in coordination and harmonization remains well below what is possible, and that one effect of some donors focusing on fewer priority partners and sectors is to increase the risks of duplication and/or the creation of funding gaps. See <http://europa.eu.int/comm/development/body/communications/docs/eu_mdg_report.pdf#zoom=125>, sect. 2.2.2 (accessed 7 Oct. 2005).

16. In mid-2006, the Global Fund was facing a funding deficit of $5.5bn for the two-year period 2006–7 (Banati, Greene and Ferazzi 2006: 6).

17. See Gibson *et al.* (2005), which also discusses the evidence for and impact of what are called perverse incentives in aid-giving, which apply particularly to project aid. These issues are discussed further in Chapter 20.

18. These figures are from detailed work first undertaken at the Massachusetts Institute of Technology by Abhijit Banerjee and Ruimin He in 2003. See Banerjee and He (forthcoming).

19. Cox and Healey note, however, that the World Bank and UNDP developed a sharper poverty focus for their projects before the leading European bilateral donors did so (2000: 76).

20. Court of Auditors Special Report no. 2 of 2003, sect. 29.

21. Similar sorts of worries about distortions arising from donor funding priorities have been voiced about the health sector: it has been argued that an 'overemphasis' on HIV/AIDS is reducing the ability of recipient governments to implement a sufficiently rounded and effective primary health care programme. These issues are discussed in Therkildsen (2005: 32ff.).

12 The impact of programme aid, technical assistance and aid for capacity development

1. According to a recent OECD/DAC publication, programme aid is restricted to 'financial contributions not linked to specific activities' (OECD 2005i: 34). However, Lister *et al.* (2006: 6) include programme food aid under their definition of programme aid.

2. See Walford (2003) for a discussion of the different ways that SWAps are and have been defined. The World Bank's sector investment programmes have also been understood as a form of SWAp (see Jones 2000). There is a website, hosted by the Canadian International Development Agency (CIDA), updating donors and researchers on SWAps and PBAs: <http://remote4.acdi-cida.gc.ca/extranet/ExtranetHome.nsf/vluaboutdoc/SWAPSEn? OpenDocument>. See also the following website: <www.sti.ch/health-systems-support/ swap/swap-project/swapwebsite/donors-and-policies.html>.

3. Other forms of programme aid would include balance-of-payments support, including debt relief.

4. For details see Riddell (2003) and UNDG (2005b).

5. For instance, in Mozambique in mid-2005, the following donors were already providing between 65 and 90 per cent of their aid as programme aid: Canada, Denmark, Finland, France, Ireland, the Netherlands, Switzerland and the UK (see Killick *et al.* 2005: 5).

6. See Lister (2005: 5ff.) for a discussion of the definition of GBS.

7. Discussion of the important issue of policy conditionality and its linkage to the provision of different forms of aid, as well as an assessment of its impact and effectiveness, will be found in Chapter 14.

8. Other studies include Lieberson *et al.* (2004); Beasley *et al.* (2005); Hauck *et al.* (2005); and Killick *et al.* (2005). Recent studies on the relationship between aid (which is an external source of funds) and domestic taxation (an internal source of funds) by Fagernäs and Roberts (2004) and Osei *et al.* (2005) are also relevant.

9. A 2004 study conducted for USAID on GBS in Malawi broadly viewed it as a failure, largely because Malawi had neither the capacity nor, in many respects, the commitment to implement the support programme efficiently and effectively (see Lieberson *et al.* 2004).

10. See Lawson *et al.* (2003: 56) for opposing evidence and views.

11. See Killick *et al.* (2005) for Mozambique, Frantz (2004) and Lawson *et al.* (2005) for Tanzania, and Hauck *et al.* (2005) for the EC.

12. See for instance the results of the study by Fagernäs and Roberts (2004), Osei *et al.* (2005) for Uganda, Malawi, Zambia and Ghana, and Lawson *et al.* (2005) for Tanzanian evidence. In the case of Zambia, however, they report that increased aid has been associated with increased borrowing.

13. Additionally, different components of technical assistance are included in official aid provided to different sectors, including, especially, to the health and education sectors.

14. According to a 2001 study, technical cooperation expenditure of the UN alone for that year amounted to $6.5bn, accounting in that year for almost 40 per cent of all multilateral ODA

(UNDP 2001: 2), though a 2003 study by Oxford Policy Management judged UN expenditure on TA to have been between $2 and $3bn in 2001 (Williams *et al.* 2003: 21). Even the lower figure is large.

15. Some evaluations, however, have pointed to problems of incompetence. For instance, in a review analysing the poor results of its support to the banking sector in Nepal, the Asian Development Bank noted the poor quality of consultants and contractors (ADB 2001, quoted in Panday 2002: 65).

16. Many decades of work by the Commonwealth Secretariat in London confirms the continued availability of key untapped skills in developing countries which could be put to work in other countries at well less than a quarter of the cost of industrialized-world consultants.

17. The 1996 World Bank review was entitled *Partnerships for Capacity Building in Africa.* The comments from the report are directly cited in Mkandawire (2002: 161).

18. Though probably an extreme case, the data from Zimbabwe are particularly disturbing. Since 1999, 60 per cent of skilled doctors and nurses have left the country, and a survey of students in higher education colleges reported that 70 per cent of those graduating expected to have left the country within two years of graduating, the most popular destination being South Africa (Tevera 2005: 5).

19. In 1981, France paid for over 11,000 long-term TC personnel; 20 years later, it had less than 2,000 contracted technical assistants. In 2004, Germany's technical cooperation agency employed just over 1,000 expatriates and almost 2,000 nationally recruited professional and technical personnel on its projects in 130 countries. See Williams *et al.* (2003: 19); GTZ (2005: 36–8) and Morgan and Baser (1993: 25).

20. Besides the Netherlands, Sweden, Norway and Canada have made substantial changes in their approach to using TA for long-term consultancies. The UN is increasingly framing its TC within national agreements, with the UNDP, in particular, increasingly transferring the management and execution responsibilities to national governments. However, a significant amount of the TC provided by the main UN specialized agencies is not very different from that provided in the past.

21. Governance and good governance encompass a perspective to aid-giving far wider than capacity building and institutional strengthening. Very little overall assessment of the impact of governance initiatives has been undertaken. The central issues of aid and governance are discussed in Chapter 20.

22. According to the OECD, 'The building metaphor suggests a process starting with a plain surface and involving the step-by-step erection of a new structure, based on a preconceived design. Experience suggests that capacity is not successfully enhanced in this way' (OECD 2006a: 9).

23. For an initial taste of the growing literature see, for instance, Morgan and Baser (1993); Moore *et al.* (1995); Eade (1997); Bossuyt (2001); Browne (2002); and Fukuda-Parr *et al.* (2002).

24. One of these is Dindo Campilan. See the discussion in Chambers (2005: 48).

25. For details see USAID (1996) and Morgan *et al.* (2005).

26. 'IBRD7440 Civil Service Reform: A Review of World Bank Assistance 1999–08–04', available at <www.dac-evaluations-cad.org/abstracts_e.htm> (accessed 14 Oct. 2005).

13 The impact of aid at the country and cross-country level

1. See OECD 1999a; World Bank 2005c: 41; and the EC evaluation website <http://europa.eu.int/comm/europeaid/evaluation> (accessed 19 Oct. 2005).

2. An extreme case would be the 1999 evaluation of all EU development aid to Asian and Latin American states, which was only able to find 100 evaluation studies from 2,000 separate projects funded in 33 countries over a 20-year period (Società Italiana di Monitoraggio 1999: i).

3. For details see Flint *et al.* (2004: viii, 17), Backström *et al.* (2004: 23–4) and Danish cooperation reports at <www.um.dk/en/menu/DevelopmentPolicy/Evaluations/ReportsByYear/> (accessed 19 Oct. 2005).

4. This does not imply that there is agreement about the 'small print' of what macroeconomic stability and pro-poor growth mean in practice.

5. There are three significant problems. First, the outcome that is assessed turns out to be the outcome of the Bank's programmes and not the overall development outcome (2005d: 21). Secondly, it is merely the chosen evaluator who (individually) assesses the extent to which outcomes are due to the Bank's input, external influences, the recipient or other stakeholders; there is no external verification. Thirdly, in a 2005 retrospective view of the results of CAEs the Bank admitted that counterfactual assessments were made for less than half of all CAEs and the focus was on what the Bank could have done differently instead of what would have happened without the Bank interventions.

6. The proposal and background documentation are contained in Development Effectiveness at the Country Level' Bigsten *et al.* (2006). For background to this initiative see <www.sida.se/shared/jsp/download.jsp?f=34933806.pdf&a=4538> (accessed 6 July 2006).

7. Two exceptions would include a more recent macroeconomic study of aid and growth in India (Mavrotas 2002) and a DFID-funded macroeconomic assessment of 20 years of official aid to Uganda, from 1980 to 1999 (Mavrotas *et al.* 2003). In the late 1990s, the World Bank conducted research with other agencies to produce a large cross-country study that examined the relationship between aid and reform (World Bank 2001a).

8. For instance, the UK, Japan, the World Bank and the Asian Development Bank have agreed to produce a joint assistance programme for Bangladesh from 2007, and in 2001 the UK started an aid programme with Vietnam which explicitly ruled out the creation of any purely UK bilateral aid projects.

9. Initially, poverty reduction strategies were referred to as PRSPs—poverty reduction strategy papers—but increasingly they become known simply as PRSes.

10. The IMF website provides a regular update, available at <www.imf.org/external/np/exr/facts/prsp.htm>.

11. See also Hatry and Yansane (2002: 4).

12. Introducing a recent special edition of the *Economic Journal* on the theme of aid and development, Hudson observed that 'the debate on the impact of aid on the economic development of developing countries is a rapidly evolving one' (2004: F184).

13. Recent examples of both types of study are the linked papers by Rajan and Subramanian (2005a, b).

14. See Riddell (1987) for a review and discussion of the cross-country evidence to the mid-1980s.

15. A recent IMF monograph concludes, simply, that cross-country regression analyses are unable to establish any robust association between aid, growth and poverty reduction (Mourmouras and Rangazas 2006: 2).

16. Nicholas Stern, 'Aid to Africa All About Resources, Governance and Development' (letter to the editor), *Financial Times*, 2 July 2005: 10. For a more polemical and hard-hitting attack on aid and growth studies see Easterly (2006), especially ch. 2.

17. This point has been well put by two of the leading scholars on aid: 'while the econometric studies are useful in summarising regularities in the data, they cannot have the richness of institutional and historical data that one gets from a good case study' (Collier and Dollar 2004: 258).

18. A number of studies have documented the extent of corruption in poor countries and have argued that often aid fuels corruption (one rather good study of this sort is Cooksey 2003). However, few studies have documented the aggregate effects of corruption on the overall impact of aid either within or across aid-recipient countries. Some cross-country studies have strongly suggested that when aid funds are diverted into unproductive ends, they seriously erode the expected virtuous link between aid inputs and growth, but these studies also point out that aid can be used to enhance accountability and transparency and so the links between aid and corruption are complex (see, for instance, Knack 2000; Svensson 2000). The impact of corruption in the delivery of humanitarian aid has been the subject of more studies: see Chapter 19 below. A study prepared for the OECD/DAC on corruption and the lessons donors have learned drew attention to a paucity of information on the effects of anti-corruption measures (Bailey 2003).

19. It is not possible to provide here a list of all the studies which analyse the effects of aid on these different variables and influences. However a selection of some key, influential, studies and syntheses of clusters of studies would include the following: Heller (1975); Mavrotas (2000); McGillivray and Morrissey (2000, 2001); Chauvet and Guillaumont (2002); Gomanee *et al.* (2002, 2003); Clemens *et al.* (2004, 2005); Fagernäs and Roberts (2004); Killick (2004); Addison *et al.* (2005); Asra *et al.* (2005); McGillivray (2005); Osei *et al.* (2005); Baliamoune-Lutz (2006); Bulír and Hamann (2006); Collier *et al.* (2006); Fukuda-Parr (2006); Dalgaard, Hansen and Tarp (2004).

20. See 'The Dutch Disease', the *Economist*, 28 Nov. 1997, 82–3.

21. For the detailed evidence see Pack and Pack (1990: 188ff.); Mavrotas (2000: 70ff.); McGillivray and Morrissey (2000, 2001); Clemens *et al.* (2004: 23–4); Dalgaard, Hansen and Tarp (2004); Fagernäs and Roberts (2004); Adam and Bevan (2005); McGillivray (2005); Osei *et al.* (2005); Bevan (2006); Bulír and Hamann (2006); and Collier *et al.* (2006).

22. See, for instance, the following research papers presented at the WIDER aid conference held in Helsinki in June 2006: Berg *et al.* (2006); Guillaumont and Jeanneney (2006); Morrissey *et al.* (2006); and Pettersson (2006).

23. These would include policies to enhance productivity in the non-traded goods sector and to diversify the export base.

14 Assessing the impact of aid conditionality

1. For recent summaries of this work see Addison *et al.* (2005) and McGillivray (2005).

2. See also Reddy and Minoiu (2006).

3. In 2006, for the first time ever, the Bank released to the public the CPIA scores for the year 2005, but not for any earlier years. It is therefore still not possible for non-Bank staff to make comparisons over time. See <http://web.worldbank.org/WBSITE/EXTERNAL/EXTABOU-TUS/IDA/0,,contentMDK:20941028~pagePK:51236175~piPK:437394~theSitePK:73154,00.html> (accessed 11 July 2006).

4. Additionally, though it has not been easy to undertake studies on the CPIAs because the data are secret, work by Dalgaard, Hansen and Tarp (2003: 19–21) suggests that like its predecessor,

the CPIA variables suffer from endogeneity problems, thereby raising serious questions about the findings.

5. These figures for the number of conditions attached to Bank loans are not consistent with, indeed are far lower than, those provided by independent researchers. For instance, Killick's analysis leads him to conclude that the number of conditions stood at 58 in the period 1988–92, falling to 36 by the period 1998–2000 (2004: 14).

6. One of the most rigorous independent assessments of conditionality concluded thus:

Stated baldly, then, our conclusion is that in the general case, conditionality is not an effective means of improving economic policies in recipient countries. The incentive system, most notably the absence of a credible threat of punishment of non-implementation, is usually inadequate in the face of differences between donors and governments about objectives and priorities, and other factors contributing to governments' participation constraints. (Killick *et al.* 1998: 165)

7. PRSPs and the PRGF were preceded by, but have always been very closely linked to, the World Bank's Comprehensive Development Framework (CDF), which emerged from the Bank in 1998/9. As its name suggests, the CDF is meant to provide an all-embracing framework within which relations between the Bank, its clients and its policies would be placed. The four principles of the CDF are long-term, holistic vision; country ownership; country-led partnership; and a results focus. In the words of the Bank, the CDF is essentially a process, not a blueprint to be applied to all countries in a uniform manner. It is a tool to achieve greater development effectiveness. See <http://web.worldbank.org/WBSITE/EXTERNAL/PROJECTS/STRATE-GIES/CDF/0,,pagePK:60447~theSitePK:140576,00.html> (accessed 1 Feb. 2006).

8. The IMF's streamlining has made little difference to its conditionality (Wood 2004: 19). Less flatteringly, Killick suggests that the Fund is still 'in denial' (2004: 13).

9. The Bank's new Operational Policy 8.60 reduces to three its conditions: the maintenance of an adequate macroeconomic framework; the implementation of an overall programme in a manner satisfactory to the Bank; and the implementation of the policy and institutional actions deemed critical for the implementation and expected results of the programme (World Bank 2005e: 4). The Bank's new approach to policy lending was announced in a press statement of 10 Aug. 2004, 'Development Policy Lending Replaces Adjustment Lending', available at <http://web.worldbank.org/WBSITE/EXTERNAL/NEWS/0,,contentMDK:20237378% 257emenuPK:34457%257epagePK:64003015%257epiPK:64003012%257etheSitePK:4607,00 .html> (accessed 3 Nov. 2005).

10. Christian Aid (2005b) provides numerous examples.

11. See Conyers and Mellors (2005: 85), referring to the study by Bräutigam and Knack (2004).

12. The most comprehensive assessment of the World Bank was undertaken by Mosley *et al.* (1991). For a short and succinct overview of the results and findings of the major studies produced to the mid-1990s see Killick *et al.* (1998: 19–52). See also Lensink (1996) for an assessment of programmes in Africa. A recent 50-year review of Latin America concludes that the policy conditionalities of the Fund and Bank were associated with lower growth and rising inequalities, though little evidence is given to show the causal relationships (Bivens 2005). Many of the points raised here are drawn from these studies.

13. The following summary of the impact of the Bank's adjustment policies encapsulates well this particular perspective:

Structural Adjustment does not, on balance, appear to have contributed in a statically significant manner to the medium-term economic performance of most adjusting countries. Part of this failure to make a large impact may be attributable to the fact that the original design of adjustment loans did not focus enough on the microeconomic supply-side reforms. Initial World Bank loan designs also neglected the impact of various policy components on the poor, particularly in the short run. (Ferreira and Keely 2000: 188)

14. 'World Bank Conditionality Review—Nordic–Baltic Position Paper', available at <http://siteresources.worldbank.org/PROJECTS/Resources/40940-1114615847489/ConditionalityNBCposition.pdf> (accessed 4 Nov. 2005).

15. There is even disagreement about the term used to describe the WC approach, with Williamson arguing that it is mistaken to categorize it as an extreme form of neo-liberalism (2003: 11).

16. These issues are discussed in more detail in a range of publications. For some recent overviews of the key issues see Killick (1995a, b); Stiglitz (1998, 2002); Naim (1999); Lensink and White (2000); Buira (2004); Woo (2004); Bird (2005); Gunther *et al.* (2005); Martin and Bagarwi (2005); and Rowden (2005).

17. Strictly speaking, capital account liberalization did not form part of the original ten elements of the WC, though it did form an essential part of subsequent IMF policy packages (see Williamson 2004: 7).

18. There is a huge literature on this issue, of which Wade (1990) and Amsden and Chu (2003) are among the most thorough studies.

19. It is not merely that adjustment processes tend to have different effects on different ethnic groups, but aid, too, is often given disproportionately to dominant groups. See Brown and Stewart (2006) for a recent review of these issues.

20. Some bilateral donors have focused explicitly on ways in which markets could be made to work better for poor groups. See Elliott and Gibson (2004).

21. Paul Wolfowitz, 'Benn Should Be Satisfied with New Bank Policy on Loans', *Financial Times*, 29 Sept. 2006: 18.

22. In his second study of the performance and reform of the IMF, Killick (1995) provides an illuminating discussion, still relevant today, of when and why the Fund has changed its approach and when and why it has not.

23. I am indebted to Simon Maxwell for drawing my attention to this summary (Maxwell 2005: 1).

15 Does official development aid really work? A summing up

1. Strictly speaking, it also has to be shown that the additional resources which the aid provides cannot easily and effectively be obtained from non-aid sources.

2. In part, this discussion needs to be informed by an assessment of the costs and benefits involved: the greater the cost and the lower the benefit, the less easy it is to justify the provision of aid.

16 NGOs in development and the impact of discrete NGO development interventions

1. The term NGO was coined in 1945 because of the need for the United Nations to differentiate two types of international organizations, the specialized agencies and other (private) organizations. The latter were defined as NGOs, thus encompassing a wide variety of organizations, many of which, as noted in Box 16.1, are not involved in humanitarian or development work.

2. For more detailed discussion of what constitutes an NGO see World Bank (1995); Fowler (1997); Willetts (2003).

3. Some of these issues are discussed in Lewis and Wallace (2000) and by Escobar (1995).

4. The intellectual roots of this view of development are closest to those propounded by Nobel Prize winner Amartya Sen (see Sen 1999). They also have close links to the human development perspective articulated in successive *Human Development Reports* produced by the UNDP, though some recent writings from the World Bank have also highlighted the importance of power and the need to incorporate the concepts of empowerment and voice in a complete understanding of development (see World Bank 2001c, 2005a). These issues have been discussed further in Part II.

5. This sense of the term 'voice', linked together with the terms 'exit' and 'loyalty', was coined by Albert Hirschman (1970).

6. The extent to which NGOs, whose *raison d'être* is development, can legitimately operate in the political sphere is an issue that remains contested. It has been addressed in different ways in different countries, depending upon the legal definition of an NGO and how the law is interpreted. In the UK, a distinction has always been made between actions that encompass a political dimension aimed at achieving a development goal (which have often been accepted as legitimate) and actions which are overtly party-political, which have never been allowed. Nevertheless, UK NGOs have been repeatedly required to defend their lobbying, advocacy and campaign activities to the Charity Commission (which regulates the activities of NGOs), which, in turn, is required to investigate complaints made to it, especially by groups which have judged these activities to be illegal. The UK Charities Act (November 2006), under which the activities of NGOs are legally regulated, allows NGOs to pursue (any) activities for the purpose of the prevention and relief of poverty, the advancement of health, the saving of life, and community development, as well as the advancement of human rights and conflict resolution, provided these are deemed to be for public benefit. These changes have been interpreted to confirm more clearly than earlier the legitimacy of NGOs to undertake advocacy, lobbying and campaigning work—provided they can be shown to be of public benefit. For the text of the new charitable laws, see <www.publications.parliament.uk/pa/ld200506/ldbills/001/2006001.pdf> (accessed 1 Oct. 2006).

7. See <www.icco.nl/documents/pdf/jaarverslag%202005%20Engelse%20vertaling.doc> (accessed 17 July 2006).

8. The United States provides a partial exception to this generalization. For decades, all government agencies, notably USAID, which provide funds to PVOs and NGOs have required them to submit detailed project completion reports.

9. A recent review of NGOs working in development in Uganda found that only two-thirds were able to provide revenue and expenditure accounts, and only one-third could match revenues with expenditures (Barr *et al.* 2004: 16).

10. Some larger NGOs have undertaken their own thematic assessments to attempt to learn lessons for themselves from the project interventions they implement or fund in particular sub-sectors.

11. These strong conclusions are made against the backdrop of some attempts to assess the overall impact of aid, such as Masud and Yontcheva 2005. This study was based on such crude assumptions and the omission of so much data on NGO aid as to cast serious doubt on the veracity of many of the sweeping generalizations made (set out on p. 10).

12. Recently, an attempt has been made to assess the contribution of Norwegian NGOs in Sri Lanka and Ethiopia. The methodological challenges involved in undertaking this work are discussed in Baklien *et al.* (2004).

13. Writing just over a decade ago, Hulme and Edwards argued that what NGOs release to the public 'comes closer to propaganda than rigorous assessment' (1995: 6).

14. BRAC's evaluations can be found at <www.bracresearch.org>.

15. Not all NGOs report on the numbers of people directly affected by their programmes. But the number of beneficiaries claimed in the 2005 annual reports of the following six NGOs—ActionAid, ADRA, BRAC, CARE, Proshika and World Vision—totals some 290mn in all. The combined expenditure of these NGOs was around $2.6bn. Thus a worldwide estimate of 600mn people directly assisted by NGO development projects and programmes is likely to be an underestimate.

16. The term 'NGO umbrella' refers to organizations like the Inter-American Foundation (IAF), established in 1969 by the United States Congress to channel funds to grassroots communities in Latin America and the Caribbean. From 1971, it has spent almost $600mn in over 4,500 projects in 32 countries. See <www.iaf.gov/index/index_en.asp> (accessed 28 Nov. 2005).

17. To try to eliminate the influence of selection bias, the Canadian and Australian donor-based impact studies undertook verification studies, comparing the assessments of project impact made by NGOs and by external evaluators. Though disagreements did arise in relation to the financial viability and cost-effectiveness of projects as well as the effects on the overall allevi-ation of poverty, they did not disagree in their assessment of whether project outputs had been successfully delivered (see Riddell *et al.* 1997: 71ff.).

18. The study of Ugandan NGOs (see note 9) reports that virtually no NGO sees itself solely as a provider of services (Barr *et al.* 2004: 38).

19. The evaluation examined four projects supported by CAFOD; the other two—a water project and an HIV/AIDS project—were both found to have been successful (Davies *et al.* 1994).

20. In common with a number of many large NGOs, Christian Aid has developed a formal system requiring all members of staff to report to senior management any cases not merely where a diversion of funds has come to light, but also where there is any suspicion that funds have not been used for the purpose intended. The default position is for all cases of fraud to be brought into the open and where sufficient evidence is available for cases to pass through the law courts.

21. The head of BRAC, the large NGO in Bangladesh, widely known for its innovative work in informal education (see Box 16.1), has argued that BRAC's project success has been predom-inantly due to its replicating and using the ideas of others (Hailey 2002: 72). In contrast, Ian Smillie (1995, 2000) is of the view that much of what the international community knows about the informal sector, micro-enterprise, public health, non-formal child and adult edu-cation, gender and environment has been due to the pioneering work of NGOs.

22. Increases in official aid to enhance the provision of minimal standards of basic health and education services as part of the wider effort to achieve the MDGs has certainly helped to reduce the problems of sub-standard government health and primary education facilities across more and more poor countries, even though significant problems of quality still remain unaddressed.

23. Clearly, for some projects, such as those in the micro-credit sector, or the costs of medicines distributed to patients, it is easier to obtain data on funds used by or provided directly to the ultimate beneficiaries.

24. Part of the reason for high costs is that salaries paid to NGO staff in poor countries are usually significantly higher than those of comparable jobs in the public sector, and salaries of north-ern NGO staff are far higher than salaries paid to staff by local NGOs (for some comparisons, see Telford and Cosgrave 2006: 65, 127–8). However, the salaries of staff working full-time for northern NGOs are usually significantly lower than for comparable jobs in both the public

and private sectors, though the differentials are larger in the UK than they are in Scandinavian countries.

25. I am grateful to David Lewis for this quotation (see Lewis 2001: 9).

26. A recent IMF study concluded that NGO aid does go to the poor (Nancy and Yontcheva 2006), but the study was based on partial figures of aid provided to NGOs by the European Commission, and on project proposal documents, not on field-based evidence of the socio-economic status of the beneficiaries.

27. All three of these NGOs are ready to admit that they still have much to learn. For instance, in its 2005 annual report, Oxfam acknowledges that it still has 'a long way to go in developing new patterns of work and relationships drawing on existing livelihoods and humanitarian strategies, to provide more effective responses to chronic poverty and vulnerability in many countries where we work' (2005: 41).

28. In some countries, some NGOs have (often deliberately) targeted the wealthier strata (Oakley *et al.* 1999: 36–43).

29. According to Lewis (2001: 180ff.), the discourse about NGO capacity building arose in the context of changing relationships between donor-country–based and developing-country-based NGOs. Some donor-country-based NGO approaches to capacity building have been sharply criticized because of their paternalistic assumption that knowledge about how best to build capacity is assumed to reside in the northern NGOs.

30. See James (2005) for a recent example of where this has—quite successfully—been tried.

31. A number of Scandinavian agencies regularly undertake, in particular, 'capacity assessments' of NGOs to whom they provide substantial funds in order to ensure they have the minimum skills and competencies required, making recommendations when shortfalls are assessed.

32. A number of authors have argued that failures of NGOs to build institutional capacities have been due to a reluctance of donors to fund such initiatives, in part because of an unwillingness to provide funding over a long time period (Edwards and Hulme 1995: 8).

33. As discussed in Chapter 12, the impact of official donor efforts in this area has been extremely limited.

34. For further details see Pact's website, <www.pactworld.org/>.

35. Pact was asked to evaluate the impact of the World Bank's small grants programme (see World Bank 2005h: 22).

17 The wider impact of non-governmental and civil society organizations

1. It was only after the EAA was formed that it decided on the first two issues it would campaign on, namely trade and HIV/AIDS.

2. For a review of the evolution of NGO and CSO activities at UN summits, see Pianta (2005).

3. In John Clark's view, NGOs and CSOs have done an invaluable service in elevating issues of trade and economic justice onto the world stage, challenging parochialism with internationalism (2003: 40).

4. See, for instance, Bratton (1990); Roche (1999); Jordan and Tuijl (2000); Pianta (2005); Pitt *et al.* (2005); Pollard and Court (2005); Robinson and Friedman (2005); and Tabbush (2005).

5. To be fair, the study by Court and colleagues was focused largely on national policies and not on impact at the local and grassroots level.

6. The conclusions drawn by Edwards (1993) were influential and, although made many years ago in a very different climate and context, they are still cited to confirm the limits of NGO advocacy.

7. Sadly, this is not an isolated incident. From 2000 to 2005, over 271 international aid workers were murdered (DFID 2006b: 10). The number of nationals killed has been far higher. For instance, in Afghanistan, in April 2006, five medical personnel of a local NGO working with Christian Aid the Rural Rehabilitation Association of Afghanistan, were murdered. The following month, three female staff members of ActionAid were murdered in Afghanistan, and in July 2006 two of World Vision's male health workers were killed. Finally, at the end of August 2006, in the worst individual incident ever recorded, 17 aid workers were murdered in northern Sri Lanka.

8. Monitoring can often be accompanied by advocacy aimed at increasing the allocation of resources to poor communities and to localities where poor people reside.

9. This work has been led by Transparency International (TI), which has played a pivotal role in getting mainstream organizations to take corruption in development seriously—convincing, for instance, an initially reluctant World Bank of the need to understand, and work with official donors to take positive steps to reduce the negative impact of corruption in poor countries, thereby contributing to the effectiveness of aid.

10. See Najam (1999: 156ff.), Lewis (2001: 123ff.), and Anderson (2002: 84ff.) for a fuller list and description of these and other concrete examples of NGO advocacy and campaigning initiatives.

11. Historically, it has been conventional to distinguish between development NGOs which (confusingly) have worked in both the emergency and development fields, environmental NGOs, and human rights NGOs, the last traditionally focusing predominantly on civil and political rights. In recent years, however, especially since the close link between development and the environment has been accepted under the rubric of sustainable development, and since the 1993 Vienna Declaration, when it was formally agreed that all human rights were mutually interrelated and inseparable and that one category cannot take priority over another, this distinction has become extremely blurred. A growing number of development NGOs now undertake their work within a human rights perspective, viewing their activities as different ways of achieving the fulfilment of social, economic, cultural, political and civil rights.

12. Quite early on in a trade campaign supported by all the main UK NGOs, a report produced by Oxfam on trade issues (Oxfam 2002) was bitterly attacked by some NGOs, who claimed it was too closely aligned with the trade-liberalization paradigm, which they viewed as the core of the problem.

13. The government was also influenced by wider and often more rigorous research undertaken well beyond the UK NGO community. NGOs appeared to have been successful in influencing the DFID to take more notice and attach more weight to research which provided a more nuanced and less simplistic view of the benefits of liberalization, not least by focusing more on supply-side constraints.

14. John Clark judges that the Jubilee 2000 campaign probably contributed more to poor countries financially than all operational NGOs combined (2003: 137), whereas Pitt *et al.* argues (2005: 5) that it largely failed to create mechanisms to ensure implementation and monitoring once the campaign had come to an end.

15. Cooperation among NGOs has never been easy. Smillie, quoting the words of David Korten, graphically describes the difficulties: jealousies among them are often intense and efforts at collaboration all too often break down into internecine warfare that paralyses efforts to work together towards the achievement of shared purposes (1994: 23).

16. In most countries, laws and regulations prevent NGOs from undertaking illegal activities, including damage to property and other forms of violent confrontation. It is thus not surprising that all large international and national NGOs have publicly condemned this form of 'influence', which most NGOs, privately, also believe undermines rather than contributes to the changes of policy and approach which their advocacy, lobbying and campaigning are trying to achieve.

17. This is not the place to discuss these important issues further. Suffice it to say that there are a number of different ways in which NGOs can represent the views of those on whose behalf they claim to speak. Rarely is there any form of advocacy more powerful than that provided by those who are themselves aggrieved. If NGOs ('advocacy' NGOs) have no links with or knowledge of the particular views of any groups of poor people upon whose behalf they claim to be speaking, then such NGOs are more akin to political lobbying groups. Most NGOs undertaking substantial advocacy work do so by means of what they call 'rooted advocacy', where what they say is based upon the views and perspectives of those for whom they speak.

18. Matthew Lockwood discusses these sorts of distortions in NGO advocacy and campaigning work (2005: 140ff.).

19. The (deliberately loose) definition given here is drawn from Riddell and Bebbington (1993), Edwards (2004), Sida (2004) and UNDP (1993). See also Van Rooy (1998).

20. USAID opened civil-society funding windows that have provided millions of dollars to NGOs. In 2003, the UK's Foreign and Commonwealth Office launched a $100mn Global Opportunities Fund, part of which was to be channelled through NGOs to support sustainable development by targeting support for good governance and respect for human rights and democracy. For further information, see <www/fco/gov/uk/servlet/Front??pagename= OpenMarket/Xcelerate/ShowPage&c> (accessed 30 Nov. 2005).

21. A recent review for USAID concluded that it had well-documented experience of building, but not strengthening, civil society in Eastern Europe (Buzzard and Webb 2004: 7). The two are not the same.

22. See <www.dfid.gov.uk/aboutdfid/intehuk/workwithcs/cs-how-to-work-understand2.asp> (accessed 9 Dec. 2005).

23. Those authors mentioned in the previous paragraphs in the text, and most scholars who have studied NGOs closely, would almost certainly agree that it is neither possible, nor particularly helpful, to try to draw simple and sweeping across-the-board conclusions about the impact of NGO development interventions.

18 The growth of emergencies and the humanitarian response

1. Though the Red Cross, or more formally the International Federation of Red Cross and Red Crescent Societies (IFRC), is widely assumed to be an NGO, strictly speaking it is not, having instead the status of an international organization (see Stoddard 2003: 27).

2. This definition of humanitarian aid comes from UN General Assembly resolution 46/182 and has been agreed by the OECD/DAC.

3. The principle of neutrality is the one around which there has recently been considerable debate, not least in situations perceived to be, or verging on, genocide: see Macrae and Leader (2000) and Macrae (2002b). There is no requirement under the Geneva Conventions and additional protocols for humanitarian assistance to be given to the military of either side of a conflict (see ICRC 1949, 1966).

4. See the discussion in Chapter 19 of the ALNAP reviews, in the section entitled 'The ALNAP data-base'.

5. Sometimes the issues are not so clear-cut. For instance, a year after the 2004 Asian tsunami, an evaluation of the emergency work of the leading UK humanitarian agencies revealed that only £128mn (36 per cent) of the total £350mn raised from the public had been spent and that tens of thousands of people were still living in inadequate temporary shelter. While the agencies acknowledged that it was unacceptable that so many people were living in temporary accommodation, they firmly defended their decision only to budget first-year expenditure at $151mn, well less than half the money raised. What is more, the evaluators recommended that the agencies take five years, rather than the three years agreed, to spend their emergency funds (Vaux *et al.* 2005: 57; see also 11, 50, 55). However, the wording of the Disasters Emergency Committee (DEC) Tsunami appeal gave no indication to counter the (very strongly held) public perception that the funds would be used as rapidly as possible. It read as follows (e.g. in The *Guardian*, 3 Jan. 2005):

Hundreds and thousands of people across a dozen countries have been affected by the major disaster and devastation caused by the earthquake in the Indian Ocean and the Tsunamis that followed. Aid agencies are working to provide emergency relief and need your support.

6. For a discussion of humanitarian aid in Biafra see Smillie (1995) and de Waal (2002).

7. Figures from Emergency Events Data-Base (EM-DAT), 'Total Number of Country-Level Disasters Reported. World: 1990–2005', available at <www.em-dat.net/documents/figures/global_trends/nb_dis_global.jpg> (accessed 4 Oct. 2006).

8. Figures from ODI (2005: 1) and Christian Aid (2005b: 7).

9. Especially in war zones and in complex emergencies, the figures of people killed tend to vary enormously. Nowhere is this better illustrated than with respect to the Darfur region of the Sudan. Early to mid-2005 reports gave estimates of the numbers killed ranging from 60,000 to over 400,000 (Bercow 2005: 20; *Washington Post*, 24 Apr. 2005: B06).

10. Figures from WHO (2005: pp. ii-iii, 9, 15–19) and the International Rescue Committee (IRC), available at <www.theirc.org/news/irc_study_reveals_31000_die_monthly_in_congo_conflict_and_38_million_died_in_past_six_years_when_will_the_world_pay_attention.html? print=t> (accessed 12 Jan. 2006).

11. On average, the OECD/DAC donors provide about 10 per cent of their total aid (ODA) in the form of emergency and distress relief. However, for some donors, such as Sweden and Norway, emergency aid amounts to over 20 per cent of total ODA, while for others, such as Germany and Japan, the ratio is less than 6 per cent. The United States, the largest provider of humanitarian aid by far, provides around 17 per cent of ODA in the form of emergency aid.

12. For further details see the websites of OCHA and the IASC, available at <http://ochaonline.un.org/org/> and <www.humanitarianinfo.org/iasc/>.

13. More details are provided on the IFRC and ICRC websites: <www.ifrc.org/> and <www.icrc.org/eng>.

14. Since 1995, the figure for overall humanitarian aid has included emergency food aid, and since 1992 it has also included (most) funds spent on refugees within DAC donor countries. Surprisingly, however the OECD/DAC has still not established an agreed definition for official humanitarian assistance (OHA).

15. These estimates are arrived at by adding together the OECD/DAC data on bilateral ODA for emergency and distress reported by bilateral donors and the European Commission, plus the multilateral contributions to UNHCR and UNRWA, plus the multilateral contributions to the WFP in proportion to the share of the WFP's operational expenditure allocated to relief

each year. These figures are derived from both the OECD/DAC data-base and from the Financial Tracking System used by OCHA (see Randel and German 2002).

16. The $12.4bn figure is my own estimate based on the assumptions and methodologies used by the DI in earlier years. This figure is probably a significant underestimate of the total flow of all humanitarian assistance, as it is likely seriously to underestimate the scale of private flows, including that provided by donations to NGOs. According to OECD/DAC data, total grants made by NGOs in 2004 amounted to over $11mn, consisting largely of funds raised privately. If only one-quarter of these funds are used to fund NGOs' emergency programmes (probably an underestimate), then this would add almost $4mn to total emergency aid (double the amount assumed by DI), increasing total humanitarian flows from $12.4bn to more than $15bn. The OECD/DAC gives a 2004 figure of $7.3bn for bilateral emergency aid, almost 13 per cent of all bilateral ODA provided by DAC donors in that year: see <www.oecd.org/dataoecd/52/9/1893143.xls> (accessed 12 Jan. 2006).

17. Figures from latest annual reports: for ECHO, <www.eu.int/comm/echo/statistics/echo_en.htm> (accessed 16 Jan. 2006); for USAID, <www.usaid.gov/our_work/humanitarian_assistance/disaster_assistance/publications/annual_reports/pdf/AR2004.pdf> (accessed 16 Jan. 2006).

18. See ICRC (2005: 350ff.).

19. Figures quoted in a speech by the UK's Secretary of State for International Development, Hilary Benn, on the need for reform of the international humanitarian system: <www.dfid.gov.uk/news/files/Speeches/bennaidsystemreform.asp> (accessed 16 Jan. 2006).

20. This happened in Kosovo in 1999; see Porter (2002: 35).

21. These points are expanded upon, with specific examples, in the ten-year evaluation of the CAP (see Porter 2002).

22. These gaps in funding are confirmed by analysis undertaken each year by ECHO. Its annual analysis of 'forgotten crisis' assessment pinpoints, on a range of criteria, a list of countries where needs remain high but donors have failed adequately to assist. For instance, in the year 2005 ECHO's list contained the names of nine forgotten crisis countries and a further 41 where needs were not sufficiently met, which together amounts to almost 80 per cent of all countries where emergency aid was, or was not, provided. See ECHO, *Forgotten Crises Assessment 2005*, available at <http://europa.eu.int/comm/echo/pdf_files/strategic_methodologies/forgotten_crisis_data_2005_en.pdf> (accessed 16 Jan. 2006). It has been argued that the ECHO assessment is more an assessment of vulnerability than of need (see Darcy and Hoffman 2003: 58).

23. For the text of this brief, see <www.wfp.org/operations/emergency_needs/EFSA_Communication_brief.pdf>. In recent years the UN and other agencies have produced 'how-to' manuals, running to hundreds of pages, to improve the quality of needs assessments. See, for instance, WFP (2005), totalling 370 pages, and UNHCR and WFP (2004), 216 pages.

24. This is true even in the case of food; see WFP (2005), esp. chs. 3 and 5.

25. See Buchanan-Smith and Fabbri (2005) for a succinct summary of the ongoing debate on this issue.

26. As Willetts-King and Faint put it (2005: 13–14), 'There is also at least anecdotal evidence that some appeals reflect a "kitchen sink" approach where agencies submit every project they have ever thought of, with a generous budget, on the assumption that donors will only fund a certain proportion anyway, so that more projects and larger budgets will maximise that agency's funding.'

27. In addition to the $5.9bn pledged by donor governments, the international financial institutions pledged a further $2bn and the governments in the affected countries a further $3.4bn, giving a total of $11.3bn provided by governments and institutional donors.

28. However, the OCHA data record additional humanitarian funding for the tsunami outside the CAP of a further $5bn, giving a total expenditure of just over $6bn. This accounted for 66 per cent of total humanitarian spending for the whole of 2005.

29. Given these huge amounts of funds raised for the tsunami, it might be assumed that less would be available for other emergencies. Though the early figures may not prove to be a good guide to subsequent funding levels and allocations, they did indeed suggest that compared with 2004, funding levels for consolidated Appeals did fall off markedly for most sectors, and that, excluding the tsunami, six months after appeals were launched no appeal had raised more than 52 per cent of the funds required (OCHA 2006: 15).

30. The Principles and Good Practice can be downloaded from <www.reliefweb.int/ghd/a%2023%20Principles%20EN-GHD19.10.04%20RED.doc> (accessed 19 July 2006).

31. The GHD website, launched in 2006, provides regular updates on its activities: <www.goodhumanitariandonorship.org/default.asp>.

32. There is a small but growing literature, some (understandably) polemical in style, describing the inadequacies of the current global system at responding effectively to the needs arising from successive emergencies including large ones. An example would be Rieff (2002).

19 **The impact of emergency and humanitarian aid**

1. There is a growing literature on these important issues. For useful overviews see de Waal (2002), Macrae (2002a, b), Tirman (2003) and Duffield (2004).

2. A 2003 study commissioned by the United Nations on humanitarian activities noted the 'ambiguities surrounding the role and responsibilities of the UN system', in part because of a lack of agreement on the parameters of humanitarian assistance (Dalton *et al.* 2003: 14).

3. Some have argued that the political dimension of humanitarian aid is a new phenomenon, others that the change lies more in the scale of political action. These issues are discussed in Slim (2001).

4. Brubacher refers to some agencies taking what she terms a 'utilitarian approach', by which she means that they present themselves as neutral when carrying out humanitarian work but actually engage in advocacy and influence the conflict (2004: 2).

5. The Dunanist tradition is named after Henri Dunant, who launched the Red Cross in the late nineteenth century (see Stoddard 2003: 27).

6. See Wagner (2006) for a recent and succinct articulation of this perspective.

7. This assessment of the Rwandan genocide was the initiative of the Danish government, and was then commissioned by an international steering committee consisting of all the official OECD bilateral donors, the European Union, the OECD/DAC, nine of the largest multilatenal agencies, the Red Cross, and five of the largest international NGOs. The overall evoluation was conducted with a team of 52 researchers and consultants, at a cost of $1.7mn. It is probably the most authoritative evaluation of a large emergency ever undertaken. The ICRC also made public in late 2005 some of its concerns about the treatment of prisoners at Guantanamo Bay. See <http://news.bbc.co.uk/2/hi/americas/4321324.stm>.

8. In 2001, the influential International Commission on Intervention and State Sovereignty's report *The Responsibility to Protect* articulated the principle that when a state is unable or

unwilling to ensure the human security of its citizens, the principle of non-interference yields to the international responsibility to protect (ICISS 2001: ix). Earlier, the additional protocols to the 1949 Geneva Convention expanded on the nature of protection and what it means in practice, including the prohibition of the destruction of objects necessary for sustenance (ICRC 1996: 37ff.).

9. See <www.un.org/summit2005/documents.html> (accessed 29 Jan. 2006).

10. The 2004 list of minimum standards in education are not prescriptive but (at this stage) have been produced as standards which provide 'guidance on how national governments, other authorities and national and international agencies *may* respond and establish education programmes in emergency settings' (INEE 2004: 7–8; emphasis added).

11. Principle 7 of the Good Humanitarian Donorship (GHD) initiative states that implementing humanitarian agencies should ensure 'to the greatest extent possible, adequate involvement of beneficiaries in the design, implementation, monitoring and evaluation of humanitarian response'.

12. For a complete version of the Code see <www.icrc.org/Web/Eng/siteeng0.nsf/html/57JMNB?OpenDocument> (accessed 19 Jan. 2006).

13. As de Waal asks (2002: 220), can humanitarian agencies save lives in the absence of any form of political contract, since claims to being neutral or politically inoffensive can no longer be taken at face value?

14. The confusion about where humanitarian aid ends and development aid begins and the role of different agencies in providing assistance is highlighted in a 2003 review of the UN's Inter-Agency Standing Committee (IASC). See Jones and Stoddard (2003: 15) and Buchanan-Smith and Fabbri (2005).

15. The GHD principles provide little guidance, stating simply that humanitarian assistance should be provided in ways which are 'supportive of recovery and long-term development' (no. 9).

16. It was only in 1997 that a group of leading donors formally met and agreed to set up the Active Learning Network for Accountability and Performance in HumanitarianAction (ALNAP), whose work led to the OECD/DAC document.The membership of ALNAP includes all leading bilateral donors, all leading UN humanitarian agencies, the ICRC and many leading international NGOs. See Hallam (1998) and the ALNAP website, <www.alnap.org/alnapabout.html#what> (accessed 19 Jan. 2006).

17. The guidelines use the term 'policy evaluations' to refer to that part of the assessment which seeks to understand the rationale and objective for particular humanitarian objectives and the assumptions which lie behind donors pursuing particular actions (OECD 1999b: 24ff.).

18. A recent guide to the how and why of undertaking protection work which develops these themes has been produced: see Slim and Bonwick (2005).

19. For a useful summary of real-time evaluations see Herson and Mitchell (2006).

20. See Checchi and Roberts (2005), and the Standardized Monitoring and Assessment of Relief and Transitions (SMART) programme, an interagency initiative to improve monitoring and evaluation of humanitarian assistance interventions, which is piloting an approach to routinely collect, analyse and disseminate information on the nutrition and mortality experience of populations served by humanitarian interventions. The SMART website is at <www.smartindicators.org/about.htm#overview> (accessed 19 Jan. 2006).

21. The following provides some agency examples. In its 2005/6 work programme, ECHO planned ten evaluations a year, and in its 2004/5 programme, WFP planned to undertake some

64 evaluations. In the period 2004–5, the UNHCR doubled the number of evaluations it undertook to 17 a year, compared to half that number in the period 2000–1. In the period 2002–5, UNICEF undertook three or four emergency or emergency-related evaluations each year. However, not all of these constitute rigorous assessments. From 1997 to 2000, USAID recorded six impact assessments of its emergency and food programmes; since then it has undertaken five more evaluations of emergency or emergency-linked assistance in most years.

22. However, as discussed in Chapter 16, a number of NGOs, such as Care, Oxfam, and more recently Save the Children (UK), now produce annual reviews of their work which include their humanitarian interventions.

23. Following some adverse media coverage of the findings of the evaluation of the DEC response to the food crisis in southern Africa, the DEC Board decided that after September 2004 it would publish only the summary of evaluations it commissions.

24. The DEC launches appeals in response to major disasters on behalf of as many of the 13 NGO members who wish to participate. It distributes the funds raised to participating agencies and commissions external evaluations to assess the impact of the funds provided. Confusingly, however, even while a DEC appeal is in operation, individual agencies are free to raise funds directly from their own members to be spent as each sees fit, though DEC rules do not permit agencies to advertise in the press and media for the duration of the DEC appeal. To add to the confusion, there are numerous NGOs in the UK who are not members of the DEC. In times of large emergencies, they solicit for funds in the press and media, alongside the DEC, reaping financial benefits from the publicity which the DEC appeals usually attract.

25. The following gives a breakdown of which agencies provided ALNAP with their evaluations. ECHO has provided the largest number, submitting 60 by the end of 2005. Between them, 12 of the largest NGOs and NGO groupings produced a further 70, the most prominent being the DEC, Oxfam, Save the Children, Care, Tearfund, the Catholic Agency for Overseas Development (CAFOD) and the Catholic federation Caritas Internationalis. Between them, some ten bilateral donors submitted about 40 evaluations, averaging less than two each per year, the most prominent being Denmark, Switzerland and the United States. For their part, different UN agencies submitted about 60 evaluations, the most prominent of which were UNHCR, WFP and OCHA. The ICRC submitted ten evaluations over the period.

26. Most of the comments in this paragraph are also drawn directly from ALNAP's synthesis of the Kosovo evaluations. See ALNAP 2002, Chapter 3.

27. Assessing performance on the basis of aggregating the score obtained from the evaluations submitted to ALNAP is clearly very different from concluding that about half of all humanitarian interventions are successful and half are not: the ALNAP data-base makes no assumption as to how representative of the overall humanitarian aid effort the evaluations submitted are.

28. In an early assessment of humanitarian action in Darfur, the 2005 ALNAP review noted the efforts of some agencies (particularly NGOs) in highlighting the lack of protection faced by tens of thousands of people in the Sudan, including the positive role that 'highly visible expatriates' had played, though overall the effects fell far short of what was needed (2005: 110).

29. In general, refugees have received far more protection than have the growing number of internally displaced persons (IDPs), due in no small measure to the absence of a UN agency with a remit effectively to oversee and lead activities to address the problems of IDPs.

30. In the case of Hurricane Mitch in Central America in the late 1990s the timely provision of agricultural inputs to many affected communities made a major difference in radically reducing the numbers of people who were forced to move—something unseen by the cameras (see ALNAP 2002: 121).

31. A relatively new area of controversy relates to the provision of food aid in the form of genetically modified grains, an issue which was the subject of much debate in the 2003 emergency in southern Africa (see ALNAP 2004: 96).

32. Between 1999 and 2002, the United States provided food aid to Afghanistan which cost $156mn to purchase. However, it cost a further $111mn to ship it from the United States. See <www.cgdev.org/doc/event%20docs/12.9.05_Food_Aid/food%20aid%20transcript.pdf> (accessed 31 Jan. 2006).

33. The comments in this paragraph are drawn heavily from the 2003 ALNAP annual review of food aid, based on 18 evaluations reviewed in that year, as well as drawing on earlier findings (see ALNAP 2004: 62ff.).

34. In a comparatively rare case which reached the courts, in February 2006, a senior US official admitted taking bribes and stealing more than $2mn from aid funds in Iraq, which were flown home in suitcases. See <http://newsvote.bbc.co.uk/2/hi/middle_east/4675902.stm> (accessed 3 Feb. 2006).

35. In all but the most transitory camps and settlements for refugees and internally displaced people, thriving commercial activity is usually quickly established.

36. In spite of these problems, the overall conclusions of this evaluation are that US humanitarian relief efforts have saved many Congolese lives and prevented, to some extent, still more chaos and suffering: 'Despite some discrete findings to the contrary, well to be expected in such an environment, their overall efforts have been efficient, focused and, above all, courageous' (Reed *et al*. 2004: xi).

37. This comment is based on the view that if there were massive diversions of humanitarian aid, it would not be easy to conceal.

38. See 'Fraudsters Stole $1bn in Hurricane Katrina Relief Cash, Congress Told', The *Guardian*, 15 June 2006, and US Government Accounting Office, 'Hurricanes Katrina and Rita Disaster Relief: Improper and Potentially Fraudulent Payments Estimated to be between $600 Million and $1.4 Billion', available at <www.gao.gov/new.items/d06844t.pdf> (accessed 20 July 2006).

39. For details see the TEC web page: <www.alnap.org/tec/index.htm>.

40. The points made here are based largely on the evaluations of the TEC, evaluations submitted to the TEC by different UN agencies and NGOs, and by the summary of the evaluation of the DEC response: Vaux *et al.* (2005); Cosgrave (2005); and Telford and Cosgrave (2006).

41. Shawn Donnan, 'Little Clarity on How Aid Gets Spent', *Financial Times*, 29 Dec. 2005.

42. In their report on the WFP, Goyder *et al.* (2005) highlight this as a major weakness.

43. A website has been set up as a focus for lobbying and advocacy work on Darfur, available at <www.savedarfur.org> (accessed 24 Jan. 2006).

20 Why aid isn't working

1. The details are in Chapter 6.

2. The word 'potential' is used here because it cannot be assumed that increasing the total amount of aid would automatically result in its being used effectively. The issue of absorptive capacity and the ability of countries to make good use of rising amounts of development aid are discussed later in the chapter.

3. A range of informal domestic and international pressures have been put on donors to provide aid up to a certain level (0.7 per cent of gross national income) and these pressures have been growing in recent years. However, as discussed in Chapter 9, there are no national or international binding or legal obligations on donors either to provide aid to poor countries or to provide it in any specified amounts.

4. For a discussion of the origin of silent partnerships, and some examples of where silent partnerships (also called delegated cooperation) have been operating, see <http://portal.unesco. org/education/en/file_download.php/285ee0d0f5306ef4f53862c06785fec3Koopman_H. doc> (accessed 15 May 2006).

5. Though the Paris Declaration targets are very significant when set against prevailing donor practice, they are far less ambitious than the achievement of full harmonization and alignment of policies. Two key Declaration alignment targets are merely to halve the proportion of aid flows to the government sector not reported on aid-recipient government budgets and for only 50 per cent of technical cooperation flows to be consistent with national development strategies. Four of the harmonization targets for 2010 are for (only) 60 per cent of aid flows to be provided in the context of programme-based approaches, for (only) 25 per cent of such aid to use common arrangements and procedures, for (only) 40 per cent of donor aid missions to be joint missions, and (only) 66 per cent of country-specific analytic work to be a joint activity of all donors (OECD 2006a: 64–5.)

6. A shortened version of the study was published in 2005, entitled *The Samaritan's Dilemma* (Gibson *et al.* 2005). The study analyses aid through the perspective of a 'collective action' framework, applied to situations in which a desired joint outcome requires the input of several individuals. Collective action problems arise when actors choose actions producing outcomes assessed as less desirable than other actions available to them (see Ostrom *et al.* 2002: 9ff.; Gibson *et al.* 2005: 15ff.).

7. These problems are not confined to the donor end of the aid relationship: at the recipient end, too, key staff tend not to be judged or rewarded on the basis of the impact of the aid projects and programmes they oversee or manage (see Gibson *et al.* 2005: 131–219).

8. The final chapter of *The Samaritan's Dilemma* outlines ways in which the problems within aid agencies might be addressed to enhance the effectiveness of aid. The authors end on an optimistic note: 'We hope that this book has provided an analysis of development assistance that helps those in its creation and delivery to reach better outcomes. We believe such a goal is more possible than it was a generation ago' (Gibson *et al.* 2005: 234).

9. For the details see <www.dh.gov.uk/PublicationsAndStatistics/PressReleases/PressReleases Notices/fs/en?CONTENT_ID=4133545&chk=GIqDtl> (accessed 27 Apr. 2006). In sharp contrast, the Immigration Bill that was passing through the US Senate in mid-2006 would have precisely the opposite effect, making it easier for nurses, especially from India and the Philippines, to obtain visas to work in the United States.

10. At the end of July the talks 'collapsed into indefinite suspension' (*Financial Times*, 25 July 2006: 6).

11. This issue is discussed later in the chapter.

12. The way that governance is understood and defined is discussed later in the chapter. See also Box 20.1.

13. The way that weaknesses are assessed differ, and for some groupings, notably for the LICUS group (now also renamed fragile states), governance assessments include judgements about specific economic policies.

14. Contemporary discourse about aid and aid effectiveness continues to be influenced by an often superficial reading of the publication *Assessing Aid: What Works, What Doesn't and Why*

(World Bank 1998), which has been used to suggest that aid should be channelled to those countries able to use it well, characterized by what are assessed to be 'good economic policies and institutional capacities'. However, donors have tended not to do this (see Jones *et al.* 2005). For a succinct summary and critique of *Assessing Aid* see Degnbol-Martinussen and Engberg-Pedersen (2003: 242–51).

15. In their worldwide study of governance, Goran Hyden and colleagues show the ways that good governance and democracy overlap, but conclude that good governance is a prerequisite for democracy and development rather than the other way round (Hyden *et al.* 2004: 192–3).

16. In its 1992 policy paper *Governance and Development*, the World Bank isolated three aspects of governance: (1) the form of the political regime; (2) the process by which authority is exercised in the management of a country's economic activities and relations to other economies; and (3) the capacity of governments to design, formulate and implement policies and discharge functions. In formulating its own policy, the Bank formally confines itself solely to (2) and (3) (Hyden *et al.* 2004: 15).

17. In 1997, the OECD/DAC published a synthesis report, *Evaluation of Programs Promoting Participatory Development and Good Governance* (OECD 1997). However, this consisted only of a summary of studies which focused on different components of good governance, such as efforts to enhance the rule of law and human rights. The synthesis report cited no evaluation which had examined the overall efforts and impact of any single aid agency, or group of aid agencies, to promote good governance in an aid-recipient country. Indeed, most studies summarized were reviews of the issues and not field-based evaluations (OECD 1997: 5). See also Jenkins and Plowden (2006) for an overall critique of the way that donors have tried (unsuccessfully) to transfer governance models to recipient countries; their critique is based, in part, on a review of discrete evaluations of different dimensions of the governance agenda.

18. The tone of some studies and donor reviews suggests that the importance of politics on the impact of aid is a recent discovery. It is not. As discussed in Chapter 3, the political economy of aid was central to discussions on aid-giving in the mid-1970s.

19. For further information about these analyses, see <www.gsdrc.org/go/topic-guides/drivers-of-change#start> (accessed 6 Oct. 2006); and see also van de Walle (2005).

20. Similar conclusions have been drawn in recent studies by both Lockwood (2005) and Van de Walle (2005).

21. Furthermore, the more donors that provide aid in a single country, the more likely is this to happen (see Knack and Rahmann 2004: 24).

22. These points are drawn largely from Unsworth (2005b), itself a synthesis of a five-year research programme with case studies undertaken in both fragile states and others.

21 Making aid work better by implementing agreed reforms

1. Using aid to engineer political change is far from new, and is seen by many as anything but benign. It was an approach used widely in the Cold War era. It is clearly an area fraught with dangers.

2. Donors have always suspended aid programmes, and continue to do so. For example, in April 2006, the Dutch government announced that it had decided, with immediate effect, to suspend the provision of $150mn in aid to Kenya. Earlier in the year, the British government announced that it had suspended the provision of $88mn in aid promised to the Ethiopian government, and would channel some of this aid to and through NGOs and local authorities. In 2005, the British government suspended payment of $23mn promised to the government

of Uganda. In its Memorandum of Understanding with the government of Rwanda signed in early 2006, the British government agreed always to discuss with the government of Rwanda any concerns it had which might lead to an interruption of aid flows, except in 'extreme circumstances'.

3. See Whitfield (2006: 5ff.) for a recent discussion of recipient views on partnership.

22 Making aid work better by recasting aid relationships

1. The proposals made here have been drawn particularly from and influenced by the following studies and reports: Pearson *et al.* (1969); Brandt *et al.* (1980); Hyden (1995); Griffin and McKinley (1996); de Waal (1997); Hyden (1997); Kanbur and Sandler (1999); the South Centre (1999); Martens (2001); Zedillo (2001); Easterley (2002); Macrae *et al.* (2002); the South Centre (2002); Darcy and Hoffmann (2003); Degnbol-Martinussen and Engberg-Pedersen (2003); Griffin (2003); Birdsall (2004); Griffin (2004); Pogge (2004); Pronk (2004); Smillie and Minear (2004); AAI (2005); Adinolfo *et al.* (2005); Alston (2005); Lockwood (2005); UN Millennium Project (2005); Unsworth (2005a); van de Walle (2005); Arndt *et al.* (2006: 80); Browne (2006); and Ranis (2006).

2. Griffin and McKinley do not make the distinction between earmarked and allocated aid, proposing that all poor-country governments should receive all aid 'due' to them (1996: 25).

3. A great advantage of such a system is that, at a stroke, tied aid, and the reduction to aid's potential impact that it creates and perpetuates, would be eliminated.

4. Until agreement is reached on some form of assessed compulsory contributions to be made by donor countries, debates about raising additional aid funds through other means are likely to continue to be championed, and challenged. Recent initiatives have included the following: the introduction of a levy/tax on international air travel (France); proposals (by the UK) to establish an International Finance Facility (IFF) which expands current aid levels by creating and cashing in bonds that have to be repaid (with aid funds); and the linked establishment, in November 2006, of the IFF for Immunisation (IFFm), creating bonds to provide funds for immunization programmes, and supported by the UK, France, Sweden, Italy, Spain and the Gates Foundation. Relatedly, a series of major new aid funds, such as the Global Alliance for Vaccines and Immunization (GAVI), and the Global Fund to Fight AIDS, TB and Malaria (GFATM), have been set up with the hope that they would lead to new pledges of aid rather than the diversion of ODA funds to these new uses. These initiatives sit alongside the proposals made some years ago (but not yet implemented) to tax/levy international financial transactions (the so-called Tobin Tax) using the funds raised to enhance overall aid levels. The main reason why these funds have been set up, or are under active discussion, is because of the failure of donor governments to provide sufficient overall amounts of ODA. Their purpose is to contribute to overcoming shortfalls in aid funding, rather than to address head-on the overall, core problem of insufficient funding. For an overview of different funding initiatives see Reisen (2004).

5. Potential problems could arise for those countries which just fail to qualify for aid under the agreed criteria, especially those characterized by wide inequalities in wealth and income. The historical record suggests that it is highly unlikely that such countries would be left unassisted by donors.

6. This is slightly different from the common pool approach suggested by Kanbur and Sandler (1999: 28ff.), which proposes that the aid needs assessment be undertaken entirely in-country without any reference to a common template.

7. However, Lockwood does not provide details indicating what share of total aid would be provided with very minimal conditions and what share would require far more stringent conditions.

8. Hyden (1995) provides further details of how such a body might function in practice.

9. The implication is that aid would continue to flow to countries regardless of their human rights record, and aid could not be withdrawn from countries which are responsible for extreme violations of human rights. However, in such countries, it would be the National Agency (with strong links to wider civil society) and not the government which would be in control of, and thus which would determine, the uses to which aid is put. Thus, the risk of aid being used to support and strengthen a government widely regarded as an abuser of human rights would be minimal. For instance, if a recipient-country government was diverting line ministry (health and education) funds for military or corrupt purposes, the proposed National Agency would be likely to consider channelling aid through parallel agencies to ensure core services were provided. Additionally, the political necessity of bilateral donors having to withdraw or suspend aid from a country because of human rights abuses would no longer be the sensitive issue it now is for donor governments, precisely because the link between aid and particular donors will have been severed: the channelling of aid to a country would not provide any signal of the political acceptability to donors of the government receiving such aid.

10. Stephen Browne's view is that in very weak and fragile states, bilateral agencies should not provide aid. Rather it should be channelled exclusively through multilateral channels (2006: 144–7).

11. The status of the proposed NAIAs would need to be thought through carefully. There is a strong argument for their being viewed as either 'international' agencies or as hybrid national/international agencies, both as a form of 'quality control' and so that they could more easily attract key staff to work for them for attractive salaries. This, and the status the jobs would likely attract, would be likely to stimulate the return home of skilled nationals, notably those who currently work for international aid agencies, providing important added benefits.

12. For a discussion of the role of aid in the provision of international and regional public goods see, for instance, Griffin and McKinley (1996); Kaul *et al.* (1999, 2003); Kanbur and Sandler (1999); Birdsall (2004); Browne (2006); Velde *et al.* (2006); and the website <www.sdnp.undp.org/gpgn>.

13. A major study on aid for trade has been undertaken by the International Lawyers and Economists Against Poverty (ILEAP). For references see <www.ileap-jeicp.org>.

14. In early 2006, the Netherlands put forward ideas as part of a coalition of 13 'like-minded' donors to propose the closing down of at least a third of UN agencies, and a merging of the rest into three 'strong pillars', to begin to address the multiplicity of problems in the multilateral agencies. However, it acknowledged that its efforts would not succeed unless supported by all major donor governments. See the speech by Agnes van Ardenne-van der Hoeven, Minister of Development Cooperation, 31 Jan. 2006; available at <www.minbuza.nl/default.asp?CMS_ITEM=4DADB075E1AA41AA9B00B1ECC8E58F02X3X40032X8> (accessed 20 May 2006).

15. This proposal is refined later in the chapter to expand the proposed Commission's remit from aid and development explicitly to include emergency as well as development aid, and the link between the two.

16. Regular reports on the implementation of the reforms being led by the UN appear on the OCHA website. See, for instance, the March 2006 report, available at <www.reliefweb.int/library/documents/2006/ocha-gen-31mar.pdf> (accessed 26 May 2006).

17. The first Good Humanitarian Donorship meeting, in 2003, discussed the vision of 90 per cent of the basic humanitarian needs of people affected by conflict and disasters being met by the year 2015. Against this backdrop, such a proposal does not appear to be far-fetched. When large emergencies occur in the context of a revamped and far larger Global Emergency Fund, especially those given extensive media coverage, governments and individuals will (rightly) want to contribute to these high-profile emergencies. Clearly, if governments or individuals provide additional money for particular high-profile emergencies, there would be less need to call on funds from the proposed enlarged Global Emergency Fund to meet the humanitarian needs of such emergencies.

18. Though the CAP remains possibly the best mechanism that currently exists to raise emergency funds, even the 2002 in-depth review recognized its fundamental and systemic weaknesses (Porter 2002).

19. In 1998, OCHA was created with a mandate which includes the coordination of humanitarian response, advocacy and policy development. However, the IASC, which is chaired by the Head of OCHA, and which is made up of UN agencies, the Red Cross and representatives of NGOs, also has a mandate of coordination as well as of policy development. As the ten-year review of the IASC confirmed, there remains a lack of clarity over the roles and responsibilities of OCHA and the IASC as well as over how the problem of overlapping roles ought to be addressed (see Jones and Stoddard 2003: iv, 26ff.).

20. The most important problem identified by the *Humanitarian Response Review* was the low level of preparedness of humanitarian organizations (Adinolfi *et al.* 2005: 9).

21. Clearly, for complex emergencies, this sort of approach will not always be appropriate.

22. In a recent report to the Economic and Social Council of the UN (ECOSOC), the UN Secretary General criticizes donors not merely for failing to help strengthen the resident coordinator system but for deliberately setting up parallel structures which further undermine the system (ECOSOC 2005: para. 44).

23. There is clearly far more that could be done by NGOs to enhance their accountability and transparency. See the website of One World Trust for a wide range of references on NGO accountability, including those related to its own initiative, *Pathways to Accountability*: <www.oneworldtrust.org>.

24. A 2006 survey (though not representative) of quality standards among British NGOs found that almost a quarter (26 per cent) did not use any kind of quality standards when undertaking project work in poor countries, almost 70 per cent agreed that quality standards for their projects constituted the biggest challenge, while less than 2 per cent had systems in place to learn lessons on quality issues and were actively training staff. See 'BOND Survey to BOND Members on Quality Standards', available at <www.bond.org.uk/pubs/lte/standards/surveyresults.pdf> (accessed 30 May 2006).

25. As discussed in Chapter 18, the Code of Conduct for NGOs involved in humanitarian activities is merely a list of general (though important) principles which agencies sign. What is being proposed here is not a one-off agreement to abide by the principles (which have been externally generated), but a set of norms against which performance is assessed on an ongoing basis.

26. In mid-2006, Oxfam, Greenpeace and Amnesty International formally agreed to adhere to a code of conduct governing their overall operations, laying down standards to which they wished to be held accountable.

27. One criticism of the Sphere initiative is that it has developed such detailed standards that it has become too burdensome a tool to use effectively.

28. For recent overviews see Harvey (2005), Harvey *et al.* (2005) and IDS (2006).

29. For some recent examples from Africa, South America and South Asia, see Hanlon (2004), Barrientos and Dejong (2004) and the following webpage: <www.ids.ac.uk/ids/pvty/pdf-files/SocialProtectionPublications.pdf> (accessed 1 June 2006).

30. It may, at first, appear strange that the OECD/DAC is being proposed to lead on this work when official donors' reluctance to provide aid in these forms has been so significant. The reason is that the OECD/DAC has achieved major successes in changing donor practice through its syntheses and best-practice work, and as a result of the integrity and quality of the research and linked work it has commissioned and championed.

31. These issues have recently been aired, for example, in Birdsall (2004), Easterly (2006) and Savedoff *et al.* (2006).

32. There are clearly dangers in associating this sort of initiative with any aid agency or group of agencies. It has to be independent. Thus it could be argued that associating it with the UN would unduly compromise its independence. If an independent commission on aid and development were to be set up, then this commission could at least begin this work.

33. For instance, Emmerij dismisses Griffin's proposal that voluntary aid-giving should be replaced by compulsory contributions as 'pie in the sky' (Griffin 2004: 1090).

34. In the United Kingdom, organizations like the World Development Movement (WDM) were set up precisely in order to free themselves from the constraints which NGOs with their own development programmes face in 'speaking out'. However, ironically, many such organizations (especially outside the United Kingdom) have in practice often tended to have their work challenged by donors, politicians and other decision-makers, who have argued (often wrongly) that because they have no direct links to poor people and poor communities, they do not need to take so much notice of their views.

35. In their joint submission to the 2005 aid conference, ActionAid and Oxfam correctly observed that 'so far donors have been keen to keep ... systemic issues off the agenda for Paris, and talked about aid effectiveness as if it is disembodied and can be tackled separately from underlying objectives, incentives and institutions. Instead, they need to kick start a structured discussion with recipients and civil society about how best to reform the aid architecture' (2006: 9).

36. It has been argued that the (path-breaking) creation of the International Criminal Court and the Treaty on Landmines owed its success to the leadership and commitment of the governments of Italy and Canada (Archibugi and Marchetti 2005).

37. It might be thought that the proposals for fundamental change in the way that official aid funds are raised and allocated would be resisted most in the United States, given the dominance of national interests and the importance that short-term political considerations have had in aid decisions. However, some substantial changes have already occurred, and others may well unfold after the Bush Presidency. Two can be highlighted here.

    The first is the elevation of development to equal status and independent standing alongside defense and diplomacy that formally occurred in 2002 under the President's National Security Strategy (p. 57). A key challenge for the new Administration is for this new principle to become operational in practice, an objective which has significant support from influential quarters, such as the Brookings Institution. As Lael Brainard has argued, "while complementary, development and diplomacy are fundamentally different missions. . . . Importantly, maintaining the integrity of independent diplomatic and development functions makes it far easier to manage the frequent tension between short-term political objectives - which often require working with undemocratic regimes - and longer term economic and political reform objectives" http://www.brookings.edu/testimony/2008/0123_foreign_assistance_reform_brainard.aspx?emc=lm&m=212252&l=33&v=27828 (accessed 1 February 2008).

The second change relates to what is happening in the politics of aid within the United States, and whether this not only explains the dramatic growth in American aid in the first years of the 21st century but also marks a rupture in the historical dualism of diplomacy and development that has characterized official aid-giving from its origins in the late 1940s. In the view of Carol Lancaster, one of the leading scholars of the politics of aid, it might, and, if it does, the consequences are likely to be profound. "In sum, the politics of US aid may be in the process of fundamental political change, with potentially enormous implications for the future amount and direction of that aid. These changes may take US aid in directions quite different from the past - a greater emphasis in aid-giving on development and related issues, a broader basis of domestic support for development aid, drawing together an unexpected coalition of the Christian right and the secular left and possibly leading to higher aid levels over time. If these changes come to pass, they could be the most important shift in the politics of US foreign aid since its creation in 1947." (Lancaster, 2006: 107-9.)

■ REFERENCES

AAI (ActionAid International) (2005), *Real Aid: An Agenda for Making Aid Really Work* (Johannesburg: ActionAid International).

—— (2006), *Tsunami Response: A Human Rights Assessment* (Johannesburg: AAI).

—— and Oxfam International (2005), *Millstone or Milestone: What Rich Countries Must Do in Paris to Make Aid Work for Poor People* (London: AAI).

Acharya, A., A. de Lima, and M. Moore (2004), *Aid Proliferation: How Responsible are the Donors?*, IDS Working Paper no. 21 (Brighton: Institute of Development Studies).

Adam, C. S., and D. Bevan (2005), *Aid and the Supply Side: Public Investment, Export Performance and Dutch Disease in Low Income Countries*, Discussion Paper Series (Oxford: Department of Economics, University of Oxford).

—— A. Bigsten, P. Collier, E. Julin, and S. O'Connell (1994), *Evaluation of Swedish Development Co-operation with Tanzania* (Stockholm: Ministry for Foreign Affairs).

ADB (Asian Development Bank) (1991), *Nepal Background Paper for the 2001 Country Portfolio Review Mission* (Kathmandu: ADB).

—— (2005), *Annual Evaluation Review* (Manila: ADB).

Addison, T. (2000), 'Aid and Conflict', in Tarp and Hjertholm (2000), 393–407.

—— G. Mavrotas, and M. McGillivray (2005), *Development Assistance and Development Finance: Evidence and Global Policy Agendas*, WIDER Research Paper no. 23 (Helsinki: WIDER).

Adelman, C. C., J. Norris, and J. Weicher (2005), *America's Total Engagement with the Developing World: Rethinking the Nature and Uses of Foreign Aid* (Washington, DC: Hudson Institute).

Adinolfo, C., D. S. Bassiouni, H. F. Lauritzsen, and H. R. Williams (2005), *Humanitarian Response Review: An Independent Report Commissioned by the United Nations' Emergency Relief Coordinator and Under-Secretary-General for Humanitarian Affairs* (New York and Geneva: United Nations).

AfDB (African Development Bank) (2004), *Review of 2001–2002 Evaluation Results* (Tunis Belvedère: AfDB).

Ahmed, R. (2003), 'DSK: a model for securing access to water for the urban poor', available at <www.wateraid.org.uk/documents/bangladesh_dsk.pdf> (accessed 17 July 2006).

Alesina, A., and D. Dollar (2000), 'Who Gives Foreign Aid to Whom and Why?', *Journal of Economic Growth*, 5: 33–63.

ALNAP (Active Learning Network for Accountability and Performance) (2001, 2002, 2003), *ALNAP Review* (London: ODI).

—— (2004), *ALNAP Review of Humanitarian Action in 2004* (London: ODI).

—— (2005), *ALNAP Review of Humanitarian Action in 2005* (London: ODI).

Alonso, J. A. (2005), 'Spanish Foreign Aid: Flaws of an Emerging Framework', in Hoebink and Stokke (2005), 493–517.

Alston, P. (2005), 'Ships Passing in the Night: The Current State of the Human Rights and Development Debate Seen through the Lens of the Millennium Development Goals', *Human Rights Quarterly*, 27.3: 755–829.

—— and G. Quinn (1987), 'The Nature and Scope of States Parties' Obligations under the International Covenant on Economic, Social and Cultural Rights', *Human Rights Quarterly*, 9.2: 156–229.

Amsden, A. and W-W. Chu (2003), *Beyond Late Development: Taiwan's Upgrading Policies* (Boston: MIT Press).

Anderson, M. B. (1999), *Do No Harm: how aid can support peace—or war* (Boulder, CO: Lynne Rienner).

Anderson, I. (2002), 'Northern NGO Advocacy: Perceptions, Reality and the Challenge', in Eade (2002), 84–112.

Anderson, E., and H. Waddington (2006), 'Aid and the MDG Poverty Target: How Much is Required and How Should it be Allocated?', paper presented to the WIDER Conference on Aid, Helsinki, June 2006; available at <www.wider.unu.edu/conference/conference-2006-1/conference-2006-1.htm> (accessed 14 June 2006).

Andersson, C. (1986), 'Breaking Though', in Frühling (1986), 27–44.

Anheier, H., M. Glasius, and M. Kaldor (2004), *Global Civil Society 2004/5* (London: Sage).

Annan, K. (2005), 'In Larger Freedom: Decision Time at the UN', *Foreign Affairs*, 84.3: 63–74.

Archibugi, D., and R. Marechetti (2005), 'What to do with the United Nations?', <www.opendemocracy.net/democracy-institutions_government/UN_2816.jsp> (accessed 29 May 2006).

Arndt, C., S. Jones, and F. Tarp (2006), 'Aid and Development in Mozambique', paper presented to the WIDER Conference on Aid, Helsinki, June 2006; available at <www.wider.unu.edu/conference/conference-2006-1/conference-2006-1.htm> (accessed 14 June 2006).

Asra, A., G. Estrada, Y. Kim, and M. G. Quibria (2005), *Poverty and Foreign Aid: Evidence from Recent Cross-Country Data*, ADB Economic Research Department Working Paper no. 65 (Manila: ADB).

AusAID (Australian Agency for International Development) (2000), *Good Governance: Guiding Principles for Implementation* (Canberra: AusAID).

—— (2004), *AusAID Annual Report 2003–2004* (Canberra: AusAID).

—— (2005), *Overseas Aid Study* (Canberra: AusAID).

—— (2006), *Australian Aid: Promoting Growth and Stability* (Canberra: AusAID).

Aziz, S., L. D. Diogo, and J. Stoltenberg (co-chairs) (2006), *Delivering as One. Report of the Secretary-General's High-Level Panel.* (New York: United Nations), available at <http://www.un.org/events/panel/resources/pdfs/HLP-SWC-FinalReport.pdf> (accessed 17 November 2006).

Backström, J., C. Malmerius, and R. Sandahl (2004), *Sida's Performance Analyses* (Stockholm: Swedish International Cooperation Development Agency).

Bailey, B. (2003), *Synthesis of Lessons Learned of Donor Practices in Fighting Corruption* (Paris: Organisation for Economic Cooperation and Development).

Baklien, B., D. Getachew, M. Haug, J. Helland, and C. Weerackody (2004), 'Study of the impact of Norwegian NGOs on civil society: FORUT (Sri Lanka) and Save the Children Norway (Ethiopia)', <www.norad.no/items/2784/38/5063637394/NIBR%201%20delrapport.doc> (accessed 17 July 2006).

Baliamoune-Lutz, M. (2006), 'Aid Effectiveness: The Aid–Social Capital–Growth Nexus', paper presented to the WIDER Conference on Aid, Helsinki, June 2006; available at <www.wider.unu.edu/conference/conference-2006-1/conference-2006-1.htm> (accessed 14 June 2006).

Banati, P., G. Greene, and S. Ferazzi (2006), *Funding the Global Fight Against HIV/AIDS, Tuberculosis and Malaria: Resource Needs for the Global Fund* (Geneva: The Global Fund).

Banerjee, A., and R. He (forthcoming), 'Making Aid Work', in Easterly (forthcoming).

Barclay, A. H., M. W. Hoskis, W. K. Njenga, and R. B. Tripp (1979), *The Impact of Private Voluntary Organizations: Kenya and Niger* (Washington, DC: Development Alternatives).

Barder, O. (2006), *A Policymaker's Guide to Dutch Disease* (Washington, DC: Center for Global Development).

Barr, A., M. Fafchamps, and T. Owens (2004), *The Resources and Governance of Non-Governmental Organizations in Uganda*, CSAE Working Paper no. 6 (Oxford: Centre for the Study of African Economies).

Barrientos, A., and J. Dejong (2004), *Child Poverty and Cash Transfers*, Childhood Poverty Research and Policy Centre Report No. 4 (London: Save the Children).

Bartelink, J., and J. Starkenburg (2000), *Institutional Development: Netherlands Support to the Water Sector, 1988–1998*, Policy and Operations Evaluation Department, Job-Evaluations No. 284 (The Hague: Ministry of Foreign Affairs).

Bauer, P. T. (1971), *Dissent on Development* (London: Weidenfeld and Nicolson).

Beasley, A., D. Colin, J. Malick, A. Melnyk, M. Pitter-Lunn, and D. Ray (2005), *General Budget Support: Key Findings of Five USAID Studies* (Washington, DC: United States Agency for International Development).

Bebbington, A. and D. Miltlin (1996), *NGO Capacity and Effectiveness: A Review of Themes in NGO-Related Research Recently Funded by ESCOR* (London: International Institute for Environment and Development).

Beitz, C. (2004), 'Human Rights and the Laws of Peoples', in Chatterjee (2004), 193–216.

Bercow, J. (2005), 'The Message We Must Send to the Butchers of Khartoum', *Parliamentary Briefing*, July 2005: 20–1.

Berg, E. (1993), *Rethinking Technical Cooperation* (New York: United Nations Development Programme).

Berg, A., M. Hussain, S. Aiyar, S. Roache, T. Mirzoev, and A. Mohone (2006), 'The Macroeconomics of Managing Increased Aid Inflows: Experiences of Low-Income Countries and Policy Implications', paper presented to the WIDER conference on Aid, Helsinki, June 2006; available at <www.wider.unu.edu/conference/conference-2006-1/conference-2006-1.htm> (accessed 14 June 2006).

Berthélemy, J-C. (2004), *Bilateralism and Multilateralism in Official Development Assistance Policies*, University of Paris 1.TEAM Working Paper no. 04014 (Paris: University of Paris 1.TEAM).

—— (2005), *Bilateral Donors' Interest vs Recipient's Development Motives in Aid Allocation: Do All Donors Behave the Same?*, University of Paris 1.TEAM Working Paper No. 05001 (Paris: University of Paris 1.TEAM).

—— and A. Tichit (2002), *Bilateral Donors' Aid Allocation Decisions: A Three-Dimensional Panel Analysis*, WIDER Discussion Paper No. 123 (Helsinki: WIDER).

Bevan, D. (forthcoming), 'An Analytical Overview of Aid Absorption: Recognizing and Avoiding Macroeconomic Hazards', in L. Lipschitz (ed.), *Foreign Aid and Macroeconomic Management* (Washington, DC: International Monetary Fund Institute).

Beynon, J. (2003), *Poverty-Efficient Aid Allocations: Collier/Dollar Revisited*, Economic and Statistics Analysis Unit Working Paper No. 2 (London: ODI).

Bigsten, A., J. W. Gunning, and F. Tarp (2006), 'The Effectiveness of Foreign Aid: Overview and an Evaluation Proposal', available at <www.sida.se/shared/jsp/download.jsp?f=evaluation_proposal_february_2006.pdf&a=4542> (accessed 11 July 2006).

Bird, G. (2005), 'The IMF and Poor Countries: Towards a More Fulfilling Relationship', in Teunissen and Akkerman (2005), 16–61.

Birdsall, N. (2004), *Seven Deadly Sins: Reflections of Donor Failings*, CGD Working Paper No. 50 (Washington, DC: CGD).

—— D. Rodrick, and A. Subramanian (2005), 'How to Help Poor Countries', *Foreign Affairs*, 84.4: 136–52.

—— M. Vaishnav, and R. L. Ayres (2006), *Short of the Goal: US Policy and Poorly Performing States* (Washington, DC: CGD).

Bivens, L. J. (2005), *Reclaiming an Economic Future Through Democracy: A New Direction for Economic Policy in the Americas*, Brief No. 217 (Washington, DC: Economic Policy Institute).

Black, M. (1992), *A Cause for our Times: Oxfam—The first fifty years* (Oxford: Oxfam).

Blair, H. (2000), 'Civil Society, Empowerment, Democratic Pluralism and Poverty Reduction: Delivering the Goods at the National and Local Levels', in Lewis and Wallace (2000), 109–20.

BMZ (Bundesministerium Für Wirtschaftliche Zusamenarbeit und Entwicklung) (2001), *Poverty Reduction—A Global Responsibility. Program of Action 2015—The German Government's Contribution to Halving Extreme Poverty Worldwide*, BMZ Informational Materials No. 108 (Bonn: Bundesministerium Für Wirtschaftliche Zusamenarbeit und Entwichlung).

Bøås, M. (2002), *Public Attitudes to Aid in Norway and Japan*, CDE Working Paper No. 02 (Oslo: Centre for Development and the Environment, University of Oslo).

Bond, M. (2000), 'The Backlash Against NGOs', *Prospect Magazine*, April 2000, available at <www.globalpolicy.org/ngos/backlash.htm> (accessed 1 Dec. 2005).

Boone, P. (1994), *The Impact of Foreign Aid on Savings and Growth*, Centre for Economic Performance Working Paper No. 1265. (London: London School of Economics).

—— (1996), 'Politics and the Effectiveness of Foreign Aid', *European Economic Review*, 40: 289–329.

Booth, D. (2005) 'The Africa Commission Report: What About the Politics?' *Development Policy Review*, 23, 4, 493–98.

—— D. Cammack, J. Harrigan, E. Kanyongolo, M. Mataure, and N. Ngwira (2006), *Drivers of Change and Development in Malawi*, ODI Working Paper No. 261 (London: ODI).

—— R. Crook, E. Gyimah-Boadi, T. Killick, R. Luckham, and N. Boateng (2005), *What are the Drivers of Change in Ghana?*, ODI Policy Brief No. 1 (Nov.) (London: ODI).

Borton, J., E. Brusset, and A. Hallam (1996), *International Response to Conflict and Genocide: Lessons from the Rwandan Experience* (London: ODI).

—— M. Buchanan-Smith, and R. Otto (2005), *Support to Internally Displaced Persons: Learning from Evaluations. Synthesis Report of a Joint Evaluation Programme* (Stockholm: Sida).

Bossuyt, J. (2001), *Mainstreaming Institutional Development: Why it is Important and How it Can be Done* (Maastricht: European Centre for Development Policy Management).

Boughton, J. M. (2003), *Who's in Charge? Ownership and Conditionality in IMF-Supported Programmes*, IMF Working Paper No. 02/72 (Washington, DC: International Monetary Fund).

Brandt, W. (1980), *North–South: A Programme for Survival*, the Report of the Independent Commission on International Development (London: Pan Books).

—— (1983), *Common Crisis. North–South: Cooperation for World Recovery* (London: Pan Books).

Bratton, M. (1990), 'Non-Governmental Organizations in Africa: Can They Influence Public Policy?', *Development Policy Review*, 21: 87–118.

Bräutigam, D. A. (2004), 'The People's Budget? Politics, Power, Popular Participation and Pro-Poor Economic Policy', paper prepared for the Expert Group meeting on Participation of Civil Society in Fiscal Policy, United Nations, New York, March 2004 (mimeo).

—— and S. Knack (2004), 'Foreign Aid, Institutions and Governance in Sub-Saharan Africa', *Economic Development and Cultural Change*, 52: 255–85.

Brown, C. (2002), *Sovereignty, Rights and Justice: International Political Theory Today* (Cambridge: Polity Press).

Brown, L. D., and J. Fox (2001), 'Transnational Civil Society Coalitions and the World Bank: Lessons from Project and Policy Influence Campaigns', in Edwards and Gaventa (2001), 43–58.

Brown, G., and F. Stewart (2006), 'The Implications of Horizontal Inequality in Aid', paper presented to the WIDER Conference on Aid, Helsinki, June 2006: available at <www.wider.unu.edu/conference/conference-2006-1/conference-2006-1.htm> (accessed 14 June 2006).

Browne, S. (1990), *Foreign Aid in Practice* (London: Pinter Reference).

—— (2002), *Developing Capacity through Technical Cooperation* (London: Earthscan).

—— (2004), *Poverty Reduction Strategies in Africa: The Limits of Expectations* (Harare: African Capacity Building Foundation).

—— (2006), *Aid and Influence: Do Donors Help or Hinder?* (London: Earthscan).

Brubacher, B. (2004), 'Moral and Practical Challenges to NGO Neutrality', *Ontrac*, 28.1–2 (Sept.).

Buchanan-Smith, M. and P. Fabbri (2005), 'Linking Relief, Rehabilitation and Development: A Preliminary Review of the Debate', available at <www.alnap.org/tec/pdf/lrrd_tor_annex.pdf> (accessed 17 Jan. 2006).

Buira, A. (2004), 'The Dogmatism of the Washington Consensus', in Teunissen and Akkerman (2004), 44–52.

Bulír, A., and A. J. Hamann (2006), *Volatility of Development Aid: From the Frying Pan into the Fire?*, IMF Working Paper No. 06/65 (Washington, DC: IMF).

Burnside, C. and D. Dollar (2000), *Aid, Policies and Growth*, World Bank Policy Research Paper No. 1777 (Washington, DC: World Bank).

Buzzard, S. and A. K. Webb (2004), 'Summary of Mechanisms for PVO–NGO Collaboration: The Development Community', paper prepared for the Bureau for Democracy, Conflict and Humanitarian Assistance (mimeo).

Cabezas, M., and R. Vos (2004), *Illusions and Disillusions with Pro-Poor Growth* (Stockholm: Sida).

Carroll, T. F. (1992), *Intermediary NGOs: The Supporting Link in Grassroots Development* (West Hartford, CT: Kumarian Press).

Cassels, A. and Watson, J. (2001), *ODA/DFID Support to Health Sector Reform and Health Sector Management: Synthesis Study*, Evaluation Report EV 594 (London: Department for International Development).

Cassen, R. H. and Associates (1986), *Does Aid Work? Report to an Intergovernmental Task Force*, 1st edn (2nd edn 1994) (Oxford: Oxford University Press).

Catterson, J. and C. Lindahl (1999), *The Sustainability Enigma: Aid Dependency and the Phasing Out of Projects. The Case of Swedish Aid to Tanzania* (Stockholm: Expert Group on Development Issues).

CBO (Congressional Budget Office) (2005), *Remittances: International Payments by Migrants* (Washington, DC: Congressional Budget Office).

Chambers, R. (2005), *Ideas for Development* (London: Earthscan).

Chapman, D. W. (2002), *Global 2002: A Review of Evaluations of UNICEF's Education Activities, 1994–2000* (New York: United Nations Children's Fund).

Chatterjee, D. K. (ed.) (2004), *The Ethics of Assistance: Morality and the Distant Needy* (Cambridge: Cambridge University Press).

Chauvet, L. and P. Guillaumont (2002), 'Aid and Growth Revisited: Policy, Economic Vulnerability and Political Stability', available at <http://wbln0018.worldbank.org/eurvp/web.nsf/Pages/Paper+ by+Guillaumont/$File/GUILLAUMONT.PDF> (accessed 27 Oct. 2005).

Checchi, F. and L. Roberts (2005), *Interpreting and Using Mortality Data in Humanitarian Emergencies*, Humanitarian Practice Network (HPN) Network Paper (London: ODI).

Chenery, H., and A. M. Strout (1966), 'Foreign Assistance and Economic Development', *American Economic Review*, 56: 679–733.

—— M. T. Ahluwalia, C. L. G. Bell, J. H. Duloy, and R. Jolly (1974), *Redistribution with Growth* (Oxford: Oxford University Press).

Christian Aid (2005a), *Business as Usual: The World Bank, the IMF and the Liberalisation Agenda* (London: Christian Aid).

—— (2005b), *Don't be Scared, be Prepared: How Disaster Preparedness can Save Lives and Money* (London: Christian Aid).

Clark, J. (2003), *Worlds Apart: civil society and the battle for ethical globalization* (London: Earthscan).

Clark, D. A. (2005), *The Capability Approach: Its Development, Critique and Recent Advances*, ESRC Global Policy Research Group Working Paper No. 32 (Oxford: Economic and Social Research Council, Global Policy Research Group).

Clay, E. J. (2005), *The Development Effectiveness of Food Aid and the Effects of its Tying Status* (Paris: OECD).

Clemens, M. A., and T. J. Moss (2005), *Ghost of 0.7%: Origins and Relevance of the International Aid Target*, CGD Working Paper No. 68 (Washington, DC: CGD).

—— S. Radlett, and R. Bhavnani (2004), *Counting Chickens When They Hatch: The Short Term Effect of Aid on Growth*, CGD Working Paper No. 44 (Washington, DC: CGD).

Cogneau, D. and D. Naudet (2004), *Who Deserves Aid? Equality of opportunity, International Aid and Poverty Reduction*, DIAL Document de Travail No. 10 (Paris: Institut de recherche pour le développement et Analyses de Long Terme).

Cohen, D., P. Jacquet, and H. Reisen (2005), 'Beyond "Grants versus Loans": How to Use ODA and Debt for Development', paper presented to WIDER conference on aid, Helsinki, June 2006; available at <www.wider.unu.edu/conference/conference-2006-1/conference-2006-1.htm> (accessed 15 June 2006).

Collier, P., and D. Dollar (1999), *Aid Allocation and Poverty Reduction*, World Bank Policy Research Working Paper No. 2041 (Washington, DC: World Bank).

—— (2002), 'Aid Allocation and Poverty Reduction', *European Economic Review*, 26: 1475–1500.

Collier, P., and D. Dollar (2004), 'Development Effectiveness: What Have We Learned?', *Economic Journal*, 114: F244–71.

—— and A. Hoeffler (2004), 'Aid, Policies and Growth in Post-Conflict Societies', *European Economic Review*, 48: 1125–45.

—— B. Goderis, and A. Hoeffler (2006), 'Shocks and Growth: Adaptation, Precaution and Compensation', paper presented to the WIDER Conference on Aid, Helsinki, June 2006; available at <www.wider.unu.edu/conference/conference-2006-1/conference-2006-1.htm> (accessed 20 June 2006).

Commission for Africa (2005), *Our Common Interest: Report of the Commission for Africa* (London: Penguin Books).

Conyers, D. and R. Mellors (2005), 'Aid Ineffectiveness in Sub-Saharan Africa: The Problem of Donor Capacity', *IDS Bulletin*, 36.3: 83–9.

Cooksey, B. (2003), 'Aid and Corruption: A Worm's-Eye View of Donor Policies and Practices', paper presented to the Eleventh International Anti-Corruption Conference, Seoul, South Korea, May 2003; available at <www.11iacc.org/download/paper/WS_5.6_Cooksey_Final_Paper.doc> (accessed 1 Feb. 2006).

Cooray, R., R. Gottschalk, and Md Shahiduzzaman (2005), *Will Japan Increase Aid and Improve its Allocation to Help the Poorer Countries Achieve the Millennium Development Goals?*, IDS Working Paper No. 243 (Brighton: IDS).

Cornia, G., R. Jolly, and F. Stewart (1998), *Adjustment with a Human Face*, 2nd edn (Oxford: Oxford University Press).

Cosgrave, J. (2005), *Tsunami Evaluation Coalition: Initial Findings* (London: ODI).

Cotterrell, L. and A. Harmer (2005), *Diversity in Donorship: The Changing Landscape of Official Humanitarian Aid* (London: ODI).

Court, J., E. Mendizabal, D. Osborne, and J. Young (2006), *Policy Engagement: How Civil society Can be More Effective* (London: ODI).

Court of Auditors (of the European Commission) (2001), 'Special Report Concerning the Management of Emergency Humanitarian Aid for the Victims of the Kosovo Crisis', *Journal of the European Union Information and Notices*, 44.C168 (12 June).

Covey, J. (1994), *Accountability and Effectiveness of NGO Policy Alliances*, IDR Reports, 11.8 (Boston: Institute for Development Research).

Cox, A. and J. Healey (2000), *European Development Cooperation and the Poor* (London: ODI).

Crocker, D. A. and S. Schwenke (2005), *The Relevance of Development Ethics for USAID* (Washington, DC: USAID).

Dabelstein, N., V-H. M. Melendez, A. B. Khan, L. Caviezel, O. Feinstein, G. Lombin, and R. van den Berg (2002), *External Review of the Results and Impact of IFAD Operations* (Copenhagen: Ministry of Foreign Affairs).

Dalgaard, C-J. and H. Hansen (2005), *The Return to Foreign Aid*, University of Copenhagen Institute of Economics Discussion Paper No. 4 (Copenhagen: University of Copenhagen).

—— —— and F. Tarp (2003), *On the Empirics of Foreign Aid and Growth*, Economic Policy Research Unit Working Paper No. 03-13 (Copenhagen: Institute of Economics, University of Copenhagen).

—— and H. Hansen (2004), 'On the Empirics of Foreign Aid and Growth', *Economic Journal*, 114: 191–215.

Dalton, M., K. von Hippel, R. Kent, and R. Maurer (2003), 'Changes in Humanitarian Financing: Implications for the United Nations', available at <www.reliefweb.int/rw/lib.nsf/db900SID/LGEL-5UQMT7?OpenDocument> (accessed 18 Jan. 2006).

Danielsen, A. and L. Wohlgemuth (2005), 'Swedish Development Co-operation in Perspective', in Hoebink and Stokke (2005), 518–45.

Darcy, J., and Hofman, C-A. (2003), *According to Need? Needs Assessment and Decision-Making in the Humanitarian Sector*, HPG Research Report No. 15 (London: ODI).

Dasgupta, D. and S. Pezzini (1999), 'The Determinants of Aid Flows and Their Effects', background paper for Global Development Finance 2000 (mimeo).

Davies, R. (1994), *ODA Co-funded CAFOD Projects in Kenya*, Evaluation Report EV 556 (London: Overseas Development Administration).

Deaton, A. (2005), 'Measuring Poverty in a Growing World', *Review of Economics and Statistics*, 87.1: 1–19.

Degnbol-Martinussen, J. and P. Engberg-Pedersen (2003), *Aid: Understanding International Development Co-operation* (London: Zed Books).

Denning, S. (2002), 'Technical Cooperation and Knowledge Networks', in Fukuda-Parr, Lopes, and Malik (2002), 229–46.

Devarajan, S., D. Dollar, and T. Holmgren (2001), *Aid and Reform in Africa: Lessons from 10 Case Studies* (Washington, DC: World Bank).

—— M. J. Miller, and E. V. Sawnson (2002), *Goals for Development: History, Prospects and Costs*, World Bank Policy Research Paper No. 2819 (Washington, DC: World Bank).

—— and V. Swaroop (2000), 'The Implications of Foreign Aid Fungibility for Development Assistance', in Gilbert and Vines (2000), 196–209.

Devereux, S., J. Marshall, J. MacAskill, and L. Pelham (2005), *Making Cash Count* (London and Brighton: Help Age International, SCF and IDS).

DFID (Department for International Development) (1997), *Eliminating World Poverty: A Challenge for the 21st Century* (Norwich: The Stationery Office).

—— (2002), *Supporting Agriculture: An Evaluation of DFID's Support for Sustainable Agriculture Since the Early 1990s*, Ev Sum EV638 (London: DFID).

—— (2005a), *Departmental Report 2005* (Norwich: Stationery Office).

—— (2005b), *Partnerships for Poverty Reduction: Rethinking Conditionality* (London: DFID).

—— (2005c), *Why We Need to Work More Effectively in Fragile States* (London: DFID).

—— (2006a), *Development Aid Works 52 Weeks a Year* (London: DFID).

—— (2006b), *Eliminating World Poverty: Making Governance Work for the Poor* (Norwich: The Stationery Office).

—— (2006c), *Saving Lives, Relieving Suffering, Protecting Dignity: DFID's Humanitarian Policy* (London: DFID).

DI (Development Initiatives) (2005), *Global Humanitarian Assistance Update 2004–2005* (Evercreech, Somerset: Development Initiatives).

Dichter, T. W. (2003), *Despite Good Intentions: Why Development Assistance has Failed the Third World* (Amherst, MA and Boston: University of Massachusetts Press).

Dorsey, B-J. (1975), 'The African Secondary School Leaver', in Murphree (1975), 13–174.

Doucouliagos, H. and M. Paldam (2005), *The Aid Effectiveness Literature: The Sad Result of 40 Years of Research*, University of Aarhus Department of Economics Working Paper No. 15 (Aarhus: Department of Economics, University of Aarhus).

Dower, N. (1998), *World Ethics—The New Agenda* (Edinburgh: Edinburgh University Press).

Driscoll, R., K. Christiansen, and D. Booth (2005), *Progress Reviews and Performance Assessment in Poverty-Reduction Strategies and Budget Support: A Survey of Current Thinking* (London: ODI).

Duffield, M. (2004), *Carry on Killing: Global Governance, Humanitarianism and Terror,* Danish Institute for International Studies Working Paper No. 23 (Copenhagen: Danish Institute for International Studies).

Duflo, E. and M. Kremer (2003), 'Use of Randomization in the Evaluation of Development Effectiveness', paper prepared for the World Bank Operations Evaluation Department Conference on Evaluation and Development Effectiveness (mimeo).

Dworkin, R. (2000), *Sovereign Virtue: The Theory and Practice of Equality* (Cambridge, MA: Harvard University Press).

Eade, D. (1977), *Capacity-Building: An Approach to People-Centred Development* (Oxford: Oxfam).

—— (2002), *Development and Advocacy* (Oxford: Oxfam).

Easterly, W. (2001a), *The Elusive Quest for Growth* (Cambridge, MA: MIT Press).

—— (2001b), *IMF and World Bank Structural Adjustment Policies and Poverty* (Washington, DC: World Bank).

—— (2002), *The Cartel of Good Intentions: Markes vs. Bureaucracy in Foreign Aid,* CGD Working Paper No. 2 (Washington, DC: CGD).

—— (2006), *The White Man's Burden: Why the West's Efforts to Aid the Rest have Done so Much Ill and So Little Good* (Oxford: Oxford University Press).

—— (forthcoming), *Reinventing Foreign Aid* (Boston: MIT Press).

—— R. Levine, and D. Roodman (2003), *New Data, New Doubts: Revisiting 'Aid, Policies and Growth',* CGD Working Paper No. 26 (Washington, DC: CGD).

EC (2000a), *EC Communication: Council Statement on Development Policy* (Brussels: EC).

—— (2000b), *The EC's Development Policy,* COM (2000) 212 (Brussels: EC).

—— (2005a), *Attitudes Towards Development Aid,* Special Eurobarometer 222 (Brussels: EC).

—— (2005b), *EU Report on Millennium Development Goals 2000–2004* (Brussels: EC).

ECA (Economic Commission for Africa) and OECD (Organisation for Economic Cooperation and Development) (2005), 'Development Effectiveness in Africa: Promise and Performance: Applying Mutual Accountability in Practice' (mimeo).

ECOSOC (United Nations General Assembly Economic and Social Council) (2005), *Strengthening of the Coordination of Emergency Humanitarian Assistance of the United Nations. Report of the Secretary General,* No. 05-39642 (E) (New York: United Nations).

Edwards, M. (1993), 'Does the Doormat Influence the Boot? Critical Thoughts on UK NGOs and International Advocacy', *Development in Practice,* 3.3: 163–75.

—— (2004), *Civil Society* (Cambridge: Polity Press).

—— (2005), *Have NGOs 'Made a Difference'? From Manchester to Birmingham with an Elephant in the Room,* Global Poverty Research Group Working Paper No. 28 (Oxford: Global Poverty Research Group).

—— and J. Gaventa (2001), *Global Citizen Action* (Boulder, CO: Lynne Rienner).

—— and D. Hulme (1995), *Non-Governmental Organisations—Performance and Accountability Beyond the Magic Bullet* (London: Save the Children and Earthscan).

Eilor, J. (2004), *Education and the Sector-Wide Approach in Uganda* (Paris: International Institute for Educational Planning).

Elliott, D. and A. Gibson (2004), *'Making Markets Work for the Poor' as a Core Objective for Governments and Development Agencies* (Gallo Manor, South Africa: Commark Trust).

Erixon, F. (2005), *Aid and Development: Will It Work This Time?* (London: International Policy Network).

Escobar, A. (1995), *Encountering Development: The Making and Unmaking of the Third World* (Princeton, NJ: Princeton University Press).

Europa (2005), 'Towards a European Consensus for Development: The European Commission Approves a Proposal for an Ambitious Development Policy', <http://europa.eu.int/rapid/pressReleasesAction.do?reference=IP/05/902&format=HTML&aged=0&language=en&guiLanguage=en> (accessed 7 Sept. 2005).

Eyben, R. (2005), 'Donor's Learning Difficulties: Results, Relationships and Responsibilities', *IDS Bulletin,* 36.3: 98–107.

Fagernäs, S. and J. Roberts (2004), *Fiscal Impact of Aid: A Survey of Issues and Synthesis of Country Studies of Malawi, Uganda and Zambia,* ODI Economic and Statistics Analysis Unit Working Paper No. 11 (London: ODI).

Fallon, J., C. Sugden, and L. Pieper (2003), *The Contribution of Australian Aid to Papua New Guinea's Development 1975–2000,* AusAID Evaluation and Review Series No. 34 (Canberra: AusAID).

Ferreira, F. H. G., and L. C. Keely (2000), 'The World Bank and Structural Adjustment: Lessons from the 1980s', in Gilbert and Vines (2000), 159–96.

Ffrench-Davis, R. (2004), 'Reforming the Reforms of the Washington Consensus', in Teunissen and Akkerman (2004), 100–15.

Flint, M., C. Cameron, S. Henderson, S. Jones, and D. Ticehurst (2002), *How Effective is DFID? An Independent Review of DFID's Organisational and Development Effectiveness,* DFID Evaluation Report EV 640. (London: DFID).

—— J. Gray, and S. Jones (2004), *Evaluation of DFID Country Programmes: Synthesis Report,* DFID Evaluation Report EV 652 (London: DFID).

Flinterman, C., M. Mkosi, Th. C. van Banning, and J. van Soest (1992), *Sinakho: 'We can do it',* Programme Evaluation Report No. 48 (The Hague: DGIS/CEBEMO and ICCO).

Foster, M. (2003), *The Case for Increased Aid,* Report to the Department for International Development (Chelmsford: Mick Foster Associates Ltd).

—— and T. Killick (2006), *What Would Doubling Aid Do for Macroeconomic Management in Africa?* (London: ODI).

—— and S. Mackintosh-Walker (2001), *Sector-Wide Programmes and Poverty Reduction* (London: ODI).

Fowler, A. (1997), *Striking a Balance: A Guide to Enhancing the Effectiveness of Non-Governmental Organizations in International Development* (London: Earthscan).

—— (2005), *Aid Architecture: Reflections on NGDO Futures and the Emergence of Counter-Terrorism,* INTRAC Occasional Paper No. 45 (Oxford: International NGO Training and Resource Centre).

Fox, J. W. (1999), 'Real Progress: Fifty years of USAID in Costa Rica', in OECD (1999a), 231–70.

Foy, C and H. Helmich (1996), *Public Support for International Development* (Paris: Development Centre, OECD).

Frantz, B. (2004), 'General Budget Support in Tanzania: A Snapshot of its Effectiveness', paper prepared for USAID/Tanzania Country Strategic Plan, 2005–2014 (mimeo).

Freedman, J. (ed.) (2000), *Transforming Development: Foreign Aid for a Changing World* (Toronto: University of Toronto Press).

Freeman, T. and S. Faure (2003), *Local Solutions to Global Challenges: Towards Effective Partnership in Basic Education*, Joint Evaluation of External Support to Basic Education in Developing Countries (The Hague: Ministry of Foreign Affairs).

Frühling, P. (ed.) (1986), *Swedish Development Aid in Perspective: Policies, Problems and Results Since 1952* (Stockholm: Almqvist and Wiksell International).

Führer, H. (1994), *The Story of Development Assistance: A History of the Development Assistance Committee and the Development Co-operation Directorate in Dates and Figures* (Paris: OECD).

Fukuda-Parr, S. (2006), 'Rethinking the Policy Objectives of International Development Cooperation: from Economic Growth to an Integrated Agenda of Development and Security', paper presented to the WIDER Conference on Aid, Helsinki, June 2006; available at <www.wider.unu.edu/conference/conference-2006-1/conference-2006-1.htm> (accessed 14 June 2006).

—— C. Lopes, and K. Malik (2002), *Capacity for Development: New Solutions to Old Problems* (London: Earthscan).

Gasper, D. (1997), 'Development Ethics—An Emergent field?', in Hamelink (1997), 25–43.

—— (1999), 'Ethics and the Conduct of International Development Aid: Charity and Obligation', *Forum for Development Studies*, 1: 23–57.

—— (2004), *The Ethics of Development: From Economism to Human Development* (Edinburgh: Edinburgh University Press).

Gayfer, J. (2005), *An Independent Evaluation of SDC Nepal Country Programmes 1993–2004. Building Bridges in Nepal—Dealing with Deep Divides* (Berne: Swiss Agency for Development and Cooperation).

German, T. (1996), 'Who Shapes and Leads Public Attitudes on Development Cooperation?', in Foy and Helmich (1996), 93–108.

Ghai, D., and E. Lee (1980), *The Basic-Needs Approach to Development: Some Issues Regarding Concepts and Methodology* (Geneva: International Labour Office).

Gibson, C. G., K. Andersson, E. Ostrom, and S. Shivakumar (2005), *The Samaritan's Dilemma: The Political Economy of Development Aid* (Oxford: Oxford University Press).

Gilabert, P. (2004), 'The Duty to Eradicate Poverty: Positive or Negative?', *Ethical Theory and Moral Practice*, 7: 537–50.

Gilbert, C. L. and D. Vines (2000), *The World Bank: Structure and Policies* (Cambridge: Cambridge University Press).

Goldenberg, D. A. (2001), *CARE: The Mega Evaluation. A Review of Findings and Methodological Lessons from CARE Final Evaluations, 1994–2000* (Atlanta: CARE USA).

—— (2003), *CARE: The Mega 2002 Evaluation. A Review of Findings and Methodological Lessons from CARE Final Evaluations, 2001–2002* (Atlanta: CARE USA).

Goldin, I., H. Rogers, and N. Stern (2002), *The Role and Effectiveness of Development Experience: Lessons from World Bank Experience* (Washington, DC: World Bank).

Gomanee, K., S. Girma, and O. Morrissey (2002), *Aid and Growth in Sub-Saharan Africa: Accounting for Transmission Mechanisms*, Centre for Research in Economic Development and International Trade (Credit) Research Paper No. 02/05 (Nottingham: University of Nottingham).

—— —— —— (2003), *Searching for Aid Threshold Effects*, Credit Research Paper No. 03/15 (Nottingham: University of Nottingham).

Government of Sweden (2003), *Shared Responsibility: Sweden's Policy for Global Development*, Government Bill 2002/3: 122 (Stockholm: Ministry of Foreign Affairs).

Government of Uganda (1994), *Capacity Building Plan* (Kampala: Government of Uganda).

Goyder, H., E. Girerd-Barclay, A. Jones, J. Lefevre, and A. Larmoyer (2005), *Full Report of the 'Real Time' Evaluation of WFP's Response to the Indian Ocean Tsunami* (Rome: World Food Programme).

Griffin, K. (2003), 'Economic Globalization and Institutions of Global Governance', *Development and Change*, 34.5: 789–807.

—— (2004), 'Globalization and Global Governance: A Reply to the Debate', *Development and Change*, 35.5: 1081–91.

—— and T. McKinley (1996), *New Approaches to Development Cooperation*, UNDP Discussion Paper No. 7 (New York: United Nations Development Programme).

Grindle, M. (2004), 'Good Enough Governance: Poverty Reduction and Reform in Developing Countries', *Governance*, 17: 525–48.

—— (2005), *Good Enough Governance Revisited*, (London: DFID).

GTZ (Deutsche Gesellschaft Für Technische Zusamenarbeid) (2005), *Annual Report 2004* (Eshborn, Germany: Deutsche Gesellschaft Für Technische Zusamenarbeid).

Guillaumont, P. and S. G. Jeanneney (2006), 'Big Push versus Absorptive Capacity: How to Reconcile the Two Approaches', paper presented to the WIDER Conference on Aid, Helsinki, June 2006; available at <www.wider.unu.edu/conference/conference-2006-1/conference-2006-1.htm> (accessed 20 June 2006).

Gunter, B. G., M. J. Cohen, and H. Lofgren (2005), 'Analysing Macro-Poverty Linkages', *Development Policy Review*, 23.3: 243–65.

Haan, A. de, and M. Everest-Phillips (2006), 'Can New Aid Modalities Handle Politics?', paper presented to the WIDER Conference on Aid, Helsinki, June 2006; available at <www.wider.unu.edu/conference/conference-2006-1/conference-2006-1.htm> (accessed 15 June 2006).

Hailey, J. (2002), 'Learning for Growth: Organizational learning in South Asian NGOs', in Lewis and Wallace (2002), 64–72.

—— R. James, and R. Wrigley (2005), *Rising to the Challenges: Assessing the Impacts of Organisational Capacity Building* (Oxford: INTRAC).

Hallam, A. (1998), *Evaluating Humanitarian Assistance Programmes in Complex Emergencies*, ODI Good Practice Review No. 7 (London: ODI).

Hamelink, C. J. (ed.) (1997), *Ethics and Development: On Making Moral Choices in Development Co-operation* (Kampen: Uitgeverij Kok).

Hancock, G. (1989), *Lords of Poverty: The Power, Prestige and Corruption of the International Aid Business* (New York: Atlantic Monthly Press).

Hanlon, J. (2004), 'It is Possible to Just Give Money to the Poor', in Pronk (2004), 181–200.

Hansen, H. and F. Tarp (2000), 'Aid Effectiveness Disputed', *Journal of International Development*, 12: 375–98.

—— —— (2001), 'Aid and Growth Regressions', *Journal of Development Economics*, 64.2: 547–70.

Harmer, A. and L. Cotterrell (2005), *Diversity in Donorship: The Changing Landscape of Official Humanitarian Aid*, HPG Report No. 20 (London: ODI).

Harriss, J. (2005), *Middle Class Activism and Poor People's Politics: An Exploration of Civil Society in Chennai*, Development Studies Institute Working Paper No. 05-72. (London: London School of Economics).

Harvey, P. (2005), *Cash and Vouchers in Emergencies: An HPG Discussion Paper* (London: ODI).

—— R. Slater, and J. Farringdon (2005), *Cash Transfers—Mere 'Gadaffi Syndrome', or Serious Potential for Rural Rehabilitation and Development?*, ODI Natural Resource Perspectives No. 97 (London: ODI).

—— (2006), *Governance, Development and Aid Effectiveness: A Quick Guide to a Complex Relationship*, ODI Briefing Paper (London: ODI).

Hatry, H. and K. Yansane (2002), *Comprehensive Development Framework Evaluation Results Orientation: An Early Look* (Washington, DC: World Bank).

Hauck, V. (2004), *Resilience and High Performance Amidst Conflict, Epidemics and Extreme Poverty: the Lacor Hospital, Northern Uganda*, ECDPM Discussion Paper No. 57A (Maastricht: ECDPM).

—— O. Hasse, and M. Koppensteiner (2005), *EC Budget Support: Thumbs Up or Down?*, ECDPM Discussion Paper No. 63 (Maastrict: ECDPM).

Heller, P. (1975), 'A Model of Public Fiscal Behavior in Developing Countries: Aid, Investment and Taxation', *American Economic Review*, 65: 429–45.

Herson, M., and J. Mitchell (2006), 'Real-Time Evaluation: Where Does its Value Lie?', available at <www.odihpn.org/report.asp?ID=2772> (accessed 19 Jan. 2006).

Heymans, C. and C. Pycroft (2005), 'Drivers of Change in Nigeria: Towards Restructuring the Political Economy'. (Mimeo (London: DFID).

Hills, J. (2004), *Inequality and the State* (Oxford: Oxford University Press).

Hirschman, A. O. (1970), *Exit, Voice and Loyalty* (Cambridge, MA: Harvard University Press).

Hodges, J. (1992), *Report of the Working Group on ODA/NGO Collaboration* (London: Overseas Development Administration).

Hodges, T. and R. Tibana (2004), 'Political Economy of the Budget in Mozambique', Oxford Policy Management (mimeo).

Hoebink, P. (2005), 'A New Member of the G-0.7: Luxembourg as the Smallest and largest Donor', in Hoebink and Stokke (2005), 378–405.

—— and O. Stokke (2005), *Perspectives on European Development Co-operation: Policy and Performance of Individual Countries and the EU* (London: Routledge).

Hofmann, C-A., L. Roberts, J. Shoham, and P. Harvey (2004), *Measuring the Impact of Humanitarian Aid: A Review of Current Practice*, HPG Research Report No. 17 (London: ODI).

Hoover, D. and M. McPherson (1999), *Capacity Building in the Ministry of Finance, Zambia* (Cambridge, MA: Harvard Institute for International Development).

Hopkins, R. (2000), 'Political Economy of Foreign Aid', in Tarp and Hjertholm (2000), 422–46.

Howell, J., and J. Pearce (2000), 'Civil Society: Technical Instrument or Social Force for Change?', in Lewis and Wallace (2000), 75–88.

Hudson, J. (2004), 'Introduction: Aid and Development', *Economic Journal*, 114: F184–F185.

—— and P. Mosley (2006), 'Aid Volatility, Policy and Development', paper presented to the WIDER Conference on Aid, Helsinki, June 2006; available at <www.wider.unu.edu/conference/conference-2006-1/conference-2006-1.htm> (accessed 20 June 2006).

Hulme, D. and M. Edwards (1995), *Non-Governmental Organisations. Performance and Accountability: Beyond the Magic Bullet* (London: Earthscan).

—— and P. Mosley (1996), *Finance Against Poverty*, 2 vols (London: Routledge).

Huntingdon, R. (1987), *Accelerating Institutional Development: PVO Institutional Development Evaluation Series* (Washington, DC: International Science and Technology Institute).

Hyden, G. (1995), 'Reforming Foreign Aid to African Development: A Proposal to Set Up Politically Autonomous Development Funds', *Development Dialogue*, 2: 35–52.

—— (1997), 'The Battles for New Formulas: Foreign Aid in Longer Term Perspective', in Sida, *Project 2015: Development Cooperation in the 21st Century* (Stockholm: Sida, pp. 55–68).

—— and J. Court (2002), *Governance and Development*, UNU World Governance Discussion Paper No. 1 (Helsinki: United Nations University).

—— —— and K. Mease (2004), *Making Sense of Governance: Empirical Evidence from 16 Developing Countries* (Boulder, CO: Lynne Rienner).

ICHRP (International Council on Human Rights Policy) (2002), *Beyond Voluntarism: Human Rights and the Developing International Legal Obligations of Companies* (Geneva: International Council on Human Rights Policy).

—— (2003), *Duties sans frontiers: Human Rights and Global Social Justice* (Geneva: ICHRP).

ICISS (International Commission on Intervention and State Sovereignty) (2001), *The Responsibility to Protect* (Ottawa: International Development Research Centre).

ICRC (International Committee of the Red Cross) (1949), *The Geneva Conventions of August 12 1949* (Geneva: International Committee of the Red Cross).

—— (1996), *Protocols Additional to the Geneva Conventions of 12 August 1949* (Geneva: ICRC).

—— (2005), *Annual Report 2004* (Geneva: ICRC).

IDS (Institute of Development Studies) (2006), *Social Protection, No. 1* (Brighton: ICRC).

IFRC (International Federation of Red Cross and Red Crescent Societies), *World Disasters Report 2005* (Geneva: International Federation of Red Cross and Red Crescent Societies).

INEE (Inter-Agency Network for Education in Emergencies) (2004), *Minimum Standards for Education in Emergencies, Chronic Crises and Early Reconstruction* (Paris: Inter-Agency Network for Education in Emergencies).

Isham, J. and D. Kaufmann (1995), *The Forgotten Rationale for Policy Reform: The Productivity of Investment Projects*, World Bank Policy Research Working Paper No. 1549 (Washington, DC: World Bank).

James, R. (2005), *'Quick and Dirty' Evaluation of Capacity Building*, INTRAC Praxis Note No. 15 (Oxford: INTRAC).

Jayasinghe, K. and D. Wickramasinghe (2005), 'Can NGOs Deliver Accountability? Predication, Realities and Difficulties: The Case of Sri Lanka', paper presented to the Manchester Conference on NGOs; available at <www.sed.manchester.ac.uk/idpm/research/events/ngo2005/documents/Jayasinghe.pdf> (accessed 7 July 2006).

Jaycox, E. (1993), 'Capacity Building: The Missing Links in Africa', transcript of address to the African-American Institute Conference on African Capacity Building, Reston, VA.

Jeffreys, E. and V. Walford (2003), *Mapping of Sector-Wide Approaches in Health* (London: Institute for Health Sector Development).

Jenkins, K. and W. Plowden (2006), *Governance and Nation-Building: The Failure of International Intervention* (Cheltenham: Edward Elgar Publishing).

Jepma, C. J. (1991), *The Tying of Aid* (Paris: Development Centre OECD).

Johnson, D. H. (2004), *The Root Causes of Sudan's Civil Wars* (Oxford: James Currey).

Johnson, S., K. Doyle, M. Emrul Hasan, E. Jimenez, and T.G. Kidder (2000), 'Stormy Weather: Microfinance, Shocks and the Prospects for Sustainability', in Lewis and Wallace (2000), 121–30.

Jolly, R., L. Emmerij, and T. G. Weiss (2005), *The Power of UN Ideas: Lessons from the First 60 Years* (New York: United Nations Intellectual History Project Series).

Jones, S. (2000), 'Increasing Aid Effectiveness in Africa? The World Bank and Sector Investment Programmes', in Gilbert and Vines (2000), 266–81.

—— R. Riddell and K. Kotoglou (2005) *Aid Allocation Criteria: Managing for Development Results and Difficult Partnerships* (Paris: OECD)

—— (2006) and Associates, *Developing Capacity? An Evaluation of DFID-Funded Technical Cooperation for Economic Management in Sub-Saharan Africa* (Oxford: OPM).

Jones, B. D. and A. Stoddard (2003), *External Review of the Inter-Agency Standing Committee* (New York: New York University).

Jones, P. W. and D. Colman (2005), *The United Nations and Education: Multilateralism, Development and Globalisation* (London: Routledge Falmer).

Jordan, L. and P. van Tuijl (2000), 'Political Responsibility in Transnational NGO Advocacy', *World Development*, 28.12: 2051–65.

Kanbur, R. and T. Sandler (1999), *The Future of Development Assistance: Common Pools and International Public Goods*, ODC Policy Essay No. 25 (Washington, DC: Overseas Development Council).

Katila, M., P. J. Williams, R. Ishengoma, and S. Juma (2003), *Three Decades of Swedish Support to the Tanzanian Forestry Sector, 1969–2002*, Sida Evaluation No. 03/12 (Stockholm: Sida).

Kaufmann, D. (2005), '10 Myths about Governance and Corruption', *Finance and Development*, 42.3: 41–3.

—— A. Kraay, and M. Mastruzzi (2003), *Governance Matters III: Governance Indicators for 1996–2002* (Washington, DC: World Bank).

Kaul, I., P. Conceicao, K. Le Goulven, and R. U. Mendoza (2003), *Providing Global Public Goods: Managing Globalization* (Oxford: Oxford University Press).

—— I. Grunberg, and M. A. Stern (eds) (1999), *Global Public Goods: International Development Co-operation in the 21st Century* (New York: Oxford University Press).

Kay, J. (2004), *The Truth about Markets* (London: Penguin Books).

Keet, D. (2002), 'The International Debt Campaign: A Southern Activist View for Activists in "the North" and "the South" ', in Eade (2002), 23–46.

Khandker, S. R. (2003), *Microfinance and Poverty: Evidence Using Panel Data from Bangladesh*, Development Research Group Working Paper No. 2945, (Washington, DC: World Bank).

Killick, T. (1993), *The Adaptive Economy: Adjustment Policies in Small Low-Income Countries* (Washington, DC: World Bank).

—— (ed.) (1995a), *The Flexible Economy: Causes and Consequences of the Adaptability of National Economies* (London: Routledge).

—— (1995b), *IMF Programmes in Developing Countries: Design and Impact* (London: Routledge).

—— (2004), 'Politics, Evidence and the New Aid Agenda', *Development Policy Review*, 22.1: 5–29.

—— (2005), 'Don't Throw Money at Africa', *IDS Bulletin*, 36.3: 14–19.

—— R. Gunatilaka, and A. Marr (1998), *Aid and the Political Economy of Policy Change* (London: Routledge).

—— C. N. Castel-Branco, and R. Gerster (2005), *Perfect Partners? The Performance of Programme Aid Partners in Mozambique 2004*, report to the Programme Aid Partners and Government of Mozambique (London: DFID).

Klein, M. and T. Harford (2005), 'Aid Effectiveness: Can Aid Agencies be Smarter than the Invisible Hand?', Public Policy for the Private Sector Note No. 292 (Washington, DC: World Bank).

Knack, S. (2000), *Aid Dependence and the Quality of Governance: A Cross-Country Empirical Analysis*, World Bank Policy Research Paper No. 2396 (Washington, DC: World Bank).

—— (2001), *Aid Dependence and the Quality of Governance: A Cross-Country Empirical Analysis* (Washington, DC: World Bank).

—— and A. Rahman (2004), *Donor Fragmentation and Bureaucratic Quality in Aid Recipients*, World Bank Policy Research Working Paper No. 3186 (Washington, DC: World Bank).

Korten, D. (1987), 'Third Generation NGO Strategies: A Key to People-Centred Development', *World Development*, supp. to vol. 15: 145–59.

Krueger, A. O., C. Michalopoulos, and V. Ruttan (1989), *Aid and Development* (Baltimore and London: Johns Hopkins University Press).

Lall, S. and S. Urata (2003), *Competitiveness, FDI and Technological Activity in East Asia* (Cheltenham: Edward Elgar).

Lancaster, C. (1999a), 'Aid Effectiveness: The Problem of Africa', *Development Outreach*, 1.2: 22–4.

—— (1999b), *Aid to Africa: so much to do, so little done.* Chicago: University of Chicago Press.

—— (2006), *Foreign Aid: Diplomacy, Development, Domestic Politics* (Chicago: University of Chicago Press).

—— K. Nuamah, M. Lieber, and T. Johnson (2006), *Foreign Aid and Private Sector Development* (Providence, RI: Brown University).

Landman, T. and M. Abraham (2004), *Evaluation of Nine Human Rights Organisations* (The Hague: Ministry of Foreign Affairs).

Lavalle, A., P. Houtzager, and G. Castello (2005), *In Whose Name? Political Representation and Civil Organisations in Brazil*, IDS Working Paper No. 249 (Brighton: IDS).

Lawson, A. and D. Booth (2004), *Evaluation Framework for General Budget Support* (London: ODI).

—— —— A. Harding, D. Hoole, and F. Naschold (2003), *General Budget Support Evaluability Study Phase 1*, Evaluation Report EV 643, 2 vols (London: DFID).

—— —— M. Msuya, S. Wangwe, and T. Williamson (2005), *Does General Budget Support Work? Evidence from Tanzania* (London: ODI).

Leandro, J. E., H. Schafer, and G. Frontini (1999), 'Towards a More Effective Conditionality: An Operational Framework', *World Development*, 27.2: 285–300.

Lehman, H. P. (2006), 'Japan's Foreign Aid Policy to Africa', paper presented to the Helsinki WIDER Conference on Aid, June 2006; available at <www.wider.unu.edu/conference/conference-2006-1/conference-2006-1.htm> (accessed 21 June 2006).

Lensink, R. (1996), *Structural Adjustment in Sub-Saharan Africa* (London: Longman).

—— and H. White (2000), 'Assessing Aid: A Manifesto for the 21st Century', *Oxford Development Studies*, 28.1: 5–18.

Levin, V., and Dollar, D. (2005), 'The Forgotten States: Aid Volumes and Volatility in Difficult Partnership Countries (1992–2002)', available at <www.oecd.org/dataoecd/32/44/34687926.pdf> (accessed 20 July 2006).

Levine, R., and the What Works Working Group (2004), *Millions Saved: Proven Successes in Global Health* (Washington, DC: CGD).

Lewis, W. A. (1954), 'Economic Development with Unlimited Supplies of Labour', *The Manchester School*, 22.2: 139–91.

Lewis, D. (2001), *The Management of Non-Governmental Organizations* (London: Routledge).

Lewis, D. and T. Wallace (2000), *New Roles and Relevance: Development NGOs and the Challenge of Change* (Bloomfield, CT: Kumarian Press).

Lieberson, J., D. Ray, and B. Franz (2004), *General Budget Support and Sector Program Assistance: Malawi Country Case Study*, USAID Evaluation Working Paper No. 19 (Washington, DC: USAID).

Lipumba, N. H. I. (2006), 'Aid, Growth and Achieving the Millennium Development Goals in Tanzania', paper presented to the WIDER Conference on Aid, Helsinki, June 2006; available at <www.wider.unu.edu/conference/conference-2006-1/conference-2006-1.htm> (accessed 14 June 2006).

Lister, S. (2005) *Joint Evaluation of General Budget Support 1994–2004: Final Inception Report* (London: DFID).

—— (2006) *Evaluation of General Budget Support: Synthesis Report* (Birmingham: International Development Department, University of Birmingham).

Llavador, H. G., and J. E. Roemer (2001), 'An Equal Opportunity Approach to the Allocation of International Aid', *Journal of Development Economics*, 64: 147–71.

Lockwood, M. (2005), *The State They're In: An Agenda for International Action on Poverty in Africa* (Bourton-on-Dunsmore: Intermediate Technology Development Group).

Lumsdaine, D. H. (1993), *Moral Vision in International Politics: The Foreign Aid Regime 1949–1989* (Princeton, NJ: Princeton University Press).

McDonnell, I. (2006), 'A Literature Review of Public Perceptions of Aid Effectiveness in OECD and Developing Countries', OECD Development Centre (mimeo).

—— H-B. Silognac Lecomte, and L. Wegimont (2003a), *Public Opinion and The Fight Against Poverty* (Paris: Development Centre, OECD).

—— —— —— (2003b), *Public Opinion Research, Global Education and Development Co-operation Reform: In Search of a Virtuous Circle*, OECD Working Paper No. 222 (Paris: Development Centre, OECD).

McGillivray, M. (2003a), 'Aid Effectiveness and Selectivity: Integrating Multiple Objectives into Aid Allocations', *Aid Effectiveness and Selectivity: DAC Journal*, 4.33: 23–36.

—— (2003b), *Descriptive and Prescriptive Analyses of Aid Allocation: Approach, Issues and Consequences*, WIDER Discussion Paper No. 49 (Helsinki: UNU).

—— (2005), 'Aid Allocation and Fragile States', background paper for the Senior Level Forum on Development Effectiveness in Fragile States, <www.oecd.org/dataoecd/32/43/34256890.pdf> (accessed 27 Oct. 2005).

McGillivray, M. and H. White (1994), *Development Criteria for the Allocation of Aid and Assessment of Donor Performance*, Credit Research Paper No. 7 (Nottingham: University of Nottingham).

—— and O. Morrisey (2001a), *Aid Illusion and Public Sector Fiscal Behaviour*, Credit Research Paper No. 00/9 (Nottingham: University of Nottingham).

—— —— (2001b), *A Review of Evidence on the Fiscal Effects of Aid*, Credit Research Paper No. 01/13 (Nottingham: University of Nottingham).

McHugh, G. and L. Gostelow (2004), *Provincial Reconstruction Teams and Humanitarian-Military Relations in Afghanistan* (London: Save the Children).

McKay, A. and Baulch, B. (2004), *How Many Chronically Poor People are There in the World? Some Preliminary Estimates*, Chronic Poverty Research Centre Working Paper No. 45 (Manchester: University of Manchester).

McMurrin, S. M. (1980), *The Tanner Lectures on Human Values* (Salt Lake City: University of Utah Press).

Macrae, J. (2002a), *Aiding Recovery: The Crisis of Aid in Chronic Political Emergencies* (London: Zed Books).

—— (2002b), *The New Humanitarianism: A Review of Trends in Global Humanitarian Action*, HPG Report No. 11 (London: ODI).

—— and A. Harmer (2003), *Humanitarian Action and the 'Global War on Terror': A Review of Trends and Issues*, HPG Report No. 14 (London: ODI).

—— and N. Leader (2000), *Shifting Sands: The Theory and Practice of 'Coherence' Between Political and Humanitarian Responses to Conflict*, HPG Report No. 8 (London: ODI).

—— S. Collinson, M. Buchanan-Smith et al. (2002), *Uncertain Power: The Changing Role of Official Donors in Humanitarian Action*, HPG Report No. 12 (London: ODI).

—— A. Shepherd, O. Morrissey et al. (2004), *Aid to 'Poorly Performing' Countries: A Critical Review of Debates and Issues* (London: ODI).

Madsen, H. L. (1999), *Impact Assessments Undertaken by Danish NGOs*, CDR Working Paper No. 99–10 (Copenhagen: Centre for Development Research).

Maizels, A. and M. K. Nissanke (1984), 'Motivations for Aid to Developing Countries', *World Development*, 12.9: 879–900.

Mansfield, D. (1997), 'Country Case Study: The United States', in Riddell, Kruse, Kyllönen *et al.* (1997), vol. ii, app. 8.

Martens, J. (2001), *Rethinking ODA: Towards a Renewal of Official Development Assistance*, WEEDA Working Paper (Bonn: World Economy, Ecology and Development Association).

—— (2005), 'Why Do Aid Agencies Exist?', *Development Policy Review*, 23.6: 643–63.

Martin, M. and H. Bargawi (2005), 'A Changing Role for the IMF in Low-Income Countries', in Teunissen and Akkerman (2005), 68–126.

Masud, N., and B. Yontcheva (2005), *Does Foreign Aid Reduce Poverty? Empirical Evidence from Nongovernmental and Bilateral Aid*, IMF Working Paper No. 05/100 (Washington, DC: IMF).

Mavrotas, G. (2000), *The Impact of Aid on Private Savings and Investment* (Oxford: OPM).

—— (2002), 'Aid and Growth in India: Some Evidence from Disaggregated Aid Data', *South Asia Economic Journal*, 3.1: 19–49.

—— S. Jones, and E. Mutebile (2003), *Assessing Aid Effectiveness in Uganda: An Aid Disaggregation Approach* (Oxford: OPM).

Maxwell, S. (2005), *The Washington Consensus is Dead: Long Live the Meta-Narrative!*, ODI Working Paper No. 243 (London: ODI).

Mercer, M., P. Gosparini, P. Melchiori, F. Orivel, M. Sirtori, and T. Steinback (2002), *Evaluation of EC Support to the Education Sector in ACP Countries* (Brussels: Development Researchers' Network).

Milanovic, B. (2005), *Global Income Inequality: What It is and Why It Matters* (Washington, DC: World Bank).

Miller, V. (1994), *NGO and Grassroots Policy Influence: What is Success?*, IDR Reports 11.5 (Boston: IDR).

Miller, D. (2004), 'National Responsibility and International Justice', in Chatterjee (2004), 123–46.

Millikan, M. F. and W. W. Rostow (1957), *A Proposal: Key to an Effective Foreign Policy* (New York: Harper and Brothers).

Minear, L. (2002), *The Humanitarian Enterprise: Dilemmas and Discoveries* (Bloomfield, CT: Kumarian Press).

Ministry of Foreign Affairs (2003), *Japan's Official Development Assistance Charter* (Tokyo: Ministry of Foreign Affairs); English translation available at <www.mofa.–go.jp/policy/oda/reform/revision0308.pdf>.

Ministry of Foreign Affairs and Danida (2000), *Denmark's Development Policy: Partnership 2000* (Copenhagen: Ministry of Foreign Affairs).

Mitlin, D., S. Hickey, and A. Bebbington (2005), 'Reclaiming Development? NGOs and the Challenge of Alternatives', background paper for Third Manchester Conference on NGOs; available at <www.sed.manchester.ac.uk/idpm/research/events/ngo2005/documents/Mitlin.doc> (accessed 10 July 2006).

Ministry for Overseas Development (1975), *Overseas Development, The Changing Emphasis in British Aid Policies. More Help for the Poorest*, Cmnd 6270 (London: HMSO).

Mkandawire, T. (2002), 'Incentives, Governance and Capacity Building in Africa', in Fukuda-Parr, Lopes, and Malik (2002), 147–68.

Moellendorf, D. (2002), *Cosmopolitan Justice* (Boulder, CO: Westview Press).

Moore, M., M. Stewart, and A. Hudock (1995), *Institution Building as a Development Assistance Method*, Sida Evaluation Report No. 1 (Stockholm: Sida).

Morgan, P. and H. Baser (1993), *Making Technical Co-operation More Effective: new approaches by the international development community* (Quebec: Canadian International Development Agency).

—— T. Land, and H. Baser (2005), *Study on Capacity, Change and Performance: interim report*, ECDPM Discussion Paper No. 59A (Maastricht: ECDPM).

Morgenstern, O. (1963), *On the Accuracy of Economic Observations*, 2nd edn (Princeton, NJ: Princeton University Press).

Morrissey, O. (1993), 'The Mixing of Aid and Trade Policies', *World Economy*, 16.1: 69–84.

—— (2005), 'British Aid Policy in the 'short-Blair' Years', in Hoebink and Stokke (2005), 161–83.

Mosley, P., J. Harringan, and J. Toye (1991), *Aid and Power: The World Bank and Policy Lending*, 2 vols (London: Routledge).

—— J. Hudson and A. Verschoor (2004), 'Aid, Poverty Reduction and the "New Conditionality" ', *Economic Journal*, 114: F217–43.

Moss, T., D. Roodman, and S. Standley (2005), *The Global War on Terror and US Development Assistance: USAID Allocations by Country, 1998–2005*, CGD Working Paper No. 62 (Washington, DC: CGD).

Mourmouras, A. and P. Rangazas (2006), *Foreign Aid Policy and Sources of Poverty: A Quantitative Framework*, IMF Working Paper No. 06/14 (Washington, DC: IMF).

Muir, A. (1992), *Evaluating the Impact of NGOs in Rural Poverty Alleviation: Zimbabwe Country Case Study*, ODI Working Paper No. 52 (London: ODI).

—— (1995), 'Zimbabwe', in Riddell and Robinson (1995), 238–83.

Murphree, M. (ed.) (1975), *Education, Race and Employment in Rhodesia* (Harare: Association of Round Tables in Central Africa Publications).

MWH Consultants (2003), *Evaluation of the European Commission's Country Strategy for Bangladesh* (Brussels: EuropeAid).

Nagel, T. (2005), 'The Problem of Global Justice', *Philosophy and Public Affairs*, 33.2: 113–47.

Naim, M. (1999), 'Fads and Fashion in Economic Reforms: Washington Consensus or Washington Confusion', paper prepared for the IMF Conference on Second Generation Reforms; available at <www.imf.org/external/pubs/ft/seminar/1999/reforms/Naim.htm> (accessed 6 July 2006).

Najam, A. (1999), 'Citizen Organizations as Policy Entrepreneurs', in Lewis (1999), 142–81.

Nancy, G. and B. Yontcheva (2006), *Does NGO Aid Go to the Poor? Empirical Evidence from Europe*, IMF Working Paper No. 06/39 (Washington, DC: IMF).

NAO (National Audit Office) (2003), *Department for International Development Responding to Humanitarian Emergencies*, report by the Comptroller and Auditor General (London: National Audit Office).

Nishigaki, A. and Y. Shimomura (1999), *The Economics of Development Assistance: Japan's ODA in a Symbiotic World* (Tokyo: LTCB International Library Foundation).

Noël, A., J-P. Thérien, and S. Dallaire (2004), 'Divided over Internationalism: The Canadian Public and Development Assistance', *Canadian Public Policy*, 30.1: 29–46.

North, D. C. (1990), *Institutions, Institutional Change and Economic Performance* (Cambridge: Cambridge University Press).

Nussbaum, M. C. (2000), *Women and Human Development: The Capabilities Approach* (Cambridge: Cambridge University Press).

Oakley, P. and S. Folke (1999a), *The Danish NGO Impact Study: A Review of Danish NGO Activities in Developing Countries. Synthesis Report* (Copenhagen: Danida, Ministry of Foreign Affairs).

—— —— (1999b), *The Danish NGO Impact Study: A Review of Danish NGO Activities in Developing Countries. Overview Report* (Copenhagen: Danida, Ministry of Foreign Affairs).

O'Brien, M. (2004), *Public Attitudes Towards Development* (London: Social and Vital Statistics, Office for National Statistics).

OCHA (Office for the Coordination of Humanitarian Appeals) (2006), *Humanitarian Appeal 2006* (Geneva: Office for the Coordination of Humanitarian Appeals).

ODI (Overseas Development Institute) (2005), *Aftershocks, Natural Disaster Risk and Economic Development Policy*, ODI Briefing Paper (London: ODI).

OECD (Organisation for Economic Cooperation and Development) (1980), *Development Cooperation Report* (Paris: OECD).

—— (1985), *Development Cooperation Report. Twenty-five Years of Development Cooperation: A Review* (Paris: OECD).

—— (1996), *Shaping the 21st Century: The Contribution of Development Co-operation* (Paris: OECD).

—— (1997), *Evaluation of Programs Promoting Participatory Development and Good Governance: Synthesis Report* (Paris: OECD).

—— (1999a), *Evaluating Country Programmes* (Paris: OECD).

—— (1999b), *Guidance for Evaluating Humanitarian Assistance in Complex Emergencies* (Paris: OECD).

—— (2001a), *Evaluation Feedback for Effective Learning and Accountability* (Paris: OECD).

—— (2001b), *Germany DAC Peer Review* (Paris: OECD).

—— (2002a), *European Community DAC Peer Review* (Paris: OECD).

—— (2002b), *Glossary of Key Terms in Evaluation and Results-Based Management* (Paris: OECD).

—— (2002c), *Principles for Effective Aid* (Paris: OECD).

—— (2002d), *United States DAC Peer Review* (Paris: OECD).

—— (2003), 'Development Cooperation 2002 Report', *DAC Journal*, 4.1.

—— (2004a), *Assessment Framework for Coverage of Humanitarian Action in Peer Reviews* (Paris: OECD).

OECD (Organisation for Economic Cooperation and Development) (2004b), *France DAC Peer Review* (Paris: OECD).

—— (2004c), *Japan DAC Peer Review* (Paris: OECD).

—— (2004d), *Survey on Harmonisation and Alignment: Measuring Aid Harmonisation and Alignment in 14 Partner Countries* (Paris: OECD).

—— (2005a), *Australia DAC Peer Review* (Paris: OECD).

—— (2005b), 'Development Cooperation 2004 Report', *DAC Journal*, 6.1.

—— (2005c), *Harmonisation, Alignment, Results: Report on the Progress, Challenges and Opportunities*, background paper for OECD High Level Forum (Paris: OECD).

—— (2005d), *Making Poverty Reduction Work: OECD's Role in Development Partnership* (Paris: OECD).

—— (2005e), *Managing Aid: Practices of DAC Member Countries*, DAC Guidelines and Reference Series (Paris: OECD).

—— (2005f), *New Zealand DAC Peer Review* (Paris: OECD).

—— (2005g), *Paris Declaration on Aid Effectiveness: Ownership, Harmonisation, Alignment, Results and Mutual Accountability* (Paris: OECD).

—— (2005h), *Principles for Good International Engagement in Fragile States*, draft version (Paris: OECD).

—— (2005i), *Survey on Harmonisation and Alignment: Measuring Aid Harmonisation and Alignment in 14 Partner Countries* (Paris: OECD).

—— (2005j), *Sweden DAC Peer Review* (Paris: OECD).

—— (2006a), *The Challenge of Capacity Development: Working Towards Good Practice* (Paris: OECD).

—— (2006b), 'Development Cooperation 2005 Report', *DAC Journal*, 7.1.

—— (2006c), *Germany DAC Peer Review* (Paris: OECD).

—— (2006d), *United Kingdom DAC Peer Review* (Paris: OECD).

Ojanperä, S. (1997), 'The Bangladesh Case Study', in Riddell, Kruse, Kyllönen *et al.* (1997), vol. ii, app. 9.

Olsen, G. R. (2001), 'European Public Opinion and Aid to Africa: Is There a Link?', *Journal of Modern African Studies*, 39.4: 645–74.

—— (2005a), 'Danish Aid Policy in the Post-Cold War Period: Increasing Resources and Minor Adjustments', in Hoebink and Stokke (2005), 184–214.

—— (2005b), 'The European Union's Development Policy: Shifting Priorities in a Rapidly Changing World', in Hoebink and Stokke (2005), 573–608.

O'Neill, O. (1986), *Faces of Hunger: An Essay on Poverty, Justice and Development* (London: Allen and Unwin).

—— (1995), *Towards Justice and Virtue* (Cambridge: Cambridge University Press).

—— (2000), *Bounds of Justice* (Cambridge: Cambridge University Press).

—— (2004), 'Global Justice: Whose Obligations?', in Chatterjee (2004), 242–59.

Opeskin, B. R. (1996), 'The Moral Foundations of Foreign Aid', *World Development*, 24.1: 21–44.

Osei, B. (2004), *The Cost of Aid Tying to Ghana*, AERC Research Paper No. 11 (Nairobi: African Economic Research Consortium).

Osei, R., O. Morrissey, and T. Lloyd (2005), *The Fiscal Effects of Aid in Ghana*, WIDER Research Paper No. 2005/61 (Helsinki: WIDER).

Ostrom, E., C. Gibson, S. Shivakumar, and K. Andersson (2002), *Aid Incentives and Sustainability: An Institutional Analysis of Development Cooperation*, Sida Evaluation Study No. 02/01 (Stockholm: Sida).

Otero, M., and E. Rhyne (1994), *The New World of Microfinance: Building Healthy Financial Institutions for the Poor* (London: Intermediate Technology Publications).

Ouattara, B. and E. Strobl (2004), *Foreign Aid Inflows and the Real Exchange Rate in the CFA Franc Zone*, Credit Research Paper No. 04/07 (Nottingham: University of Nottingham).

Oxfam (2002), *Rigged Rules and Double Standards: Trade Globalisation and the Fight Against Poverty* (Oxford: Oxfam).

Oxfam GB (2005), *Programme Impact Report: Oxfam GB's Work with Partners and Allies Around the World* (Oxford: Oxfam).

Pack, H. and J. H. Pack (1990), 'Is Foreign Aid Fungible? The Case of Indonesia', *Economic Journal*, 100: 184–94.

Panday, D. P. (2002), 'Technical Co-operation and Institutional Capacity Building for Development: Back to Basics', in Fukuda-Parr, Lopes, and Malik (2002), 61–84.

Pearson, L. (1969), *Partners in Development: Report of the Commission on International Development* (New York: Praeger Publishers).

PEMconsult (2002), *Donor Support for Institutional Capacity Development in Environment: Lessons Learned* (Paris: OECD).

Pettersson, J. (2006), 'Foreign Sectoral Aid Fungibility, Growth and Poverty Reduction', paper presented to the WIDER Conference on Aid, Helsinki, June 2006; available at <www.wider.unu.edu/conference/conference-2006-1/conference-2006-1.htm> (accessed 14 June 2006).

Phelan, J. and G. Wood (2005), *Bleeding Boundaries: Civil–Military Relations and the Cartography of Neutrality* (Woking: Ockenden International).

Pianta, M. (2005), *UN World Summits and Civil Society*, UNRISD Programme Paper No. 18 (Geneva: United Nations Research Institute for Social Development).

Picciotto, R. (2006), 'Development Effectiveness at the Country Level', paper presented to the WIDER Conference on Aid, Helsinki, June 2006; available at <www.wider.unu.edu/conference/conference-2006-1/conference-2006-1.htm> (accessed 14 June 2006).

PIPA (Program on International Policy Attitudes) (2001), *Americans on Foreign Aid and World Hunger: A Study of US Public Attitudes (February, 2001)* (Washington, DC: Center on Policy Attitudes).

PIPA/Knowledge Networks Poll (2003), *Americans on Africa* (Washington, DC: Center on Policy Attitudes).

—— (2005) *Americans on World Poverty* (Washington, DC: Center on Policy Attitudes).

Pitt, C., C. Loehr, and A. Malviya (2005), *Campaigns, Evidence and Policy Influence: Lessons from International NGOs* (London: ODI).

Poate, D. (2005), *Independent External Evaluation of IFAD: Final Report* (Ditchling: ITAD).

—— R. Riddell, D. Chapman, and N. Curran (2000), *The Evaluability of Democracy and Human Rights Projects*, Sida Evaluation Study No. 00/3 (Stockholm: Sida).

Pogge, T. (2002), *World Poverty and Human Rights* (Cambridge: Polity Press).

—— (2004a), ' "Assisting" the Global Poor', in Chatterjee (2004), 260–88.

—— (2004b), 'The First United Nations Millennium Development Goal: A Cause for Celebration?', *Journal of Human Development*, 5.3: 377–97.

Pollard, A. and J. Court (2005), *How Civil Society Organisations Use Evidence to Influence Policy Processes: A Literature Review*, ODI Working Paper No. 249 (London: ODI).

Porter, T. (2002), 'An External Review of the CAP', <www.reliefweb.int/library/documents/2002/ocha-cap-ECOSOC-18apr.pdf> (accessed 17 Jan. 2006).

Pratt, C. (ed.) (1996), *Canadian International Development Assistance Policies: An Appraisal* (Montreal: McGill-Queen's University Press).

Pronk, J. P. (2004), *Catalysing Development? A Debate on Aid* (Oxford: Blackwell Publishing).

Quibria, M. S. (2004), *Development Effectiveness: What Does the Recent Research Tell Us?*, OED Working Paper No. 1 (Manila: ADB).

Radelet, S. (2006), *A Primer on Foreign Aid*, CGD Working Paper No. 92 (Washington, DC: CGD).

—— and S. Herrling (2003), *The Millennium Challenge Account: Soft Power or Collateral Damage?*, CGD Brief (Washington, DC: CGD).

—— and B. Siddiqi (2005), *US Pledges of Aid to Africa: Let's Do the Numbers*, CGD Notes (Washington, DC: CGD).

Rajan, R. G. and A. Subramanian (2005a), *Aid and Growth: What Does the Cross-Country Evidence Really Show?*, IMF Working Paper No. 127 (Washington, DC: IMF).

—— —— (2005b), *What Undermines Aid's Impact on Growth?*, IMF Working Paper No. 126 (Washington, DC: IMF).

Randel, J., and T. German (2002), 'Trends in the Financing of Humanitarian Assistance', in Macrae (2002b), 19–28.

Ranis, G. (2006), 'Towards the Enhanced Effectiveness of Foreign Aid', paper presented to the WIDER Conference on Aid, Helsinki, June 2006; available at <www.wider.unu.edu/conference/conference-2006-1/conference-2006-1.htm> (accessed 14 June 2006).

Rawls, J. (1973), *A Theory of Justice* (Oxford: Oxford University Press).

—— (2003), *The Law of Peoples* (Cambridge, MA: Harvard University Press).

Reddy, S. G. and C. Minoiu (2006), 'Development Aid and Economic Growth: A Positive Long-Run Relation', paper presented to the WIDER Conference on Aid, Helsinki, June 2006; available at <www.wider.unu.edu/conference/conference-2006-1/conference-2006-1.htm> (accessed 14 June 2006).

Reed, S., H. Weiss, and M. Mubagwa (2004), *Evaluation of USAID's Humanitarian Response in the Democratic Republic of the Congo, 2000–2004* (Washington, DC: USAID).

Reimann, K. D. (2006), 'A View from the Top: International Politics, Norms and the Worldwide Growth of NGOs', *International Studies Quarterly*, 50: 45–67.

Reisen, H. (2004), *Innovative Approaches to Funding the Millennium Development Goals*, OECD Policy Brief No. 24 (Paris: OECD Development Centre).

Renzio, P. de, D. Booth, A. Rogerson, and Z. Curran (2005), *Incentives for Harmonisation and Alignment in Aid Agencies*, ODI Working Paper No. 248 (London: ODI).

Rhi-Sausi, J. and M. Zupi (2005), 'Trends in the Debate on Italian Aid', in Hoebink and Stokke (2005), 336–77.

Rice, A. E. (1996), 'Building a Constituency for Development Co-operation: Some Reflections on the US Experience', in Foy and Helmich (1996), 67–84.

Riddell, A. R. (2003), 'Synthesis Report on Recent Developments and Issues Raised by Development Agencies Concerning Programme-Based Approaches', paper prepared for the Forum on Alignment Challenges in Program-Based Approaches (mimeo).

Riddell, R. C. (1987), *Foreign Aid Reconsidered* (London: James Currey; Baltimore: Johns Hopkins University Press).

—— (1997), 'Country Case Study: Kenya', in Riddell, Kruse, Kyllönen *et al.* (1997), ii, app. 12.

Riddell, R. C. and A. J. Bebbington (1993), *Developing Country NGOs and Donor Governments: Report to the Overseas Development Administration* (London: ODI).

—— and M. Robinson (1995), *Non-Governmental Organizations and Rural Poverty Alleviation* (Oxford: Oxford University Press).

—— and S. Stevens (1997), *Evaluation of Commonwealth Fund for Technical Co-operation (CFTC) to Uganda* (London: Strategic Planning and Evaluation Unit, Commonwealth Secretariat).

—— S. Matsvai, and S. Ncube (1995), *The Development Impact of The Swedish Government's Support to NGOs: Zimbabwe country case study* (London: ODI).

—— S-E. Kruse, T. Kyllönen, S. Ojanperä, and J-L. Vielajus (1997), *Searching for Impact and Methods: NGO Evaluation Synthesis Study*, 2 vols (Paris: OECD DAC; Helsinki, Department for International Development Cooperation, Ministry for Foreign Affairs of Finland).

Rieff, D. (2002), *A Bed for the Night: Humanitarianism in Crisis* (London: Vintage).

Risse, M. (2005), 'How Does the Global Order Harm the Poor?', *Philosophy and Public Affairs*, 33.4: 349–76.

Robinson, M. and S. Friedman (2005), *Civil Society, Democratisation and Foreign Aid in Africa*, IDS Discussion Paper No. 383 (Brighton: IDS).

Roche, C. (1999), *Impact Assessment for Development Agencies: Learning to Value Change* (Oxford: Oxfam).

Rodrik, D. (2005), *Rethinking Growth Strategies*, WIDER Annual Lecture 8 (Helsinki: UNU-WIDER).

—— (forthcoming), 'Goodbye Washington Consensus, Hello Washington Confusion?', *Journal of Economic Literature*.

—— A. Subramanian, and F. Trebbi (2002), *Institutions Rule: The Primacy of Institutions Over Geography and Integration in Economic Development*, NBER Working Paper No. 9305 (Cambridge: National Bureau of Economic Research).

Rogerson, A., A. Hewitt, and D. Waldenberg (2004), *The International Aid System 2005–2010: Forces For and Against Change*, ODI Working Paper No. 235 (London: ODI).

Roodman, D. (2004a), *The Anarchy of Numbers: Aid, Development and Cross-Country Empirics*, CGD Working Paper No. 32 (Washington, DC: CGD).

—— (2004b), *An Index of Donor Performance*, CGD Working Paper No. 42 (Washington, DC: CGD).

—— (2006), *Aid Project Proliferation and Absorptive Capacity*, CGD Working Paper No. 75 (Washington, DC: CGD).

Rosenstein-Rodan, P. (1943), 'Problems of Industrialization in Eastern and South-east Europe', *Economic Journal*, 53: 201–11.

—— (1961), 'International Aid for Underdeveloped Countries', *Review of Economics and Statistics*, 43: 107–38.

Round, J. I. and Odedokun, M. (2003), *Aid Effort and its Determinants*, WIDER Discussion Paper No. 03 (Helsinki: WIDER).

Rowden, R. (2005), *Changing Course: Alternative Approaches to Achieve the Millennium Development Goals and Fight HIV/AIDS* (Washington, DC: AAI).

Ruggeri Laderchi, C., R. Saith, and F. Stewart (2003), *Does it Matter That We Don't Agree on the Definitions of Poverty? A Comparison of Four Approaches*, QEH Working Paper No. 107 (Oxford: Queen Elizabeth House).

Sachs, J. (2005), *The End of Poverty* (New York: Penguin Press).

Sagasti, F., K. Bezanson, and F. Prada (2005), *The Future of Development Financing: Challenges and Strategic Choices*, Global Development Studies No. 1 (Stockholm: Ministry for Foreign Affairs).

Samuel, J. (ed.) (2000), *Social Action: An Indian Panorama* (New Delhi: Voluntary Action Network India).

Savedoff, W. D., R. Levine, and N. Birdsall (2006), *When Will We Ever Learn? Improving Lives through Impact Evaluation*, Report of the Evaluation Gap Working Group (Washington, DC: CGD).

Schulpen, L. (2005), 'All in the Name of Quality: Dutch Development Co-operation in the 1990s', in Hoebink and Stokke (2005), 406–47.

SDC (Swiss Agency for Development and Cooperation) (2004), *Advocacy Guidelines: Humanitarian Aid of the Swiss Confederation* (Geneva: SDC).

Sen, A. (1980), 'Equality of What?', in McMurrin (1980), 195–220.

—— (1999), *Development and Freedom* (Oxford: Oxford University Press).

—— (2005), 'Human Rights and Capabilities', *Journal of Human Development*, 6.2: 151–66.

Shue, H. (1996), *Basic Rights: Subsistence, Affluence and US Foreign Policy* (Princeton, NJ: Princeton University Press).

Sida (Swedish International Development Cooperation Agency) (1997), *Project 2015: Aid Dependency—Causes, Symptoms and Remedies* (Stockholm: Sida).

—— (2004), *Sida's Policy for Civil Society* (Stockholm: Sida).

Simkin, P. (2004), 'Evaluation of the Response to the 2002–03 Emergency in Ethiopia', available at <www.unicef.org/evaldatabase/files/Ethiopia_2004_009_ Emergency.pdf> (accessed 23 Jan. 2006).

Simmons, A. J. (2001), *Justification and Legitimacy: Essays on Rights and Obligations* (Cambridge: Cambridge University Press).

Simons, H. P., G. Hart, and C. Walsh (1997), *One Clear Objective: Poverty Reduction Through Sustainable Development*, Report of the Committee to Review the Australian Overseas Aid Program (Simons Report) (Canberra: AusAID).

Singer, P. (2004), 'Outsiders: Our Obligations to Those Beyond our Borders', in Chatterjee (2004), 7–32.

Slim, H. (2001), *Military Intervention to Protect Human Rights: the Humanitarian Agency Perspective* (Geneva: ICHRP).

—— (2004), *A Call to Alms: Humanitarian Action and the Art of War* (Geneva: Centre for Humanitarian Dialogue).

—— and A. Bonwick (2005), *Protection: An ALNAP Guide for Humanitarian Agencies* (London: ODI).

Smillie, I. (1994), 'Changing Partners: Northern NGOs, Northern Governments', in Smillie and Helmich (1994), 13–43.

—— (1995), *The Alms Bazaar. Altruism under Fire—Non-Profit Organisations and International Development* (London: Intermediate Technology Publications).

—— (2000), 'NGOs: Crisis and Opportunity in the New World Order', in Freedman (2000), 114–33.

—— and H. Helmich (1994), *Non-Governmental Organisations and Governments: Stakeholders for Development* (Paris: Development Centre, OECD).

—— and L. Minear (2003), *The Quality of Money: Donor Behaviour in Humanitarian Financing* (Somerville, MA: Tufts University Press).

—— —— (2004), *The Charity of Nations: Humanitarian Action in a Calculating World* (Bloomfield, CT: Kumarian Press).

Snodgrass, D. and J. Sebsted (2002), *Clients in Context: The Impact of Microfinance in Three Countries. Synthesis Report.* (Washington, DC: USAID).

Sobham, R. (2005), 'Increasing Aid for Poverty Reduction: Rethinking the Policy Agenda', *IDS Bulletin*, 36.3: 61–7.

Società Italiana di Monitoraggio (1999), *Evaluation of EU Development Aid to ALA States* (Brussels: EC).

Sogge, D. (2002), *Give and Take: What's the Matter with Foreign Aid?* (London: Zed Books).

Solimano, A. (2005), 'Remittance by Emigrants: Issues and Evidence', *Helsinki Process Papers on Global Economic Agenda*, 3: 104–27.

South Centre (1999), *Financing Development: Key Issues for the South* (Geneva: South Centre).

—— (2002), *Financing Development Beyond Monterrey: Contributions to a South Agenda* (Geneva: South Centre).

South Research, IDPM, INTRAC, Particip GmbH, and Prospect (2000), *Evaluation of Co-financing Operations with European Non-Governmental Development Organisations (NGOs) Budget Line B7-6000* (Leuven: South Research).

Sphere Project (2004), *Humanitarian Charter and Minimum Standards in Disaster Response* (Geneva: Sphere Project).

Stern, M. (1998), *Development Aid: What the Public Thinks*, UNDP Working Paper Series No. 4 (New York: UNDP).

Stern, N. (2002), 'Making the Case for Aid', in World Bank (2002a), 15–24.

Stewart, F. (2003), 'Evaluating Evaluation in a World of Multiple Goals, Interests and Models', paper prepared for the World Bank Operations Evaluation Department (OED) Conference on Evaluation and Development Effectiveness. (mimeo).

—— and M. Wang (2003), *Do PRSPs Empower Poor Countries and Disempower the World Bank or it is the Other Way Round?*, QEH Working Paper No. 108 (Oxford: Queen Elizabeth House).

Stiglitz, J. E. (1998), 'More Instruments and Broader Goals: Moving Towards the Post-Washington consensus', WIDER Annual Lectures No. 2 (Helsinki: UNU/WIDER).

—— (2002), *Globalization and its Discontents* (New York: A. A. Andrews).

—— (2005), *Post-Washington Consensus*, Initiative for Policy Dialogue Working Paper Series (New York: Columbia University).

—— and M. Charlton (2005), *Fair Trade for All: How Trade Can Promote Development* (Oxford: Oxford University Press).

Stoddard, A. (2003), 'Humanitarian NGOs: Challenges and Trends', in Macrae and Harmer (2003), 25–35.

Stokke, O. (2005), 'Norwegian Aid Policy: Continuity and Change', in Hoebink and Stokke (2005), 448–92.

Streeten, P. (1983), 'Why Development Aid?', *Banca Nazionale del Lavoro Quarterly Review*, 47: 378–95.

Sustainability (2003), *The 21st-Century NGO: In the Market for Change* (London: Sustainability).

Svensson, J. (2000), 'Foreign Aid and Rent-Seeking', *Journal of International Economics*, 5: 437–61.

Szekely, M., N. Lustig, J. A. Meijia, and M. Cumpa (2000), *Do We Know How Much Poverty There Is?* (Washington, DC: Inter-American Development Bank).

Szirmai, A. (2005), *The Dynamics of Socio-Economic Development* (Cambridge: Cambridge University Press).

Tabbush, C. (2005), *Civil Society in United Nations Conferences*, UNRISD Programme Paper No. 17 (Geneva: UNRISD).

Tarp, F., and P. Hjertholm (2000), *Foreign Aid and Development: Lessons Learnt and Directions for the Future* (London: Routledge).

Telford, J., and J. Cosgrave (2006), *Joint Evaluation of the International Response to the Indian Ocean Tsunami: Synthesis Report* (London: Tsunami Evaluation Coalition).

Tettey, W. J. (2002), 'Africa's Brain Drain: Exploring Possibilities for its Positive Utilization Through Networked Communities', *Mots Pluriels*, No. 20 (Feb.); available at <www.arts.uwa.edu.au/MotsPluriels/MP2002index.html> (accessed 13 Oct. 2005).

Teunissen, J. J. and A. Akkerman (2004), *Diversity in Development* (The Hague: FONDAD).

—— —— (2005), *Helping the Poor? The IMF and Low-Income Countries* (The Hague: Forum on Debt and Development).

Tevera, D. (2005), *Early Departures: The Emigration Potential of Zimbabwean Students*, Southern African Migration Project, Migration Policy Series No. 39 (Cape Town: Idasa).

Thakur, J. and N. Saxena (1999), 'Working with the Non-Profit Organisations in India', paper prepared for the Charities Aid Foundation International (mimeo).

Therkildsen, O. (2005), 'Major Additional Funding for the MDGs: A Mixed Blessing for Capacity Development', *IDS Bulletin*, 36.3: 28–39.

Tirman, J. (2003), 'The New Humanitarianism: How Military Intervention Became the Norm', *Boston Review*, December 2003–January 2004: 24–7.

Tomaševski, K. (1993), *Development Aid and Human Rights Revisited* (London: Pinter Publishers).

Torres, M., and M. Anderson (2004), *Fragile States: Defining Difficult Environments for Poverty Reduction*, Poverty Reduction in Difficult Environments (PRDE) Working Paper No. 1 (London: DFID).

UN (United Nations) (2002), *Final Outcome of the International Conference on Financing for Development* (New York: United Nations).

—— (2005), *World Economic and Social Survey* (New York: UN Department of Economic and Social Affairs).

UNCTAD (United Nations Conference on Trade and Development) (2006), *The Least Developed Countries Report 2006: Developing Productive Capacities* (Geneva and New York: United Nations).

UNDG (United Nations Development Group) (2005a), *The Role of the UN System in a Changing Aid Environment: Sector Support and Sector Programmes* (New York: UNDP).

—— (2005b), *UN Reform: Harmonisation and Alignment to Achieve the Millennium Development Goals* (New York: United Nations).

UNDP (United Nations Development Programme) (1993a), *Human Development Report 1993* (New York: UNDP).

—— (1993b), *UNDP and Organizations of Civil Society* (New York: UNDP).

—— (1999), *UNDP and Governance: Experiences and Lessons Learned*, UNDP Lessons-Learned Series No. 1 (New York: UNDP).

—— (2003), *Development Effectiveness 2003: Partnerships for Results* (New York: UNDP).

—— (2005), *Human Development Report 2005* (New York: UNDP).

—— and UN Population Fund (2001), *Financial Budgetary and Administrative Matters: Information on United Nations System Technical Cooperation Expenditure 2000* (New York: United Nations).

UNHCR (United Nations High Commissioner for Refugees) (2005), *Refugees by Numbers, 2005* (Geneva: United Nations High Commissioner for Refugees).

—— and WFP (World Food Programme) (2004), *Joint Assessment Guidelines*, 1st edn (Geneva and Rome: UNHCR and WFP).

United States Department of Defense (2006), *Quadrennial Defense Review Report* (Washington, DC: Department of Defense).

United States Department of State and USAID (2004), *Strategic Plan Fiscal Years 2004–2009: Aligning Diplomacy and Development Assistance* (Washington, DC: United States Department of State and USAID).

UN Millennium Project (2005), *Investing in Development: A Practical Plan to Achieve the Millennium Development Goals* (London and Sterling, VA: Earthscan).

Unsworth, S. (2005a), *Focusing Aid on Good Governance*, Global Economic Governance Programme, Department of Politics and International Relations, University of Oxford Working Paper No. 18 (Oxford: University of Oxford).

—— (2005b), *Signpost to More Effective States: Responding to Governance Challenges in Developing Countries* (Brighton: IDS).

USAID (United States Agency for International Development) (1996), 'Project Assistance Completion Report: project No. 515-0244.OOG—justice sector improvement (JSIP II)', available at <www.dac-evaluations-cad.org/abstracts_e.htm> (accessed 12 Oct. 2005).

—— (2004), *US Foreign Aid: Meeting the Challenges of the Twenty-First Century* (Washington, DC: USAID).

—— (2005a), *Fragile States Strategy* (Washington, DC: USAID).

—— (2005b), *On the Front Lines: Performance and Accountability. Highlights Fiscal Year 2004* (Washington, DC: USAID).

—— (2006), *2006 VOLAG Report of Voluntary Agencies Engaged in Overseas Relief and Development Registered with USAID* (Washington, DC: USAID).

Uvin, P. (1998), *Aiding Violence: The Development Enterprise in Rwanda* (West Hartford, CT: Kumarian Press).

—— (2004), *Human Rights and Development* (Bloomfield, CT: Kumarian Press).

Van Rooy A. (ed.) (1998), *Civil Society and the Aid Industry* (London: Earthscan).

Vaux, T. (2005), *Independent Evaluation of the DEC Tsunami Crisis Response* (London: Valid International).

Velde, D. W. te, A. Hewitt, and O. Morrissey (2006), *Aid financing of International Public Goods: Recent Developments* (London: ODI).

Waal, A. de (2002), *Famine Crimes: Politics and the Disaster Relief Industry in Africa* (Oxford: James Currey).

Wade, R. (1990), *Governing the Market: Economic Theory and the Role of Government in East Asian Industrialization* (Princeton, NJ: Princeton University Press).

—— (2001), *The US Role in the Malaise at the World Bank: Get Up Gulliver* (London: LSE).

Wagner, J. G. (2006), *An IHL/ICRC Perspective on Humanitarian Space* (London: ODI).

Walford, V. (2003), *Defining and Evaluating SWAps* (London: Institute for Health Sector Development).

Walle, N. van de (2005), *Overcoming Stagnation in Aid-Dependent Countries* (Washington, DC: CGD).

Watson, D. (2006), *Monitoring and Evaluation: Aspects of Capacity and Capacity Development*, ECDPM Discussion Paper No. 58B (Maastricht: ECDPM).

Weeks, J. (2002), *Supporting Ownership: Swedish Development Cooperation with Kenya, Tanzania and Uganda*, Sida Evaluation No. 33 (Stockholm: Sida).

West, R. (2003), *Education and Sector-wide Approaches in Namibia* (Paris: International Institute for Educational Planning).

WFP (World Food Programme) (2005), *Emergency Food Security Assessment Handbook*, 2 vols (Rome: WFP).

White, H. (1992), 'What Do We Know About Aid's Macroeconomic Impact? An Overview of the Aid Effectiveness Debate', *Journal of International Development*, 4: 121–37.

—— (2005a), 'The Case for Doubling Aid', *IDS Bulletin*, 36.3: 8–13.

—— (2005b), *Challenges in Evaluating Development Effectiveness*, IDS Working Paper No. 242 (Brighton: IDS).

Whitfield, L. (2006), 'Shifting Boundaries, Shifting Powers?', paper presented to the WIDER Conference on Aid, June 2006; available at <www.wider.unu.edu/conference/conference-2006-1/conference-2006-1.htm> (accessed 15 June 2006).

WHO (World Health Organization) (2005), *Health and Mortality Survey Among Internally Displaced Persons in Gulu, Kitgum and Pader Districts, Northern Uganda* (Geneva: World Health Organization).

Wiles, P. (2005), 'Meta-Evaluation', in *ALNAP Review of Humanitarian Action in 2004* (London: ODI).

Willetts, P. (2003), 'What is a Non-Governmental Organization?', in *UNESCO Encyclopaedia of Life Sciences*; available at <www.staff.city.ac.uk/p.willetts/CS-NTWKS/NGO-ART.HTM> (accessed 24 Nov. 2005).

Willetts-King, B., and T. Faint (2005), 'Study on Revised CERF Mechanism', report prepared for Development Cooperation Ireland and DFID, available at <www.reliefweb.int/ghd/CERF2005.doc> (accessed 17 Jan. 2006).

Williams, G., S. Jones, V. Amber, and A. Cox (2003), *A Vision for the Future of Technical Assistance in the International System* (Oxford: OPM).

Williamson, J. (1994), *The Political Economy of Reform* (Washington, DC: Institute for International Economics).

—— (2003), 'From Reform Agenda: A Short History of the Washington Consensus and Suggestions for What to Do Next', *Finance and Development*, September 2003: 10–13.

—— (2004), 'A Short history of the Washington Consensus', paper presented to the conference 'From the Washington Consensus towards a New Global Governance', Barcelona, Spain; available at http://iie.com/publications/papers/williamson0904-2.pdf <accessed 9 Nov. 2005>.

Woo, W. T. (2004), 'Serious Inadequacies of the Washington Consensus: Misunderstanding the Poor by the Brightest', in Teunissen and Akkerman (2004), 9–43.

Wood, A. (2004), *One Step Forward, Two Steps Back: Ownership, PRSPS and IFI Conditionality* (Milton Keynes: World Vision).

Woods, N. (2005), 'The Shifting Politics of Foreign Aid', *International Affairs*, 81.2: 393–411.

—— (2006), *The IMF, the World Bank and their Borrowers* (New York: Cornell University Press).

World Bank (1981), *Accelerated Development in Sub-Saharan Africa: An Agenda for Action* (Washington, DC: World Bank).

World Bank (1989), *Sub-Saharan Africa: From Crisis to Sustainable Growth* (Washington, DC: World Bank).

—— (1990), *World Development Report 1990* (Washington, DC: World Bank).

—— (1995), *World Bank Participation Sourcebook* (Washington, DC: World Bank).

—— (1996a), 'Lessons and Practices: Technical Assistance', available at <www.dac-evaluations-cad.org/abstracts_e.htm> (accessed 12 Oct. 2005).

—— (1996b), *Partnerships for Capacity Building in Africa* (Washington, DC: World Bank).

—— (1996c), *NGOs and the Bank: Incorporating F 95 Progress Report on Cooperation Between the World Bank and NGOs* (Washington, DC: World Bank).

—— (1998), *Assessing Aid: What Works, What Doesn't and Why* (Washington, DC: World Bank).

—— (1999a), *Civil Service Reform: A Review of World Bank Assistance* (Washington, DC: World Bank).

—— (1999b), *NGOs in World Bank-Supported Projects* (Washington, DC: World Bank).

—— (2000), *Attacking Poverty: World Development Report 2000/2001* (Washington, DC: World Bank).

—— (2001a), *Adjustment Lending Retrospective: Final Report* (Washington, DC: World Bank).

—— (2001b), *Education and Health in Sub-Saharan Africa: A Review of Sector-Wide Approaches* (Washington, DC: World Bank).

—— (2001c), *World Development Report: Attacking Poverty* (Washington, DC: World Bank).

—— (2002a), *A Case for Aid: Building Consensus for Development Assistance* (Washington, DC: World Bank).

—— (2002b), *The Next Ascent: An Evaluation of the Aga Khan Rural Support Program, Pakistan* (Washington, DC: World Bank).

—— (2003), 'Country Policy and Institutional Assessment 2003: Assessment Questionnaire' (mimeo).

—— (2005a), *2004 Annual Review of Development Effectiveness: The World Bank's Contribution to Poverty Reduction* (Washington, DC: World Bank).

—— (2005b), *Building Effective States, Forging Engaged Societies*, Report of the World Bank Task Force on Capacity Development in Africa (Washington, DC: World Bank).

—— (2005c), *Country Assistance Evaluation Retrospective: OED Self-Evaluation* (Washington, DC: World Bank).

—— (2005d), *Economic Growth in the 1990s: Learning from a Decade of Reform* (Washington, DC: World Bank).

—— (2005e), *Engaging Civil Society Organizations in Conflict-Affected and Fragile States: Three African Country Case Studies* (Washington, DC: World Bank).

—— (2005f), *Issues and Options for Improving Engagement Between the World Bank and Civil Society Organizations* (Washington, DC: World Bank).

—— (2005g), *Low-Income Countries Under Stress: Update* (Washington, DC: World Bank).

—— (2005h), *Review of World Bank Conditionality* (Washington, DC: World Bank).

—— (2005i), *The World Bank Annual Report 2004* (Washington, DC: World Bank).

—— (2005j), *World Bank–Civil Society Engagement: Review of Fiscal Years 2002–2004* (Washington, DC: World Bank).

—— (2005k), *World Bank Support for Capacity Building in Africa* (Washington, DC: World Bank).

World Bank (2005l), *World Development Indicators* (Washington, DC: World Bank).

—— (2005m), *World Development Report 2006: Equity and Development* (Washington and New York: World Bank and Oxford University Press).

—— (2006a), *Global Economic Prospects* (Washington, DC: World Bank).

—— (2006b), *Global Development Finance: The Development Potential of Surging Capital Flows* (Washington, DC: World Bank).

—— (2006c), *Global Monitoring Report 2006* (Washington, DC: World Bank).

Yankelovich, D. (1996), 'Public Judgement on Aid', in Foy and Helmich (1996), 55–66.

Zedillo, E. (2001), *Financing for Development*, Report of the High-Level Panel (New York: United Nations).

■ INDEX

Abraham, M. 292, 296
absorptive capacity 128, 227–8, 229–30
Abuom, Agnes 25
accountability 385
Acharya, A. 52
Action by Churches Together International
    (ACT) 316
Action Aid International (AAI) 9, 280, 347,
    412, 415n1, 453n1, 456n35
Active Learning Network for Accountability
    and Performance (ALNAP) 334–9,
    341–4, 346
Adam, C. 220, 229, 437n21
Addison, T. 225, 230, 232–3, 344, 437nn1, 19
Adinolfi, C. 401, 453n1, 455n20
adjustment lending 238
adjustment policies 364
advocacy 411, 412
    and humanitarian aid 313, 349–52
    awareness-raising 350
    effectiveness: local 291–4; national and
        international 294–8
    methodology 288–9
    NGOs 37, 49, 262–4, 268, 287–310
Afghanistan 7, 54, 58, 93, 95, 97–8, 102, 327,
    335, 337, 376
Africa 20, 25, 45–6, 114, 121, 199, 206, 209,
    281, 319, 371, 375
Africa Progress Panel 46
African Development Bank (AfDB) 81,
    182–3, 187
    African Development Fund 82
Aga Khan Foundation 281
agriculture 219, 281
    failure 272–3
    India 179, 270
    success 182–3, 191–2, 278
Ahmed, R. 278
aid
    absorption, absorptive capacity 128,
        227–9
    accountability 45
    administrative costs 237
    adverse effects 176–7, 228
    allocation 91–106, 382, 392, 395
    amount needed 124–5

and growth 13, 173–5, 219–20, 225
as act of beneficence 143
as cash hand-outs 406–8
context 215–16
a continuum 123
country impact 218–20
cross-country studies 222–5
data quality of 166–9
definitions 17, 18–21
dependency 38
donor self-interest 93–8
effectiveness 128, 156, 213–18, 256–7,
    belief in 114–17; criteria 170–2,
    177
ethical theories and 129–38
extent of 175
fatigue 107–8
how much is needed 123–5
human rights and 134–5, 141, 144–54
impact of donor self-interest 101–5,
    365–6
insufficient 93, 359, 386
literature 4, 5, 28
low public priority 111–13
monitoring 61
moral case for 11, 116–29, 139–62
multiplicity of donors and projects
    360–1
need for evidence 177
need for strategic thinking 215
origins 24–26
overall impact 253–8, 355–6
perverse effect 377–8
policy advice 231–52, 363–66
poor decision-making 357
problems with 13, 357–80, 386–7
recipient problems and dilemmas 369–77
recommendations for changes to 13,
    381–88, 389–414
role of 122–3
sectoral impact 219
solidarity and 139–42
targetry 28
tied 73, 99–100, 386; cost of 100–1, 358
trends 2–4
volatility 202, 228, 359, 386